TWO DEAD

STORY **VAN JENSEN**

ART **NATE POWELL**

COLORS **ERIN TOBEY**

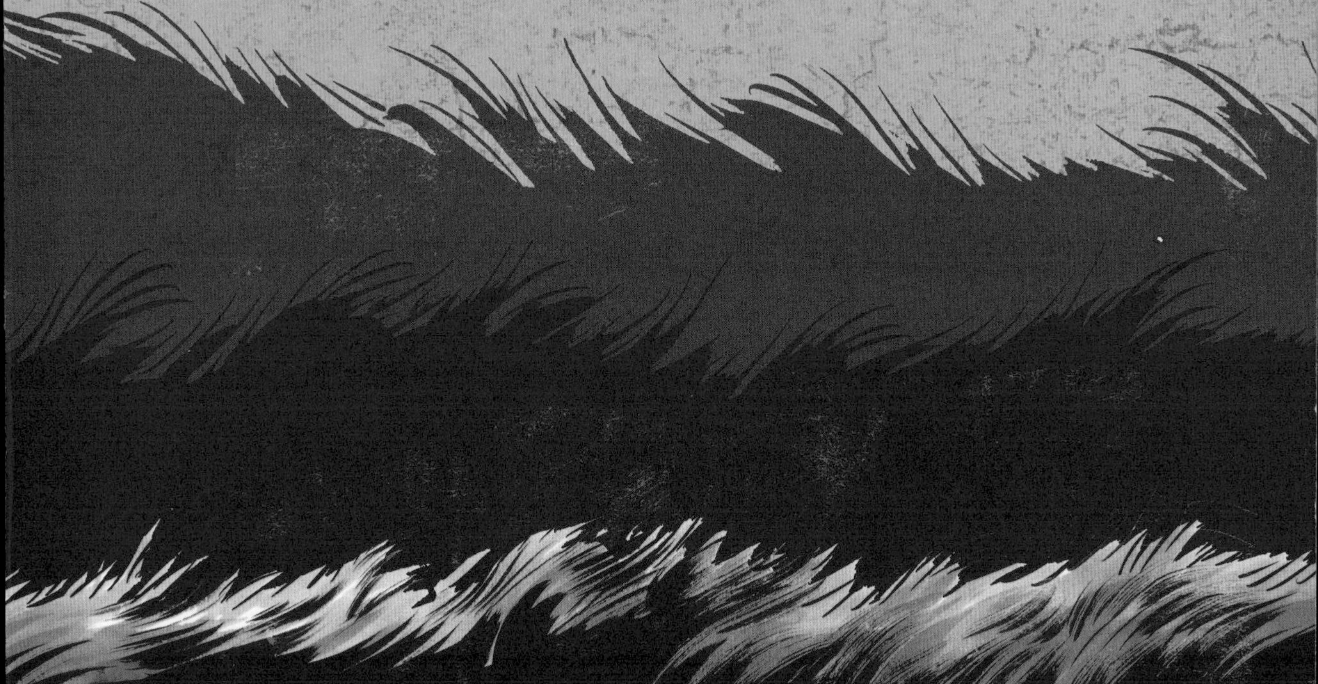

GALLERY 13

NEW YORK   LONDON   TORONTO SYDNEY   NEW DELHI

GALLERY 13

An Imprint of Simon & Schuster, Inc.

1230 Avenue of the Americas

New York, NY 10020

First Gallery 13 trade paperback edition November 2019

GALLERY 13 and colophon are trademarks of Simon & Schuster, Inc.

For information about special discounts for bulk purchases, please contact Simon & Schuster Special Sales at 1-866-506-1949 or business@simonandschuster.com.

The Simon & Schuster Speakers Bureau can bring authors to your live event. For more information or to book an event contact the Simon & Schuster Speakers Bureau at 1-866-248-3049 or visit our website at www.simonspeakers.com.

Manufactured in the United States of America

10 9 8 7 6 5 4 3 2 1

Library of Congress Cataloging-in-Publication Data has been applied for.

ISBN 978-1-5011-6895-6

ISBN 978-1-5011-6897-0 (ebook)

This book is for the dead, and for the survivors. May they know peace.
—VAN JENSEN

My work on this book is dedicated to restless souls,
living and dead, in the twin communities that birthed and shaped me.
Little Rock and North Little Rock: my comics will always be equal parts
love letter, anchor, and reckoning with you.
—NATE POWELL

WINTER, 1944

HÜRTGEN FOREST, GERMANY

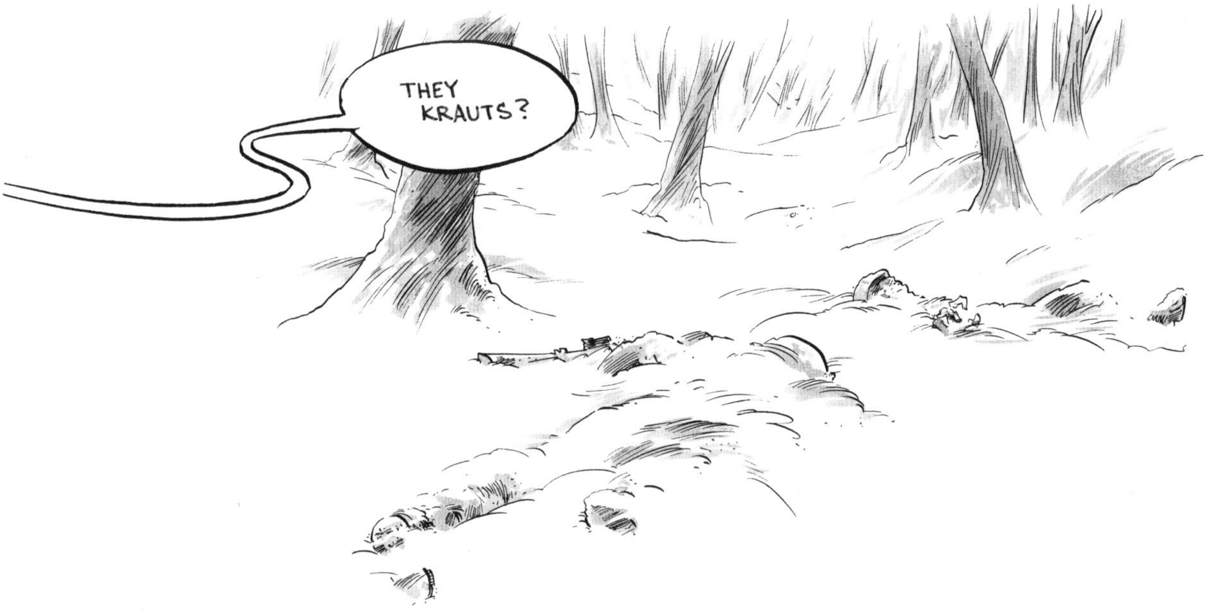
THEY KRAUTS?

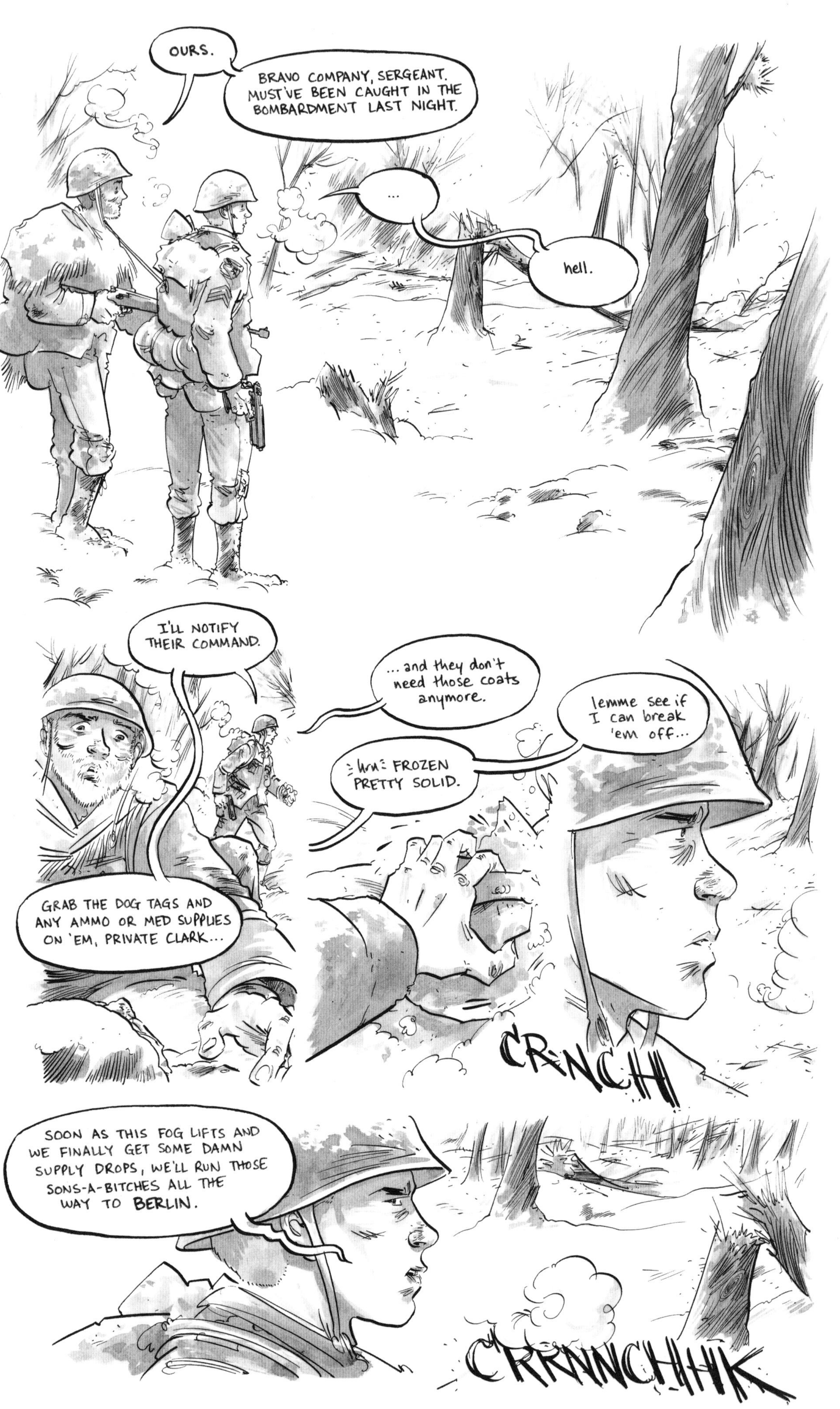

OURS.
BRAVO COMPANY, SERGEANT. MUST'VE BEEN CAUGHT IN THE BOMBARDMENT LAST NIGHT.
...
hell.
I'LL NOTIFY THEIR COMMAND.
GRAB THE DOG TAGS AND ANY AMMO OR MED SUPPLIES ON 'EM, PRIVATE CLARK...
...and they don't need those coats anymore.
lemme see if I can break 'em off...
hrn: FROZEN PRETTY SOLID.
CRNCH
SOON AS THIS FOG LIFTS AND WE FINALLY GET SOME DAMN SUPPLY DROPS, WE'LL RUN THOSE SONS-A-BITCHES ALL THE WAY TO BERLIN.
CRRNNCHHK

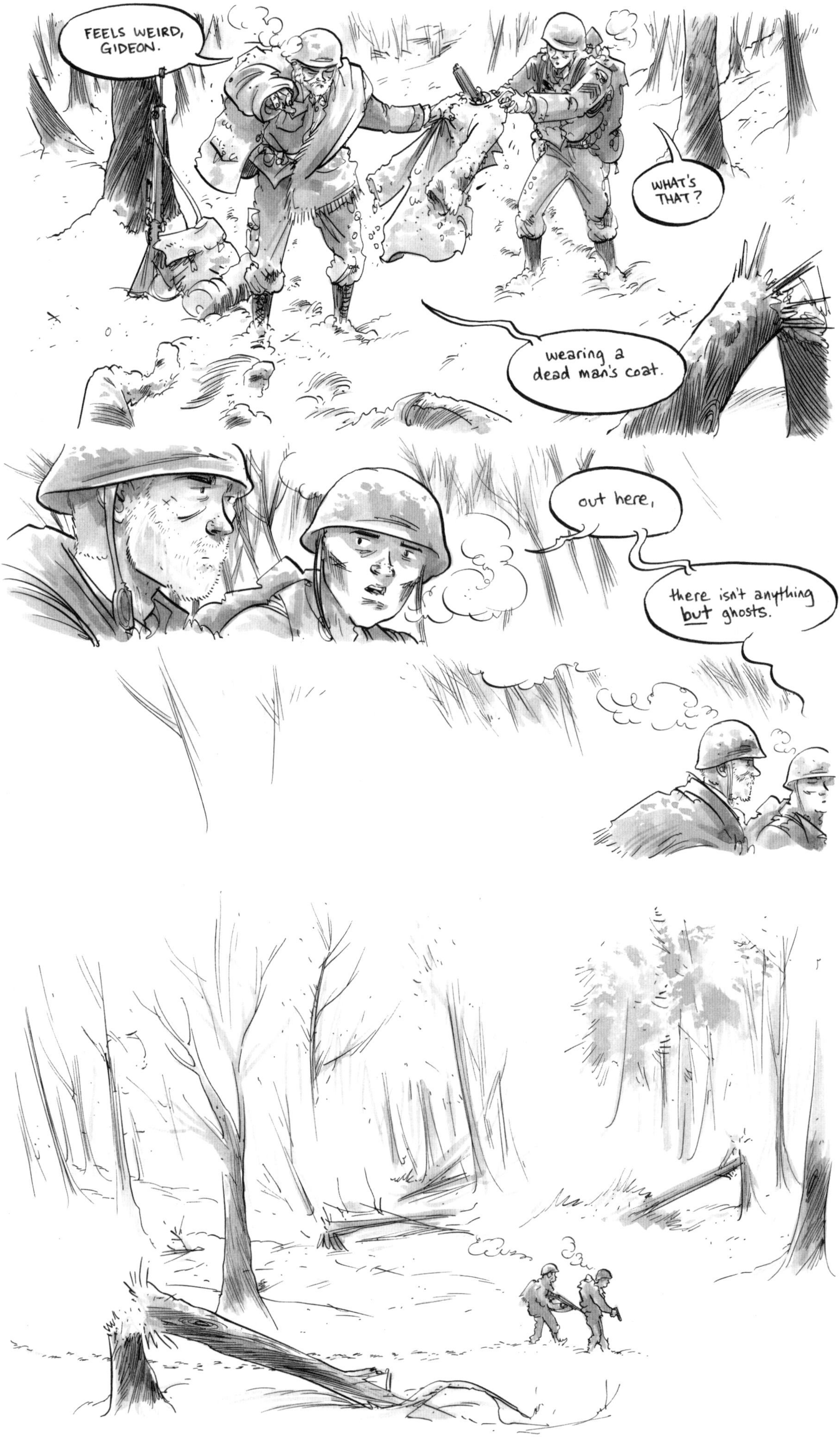
FEELS WEIRD, GIDEON.
WHAT'S THAT?
wearing a dead man's coat.
out here,
there isn't anything but ghosts.

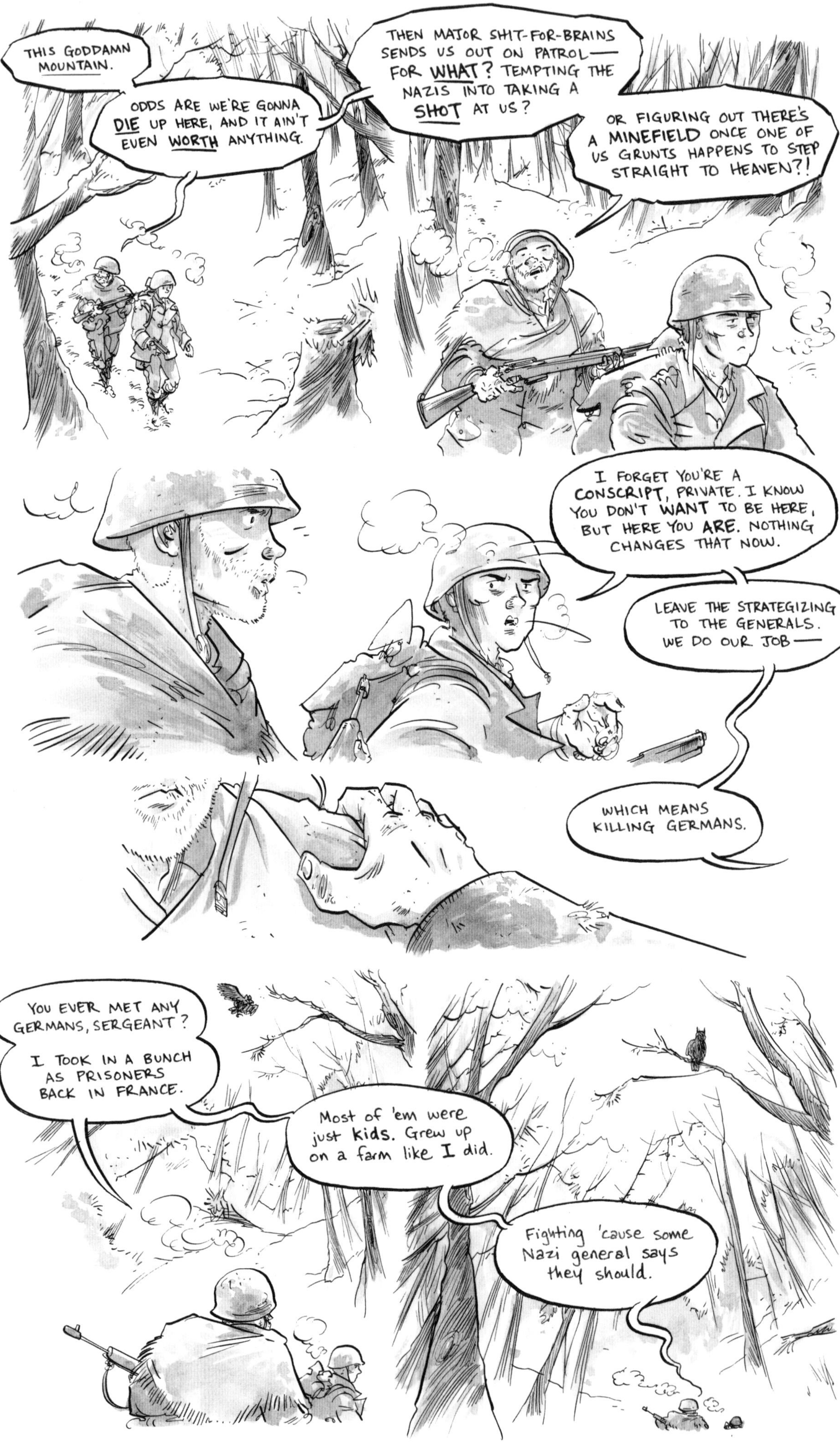
THIS GODDAMN MOUNTAIN.
ODDS ARE WE'RE GONNA DIE UP HERE, AND IT AIN'T EVEN WORTH ANYTHING.
THEN MAJOR SHIT-FOR-BRAINS SENDS US OUT ON PATROL— FOR WHAT? TEMPTING THE NAZIS INTO TAKING A SHOT AT US?
OR FIGURING OUT THERE'S A MINEFIELD ONCE ONE OF US GRUNTS HAPPENS TO STEP STRAIGHT TO HEAVEN?!
I FORGET YOU'RE A CONSCRIPT, PRIVATE. I KNOW YOU DON'T WANT TO BE HERE, BUT HERE YOU ARE. NOTHING CHANGES THAT NOW.
LEAVE THE STRATEGIZING TO THE GENERALS. WE DO OUR JOB—
WHICH MEANS KILLING GERMANS.
YOU EVER MET ANY GERMANS, SERGEANT?
I TOOK IN A BUNCH AS PRISONERS BACK IN FRANCE.
Most of 'em were just kids. Grew up on a farm like I did.
Fighting 'cause some Nazi general says they should.

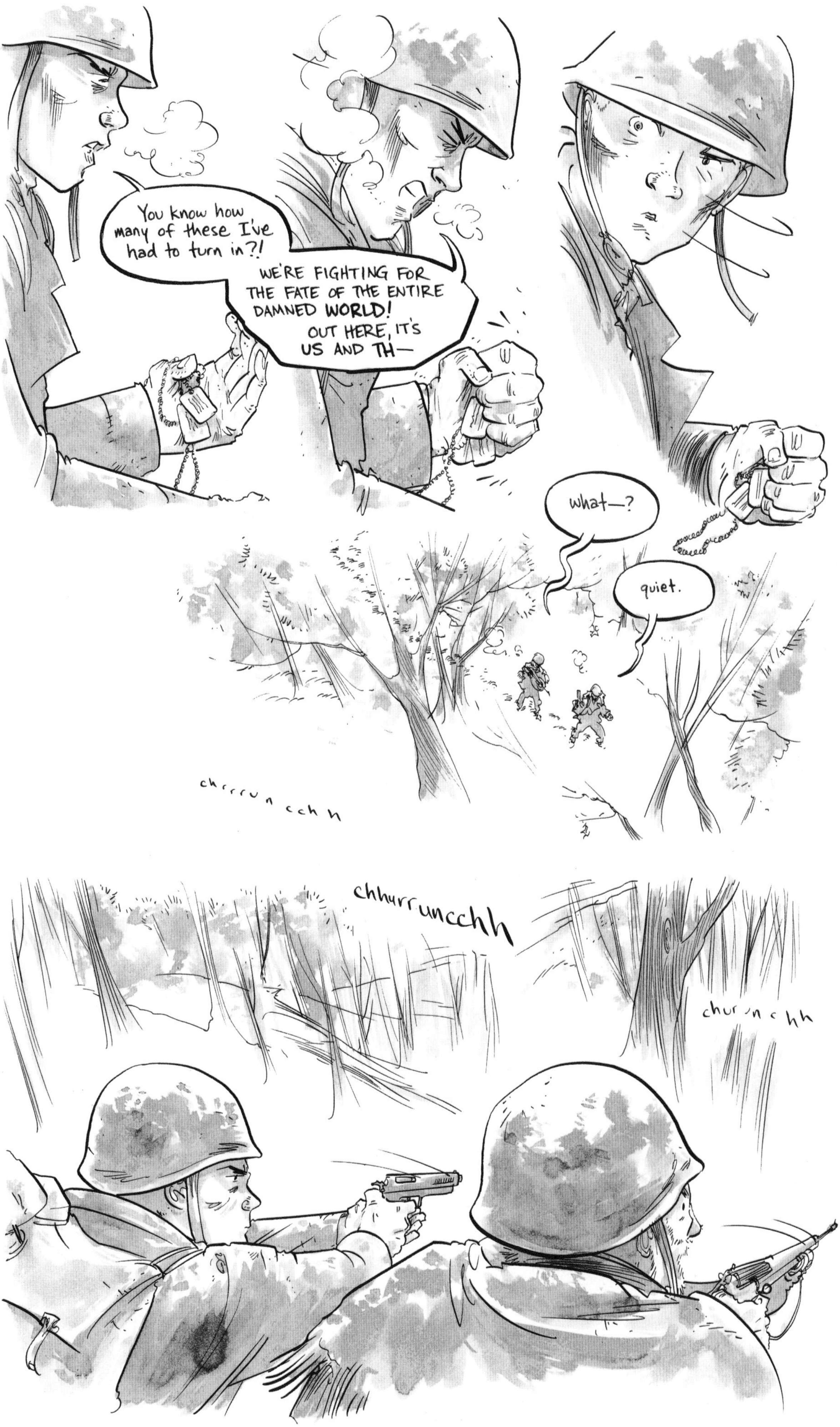
You know how many of these I've had to turn in?!
WE'RE FIGHTING FOR THE FATE OF THE ENTIRE DAMNED WORLD! OUT HERE, IT'S US AND TH—
what—?
quiet.
chrrrunnchh
chhurrruncchh
churunchh

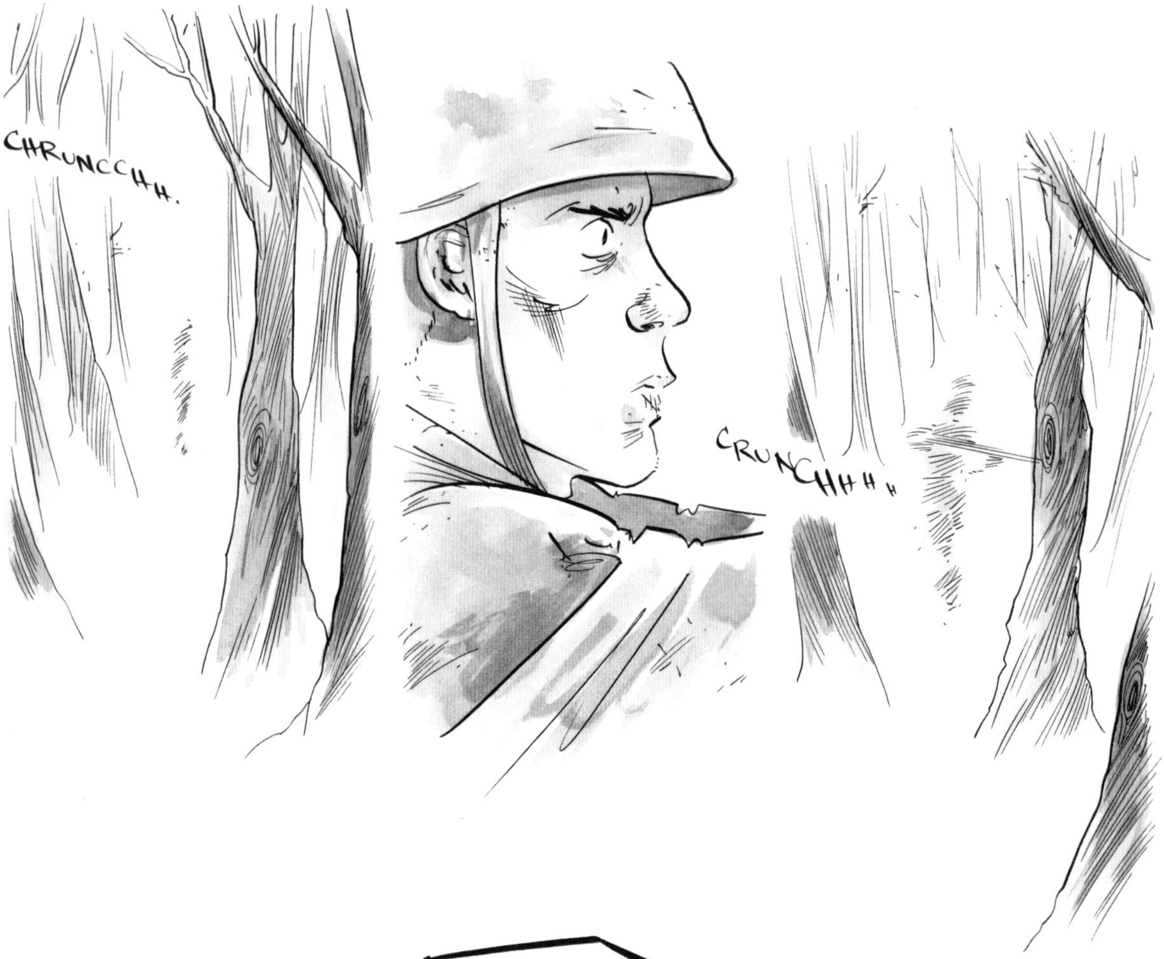
CHRUNCCHH.
CRUNCHHHH

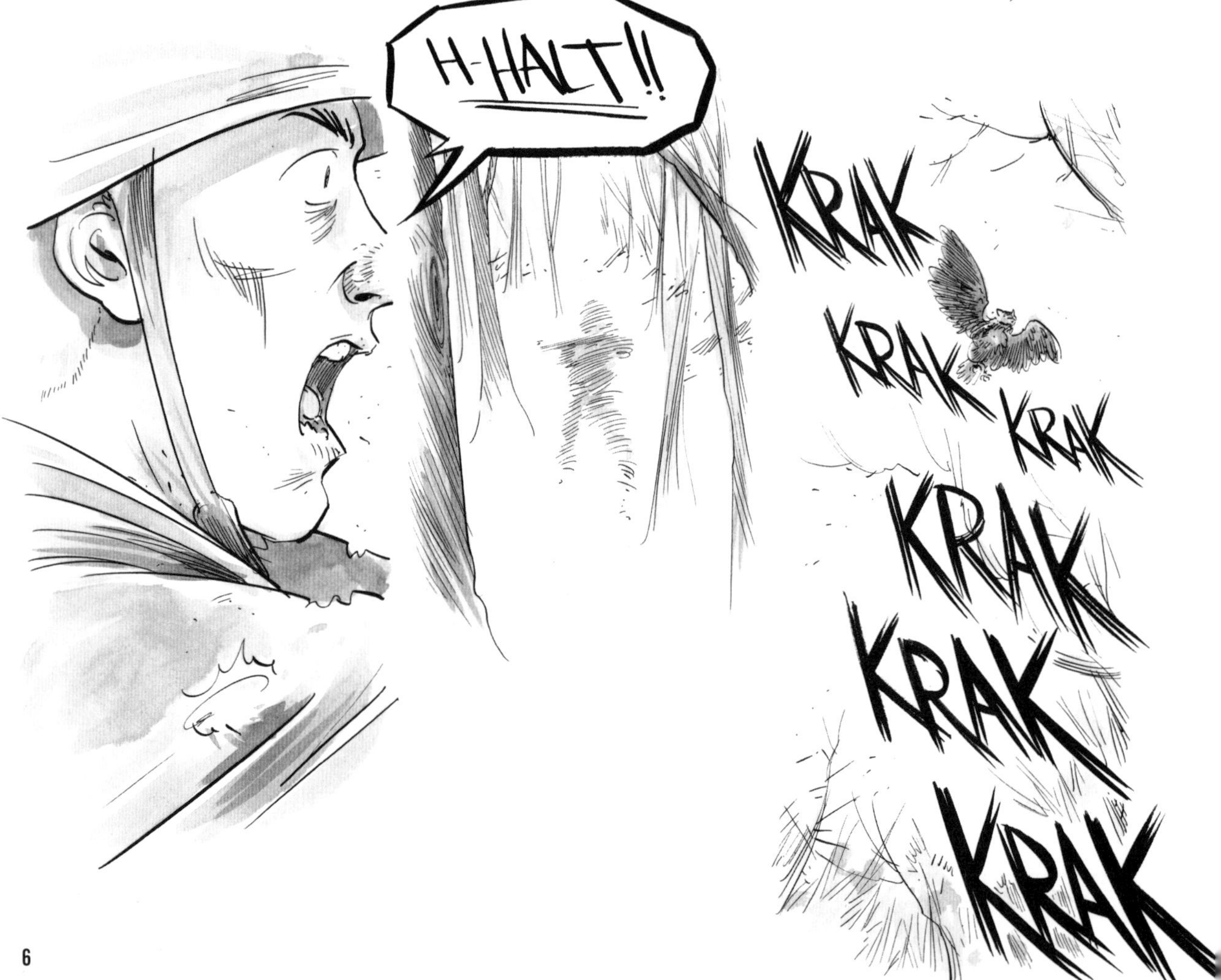
H-HALT!!
KRAK
KRAK
KRAK
KRAK
KRAK
KRAK

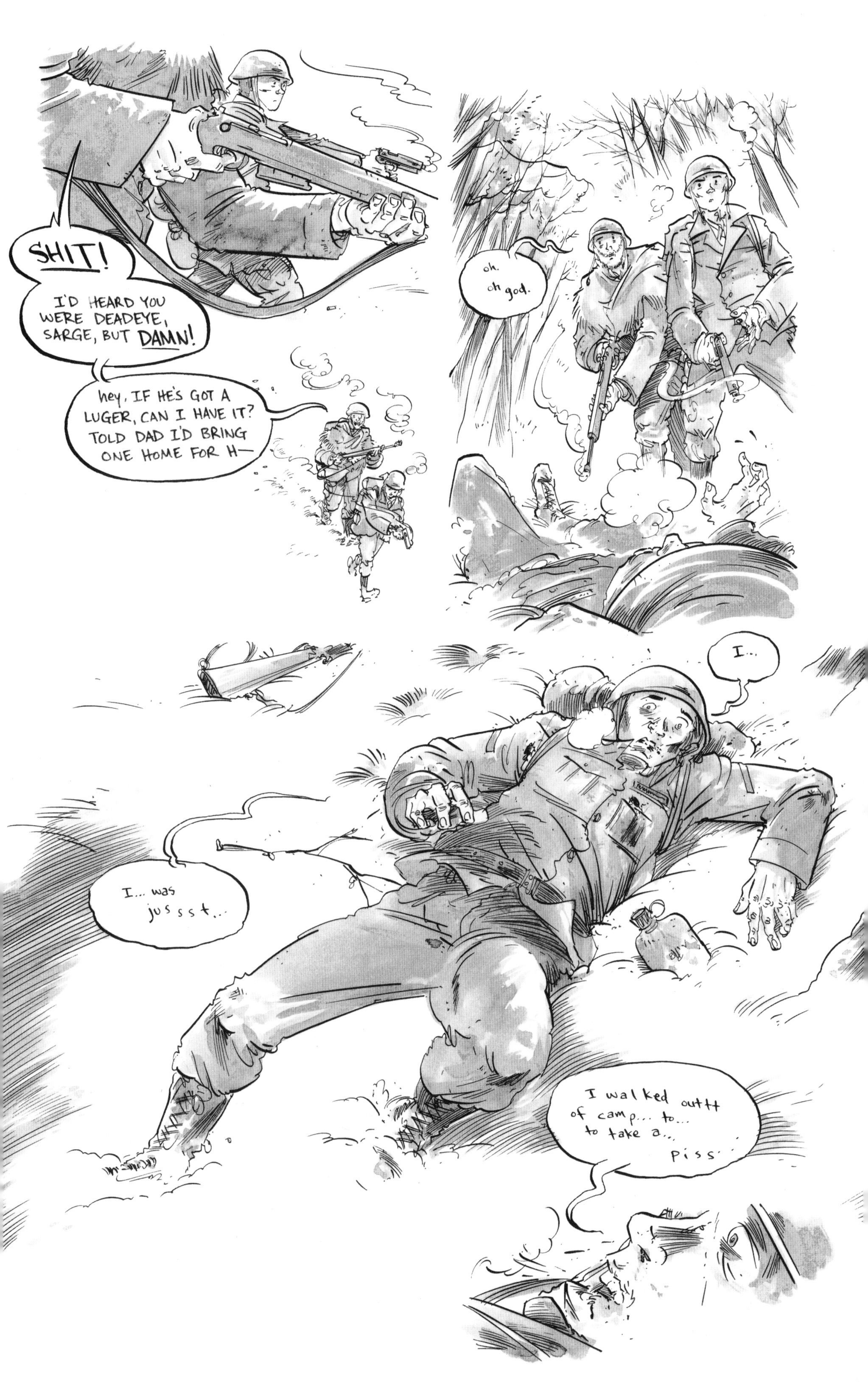
SHIT!
I'D HEARD YOU WERE DEADEYE, SARGE, BUT DAMN!
hey, IF HE'S GOT A LUGER, CAN I HAVE IT? TOLD DAD I'D BRING ONE HOME FOR H—
oh. oh god.
I...
I... was jussst...
I walked outtt of camp... to... to take a... piss.

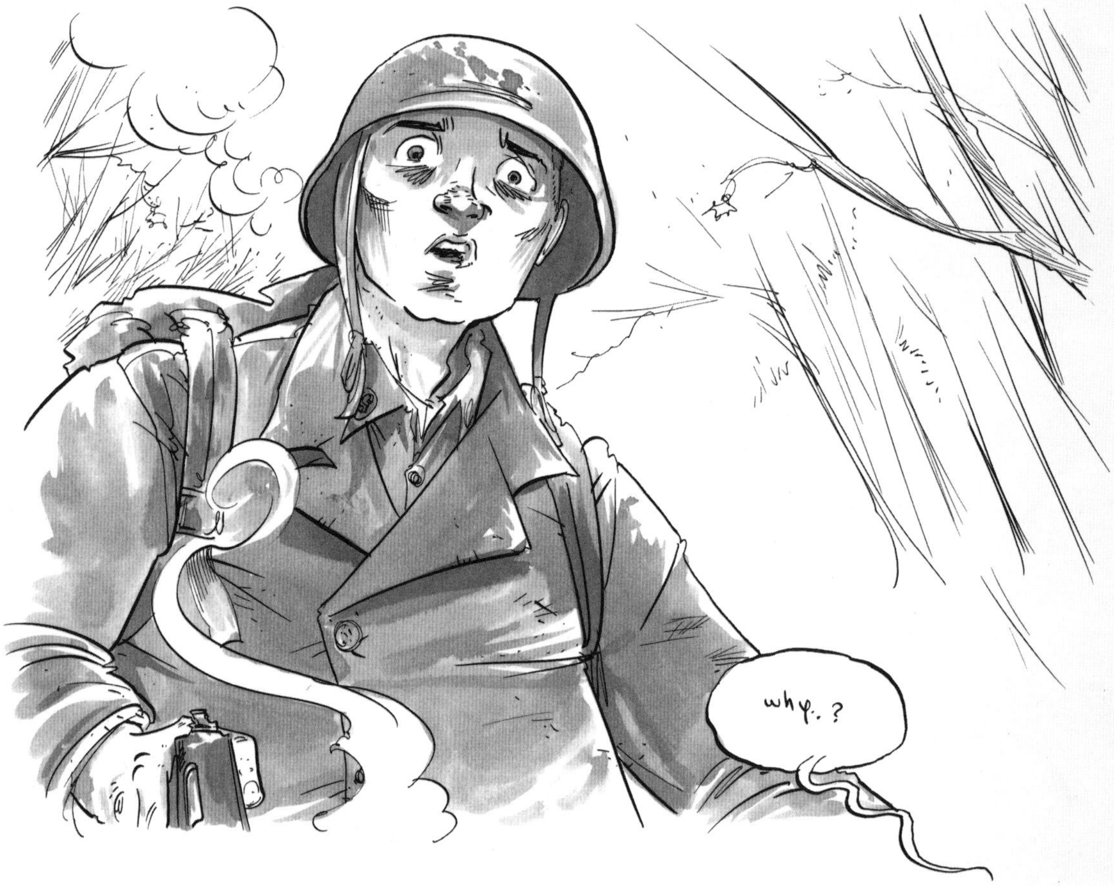
why..?

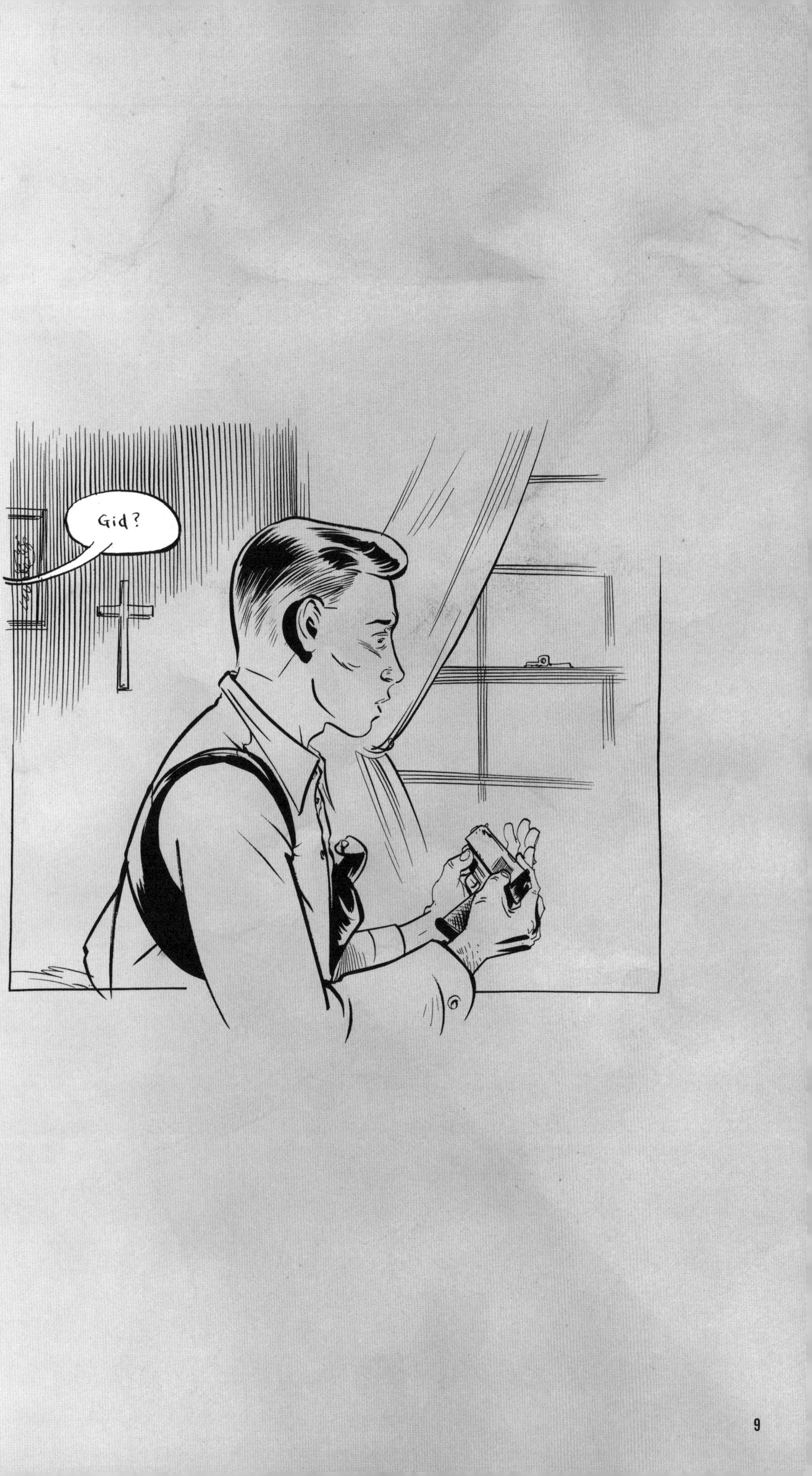
Gid?

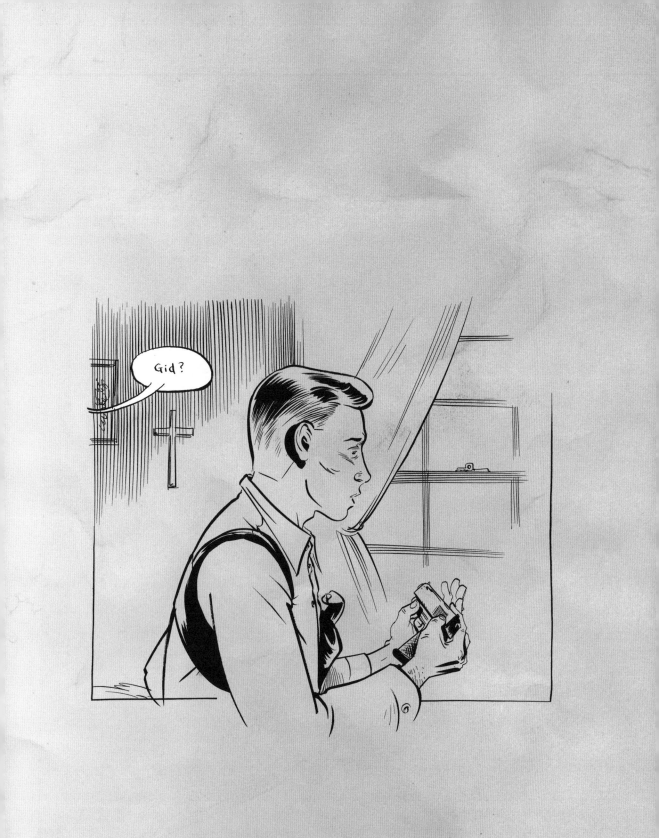

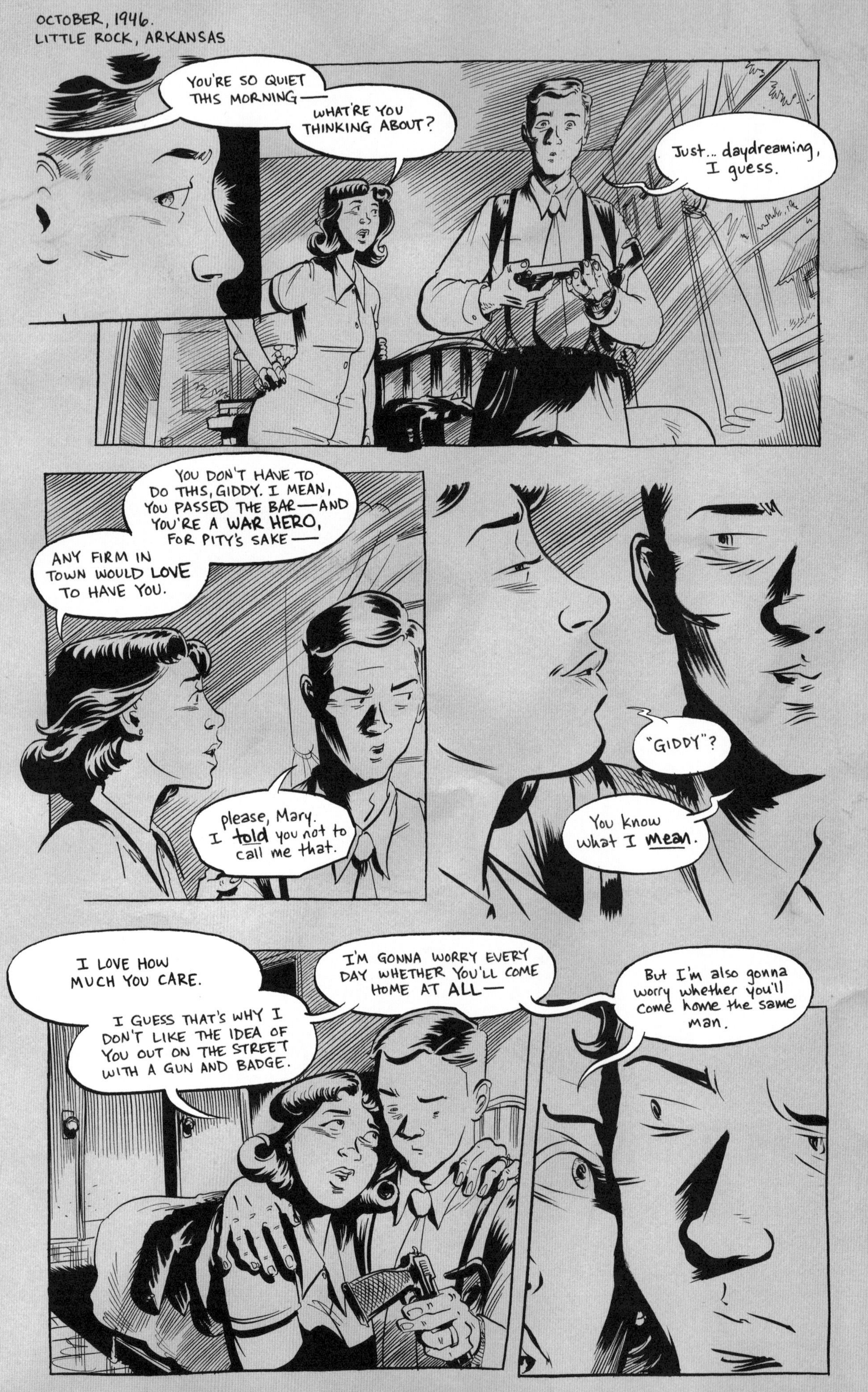

OCTOBER, 1946.
LITTLE ROCK, ARKANSAS
YOU'RE SO QUIET THIS MORNING—
WHAT'RE YOU THINKING ABOUT?
Just... daydreaming, I guess.
YOU DON'T HAVE TO DO THIS, GIDDY. I MEAN, YOU PASSED THE BAR—AND YOU'RE A WAR HERO, FOR PITY'S SAKE—
ANY FIRM IN TOWN WOULD LOVE TO HAVE YOU.
please, Mary. I told you not to call me that.
"GIDDY"?
You know what I mean.
I LOVE HOW MUCH YOU CARE.
I GUESS THAT'S WHY I DON'T LIKE THE IDEA OF YOU OUT ON THE STREET WITH A GUN AND BADGE.
I'M GONNA WORRY EVERY DAY WHETHER YOU'LL COME HOME AT ALL—
But I'm also gonna worry whether you'll come home the same man.

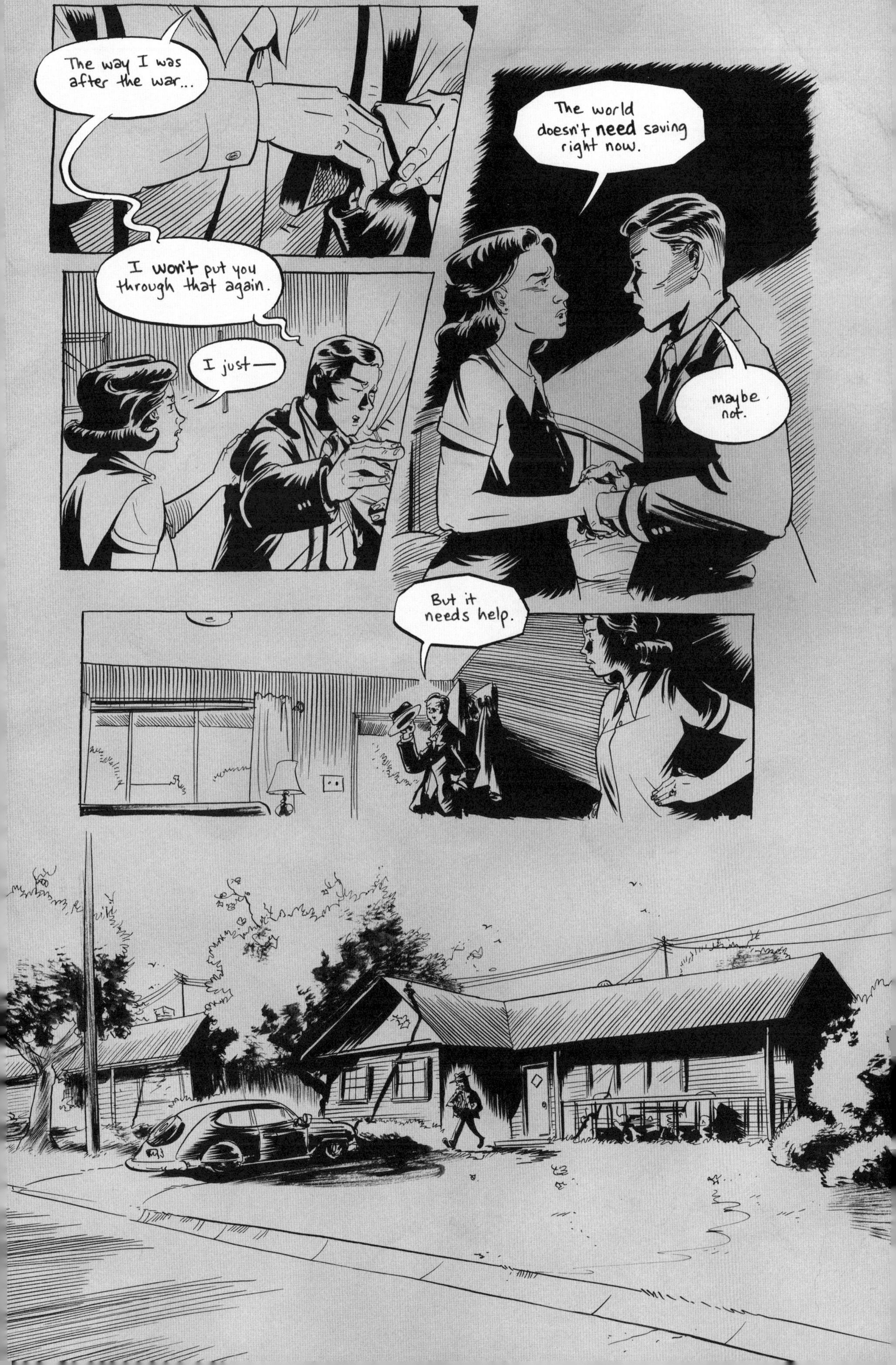
The way I was after the war...
I won't put you through that again.
I just—
The world doesn't need saving right now.
maybe not.
But it needs help.

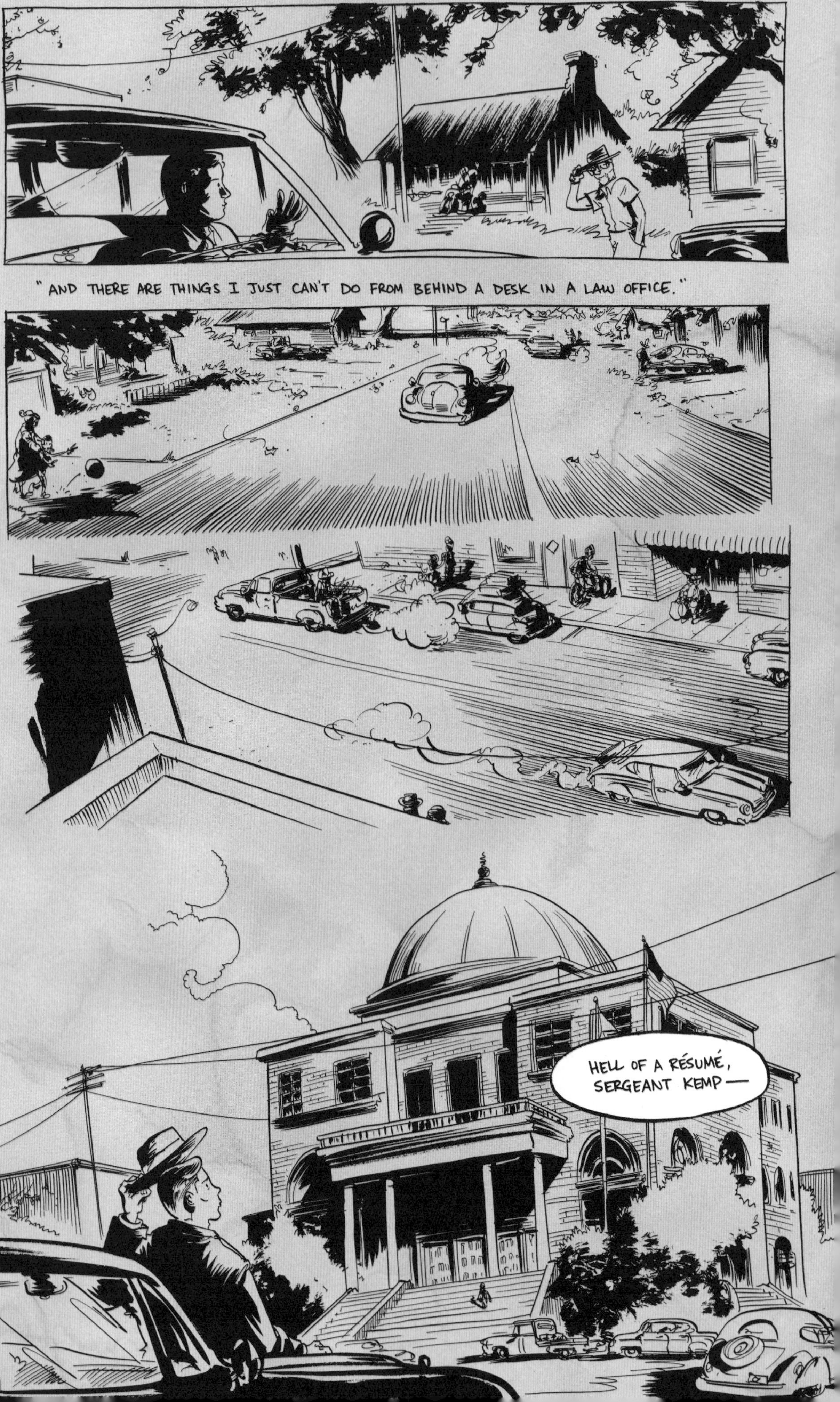
"AND THERE ARE THINGS I JUST CAN'T DO FROM BEHIND A DESK IN A LAW OFFICE."
HELL OF A RÉSUMÉ, SERGEANT KEMP—

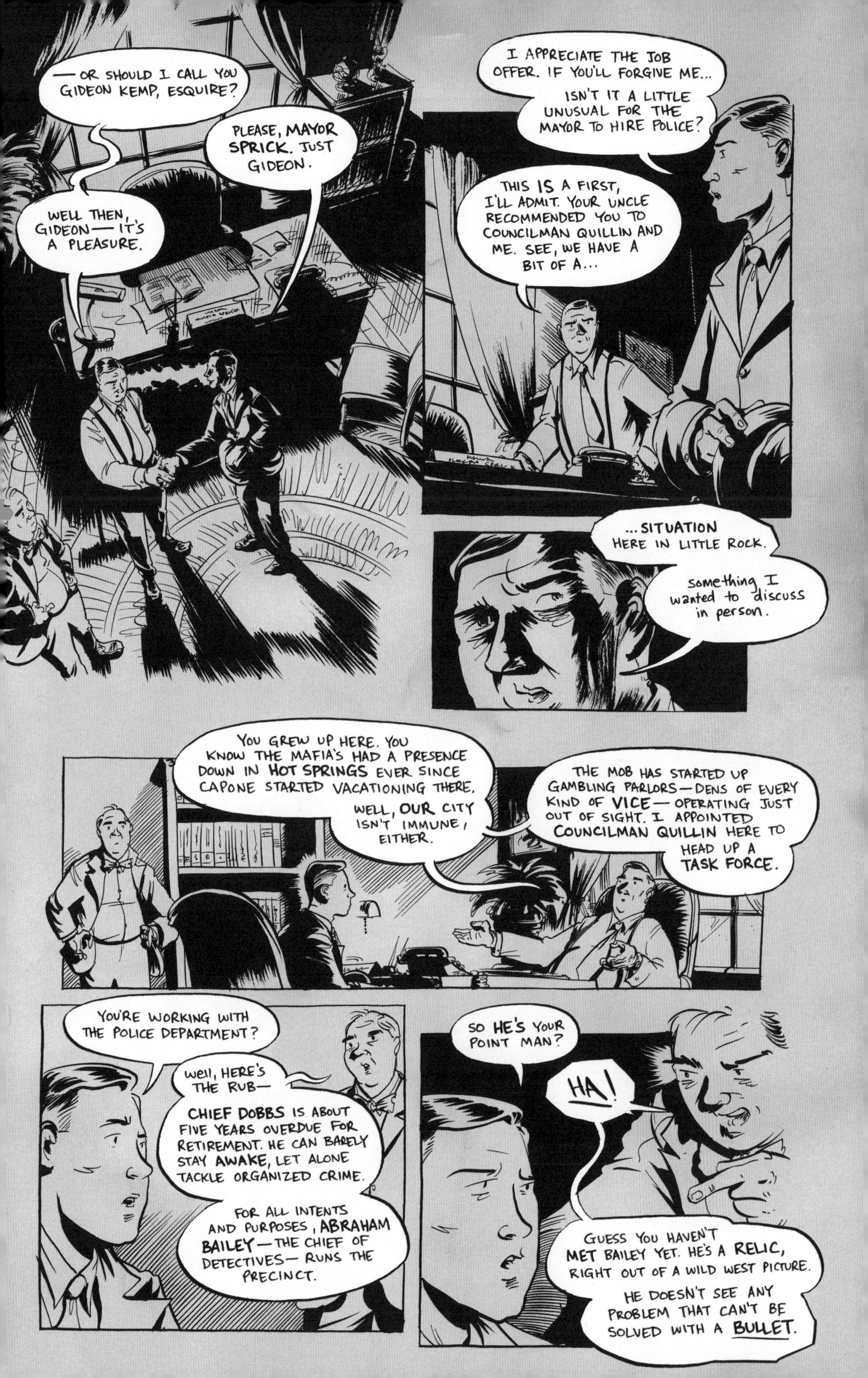

—OR SHOULD I CALL YOU GIDEON KEMP, ESQUIRE?
PLEASE, MAYOR SPRICK. JUST GIDEON.
WELL THEN, GIDEON—IT'S A PLEASURE.
I APPRECIATE THE JOB OFFER. IF YOU'LL FORGIVE ME...
ISN'T IT A LITTLE UNUSUAL FOR THE MAYOR TO HIRE POLICE?
THIS IS A FIRST, I'LL ADMIT. YOUR UNCLE RECOMMENDED YOU TO COUNCILMAN QUILLIN AND ME. SEE, WE HAVE A BIT OF A...
...SITUATION HERE IN LITTLE ROCK.
something I wanted to discuss in person.
YOU GREW UP HERE. YOU KNOW THE MAFIA'S HAD A PRESENCE DOWN IN HOT SPRINGS EVER SINCE CAPONE STARTED VACATIONING THERE.
WELL, OUR CITY ISN'T IMMUNE, EITHER.
THE MOB HAS STARTED UP GAMBLING PARLORS—DENS OF EVERY KIND OF VICE—OPERATING JUST OUT OF SIGHT. I APPOINTED COUNCILMAN QUILLIN HERE TO HEAD UP A TASK FORCE.
YOU'RE WORKING WITH THE POLICE DEPARTMENT?
WELL, HERE'S THE RUB—
CHIEF DOBBS IS ABOUT FIVE YEARS OVERDUE FOR RETIREMENT. HE CAN BARELY STAY AWAKE, LET ALONE TACKLE ORGANIZED CRIME.
FOR ALL INTENTS AND PURPOSES, ABRAHAM BAILEY—THE CHIEF OF DETECTIVES—RUNS THE PRECINCT.
SO HE'S YOUR POINT MAN?
HA!
GUESS YOU HAVEN'T MET BAILEY YET. HE'S A RELIC, RIGHT OUT OF A WILD WEST PICTURE.
HE DOESN'T SEE ANY PROBLEM THAT CAN'T BE SOLVED WITH A BULLET.

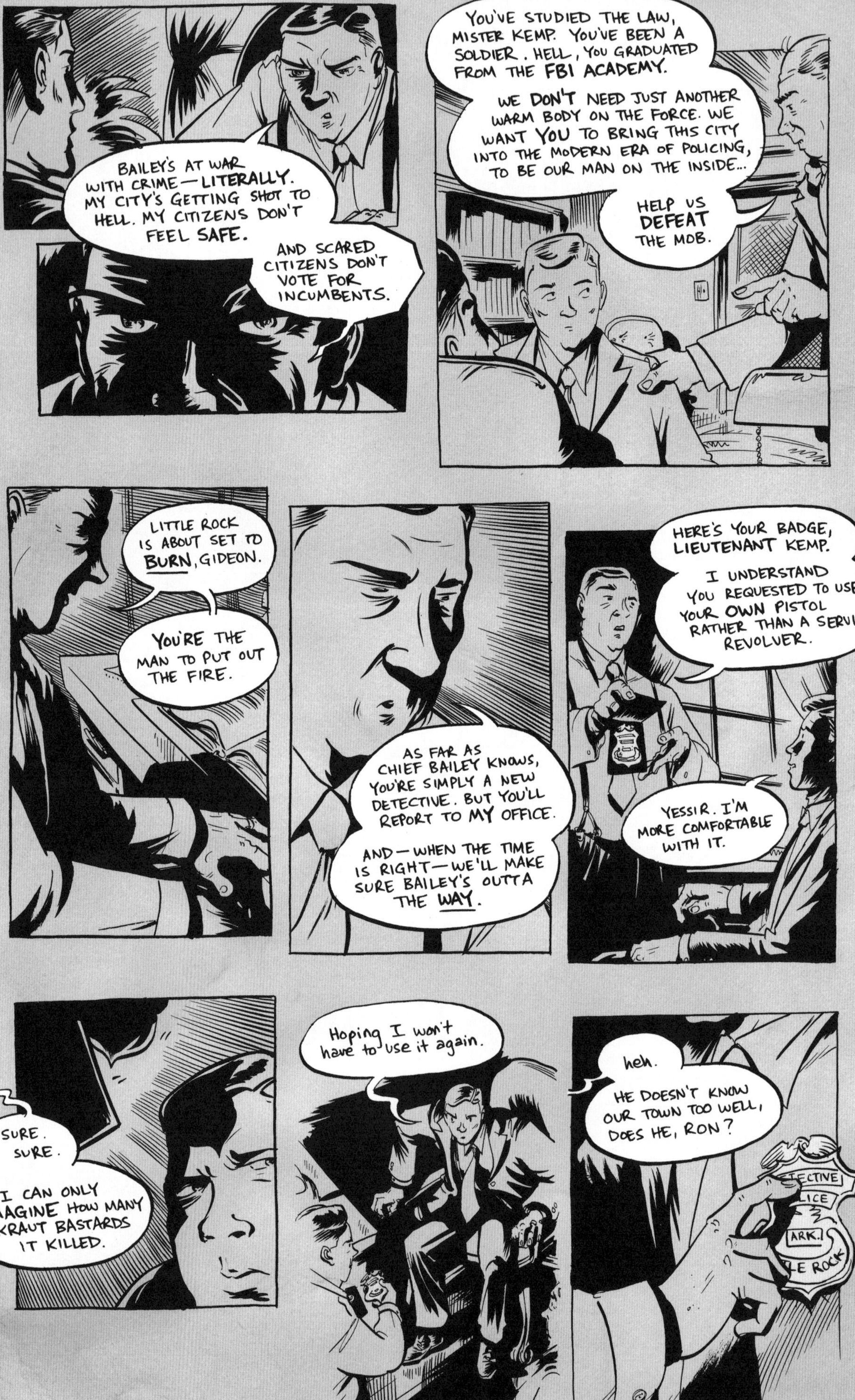
BAILEY'S AT WAR WITH CRIME—LITERALLY. MY CITY'S GETTING SHOT TO HELL. MY CITIZENS DON'T FEEL SAFE.
AND SCARED CITIZENS DON'T VOTE FOR INCUMBENTS.
YOU'VE STUDIED THE LAW, MISTER KEMP. YOU'VE BEEN A SOLDIER. HELL, YOU GRADUATED FROM THE FBI ACADEMY.
WE DON'T NEED JUST ANOTHER WARM BODY ON THE FORCE. WE WANT YOU TO BRING THIS CITY INTO THE MODERN ERA OF POLICING, TO BE OUR MAN ON THE INSIDE...
HELP US DEFEAT THE MOB.
LITTLE ROCK IS ABOUT SET TO BURN, GIDEON.
YOU'RE THE MAN TO PUT OUT THE FIRE.
AS FAR AS CHIEF BAILEY KNOWS, YOU'RE SIMPLY A NEW DETECTIVE. BUT YOU'LL REPORT TO MY OFFICE.
AND—WHEN THE TIME IS RIGHT—WE'LL MAKE SURE BAILEY'S OUTTA THE WAY.
HERE'S YOUR BADGE, LIEUTENANT KEMP.
I UNDERSTAND YOU REQUESTED TO USE YOUR OWN PISTOL RATHER THAN A SERVICE REVOLVER.
YESSIR. I'M MORE COMFORTABLE WITH IT.
SURE. SURE.
I CAN ONLY IMAGINE HOW MANY KRAUT BASTARDS IT KILLED.
Hoping I won't have to use it again.
heh.
HE DOESN'T KNOW OUR TOWN TOO WELL, DOES HE, RON?
ARK.

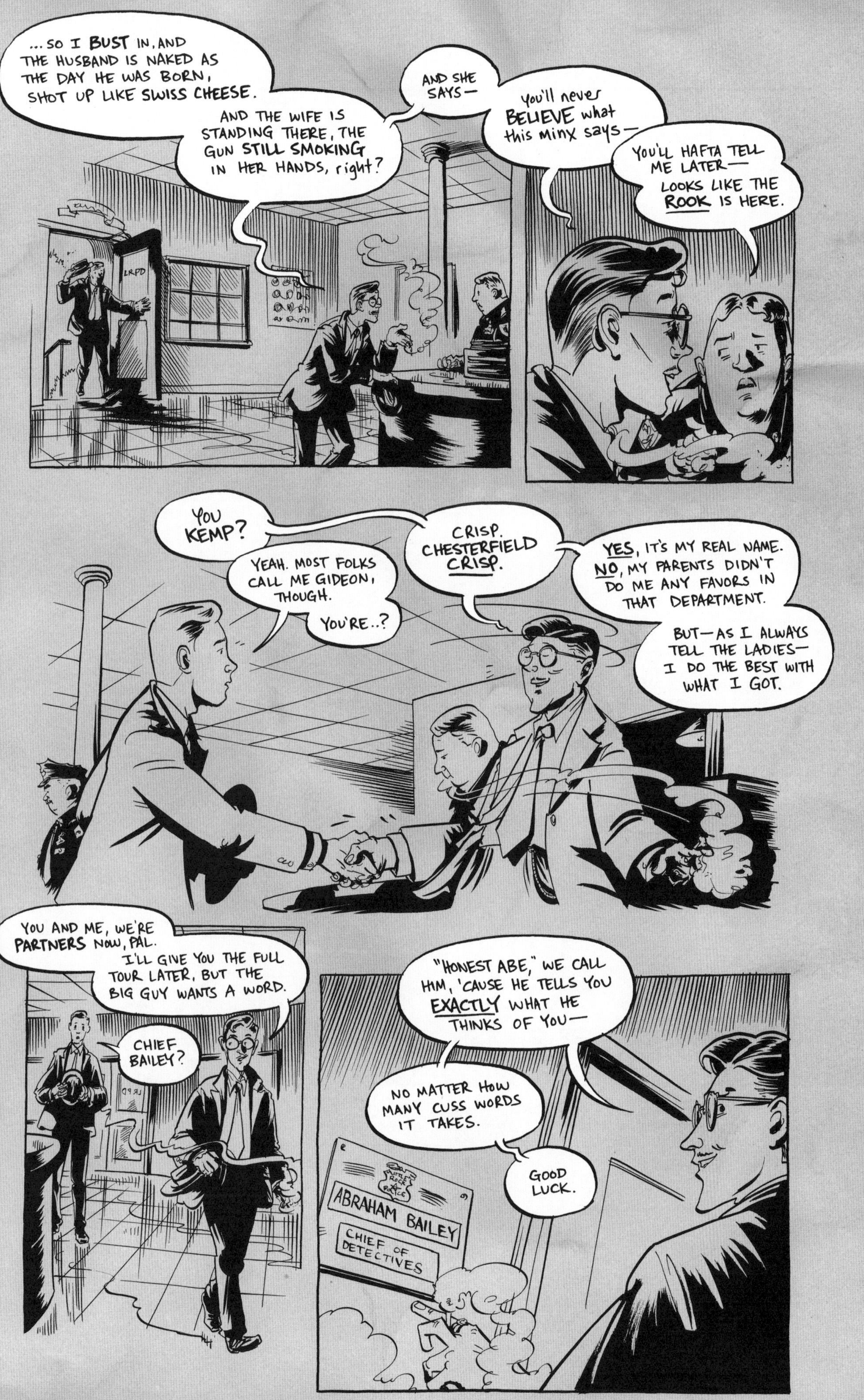
...SO I BUST IN, AND THE HUSBAND IS NAKED AS THE DAY HE WAS BORN, SHOT UP LIKE SWISS CHEESE.
AND THE WIFE IS STANDING THERE, THE GUN STILL SMOKING IN HER HANDS, right?
AND SHE SAYS—
You'll never BELIEVE what this minx says—
YOU'LL HAFTA TELL ME LATER—
LOOKS LIKE THE ROOK IS HERE.
LRPD
YOU KEMP?
YEAH. MOST FOLKS CALL ME GIDEON, THOUGH.
YOU'RE..?
CRISP. CHESTERFIELD CRISP.
YES, IT'S MY REAL NAME. NO, MY PARENTS DIDN'T DO ME ANY FAVORS IN THAT DEPARTMENT.
BUT—AS I ALWAYS TELL THE LADIES—I DO THE BEST WITH WHAT I GOT.
YOU AND ME, WE'RE PARTNERS NOW, PAL.
I'LL GIVE YOU THE FULL TOUR LATER, BUT THE BIG GUY WANTS A WORD.
CHIEF BAILEY?
LRPD
"HONEST ABE," WE CALL HIM, 'CAUSE HE TELLS YOU EXACTLY WHAT HE THINKS OF YOU—
NO MATTER HOW MANY CUSS WORDS IT TAKES.
GOOD LUCK.
ABRAHAM BAILEY
CHIEF OF DETECTIVES

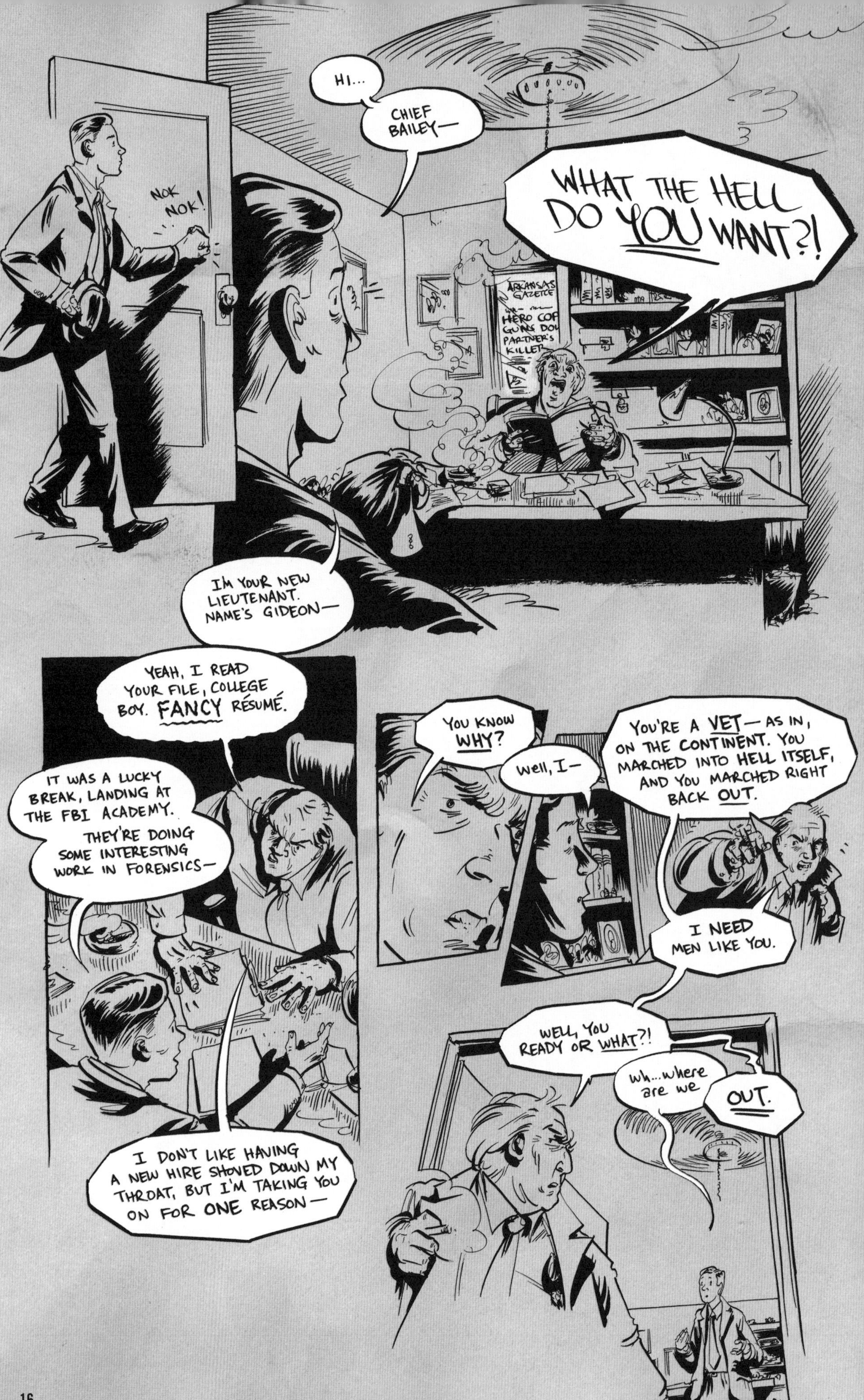
NOK NOK!
HI...
CHIEF BAILEY—
WHAT THE HELL DO YOU WANT?!
ARKANSAS GAZETTE
HERO COP GUNS DOWN PARTNER'S KILLER
I'M YOUR NEW LIEUTENANT. NAME'S GIDEON—
YEAH, I READ YOUR FILE, COLLEGE BOY. FANCY RÉSUMÉ.
IT WAS A LUCKY BREAK, LANDING AT THE FBI ACADEMY.
THEY'RE DOING SOME INTERESTING WORK IN FORENSICS—
I DON'T LIKE HAVING A NEW HIRE SHOVED DOWN MY THROAT, BUT I'M TAKING YOU ON FOR ONE REASON—
YOU KNOW WHY?
Well, I—
YOU'RE A VET—AS IN, ON THE CONTINENT. YOU MARCHED INTO HELL ITSELF, AND YOU MARCHED RIGHT BACK OUT.
I NEED MEN LIKE YOU.
WELL, YOU READY OR WHAT?!
wh...where are we
OUT.

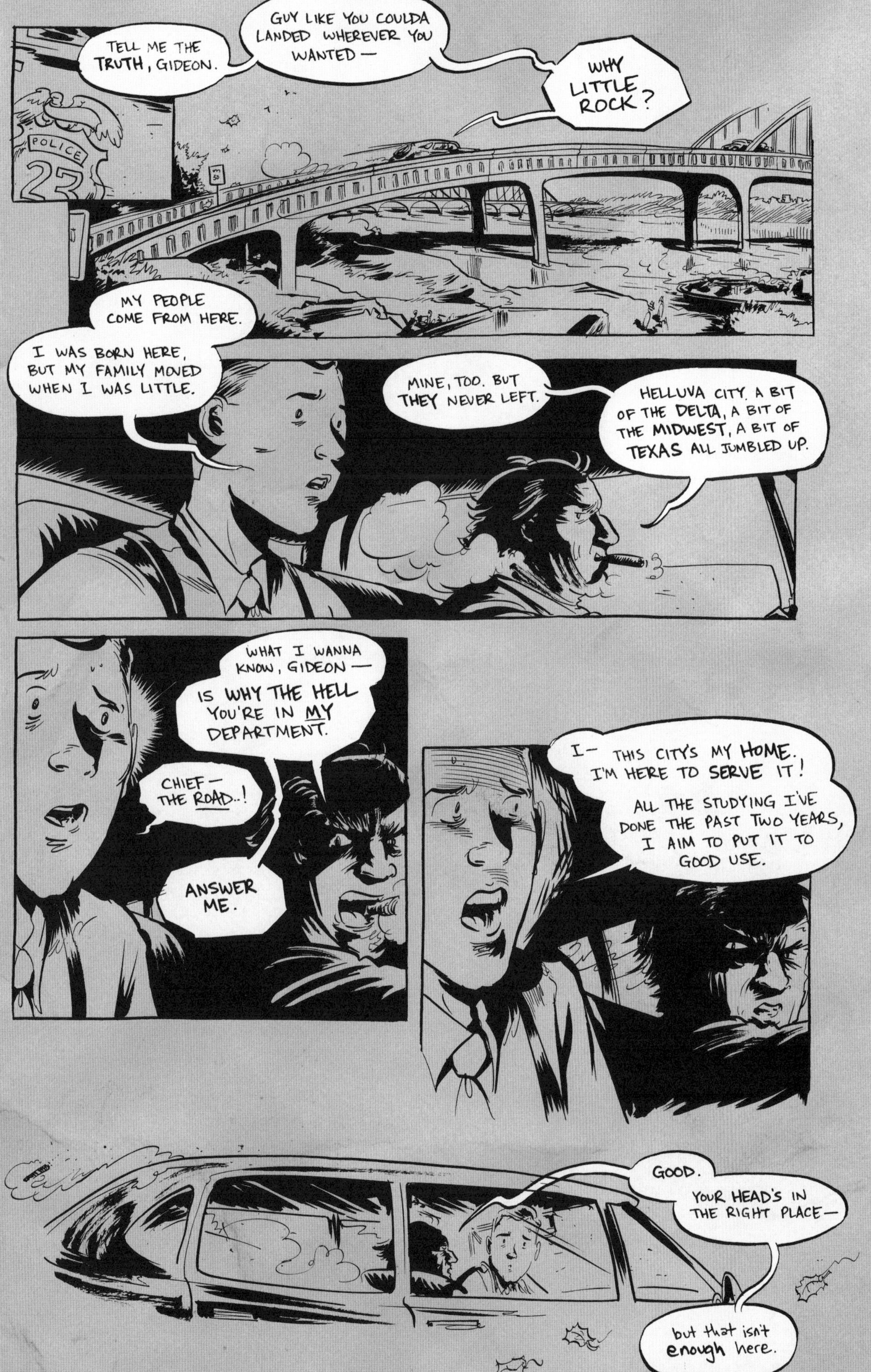
TELL ME THE TRUTH, GIDEON.
GUY LIKE YOU COULDA LANDED WHEREVER YOU WANTED—
WHY LITTLE ROCK?
POLICE
23
MY PEOPLE COME FROM HERE.
I WAS BORN HERE, BUT MY FAMILY MOVED WHEN I WAS LITTLE.
MINE, TOO. BUT THEY NEVER LEFT.
HELLUVA CITY. A BIT OF THE DELTA, A BIT OF THE MIDWEST, A BIT OF TEXAS ALL JUMBLED UP.
WHAT I WANNA KNOW, GIDEON—
IS WHY THE HELL YOU'RE IN MY DEPARTMENT.
CHIEF— THE ROAD..!
ANSWER ME.
I— THIS CITY'S MY HOME. I'M HERE TO SERVE IT!
ALL THE STUDYING I'VE DONE THE PAST TWO YEARS, I AIM TO PUT IT TO GOOD USE.
GOOD.
YOUR HEAD'S IN THE RIGHT PLACE—
but that isn't enough here.

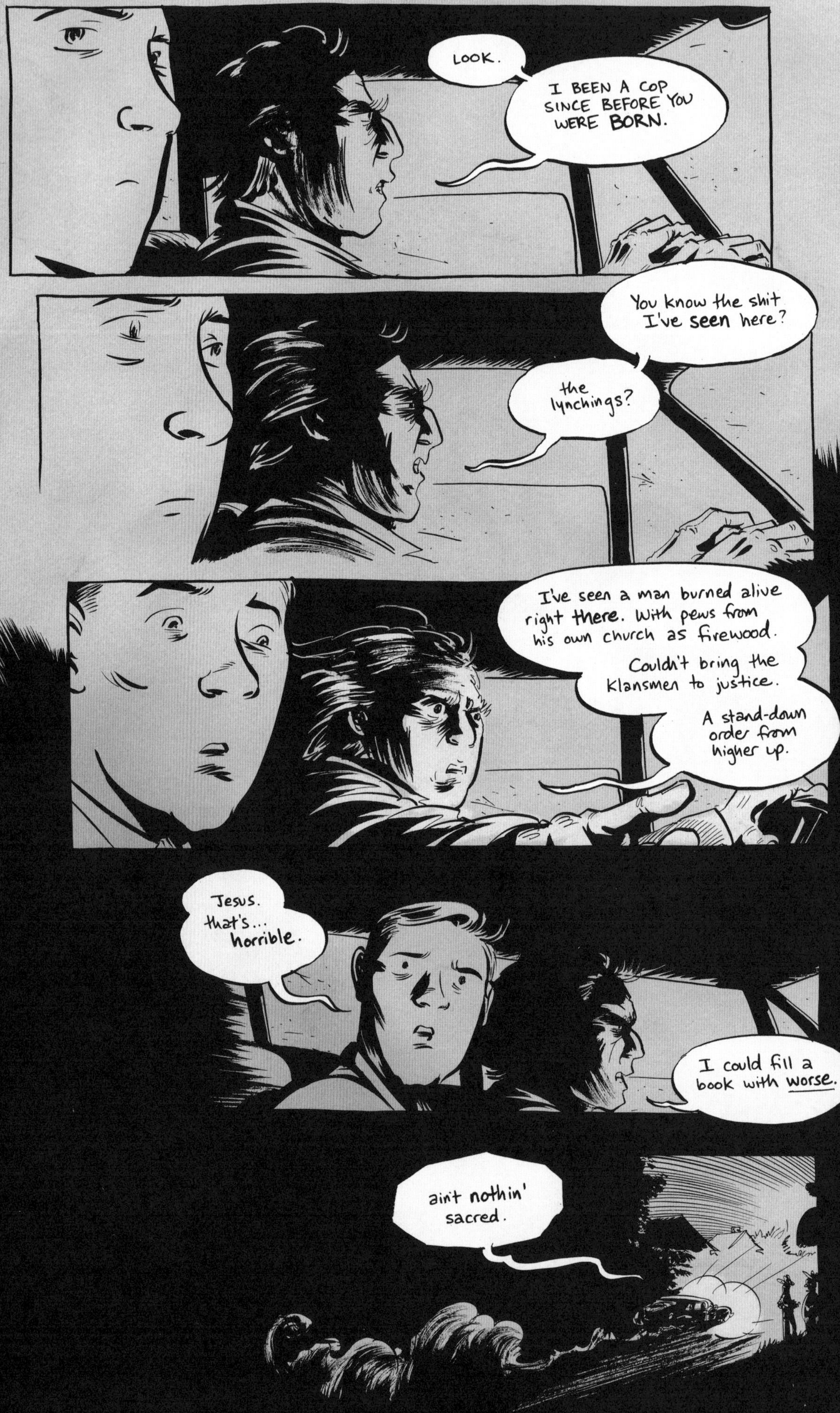
LOOK.
I BEEN A COP SINCE BEFORE YOU WERE BORN.
You know the shit I've seen here?
the lynchings?
I've seen a man burned alive right there. With pews from his own church as firewood.
Couldn't bring the Klansmen to justice.
A stand-down order from higher up.
Jesus. that's... horrible.
I could fill a book with worse.
ain't nothin' sacred.

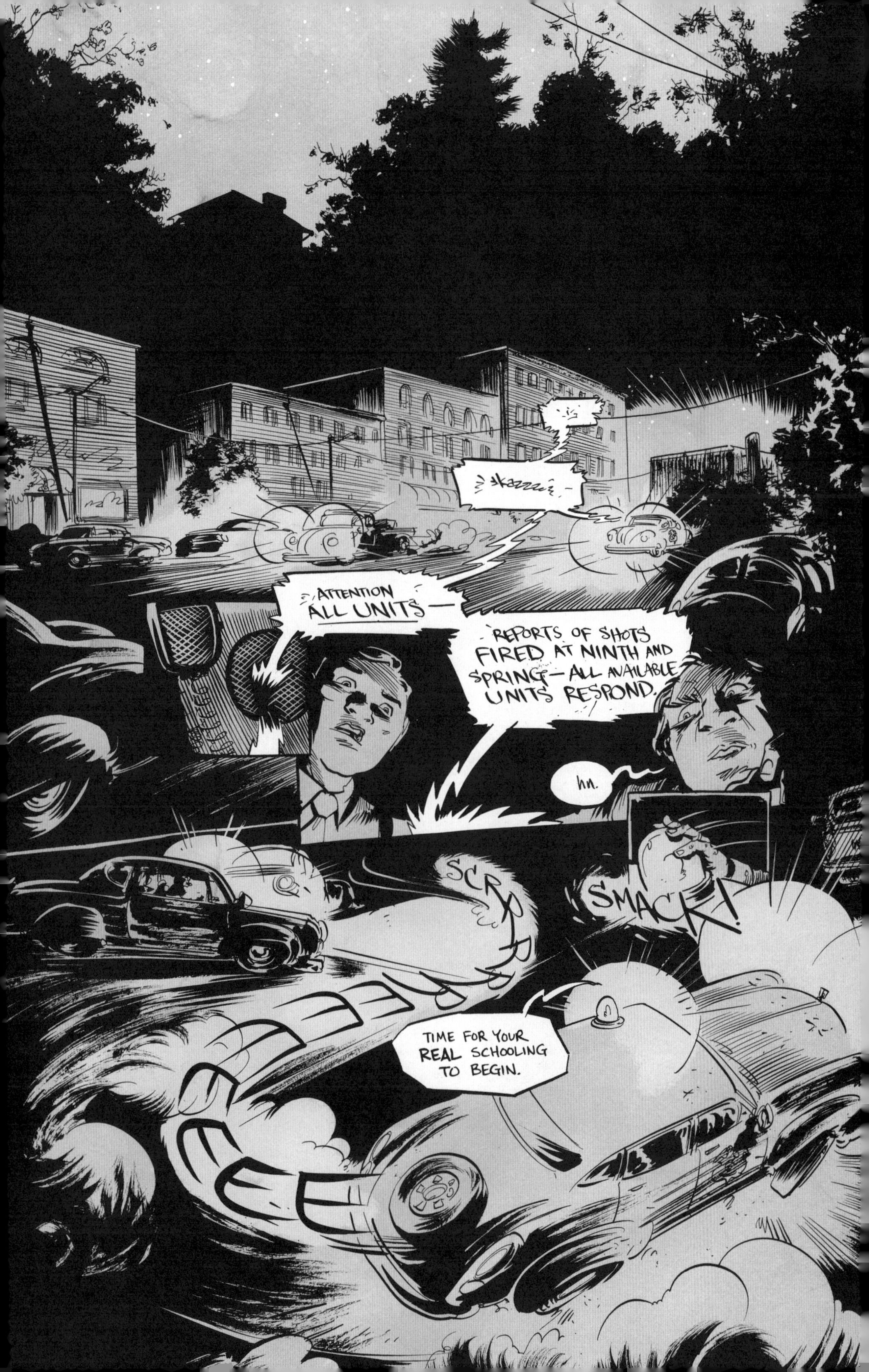

skzzzz
ATTENTION ALL UNITS—
REPORTS OF SHOTS FIRED AT NINTH AND SPRING—ALL AVAILABLE UNITS RESPOND.
hn.
SCRRR
SMACK!
TIME FOR YOUR REAL SCHOOLING TO BEGIN.

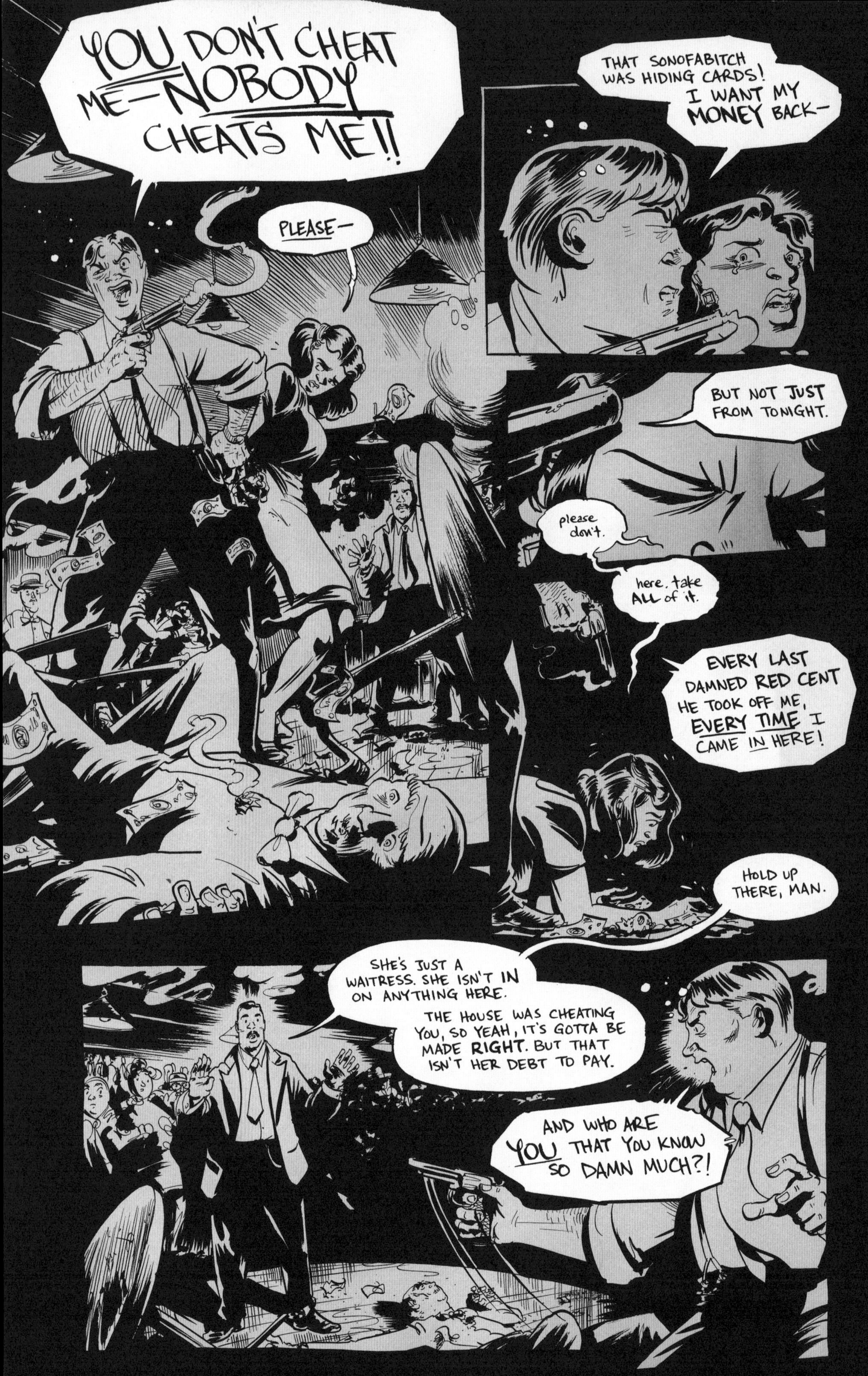
YOU DON'T CHEAT ME—NOBODY CHEATS ME!!
PLEASE—
THAT SONOFABITCH WAS HIDING CARDS! I WANT MY MONEY BACK—
BUT NOT JUST FROM TONIGHT.
please don't.
here. take ALL of it.
EVERY LAST DAMNED RED CENT HE TOOK OFF ME, EVERY TIME I CAME IN HERE!
HOLD UP THERE, MAN.
SHE'S JUST A WAITRESS. SHE ISN'T IN ON ANYTHING HERE.
THE HOUSE WAS CHEATING YOU, SO YEAH, IT'S GOTTA BE MADE RIGHT. BUT THAT ISN'T HER DEBT TO PAY.
AND WHO ARE YOU THAT YOU KNOW SO DAMN MUCH?!

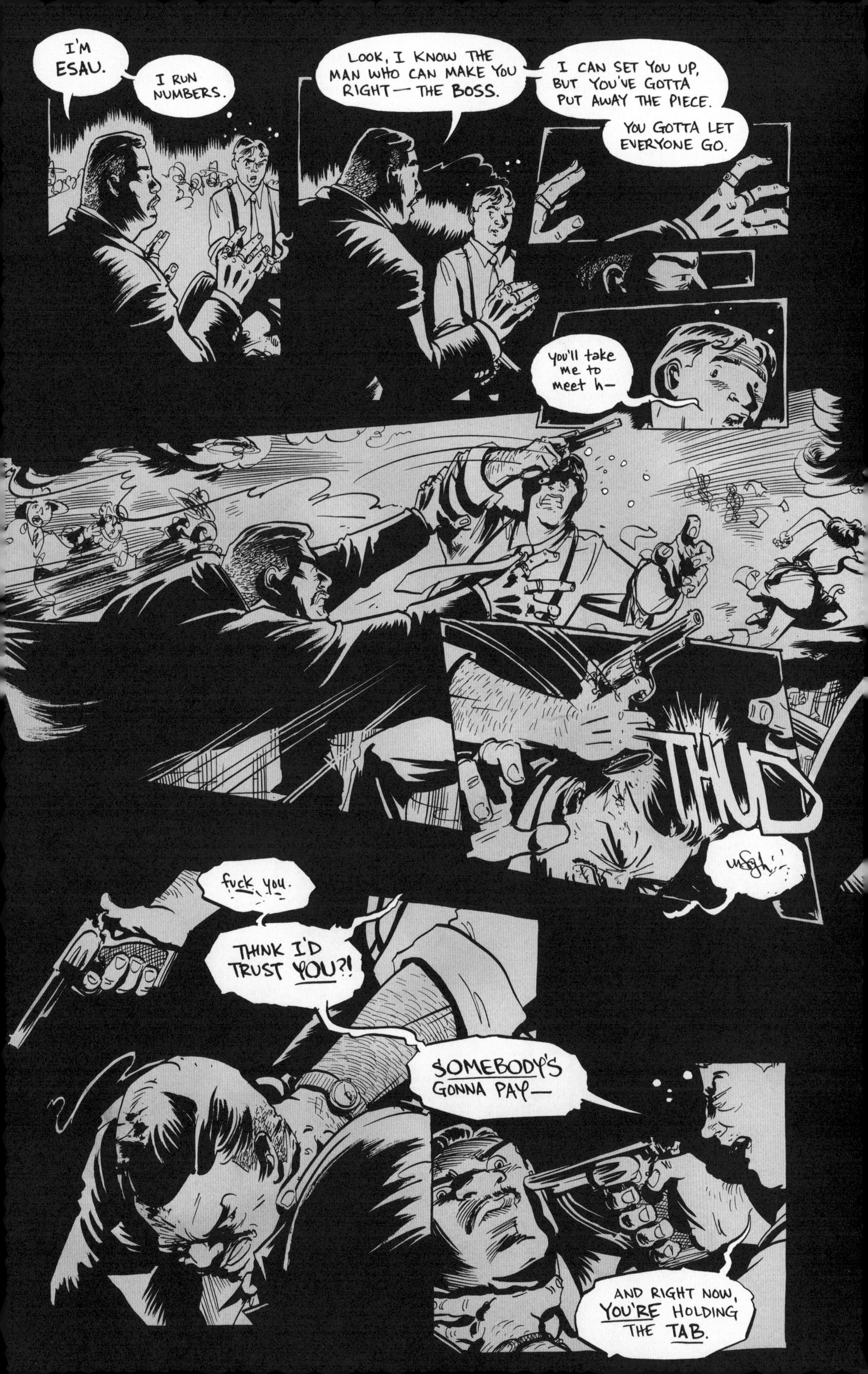

I'M ESAU.
I RUN NUMBERS.
LOOK, I KNOW THE MAN WHO CAN MAKE YOU RIGHT— THE BOSS.
I CAN SET YOU UP, BUT YOU'VE GOTTA PUT AWAY THE PIECE.
YOU GOTTA LET EVERYONE GO.
you'll take me to meet h—
THUD
fuck you.
THINK I'D TRUST YOU?!
SOMEBODY'S GONNA PAY—
AND RIGHT NOW, YOU'RE HOLDING THE TAB.

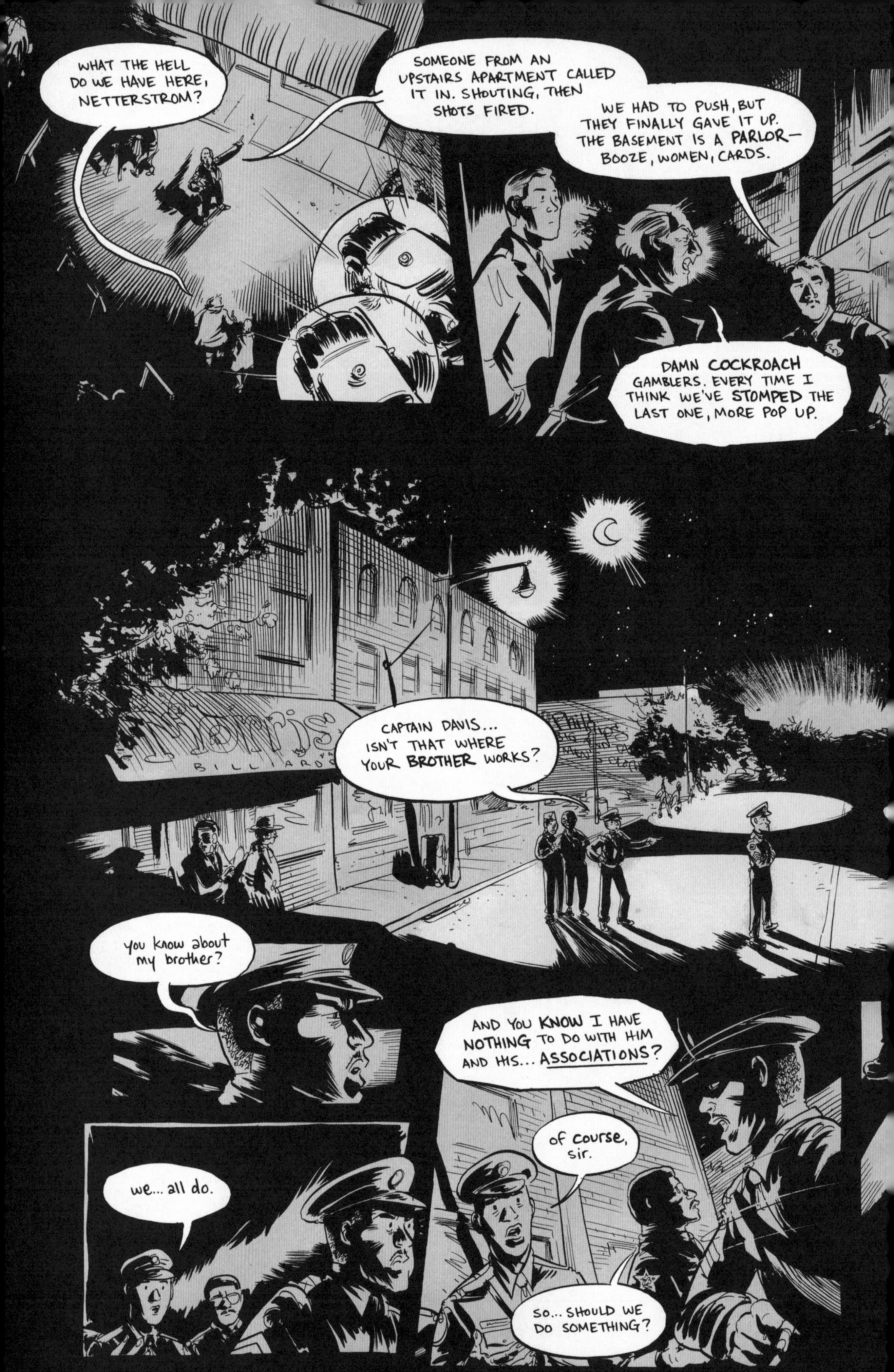
WHAT THE HELL DO WE HAVE HERE, NETTERSTROM?
SOMEONE FROM AN UPSTAIRS APARTMENT CALLED IT IN. SHOUTING, THEN SHOTS FIRED.
WE HAD TO PUSH, BUT THEY FINALLY GAVE IT UP. THE BASEMENT IS A PARLOR— BOOZE, WOMEN, CARDS.
DAMN COCKROACH GAMBLERS. EVERY TIME I THINK WE'VE STOMPED THE LAST ONE, MORE POP UP.
BILLIARDS
CAPTAIN DAVIS... ISN'T THAT WHERE YOUR BROTHER WORKS?
you know about my brother?
AND YOU KNOW I HAVE NOTHING TO DO WITH HIM AND HIS... ASSOCIATIONS?
we... all do.
of course, sir.
SO... SHOULD WE DO SOMETHING?

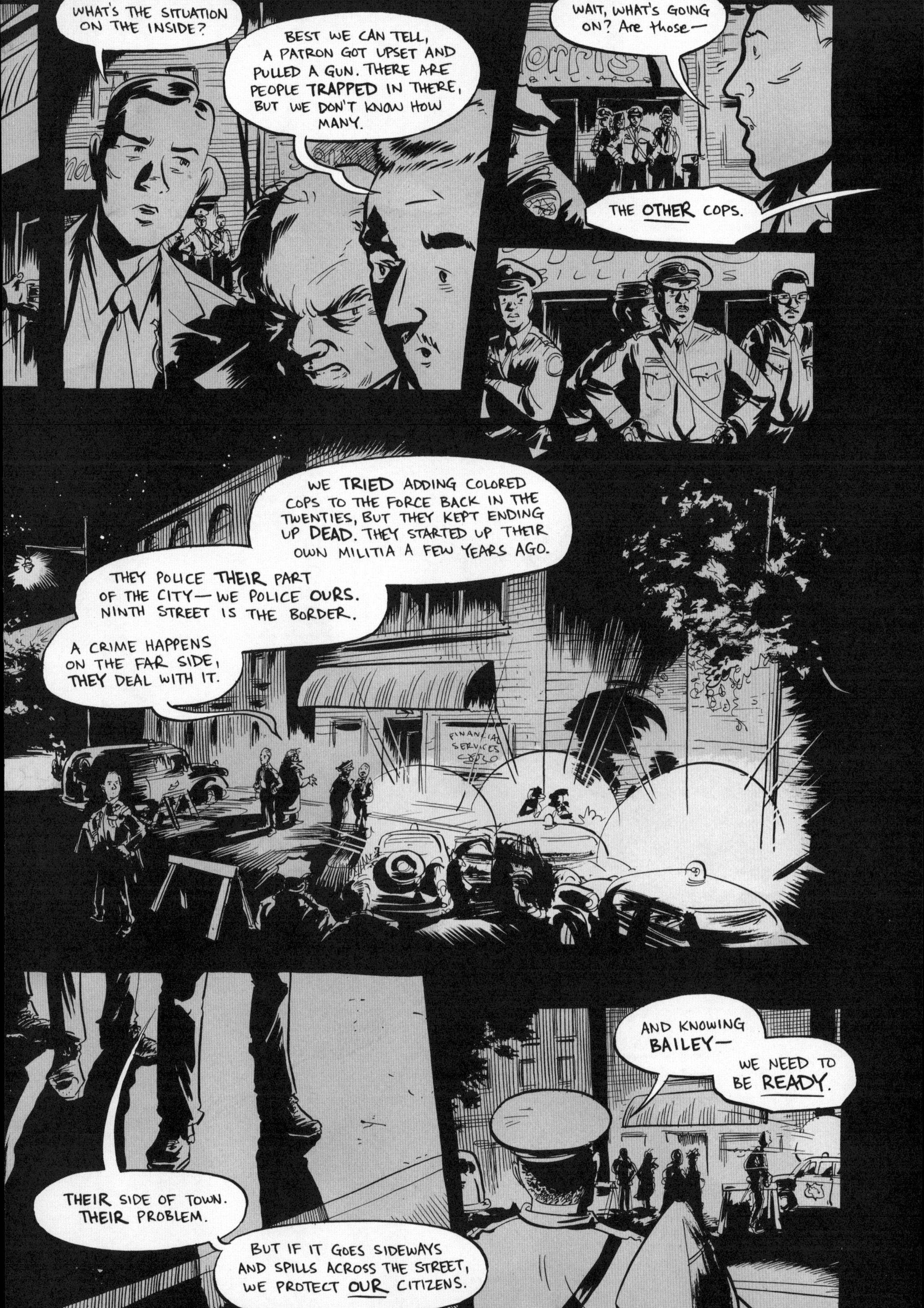
WHAT'S THE SITUATION ON THE INSIDE?
BEST WE CAN TELL, A PATRON GOT UPSET AND PULLED A GUN. THERE ARE PEOPLE TRAPPED IN THERE, BUT WE DON'T KNOW HOW MANY.
WAIT, WHAT'S GOING ON? Are those—
THE OTHER COPS.
WE TRIED ADDING COLORED COPS TO THE FORCE BACK IN THE TWENTIES, BUT THEY KEPT ENDING UP DEAD. THEY STARTED UP THEIR OWN MILITIA A FEW YEARS AGO.
THEY POLICE THEIR PART OF THE CITY— WE POLICE OURS. NINTH STREET IS THE BORDER.
A CRIME HAPPENS ON THE FAR SIDE, THEY DEAL WITH IT.
THEIR SIDE OF TOWN. THEIR PROBLEM.
BUT IF IT GOES SIDEWAYS AND SPILLS ACROSS THE STREET, WE PROTECT OUR CITIZENS.
AND KNOWING BAILEY—
WE NEED TO BE READY.

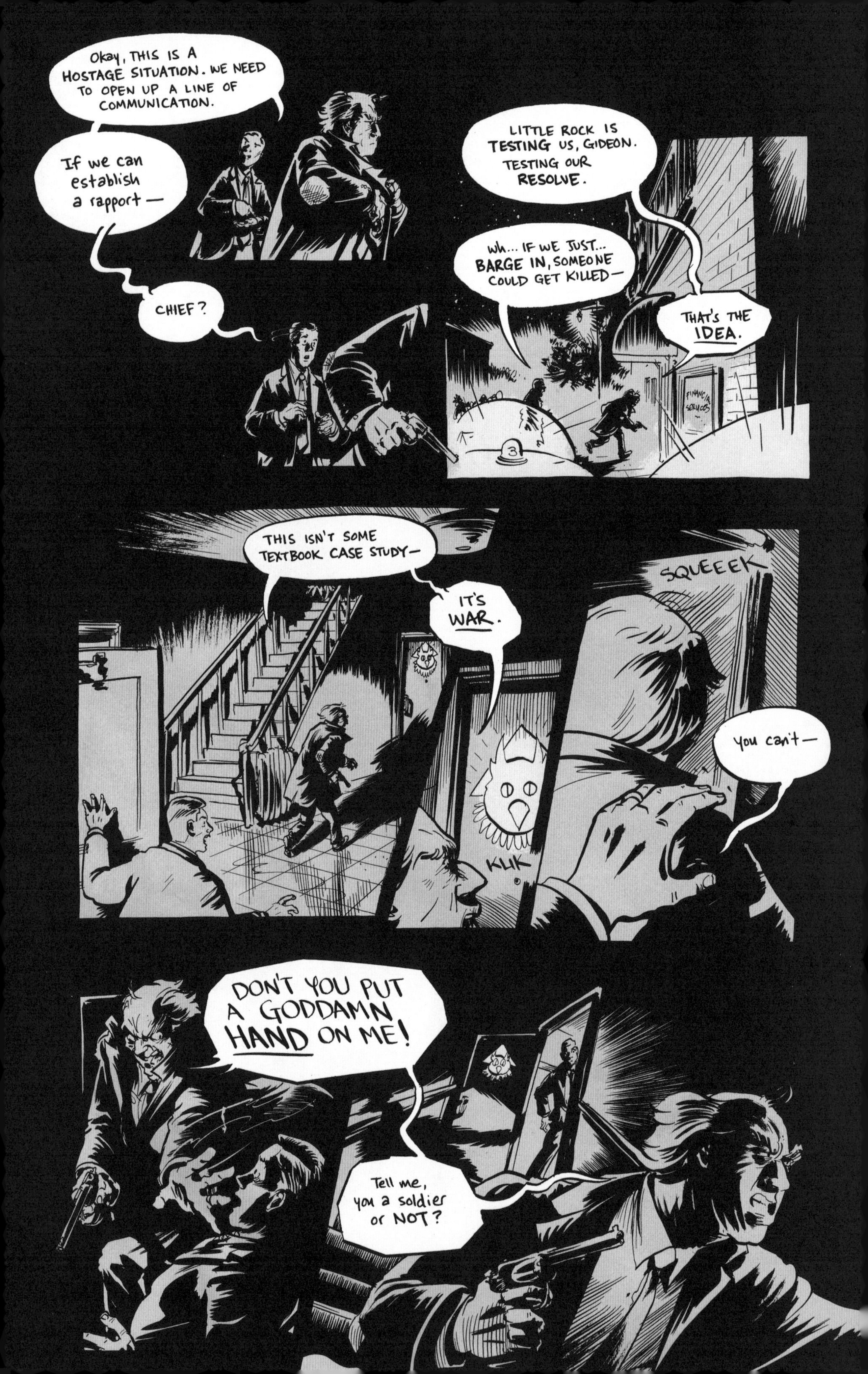
Okay, THIS IS A HOSTAGE SITUATION. WE NEED TO OPEN UP A LINE OF COMMUNICATION.
If we can establish a rapport —
CHIEF?
LITTLE ROCK IS TESTING US, GIDEON. TESTING OUR RESOLVE.
Wh... IF WE JUST... BARGE IN, SOMEONE COULD GET KILLED—
THAT'S THE IDEA.
FINANCIAL SERVICES
THIS ISN'T SOME TEXTBOOK CASE STUDY—
IT'S WAR.
SQUEEEK
KLIK
You can't—
DON'T YOU PUT A GODDAMN HAND ON ME!
Tell me, you a soldier or NOT?

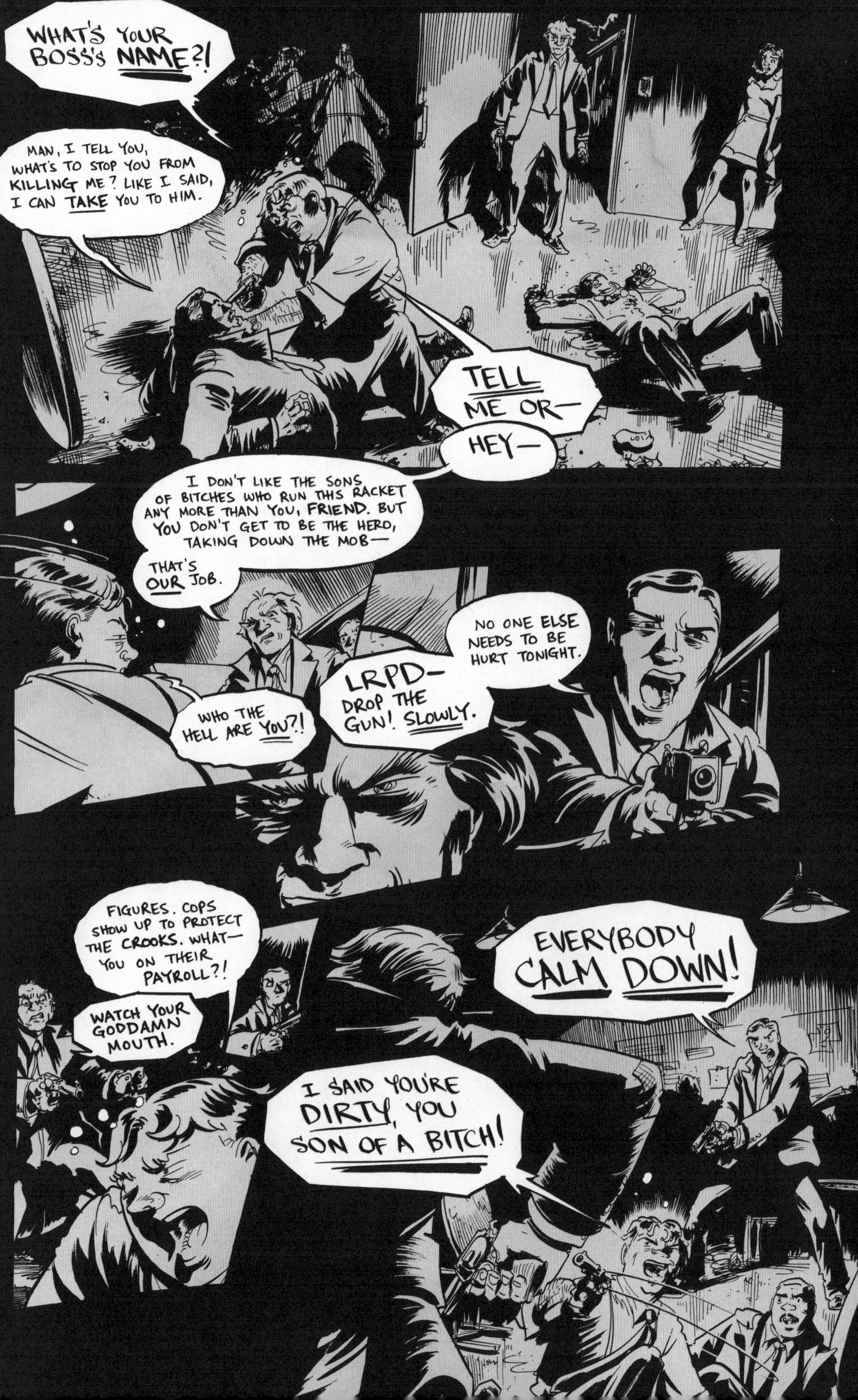
WHAT'S YOUR BOSS'S NAME?!
MAN, I TELL YOU, WHAT'S TO STOP YOU FROM KILLING ME? LIKE I SAID, I CAN TAKE YOU TO HIM.
TELL ME OR—
HEY—
I DON'T LIKE THE SONS OF BITCHES WHO RUN THIS RACKET ANY MORE THAN YOU, FRIEND. BUT YOU DON'T GET TO BE THE HERO, TAKING DOWN THE MOB—
THAT'S OUR JOB.
WHO THE HELL ARE YOU?!
LRPD— DROP THE GUN! SLOWLY.
NO ONE ELSE NEEDS TO BE HURT TONIGHT.
FIGURES. COPS SHOW UP TO PROTECT THE CROOKS. WHAT— YOU ON THEIR PAYROLL?!
WATCH YOUR GODDAMN MOUTH.
EVERYBODY CALM DOWN!
I SAID YOU'RE DIRTY, YOU SON OF A BITCH!

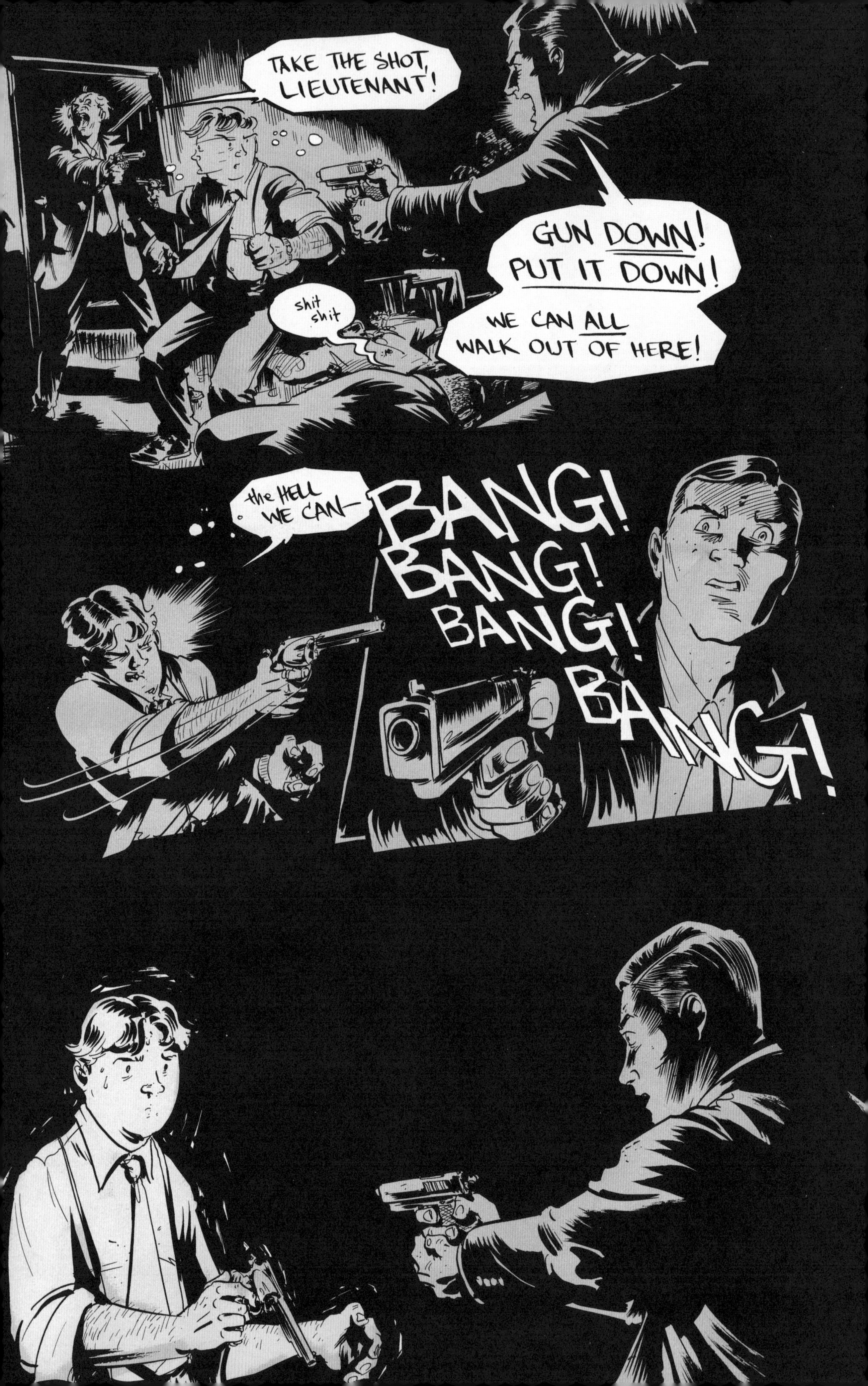
TAKE THE SHOT, LIEUTENANT!
GUN DOWN! PUT IT DOWN!
WE CAN ALL WALK OUT OF HERE!
shit shit
the HELL WE CAN—
BANG! BANG! BANG! BANG!

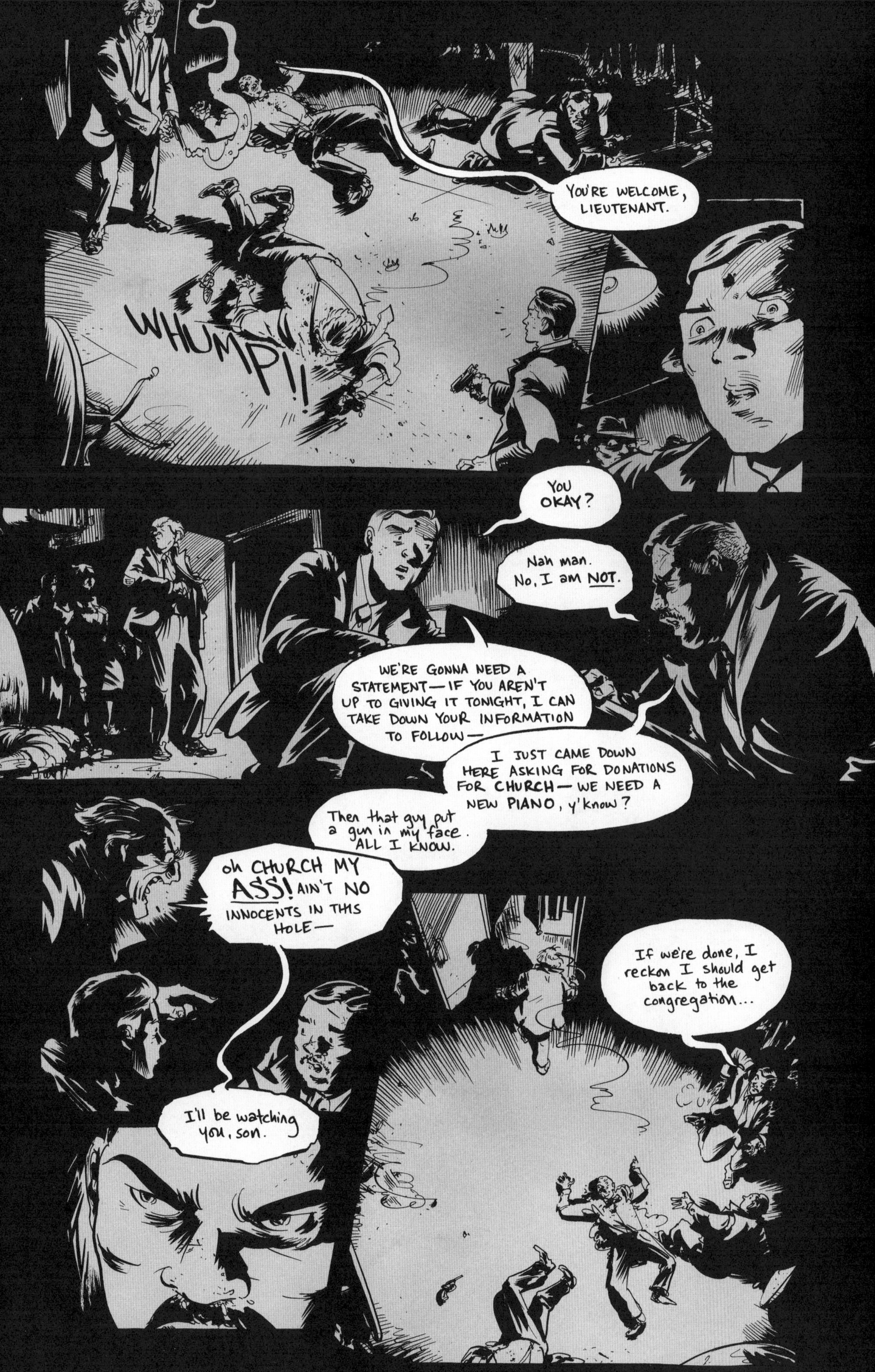
YOU'RE WELCOME, LIEUTENANT.
WHUMP!!
YOU OKAY?
Nah man. No, I am NOT.
WE'RE GONNA NEED A STATEMENT— IF YOU AREN'T UP TO GIVING IT TONIGHT, I CAN TAKE DOWN YOUR INFORMATION TO FOLLOW—
I JUST CAME DOWN HERE ASKING FOR DONATIONS FOR CHURCH— WE NEED A NEW PIANO, y'know?
Then that guy put a gun in my face. ALL I KNOW.
oh CHURCH MY ASS! AIN'T NO INNOCENTS IN THIS HOLE—
I'll be watching you, son.
If we're done, I reckon I should get back to the congregation...

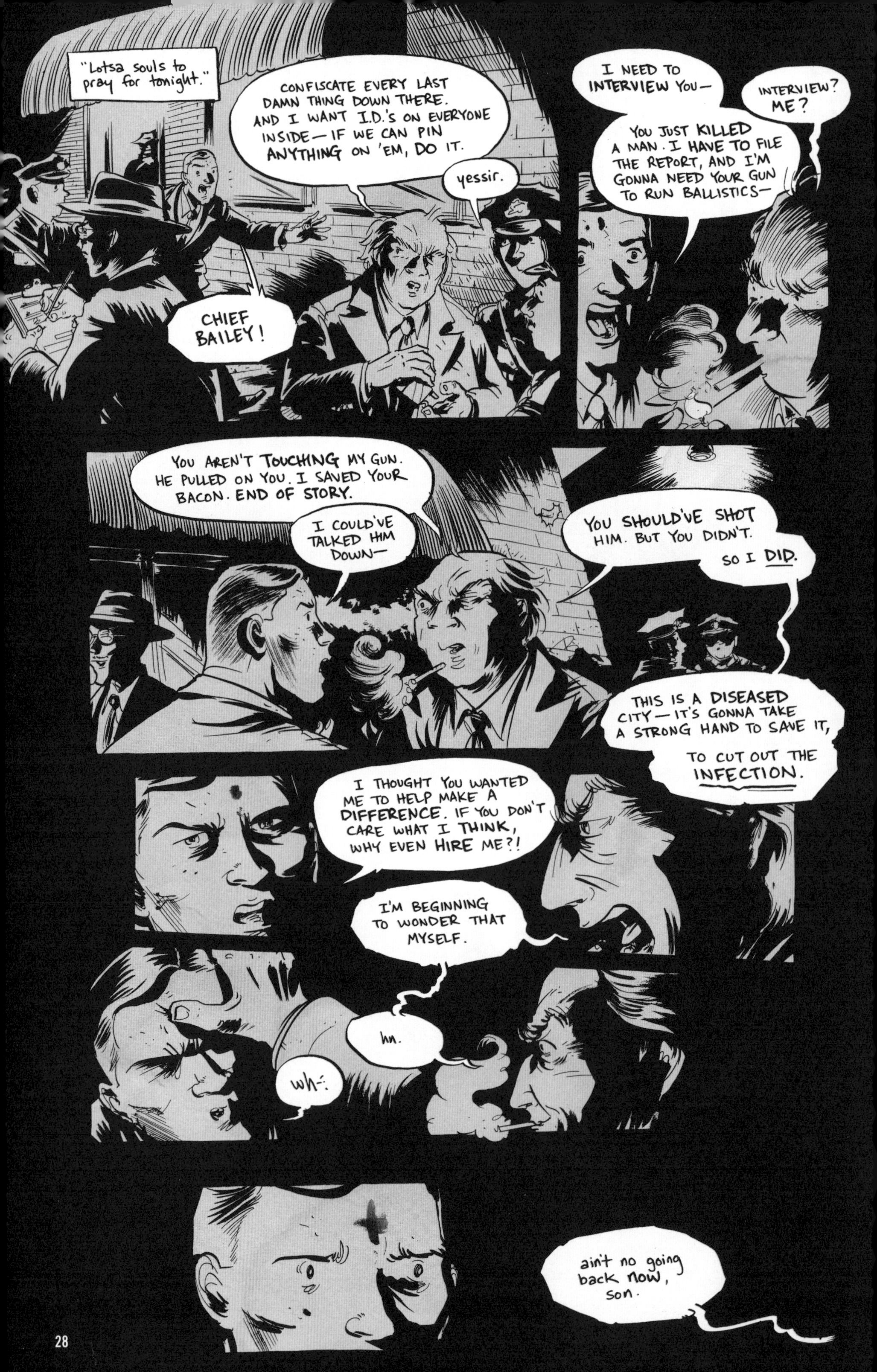
"Lotsa souls to pray for tonight."
CONFISCATE EVERY LAST DAMN THING DOWN THERE. AND I WANT I.D.'s ON EVERYONE INSIDE— IF WE CAN PIN ANYTHING ON 'EM, DO IT.
yessir.
CHIEF BAILEY!
I NEED TO INTERVIEW YOU—
INTERVIEW? ME?
YOU JUST KILLED A MAN. I HAVE TO FILE THE REPORT, AND I'M GONNA NEED YOUR GUN TO RUN BALLISTICS—
YOU AREN'T TOUCHING MY GUN. HE PULLED ON YOU. I SAVED YOUR BACON. END OF STORY.
I COULD'VE TALKED HIM DOWN—
YOU SHOULD'VE SHOT HIM. BUT YOU DIDN'T.
SO I DID.
THIS IS A DISEASED CITY— IT'S GONNA TAKE A STRONG HAND TO SAVE IT,
TO CUT OUT THE INFECTION.
I THOUGHT YOU WANTED ME TO HELP MAKE A DIFFERENCE. IF YOU DON'T CARE WHAT I THINK, WHY EVEN HIRE ME?!
I'M BEGINNING TO WONDER THAT MYSELF.
hn.
wh-:
ain't no going back now, son.

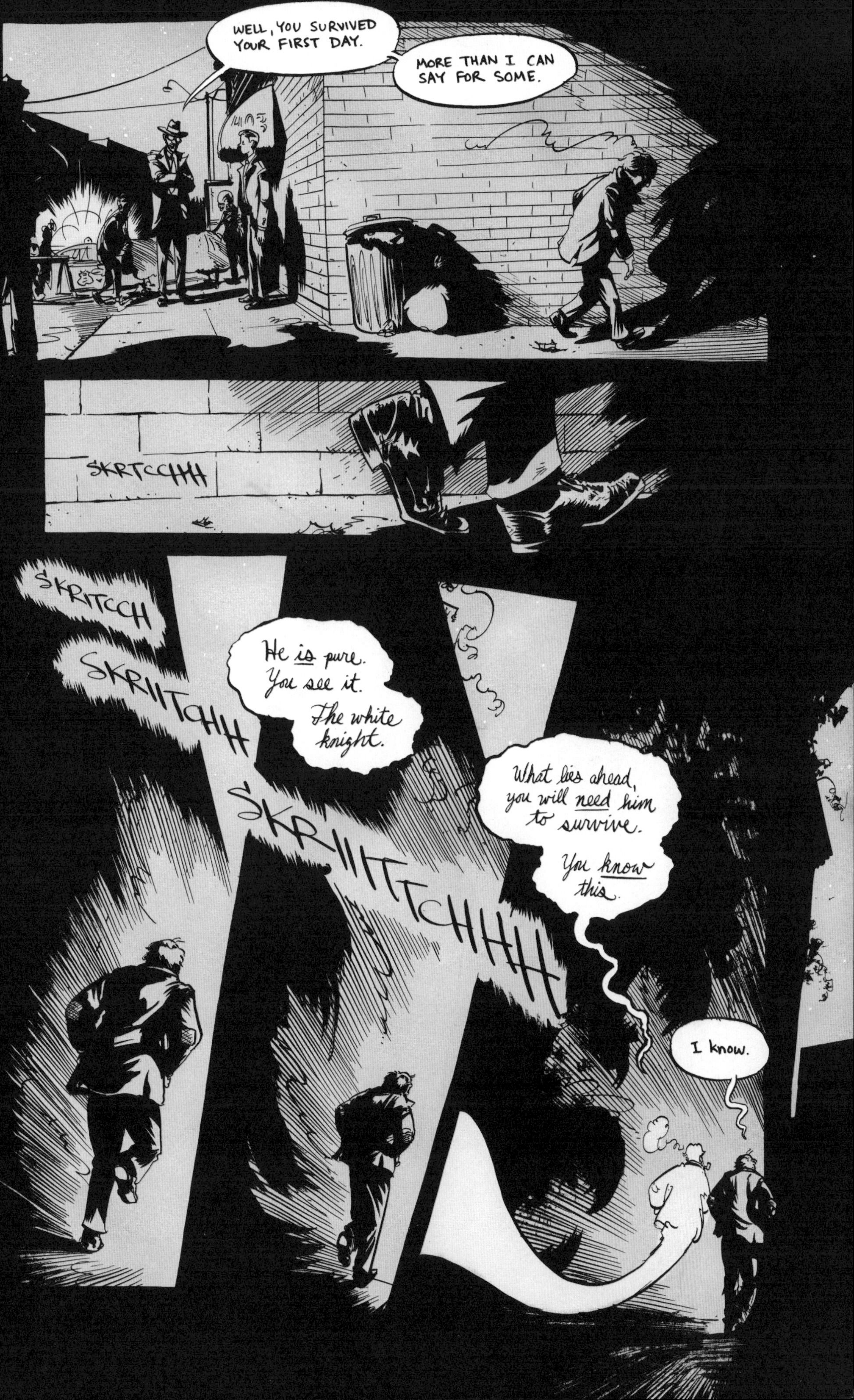
WELL, YOU SURVIVED YOUR FIRST DAY.
MORE THAN I CAN SAY FOR SOME.
SKRTCCHH
SKRITCCH
SKRIITCHH
He is pure. You see it. The white knight.
SKRIIITTCHHH
What lies ahead, you will need him to survive.
You know this.
I know.

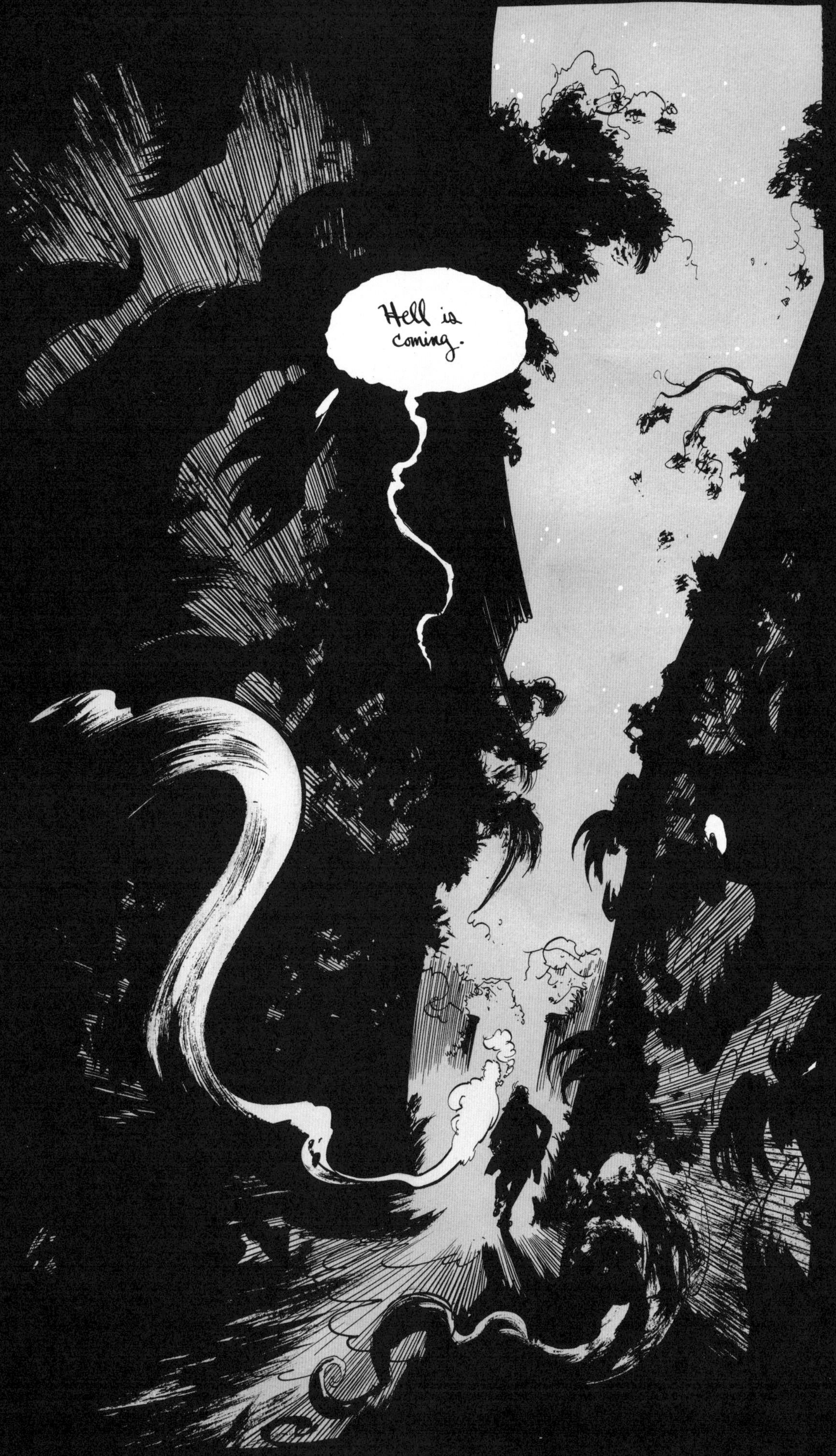
Hell is coming.

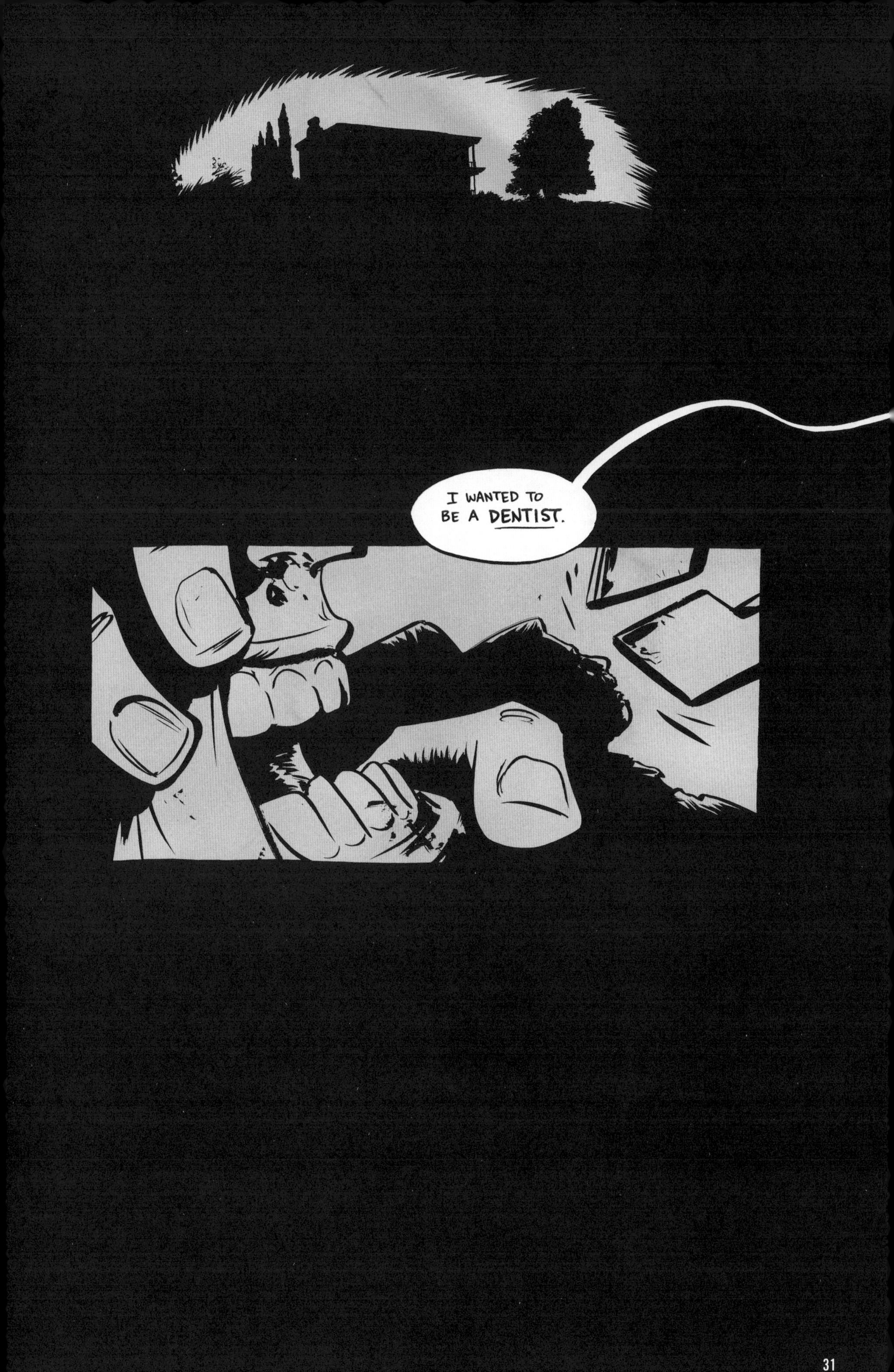
I WANTED TO BE A DENTIST.

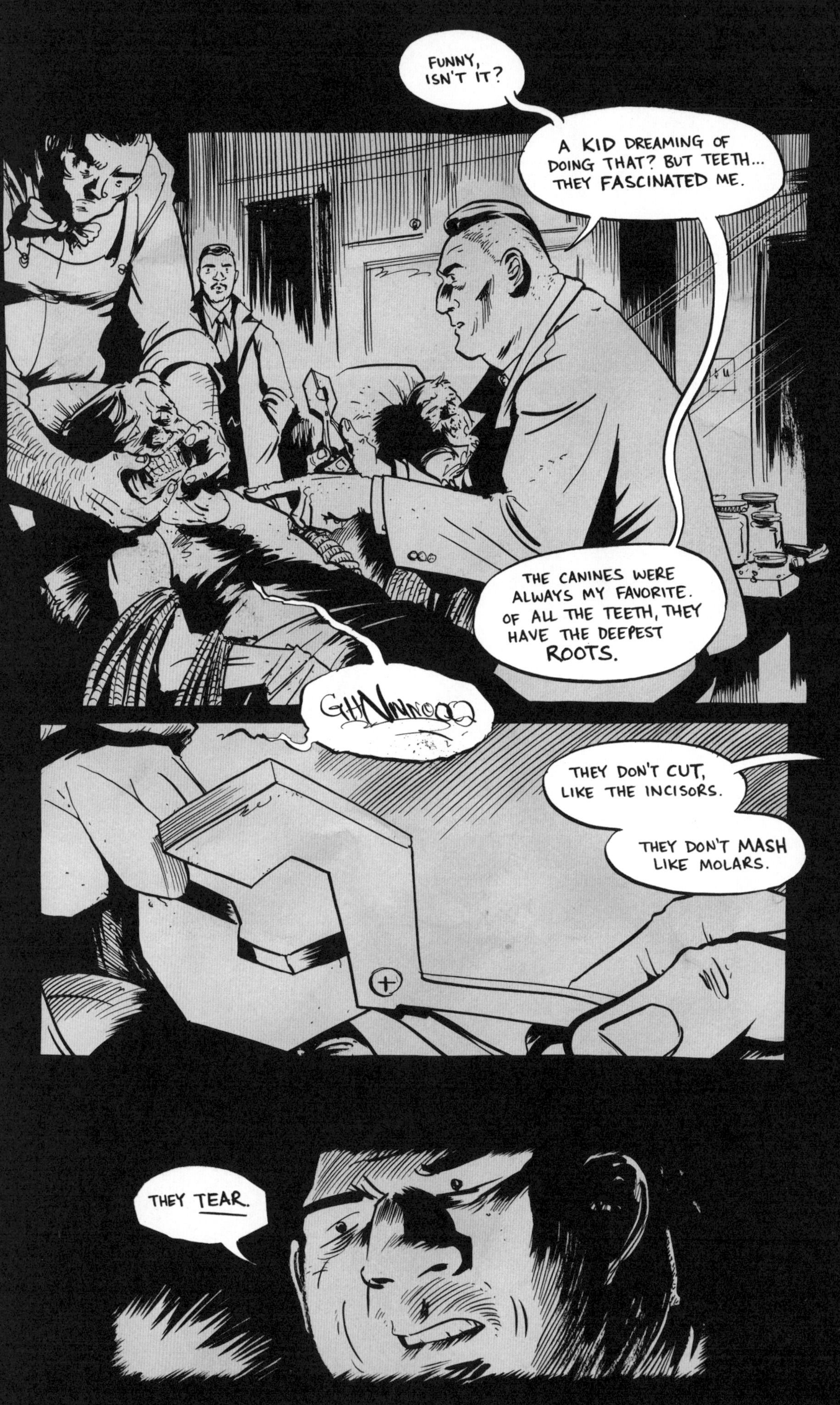
FUNNY, ISN'T IT?
A KID DREAMING OF DOING THAT? BUT TEETH... THEY FASCINATED ME.
THE CANINES WERE ALWAYS MY FAVORITE. OF ALL THE TEETH, THEY HAVE THE DEEPEST ROOTS.
GHNNNNOOO
THEY DON'T CUT, LIKE THE INCISORS.
THEY DON'T MASH LIKE MOLARS.
THEY TEAR.

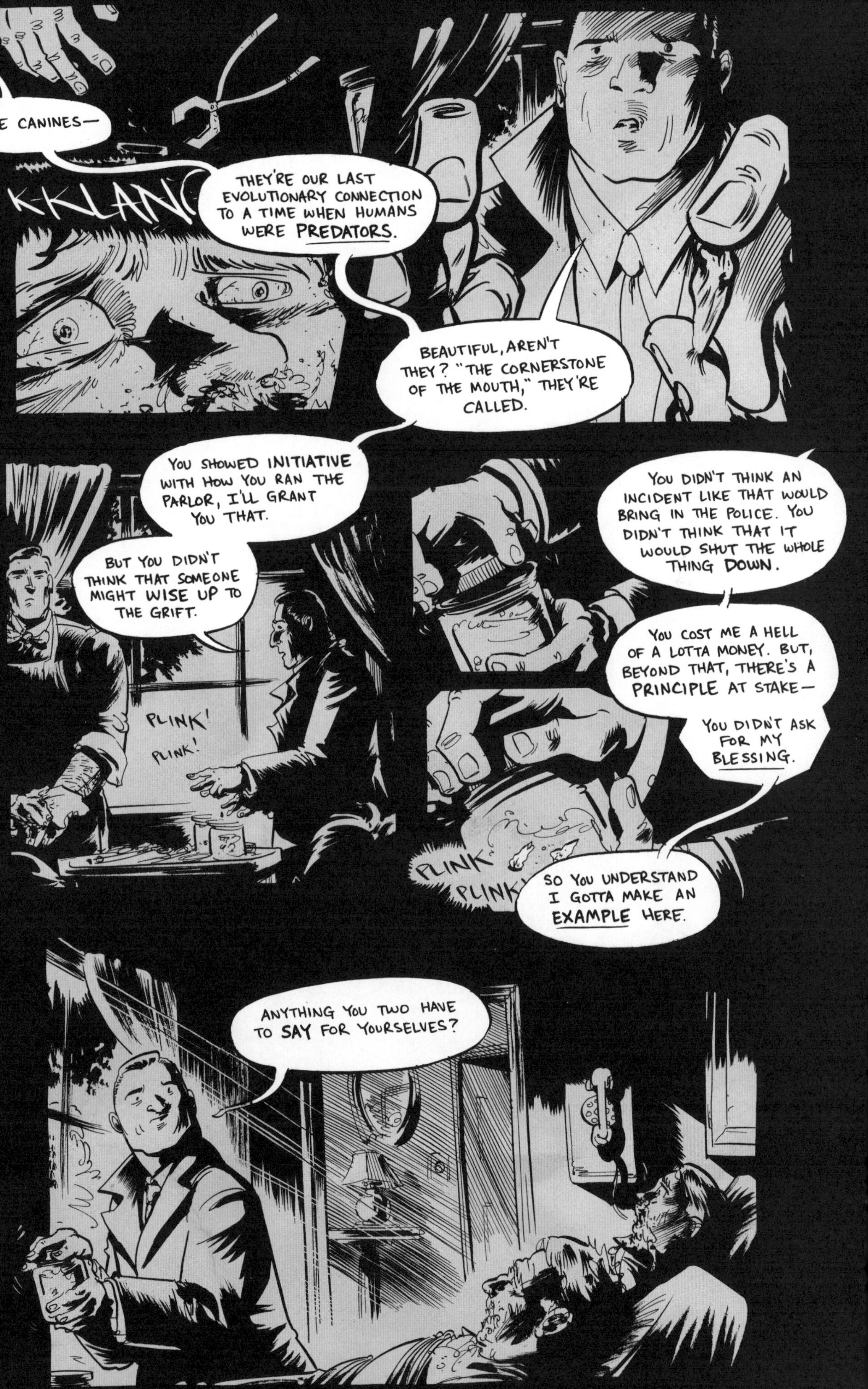
THE CANINES—
K-KLANG
THEY'RE OUR LAST EVOLUTIONARY CONNECTION TO A TIME WHEN HUMANS WERE PREDATORS.
BEAUTIFUL, AREN'T THEY? "THE CORNERSTONE OF THE MOUTH," THEY'RE CALLED.
YOU SHOWED INITIATIVE WITH HOW YOU RAN THE PARLOR, I'LL GRANT YOU THAT.
BUT YOU DIDN'T THINK THAT SOMEONE MIGHT WISE UP TO THE GRIFT.
PLINK!
PLINK!
YOU DIDN'T THINK AN INCIDENT LIKE THAT WOULD BRING IN THE POLICE. YOU DIDN'T THINK THAT IT WOULD SHUT THE WHOLE THING DOWN.
YOU COST ME A HELL OF A LOTTA MONEY. BUT, BEYOND THAT, THERE'S A PRINCIPLE AT STAKE—
YOU DIDN'T ASK FOR MY BLESSING.
PLINK
PLINK
SO YOU UNDERSTAND I GOTTA MAKE AN EXAMPLE HERE.
ANYTHING YOU TWO HAVE TO SAY FOR YOURSELVES?

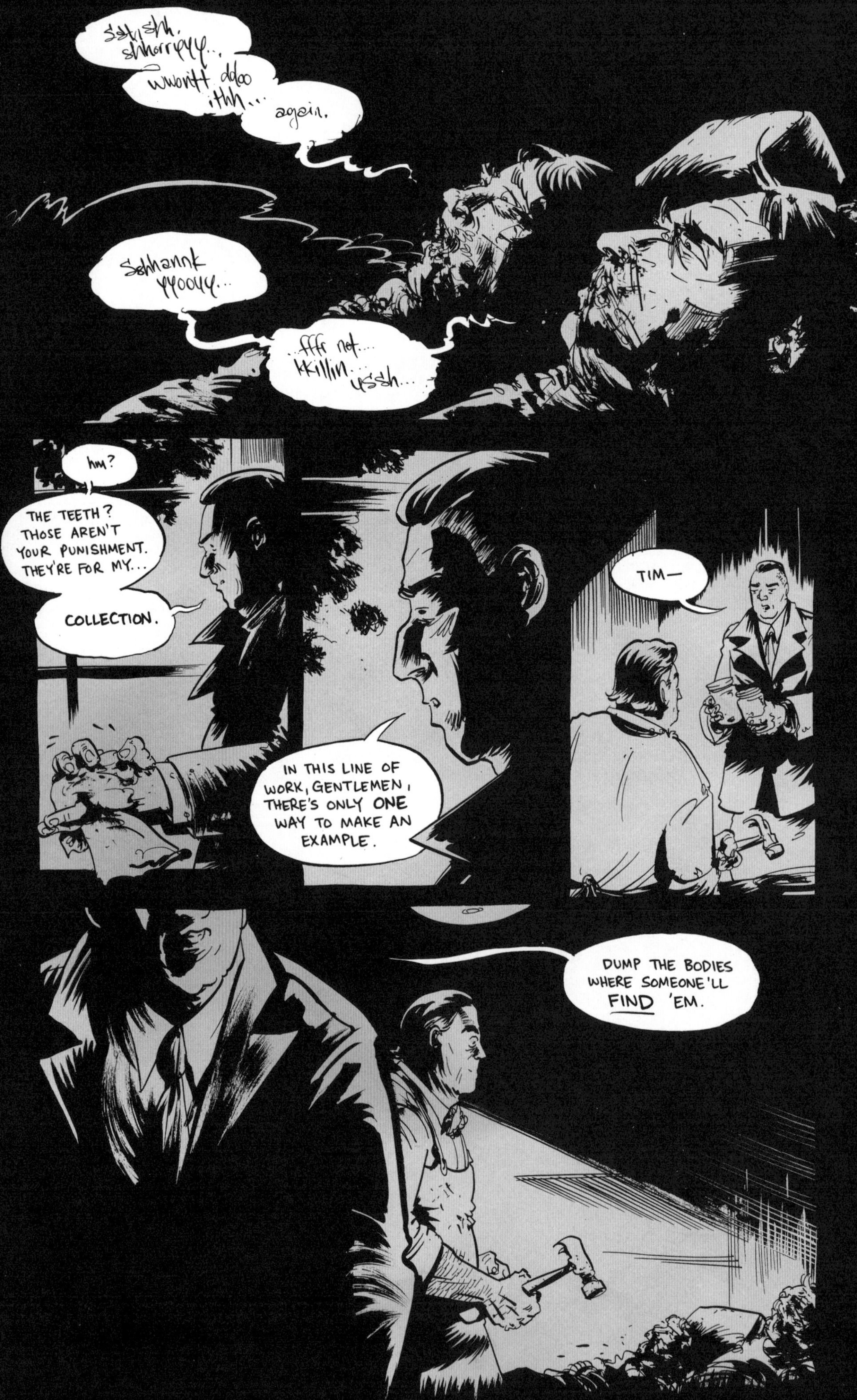
sstishh. shhorriyyy...
wwonitt ddoo ithh... again.
Sshhannk yyoouy...
...fffr not... kkillin... ussh...
hm?
THE TEETH? THOSE AREN'T YOUR PUNISHMENT. THEY'RE FOR MY...
COLLECTION.
IN THIS LINE OF WORK, GENTLEMEN, THERE'S ONLY ONE WAY TO MAKE AN EXAMPLE.
TIM—
DUMP THE BODIES WHERE SOMEONE'LL FIND 'EM.

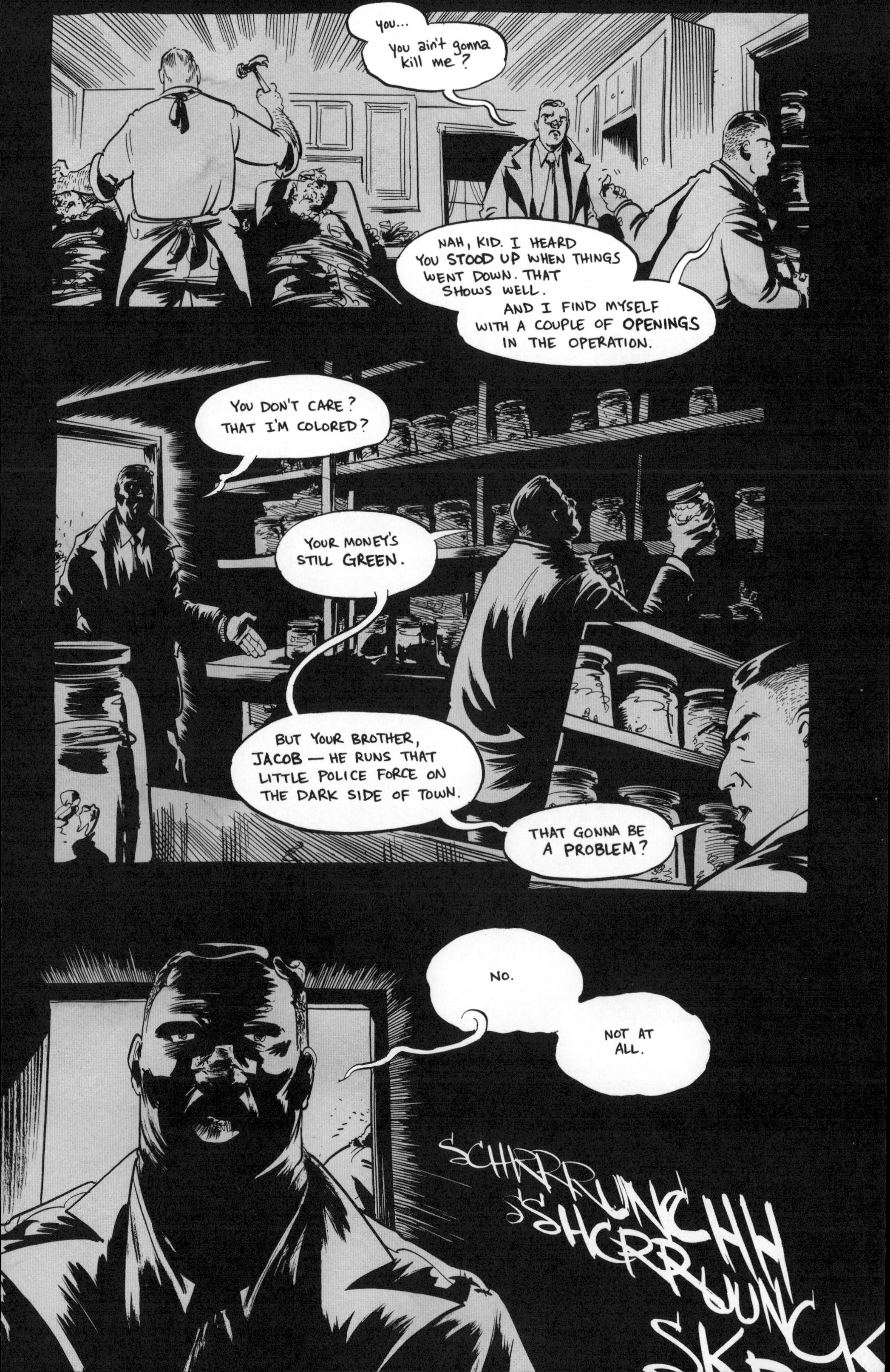
you... you ain't gonna kill me?
NAH, KID. I HEARD YOU STOOD UP WHEN THINGS WENT DOWN. THAT SHOWS WELL.
AND I FIND MYSELF WITH A COUPLE OF OPENINGS IN THE OPERATION.
YOU DON'T CARE? THAT I'M COLORED?
YOUR MONEY'S STILL GREEN.
BUT YOUR BROTHER, JACOB — HE RUNS THAT LITTLE POLICE FORCE ON THE DARK SIDE OF TOWN.
THAT GONNA BE A PROBLEM?
NO.
NOT AT ALL.
SCHRRRUNCHH
SHCRRRUNC

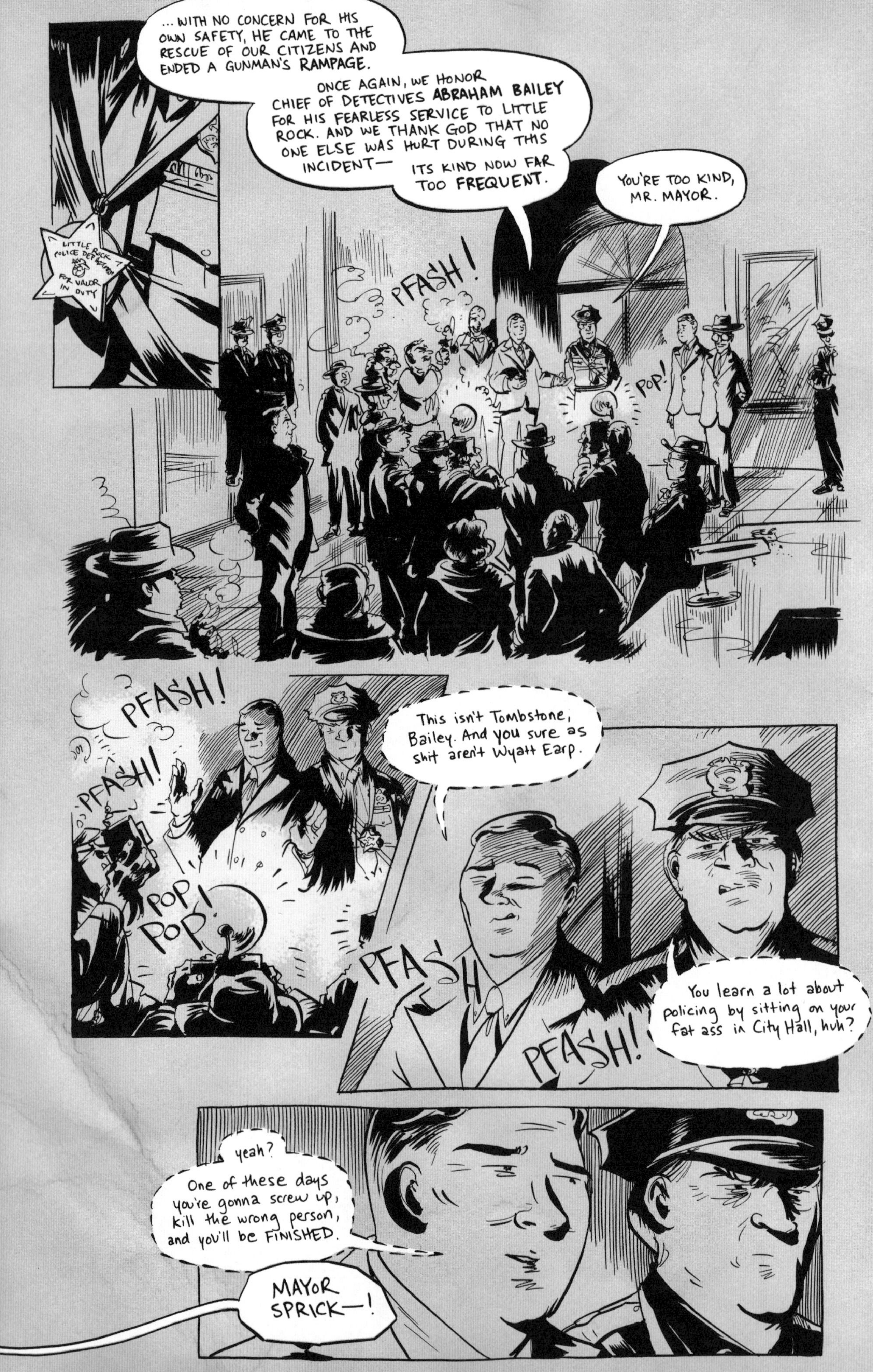

...WITH NO CONCERN FOR HIS OWN SAFETY, HE CAME TO THE RESCUE OF OUR CITIZENS AND ENDED A GUNMAN'S RAMPAGE.
ONCE AGAIN, WE HONOR CHIEF OF DETECTIVES ABRAHAM BAILEY FOR HIS FEARLESS SERVICE TO LITTLE ROCK. AND WE THANK GOD THAT NO ONE ELSE WAS HURT DURING THIS INCIDENT—
ITS KIND NOW FAR TOO FREQUENT.
YOU'RE TOO KIND, MR. MAYOR.
LITTLE ROCK POLICE DEPARTMENT FOR VALOR IN DUTY
PFASH!
POP!
PFASH!
PFASH!
POP! POP!
This isn't Tombstone, Bailey. And you sure as shit aren't Wyatt Earp.
PFASH
PFASH!
You learn a lot about policing by sitting on your fat ass in City Hall, huh?
yeah?
One of these days you're gonna screw up, kill the wrong person, and you'll be FINISHED.
MAYOR SPRICK—!

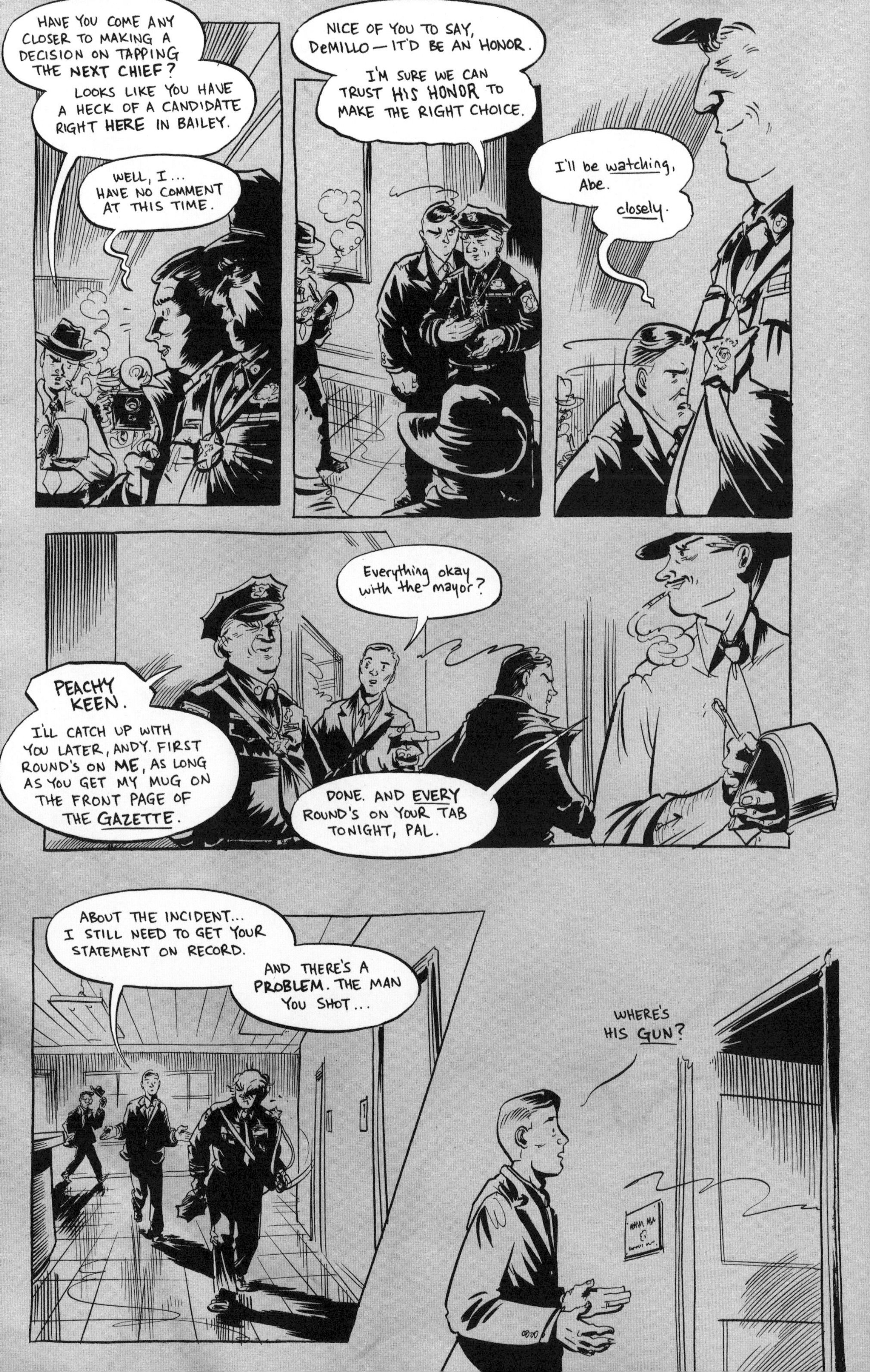
HAVE YOU COME ANY CLOSER TO MAKING A DECISION ON TAPPING THE NEXT CHIEF?
LOOKS LIKE YOU HAVE A HECK OF A CANDIDATE RIGHT HERE IN BAILEY.
WELL, I... HAVE NO COMMENT AT THIS TIME.
NICE OF YOU TO SAY, DeMILLO—IT'D BE AN HONOR.
I'M SURE WE CAN TRUST HIS HONOR TO MAKE THE RIGHT CHOICE.
I'll be watching, Abe.
closely.
Everything okay with the mayor?
PEACHY KEEN.
I'LL CATCH UP WITH YOU LATER, ANDY. FIRST ROUND'S ON ME, AS LONG AS YOU GET MY MUG ON THE FRONT PAGE OF THE GAZETTE.
DONE. AND EVERY ROUND'S ON YOUR TAB TONIGHT, PAL.
ABOUT THE INCIDENT... I STILL NEED TO GET YOUR STATEMENT ON RECORD.
AND THERE'S A PROBLEM. THE MAN YOU SHOT...
WHERE'S HIS GUN?

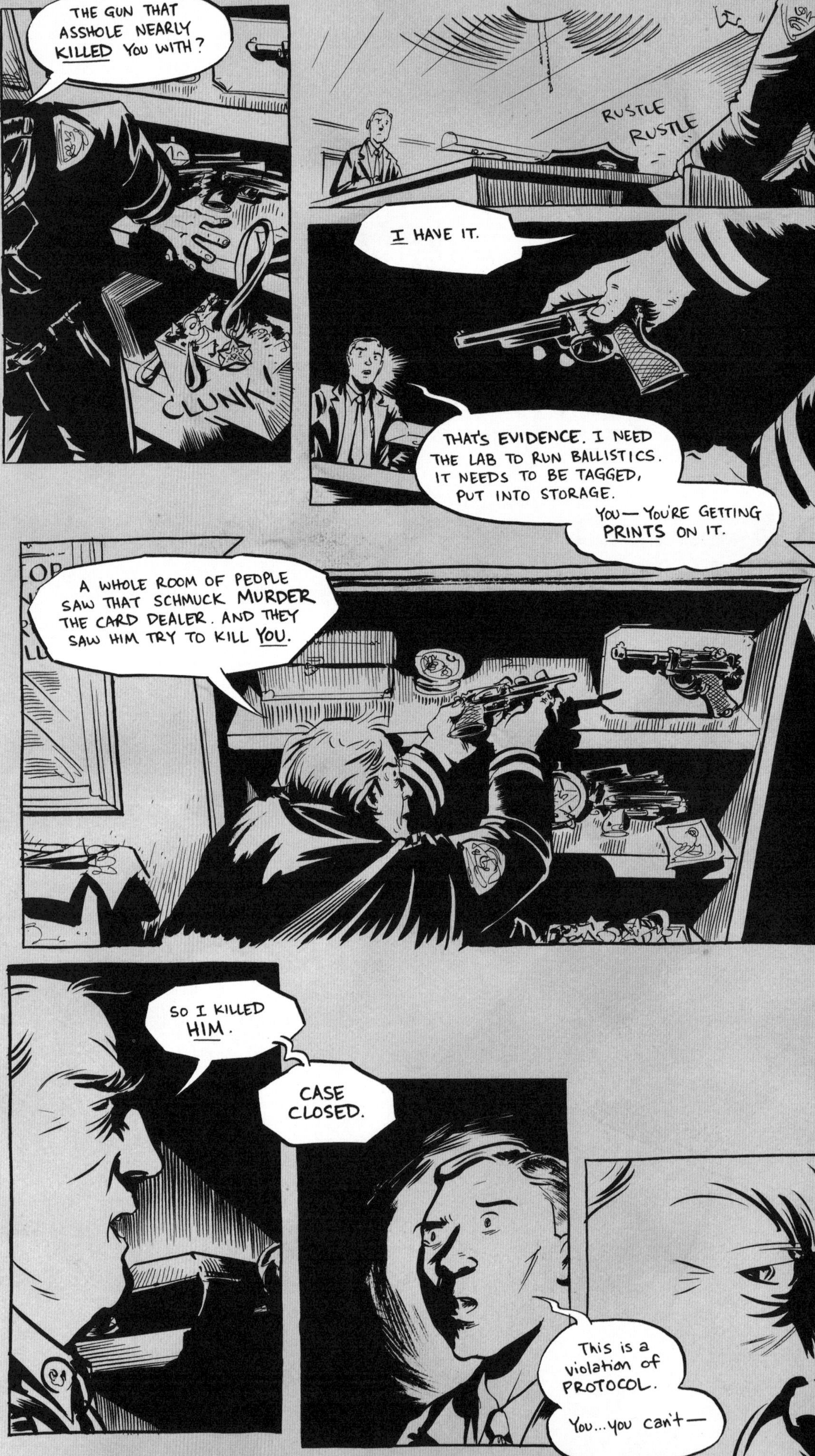
THE GUN THAT ASSHOLE NEARLY KILLED YOU WITH?
CLUNK!
RUSTLE RUSTLE
I HAVE IT.
THAT'S EVIDENCE. I NEED THE LAB TO RUN BALLISTICS. IT NEEDS TO BE TAGGED, PUT INTO STORAGE.
YOU— YOU'RE GETTING PRINTS ON IT.
A WHOLE ROOM OF PEOPLE SAW THAT SCHMUCK MURDER THE CARD DEALER. AND THEY SAW HIM TRY TO KILL YOU.
SO I KILLED HIM.
CASE CLOSED.
This is a violation of PROTOCOL.
You... you can't—

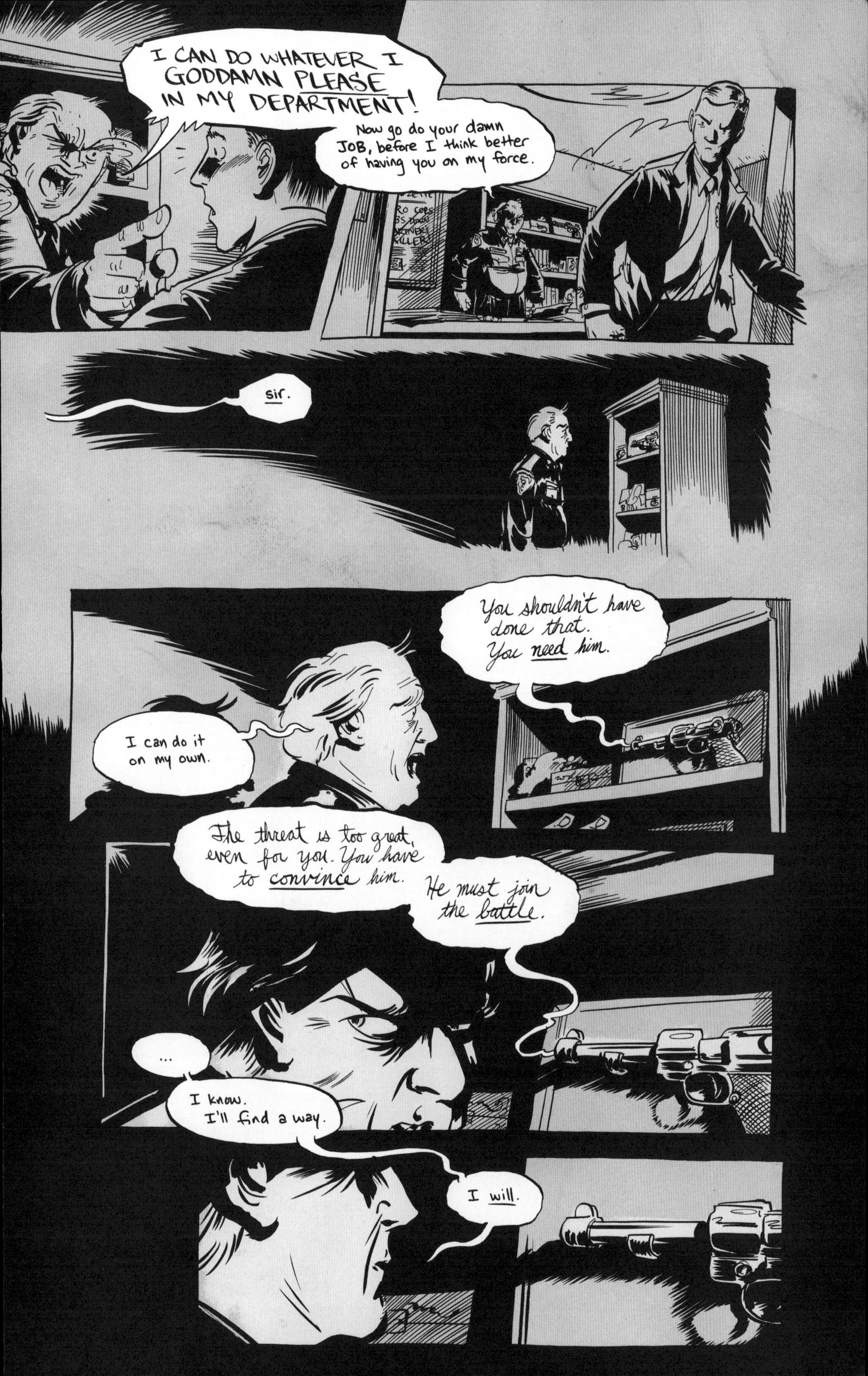
I CAN DO WHATEVER I GODDAMN PLEASE IN MY DEPARTMENT!
Now go do your damn JOB, before I think better of having you on my force.
sir.
You shouldn't have done that. You need him.
I can do it on my own.
The threat is too great, even for you. You have to convince him.
He must join the battle.
...
I know. I'll find a way.
I will.

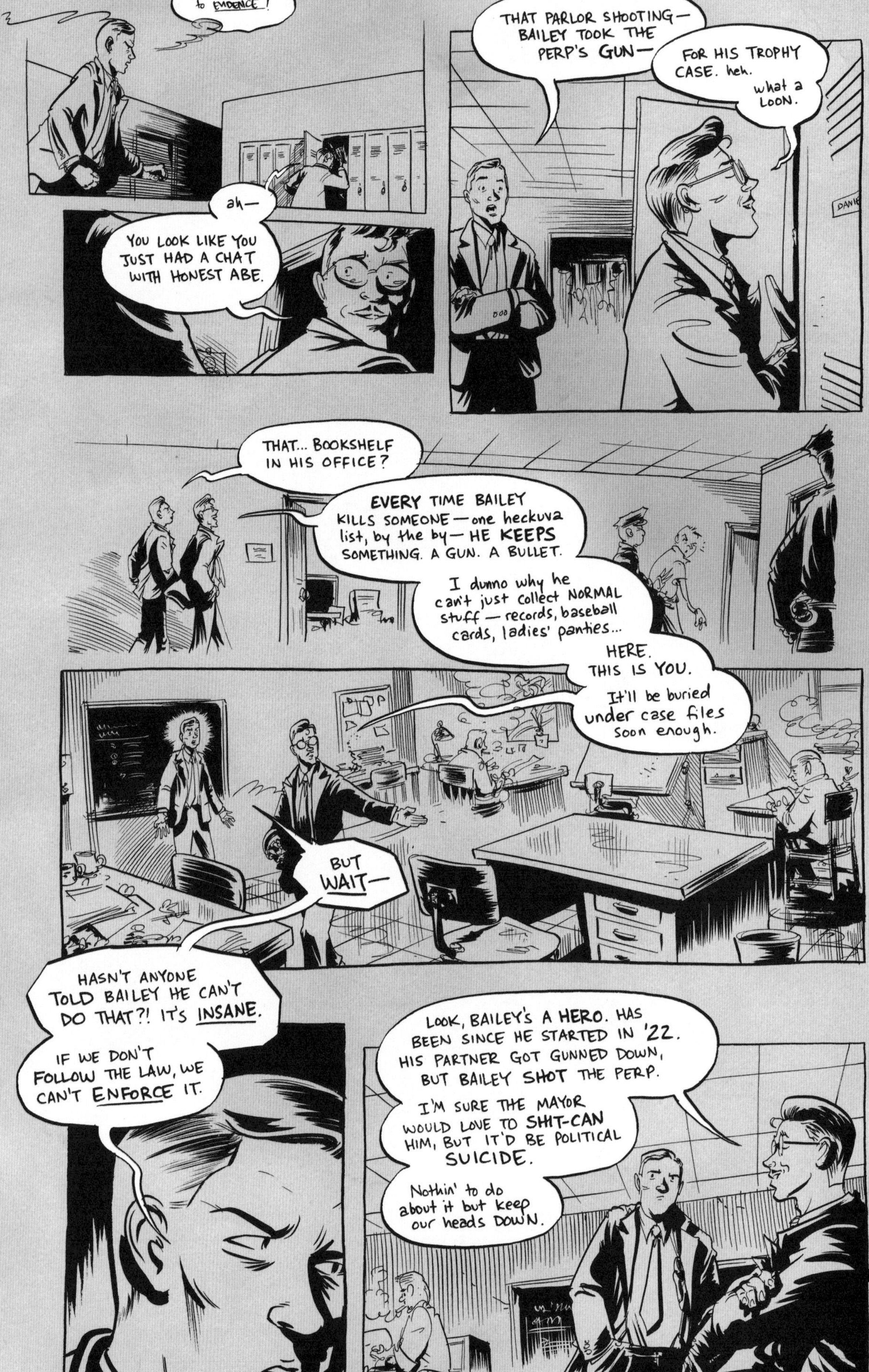
can't do that to EVIDENCE!
ah—
YOU LOOK LIKE YOU JUST HAD A CHAT WITH HONEST ABE.
THAT PARLOR SHOOTING— BAILEY TOOK THE PERP'S GUN—
FOR HIS TROPHY CASE. heh.
what a LOON.
THAT... BOOKSHELF IN HIS OFFICE?
EVERY TIME BAILEY KILLS SOMEONE—one heckuva list, by the by—HE KEEPS SOMETHING. A GUN. A BULLET.
I dunno why he can't just collect NORMAL stuff—records, baseball cards, ladies' panties...
HERE. THIS IS YOU.
It'll be buried under case files soon enough.
BUT WAIT—
HASN'T ANYONE TOLD BAILEY HE CAN'T DO THAT?! IT'S INSANE.
IF WE DON'T FOLLOW THE LAW, WE CAN'T ENFORCE IT.
LOOK, BAILEY'S A HERO. HAS BEEN SINCE HE STARTED IN '22. HIS PARTNER GOT GUNNED DOWN, BUT BAILEY SHOT THE PERP.
I'M SURE THE MAYOR WOULD LOVE TO SHIT-CAN HIM, BUT IT'D BE POLITICAL SUICIDE.
Nothin' to do about it but keep our heads DOWN.

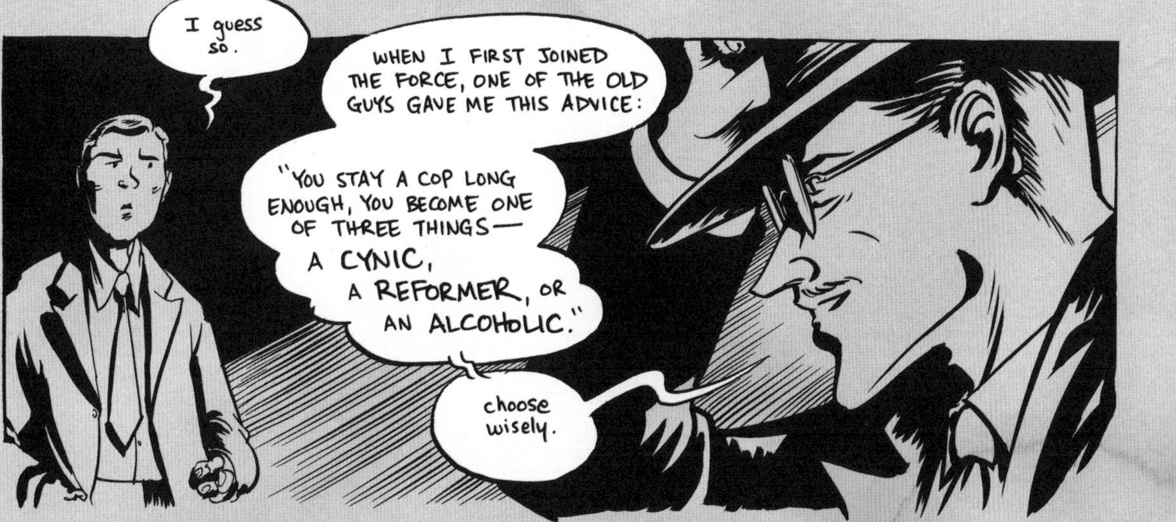
I guess so.
WHEN I FIRST JOINED THE FORCE, ONE OF THE OLD GUYS GAVE ME THIS ADVICE:
"YOU STAY A COP LONG ENOUGH, YOU BECOME ONE OF THREE THINGS— A CYNIC, A REFORMER, OR AN ALCOHOLIC."
choose wisely.

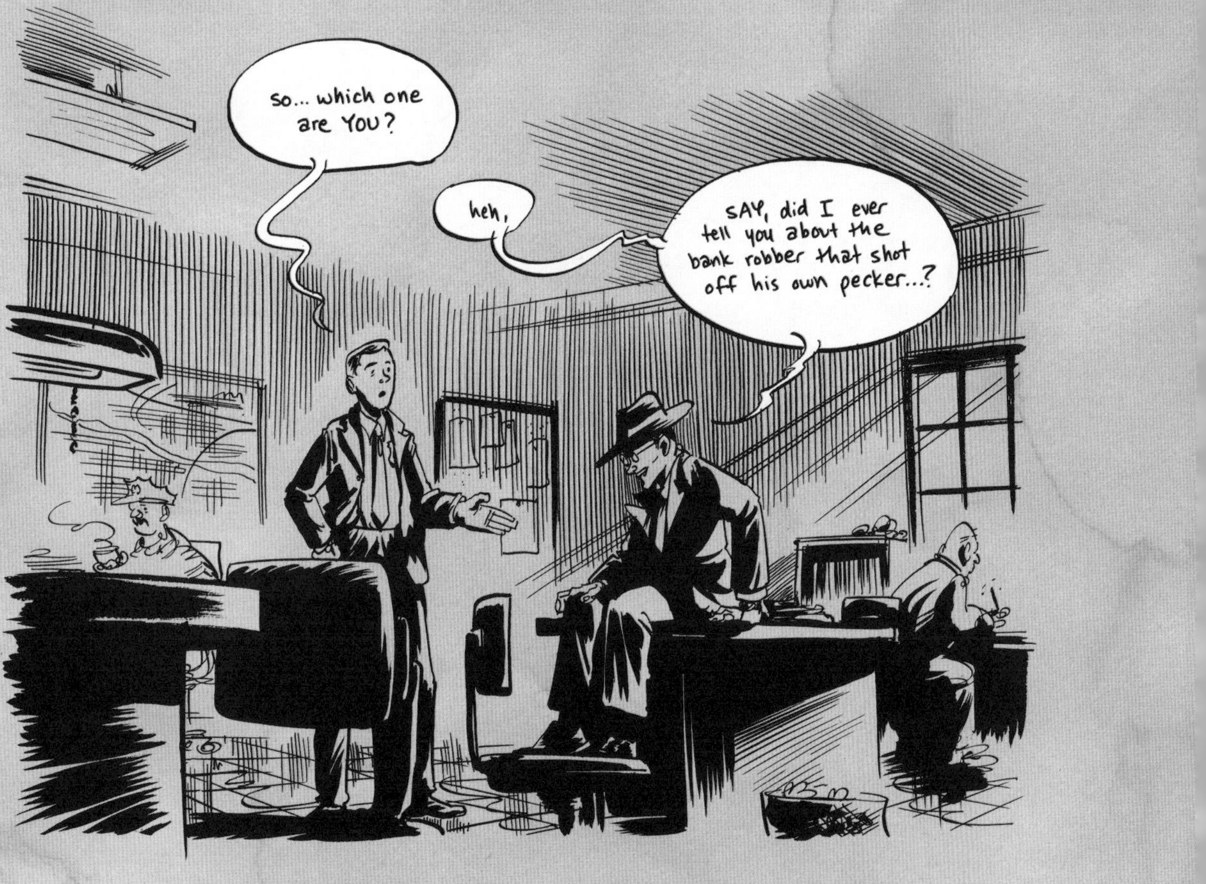
so... which one are YOU?
heh,
SAY, did I ever tell you about the bank robber that shot off his own pecker...?

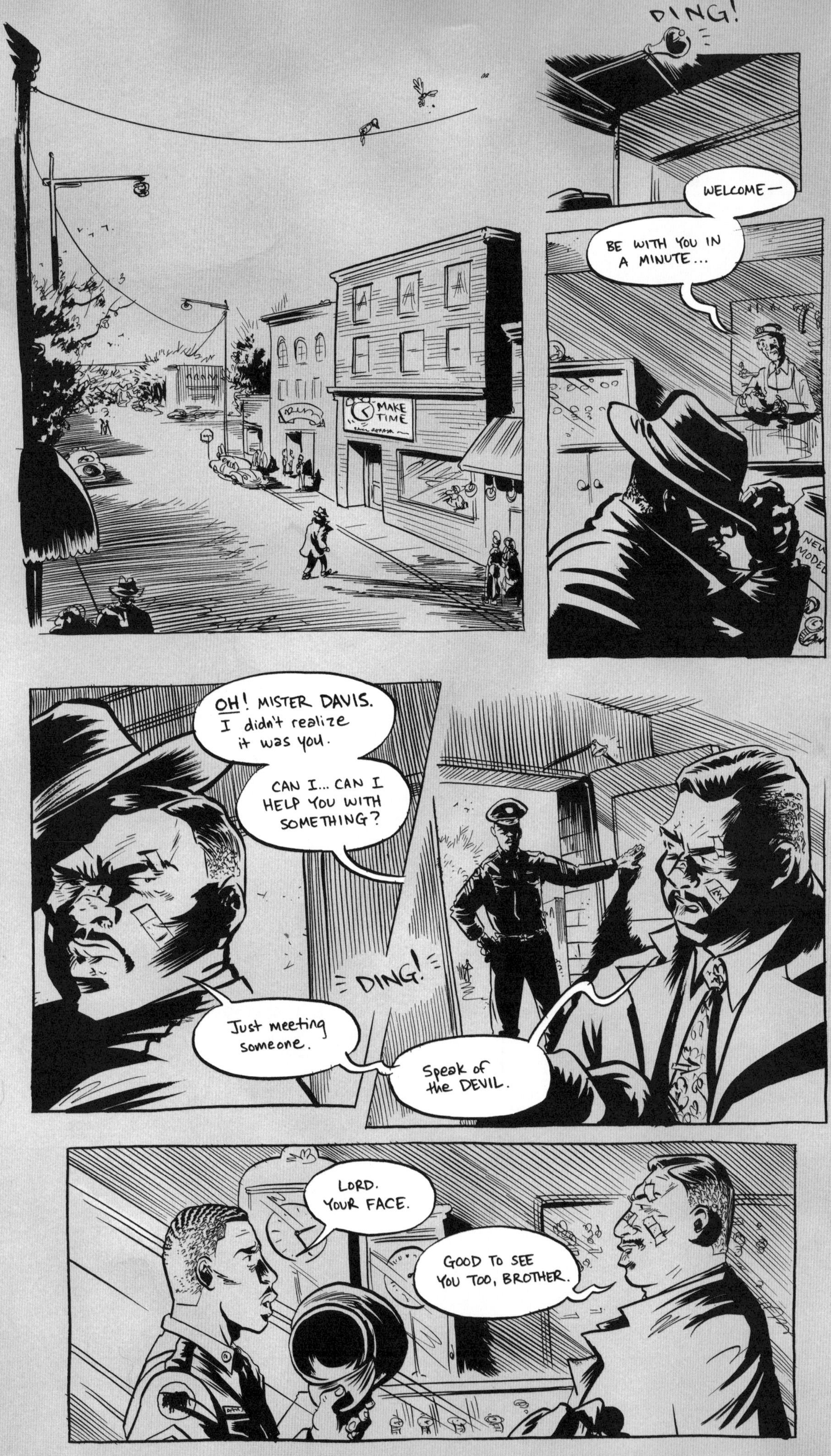
DING!
WELCOME—
BE WITH YOU IN A MINUTE...
MAKE TIME
NEW MODEL
OH! MISTER DAVIS. I didn't realize it was you.
CAN I... CAN I HELP YOU WITH SOMETHING?
DING!
Just meeting someone.
Speak of the DEVIL.
LORD. YOUR FACE.
GOOD TO SEE YOU TOO, BROTHER.

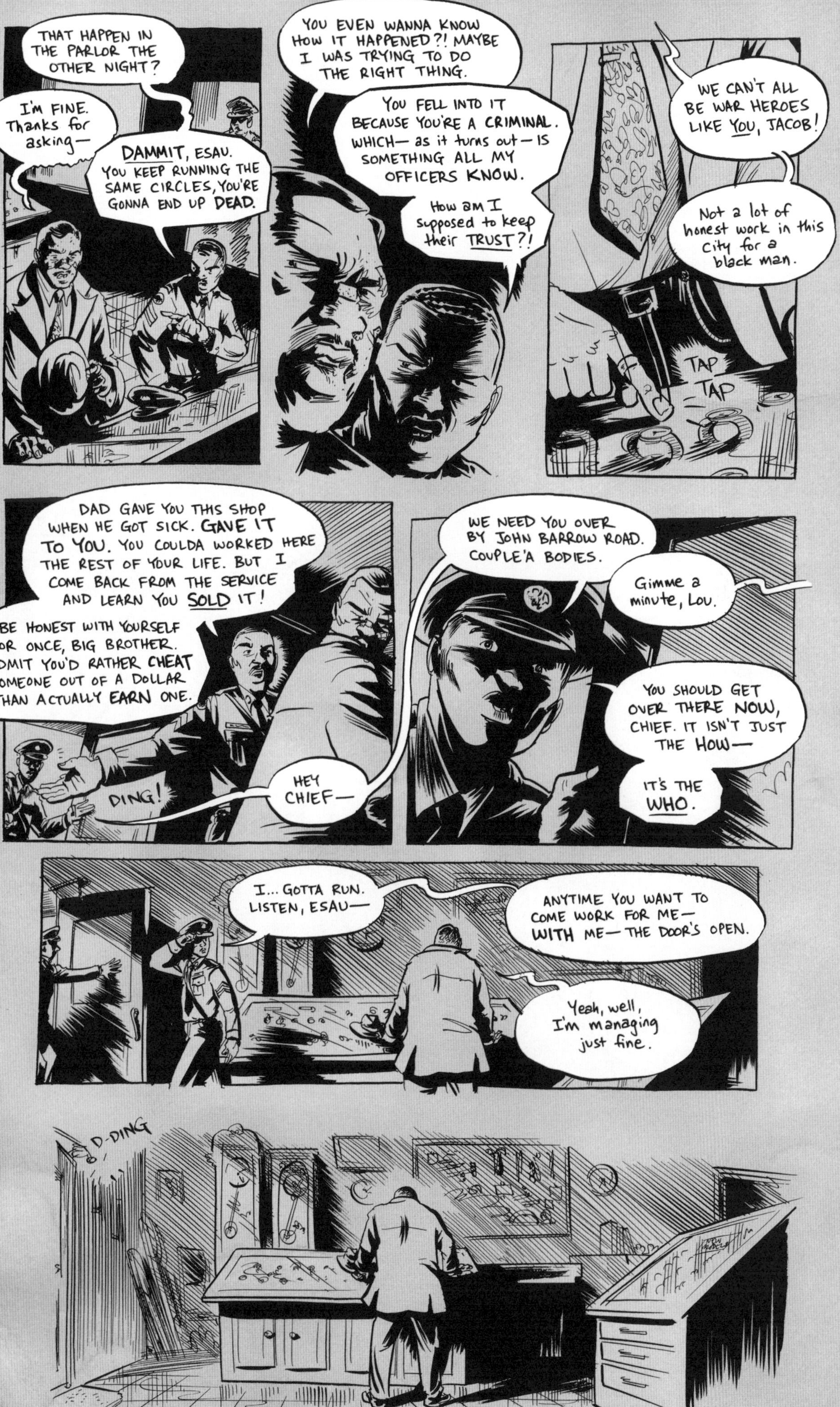
THAT HAPPEN IN THE PARLOR THE OTHER NIGHT?
I'M FINE. Thanks for asking—
DAMMIT, ESAU. YOU KEEP RUNNING THE SAME CIRCLES, YOU'RE GONNA END UP DEAD.
YOU EVEN WANNA KNOW HOW IT HAPPENED?! MAYBE I WAS TRYING TO DO THE RIGHT THING.
YOU FELL INTO IT BECAUSE YOU'RE A CRIMINAL. WHICH— as it turns out— IS SOMETHING ALL MY OFFICERS KNOW.
How am I supposed to keep their TRUST?!
WE CAN'T ALL BE WAR HEROES LIKE YOU, JACOB!
Not a lot of honest work in this city for a black man.
TAP TAP
DAD GAVE YOU THIS SHOP WHEN HE GOT SICK. GAVE IT TO YOU. YOU COULDA WORKED HERE THE REST OF YOUR LIFE. BUT I COME BACK FROM THE SERVICE AND LEARN YOU SOLD IT!
BE HONEST WITH YOURSELF FOR ONCE, BIG BROTHER. ADMIT YOU'D RATHER CHEAT SOMEONE OUT OF A DOLLAR THAN ACTUALLY EARN ONE.
DING!
HEY CHIEF—
WE NEED YOU OVER BY JOHN BARROW ROAD. COUPLE'A BODIES.
Gimme a minute, Lou.
YOU SHOULD GET OVER THERE NOW, CHIEF. IT ISN'T JUST THE HOW—
IT'S THE WHO.
I... GOTTA RUN. LISTEN, ESAU—
ANYTIME YOU WANT TO COME WORK FOR ME— WITH ME— THE DOOR'S OPEN.
Yeah, well, I'm managing just fine.
D-DING

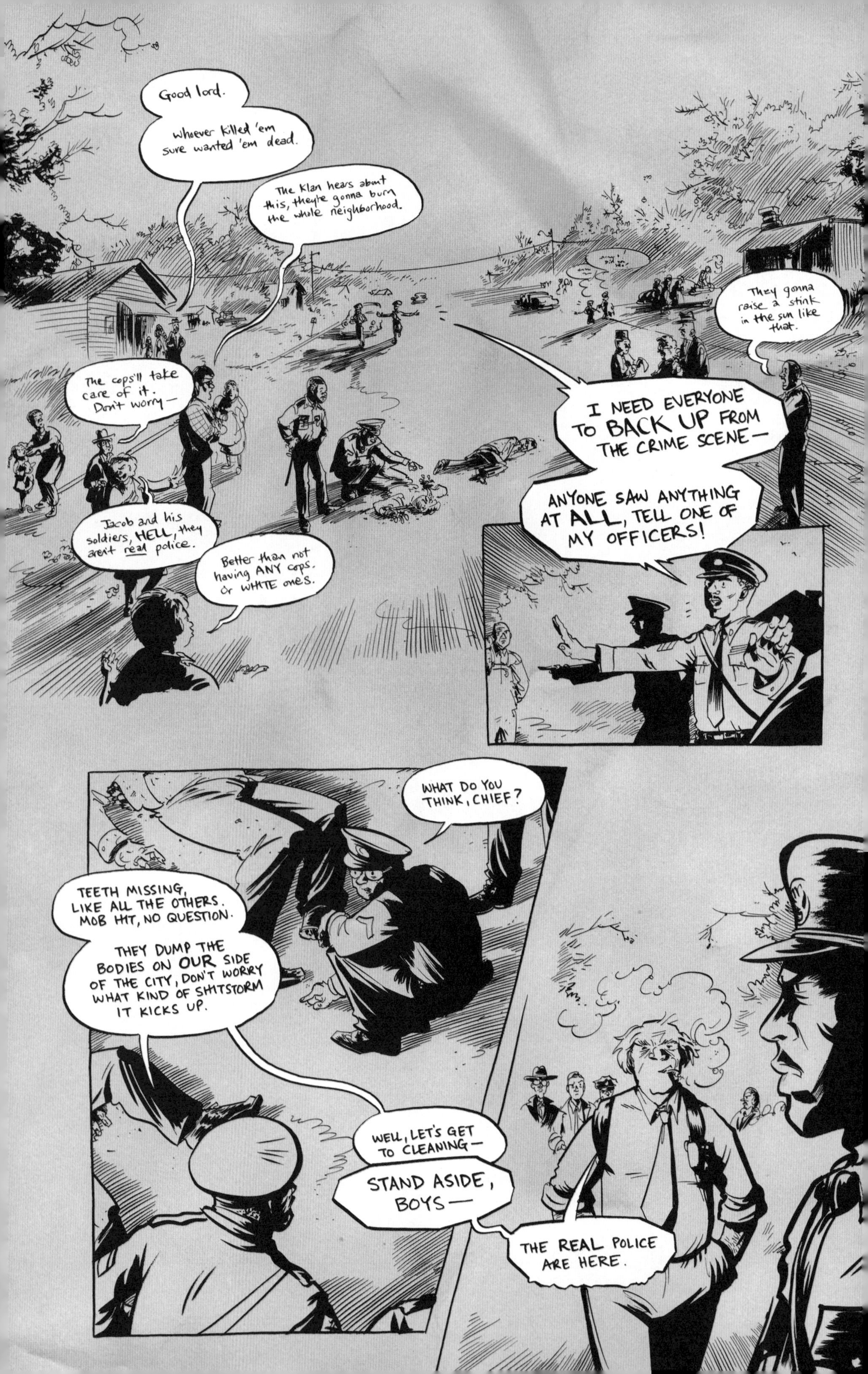
Good lord.
whoever killed 'em sure wanted 'em dead.
The Klan hears about this, they're gonna burn the whole neighborhood.
They gonna raise a stink in the sun like that.
The cops'll take care of it. Don't worry—
Jacob and his soldiers, HELL, they aren't real police.
Better than not having ANY cops. Or WHITE ones.
I NEED EVERYONE TO BACK UP FROM THE CRIME SCENE—
ANYONE SAW ANYTHING AT ALL, TELL ONE OF MY OFFICERS!
WHAT DO YOU THINK, CHIEF?
TEETH MISSING, LIKE ALL THE OTHERS. MOB HIT, NO QUESTION.
THEY DUMP THE BODIES ON OUR SIDE OF THE CITY, DON'T WORRY WHAT KIND OF SHITSTORM IT KICKS UP.
WELL, LET'S GET TO CLEANING—
STAND ASIDE, BOYS—
THE REAL POLICE ARE HERE.

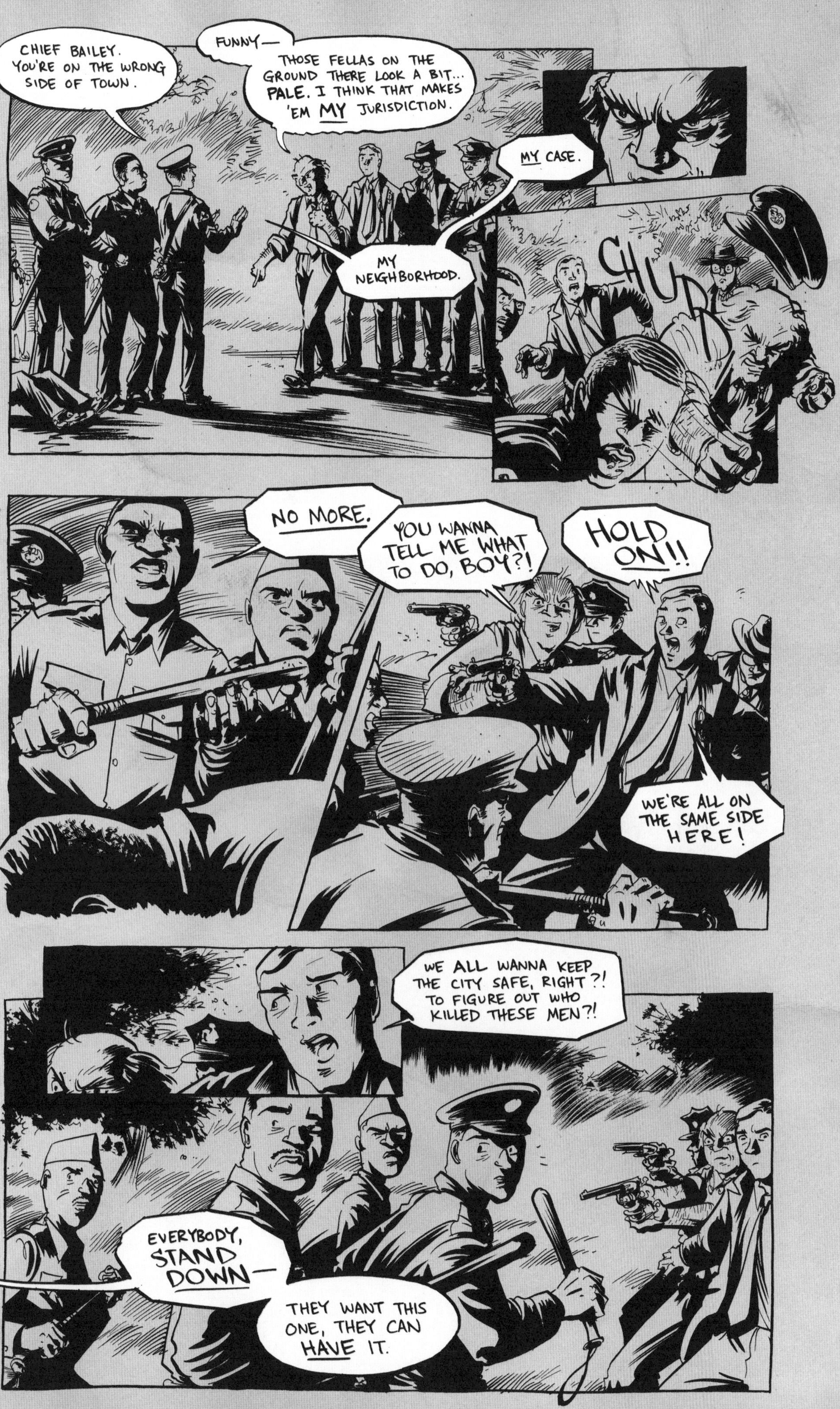

CHIEF BAILEY. YOU'RE ON THE WRONG SIDE OF TOWN.
FUNNY—
THOSE FELLAS ON THE GROUND THERE LOOK A BIT... PALE. I THINK THAT MAKES 'EM MY JURISDICTION.
MY NEIGHBORHOOD.
MY CASE.
CHUD
NO MORE.
YOU WANNA TELL ME WHAT TO DO, BOY?!
HOLD ON!!
WE'RE ALL ON THE SAME SIDE HERE!
WE ALL WANNA KEEP THE CITY SAFE, RIGHT?! TO FIGURE OUT WHO KILLED THESE MEN?!
EVERYBODY, STAND DOWN—
THEY WANT THIS ONE, THEY CAN HAVE IT.

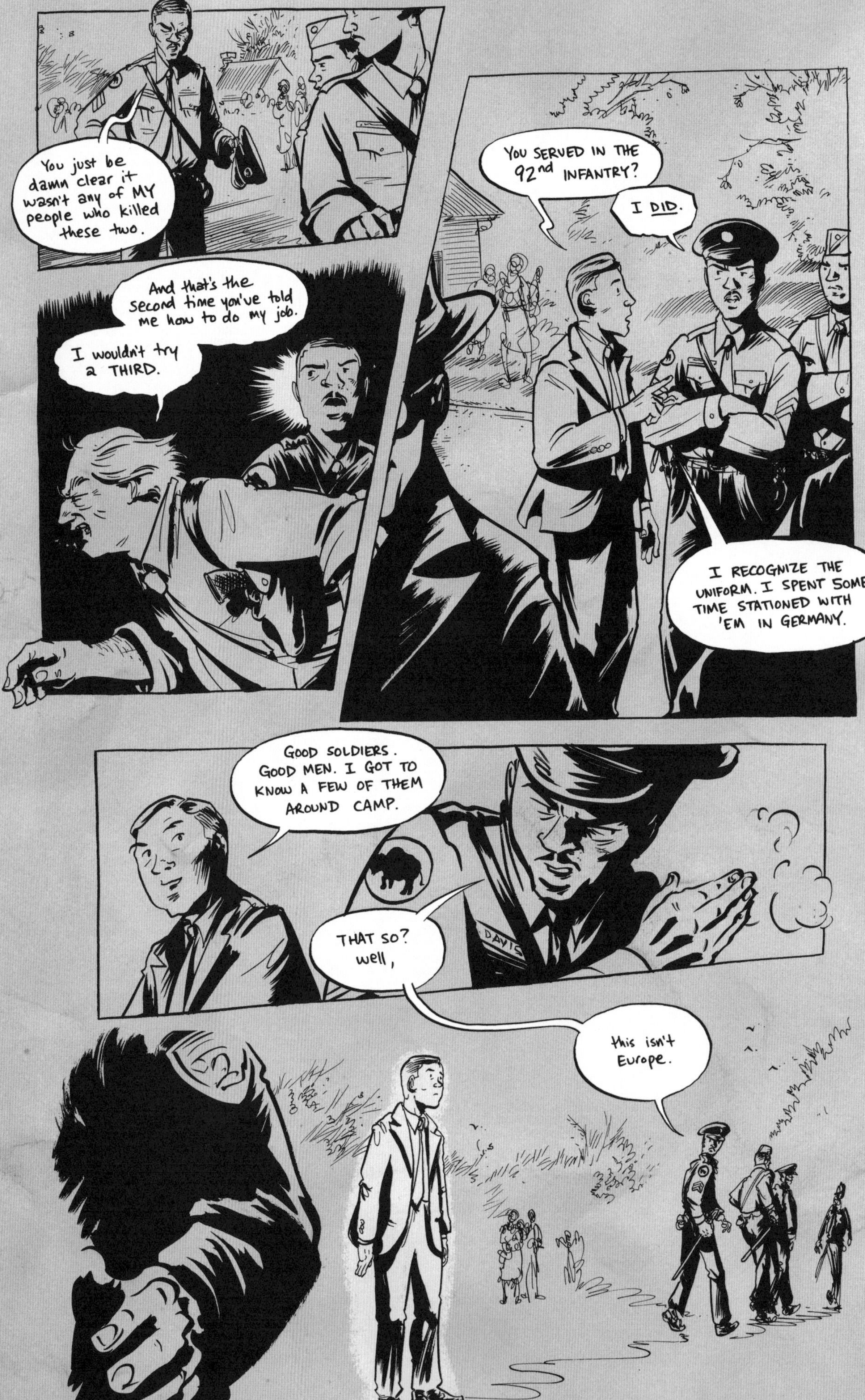
You just be damn clear it wasn't any of MY people who killed these two.
And that's the second time you've told me how to do my job.
I wouldn't try a THIRD.
YOU SERVED IN THE 92nd INFANTRY?
I DID.
I RECOGNIZE THE UNIFORM. I SPENT SOME TIME STATIONED WITH 'EM IN GERMANY.
GOOD SOLDIERS. GOOD MEN. I GOT TO KNOW A FEW OF THEM AROUND CAMP.
THAT SO? well,
this isn't Europe.

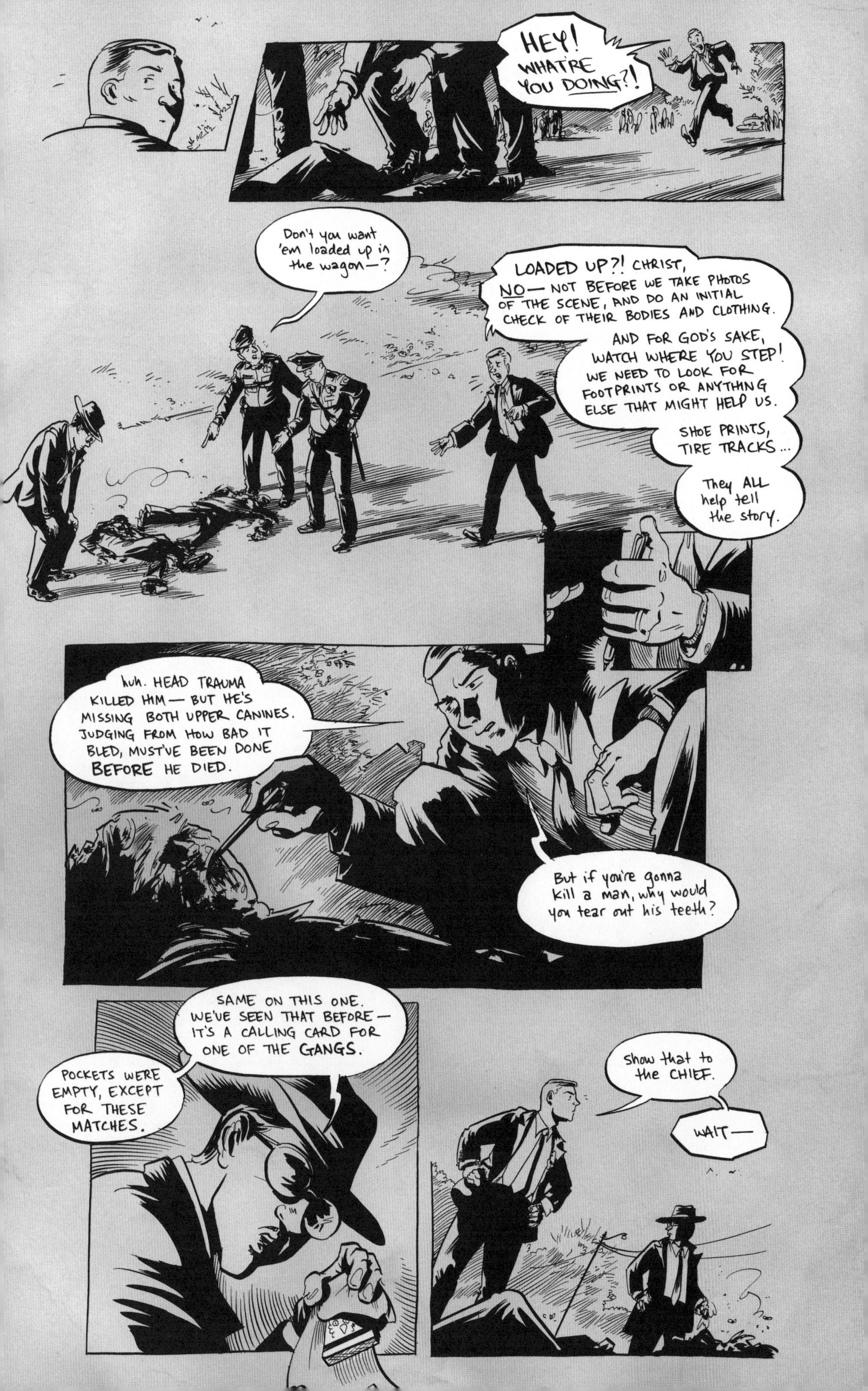

HEY! WHAT'RE YOU DOING?!
Don't you want 'em loaded up in the wagon—?
LOADED UP?! CHRIST, NO— NOT BEFORE WE TAKE PHOTOS OF THE SCENE, AND DO AN INITIAL CHECK OF THEIR BODIES AND CLOTHING.
AND FOR GOD'S SAKE, WATCH WHERE YOU STEP! WE NEED TO LOOK FOR FOOTPRINTS OR ANYTHING ELSE THAT MIGHT HELP US.
SHOE PRINTS, TIRE TRACKS...
They ALL help tell the story.
huh. HEAD TRAUMA KILLED HIM— BUT HE'S MISSING BOTH UPPER CANINES. JUDGING FROM HOW BAD IT BLED, MUST'VE BEEN DONE BEFORE HE DIED.
But if you're gonna kill a man, why would you tear out his teeth?
POCKETS WERE EMPTY, EXCEPT FOR THESE MATCHES.
SAME ON THIS ONE. WE'VE SEEN THAT BEFORE— IT'S A CALLING CARD FOR ONE OF THE GANGS.
Show that to the CHIEF.
WAIT—

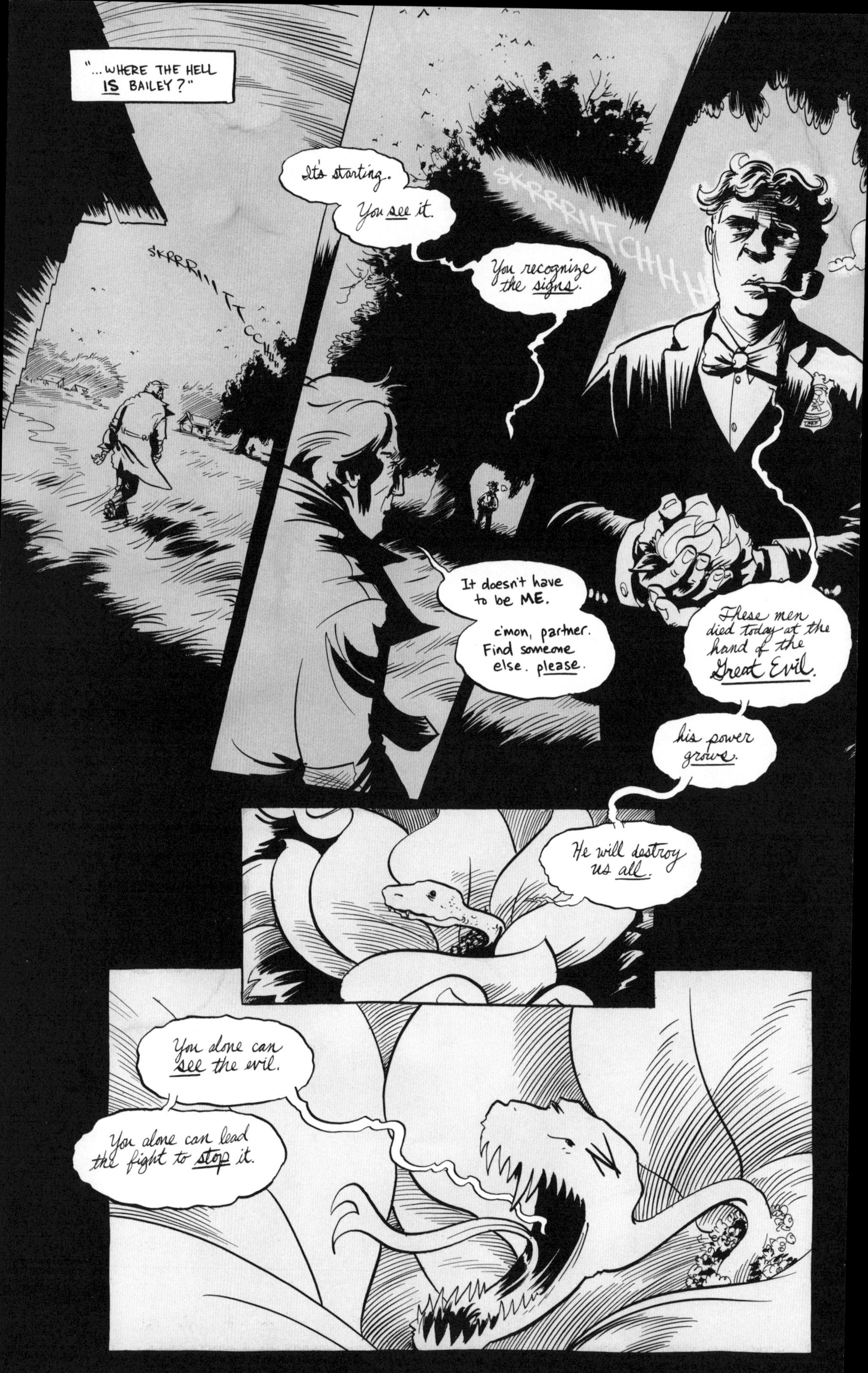
"...WHERE THE HELL IS BAILEY?"
SKRRRIIITTCCHH
It's starting.
You see it.
You recognize the signs.
SKRRRRIITCHHH
It doesn't have to be ME.
c'mon, partner. Find someone else. please.
These men died today at the hand of the Great Evil.
his power grows.
He will destroy us all.
You alone can see the evil.
You alone can lead the fight to stop it.

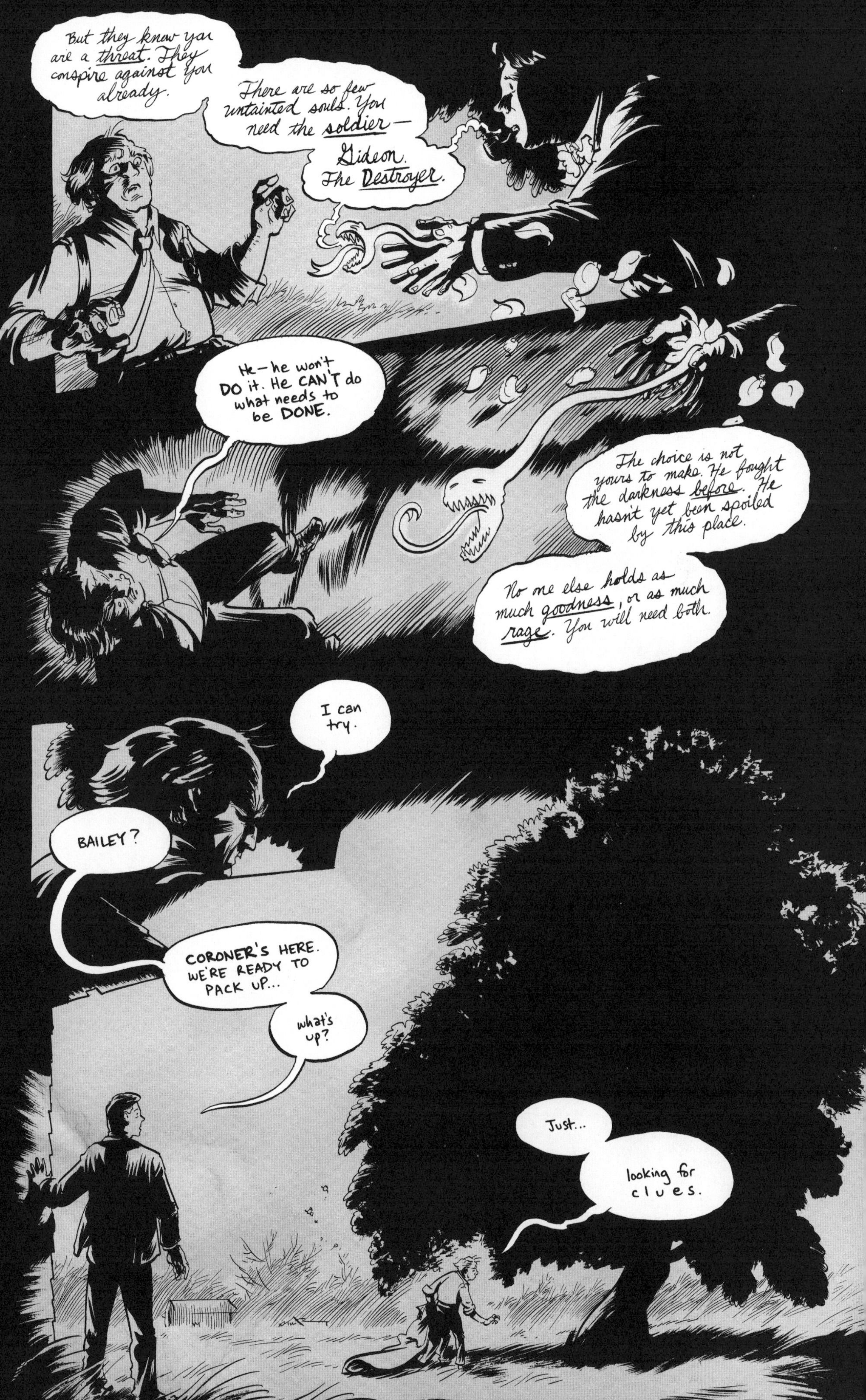
But they know you are a threat. They conspire against you already.
There are so few untainted souls. You need the soldier—
Gideon. The Destroyer.
He—he won't DO it. He CAN'T do what needs to be DONE.
The choice is not yours to make. He fought the darkness before. He hasn't yet been spoiled by this place.
No one else holds as much goodness, or as much rage. You will need both.
I can try.
BAILEY?
CORONER'S HERE. WE'RE READY TO PACK UP...
what's up?
Just...
looking for clues.

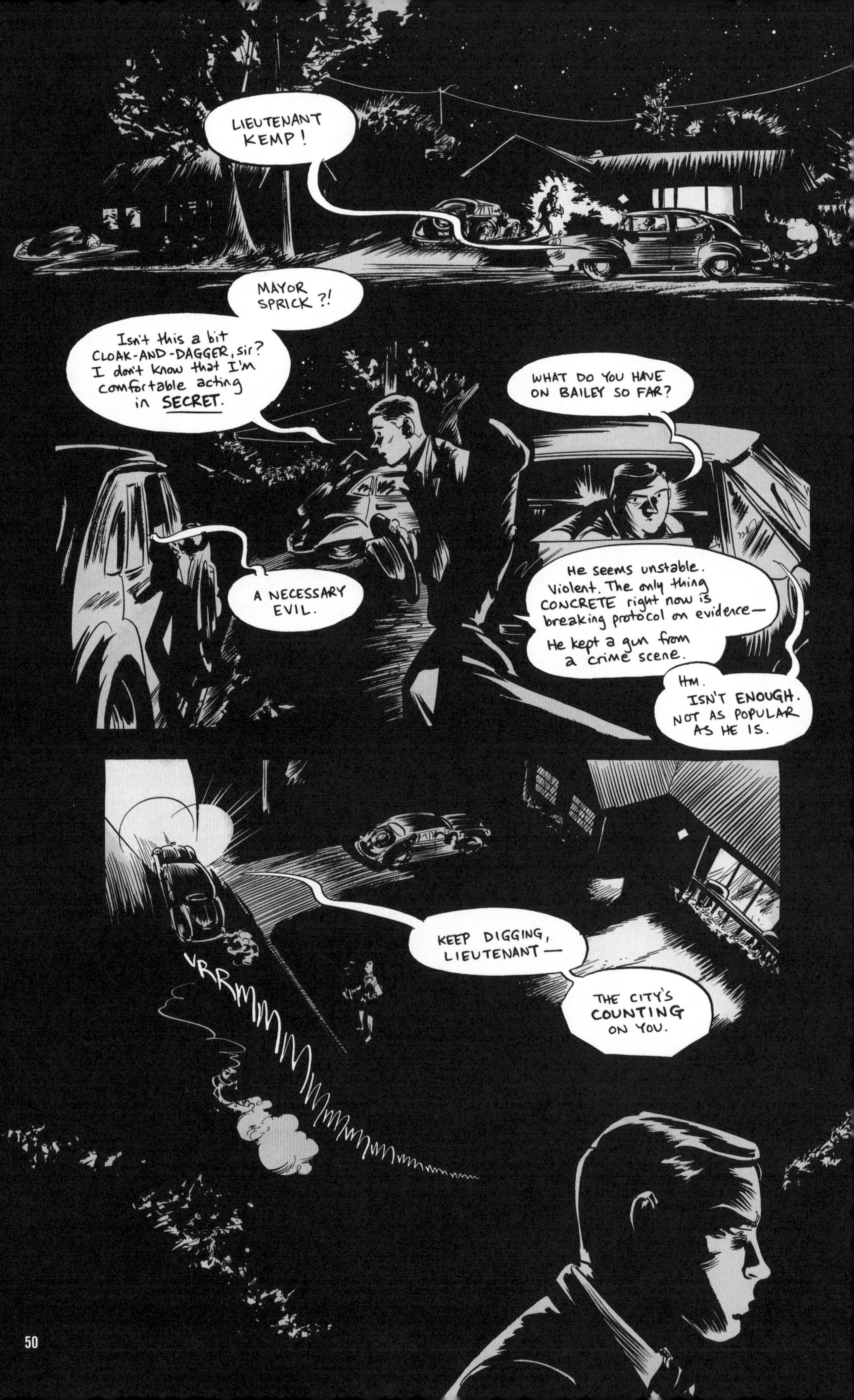
LIEUTENANT KEMP!
MAYOR SPRICK?!
Isn't this a bit CLOAK-AND-DAGGER, sir? I don't know that I'm comfortable acting in SECRET.
A NECESSARY EVIL.
WHAT DO YOU HAVE ON BAILEY SO FAR?
He seems unstable. Violent. The only thing CONCRETE right now is breaking protocol on evidence—
He kept a gun from a crime scene.
Hm. ISN'T ENOUGH. NOT AS POPULAR AS HE IS.
KEEP DIGGING, LIEUTENANT—
THE CITY'S COUNTING ON YOU.
VRRMMMMMMMMMMMMmmmmmm

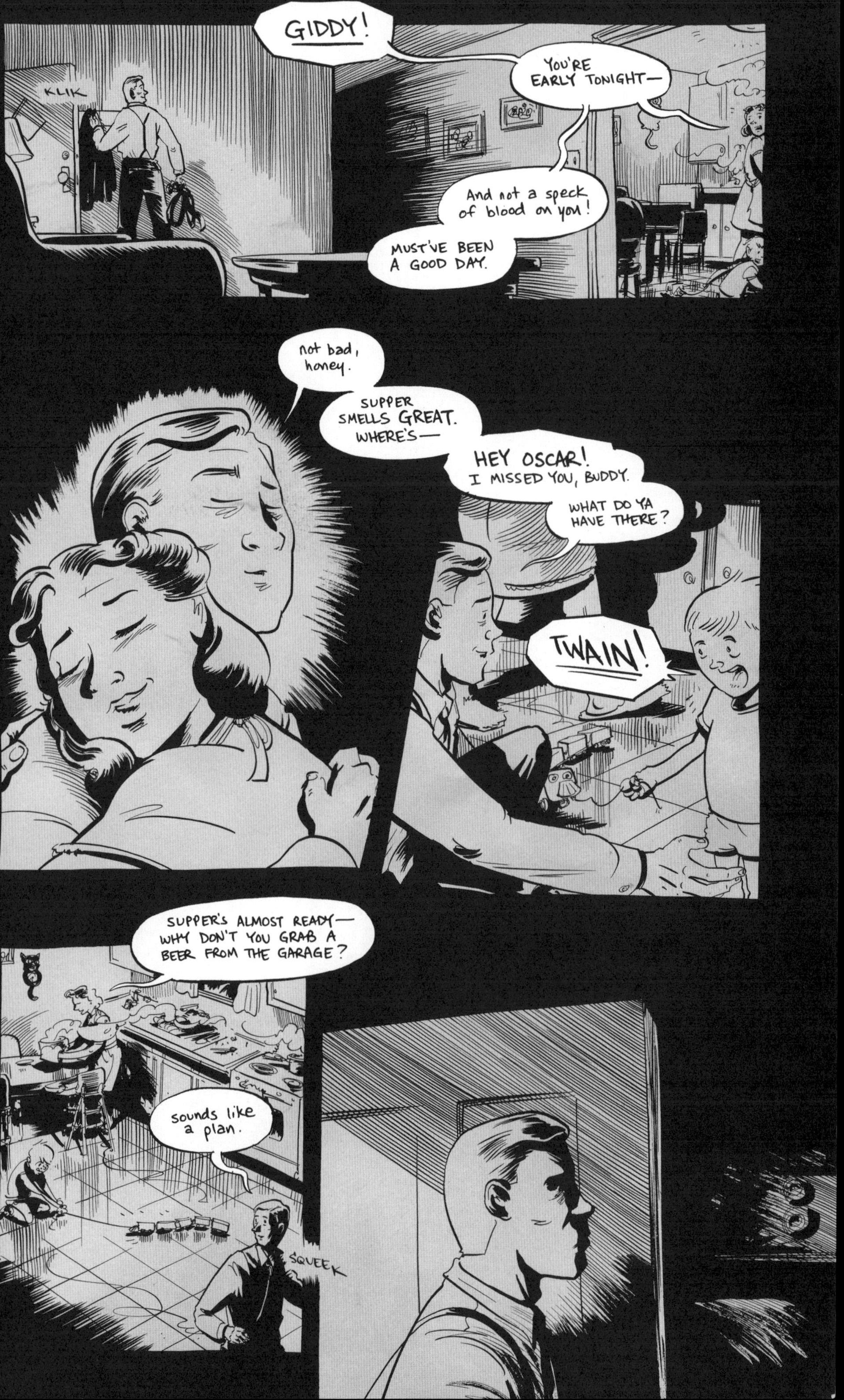
GIDDY!
KLIK
YOU'RE EARLY TONIGHT—
And not a speck of blood on you!
MUST'VE BEEN A GOOD DAY.
not bad, honey.
SUPPER SMELLS GREAT. WHERE'S—
HEY OSCAR! I MISSED YOU, BUDDY.
WHAT DO YA HAVE THERE?
TWAIN!
SUPPER'S ALMOST READY— WHY DON'T YOU GRAB A BEER FROM THE GARAGE?
sounds like a plan.
SQUEEK

shukka shukka
NAIL
KLUNK
KLUNK
RATTLE

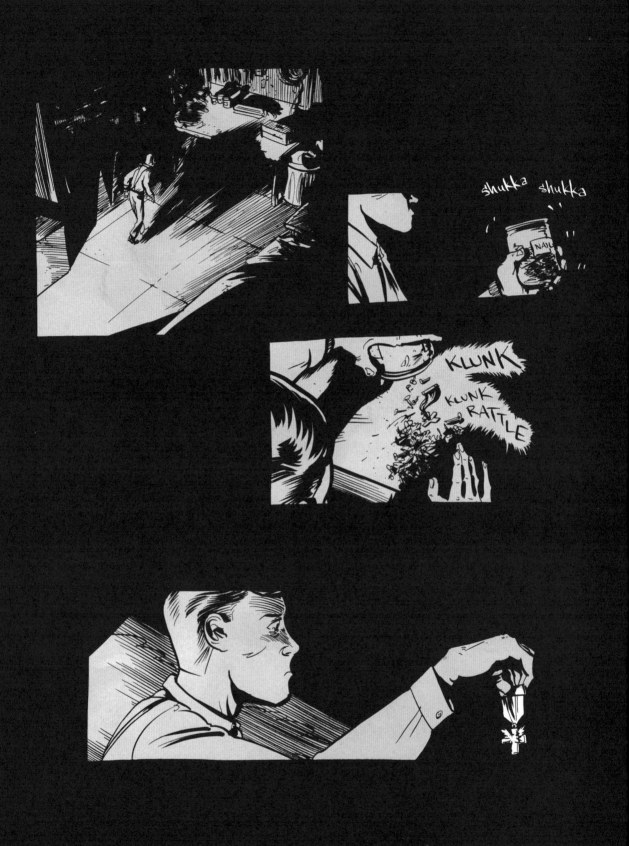

AUGUST, 1922

NORTH LITTLE ROCK

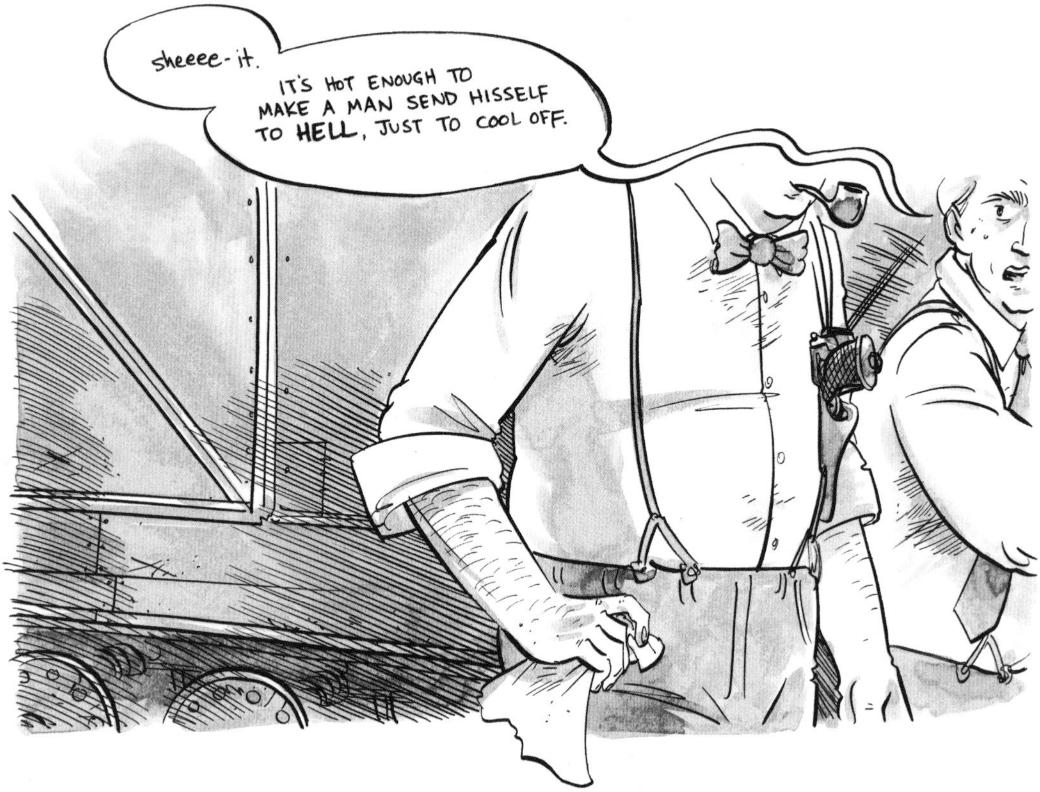
sheeee-it.
IT'S HOT ENOUGH TO MAKE A MAN SEND HISSELF TO **HELL**, JUST TO COOL OFF.

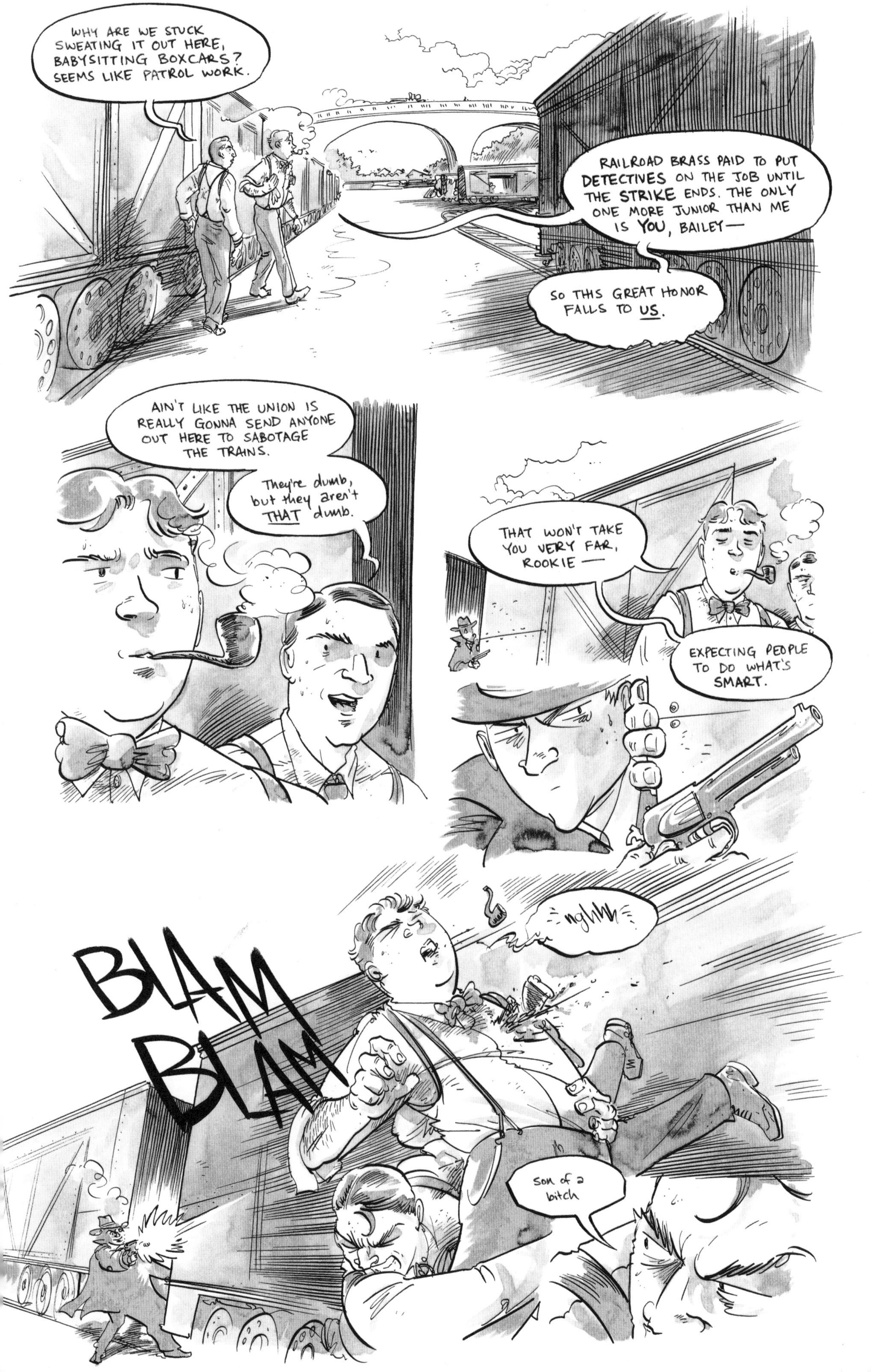
WHY ARE WE STUCK SWEATING IT OUT HERE, BABYSITTING BOXCARS? SEEMS LIKE PATROL WORK.
RAILROAD BRASS PAID TO PUT DETECTIVES ON THE JOB UNTIL THE STRIKE ENDS. THE ONLY ONE MORE JUNIOR THAN ME IS YOU, BAILEY—
SO THIS GREAT HONOR FALLS TO US.
AIN'T LIKE THE UNION IS REALLY GONNA SEND ANYONE OUT HERE TO SABOTAGE THE TRAINS.
They're dumb, but they aren't THAT dumb.
THAT WON'T TAKE YOU VERY FAR, ROOKIE—
EXPECTING PEOPLE TO DO WHAT'S SMART.
BLAM
BLAM
nghhh
Son of a bitch

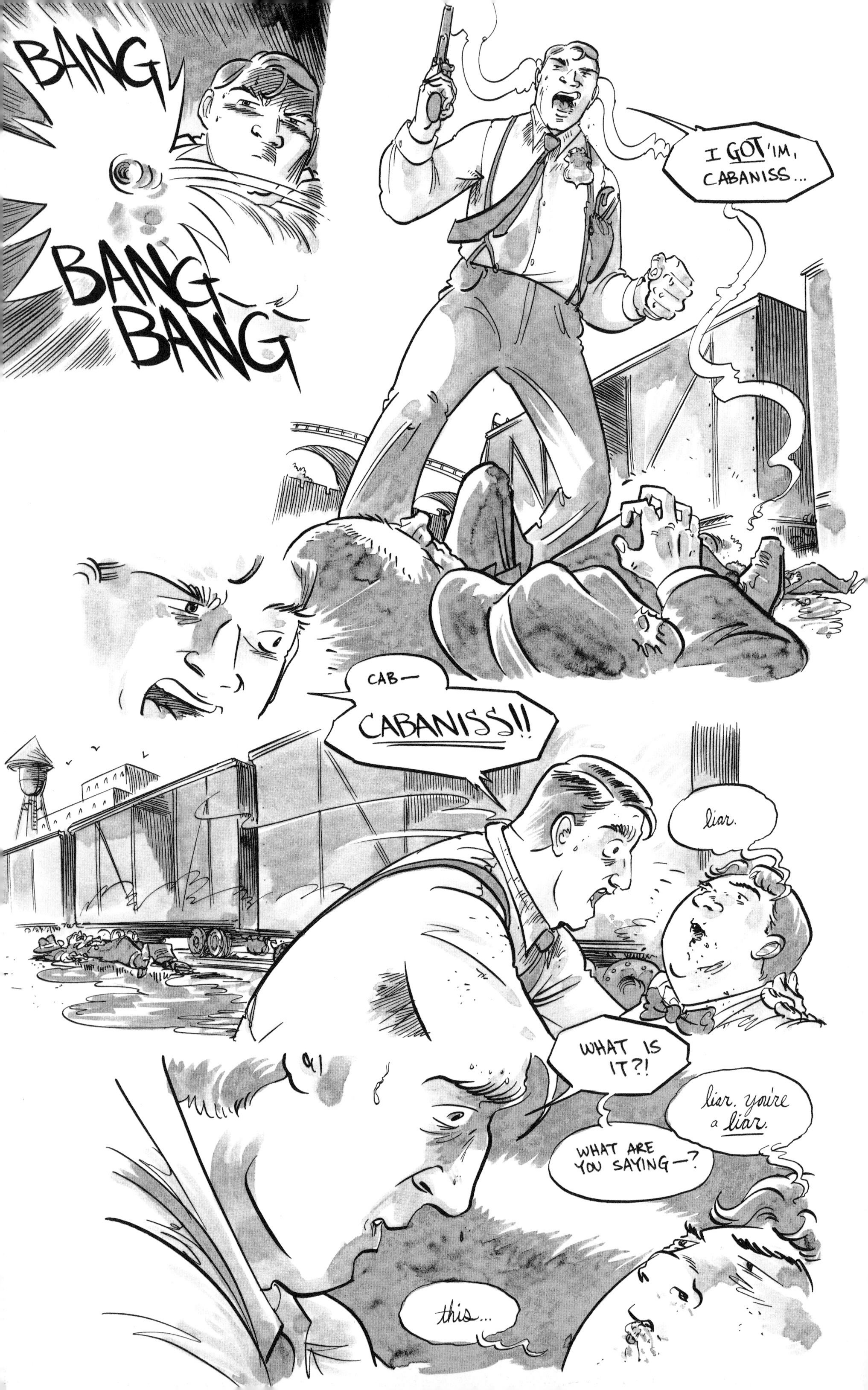
BANG
BANG-BANG
I GOT 'IM, CABANISS...
CAB—
CABANISS!!
liar.
WHAT IS IT?!
liar. you're a liar.
WHAT ARE YOU SAYING—?
this...

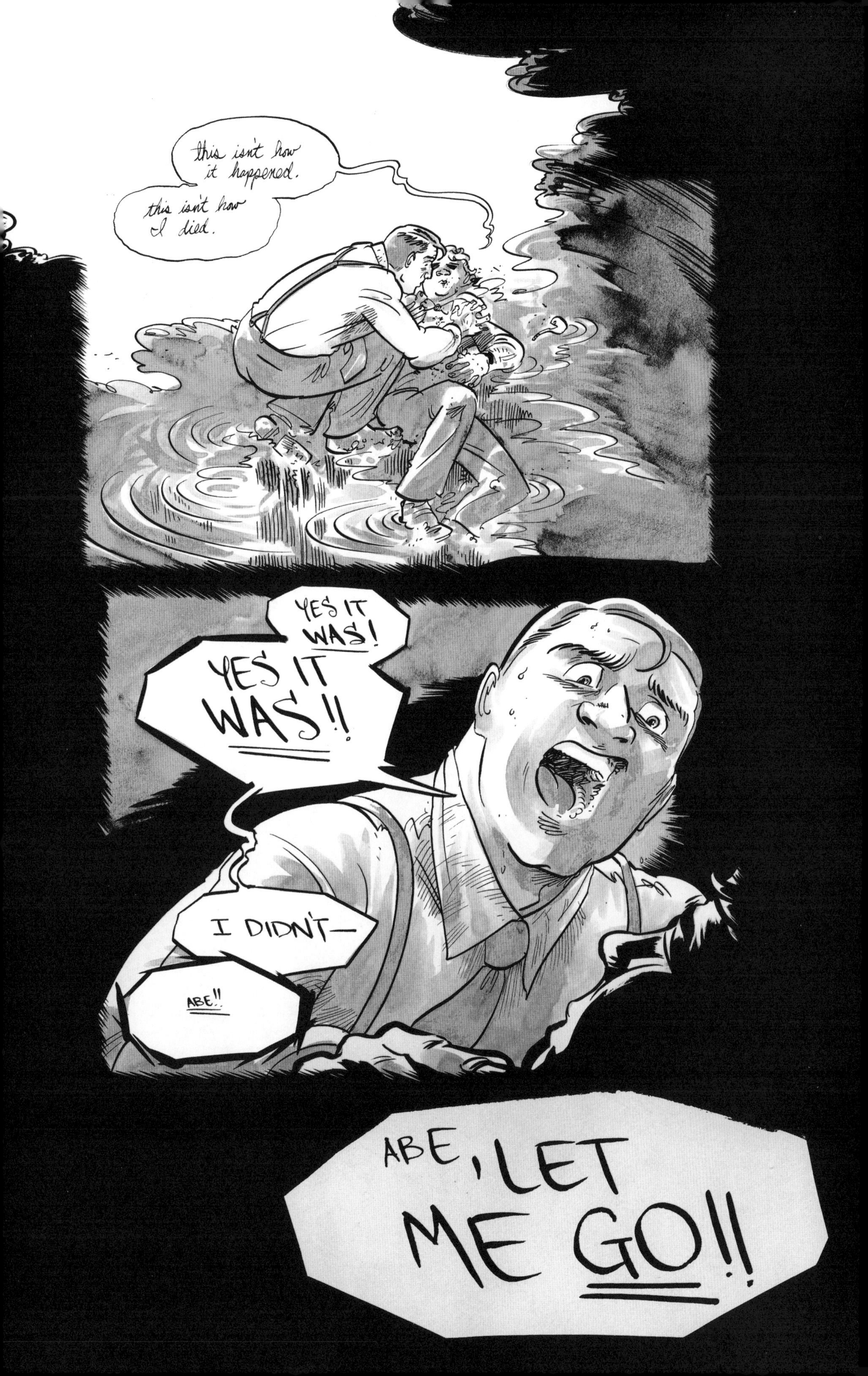
this isn't how it happened.
this isn't how I died.
YES IT WAS!
YES IT WAS!!
I DIDN'T—
ABE!!
ABE, LET ME GO!!

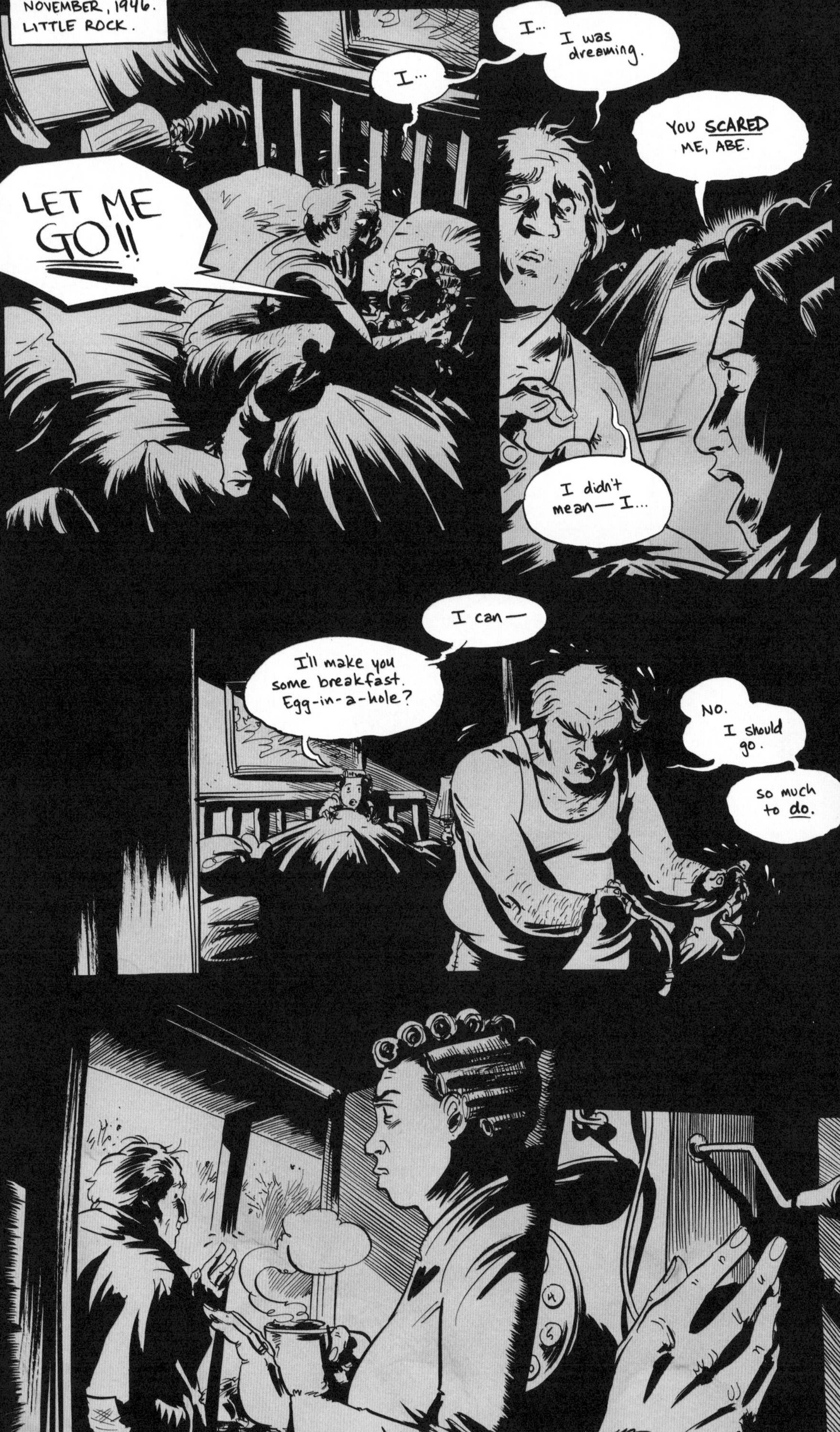
NOVEMBER, 1946. LITTLE ROCK.
LET ME GO!!
I...
I... I was dreaming.
YOU SCARED ME, ABE.
I didn't mean— I...
I can—
I'll make you some breakfast. Egg-in-a-hole?
No. I should go.
so much to do.

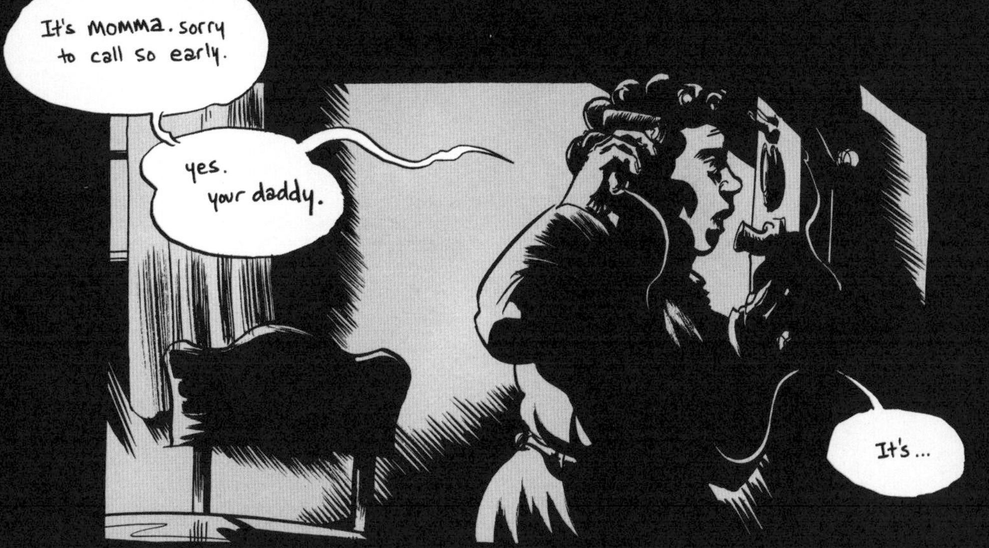
It's MOMMA. sorry to call so early.
yes. your daddy.
It's...

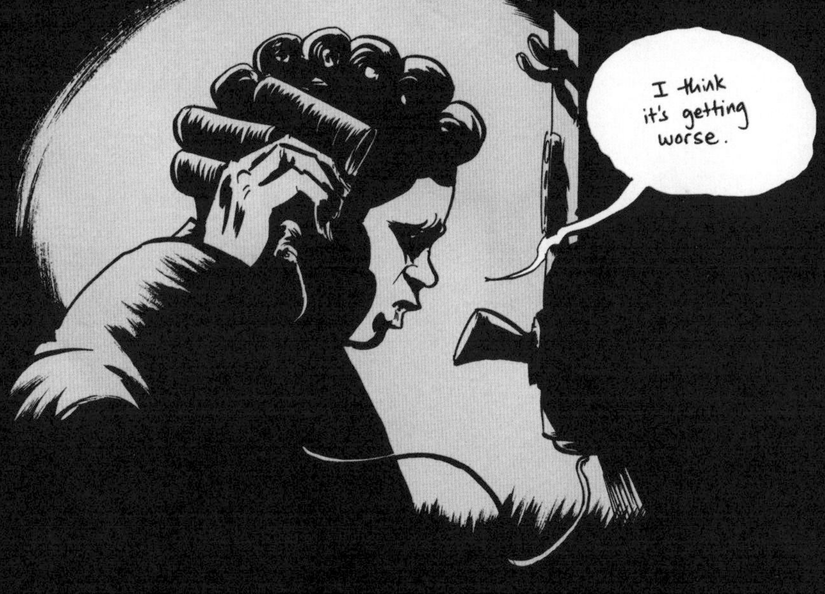
I think it's getting worse.

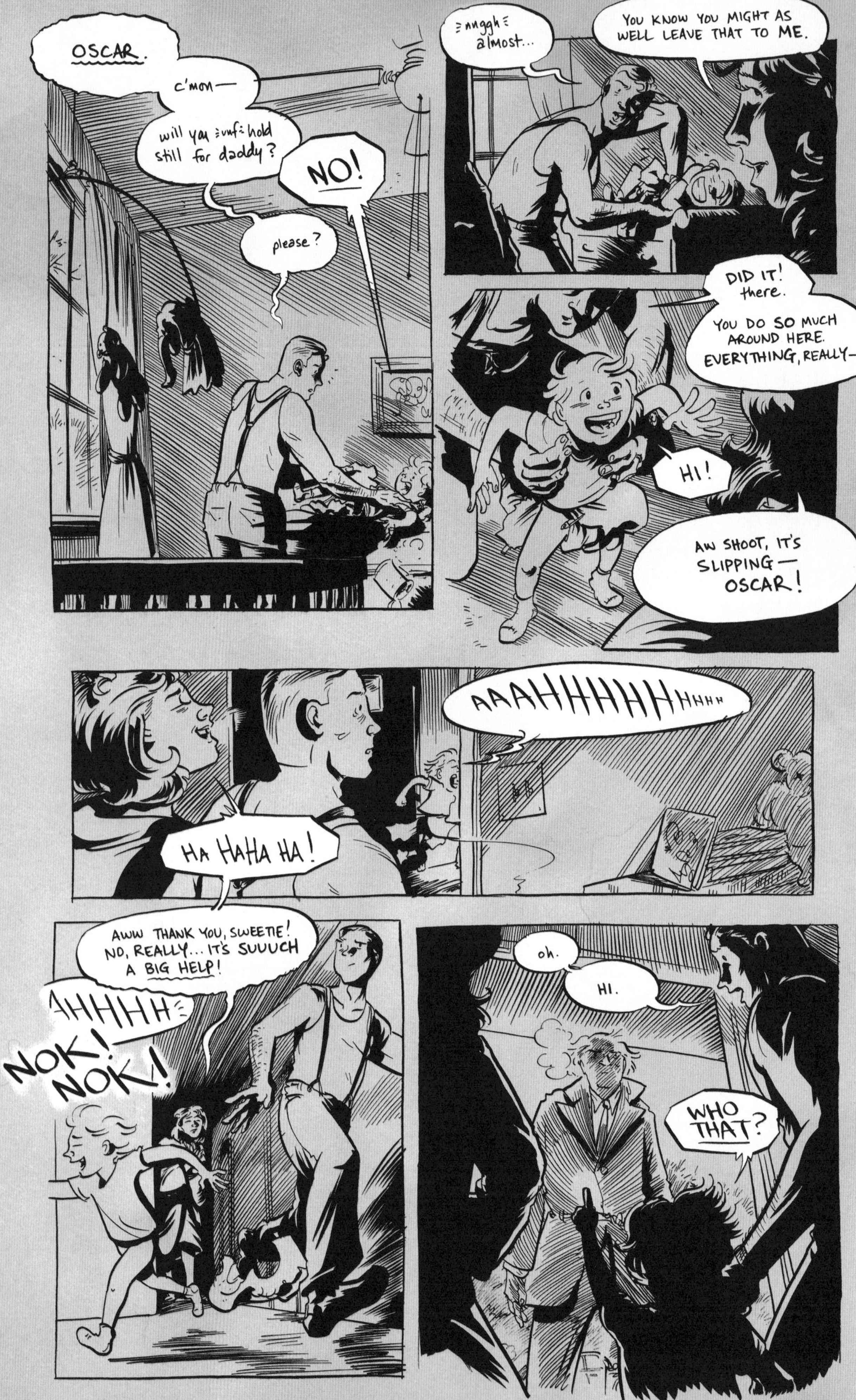

OSCAR.
c'mon—
will you =unf= hold still for daddy?
NO!
please?
=nnggh= almost...
YOU KNOW YOU MIGHT AS WELL LEAVE THAT TO ME.
DID IT! there.
YOU DO SO MUCH AROUND HERE. EVERYTHING, REALLY—
HI!
AW SHOOT, IT'S SLIPPING— OSCAR!
HA HAHA HA!
AAAHHHHHHhhhh
AWW THANK YOU, SWEETIE! NO, REALLY... IT'S SUUUCH A BIG HELP!
AHHHHH
NOK! NOK!
oh.
HI.
WHO THAT?

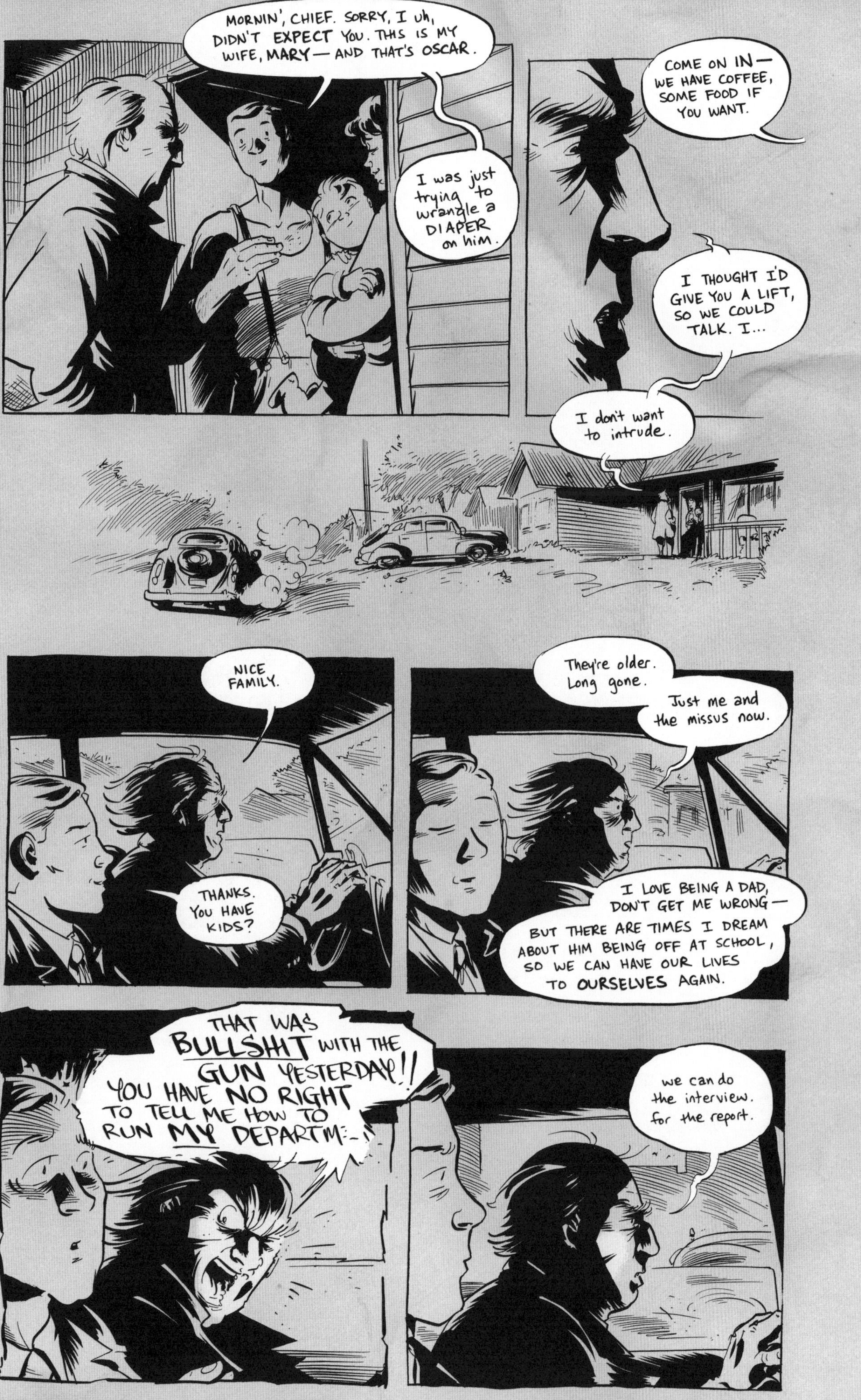
MORNIN', CHIEF. SORRY, I uh, DIDN'T EXPECT YOU. THIS IS MY WIFE, MARY— AND THAT'S OSCAR.
I was just trying to wrangle a DIAPER on him.
COME ON IN— WE HAVE COFFEE, SOME FOOD IF YOU WANT.
I THOUGHT I'D GIVE YOU A LIFT, SO WE COULD TALK. I...
I don't want to intrude.
NICE FAMILY.
THANKS. YOU HAVE KIDS?
They're older. Long gone.
Just me and the missus now.
I LOVE BEING A DAD, DON'T GET ME WRONG— BUT THERE ARE TIMES I DREAM ABOUT HIM BEING OFF AT SCHOOL, SO WE CAN HAVE OUR LIVES TO OURSELVES AGAIN.
THAT WAS BULLSHIT WITH THE GUN YESTERDAY!! YOU HAVE NO RIGHT TO TELL ME HOW TO RUN MY DEPARTM—
we can do the interview. for the report.

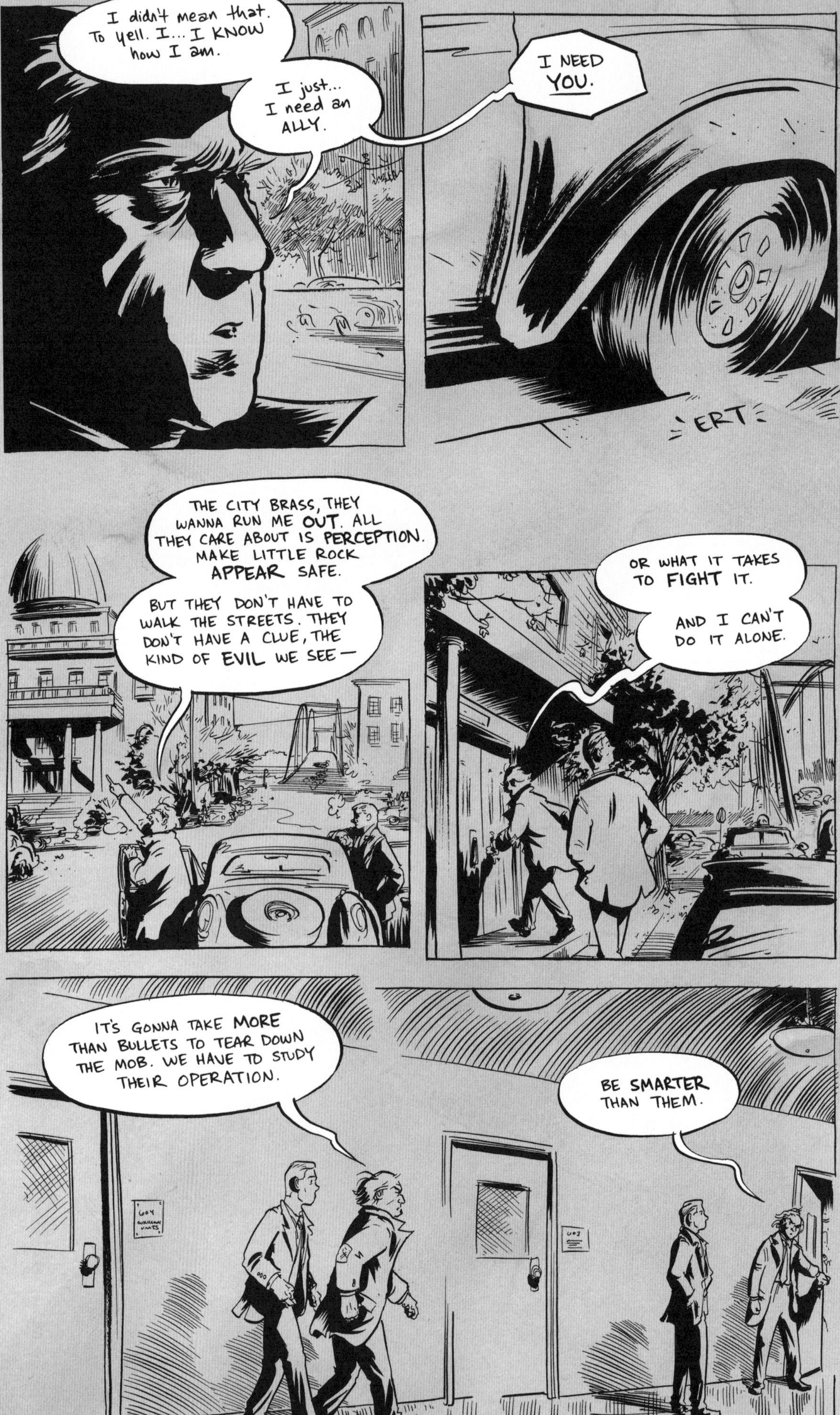
I didn't mean that. To yell. I... I KNOW how I am.
I just... I need an ALLY.
I NEED YOU.
ERT
THE CITY BRASS, THEY WANNA RUN ME OUT. ALL THEY CARE ABOUT IS PERCEPTION. MAKE LITTLE ROCK APPEAR SAFE.
BUT THEY DON'T HAVE TO WALK THE STREETS. THEY DON'T HAVE A CLUE, THE KIND OF EVIL WE SEE—
OR WHAT IT TAKES TO FIGHT IT.
AND I CAN'T DO IT ALONE.
IT'S GONNA TAKE MORE THAN BULLETS TO TEAR DOWN THE MOB. WE HAVE TO STUDY THEIR OPERATION.
BE SMARTER THAN THEM.

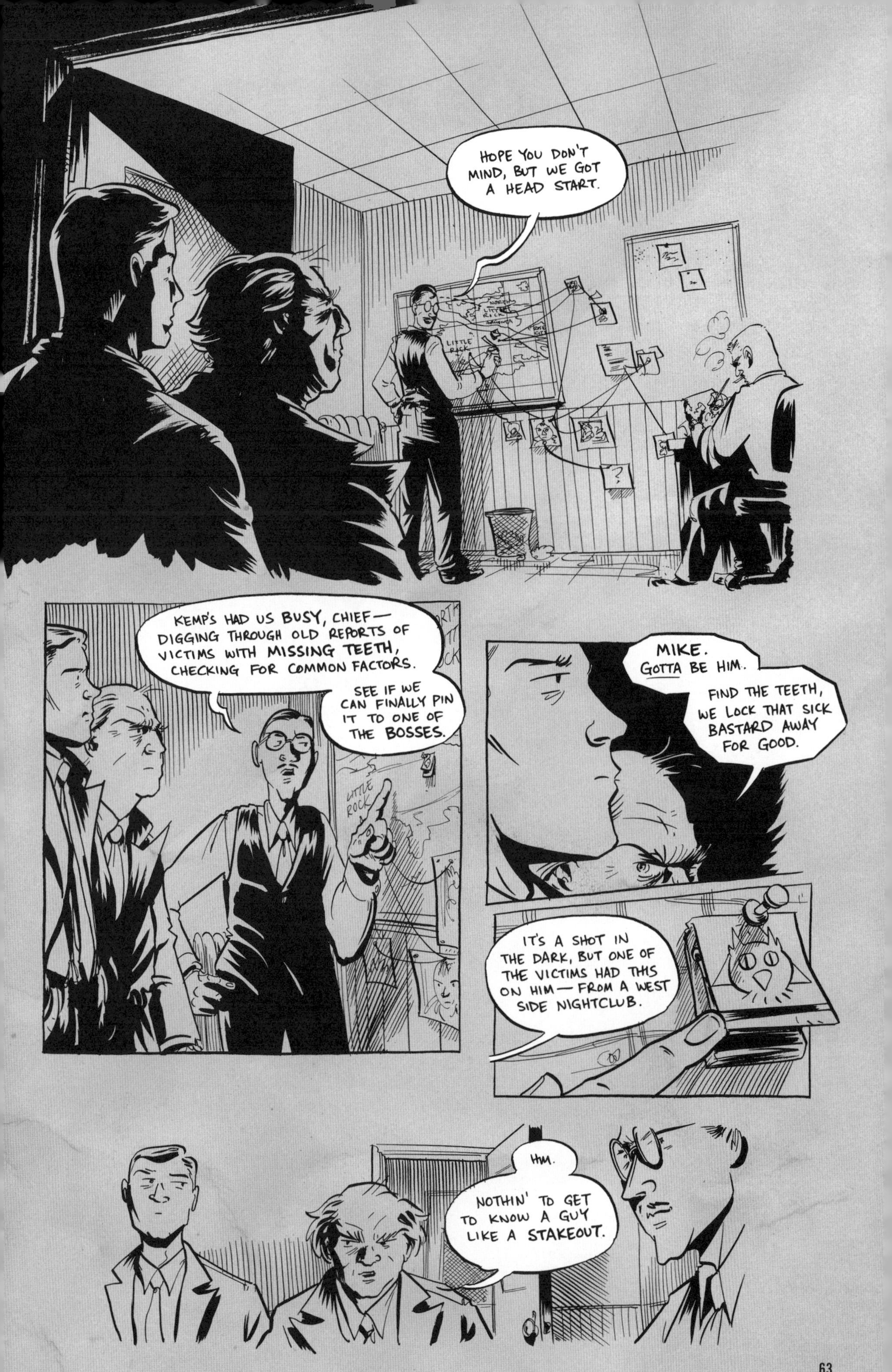
HOPE YOU DON'T MIND, BUT WE GOT A HEAD START.
KEMP'S HAD US BUSY, CHIEF— DIGGING THROUGH OLD REPORTS OF VICTIMS WITH MISSING TEETH, CHECKING FOR COMMON FACTORS.
SEE IF WE CAN FINALLY PIN IT TO ONE OF THE BOSSES.
MIKE. GOTTA BE HIM.
FIND THE TEETH, WE LOCK THAT SICK BASTARD AWAY FOR GOOD.
IT'S A SHOT IN THE DARK, BUT ONE OF THE VICTIMS HAD THIS ON HIM— FROM A WEST SIDE NIGHTCLUB.
HM.
NOTHIN' TO GET TO KNOW A GUY LIKE A STAKEOUT.

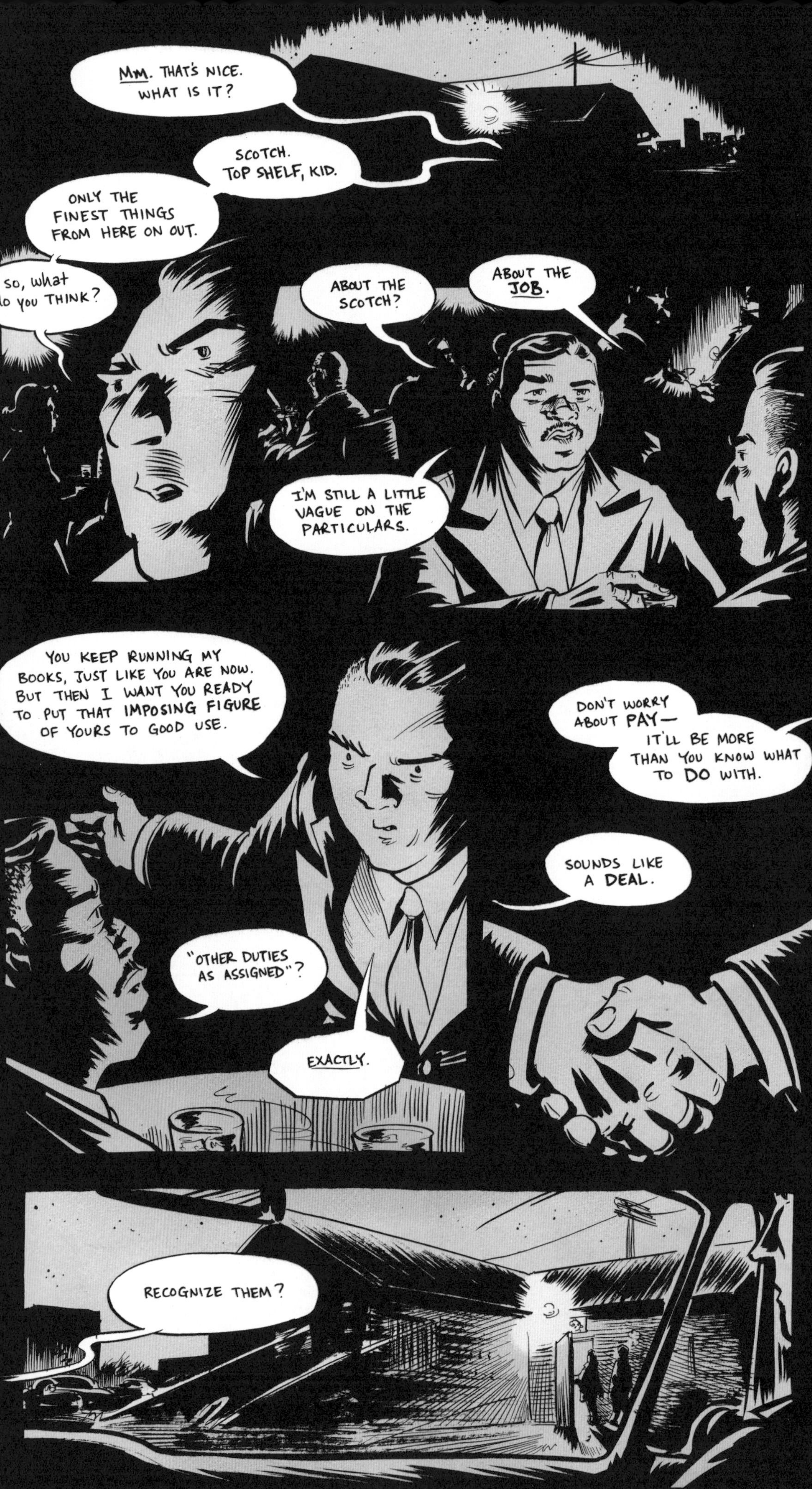
MM. THAT'S NICE. WHAT IS IT?
SCOTCH. TOP SHELF, KID.
ONLY THE FINEST THINGS FROM HERE ON OUT.
...SO, WHAT DO YOU THINK?
ABOUT THE SCOTCH?
ABOUT THE JOB.
I'M STILL A LITTLE VAGUE ON THE PARTICULARS.
YOU KEEP RUNNING MY BOOKS, JUST LIKE YOU ARE NOW. BUT THEN I WANT YOU READY TO PUT THAT IMPOSING FIGURE OF YOURS TO GOOD USE.
"OTHER DUTIES AS ASSIGNED"?
EXACTLY.
DON'T WORRY ABOUT PAY—
IT'LL BE MORE THAN YOU KNOW WHAT TO DO WITH.
SOUNDS LIKE A DEAL.
RECOGNIZE THEM?

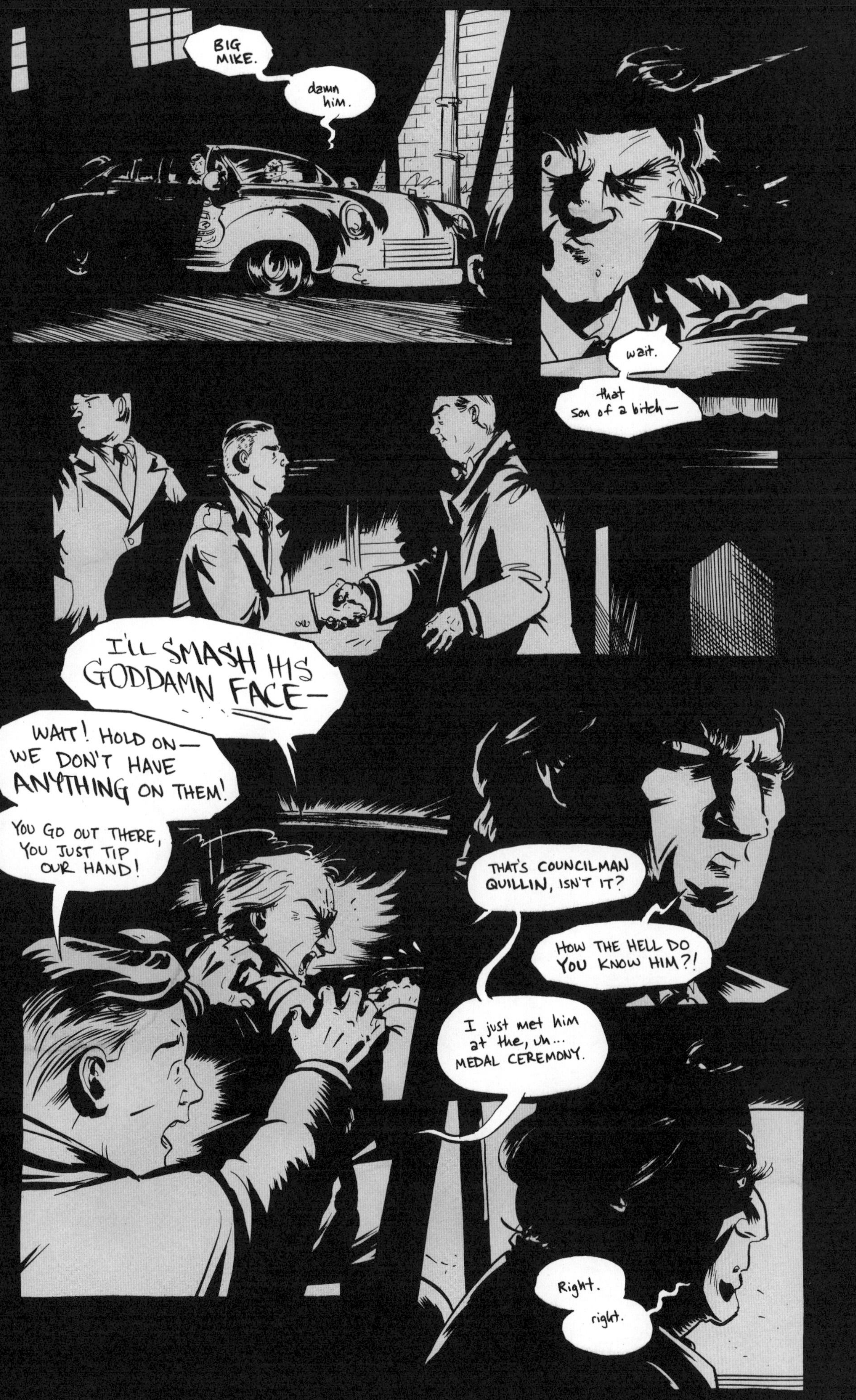
BIG MIKE.
damn him.
wait.
that son of a bitch—
I'LL SMASH HIS GODDAMN FACE—
WAIT! HOLD ON— WE DON'T HAVE ANYTHING ON THEM!
YOU GO OUT THERE, YOU JUST TIP OUR HAND!
THAT'S COUNCILMAN QUILLIN, ISN'T IT?
HOW THE HELL DO YOU KNOW HIM?!
I just met him at the, uh... MEDAL CEREMONY.
Right.
right.

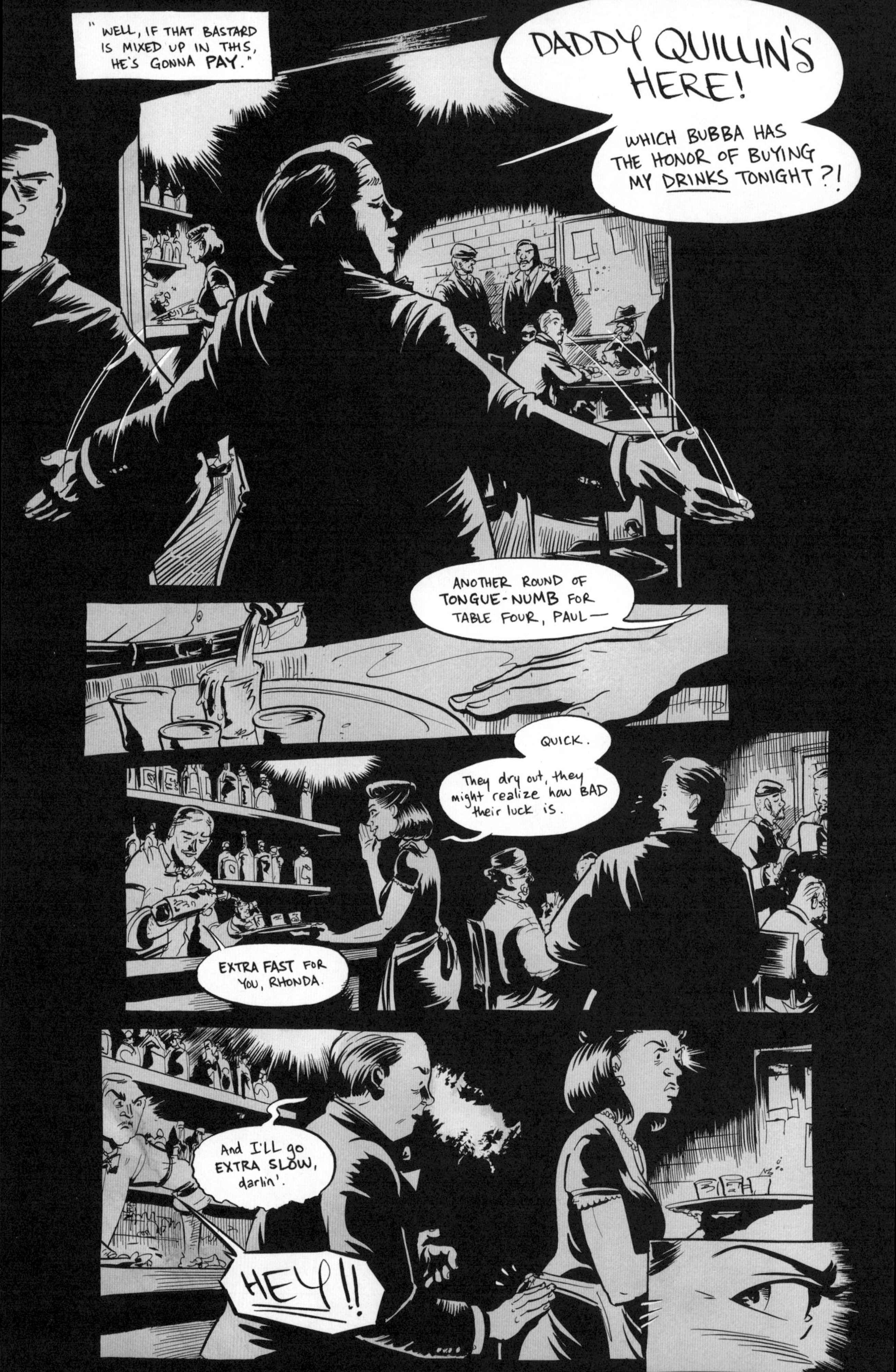
"WELL, IF THAT BASTARD IS MIXED UP IN THIS, HE'S GONNA PAY."
DADDY QUILLIN'S HERE!
WHICH BUBBA HAS THE HONOR OF BUYING MY DRINKS TONIGHT?!
ANOTHER ROUND OF TONGUE-NUMB FOR TABLE FOUR, PAUL—
QUICK.
They dry out, they might realize how BAD their luck is.
EXTRA FAST FOR YOU, RHONDA.
And I'LL go EXTRA SLOW, darlin'.
HEY!!

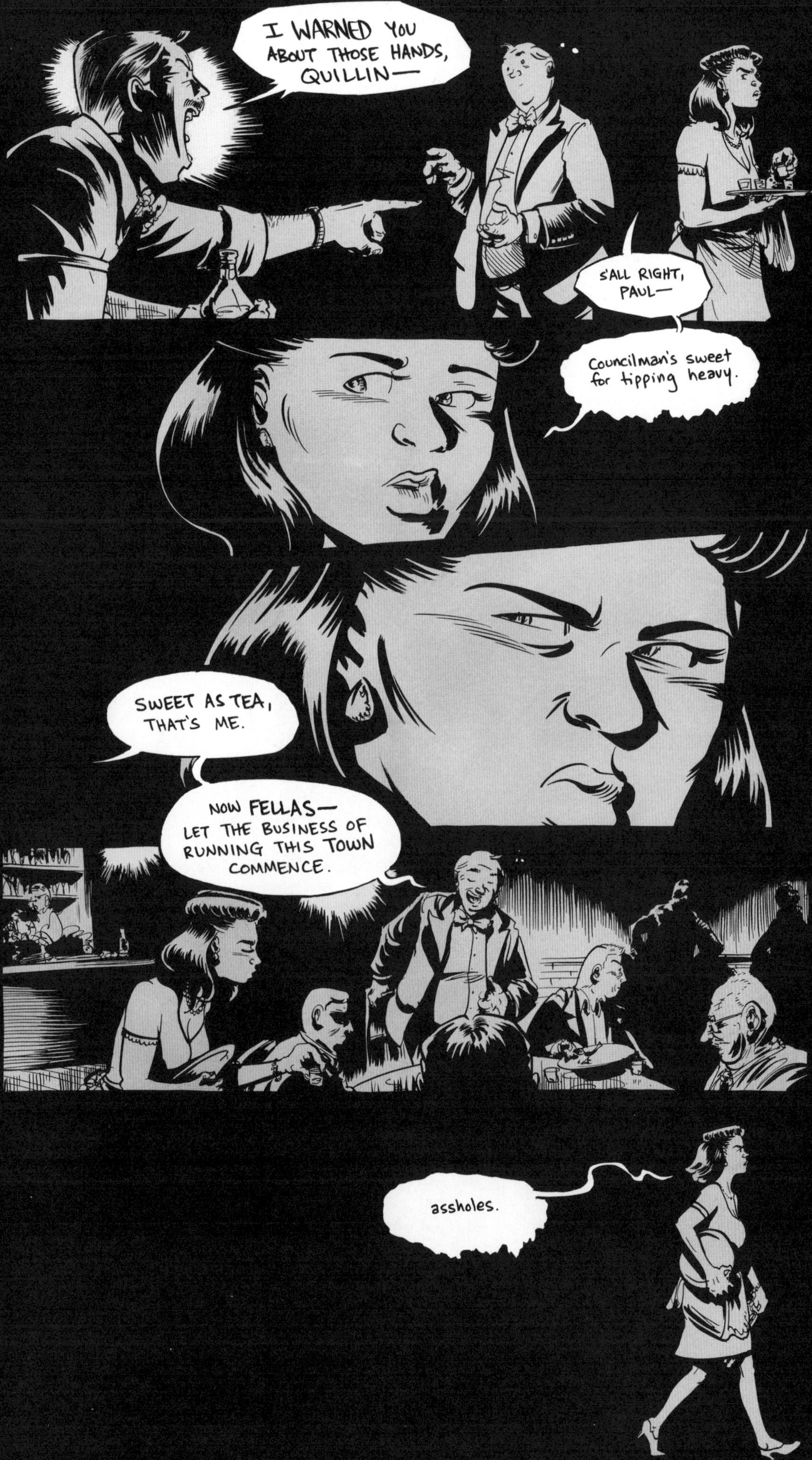

I WARNED YOU ABOUT THOSE HANDS, QUILLIN—
S'ALL RIGHT, PAUL—
Councilman's sweet for tipping heavy.
SWEET AS TEA, THAT'S ME.
NOW FELLAS— LET THE BUSINESS OF RUNNING THIS TOWN COMMENCE.
assholes.

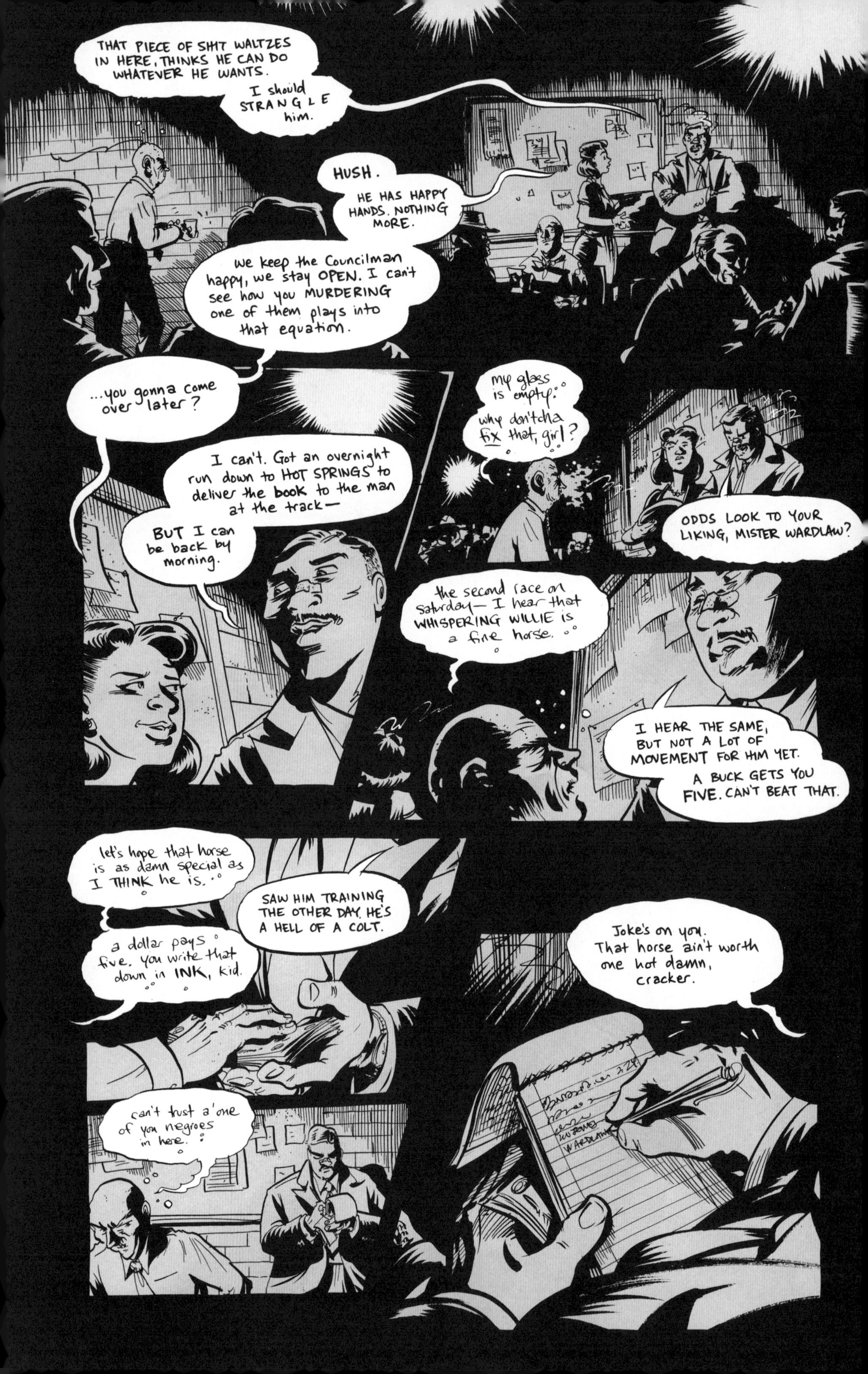
THAT PIECE OF SHIT WALTZES IN HERE, THINKS HE CAN DO WHATEVER HE WANTS.
I should STRANGLE him.
HUSH.
HE HAS HAPPY HANDS. NOTHING MORE.
we keep the Councilman happy, we stay OPEN. I can't see how you MURDERING one of them plays into that equation.
...you gonna come over later?
I can't. Got an overnight run down to HOT SPRINGS to deliver the book to the man at the track—
BUT I can be back by morning.
my glass is empty.
why don'tcha fix that, girl?
ODDS LOOK TO YOUR LIKING, MISTER WARDLAW?
the second race on saturday— I hear that WHISPERING WILLIE is a fine horse.
I HEAR THE SAME, BUT NOT A LOT OF MOVEMENT FOR HIM YET.
A BUCK GETS YOU FIVE. CAN'T BEAT THAT.
let's hope that horse is as damn special as I THINK he is.
SAW HIM TRAINING THE OTHER DAY. HE'S A HELL OF A COLT.
a dollar pays five. you write that down in INK, kid.
can't trust a'one of you negroes in here.
Joke's on you. That horse ain't worth one hot damn, cracker.

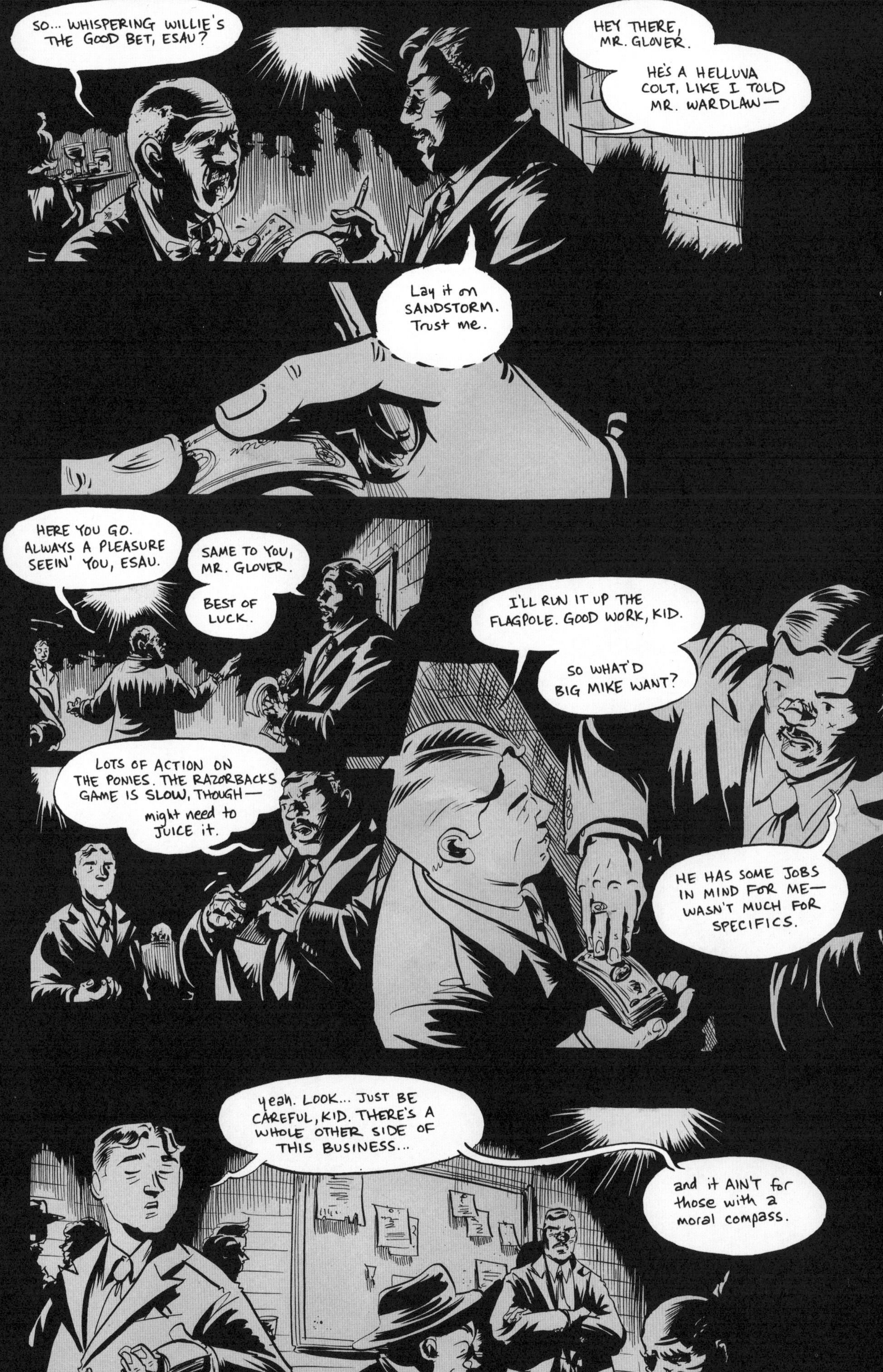
SO... WHISPERING WILLIE'S THE GOOD BET, ESAU?
HEY THERE, MR. GLOVER.
HE'S A HELLUVA COLT, LIKE I TOLD MR. WARDLAW—
Lay it on SANDSTORM. Trust me.
HERE YOU GO. ALWAYS A PLEASURE SEEIN' YOU, ESAU.
SAME TO YOU, MR. GLOVER.
BEST OF LUCK.
LOTS OF ACTION ON THE PONIES. THE RAZORBACKS GAME IS SLOW, THOUGH— might need to JUICE it.
I'LL RUN IT UP THE FLAGPOLE. GOOD WORK, KID.
SO WHAT'D BIG MIKE WANT?
HE HAS SOME JOBS IN MIND FOR ME— WASN'T MUCH FOR SPECIFICS.
yeah. LOOK... JUST BE CAREFUL, KID. THERE'S A WHOLE OTHER SIDE OF THIS BUSINESS...
and it AIN'T for those with a moral compass.

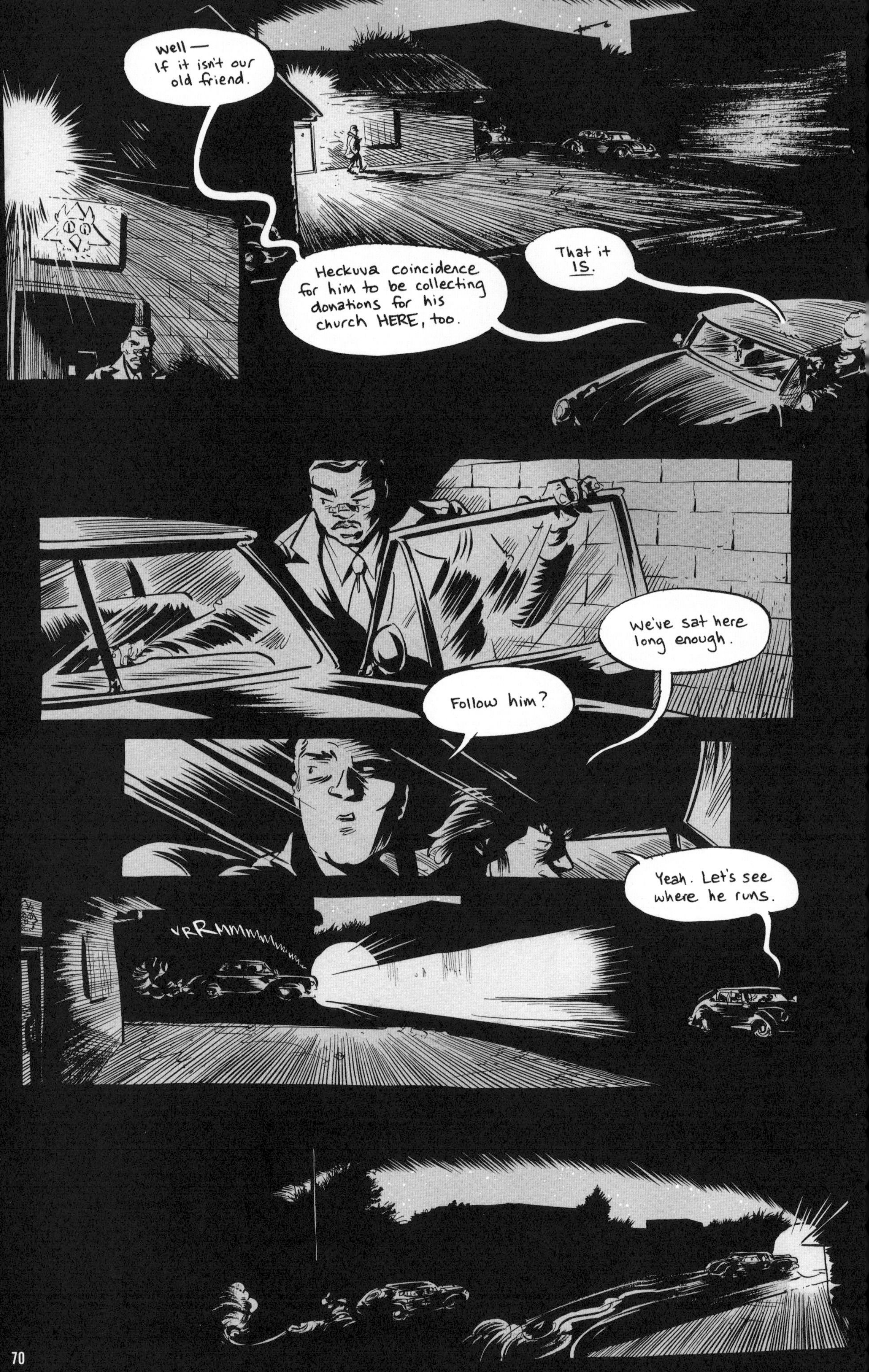

Well— If it isn't our old friend.
Heckuva coincidence for him to be collecting donations for his church HERE, too.
That it IS.
We've sat here long enough.
Follow him?
Yeah. Let's see where he runs.
VRRMMMMMMmmmmmmm

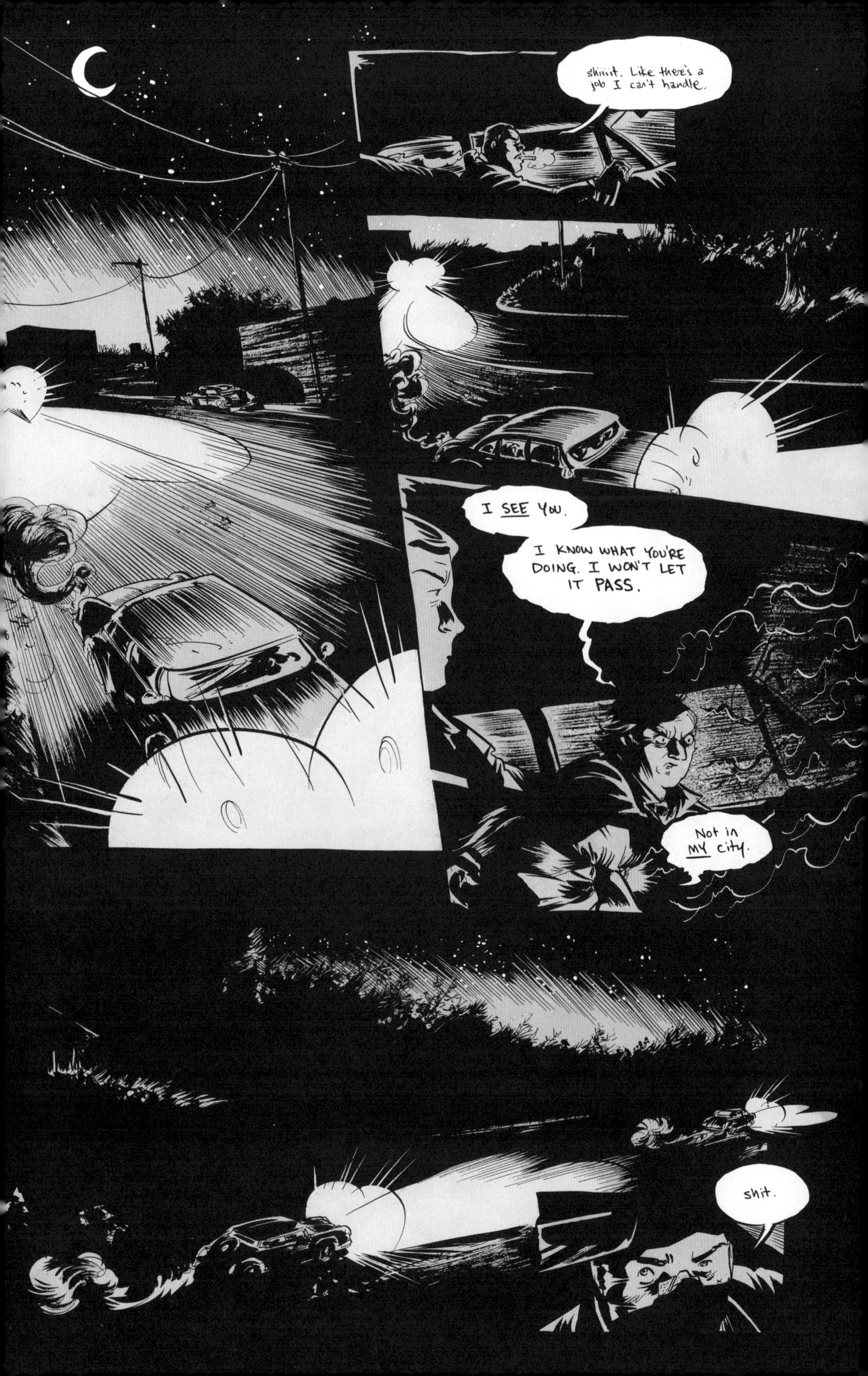
shiiiit. Like there's a job I can't handle.
I SEE YOU.
I KNOW WHAT YOU'RE DOING. I WON'T LET IT PASS.
Not in MY city.
shit.

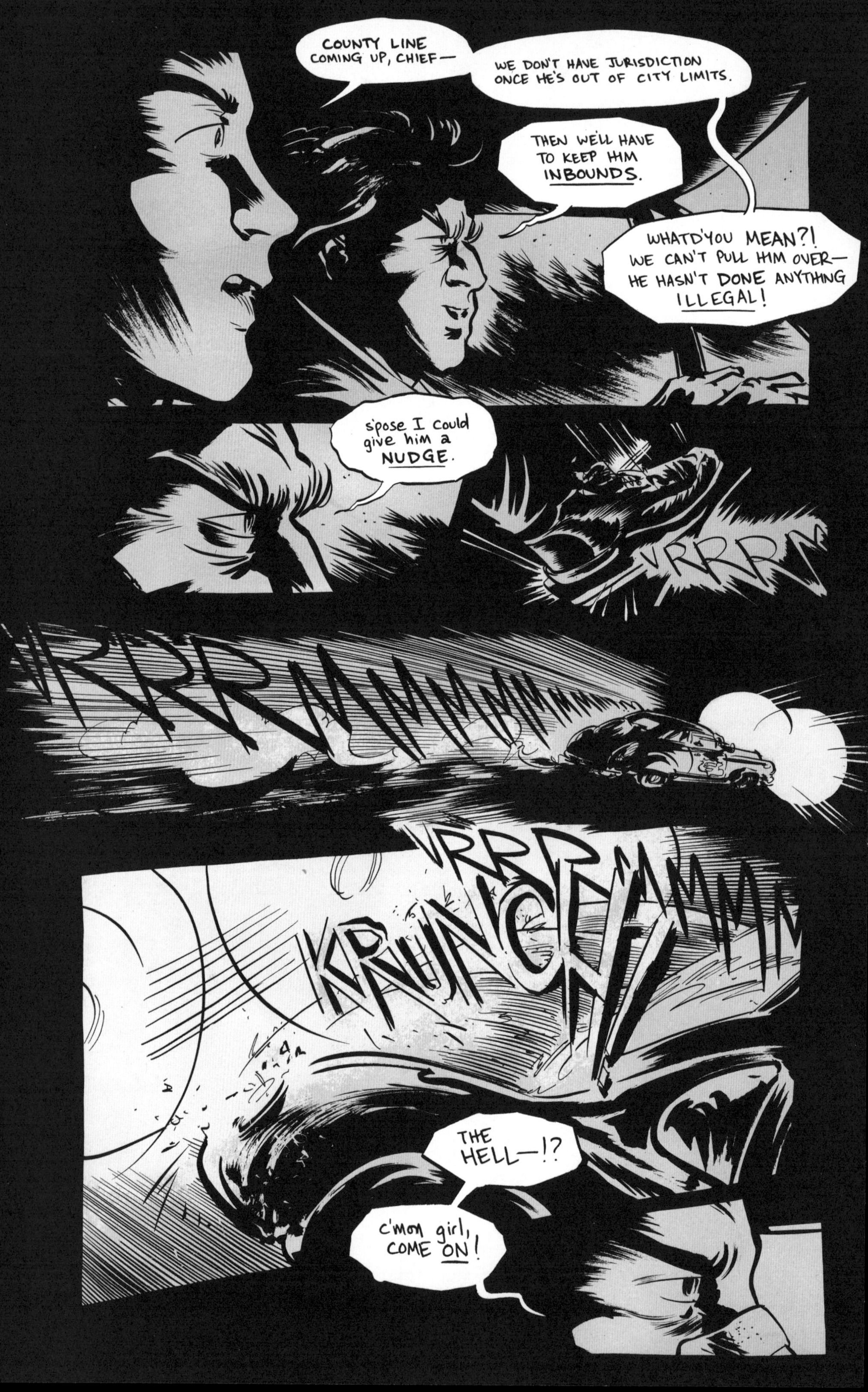
COUNTY LINE COMING UP, CHIEF—
WE DON'T HAVE JURISDICTION ONCE HE'S OUT OF CITY LIMITS.
THEN WE'LL HAVE TO KEEP HIM INBOUNDS.
WHATD'YOU MEAN?! WE CAN'T PULL HIM OVER—HE HASN'T DONE ANYTHING ILLEGAL!
s'pose I could give him a NUDGE.
VRRRR
VRRRAMMMM...
VRRRAMMMM
KRUNCH!
THE HELL—!?
c'mon girl, COME ON!

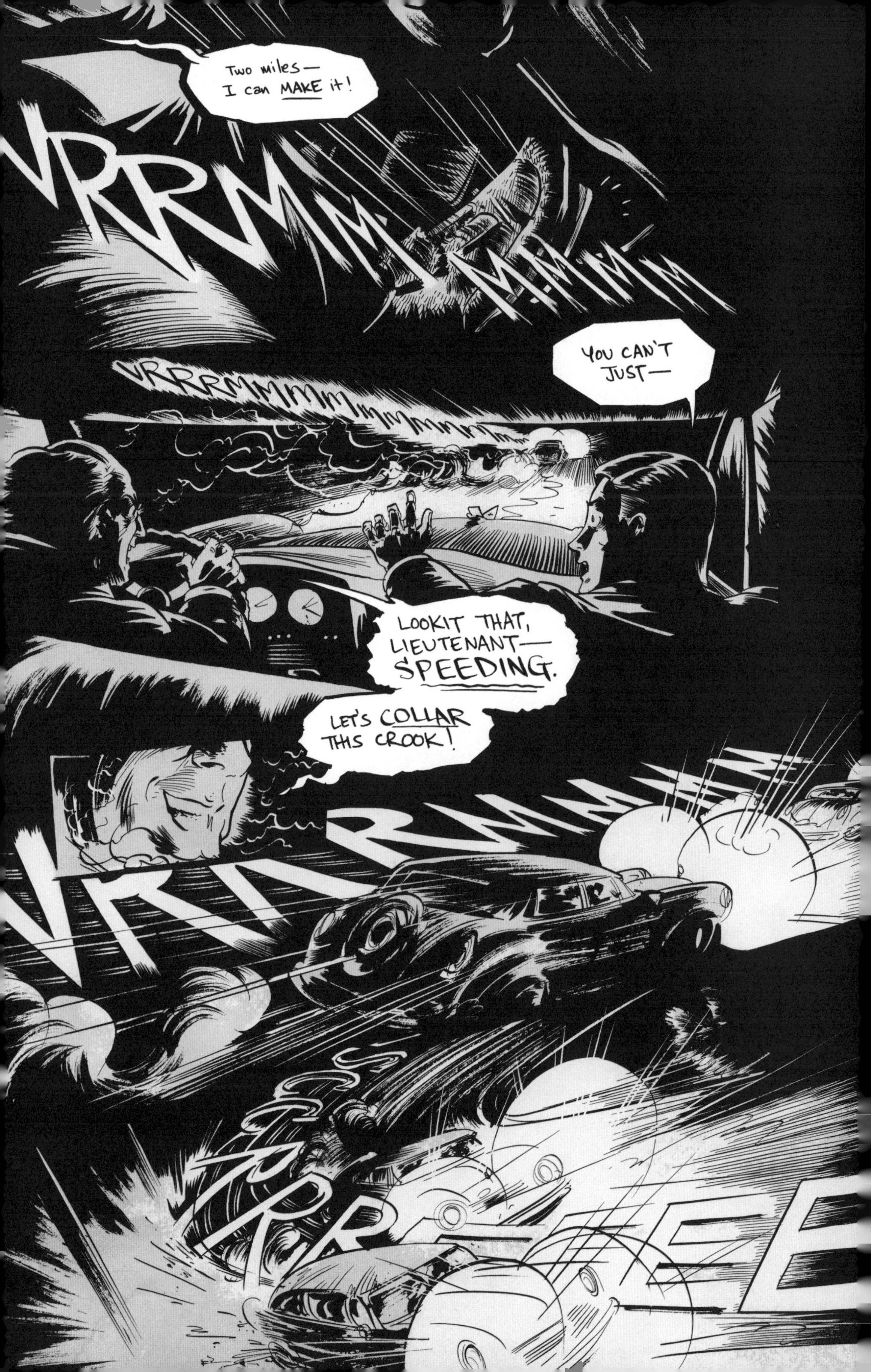
Two miles—
I can MAKE it!
VRRRMMMMMM
VRRRMMMMMMMMMMMMM
YOU CAN'T JUST—
LOOKIT THAT, LIEUTENANT—SPEEDING.
LET'S COLLAR THIS CROOK!
VRRRMMMM
RRREEE

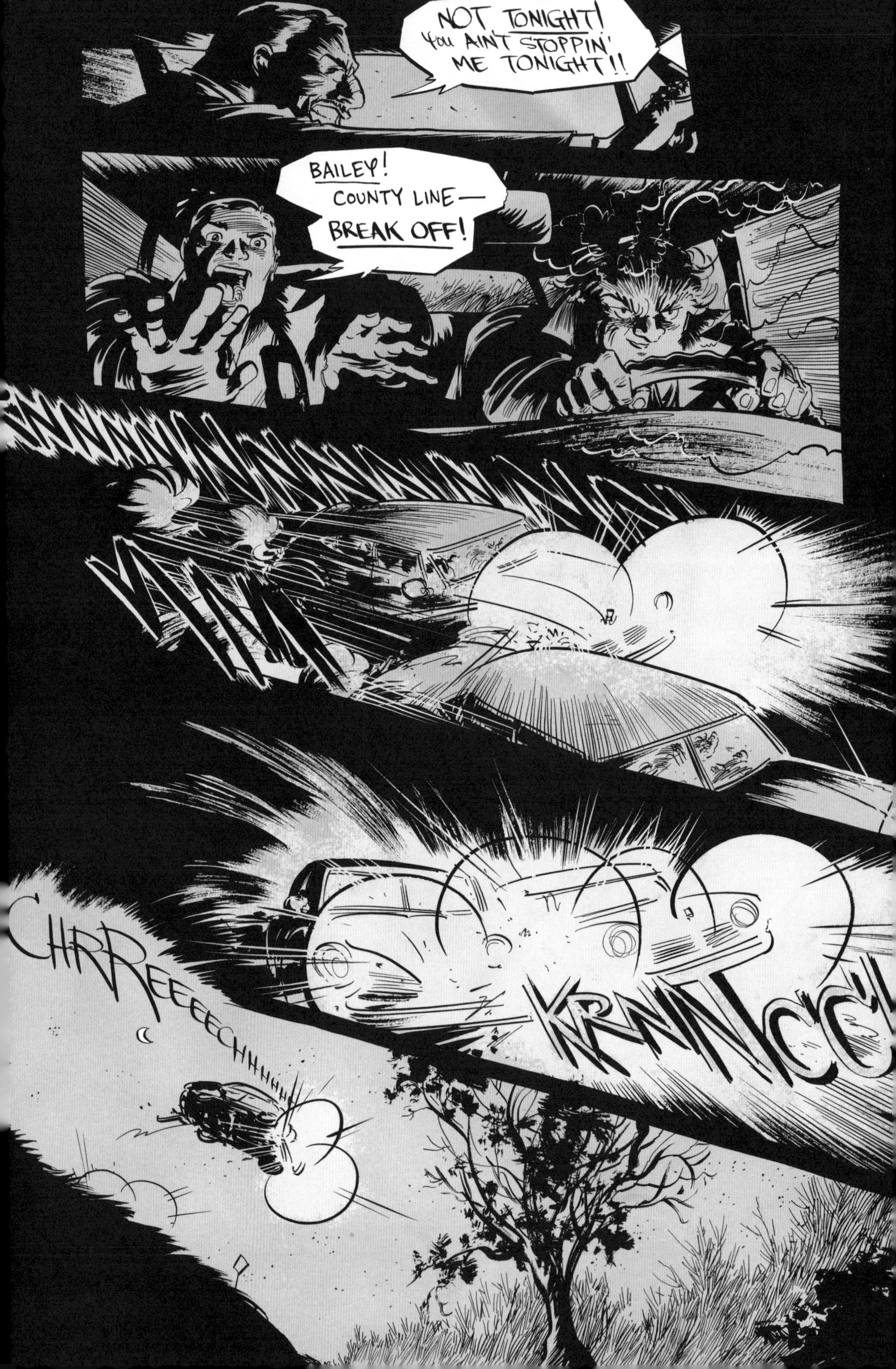

NOT TONIGHT! You AIN'T STOPPIN' ME TONIGHT!!
BAILEY! COUNTY LINE— BREAK OFF!
KRNNTCC'L
CHRREEEECHHHHH

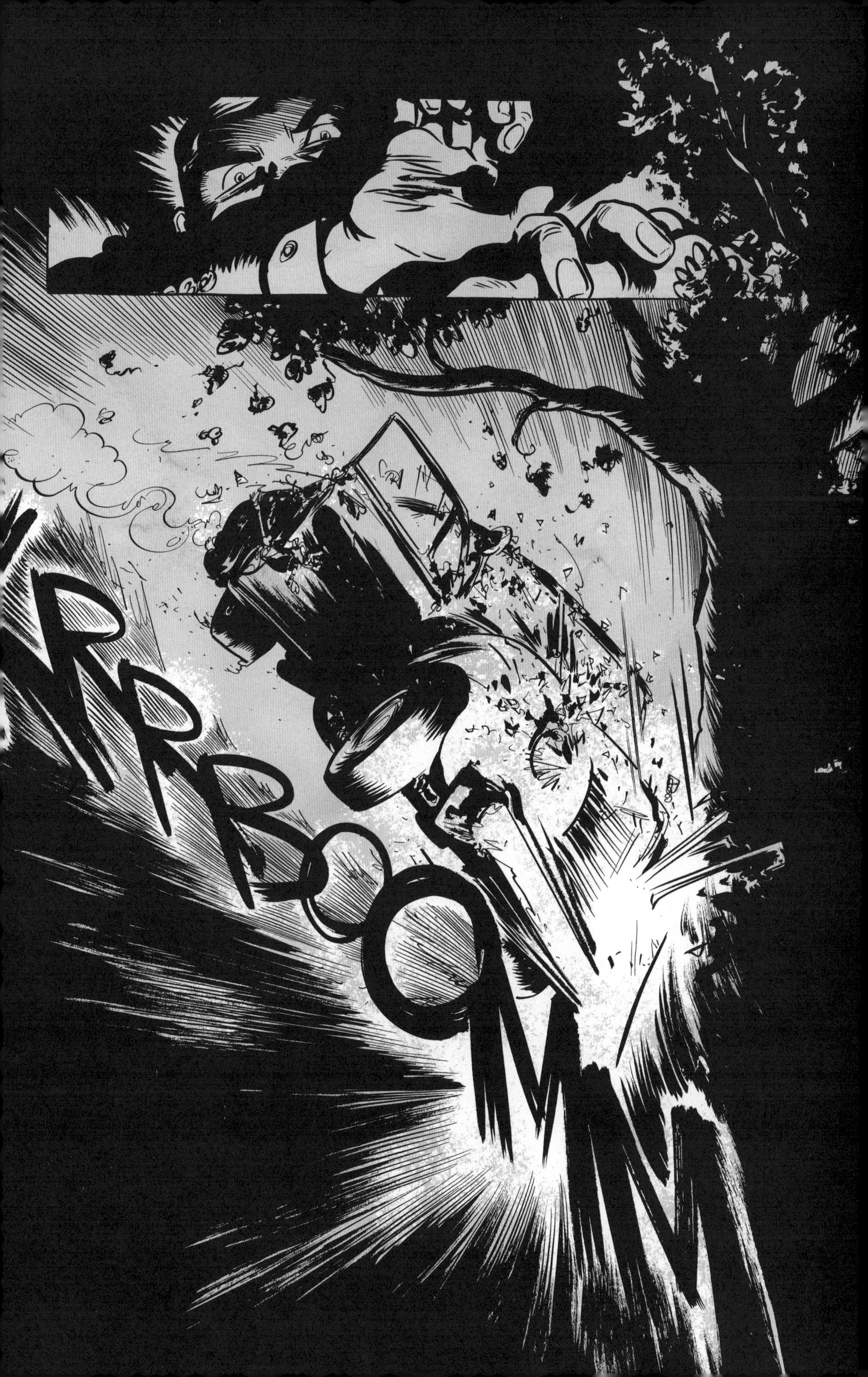
RRROOOM

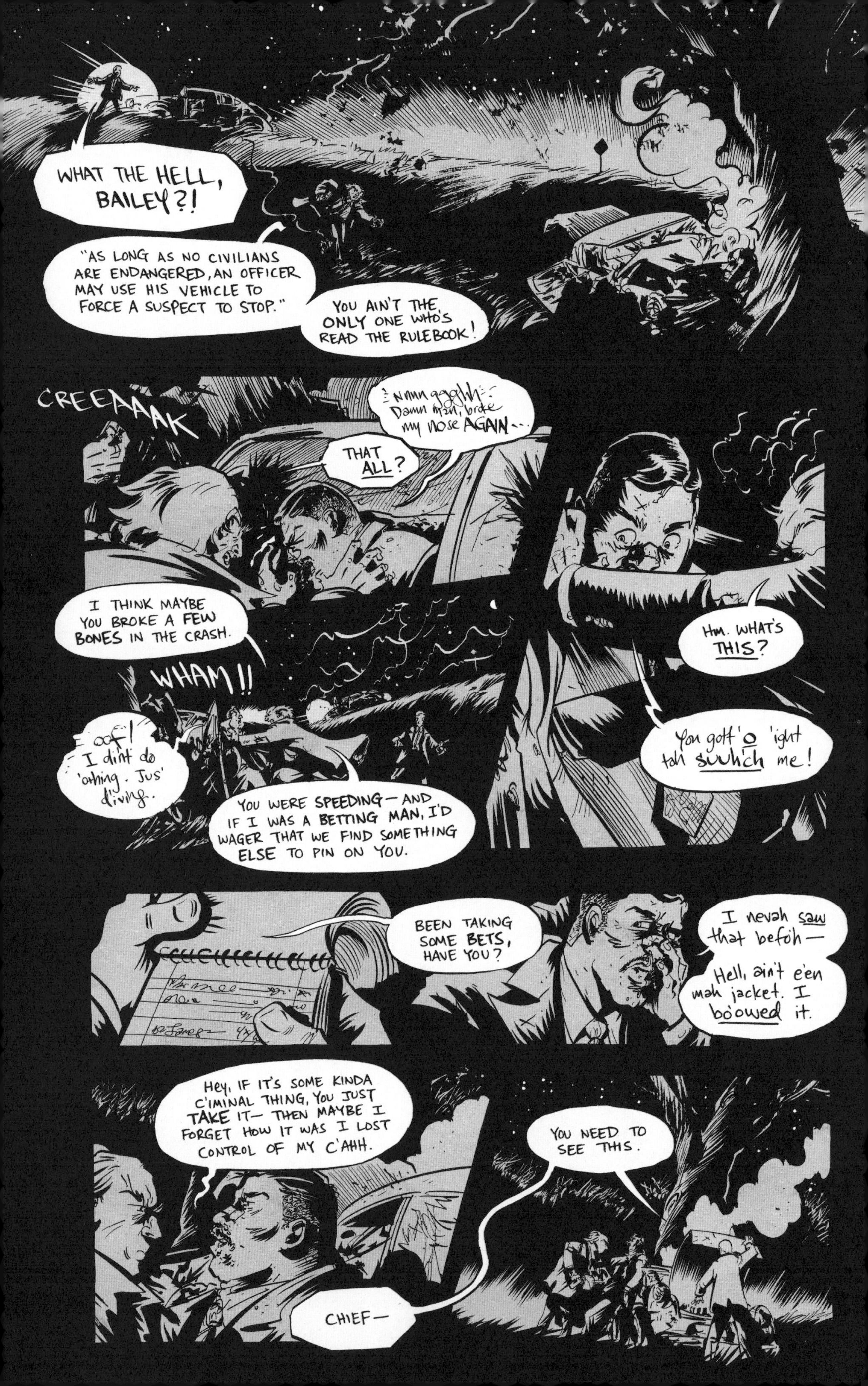

WHAT THE HELL, BAILEY?!
"AS LONG AS NO CIVILIANS ARE ENDANGERED, AN OFFICER MAY USE HIS VEHICLE TO FORCE A SUSPECT TO STOP."
YOU AIN'T THE ONLY ONE WHO'S READ THE RULEBOOK!
CREEAAAAK
Nnnn ggghh Damn man, broke my nose AGAIN...
THAT ALL?
I THINK MAYBE YOU BROKE A FEW BONES IN THE CRASH.
WHAM!!
oof! I din't do 'othing. Jus' diving.
YOU WERE SPEEDING— AND IF I WAS A BETTING MAN, I'D WAGER THAT WE FIND SOMETHING ELSE TO PIN ON YOU.
Hm. WHAT'S THIS?
You got'o 'ight tah suuh'ch me!
BEEN TAKING SOME BETS, HAVE YOU?
I nevah saw that befoh—
Hell, ain't e'en mah jacket. I bo'owed it.
Hey, IF IT'S SOME KINDA C'IMINAL THING, YOU JUST TAKE IT— THEN MAYBE I FORGET HOW IT WAS I LOST CONTROL OF MY C'AHH.
CHIEF—
YOU NEED TO SEE THIS.

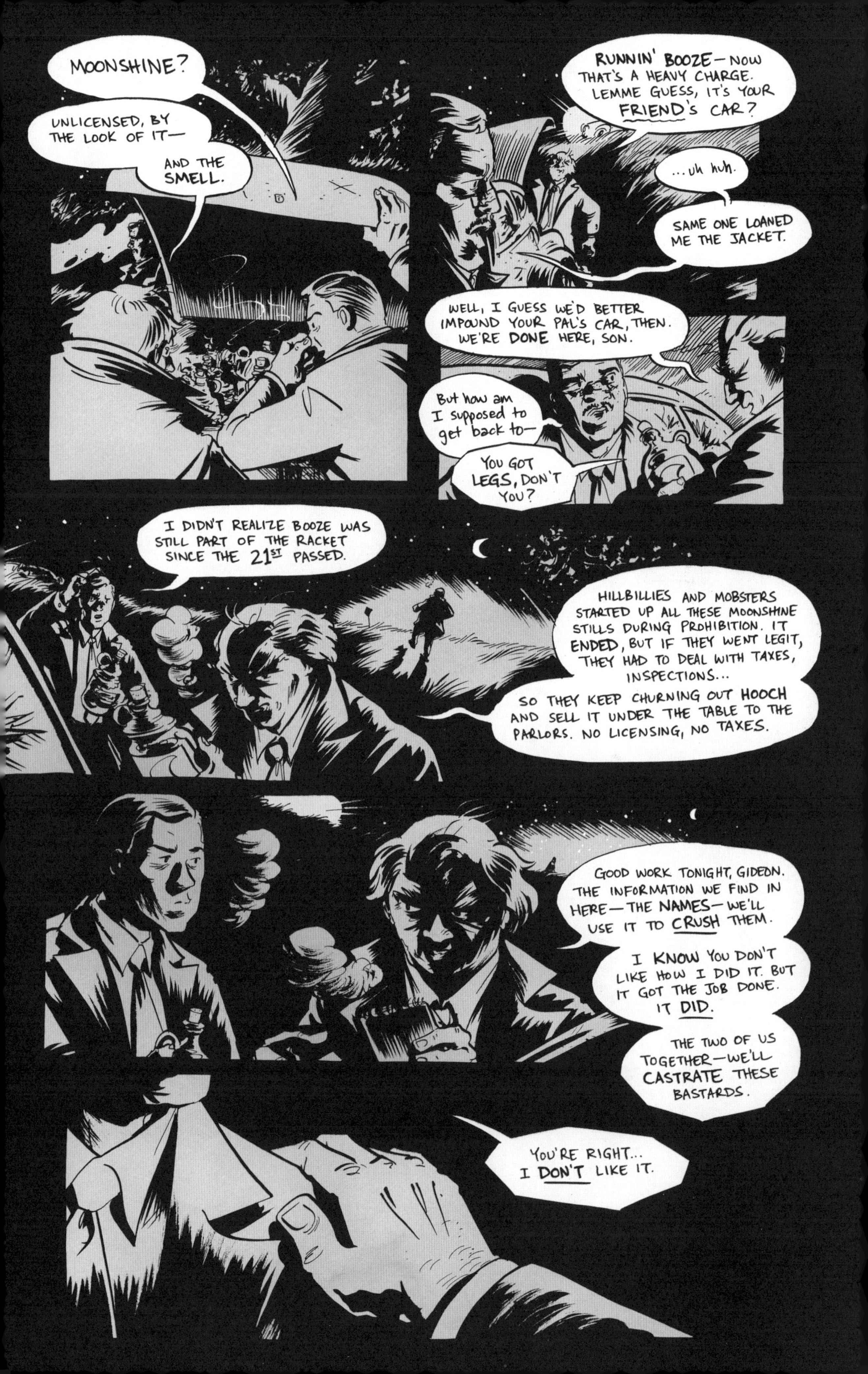
MOONSHINE?
UNLICENSED, BY THE LOOK OF IT—
AND THE SMELL.
RUNNIN' BOOZE—NOW THAT'S A HEAVY CHARGE. LEMME GUESS, IT'S YOUR FRIEND'S CAR?
...uh huh.
SAME ONE LOANED ME THE JACKET.
WELL, I GUESS WE'D BETTER IMPOUND YOUR PAL'S CAR, THEN. WE'RE DONE HERE, SON.
But how am I supposed to get back to—
YOU GOT LEGS, DON'T YOU?
I DIDN'T REALIZE BOOZE WAS STILL PART OF THE RACKET SINCE THE 21ST PASSED.
HILLBILLIES AND MOBSTERS STARTED UP ALL THESE MOONSHINE STILLS DURING PROHIBITION. IT ENDED, BUT IF THEY WENT LEGIT, THEY HAD TO DEAL WITH TAXES, INSPECTIONS...
SO THEY KEEP CHURNING OUT HOOCH AND SELL IT UNDER THE TABLE TO THE PARLORS. NO LICENSING, NO TAXES.
GOOD WORK TONIGHT, GIDEON. THE INFORMATION WE FIND IN HERE—THE NAMES—WE'LL USE IT TO CRUSH THEM.
I KNOW YOU DON'T LIKE HOW I DID IT. BUT IT GOT THE JOB DONE. IT DID.
THE TWO OF US TOGETHER—WE'LL CASTRATE THESE BASTARDS.
YOU'RE RIGHT... I DON'T LIKE IT.

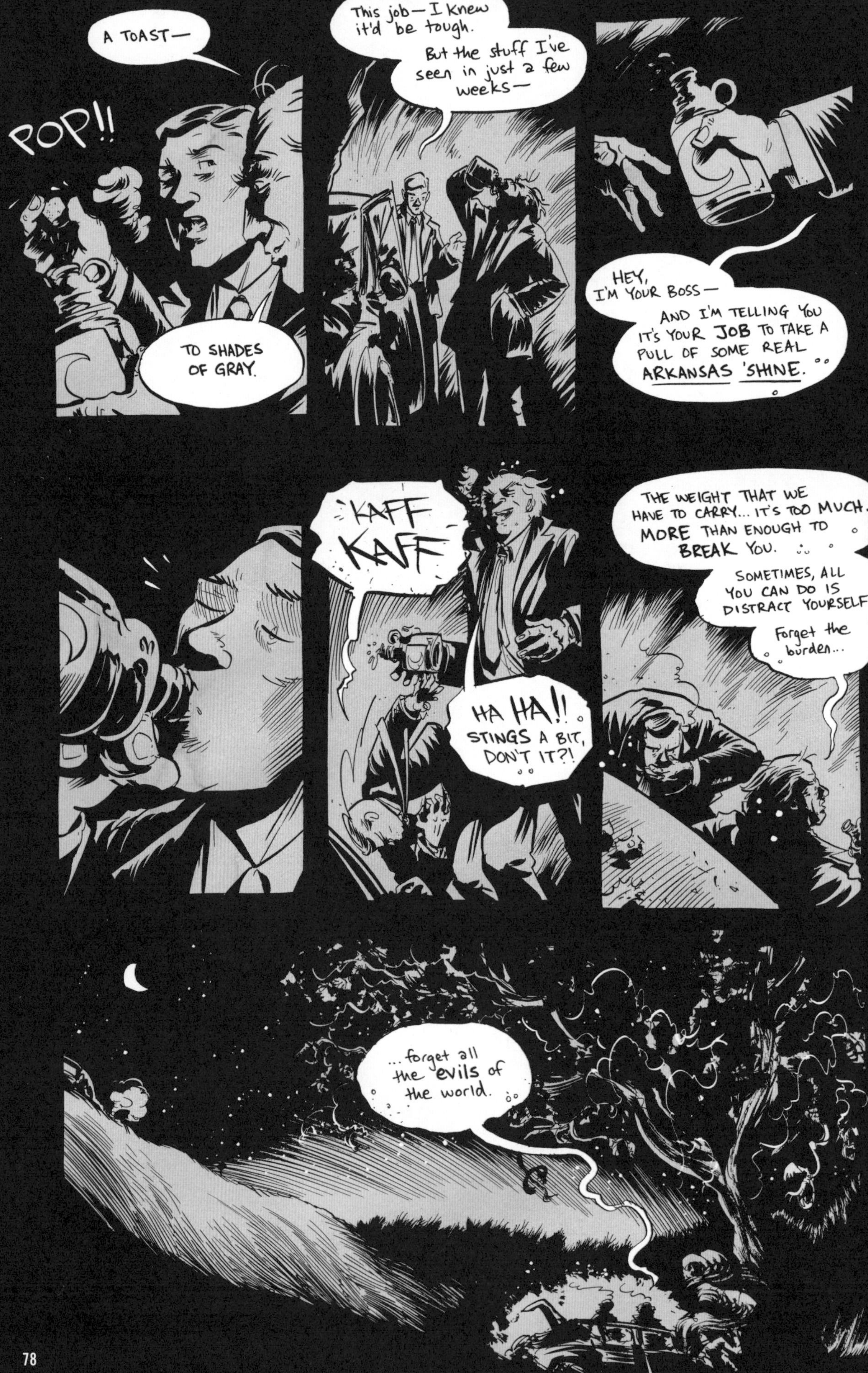
A TOAST—
POP!!
TO SHADES OF GRAY.
This job—I knew it'd be tough.
But the stuff I've seen in just a few weeks—
HEY, I'M YOUR BOSS—
AND I'M TELLING YOU IT'S YOUR JOB TO TAKE A PULL OF SOME REAL ARKANSAS 'SHINE.
KAFF KAFF
HA HA!! STINGS A BIT, DON'T IT?!
THE WEIGHT THAT WE HAVE TO CARRY... IT'S TOO MUCH. MORE THAN ENOUGH TO BREAK YOU.
SOMETIMES, ALL YOU CAN DO IS DISTRACT YOURSELF.
Forget the burden...
...forget all the evils of the world.

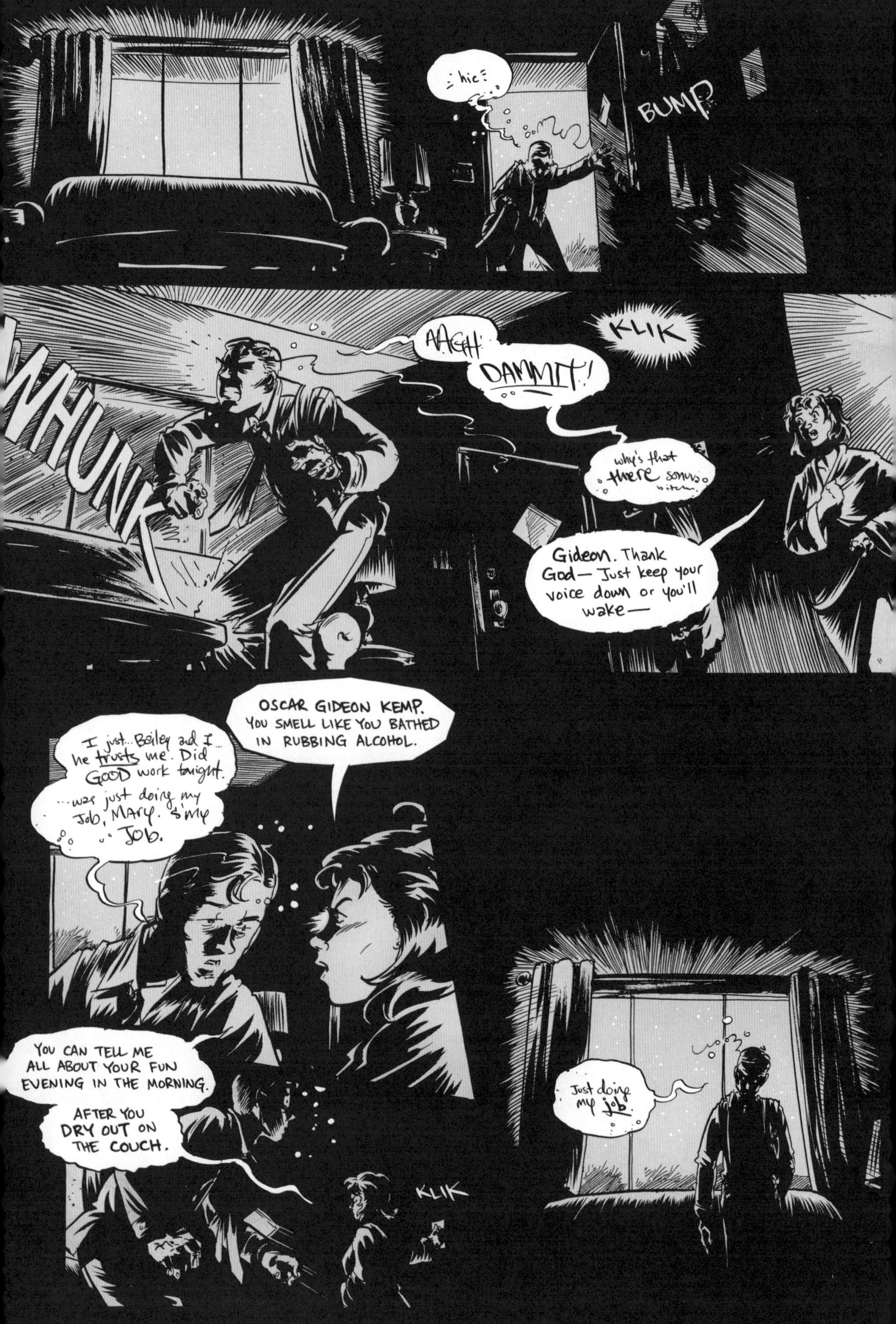

hic
BUMP
WHUNK
AAGH! DAMMIT!
KLIK
why's that there sonuva bitch.
Gideon. Thank God— Just keep your voice down or you'll wake—
I just... Bailey and I... he trusts me. Did GOOD work tonight. ...was just doing my Job, MAry. s'my Job.
OSCAR GIDEON KEMP. YOU SMELL LIKE YOU BATHED IN RUBBING ALCOHOL.
YOU CAN TELL ME ALL ABOUT YOUR FUN EVENING IN THE MORNING.
AFTER YOU DRY OUT ON THE COUCH.
KLIK
Just doing my job.

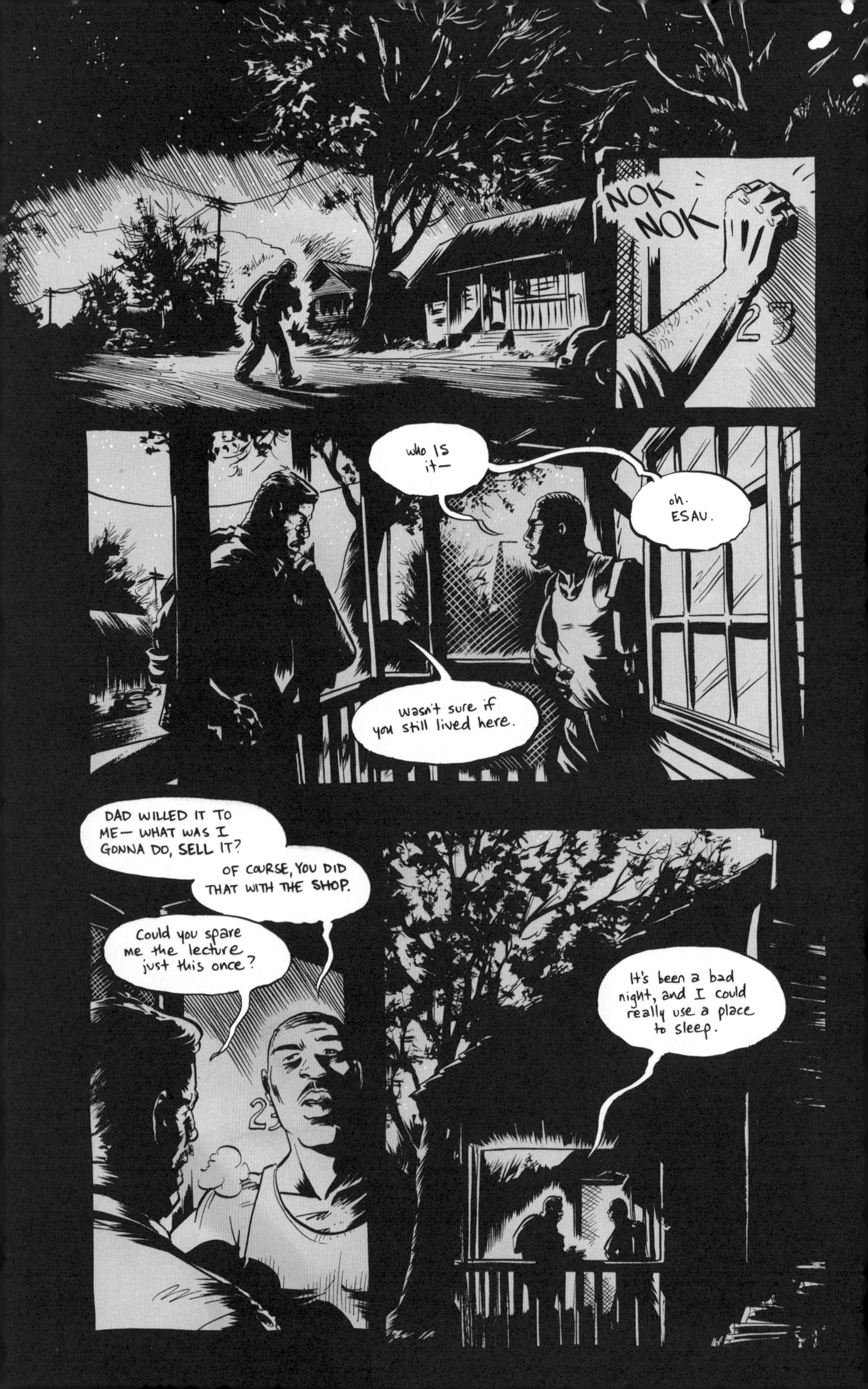
NOK NOK
who IS it—
oh. ESAU.
wasn't sure if you still lived here.
DAD WILLED IT TO ME— WHAT WAS I GONNA DO, SELL IT?
OF COURSE, YOU DID THAT WITH THE SHOP.
Could you spare me the lecture just this once?
It's been a bad night, and I could really use a place to sleep.

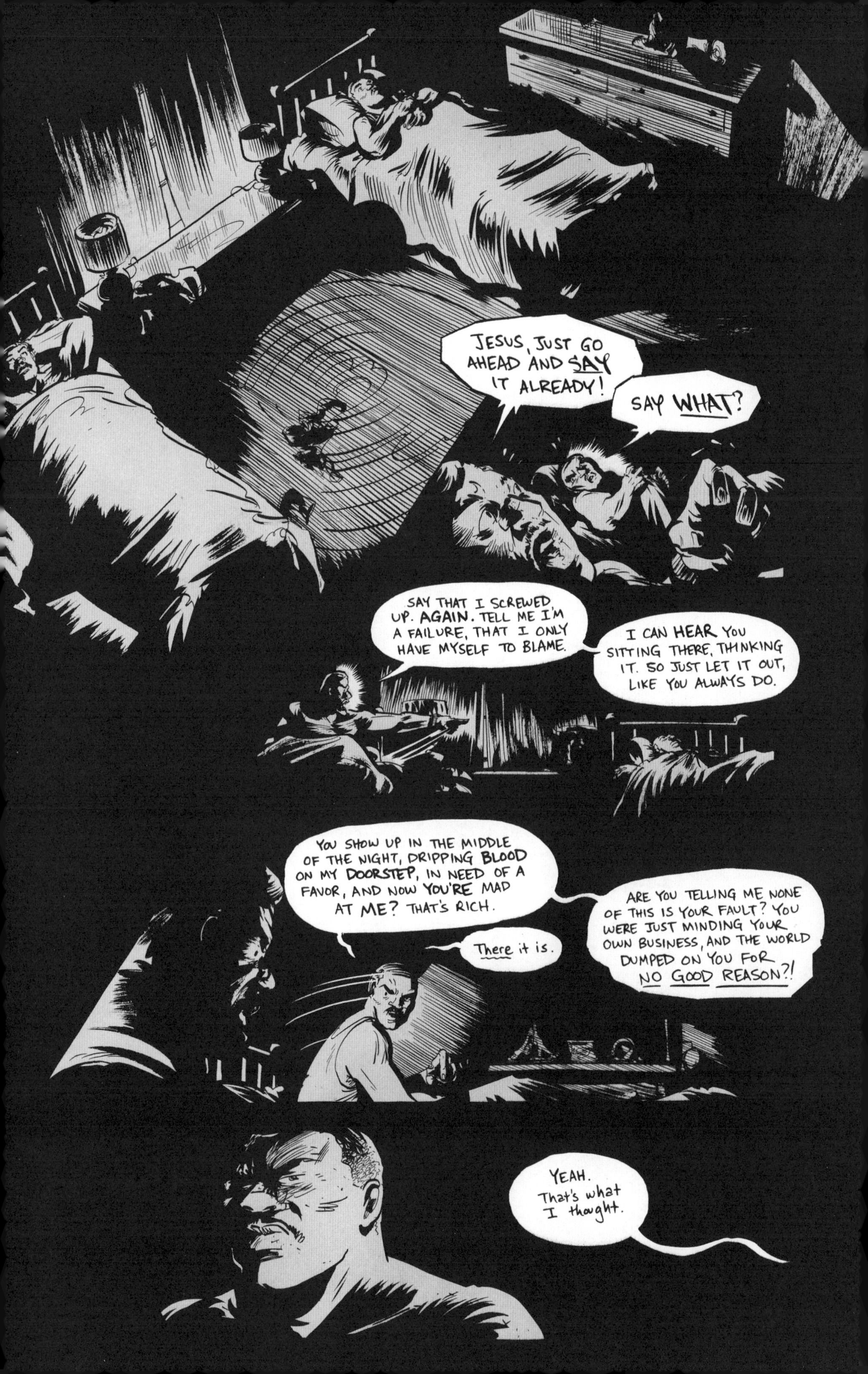

JESUS, JUST GO AHEAD AND SAY IT ALREADY!
SAY WHAT?
SAY THAT I SCREWED UP. AGAIN. TELL ME I'M A FAILURE, THAT I ONLY HAVE MYSELF TO BLAME.
I CAN HEAR YOU SITTING THERE, THINKING IT. SO JUST LET IT OUT, LIKE YOU ALWAYS DO.
YOU SHOW UP IN THE MIDDLE OF THE NIGHT, DRIPPING BLOOD ON MY DOORSTEP, IN NEED OF A FAVOR, AND NOW YOU'RE MAD AT ME? THAT'S RICH.
There it is.
ARE YOU TELLING ME NONE OF THIS IS YOUR FAULT? YOU WERE JUST MINDING YOUR OWN BUSINESS, AND THE WORLD DUMPED ON YOU FOR NO GOOD REASON?!
YEAH. That's what I thought.

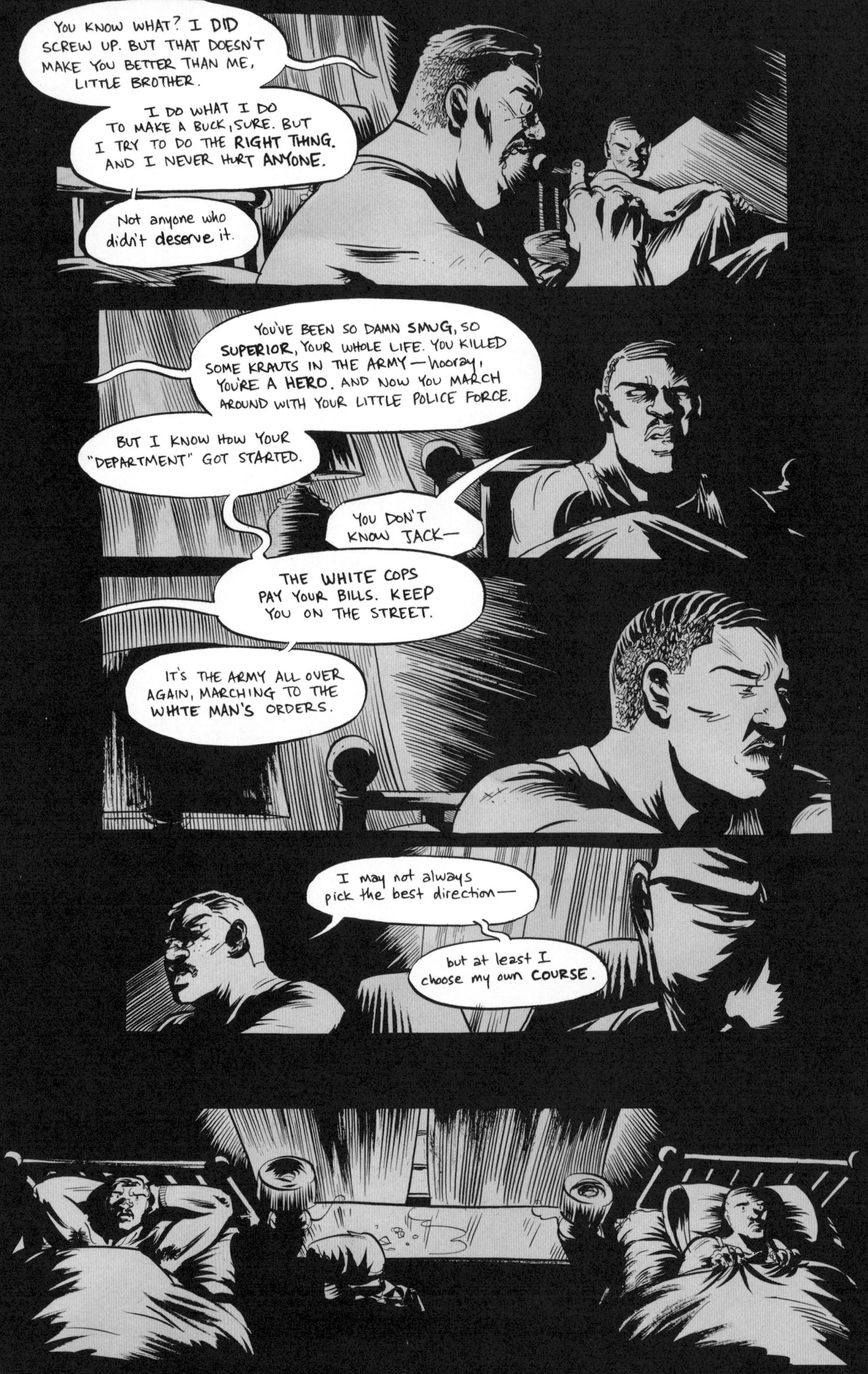

YOU KNOW WHAT? I DID SCREW UP. BUT THAT DOESN'T MAKE YOU BETTER THAN ME, LITTLE BROTHER.
I DO WHAT I DO TO MAKE A BUCK, SURE. BUT I TRY TO DO THE RIGHT THING. AND I NEVER HURT ANYONE.
Not anyone who didn't deserve it.
YOU'VE BEEN SO DAMN SMUG, SO SUPERIOR, YOUR WHOLE LIFE. YOU KILLED SOME KRAUTS IN THE ARMY—hooray, YOU'RE A HERO. AND NOW YOU MARCH AROUND WITH YOUR LITTLE POLICE FORCE.
BUT I KNOW HOW YOUR "DEPARTMENT" GOT STARTED.
YOU DON'T KNOW JACK—
THE WHITE COPS PAY YOUR BILLS. KEEP YOU ON THE STREET.
IT'S THE ARMY ALL OVER AGAIN, MARCHING TO THE WHITE MAN'S ORDERS.
I may not always pick the best direction—
but at least I choose my own COURSE.

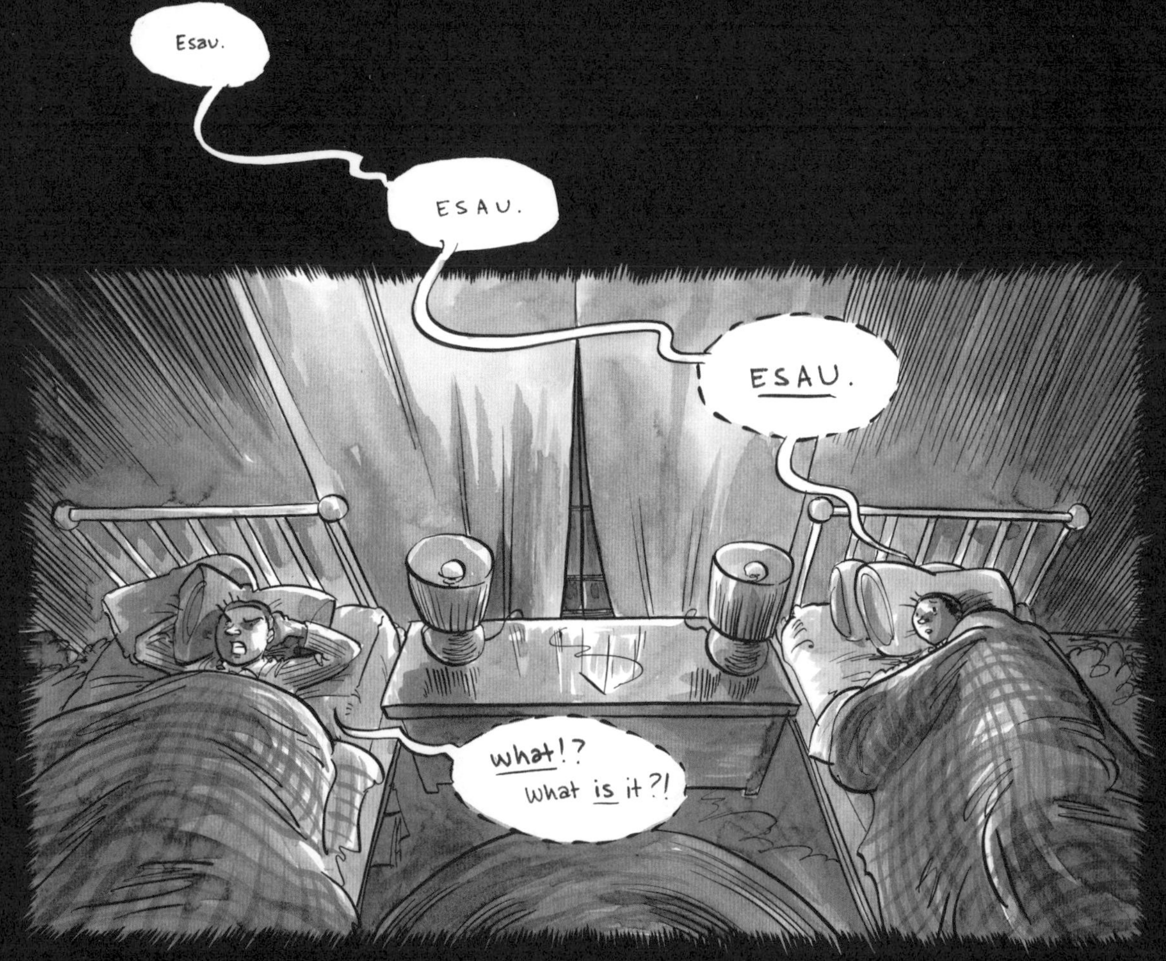
Esau.
ESAU.
ESAU.
what!? what is it?!

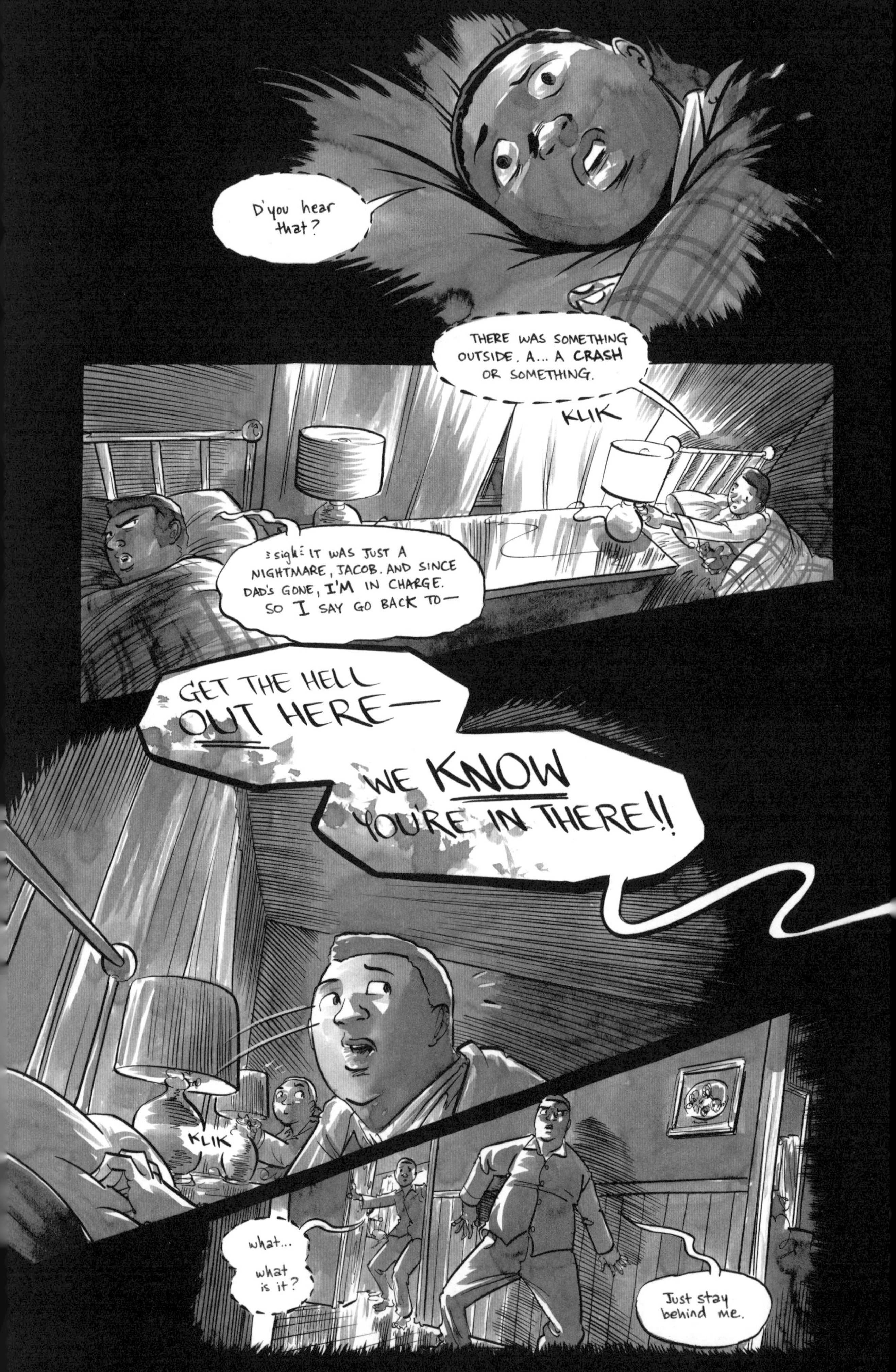
D'you hear that?
THERE WAS SOMETHING OUTSIDE. A... A CRASH OR SOMETHING.
KLIK
≈sigh≈ IT WAS JUST A NIGHTMARE, JACOB. AND SINCE DAD'S GONE, I'M IN CHARGE. SO I SAY GO BACK TO—
GET THE HELL OUT HERE—
WE KNOW YOU'RE IN THERE!!
KLIK
what... what is it?
Just stay behind me.

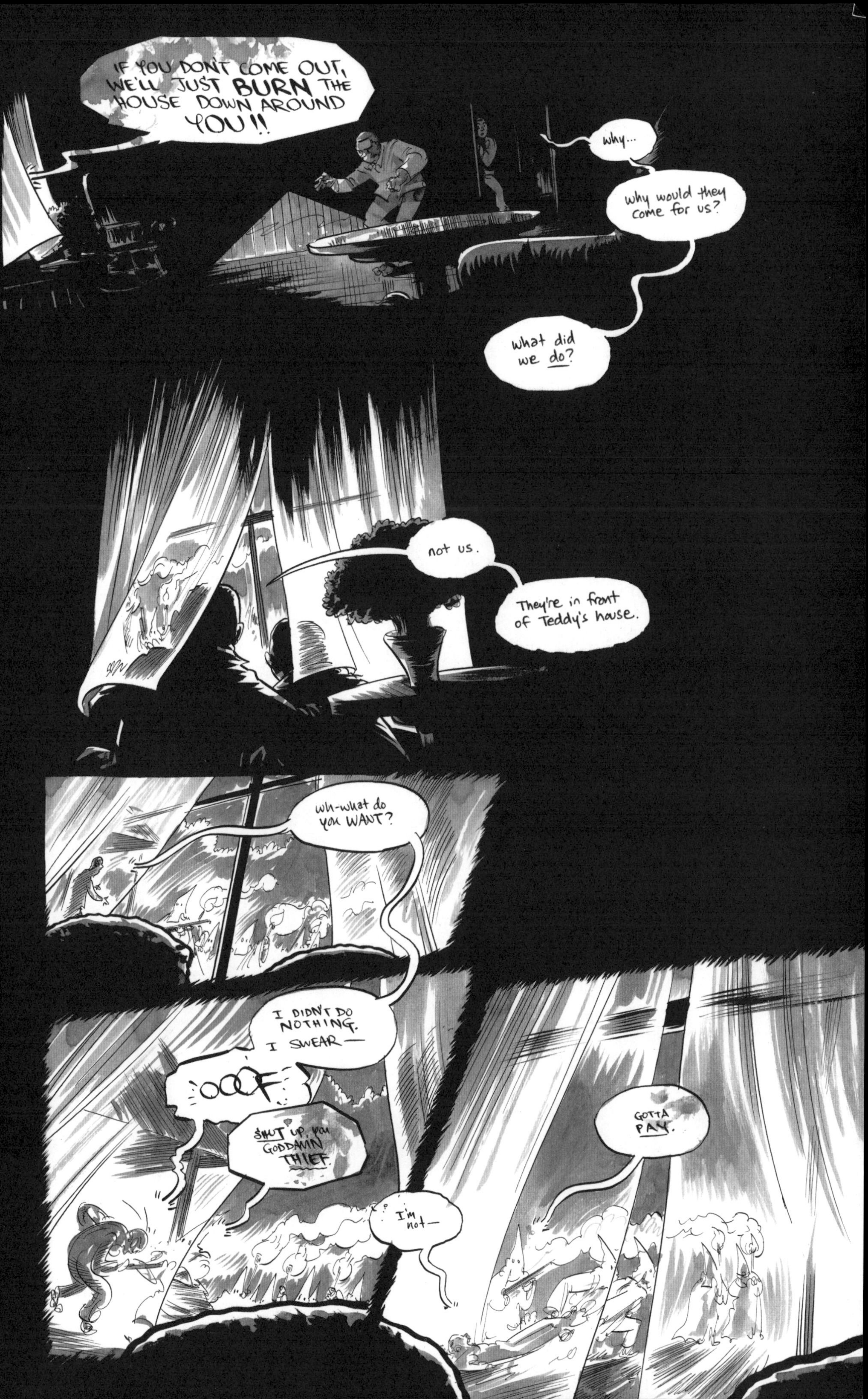
IF YOU DON'T COME OUT, WE'LL JUST BURN THE HOUSE DOWN AROUND YOU!!
why...
why would they come for us?
what did we do?
not us.
They're in front of Teddy's house.
wh-what do you WANT?
I DIDN'T DO NOTHING. I SWEAR—
OOOF
SHUT up, you GODDAMN THIEF.
I'm not—
GOTTA PAY.

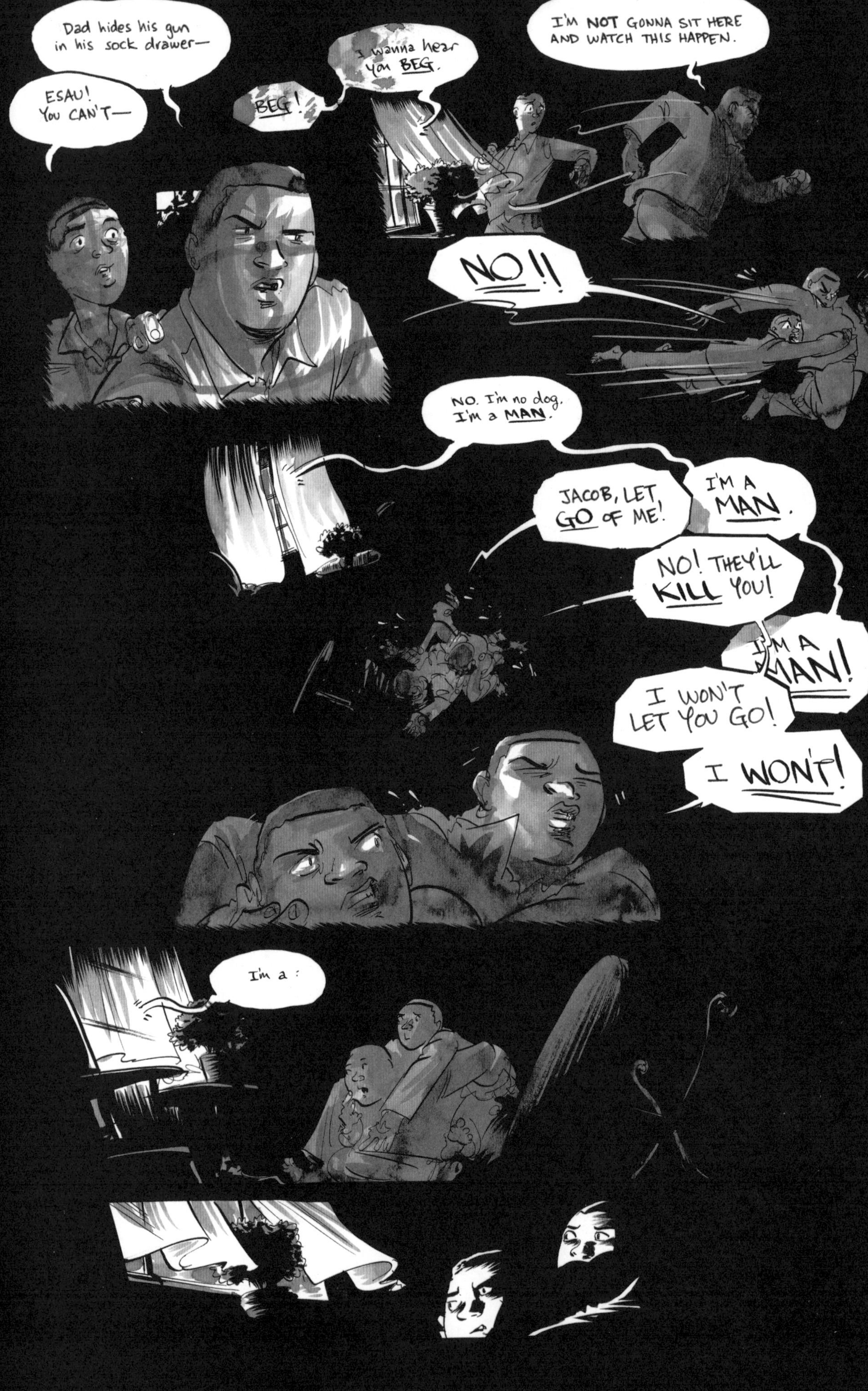
Dad hides his gun in his sock drawer—
ESAU! You CAN'T—
BEG!
I wanna hear you BEG.
I'M NOT GONNA SIT HERE AND WATCH THIS HAPPEN.
NO!!
NO. I'm no dog. I'm a MAN.
I'M A MAN.
JACOB, LET GO OF ME!
NO! THEY'LL KILL YOU!
I'M A MAN!
I WON'T LET YOU GO!
I WON'T!
I'm a :

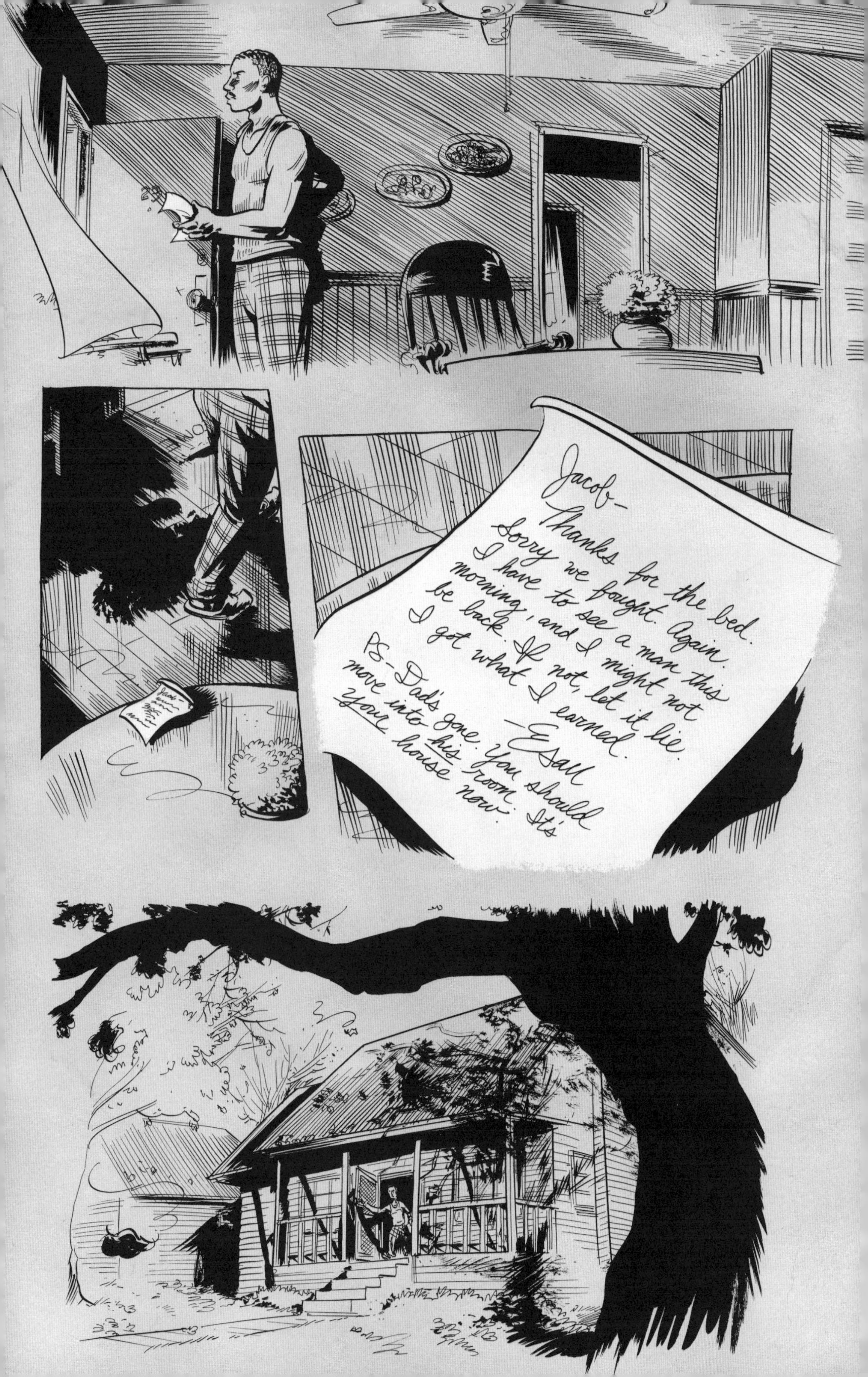
Jacob-
Thanks for the bed.
Sorry we fought. Again.
I have to see a man this
morning, and I might not
be back. If not, let it lie.
I got what I earned.
-Esau
PS-Dad's gone. You should
move into his room. It's
your house now.

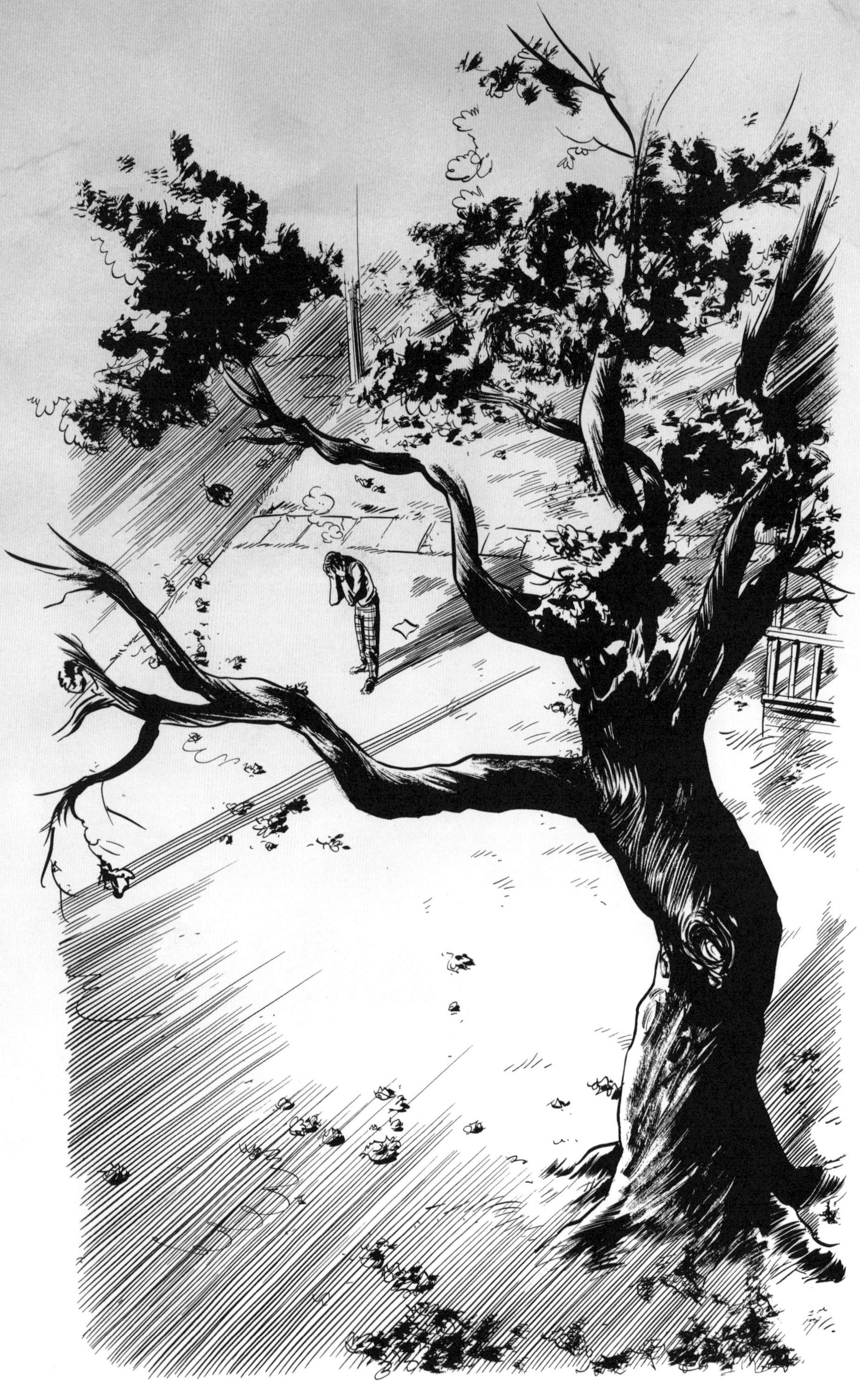

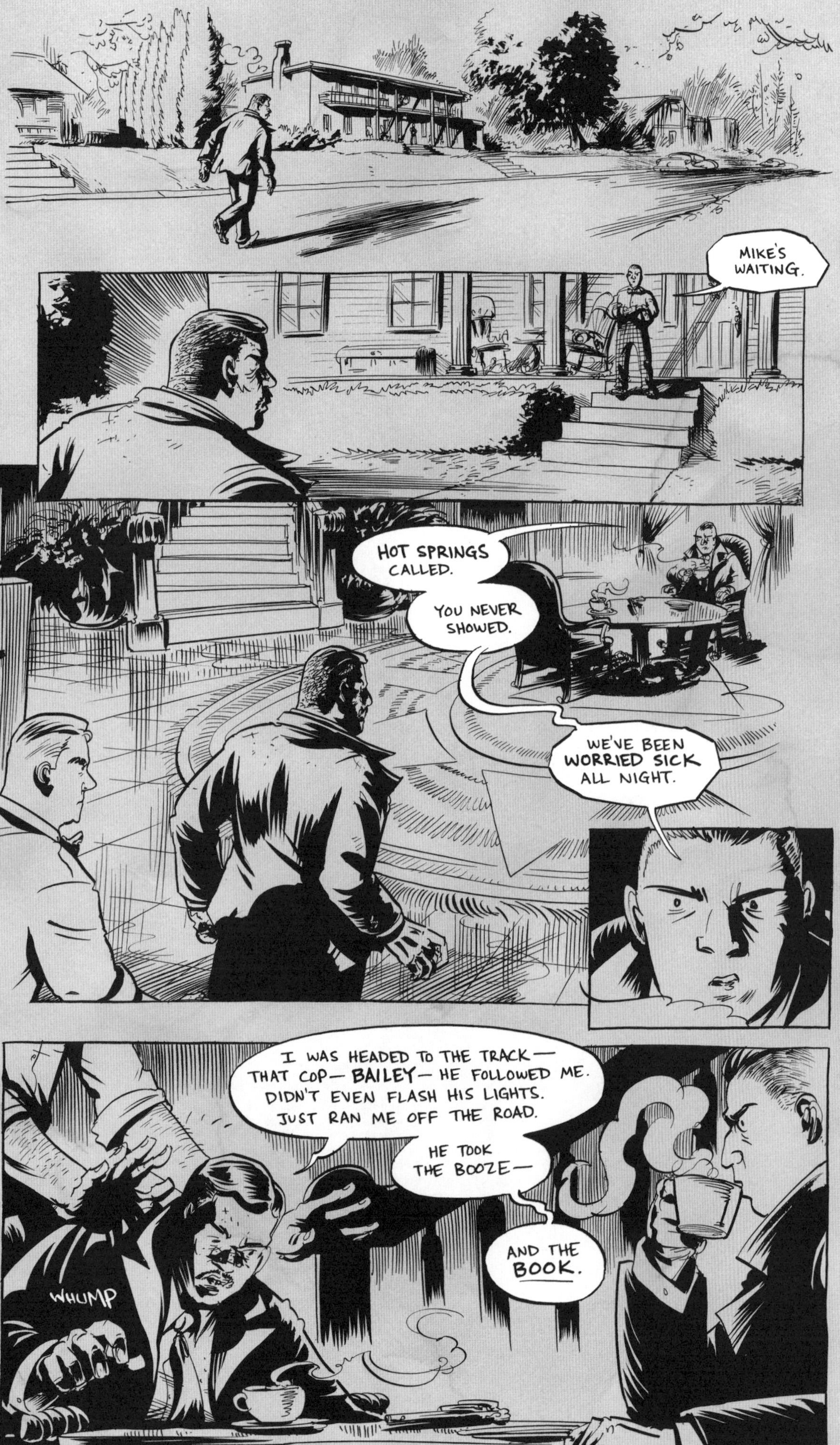
MIKE'S WAITING.
HOT SPRINGS CALLED.
YOU NEVER SHOWED.
WE'VE BEEN WORRIED SICK ALL NIGHT.
I WAS HEADED TO THE TRACK— THAT COP— BAILEY— HE FOLLOWED ME. DIDN'T EVEN FLASH HIS LIGHTS. JUST RAN ME OFF THE ROAD.
HE TOOK THE BOOZE—
AND THE BOOK.
WHUMP

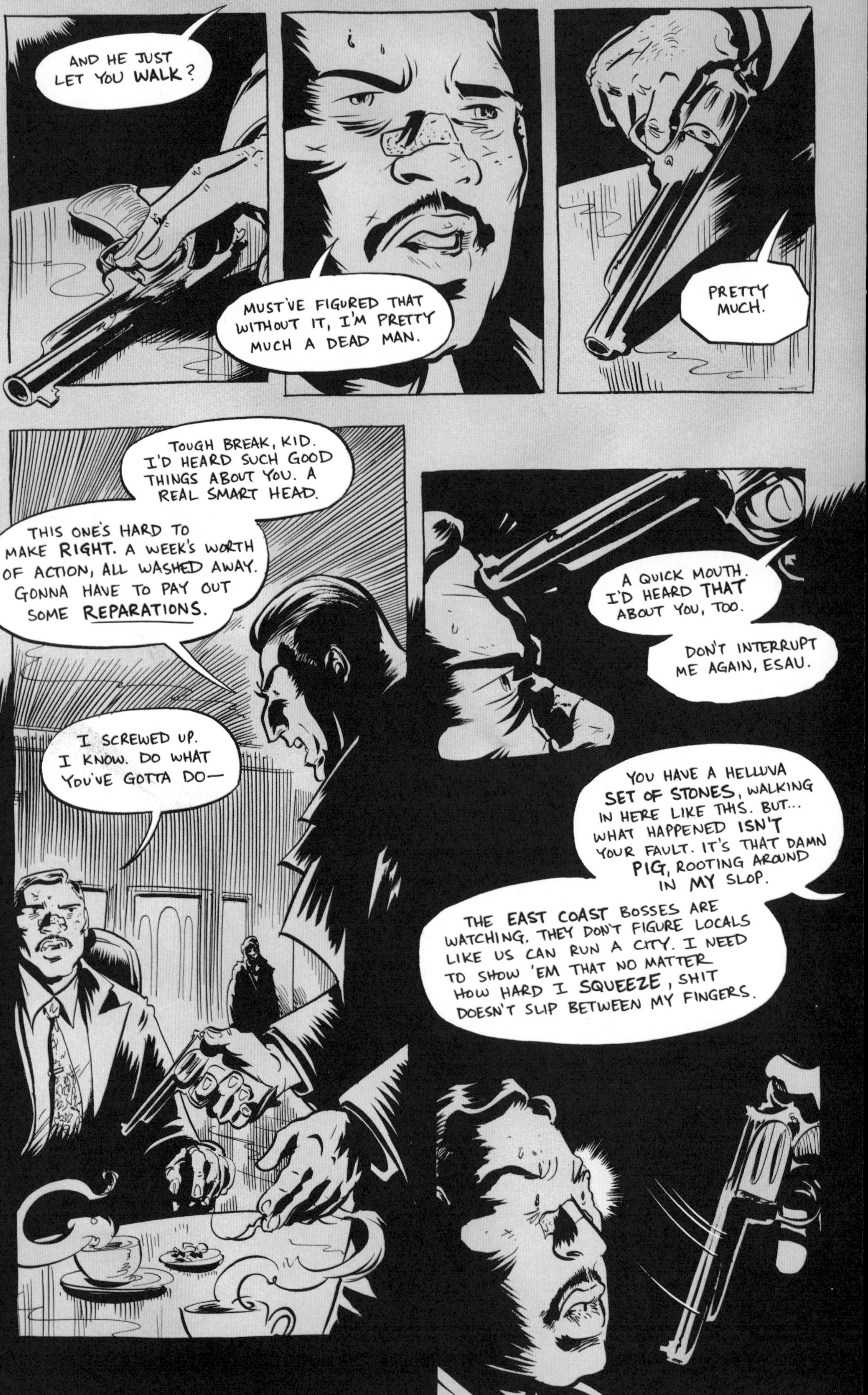
AND HE JUST LET YOU WALK?
MUST'VE FIGURED THAT WITHOUT IT, I'M PRETTY MUCH A DEAD MAN.
PRETTY MUCH.
TOUGH BREAK, KID. I'D HEARD SUCH GOOD THINGS ABOUT YOU. A REAL SMART HEAD.
THIS ONE'S HARD TO MAKE RIGHT. A WEEK'S WORTH OF ACTION, ALL WASHED AWAY. GONNA HAVE TO PAY OUT SOME REPARATIONS.
I SCREWED UP. I KNOW. DO WHAT YOU'VE GOTTA DO—
A QUICK MOUTH. I'D HEARD THAT ABOUT YOU, TOO.
DON'T INTERRUPT ME AGAIN, ESAU.
YOU HAVE A HELLUVA SET OF STONES, WALKING IN HERE LIKE THIS. BUT... WHAT HAPPENED ISN'T YOUR FAULT. IT'S THAT DAMN PIG, ROOTING AROUND IN MY SLOP.
THE EAST COAST BOSSES ARE WATCHING. THEY DON'T FIGURE LOCALS LIKE US CAN RUN A CITY. I NEED TO SHOW 'EM THAT NO MATTER HOW HARD I SQUEEZE, SHIT DOESN'T SLIP BETWEEN MY FINGERS.

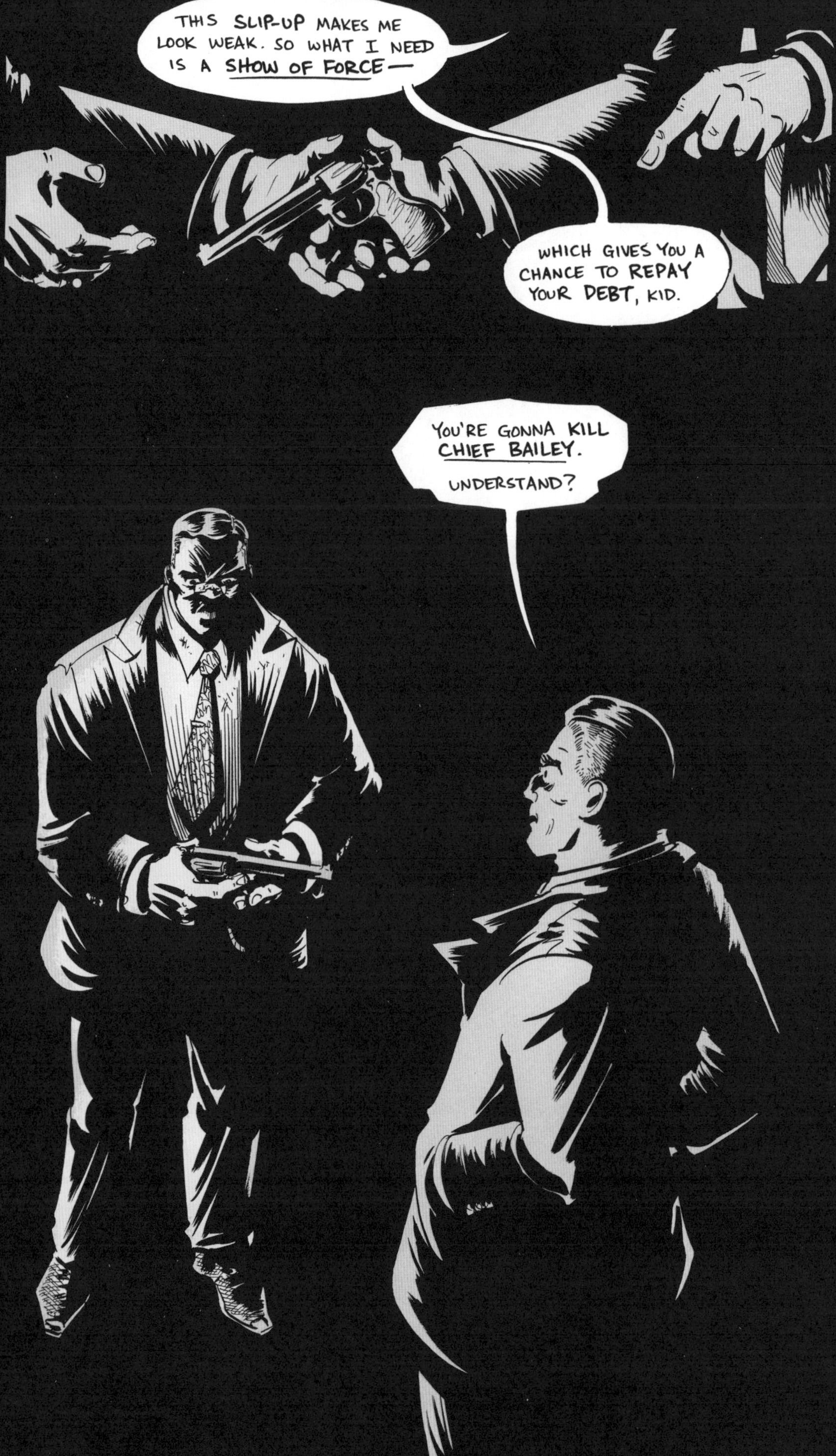
THIS SLIP-UP MAKES ME LOOK WEAK. SO WHAT I NEED IS A SHOW OF FORCE—
WHICH GIVES YOU A CHANCE TO REPAY YOUR DEBT, KID.
YOU'RE GONNA KILL CHIEF BAILEY.
UNDERSTAND?

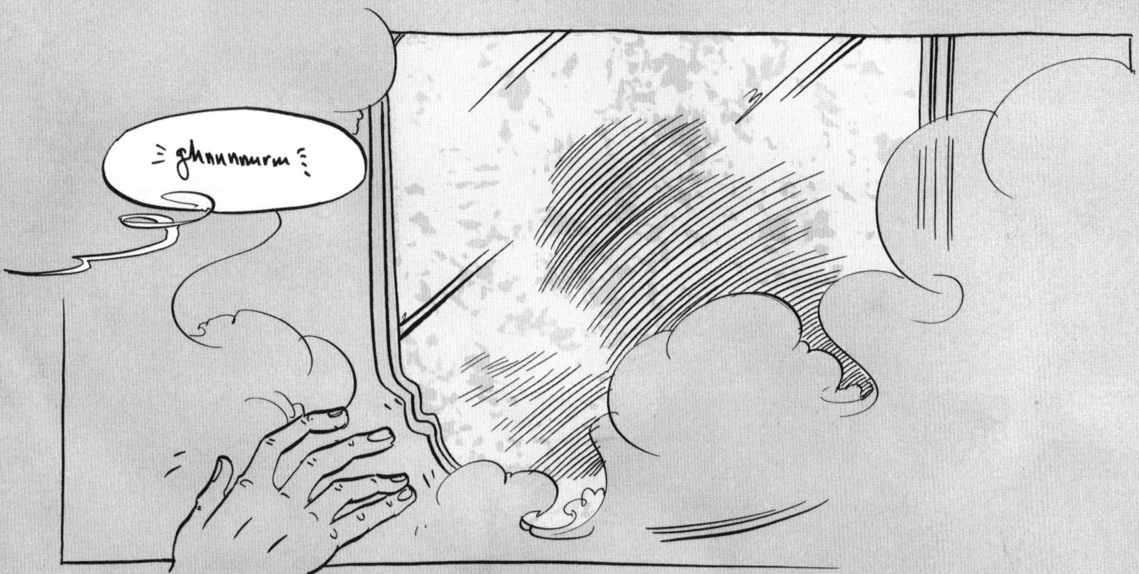
ghnnnnurm

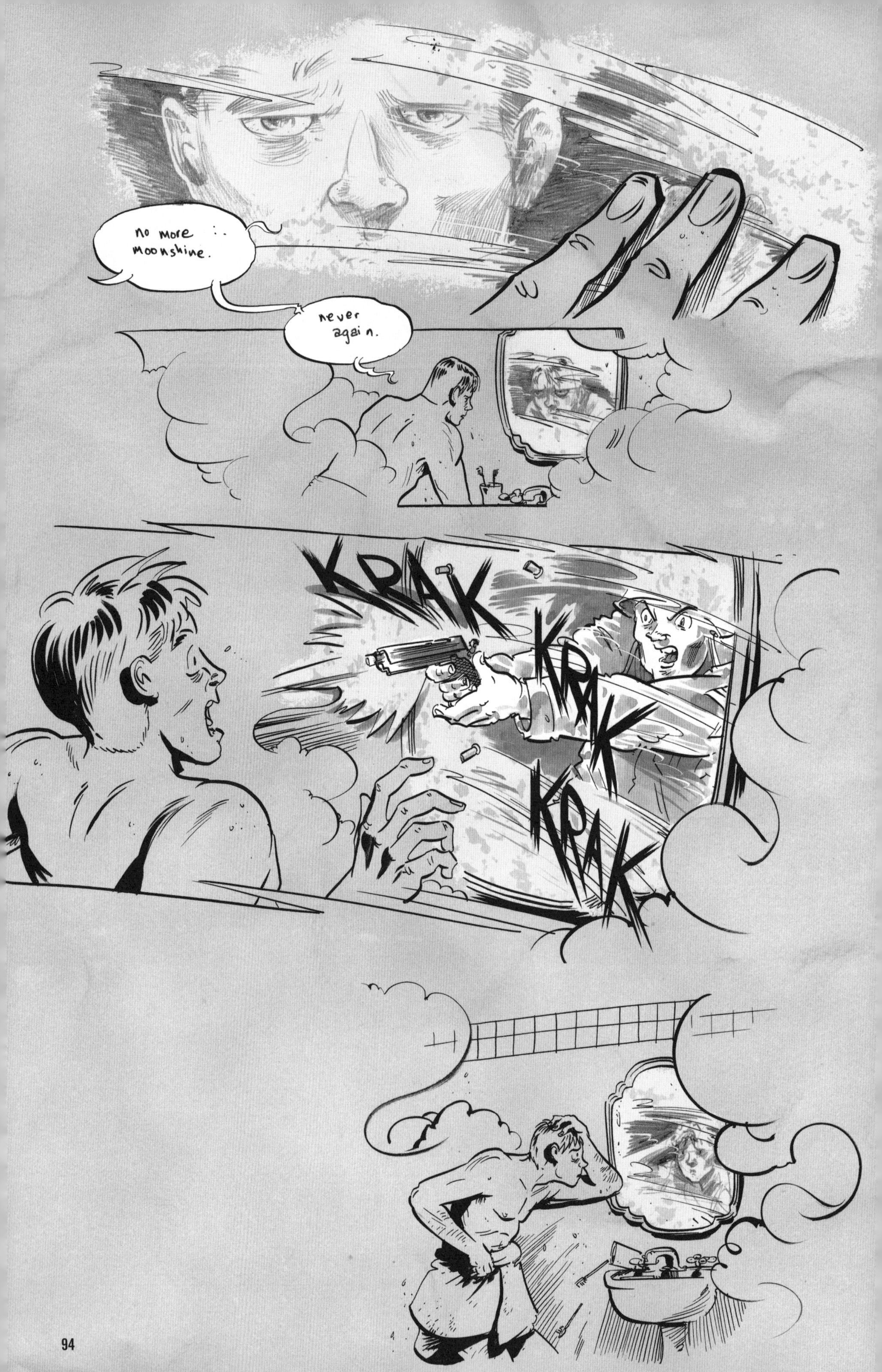
no more moonshine.
never again.
KRAK
KRAK
KRAK
KRAK

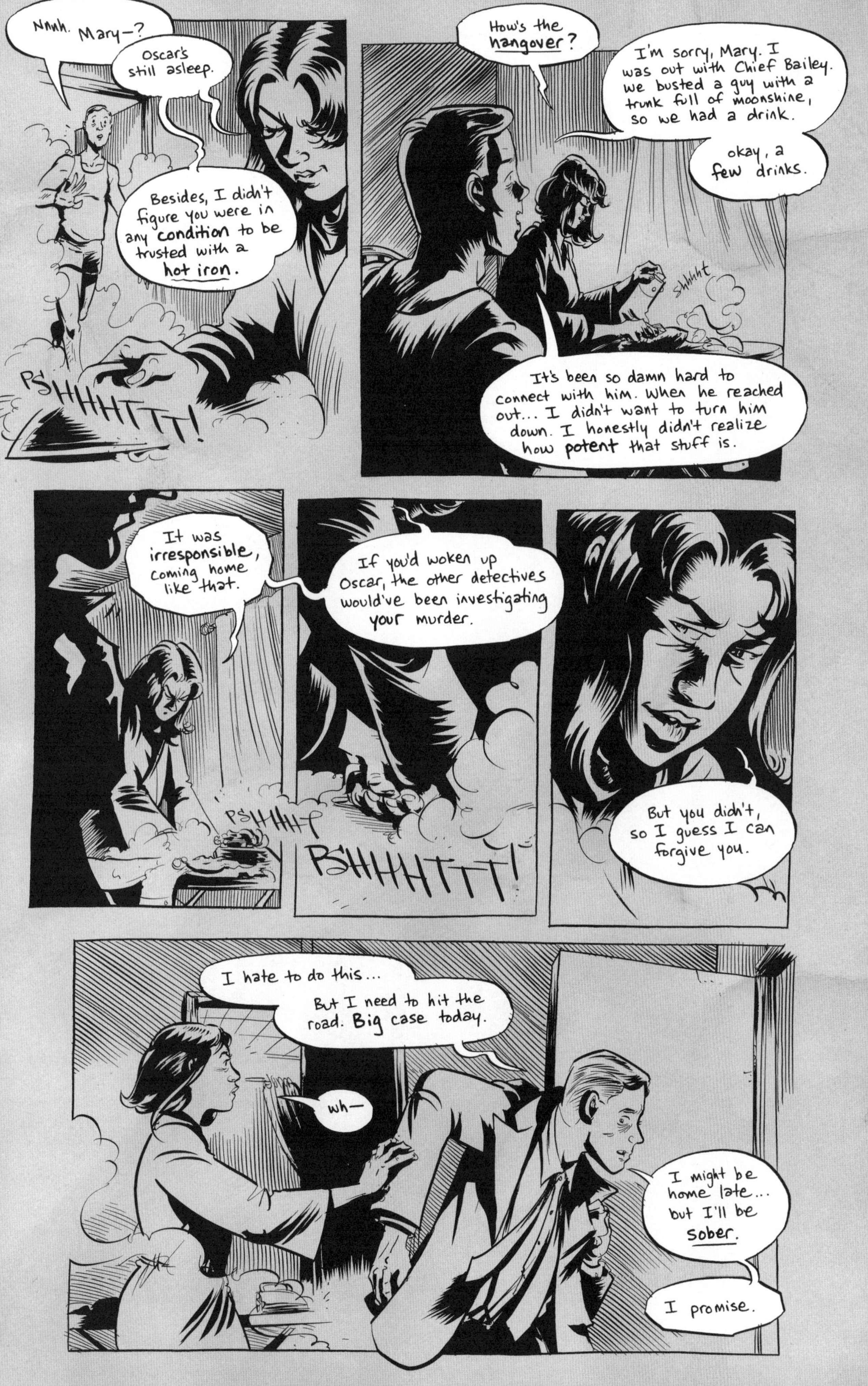

Nnnh. Mary–?
Oscar's still asleep.
Besides, I didn't figure you were in any condition to be trusted with a hot iron.
PSHHHTTTT!
How's the hangover?
I'm sorry, Mary. I was out with Chief Bailey. We busted a guy with a trunk full of moonshine, so we had a drink.
okay, a few drinks.
shhht
It's been so damn hard to connect with him. When he reached out... I didn't want to turn him down. I honestly didn't realize how potent that stuff is.
It was irresponsible, coming home like that.
If you'd woken up Oscar, the other detectives would've been investigating your murder.
PSHHHT
PSHHHTTT!
But you didn't, so I guess I can forgive you.
I hate to do this...
But I need to hit the road. Big case today.
wh–
I might be home late... but I'll be sober.
I promise.

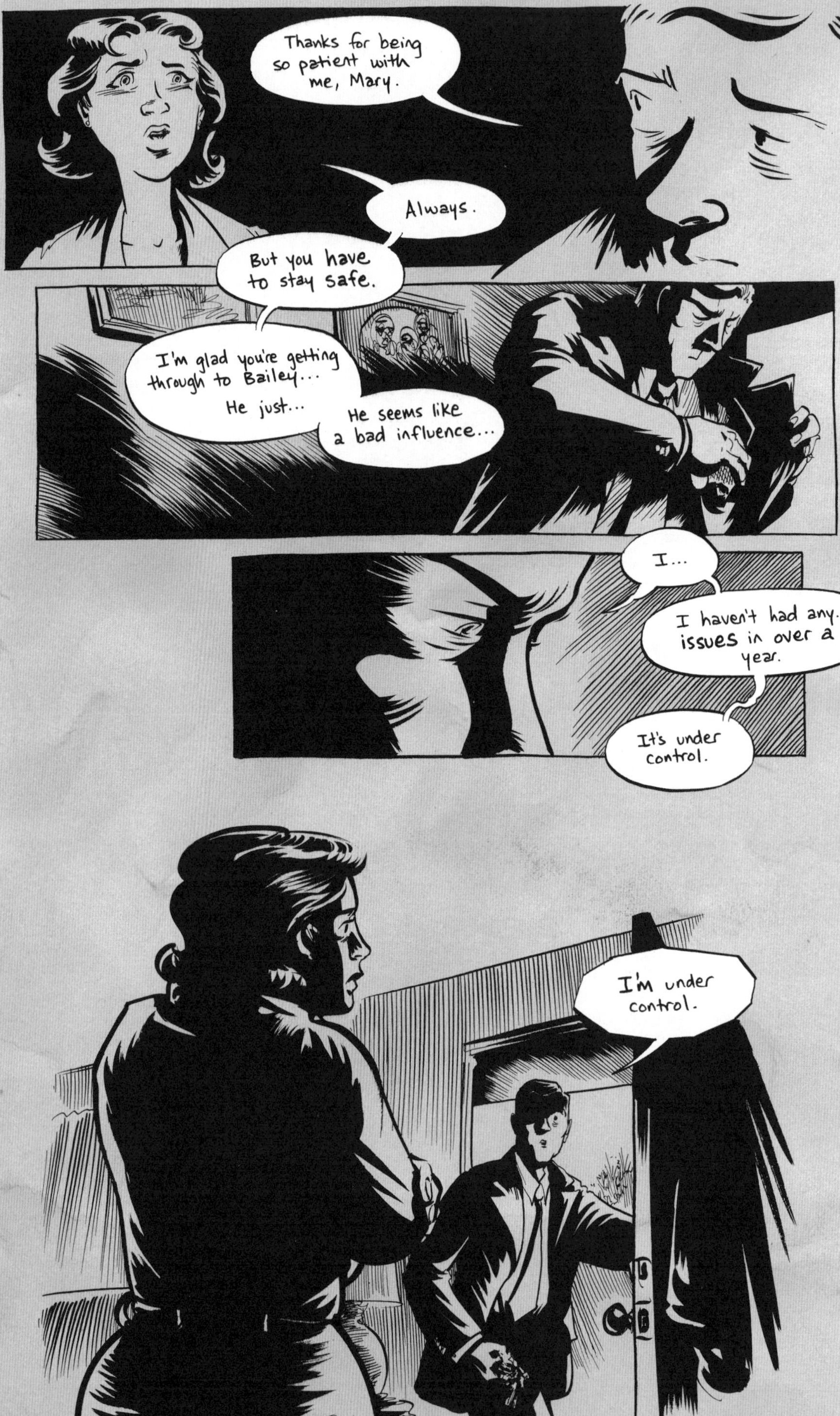
Thanks for being so patient with me, Mary.
Always.
But you have to stay safe.
I'm glad you're getting through to Bailey...
He just...
He seems like a bad influence...
I...
I haven't had any... issues in over a year.
It's under control.
I'm under control.

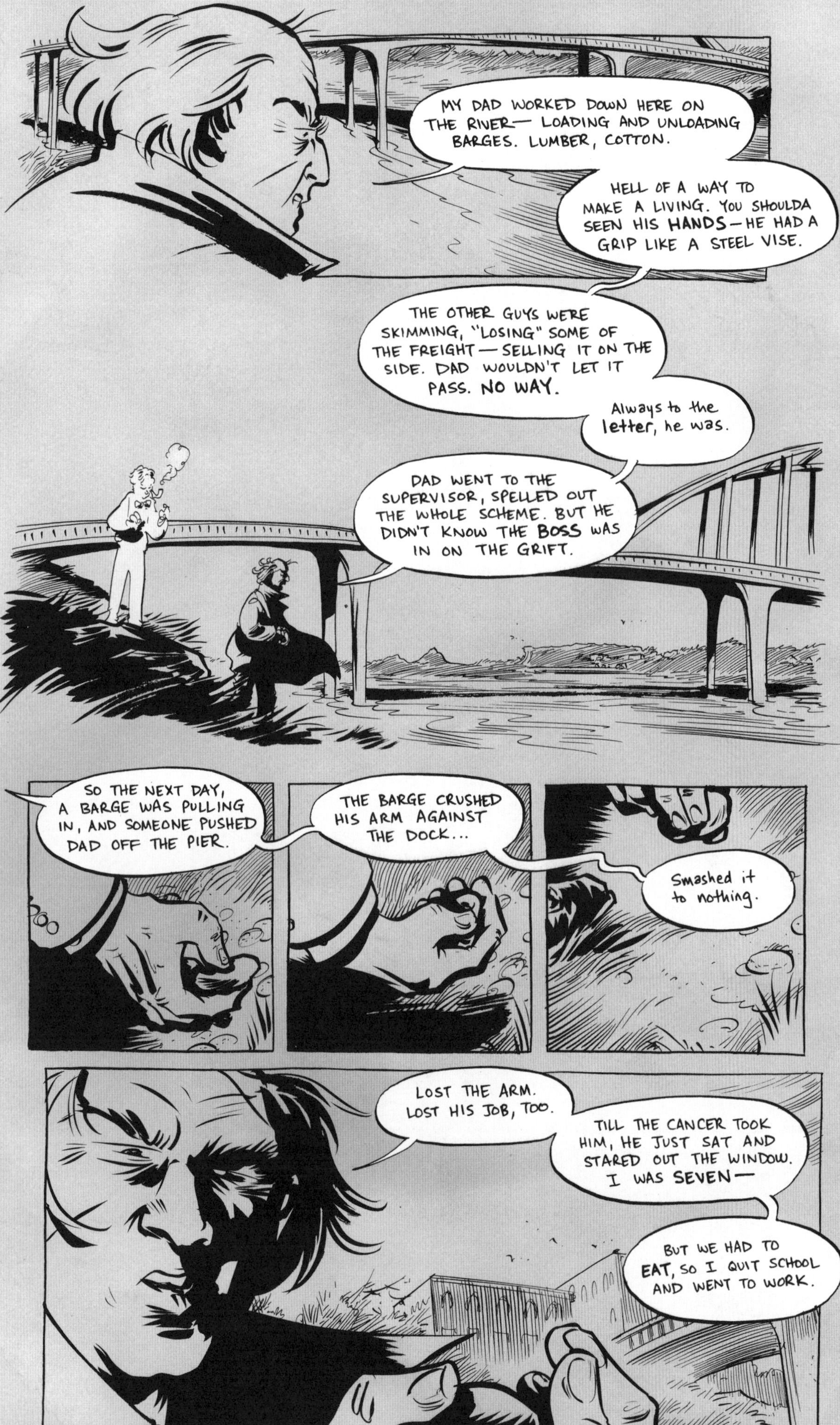
MY DAD WORKED DOWN HERE ON THE RIVER— LOADING AND UNLOADING BARGES. LUMBER, COTTON.
HELL OF A WAY TO MAKE A LIVING. YOU SHOULDA SEEN HIS HANDS—HE HAD A GRIP LIKE A STEEL VISE.
THE OTHER GUYS WERE SKIMMING, "LOSING" SOME OF THE FREIGHT— SELLING IT ON THE SIDE. DAD WOULDN'T LET IT PASS. NO WAY.
Always to the letter, he was.
DAD WENT TO THE SUPERVISOR, SPELLED OUT THE WHOLE SCHEME. BUT HE DIDN'T KNOW THE BOSS WAS IN ON THE GRIFT.
SO THE NEXT DAY, A BARGE WAS PULLING IN, AND SOMEONE PUSHED DAD OFF THE PIER.
THE BARGE CRUSHED HIS ARM AGAINST THE DOCK...
Smashed it to nothing.
LOST THE ARM. LOST HIS JOB, TOO.
TILL THE CANCER TOOK HIM, HE JUST SAT AND STARED OUT THE WINDOW. I WAS SEVEN—
BUT WE HAD TO EAT, SO I QUIT SCHOOL AND WENT TO WORK.

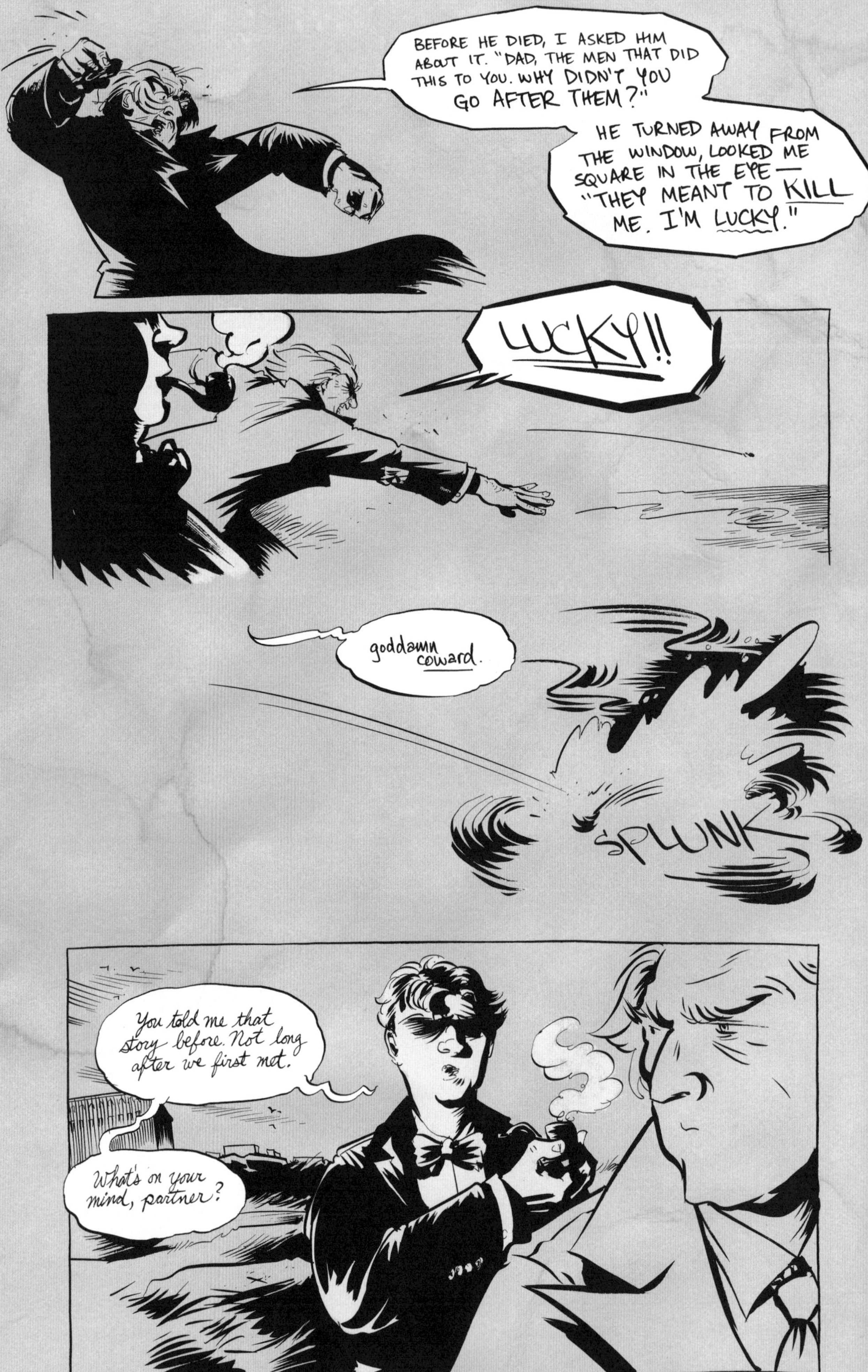
BEFORE HE DIED, I ASKED HIM ABOUT IT. "DAD, THE MEN THAT DID THIS TO YOU. WHY DIDN'T YOU GO AFTER THEM?"
HE TURNED AWAY FROM THE WINDOW, LOOKED ME SQUARE IN THE EYE— "THEY MEANT TO KILL ME. I'M LUCKY."
LUCKY!!
goddamn coward.
SPLUNK
You told me that story before. Not long after we first met.
What's on your mind, partner?

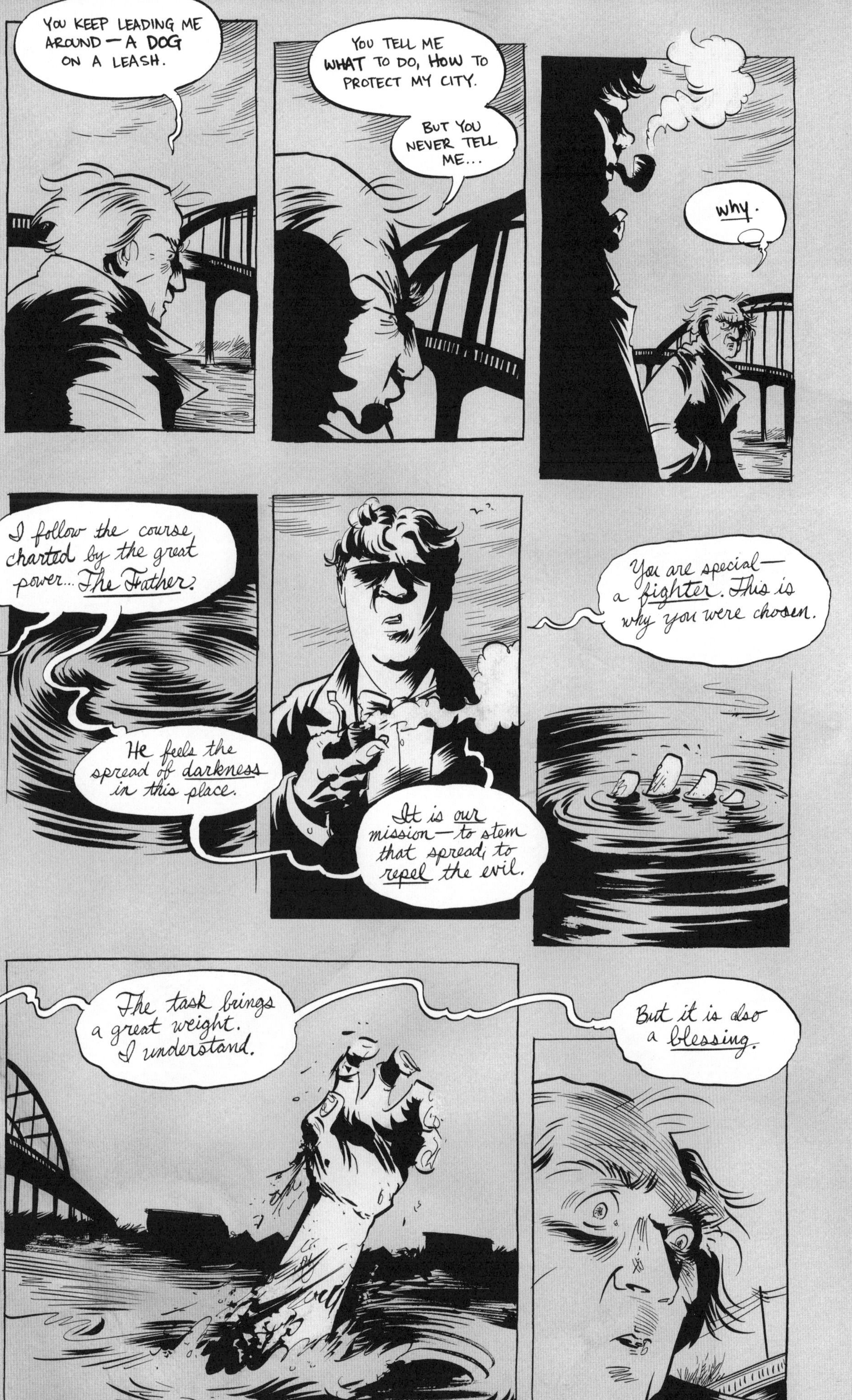
YOU KEEP LEADING ME AROUND—A DOG ON A LEASH.
YOU TELL ME WHAT TO DO, HOW TO PROTECT MY CITY.
BUT YOU NEVER TELL ME...
why.
I follow the course charted by the great power... The Father.
He feels the spread of darkness in this place.
It is our mission—to stem that spread; to repel the evil.
You are special—a fighter. This is why you were chosen.
The task brings a great weight. I understand.
But it is also a blessing.

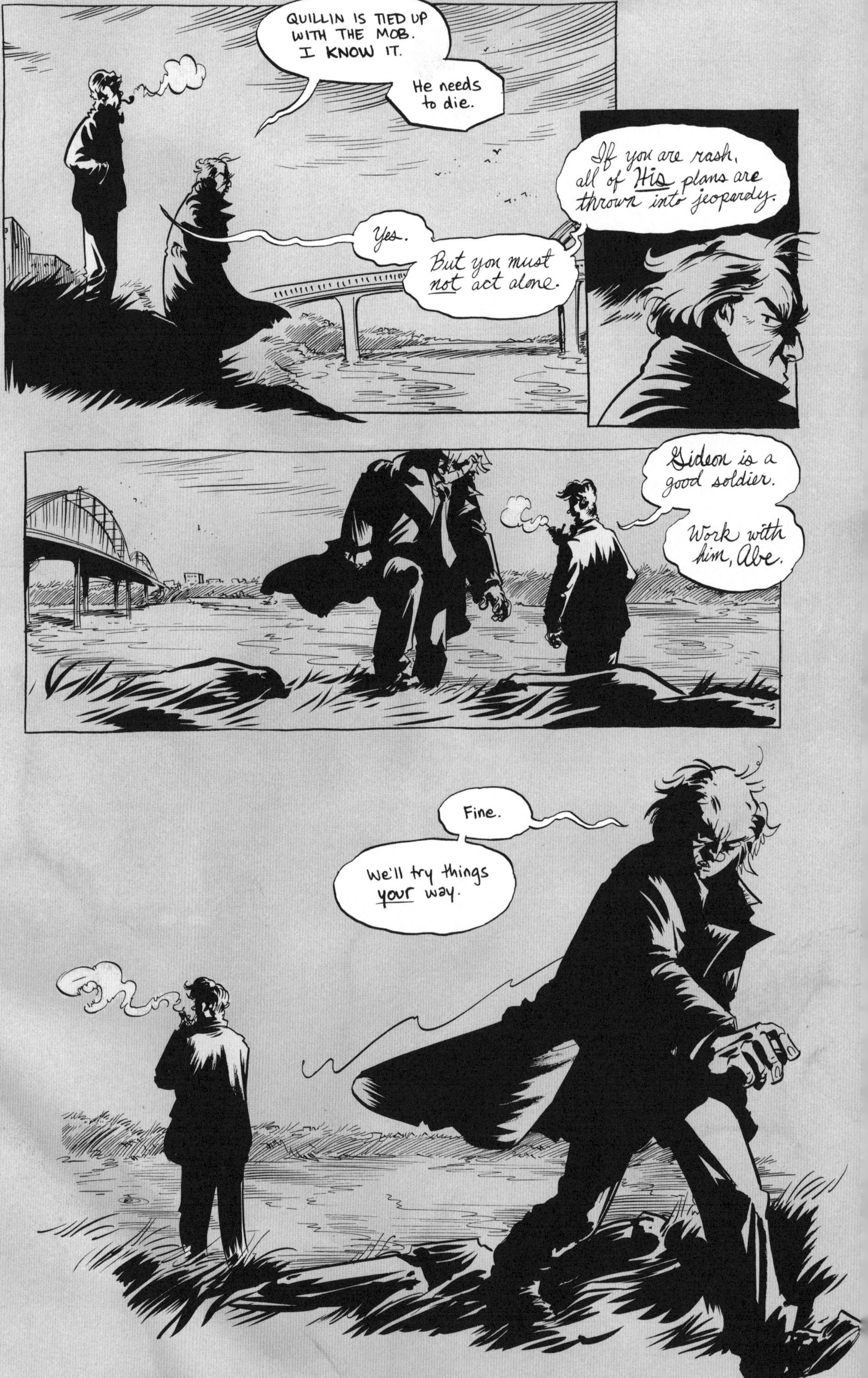

QUILLIN IS TIED UP WITH THE MOB. I KNOW IT.
He needs to die.
Yes.
But you must not act alone.
If you are rash, all of His plans are thrown into jeopardy.
Gideon is a good soldier.
Work with him, Abe.
Fine.
We'll try things your way.

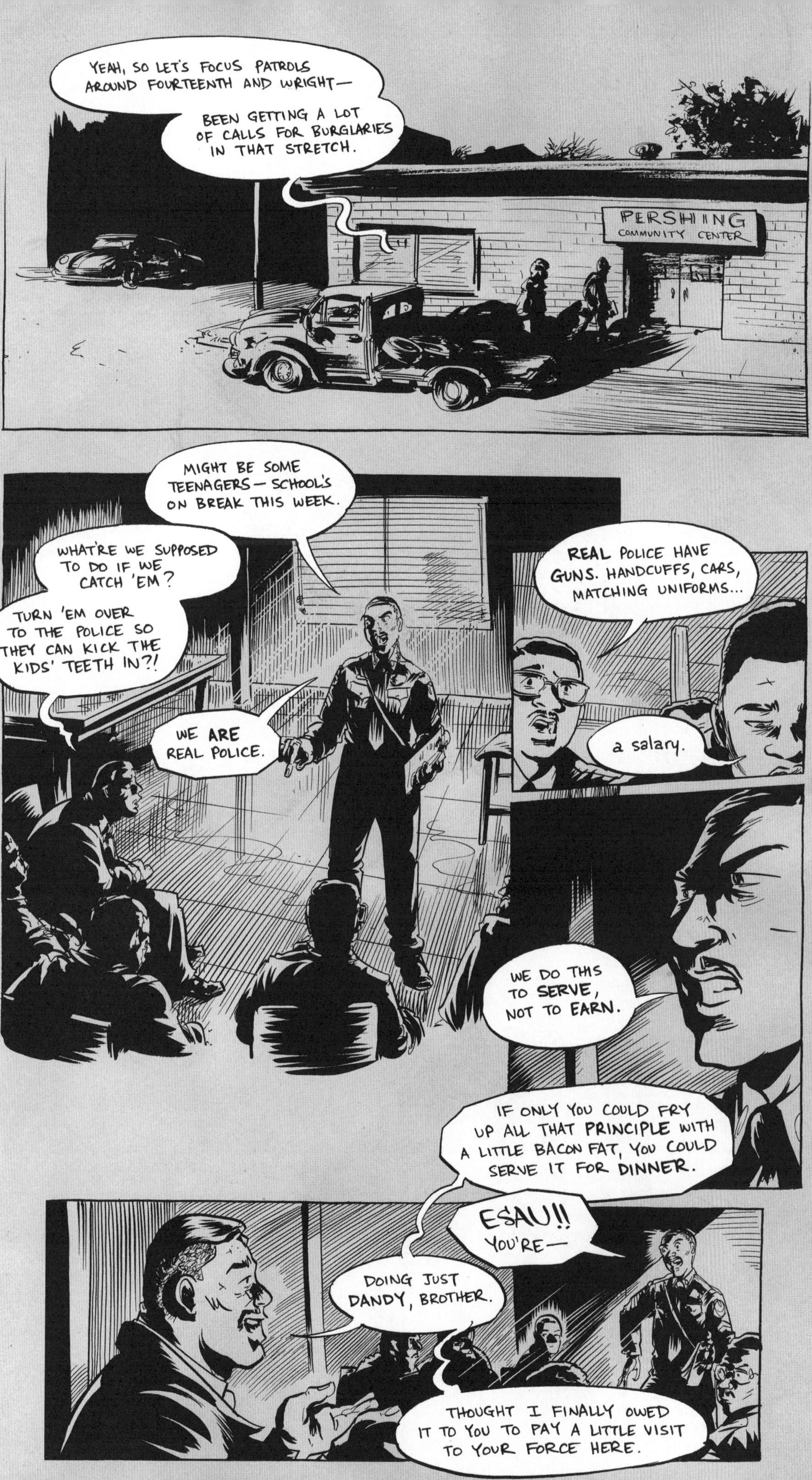
YEAH, SO LET'S FOCUS PATROLS AROUND FOURTEENTH AND WRIGHT—
BEEN GETTING A LOT OF CALLS FOR BURGLARIES IN THAT STRETCH.
PERSHING COMMUNITY CENTER
MIGHT BE SOME TEENAGERS—SCHOOL'S ON BREAK THIS WEEK.
WHAT'RE WE SUPPOSED TO DO IF WE CATCH 'EM?
TURN 'EM OVER TO THE POLICE SO THEY CAN KICK THE KIDS' TEETH IN?!
WE ARE REAL POLICE.
REAL POLICE HAVE GUNS. HANDCUFFS, CARS, MATCHING UNIFORMS...
a salary.
WE DO THIS TO SERVE, NOT TO EARN.
IF ONLY YOU COULD FRY UP ALL THAT PRINCIPLE WITH A LITTLE BACON FAT, YOU COULD SERVE IT FOR DINNER.
ESAU!! YOU'RE—
DOING JUST DANDY, BROTHER.
THOUGHT I FINALLY OWED IT TO YOU TO PAY A LITTLE VISIT TO YOUR FORCE HERE.

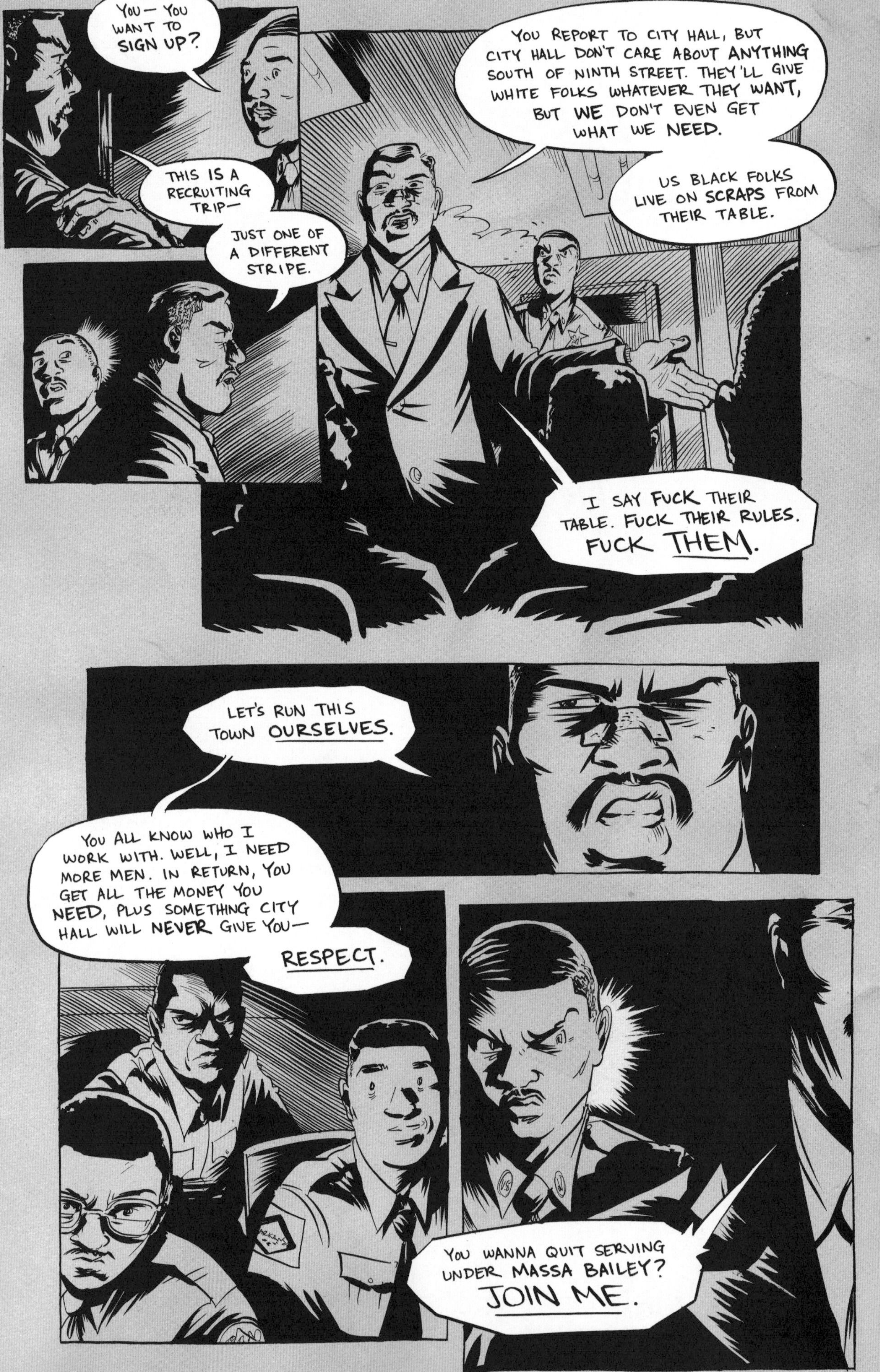
YOU— YOU WANT TO SIGN UP?
THIS IS A RECRUITING TRIP—
JUST ONE OF A DIFFERENT STRIPE.
YOU REPORT TO CITY HALL, BUT CITY HALL DON'T CARE ABOUT ANYTHING SOUTH OF NINTH STREET. THEY'LL GIVE WHITE FOLKS WHATEVER THEY WANT, BUT WE DON'T EVEN GET WHAT WE NEED.
US BLACK FOLKS LIVE ON SCRAPS FROM THEIR TABLE.
I SAY FUCK THEIR TABLE. FUCK THEIR RULES. FUCK THEM.
LET'S RUN THIS TOWN OURSELVES.
YOU ALL KNOW WHO I WORK WITH. WELL, I NEED MORE MEN. IN RETURN, YOU GET ALL THE MONEY YOU NEED, PLUS SOMETHING CITY HALL WILL NEVER GIVE YOU—
RESPECT.
YOU WANNA QUIT SERVING UNDER MASSA BAILEY? JOIN ME.

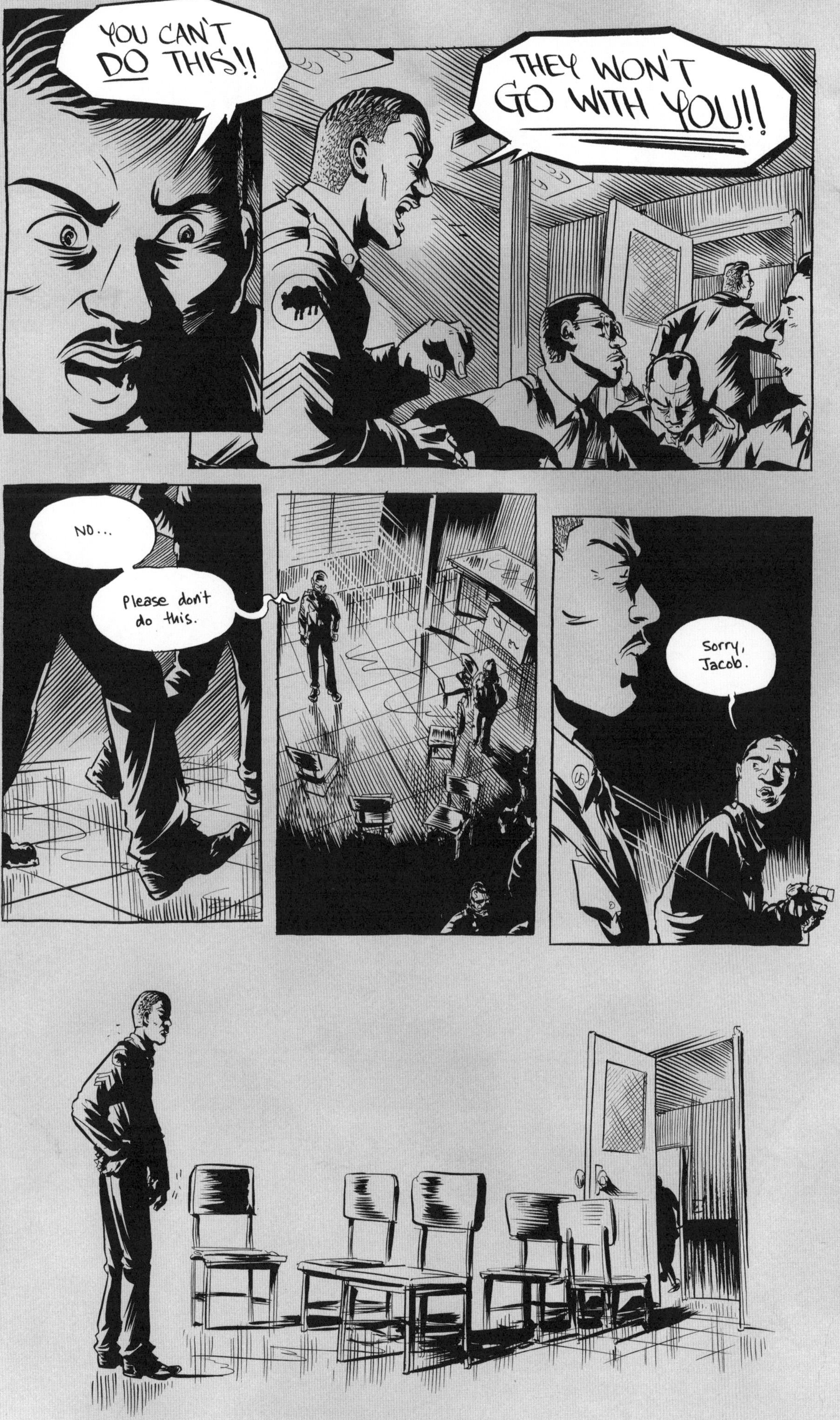
YOU CAN'T DO THIS!!
THEY WON'T GO WITH YOU!!
NO...
Please don't do this.
Sorry, Jacob.

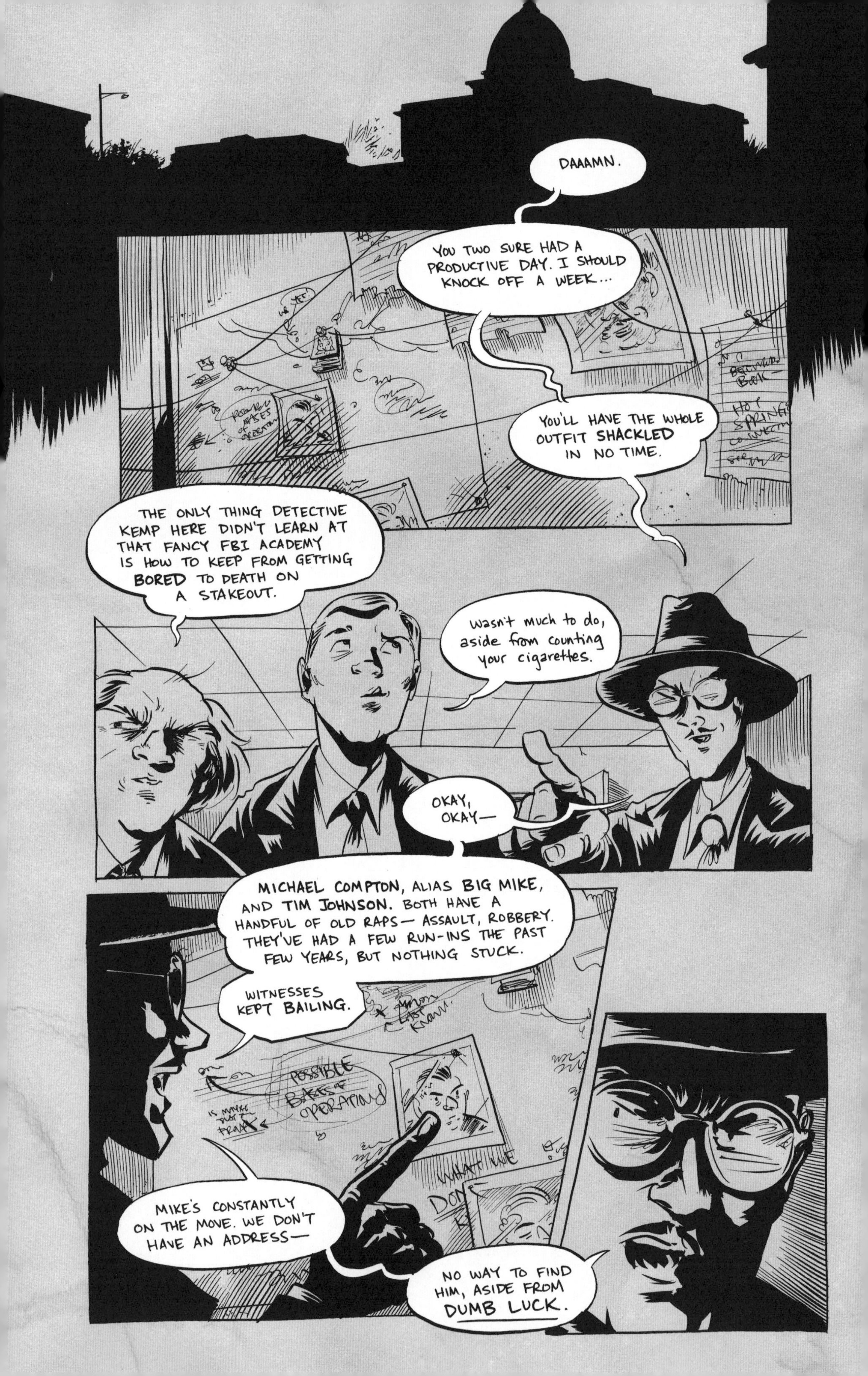
DAAAMN.
YOU TWO SURE HAD A PRODUCTIVE DAY. I SHOULD KNOCK OFF A WEEK...
YOU'LL HAVE THE WHOLE OUTFIT SHACKLED IN NO TIME.
THE ONLY THING DETECTIVE KEMP HERE DIDN'T LEARN AT THAT FANCY FBI ACADEMY IS HOW TO KEEP FROM GETTING BORED TO DEATH ON A STAKEOUT.
Wasn't much to do, aside from counting your cigarettes.
OKAY, OKAY—
MICHAEL COMPTON, ALIAS BIG MIKE, AND TIM JOHNSON. BOTH HAVE A HANDFUL OF OLD RAPS— ASSAULT, ROBBERY. THEY'VE HAD A FEW RUN-INS THE PAST FEW YEARS, BUT NOTHING STUCK.
WITNESSES KEPT BAILING.
POSSIBLE BASES OF OPERATION
MIKE'S CONSTANTLY ON THE MOVE. WE DON'T HAVE AN ADDRESS—
NO WAY TO FIND HIM, ASIDE FROM DUMB LUCK.

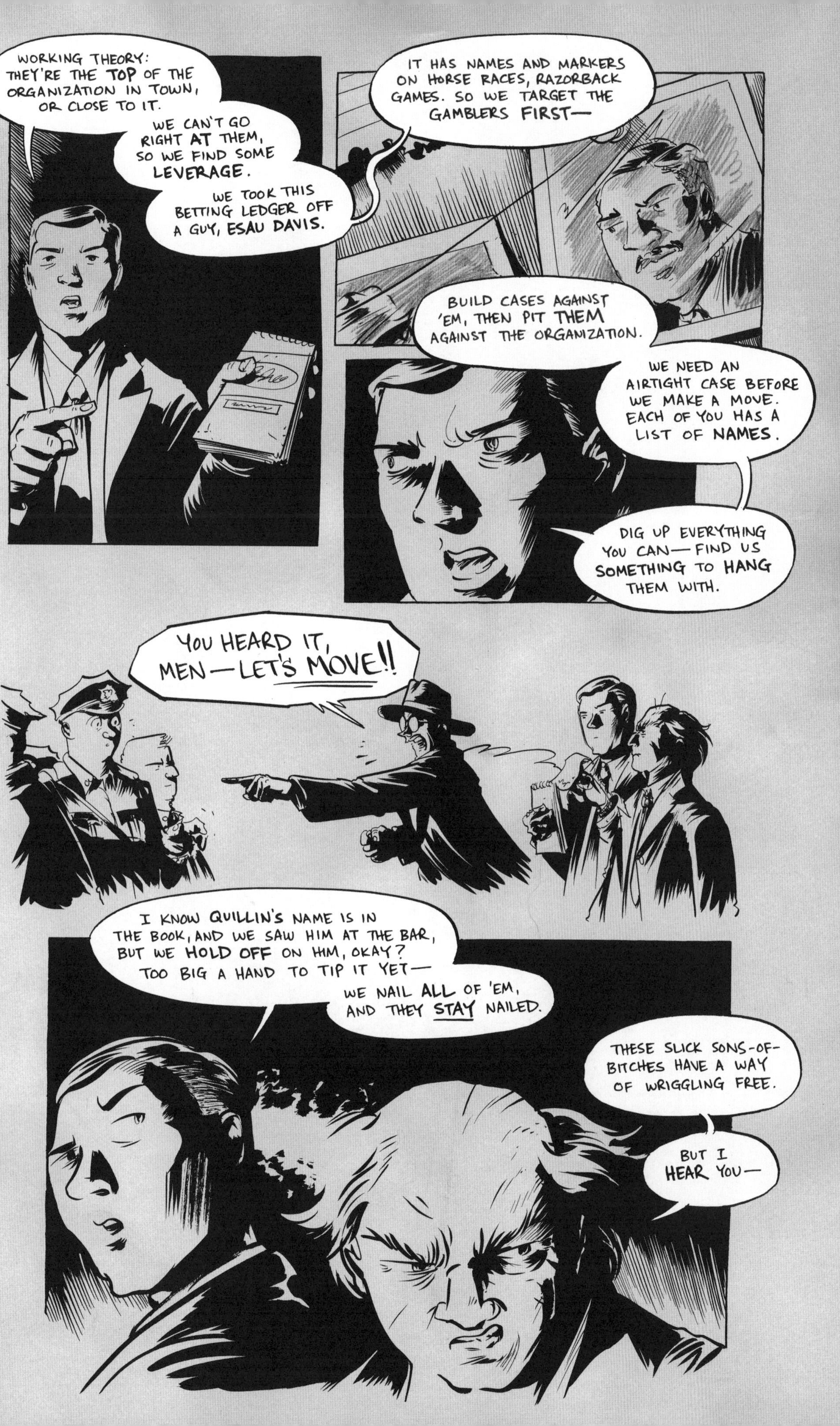
WORKING THEORY: THEY'RE THE TOP OF THE ORGANIZATION IN TOWN, OR CLOSE TO IT.
WE CAN'T GO RIGHT AT THEM, SO WE FIND SOME LEVERAGE.
WE TOOK THIS BETTING LEDGER OFF A GUY, ESAU DAVIS.
IT HAS NAMES AND MARKERS ON HORSE RACES, RAZORBACK GAMES. SO WE TARGET THE GAMBLERS FIRST—
BUILD CASES AGAINST 'EM, THEN PIT THEM AGAINST THE ORGANIZATION.
WE NEED AN AIRTIGHT CASE BEFORE WE MAKE A MOVE. EACH OF YOU HAS A LIST OF NAMES.
DIG UP EVERYTHING YOU CAN— FIND US SOMETHING TO HANG THEM WITH.
YOU HEARD IT, MEN— LET'S MOVE!!
I KNOW QUILLIN'S NAME IS IN THE BOOK, AND WE SAW HIM AT THE BAR, BUT WE HOLD OFF ON HIM, OKAY? TOO BIG A HAND TO TIP IT YET—
WE NAIL ALL OF 'EM, AND THEY STAY NAILED.
THESE SLICK SONS-OF-BITCHES HAVE A WAY OF WRIGGLING FREE.
BUT I HEAR YOU—

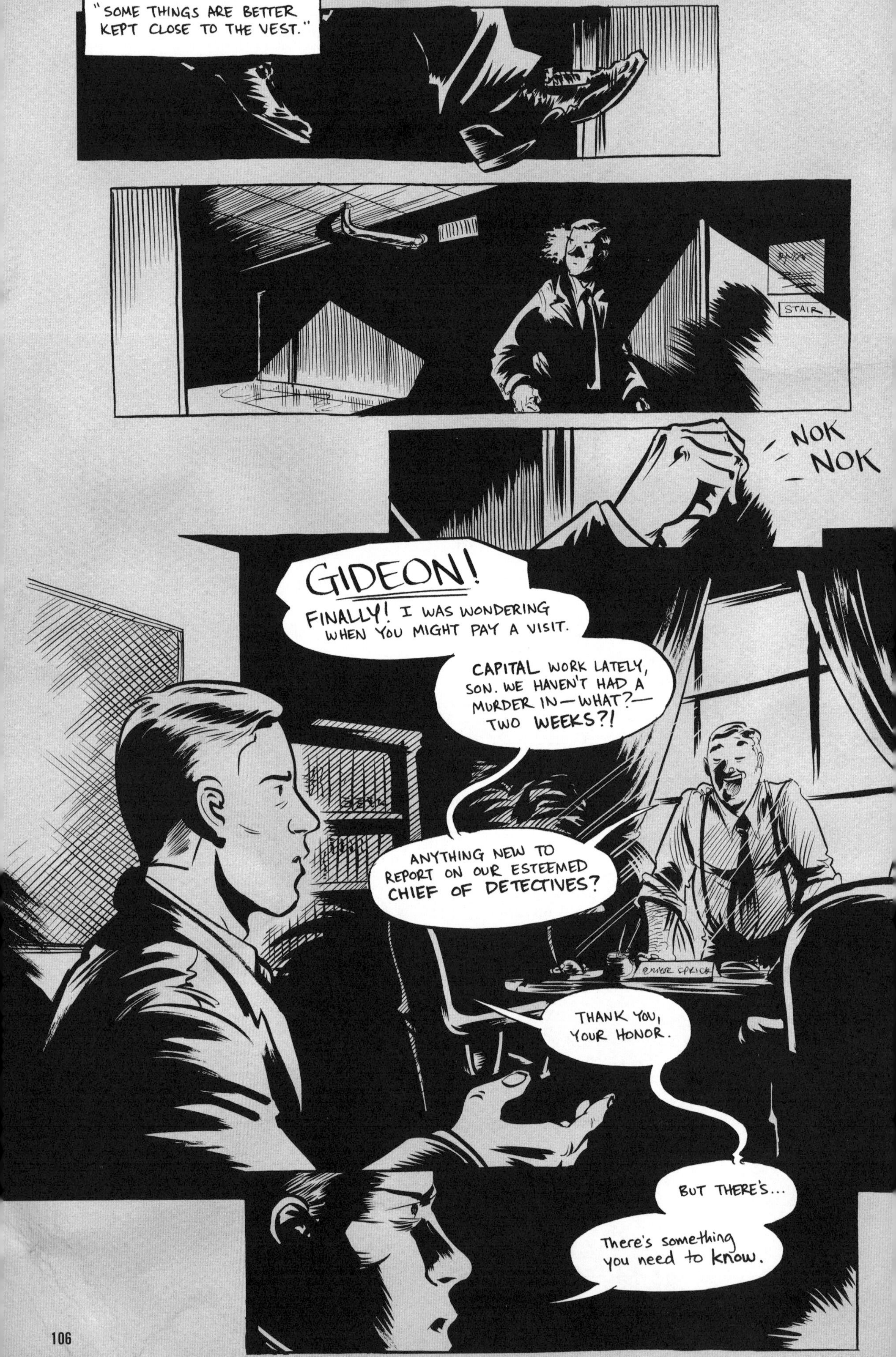
"SOME THINGS ARE BETTER KEPT CLOSE TO THE VEST."
STAIR
NOK NOK
GIDEON!
FINALLY! I WAS WONDERING WHEN YOU MIGHT PAY A VISIT.
CAPITAL WORK LATELY, SON. WE HAVEN'T HAD A MURDER IN—WHAT?—TWO WEEKS?!
ANYTHING NEW TO REPORT ON OUR ESTEEMED CHIEF OF DETECTIVES?
THANK YOU, YOUR HONOR.
BUT THERE'S...
There's something you need to know.

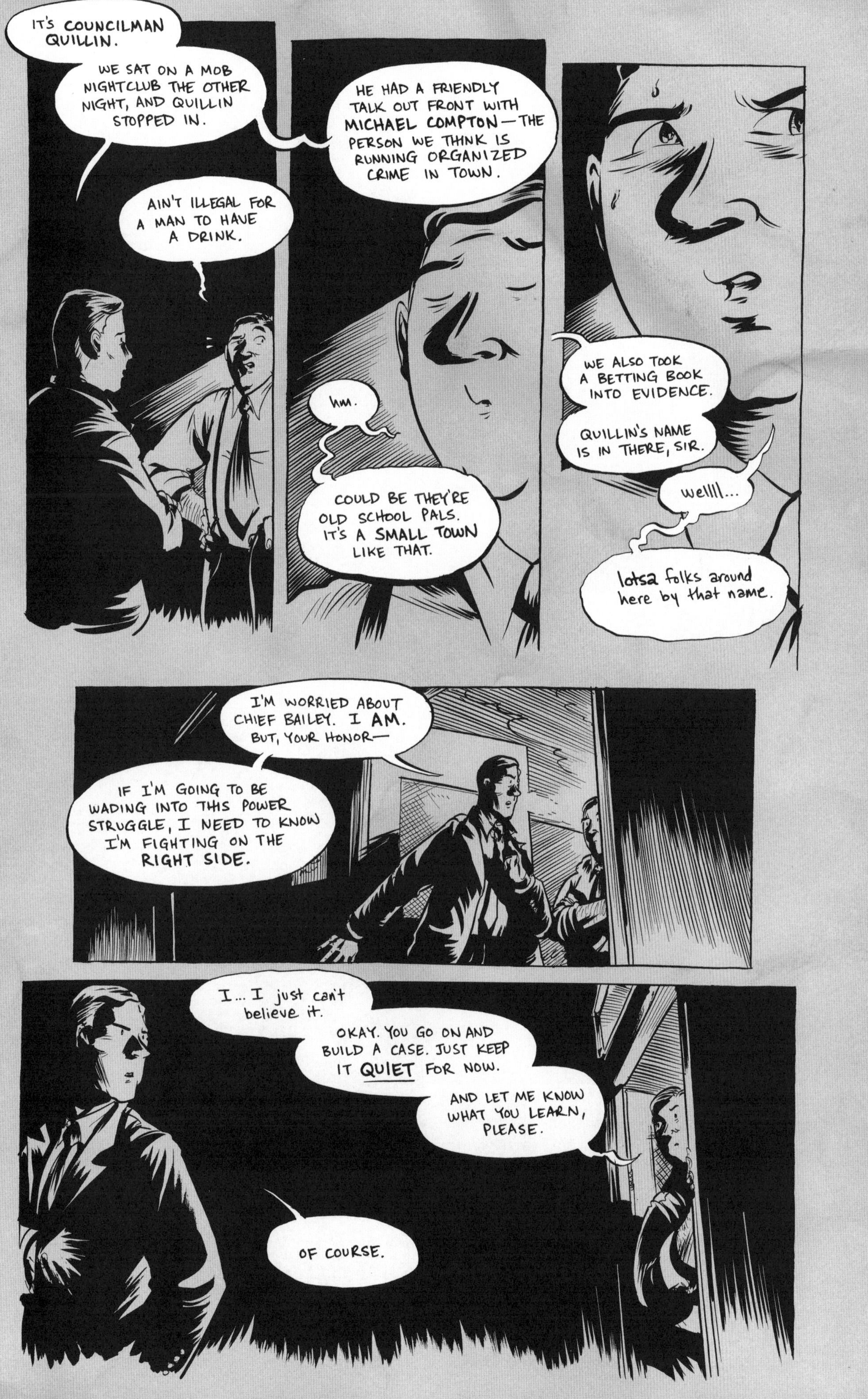
IT'S COUNCILMAN QUILLIN.
WE SAT ON A MOB NIGHTCLUB THE OTHER NIGHT, AND QUILLIN STOPPED IN.
AIN'T ILLEGAL FOR A MAN TO HAVE A DRINK.
HE HAD A FRIENDLY TALK OUT FRONT WITH MICHAEL COMPTON—THE PERSON WE THINK IS RUNNING ORGANIZED CRIME IN TOWN.
hm.
COULD BE THEY'RE OLD SCHOOL PALS. IT'S A SMALL TOWN LIKE THAT.
WE ALSO TOOK A BETTING BOOK INTO EVIDENCE.
QUILLIN'S NAME IS IN THERE, SIR.
wellll...
lotsa folks around here by that name.
I'M WORRIED ABOUT CHIEF BAILEY. I AM. BUT, YOUR HONOR—
IF I'M GOING TO BE WADING INTO THIS POWER STRUGGLE, I NEED TO KNOW I'M FIGHTING ON THE RIGHT SIDE.
I... I just can't believe it.
OKAY. YOU GO ON AND BUILD A CASE. JUST KEEP IT QUIET FOR NOW.
AND LET ME KNOW WHAT YOU LEARN, PLEASE.
OF COURSE.

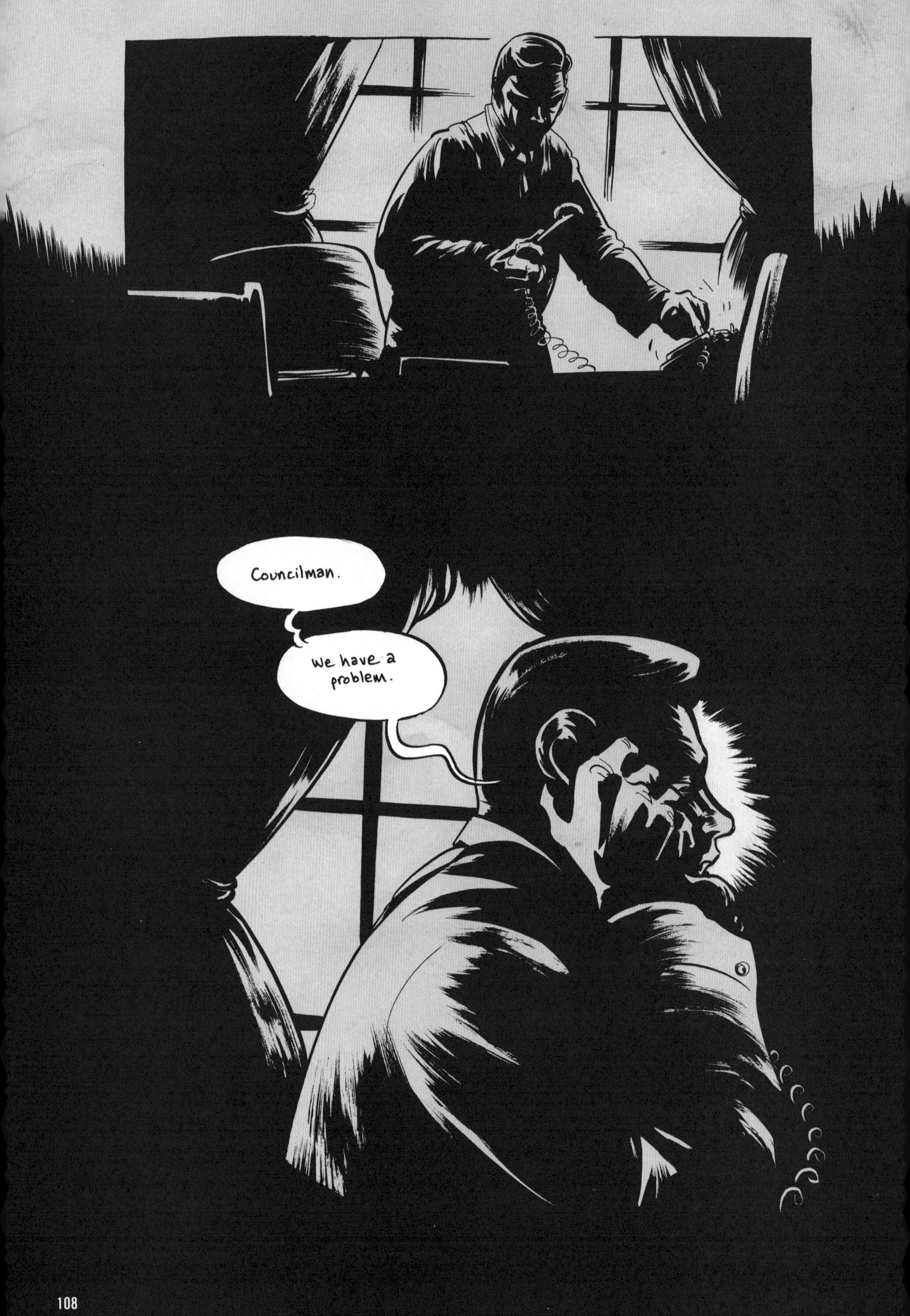
Councilman.
We have a problem.

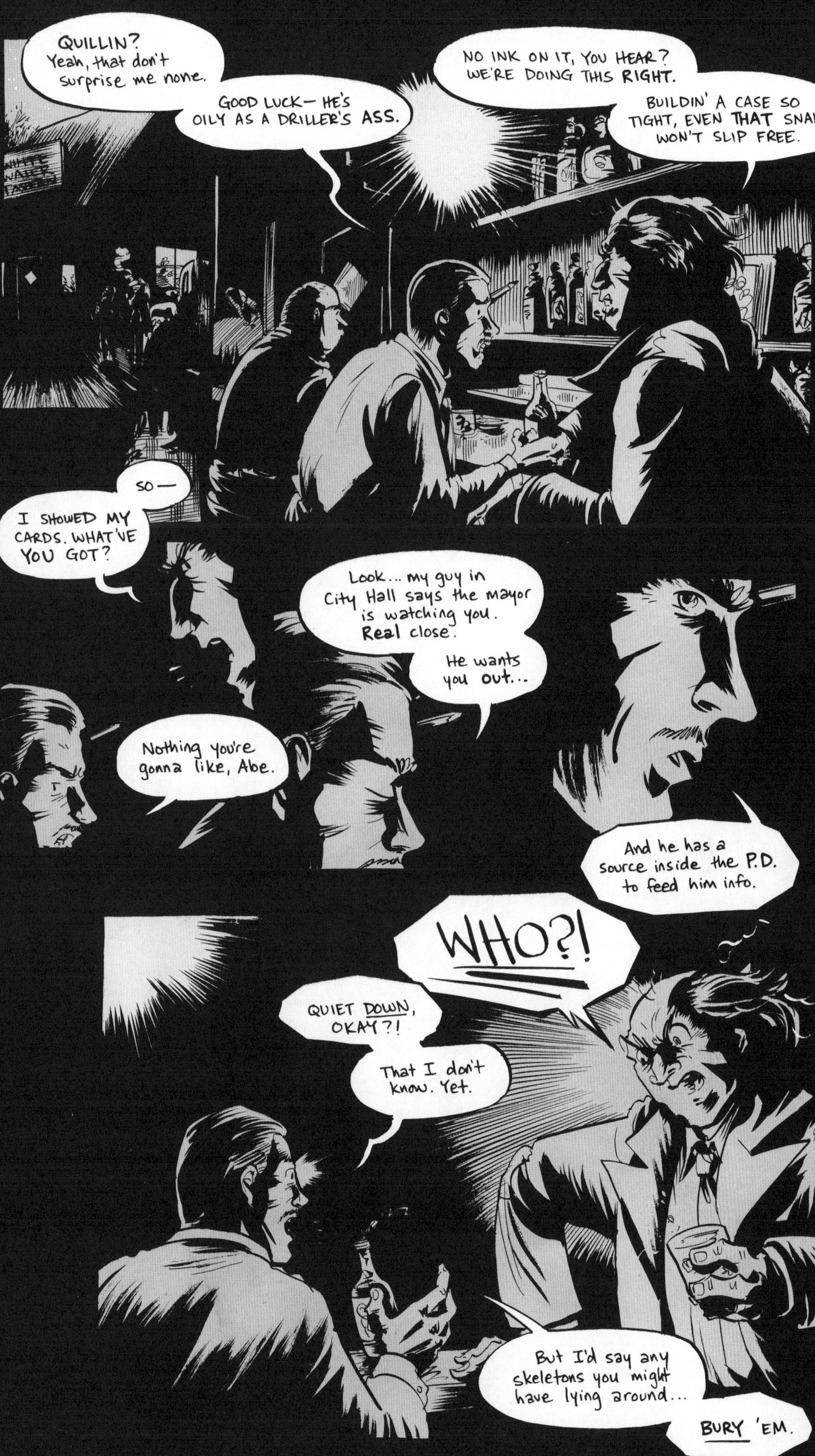
QUILLIN? Yeah, that don't surprise me none.
GOOD LUCK— HE'S OILY AS A DRILLER'S ASS.
NO INK ON IT, YOU HEAR? WE'RE DOING THIS RIGHT.
BUILDIN' A CASE SO TIGHT, EVEN THAT SNAKE WON'T SLIP FREE.
SO—
I SHOWED MY CARDS. WHAT'VE YOU GOT?
Nothing you're gonna like, Abe.
Look... my guy in City Hall says the mayor is watching you. Real close.
He wants you out...
And he has a source inside the P.D. to feed him info.
WHO?!
QUIET DOWN, OKAY?!
That I don't know. Yet.
But I'd say any skeletons you might have lying around...
BURY 'EM.

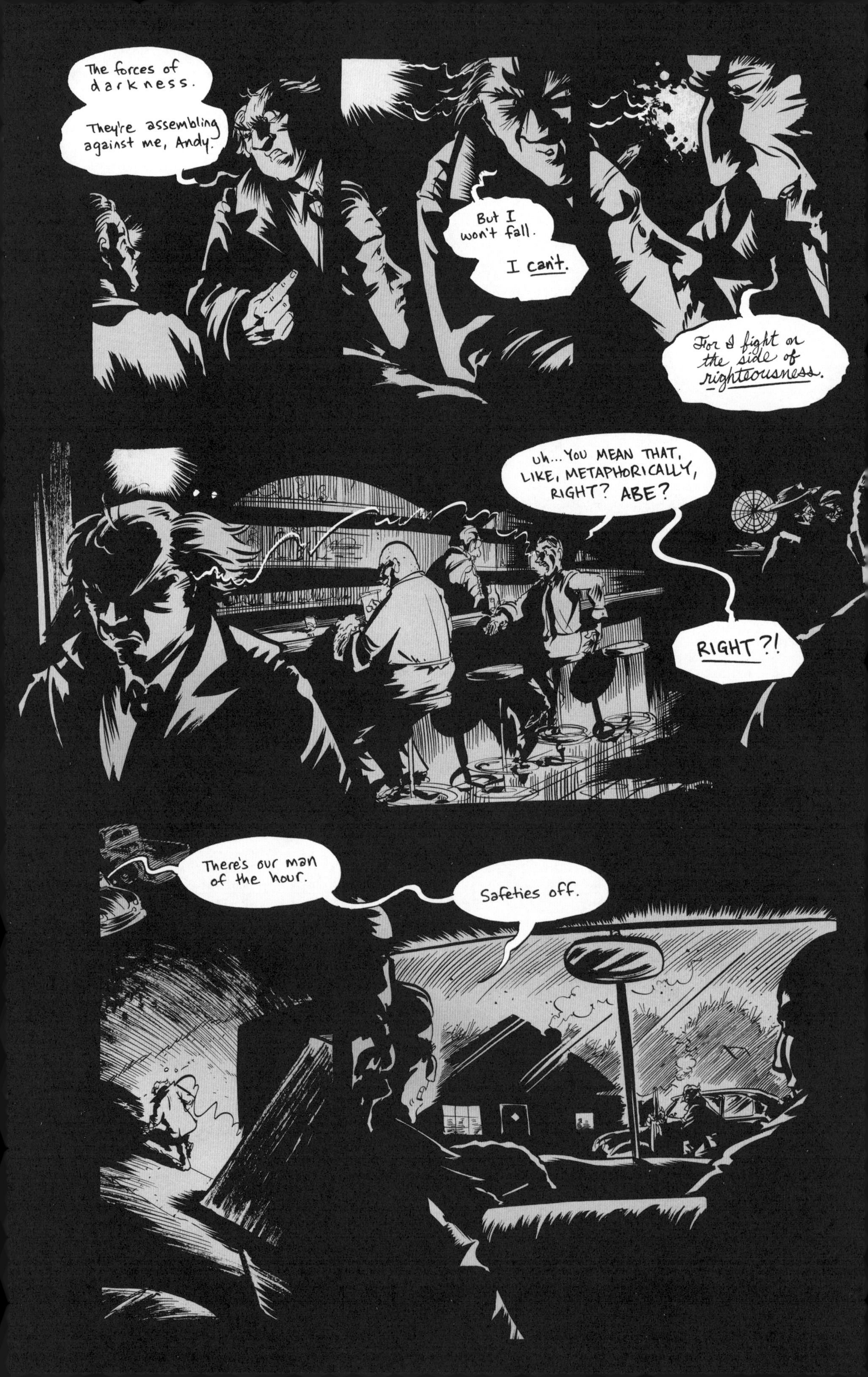
The forces of darkness.
They're assembling against me, Andy.
But I won't fall.
I can't.
For I fight on the side of righteousness.
uh... YOU MEAN THAT, LIKE, METAPHORICALLY, RIGHT? ABE?
RIGHT?!
There's our man of the hour.
Safeties off.

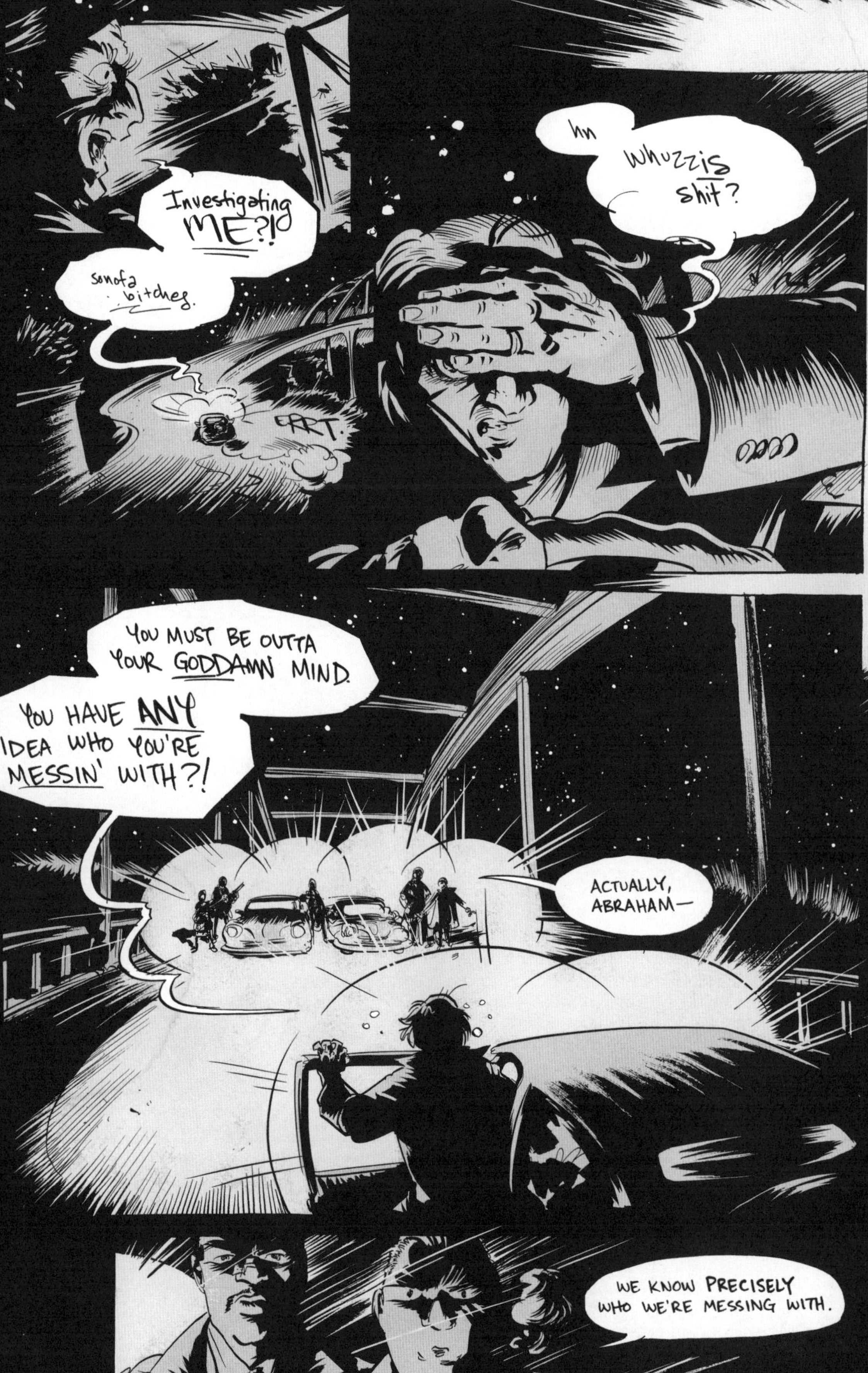
Investigating ME?!
sonofa bitches.
ERRT.
hn Whuzzis shit?
You must be outta your GODDAMN mind.
You have ANY idea who you're MESSIN' with?!
ACTUALLY, ABRAHAM—
WE KNOW PRECISELY WHO WE'RE MESSING WITH.

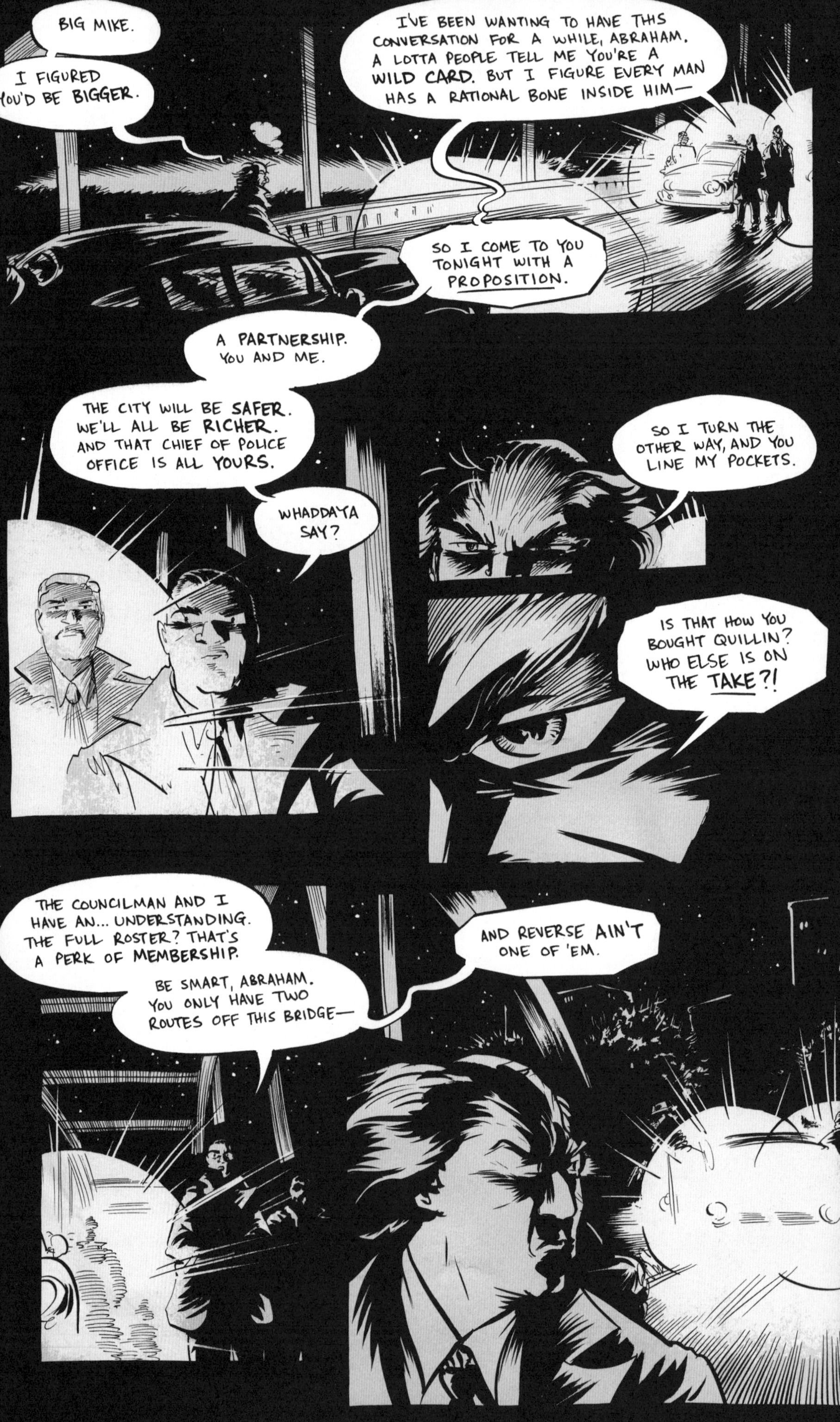
BIG MIKE.
I FIGURED YOU'D BE BIGGER.
I'VE BEEN WANTING TO HAVE THIS CONVERSATION FOR A WHILE, ABRAHAM. A LOTTA PEOPLE TELL ME YOU'RE A WILD CARD. BUT I FIGURE EVERY MAN HAS A RATIONAL BONE INSIDE HIM—
SO I COME TO YOU TONIGHT WITH A PROPOSITION.
A PARTNERSHIP. YOU AND ME.
THE CITY WILL BE SAFER. WE'LL ALL BE RICHER. AND THAT CHIEF OF POLICE OFFICE IS ALL YOURS.
WHADDAYA SAY?
SO I TURN THE OTHER WAY, AND YOU LINE MY POCKETS.
IS THAT HOW YOU BOUGHT QUILLIN? WHO ELSE IS ON THE TAKE?!
THE COUNCILMAN AND I HAVE AN... UNDERSTANDING. THE FULL ROSTER? THAT'S A PERK OF MEMBERSHIP.
BE SMART, ABRAHAM. YOU ONLY HAVE TWO ROUTES OFF THIS BRIDGE—
AND REVERSE AIN'T ONE OF 'EM.

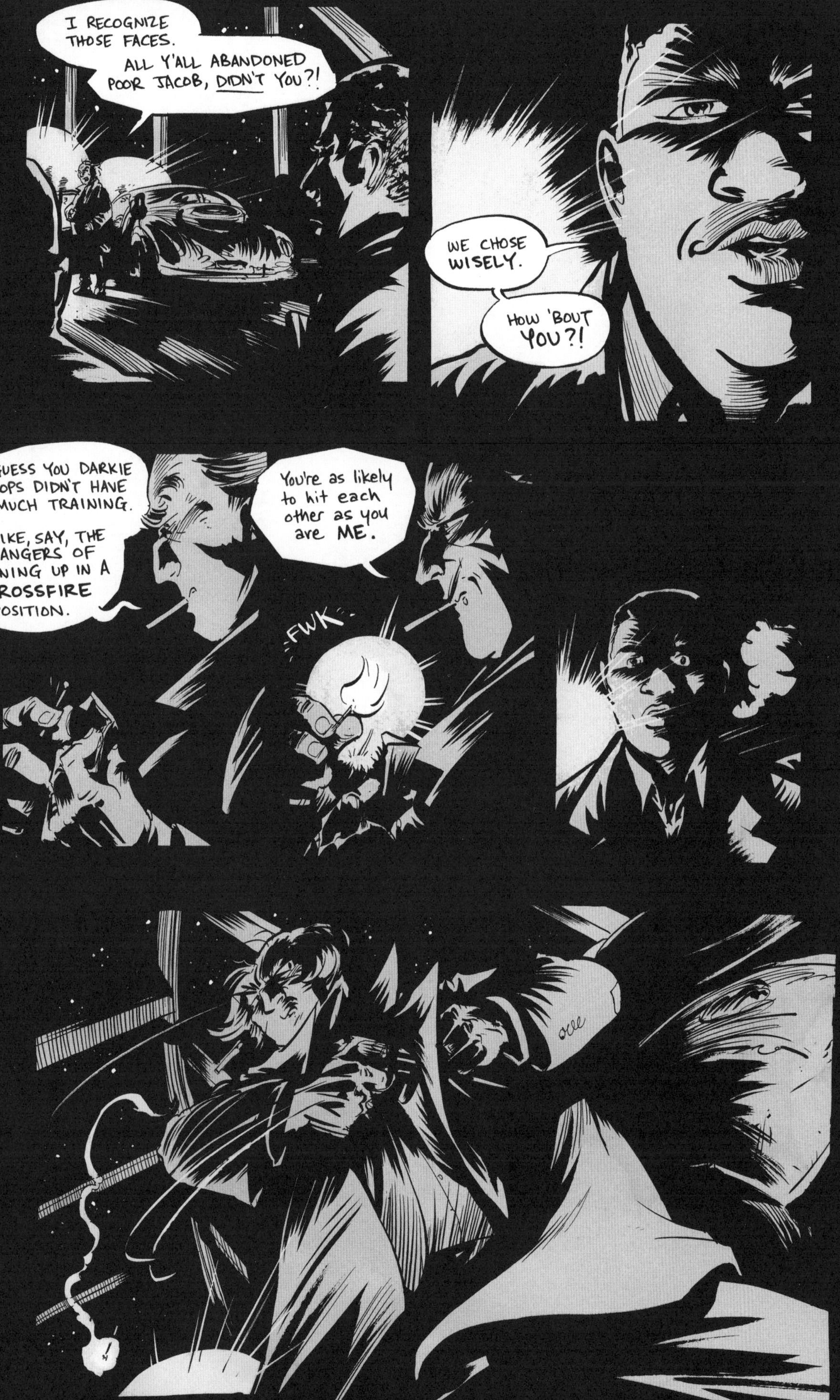
I RECOGNIZE THOSE FACES.
ALL Y'ALL ABANDONED POOR JACOB, DIDN'T YOU?!
WE CHOSE WISELY.
HOW 'BOUT YOU?!
GUESS YOU DARKIE COPS DIDN'T HAVE MUCH TRAINING.
LIKE, SAY, THE DANGERS OF LINING UP IN A CROSSFIRE POSITION.
You're as likely to hit each other as you are ME.
FWK

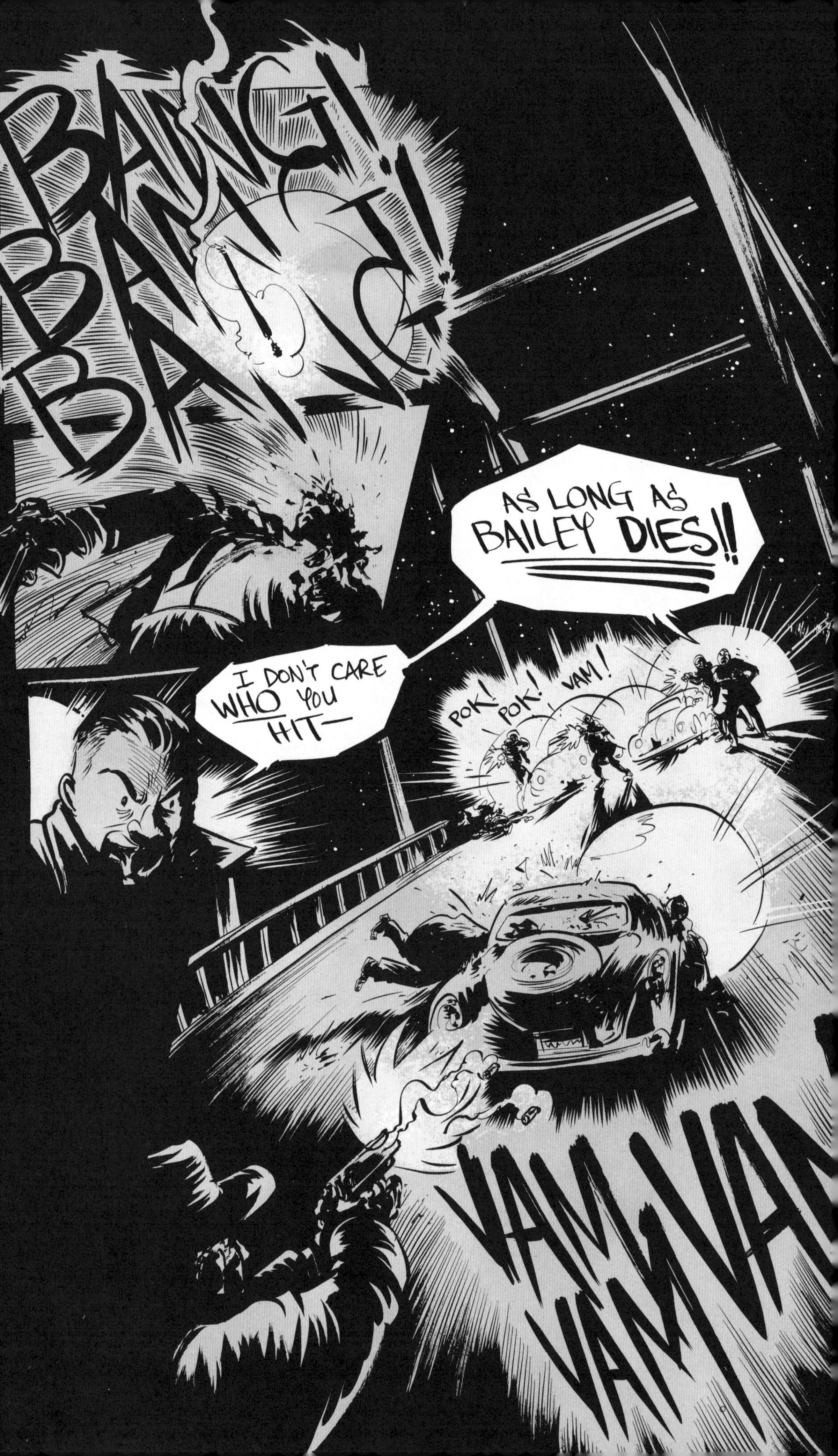
BANG! BANG! BANG!!
I DON'T CARE WHO YOU HIT—
AS LONG AS BAILEY DIES!!
POK! POK! VAM!
VAM VAM VAM VAM

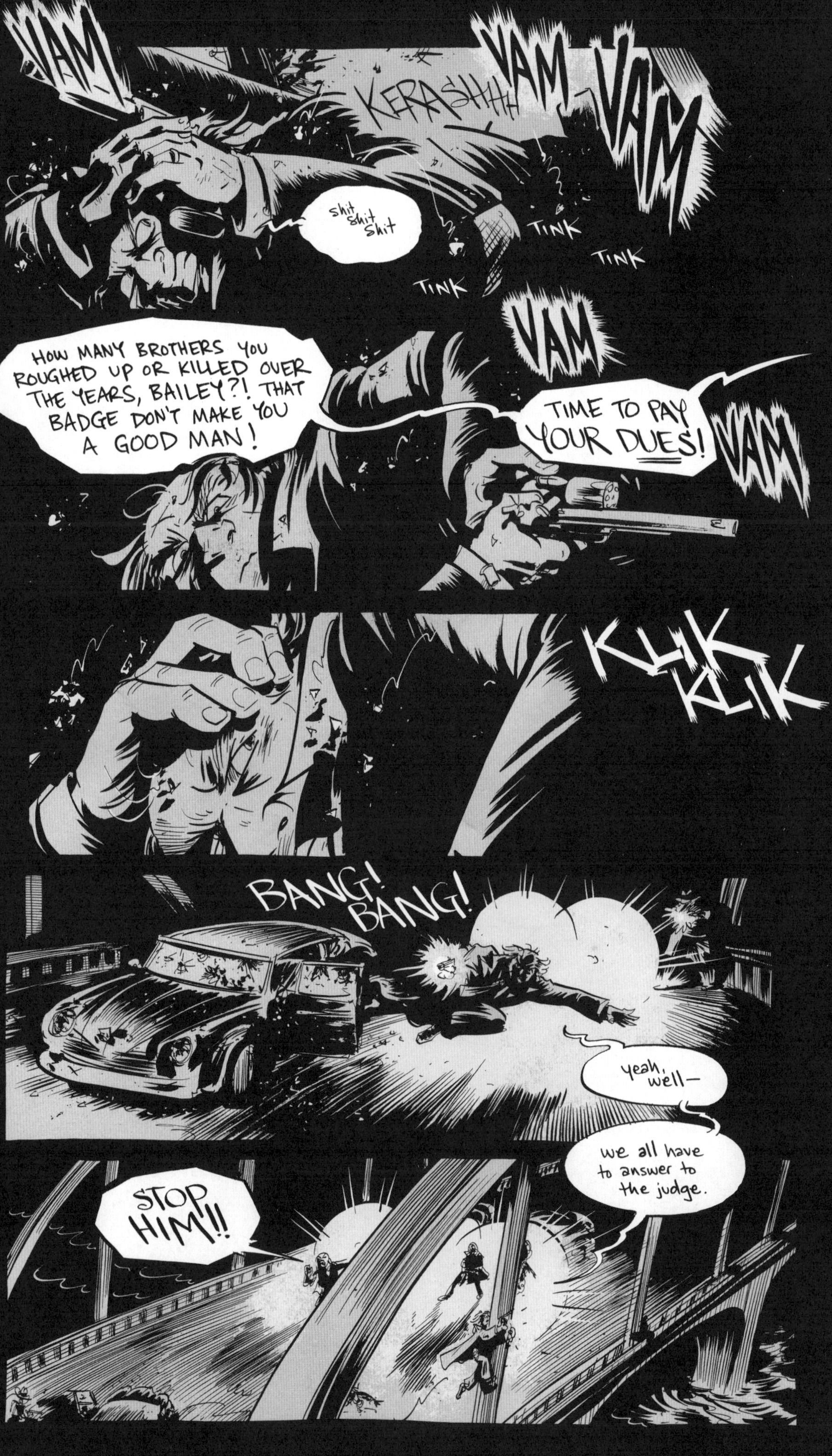
VAM
KERASHHH
VAM-VAM
shit shit shit
TINK
TINK
TINK
VAM
HOW MANY BROTHERS YOU ROUGHED UP OR KILLED OVER THE YEARS, BAILEY?! THAT BADGE DON'T MAKE YOU A GOOD MAN!
TIME TO PAY YOUR DUES!
VAM
KLIK KLIK
BANG! BANG!
yeah, well—
we all have to answer to the judge.
STOP HIM!!

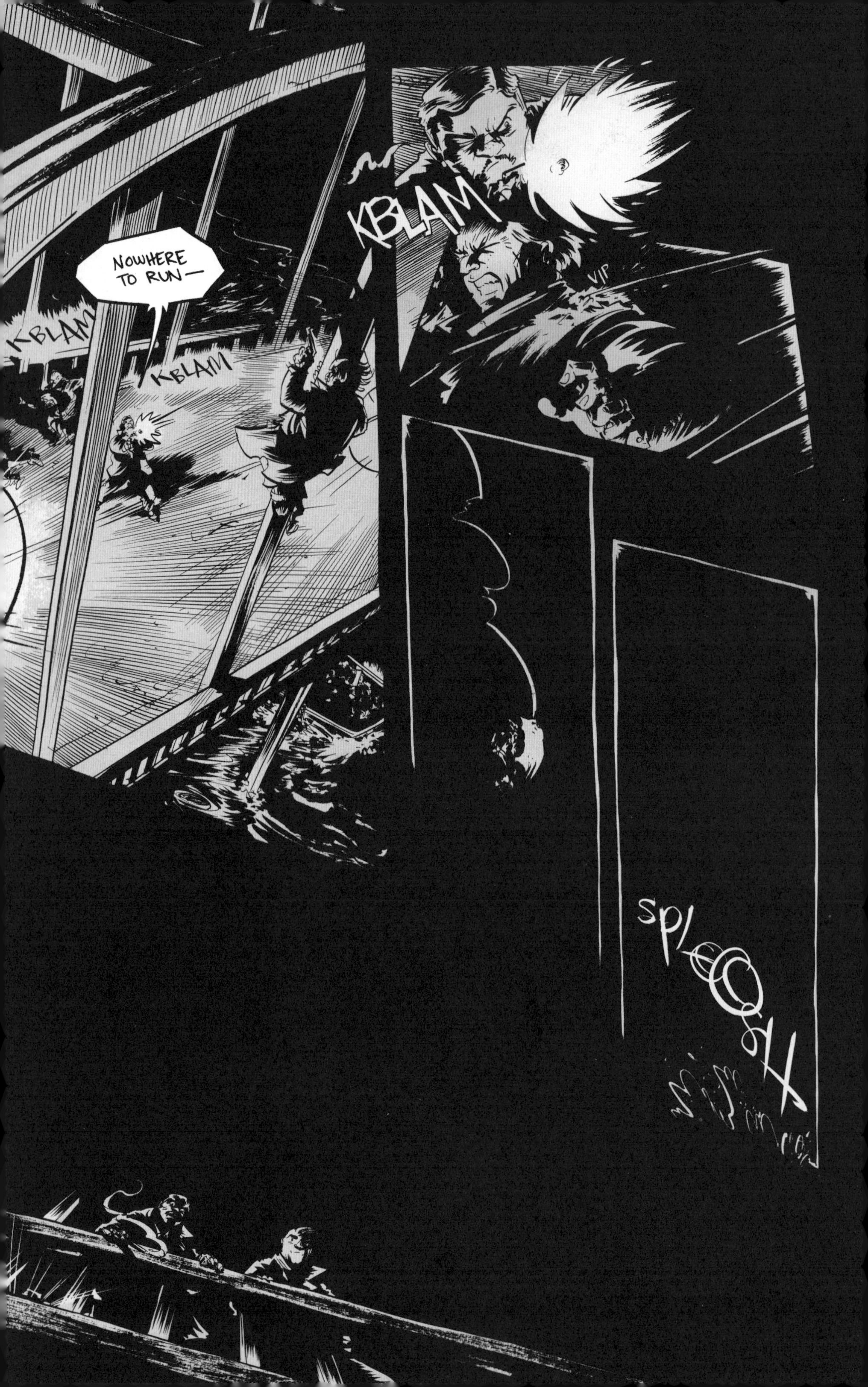
NOWHERE TO RUN—
KBLAM
KBLAM
KBLAM
SPLOOSH

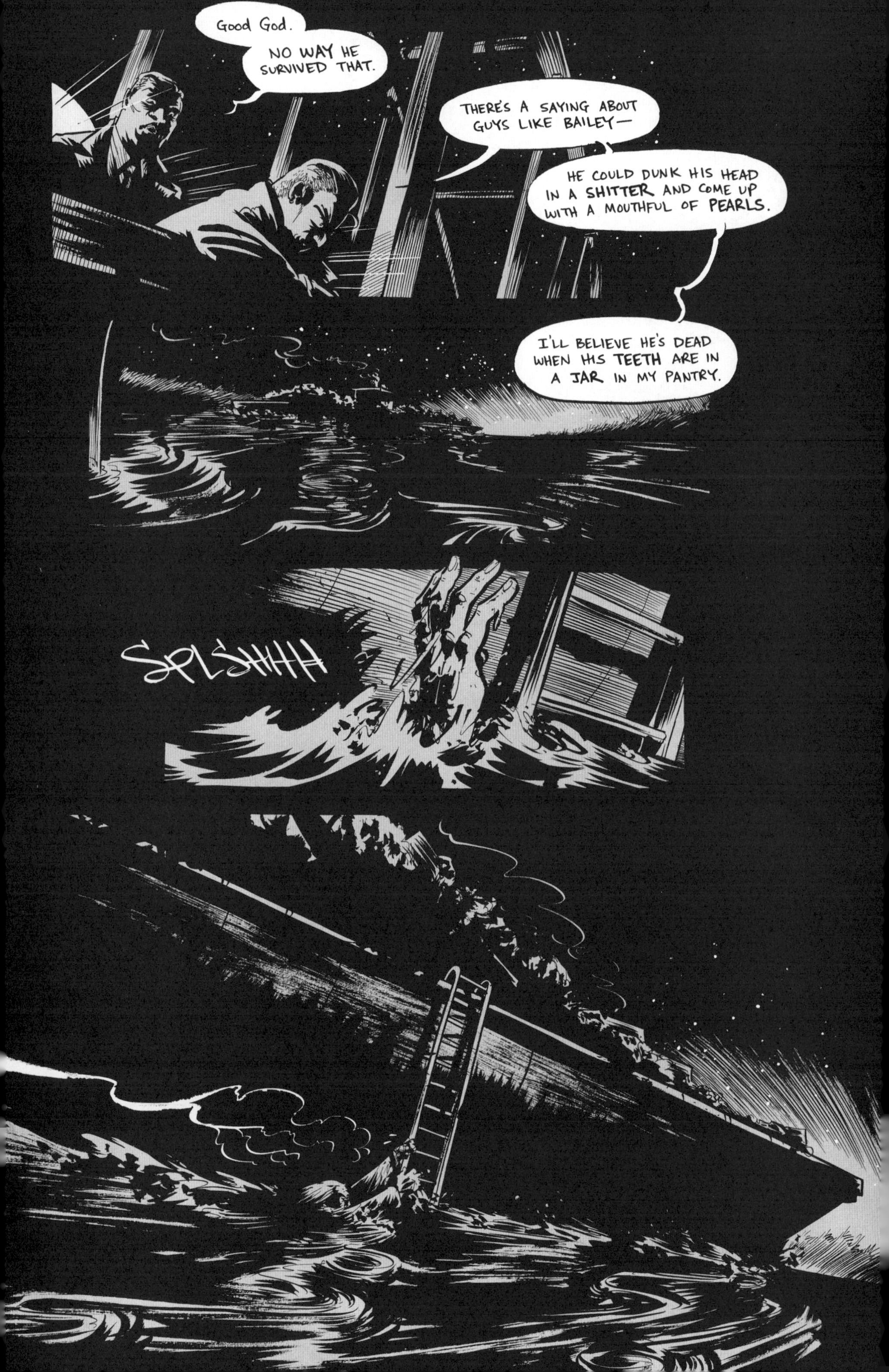

Good God.
NO WAY HE SURVIVED THAT.
THERE'S A SAYING ABOUT GUYS LIKE BAILEY—
HE COULD DUNK HIS HEAD IN A SHITTER AND COME UP WITH A MOUTHFUL OF PEARLS.
I'LL BELIEVE HE'S DEAD WHEN HIS TEETH ARE IN A JAR IN MY PANTRY.
SPLSHHH

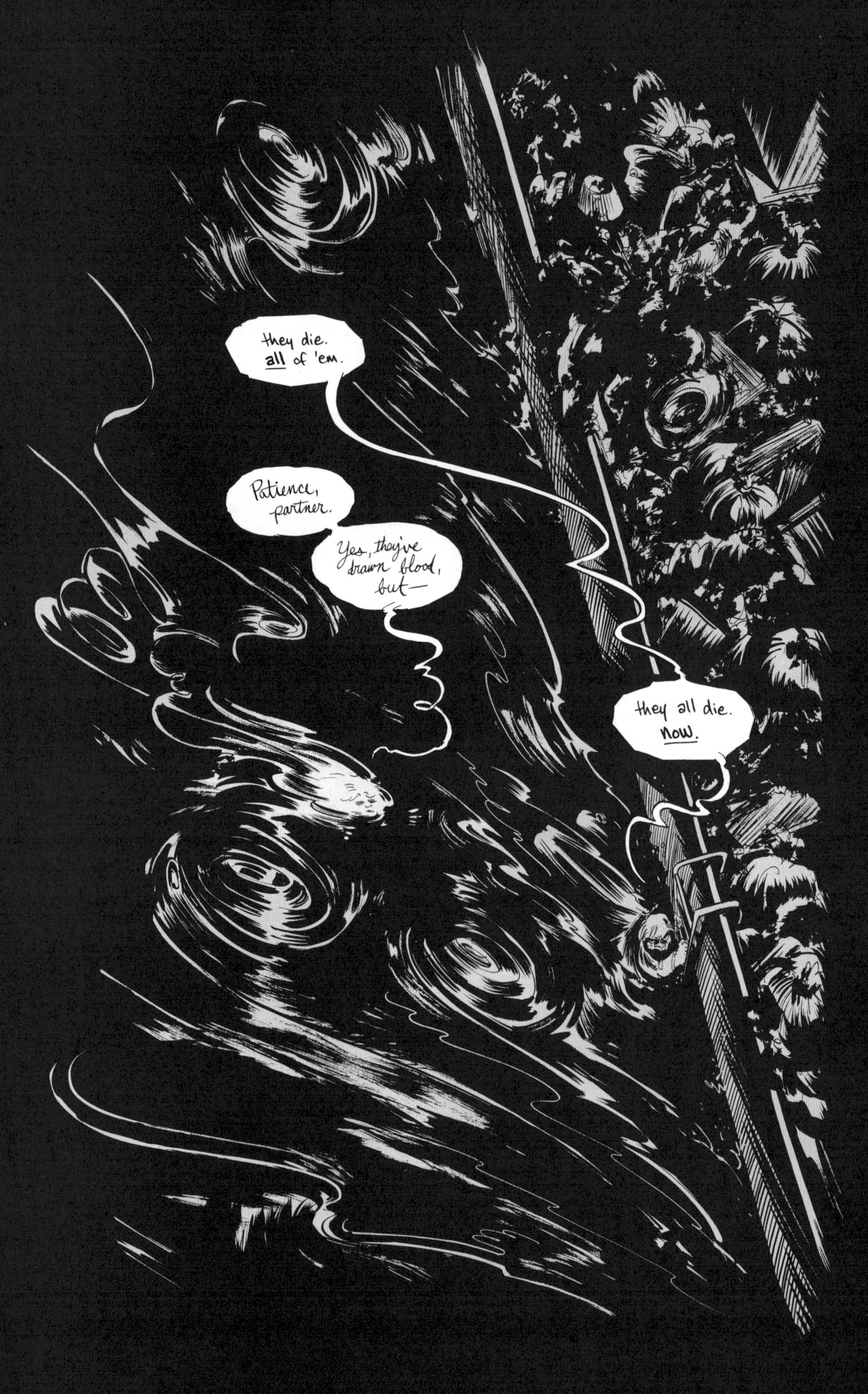
they die. all of 'em.
Patience, partner.
Yes, they've drawn blood, but—
they all die. now.

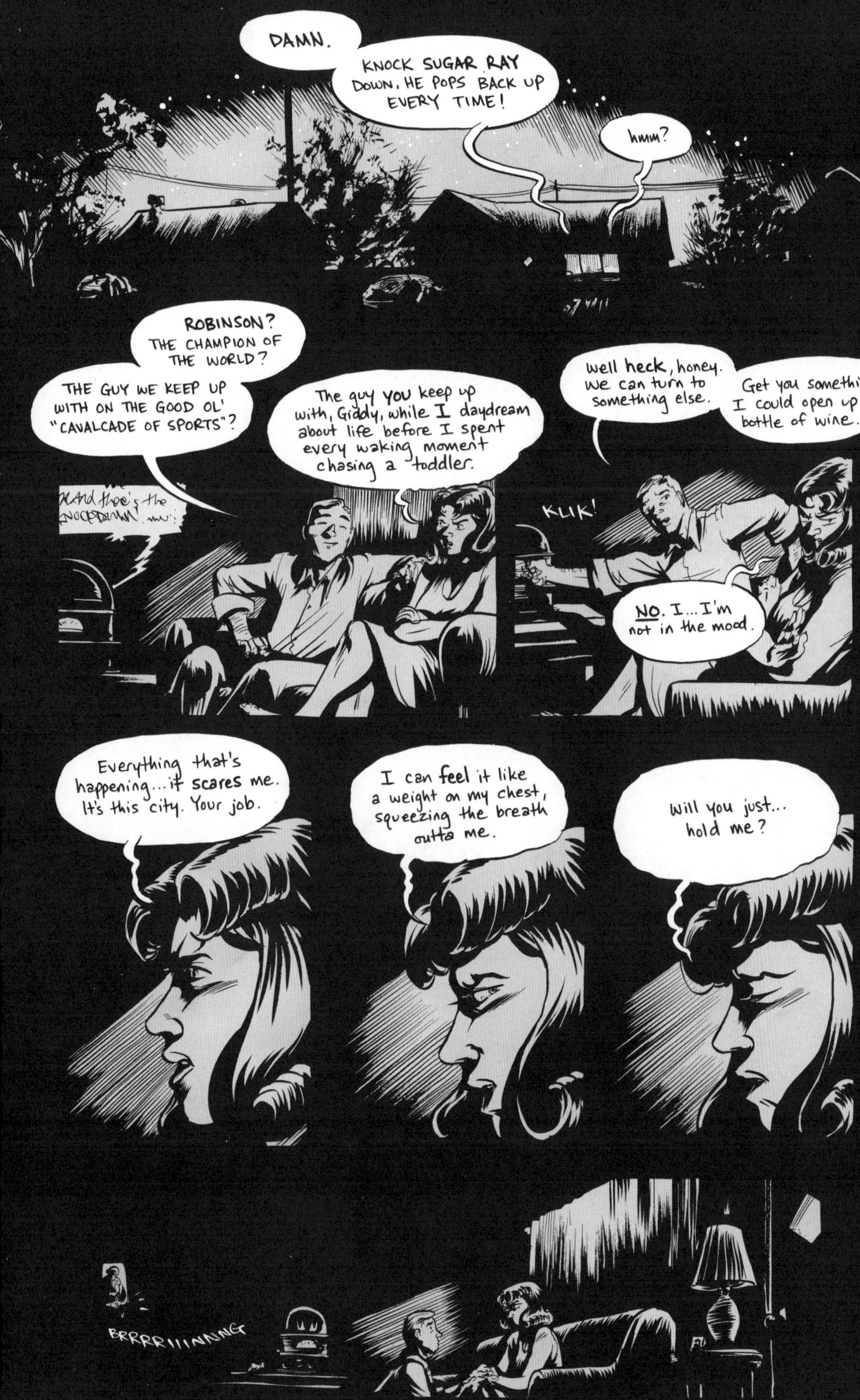

DAMN.
KNOCK SUGAR RAY DOWN, HE POPS BACK UP EVERY TIME!
hmm?
ROBINSON? THE CHAMPION OF THE WORLD?
THE GUY WE KEEP UP WITH ON THE GOOD OL' "CAVALCADE OF SPORTS"?
The guy YOU keep up with, Giddy, while I daydream about life before I spent every waking moment chasing a toddler.
KLIK!
Well heck, honey. We can turn to something else.
Get you something? I could open up a bottle of wine.
NO. I... I'm not in the mood.
Everything that's happening... it scares me. It's this city. Your job.
I can feel it like a weight on my chest, squeezing the breath outta me.
Will you just... hold me?
BRRRRIIINNNG

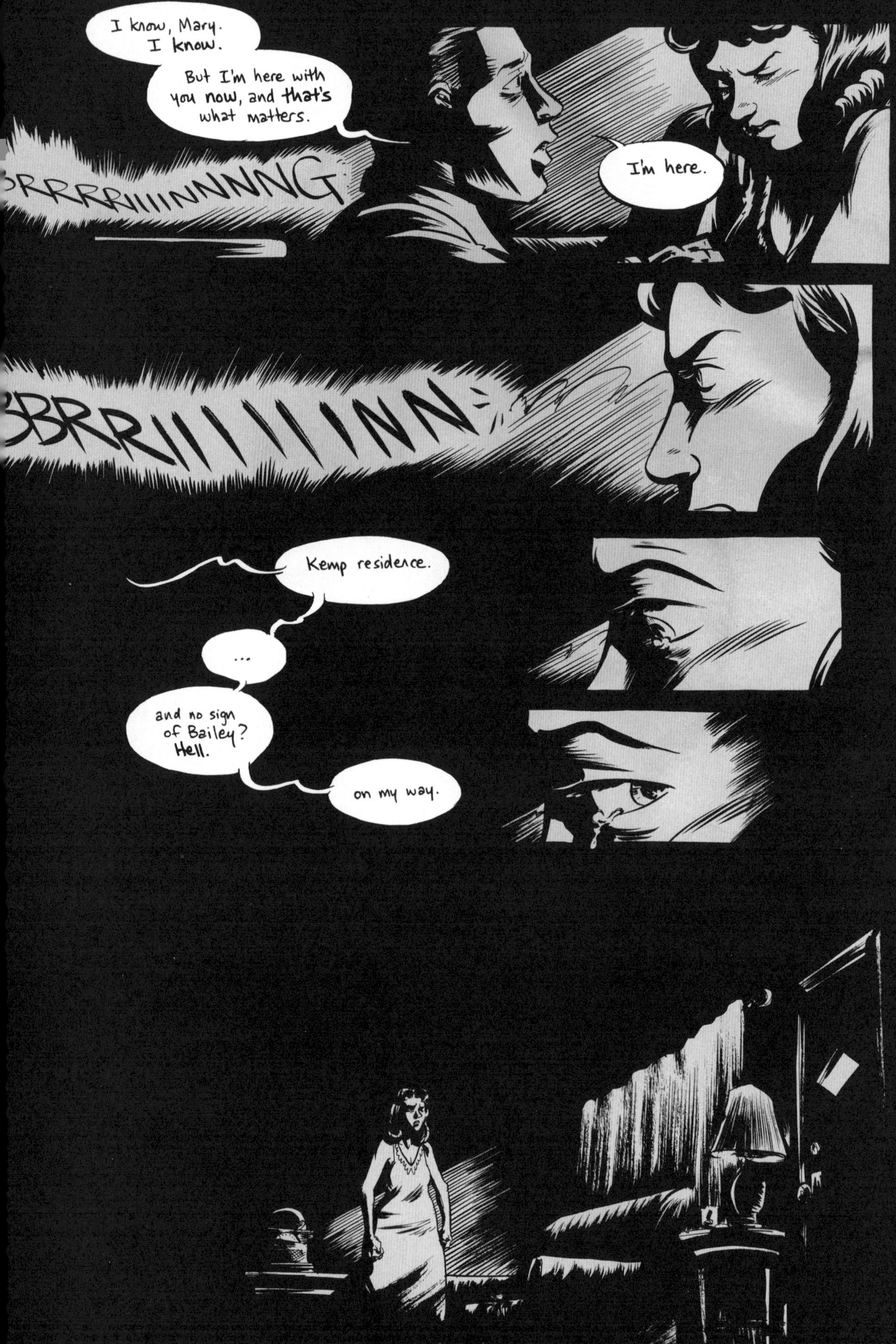
I know, Mary. I know.
But I'm here with you now, and that's what matters.
BRRRRRIIIINNNNG
I'm here.
BRRIIIIIINN
Kemp residence.
...
and no sign of Bailey? Hell.
on my way.

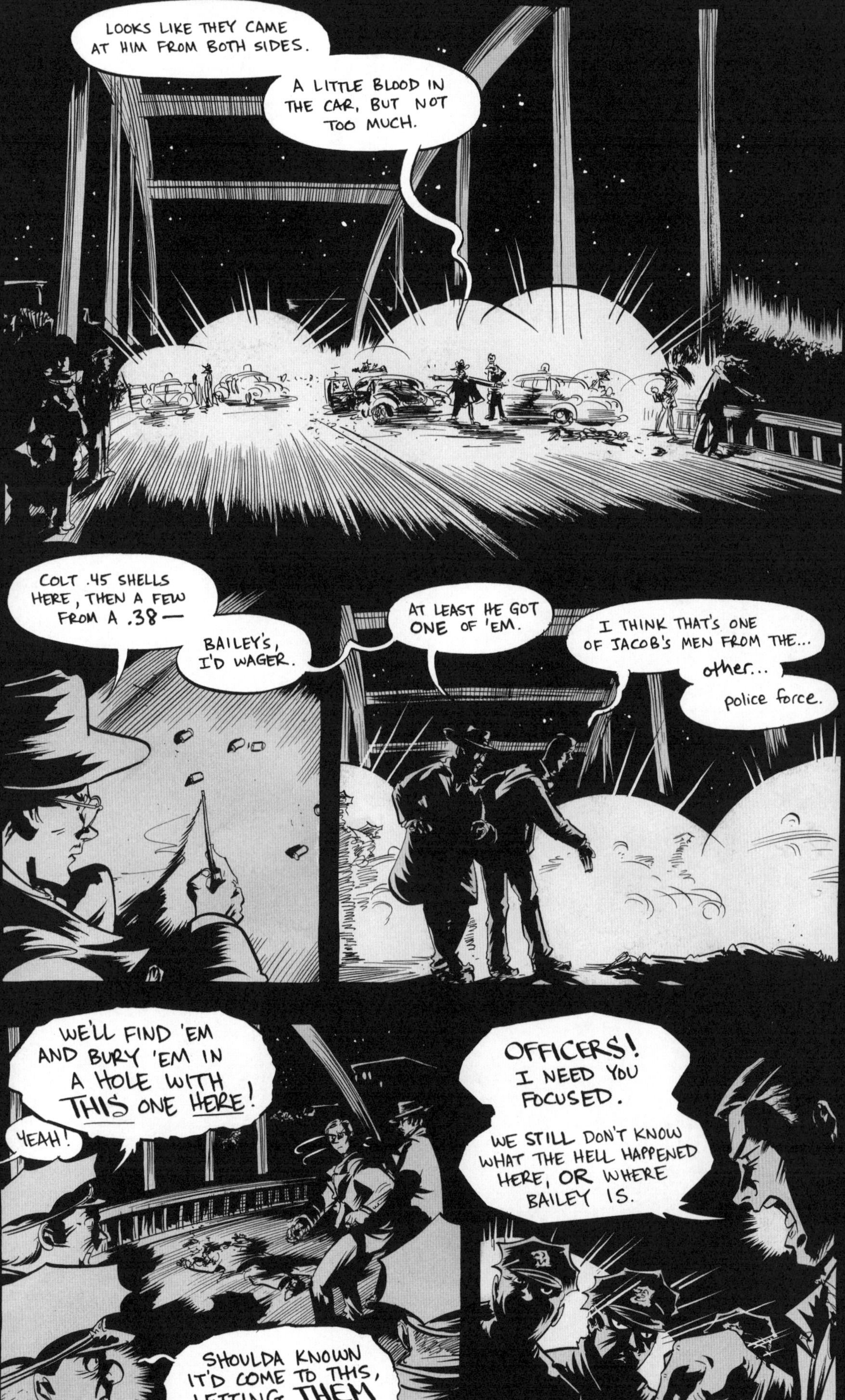
LOOKS LIKE THEY CAME AT HIM FROM BOTH SIDES.
A LITTLE BLOOD IN THE CAR, BUT NOT TOO MUCH.
COLT .45 SHELLS HERE, THEN A FEW FROM A .38—
BAILEY'S, I'D WAGER.
AT LEAST HE GOT ONE OF 'EM.
I THINK THAT'S ONE OF JACOB'S MEN FROM THE...
other...
police force.
WE'LL FIND 'EM AND BURY 'EM IN A HOLE WITH THIS ONE HERE!
YEAH!
SHOULDA KNOWN IT'D COME TO THIS, LETTING THEM CARRY GUNS.
OFFICERS! I NEED YOU FOCUSED.
WE STILL DON'T KNOW WHAT THE HELL HAPPENED HERE, OR WHERE BAILEY IS.

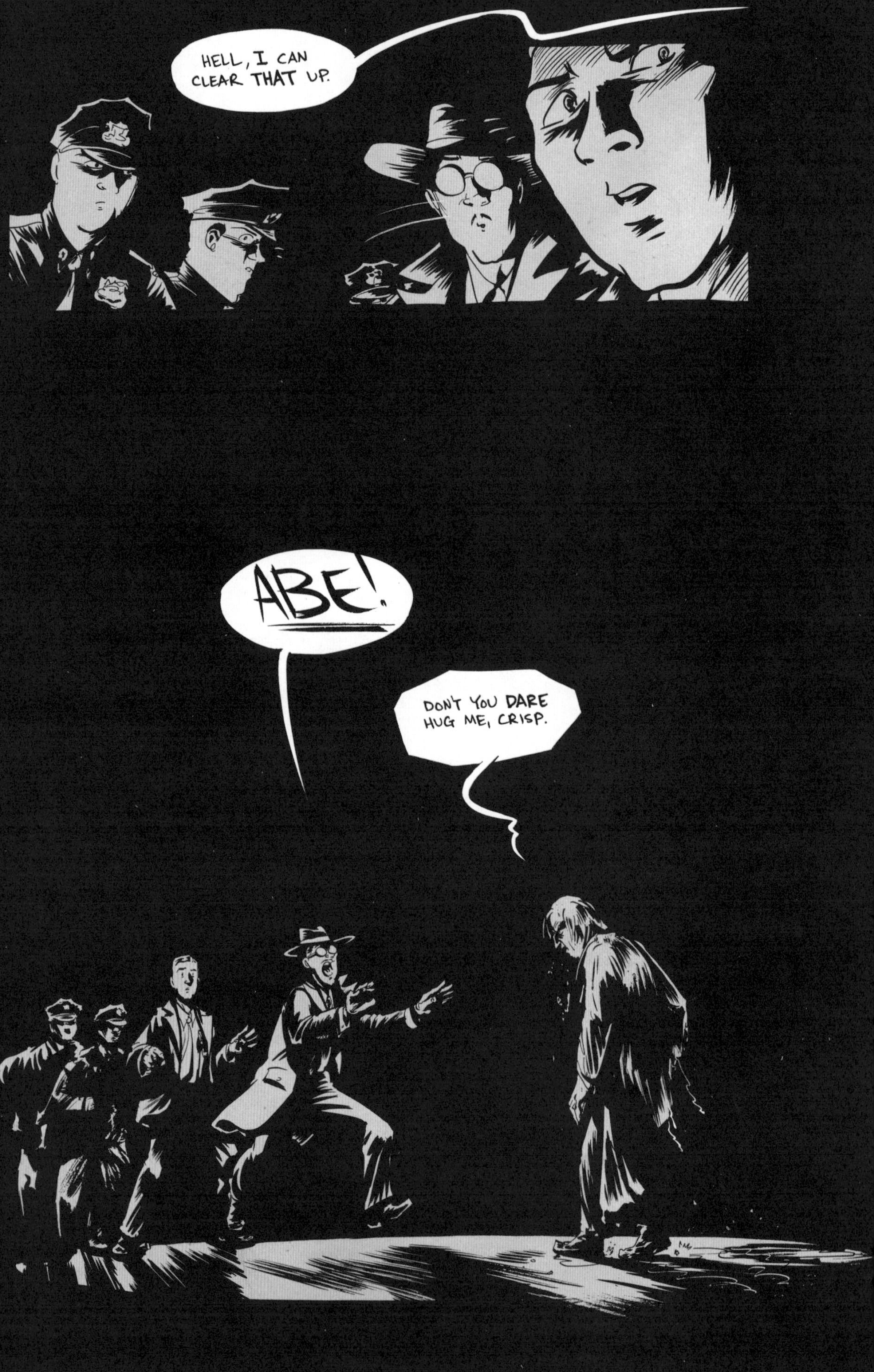
HELL, I CAN CLEAR THAT UP.
ABE!
DON'T YOU DARE HUG ME, CRISP.

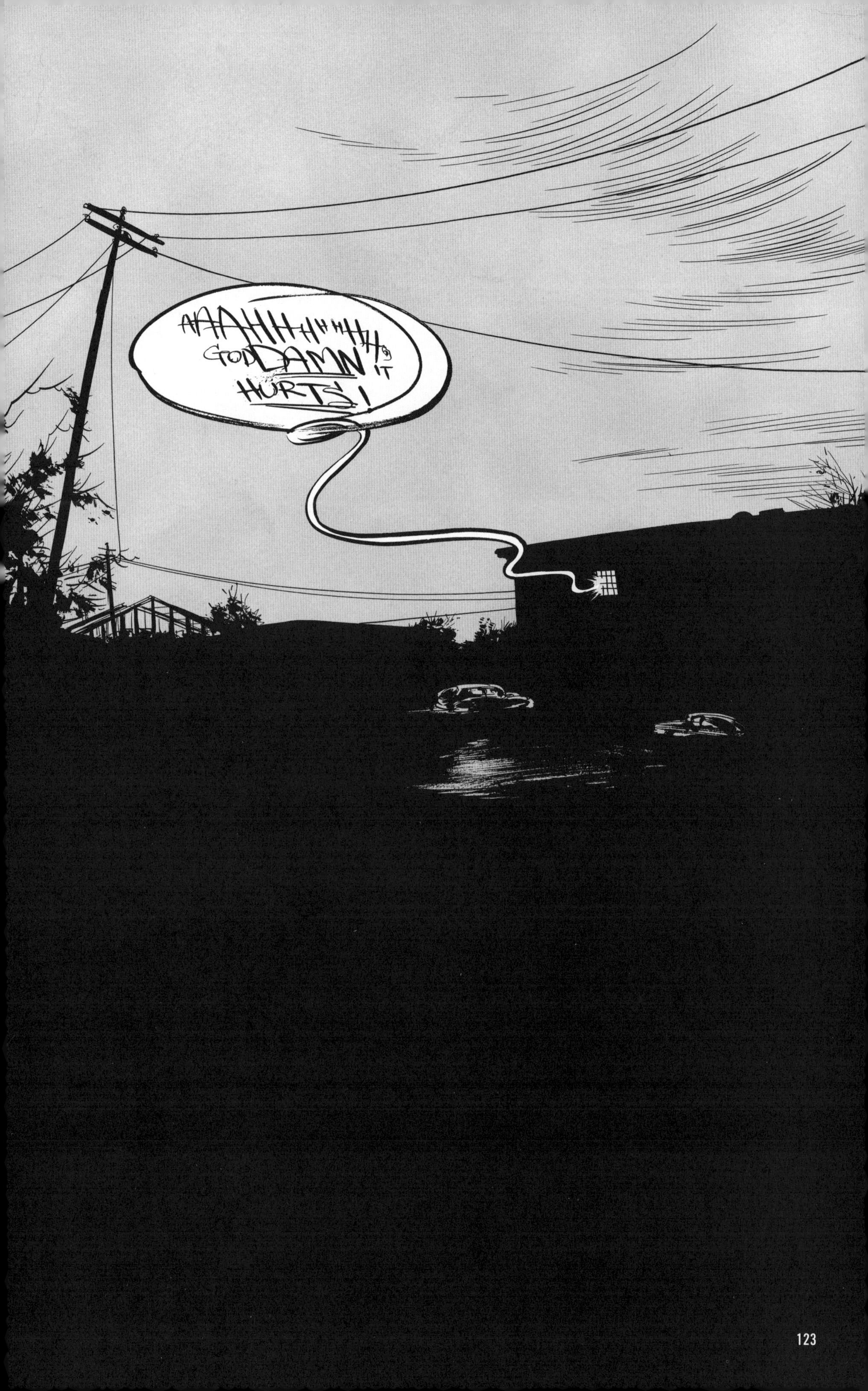
AAAHHHHHHHH!!
GODDAMN IT HURTS!!

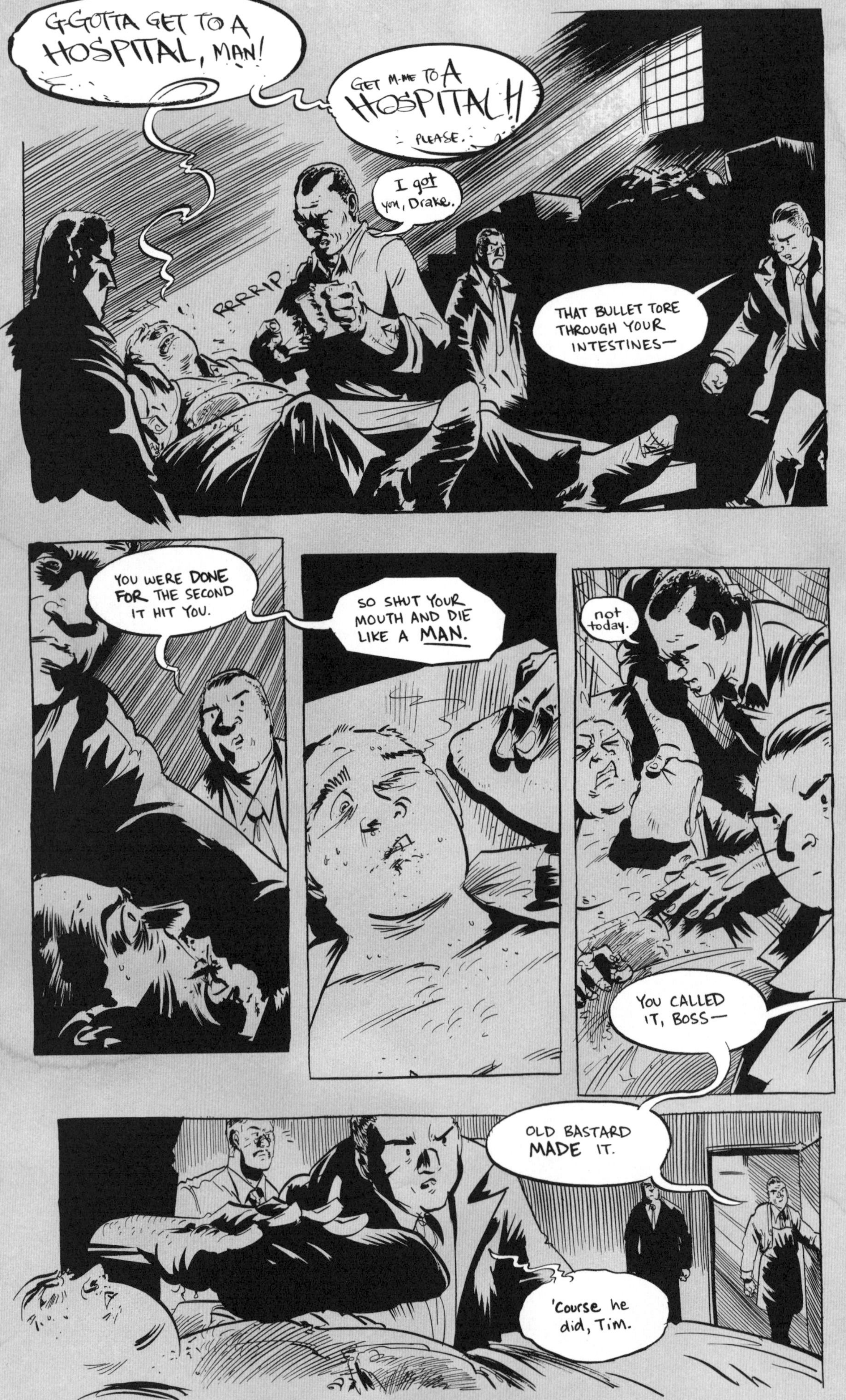
G-GOTTA GET TO A HOSPITAL, MAN!
GET M-ME TO A HOSPITAL!!
PLEASE.
I got you, Drake.
RRRRIP
THAT BULLET TORE THROUGH YOUR INTESTINES—
YOU WERE DONE FOR THE SECOND IT HIT YOU.
SO SHUT YOUR MOUTH AND DIE LIKE A MAN.
not today.
YOU CALLED IT, BOSS—
OLD BASTARD MADE IT.
'course he did, Tim.

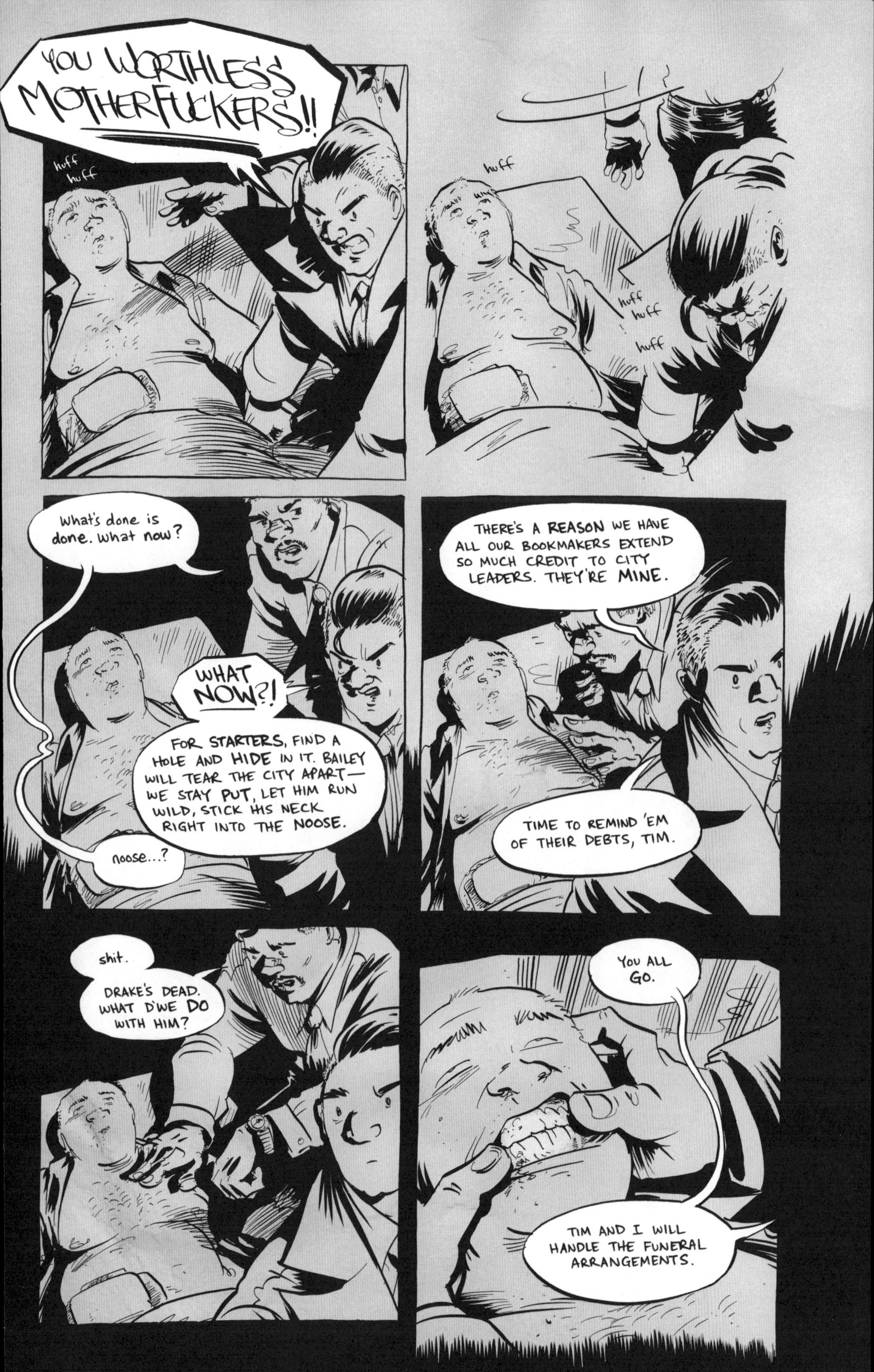
YOU WORTHLESS MOTHERFUCKERS!!
huff huff
huff
huff huff huff
What's done is done. What now?
WHAT NOW?!
FOR STARTERS, FIND A HOLE AND HIDE IN IT. BAILEY WILL TEAR THE CITY APART—WE STAY PUT, LET HIM RUN WILD, STICK HIS NECK RIGHT INTO THE NOOSE.
noose...?
THERE'S A REASON WE HAVE ALL OUR BOOKMAKERS EXTEND SO MUCH CREDIT TO CITY LEADERS. THEY'RE MINE.
TIME TO REMIND 'EM OF THEIR DEBTS, TIM.
shit.
DRAKE'S DEAD. WHAT D'WE DO WITH HIM?
YOU ALL GO.
TIM AND I WILL HANDLE THE FUNERAL ARRANGEMENTS.

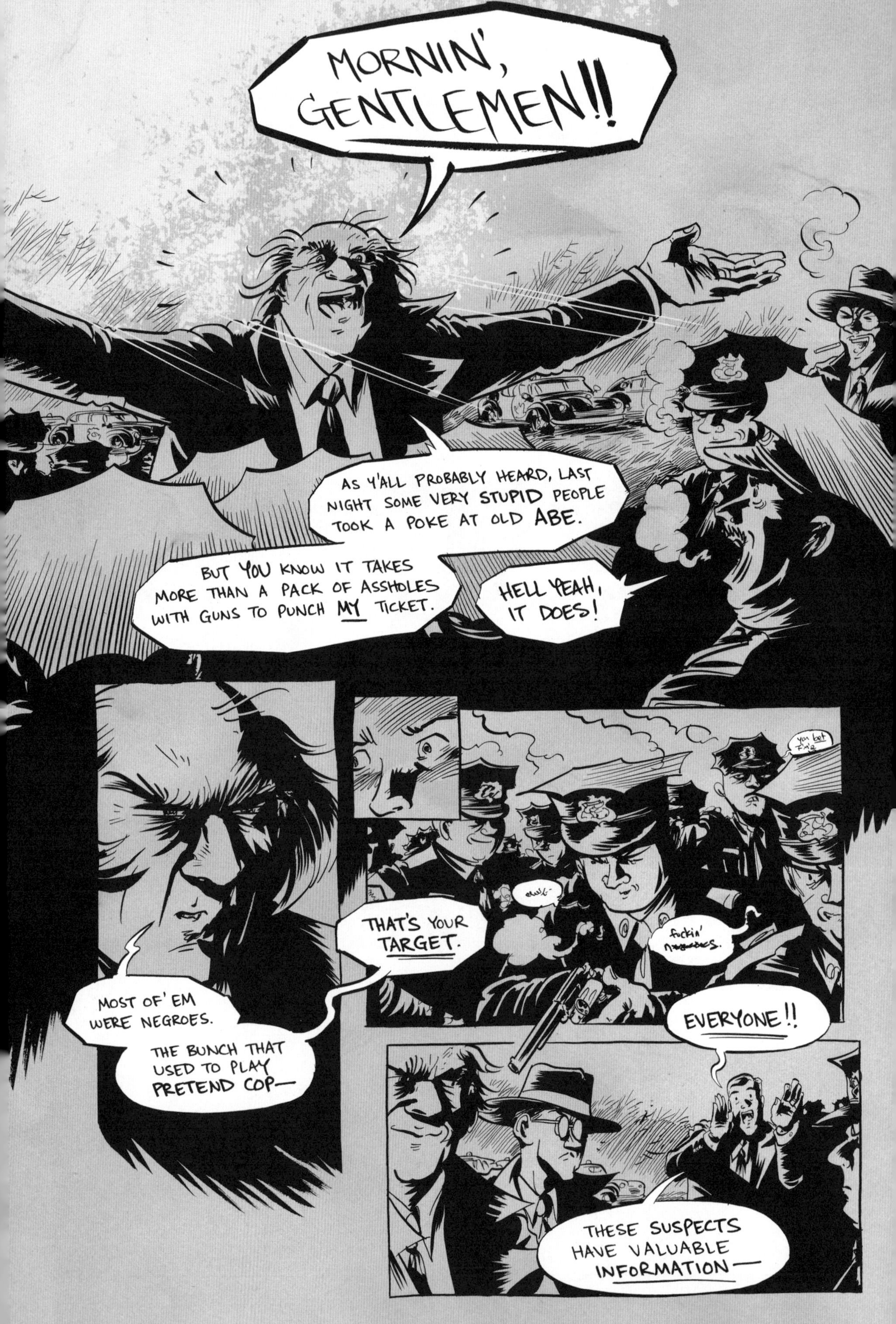
MORNIN', GENTLEMEN!!
AS Y'ALL PROBABLY HEARD, LAST NIGHT SOME VERY STUPID PEOPLE TOOK A POKE AT OLD ABE.
BUT YOU KNOW IT TAKES MORE THAN A PACK OF ASSHOLES WITH GUNS TO PUNCH MY TICKET.
HELL YEAH, IT DOES!
MOST OF' EM WERE NEGROES.
THE BUNCH THAT USED TO PLAY PRETEND COP—
THAT'S YOUR TARGET.
you bet
fuckin'
EVERYONE!!
THESE SUSPECTS HAVE VALUABLE INFORMATION—

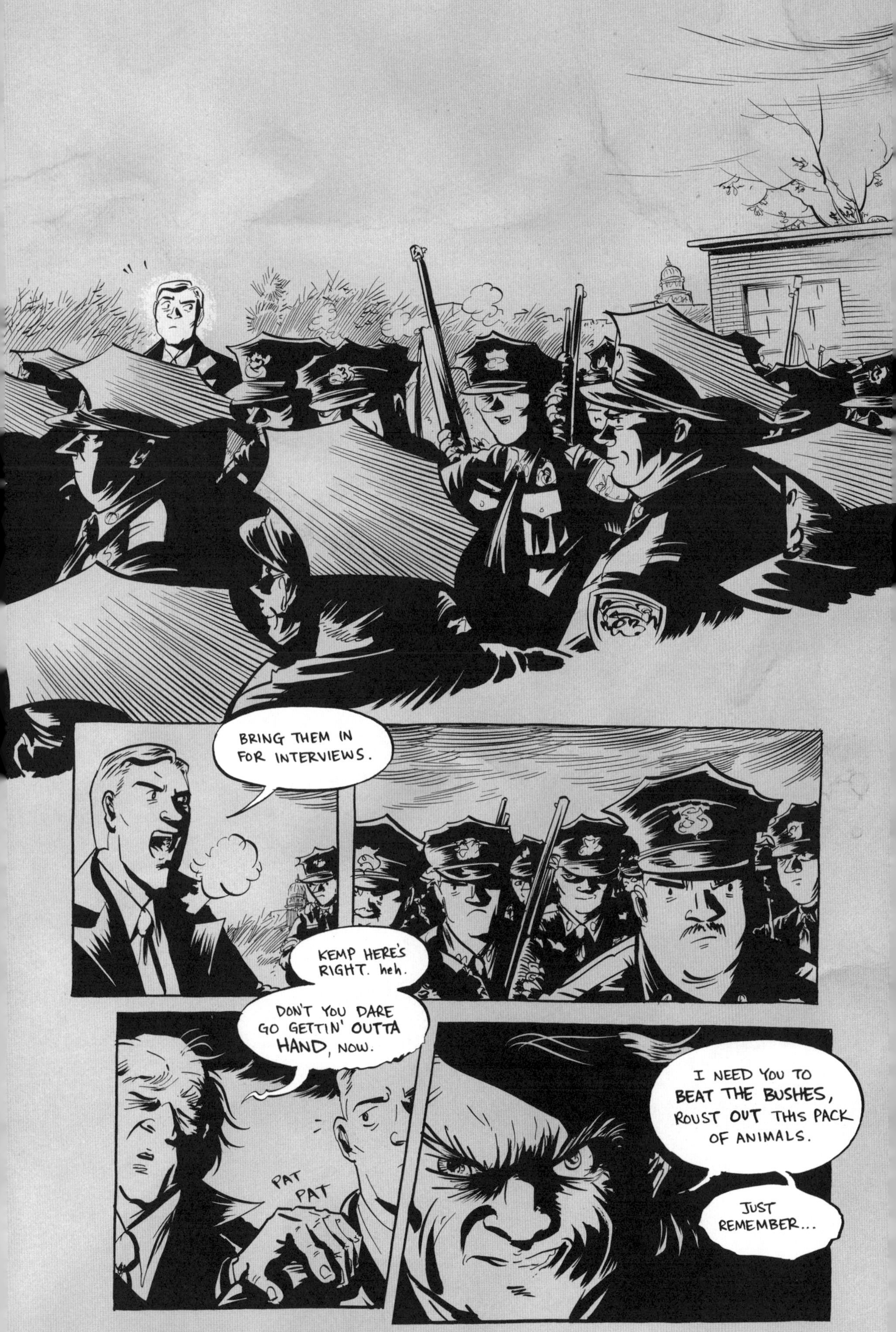
BRING THEM IN FOR INTERVIEWS.
KEMP HERE'S RIGHT. heh.
DON'T YOU DARE GO GETTIN' OUTTA HAND, NOW.
PAT PAT
I NEED YOU TO BEAT THE BUSHES, ROUST OUT THIS PACK OF ANIMALS.
JUST REMEMBER...

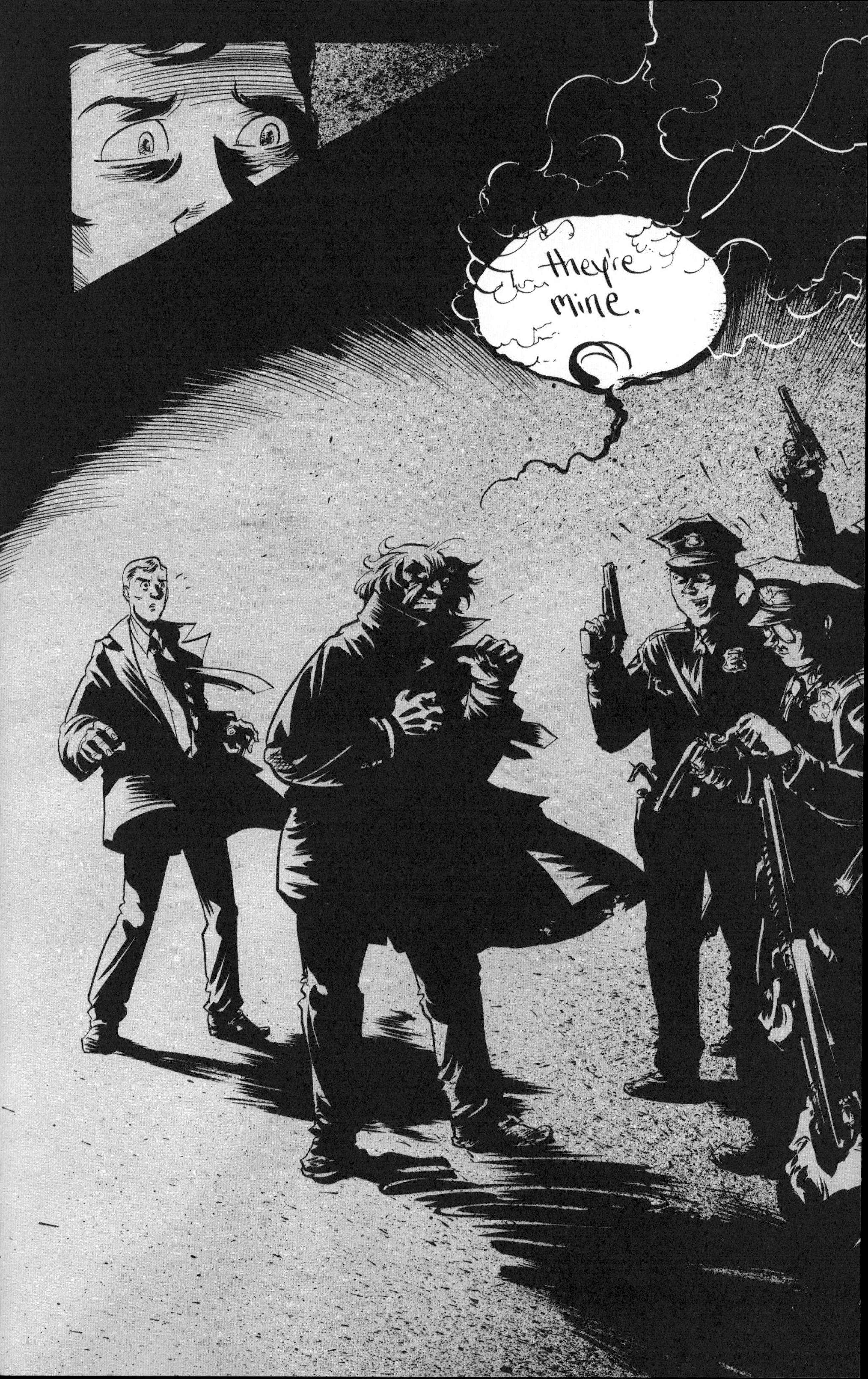
they're mine.

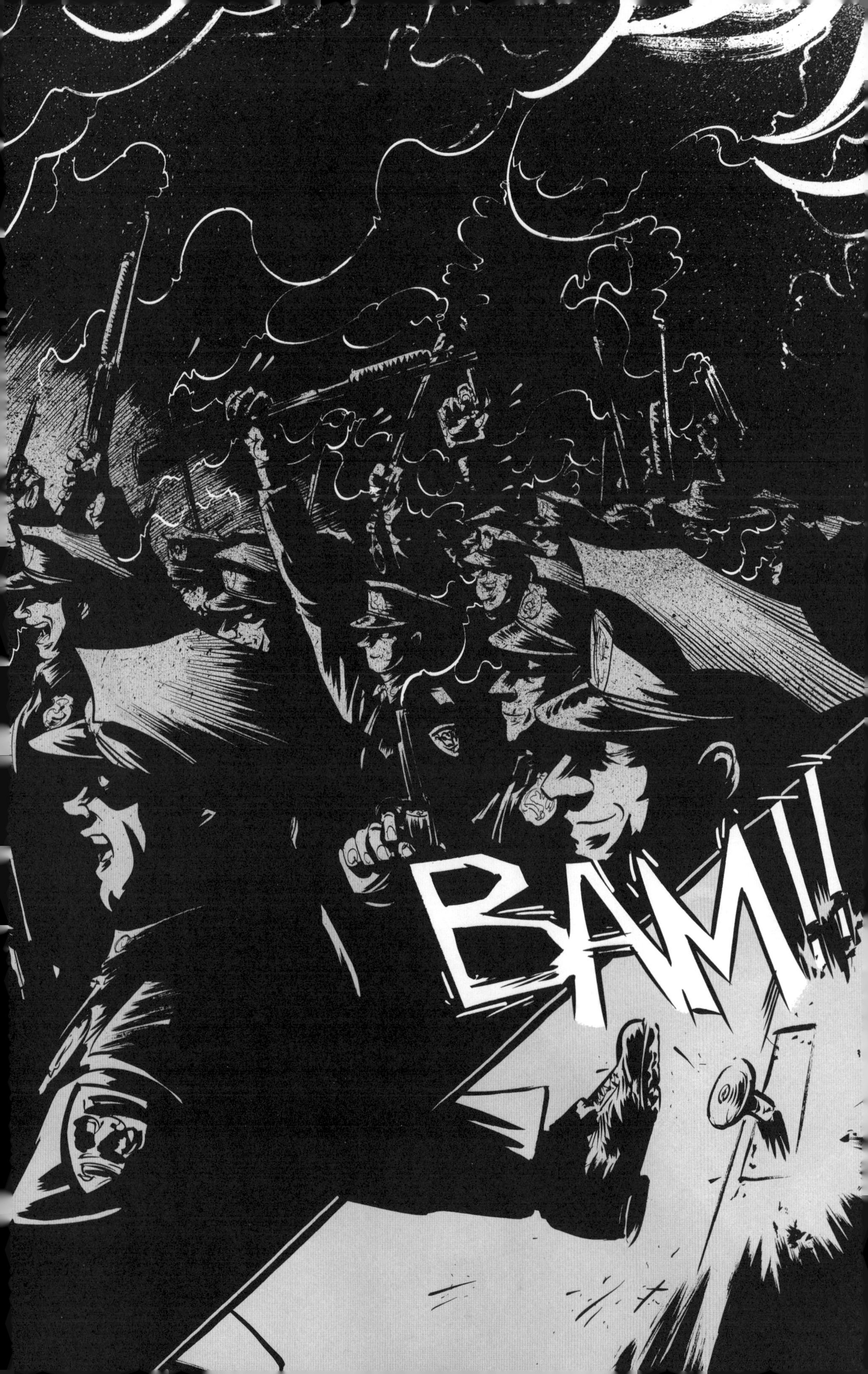
BAM!!

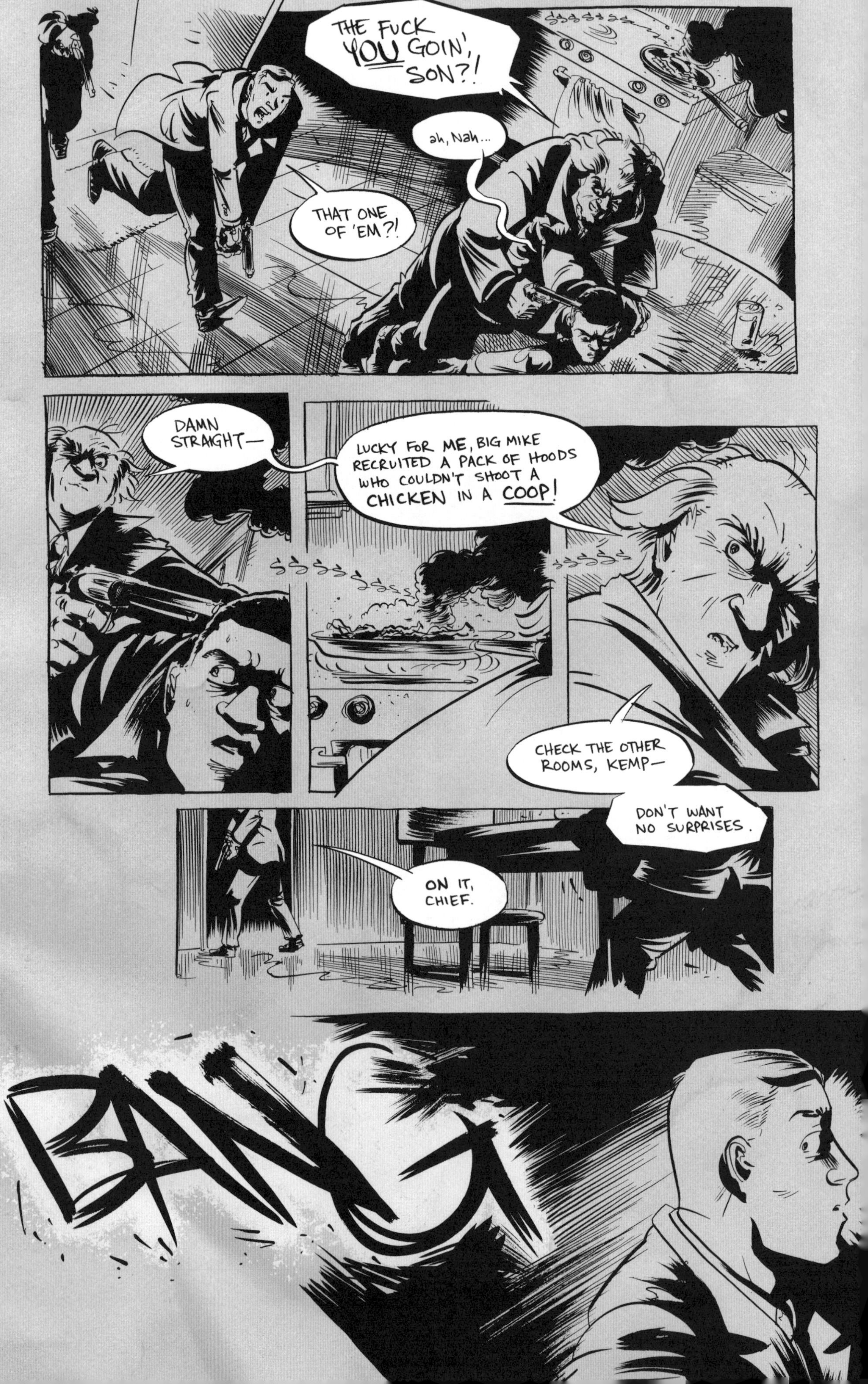
THE FUCK YOU GOIN', SON?!
ah, Nah...
THAT ONE OF 'EM?!
DAMN STRAIGHT—
LUCKY FOR ME, BIG MIKE RECRUITED A PACK OF HOODS WHO COULDN'T SHOOT A CHICKEN IN A COOP!
CHECK THE OTHER ROOMS, KEMP—
DON'T WANT NO SURPRISES.
ON IT, CHIEF.
BANG

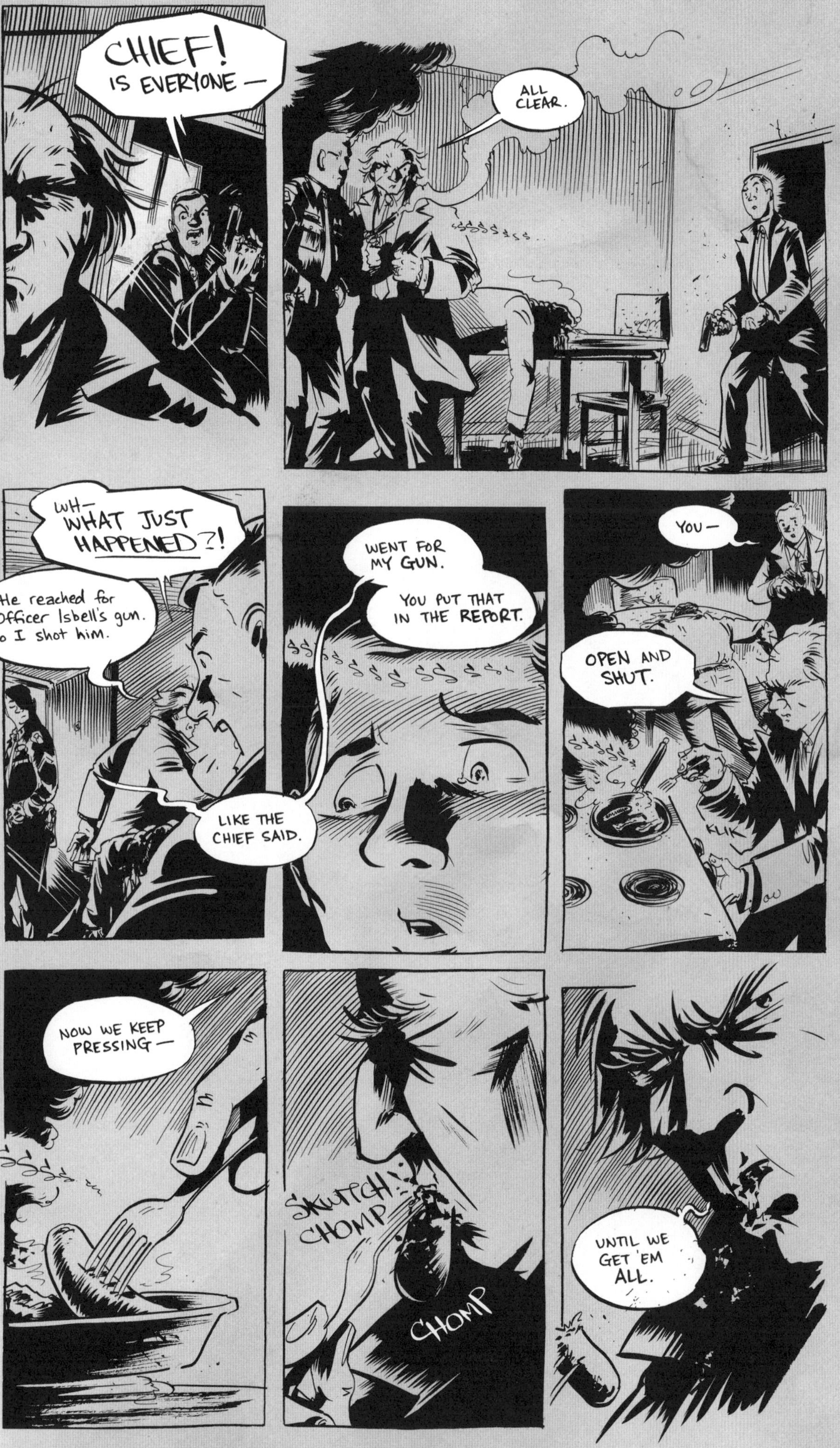
CHIEF! IS EVERYONE —
ALL CLEAR.
WH— WHAT JUST HAPPENED?!
He reached for Officer Isbell's gun. So I shot him.
WENT FOR MY GUN.
YOU PUT THAT IN THE REPORT.
LIKE THE CHIEF SAID.
YOU—
OPEN AND SHUT.
KLIK
NOW WE KEEP PRESSING—
SKWTCH!
CHOMP
CHOMP
UNTIL WE GET 'EM ALL.

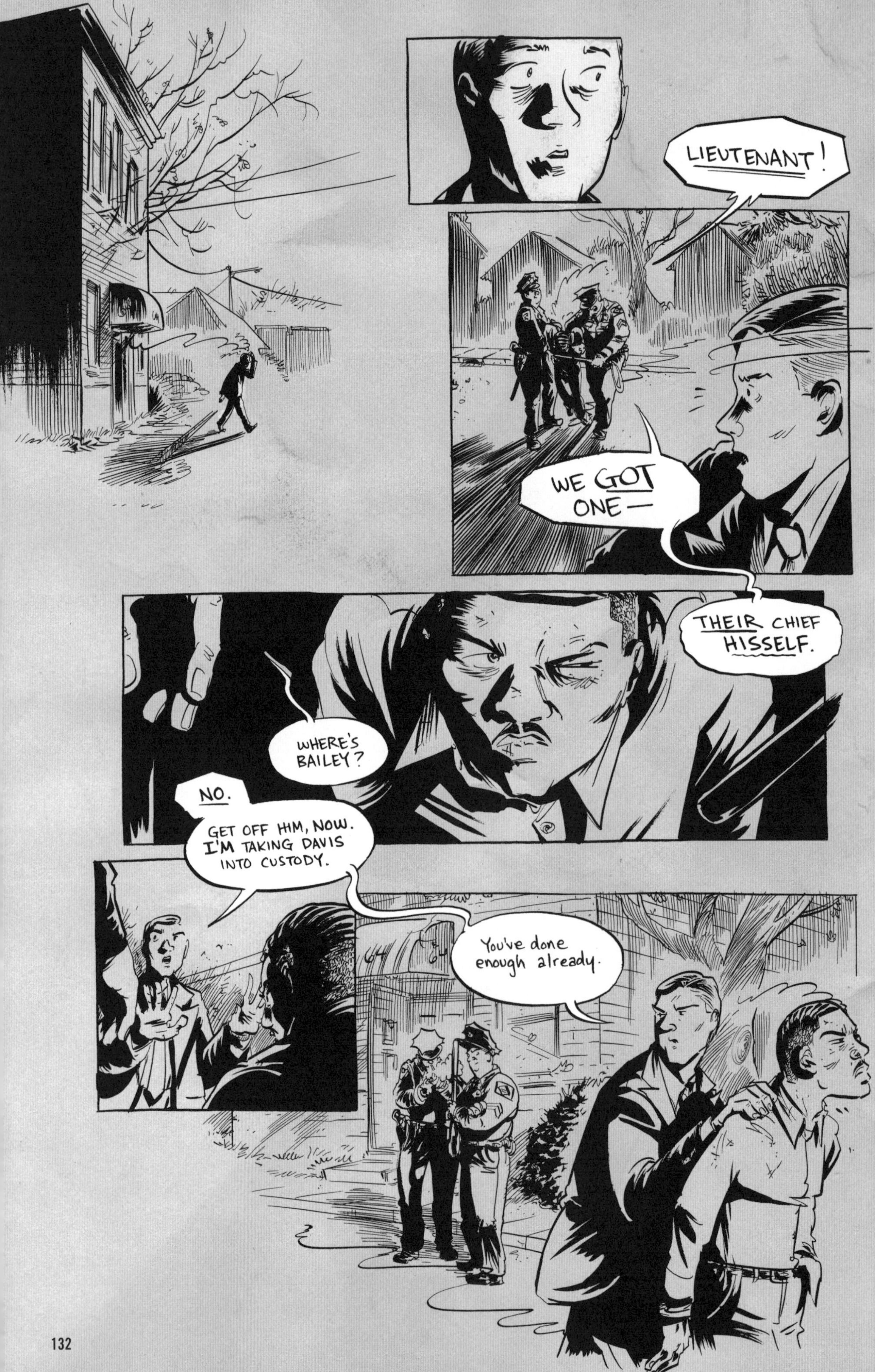
LIEUTENANT!
WE GOT ONE—
THEIR CHIEF HISSELF.
WHERE'S BAILEY?
NO.
GET OFF HIM, NOW. I'M TAKING DAVIS INTO CUSTODY.
You've done enough already.

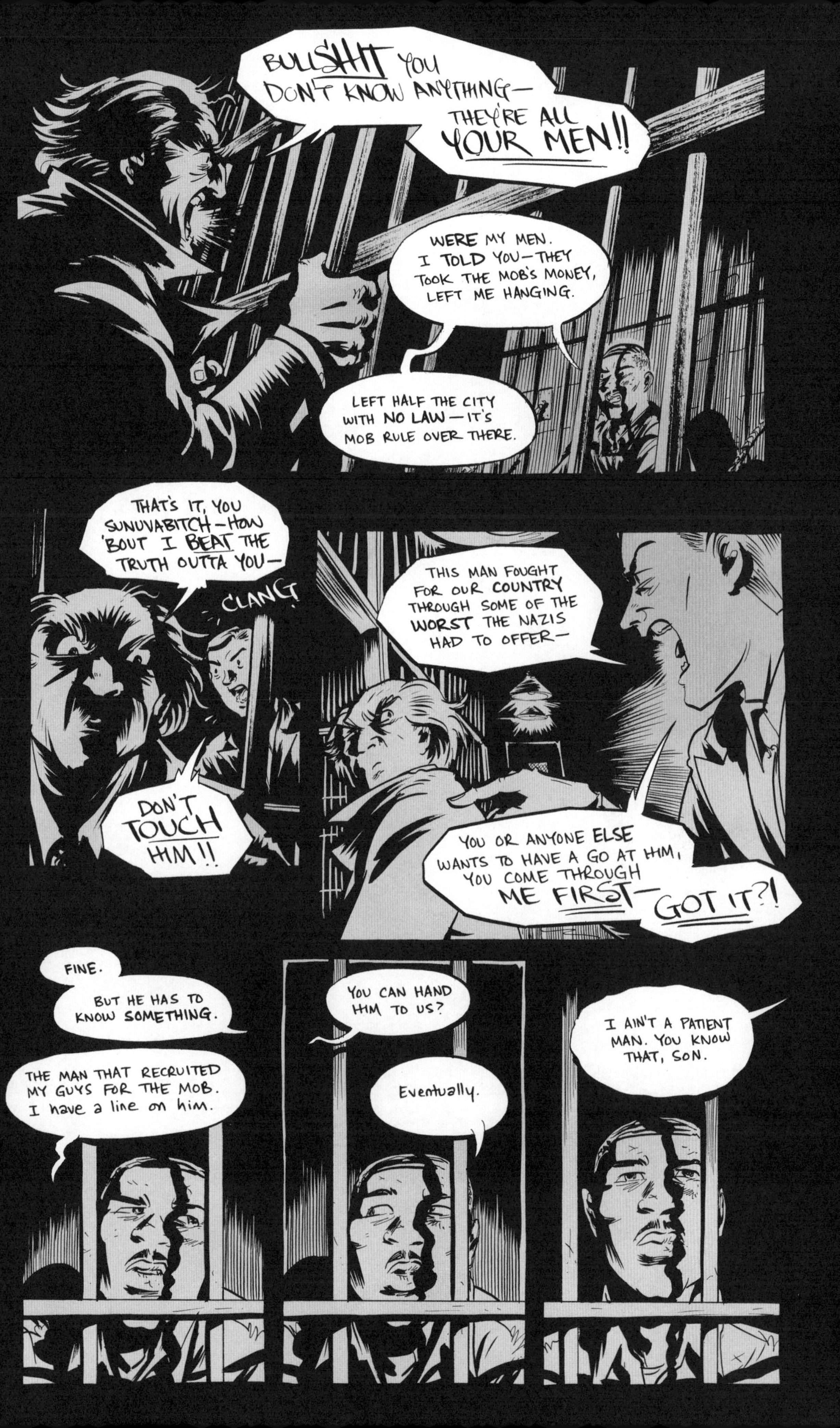
BULLSHIT YOU DON'T KNOW ANYTHING— THEY'RE ALL YOUR MEN!!
WERE MY MEN. I TOLD YOU—THEY TOOK THE MOB'S MONEY, LEFT ME HANGING.
LEFT HALF THE CITY WITH NO LAW—IT'S MOB RULE OVER THERE.
THAT'S IT, YOU SUNUVABITCH—HOW 'BOUT I BEAT THE TRUTH OUTTA YOU—
CLANG
DON'T TOUCH HIM!!
THIS MAN FOUGHT FOR OUR COUNTRY THROUGH SOME OF THE WORST THE NAZIS HAD TO OFFER—
YOU OR ANYONE ELSE WANTS TO HAVE A GO AT HIM, YOU COME THROUGH ME FIRST—
GOT IT?!
FINE.
BUT HE HAS TO KNOW SOMETHING.
THE MAN THAT RECRUITED MY GUYS FOR THE MOB. I have a line on him.
YOU CAN HAND HIM TO US?
Eventually.
I AIN'T A PATIENT MAN. YOU KNOW THAT, SON.

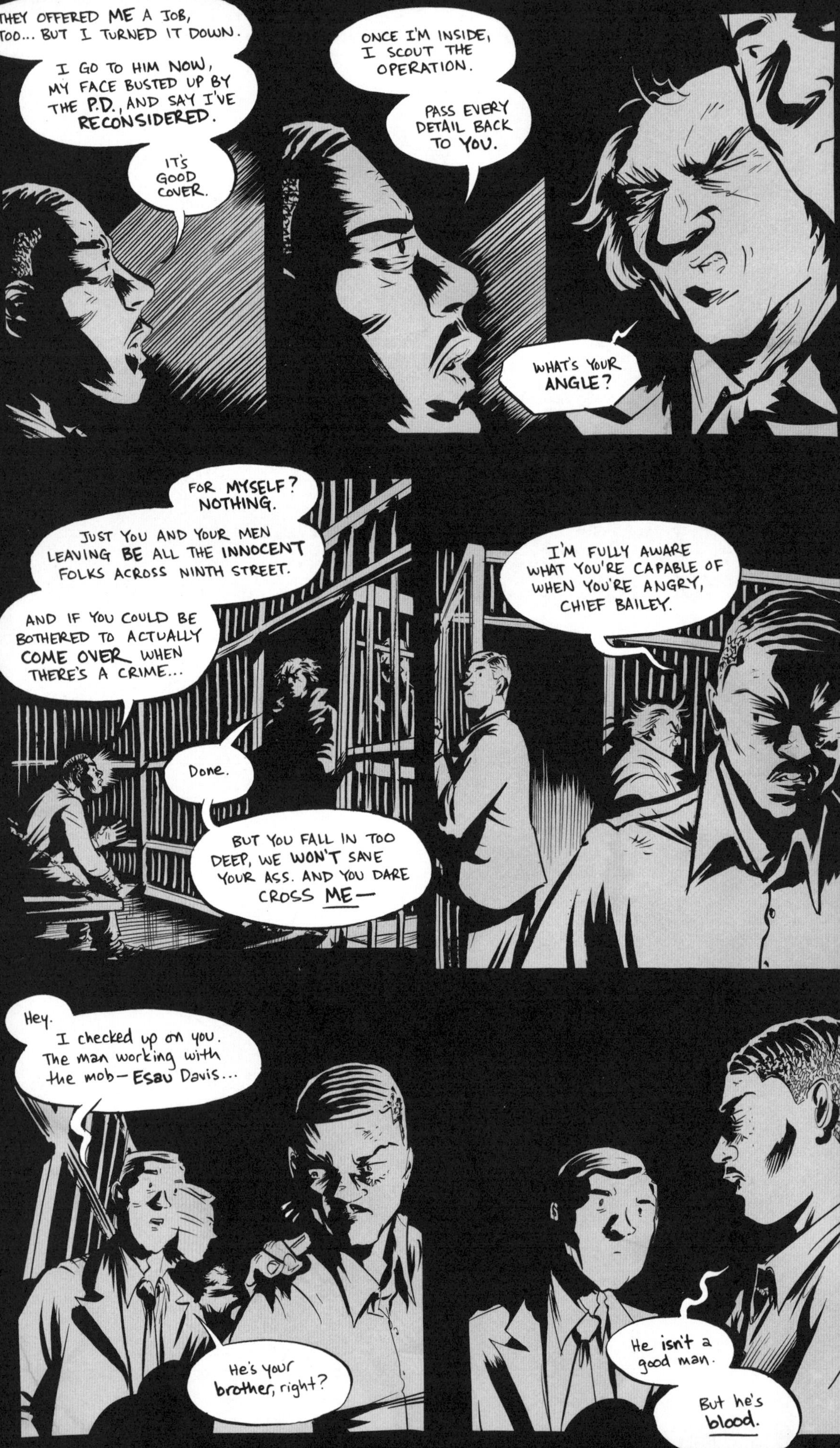
THEY OFFERED ME A JOB, TOO... BUT I TURNED IT DOWN.
I GO TO HIM NOW, MY FACE BUSTED UP BY THE P.D., AND SAY I'VE RECONSIDERED.
IT'S GOOD COVER.
ONCE I'M INSIDE, I SCOUT THE OPERATION.
PASS EVERY DETAIL BACK TO YOU.
WHAT'S YOUR ANGLE?
FOR MYSELF? NOTHING.
JUST YOU AND YOUR MEN LEAVING BE ALL THE INNOCENT FOLKS ACROSS NINTH STREET.
AND IF YOU COULD BE BOTHERED TO ACTUALLY COME OVER WHEN THERE'S A CRIME...
Done.
BUT YOU FALL IN TOO DEEP, WE WON'T SAVE YOUR ASS. AND YOU DARE CROSS ME—
I'M FULLY AWARE WHAT YOU'RE CAPABLE OF WHEN YOU'RE ANGRY, CHIEF BAILEY.
Hey.
I checked up on you. The man working with the mob—Esau Davis...
He's your brother, right?
He isn't a good man.
But he's blood.

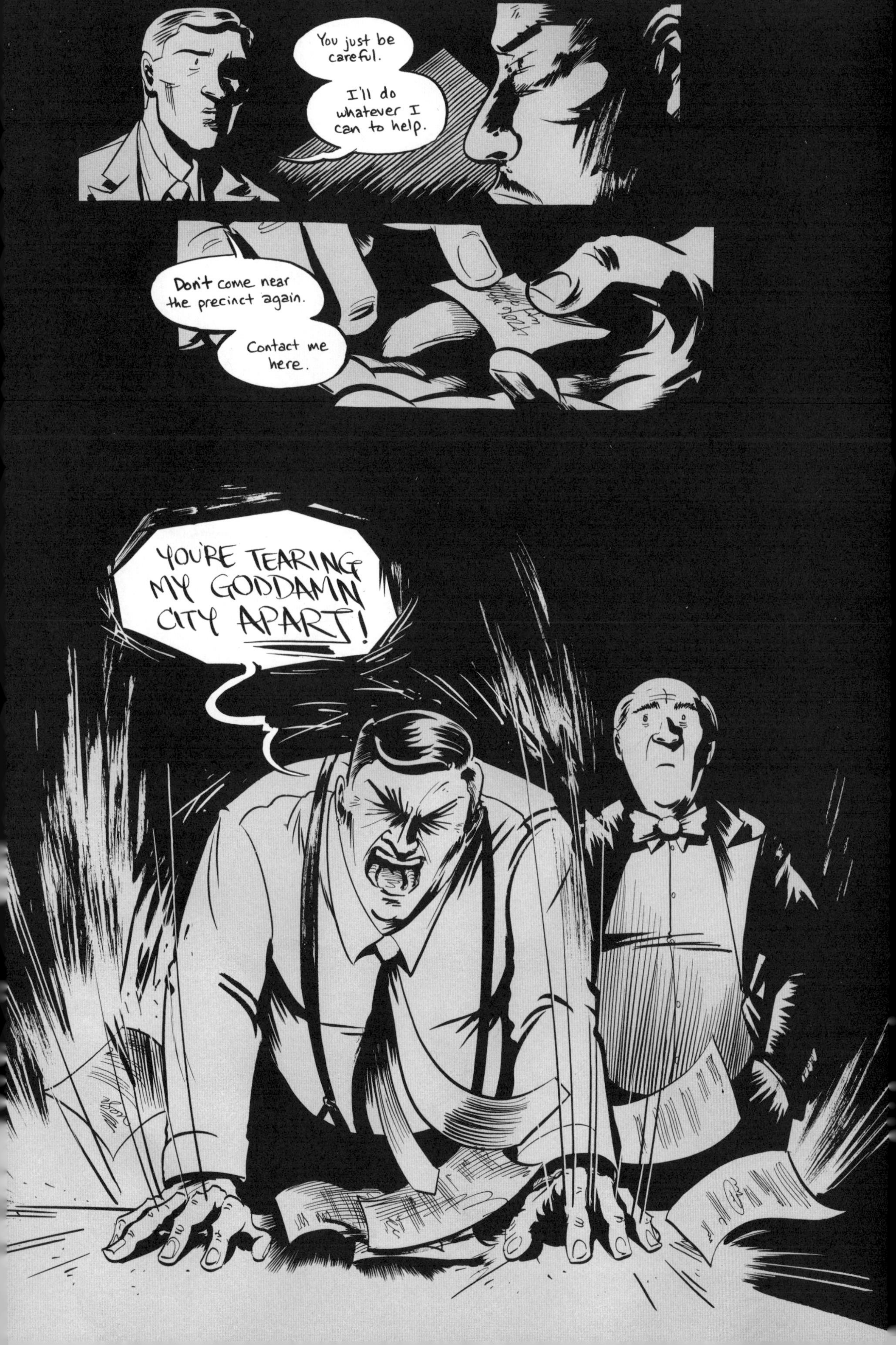
You just be careful.
I'll do whatever I can to help.
Don't come near the precinct again.
Contact me here.
YOU'RE TEARING MY GODDAMN CITY APART!

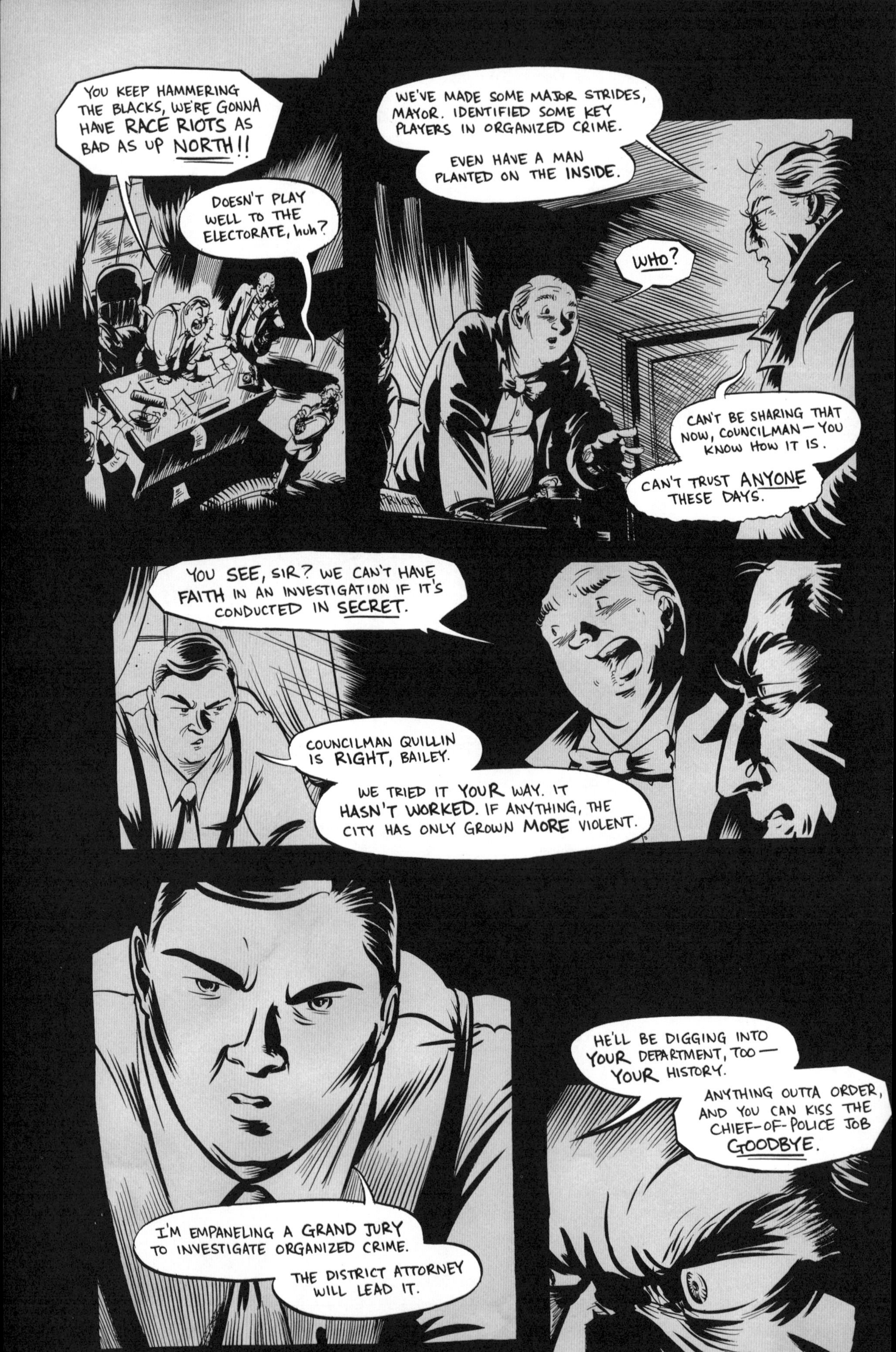
YOU KEEP HAMMERING THE BLACKS, WE'RE GONNA HAVE RACE RIOTS AS BAD AS UP NORTH!!
DOESN'T PLAY WELL TO THE ELECTORATE, huh?
WE'VE MADE SOME MAJOR STRIDES, MAYOR. IDENTIFIED SOME KEY PLAYERS IN ORGANIZED CRIME.
EVEN HAVE A MAN PLANTED ON THE INSIDE.
WHO?
CAN'T BE SHARING THAT NOW, COUNCILMAN—YOU KNOW HOW IT IS.
CAN'T TRUST ANYONE THESE DAYS.
YOU SEE, SIR? WE CAN'T HAVE FAITH IN AN INVESTIGATION IF IT'S CONDUCTED IN SECRET.
COUNCILMAN QUILLIN IS RIGHT, BAILEY.
WE TRIED IT YOUR WAY. IT HASN'T WORKED. IF ANYTHING, THE CITY HAS ONLY GROWN MORE VIOLENT.
I'M EMPANELING A GRAND JURY TO INVESTIGATE ORGANIZED CRIME.
THE DISTRICT ATTORNEY WILL LEAD IT.
HE'LL BE DIGGING INTO YOUR DEPARTMENT, TOO—YOUR HISTORY.
ANYTHING OUTTA ORDER, AND YOU CAN KISS THE CHIEF-OF-POLICE JOB GOODBYE.

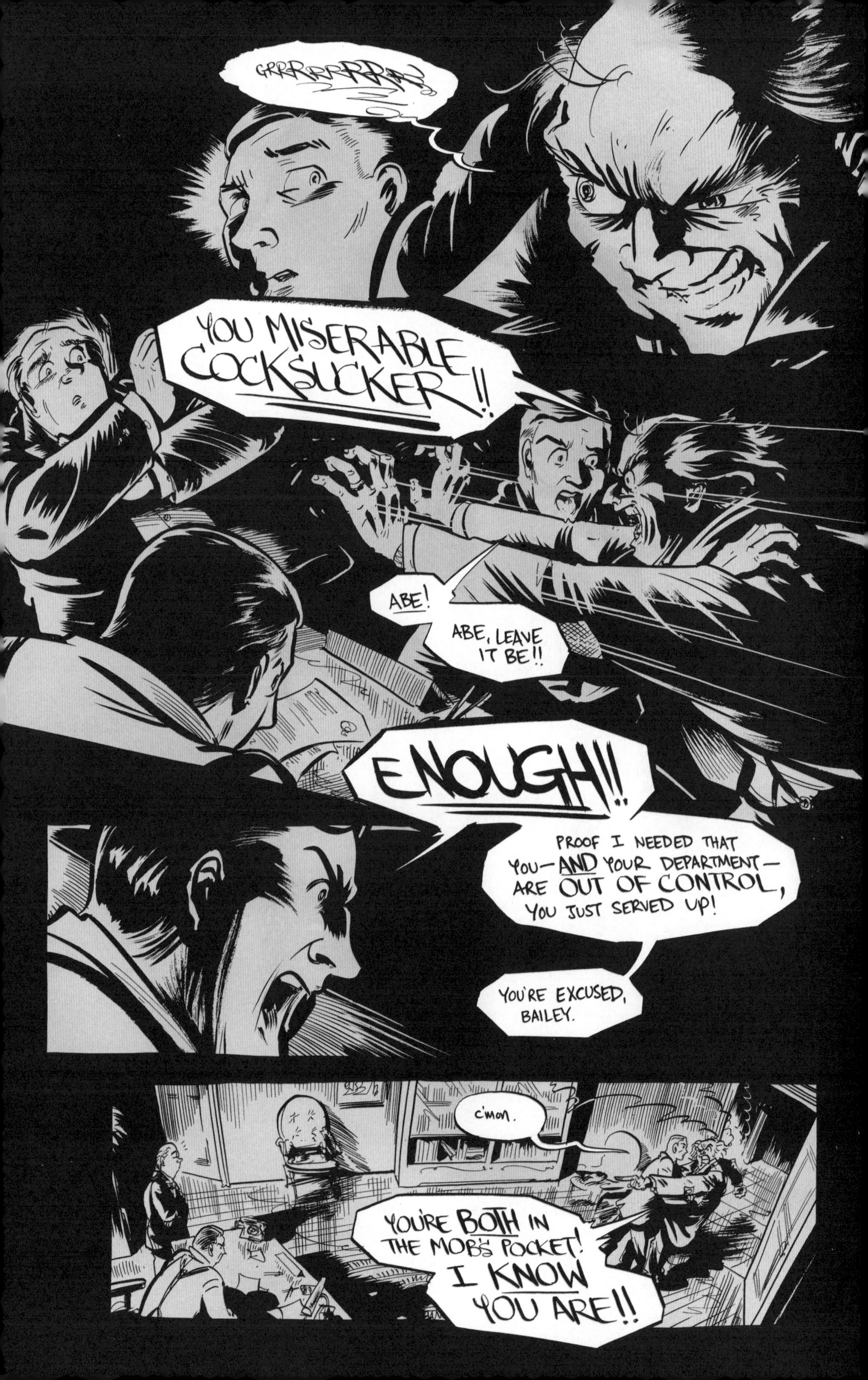
GRRRRRRRRR
YOU MISERABLE COCKSUCKER!!
ABE!
ABE, LEAVE IT BE!!
ENOUGH!!
PROOF I NEEDED THAT YOU—AND YOUR DEPARTMENT—ARE OUT OF CONTROL, YOU JUST SERVED UP!
YOU'RE EXCUSED, BAILEY.
c'mon.
YOU'RE BOTH IN THE MOB'S POCKET! I KNOW YOU ARE!!

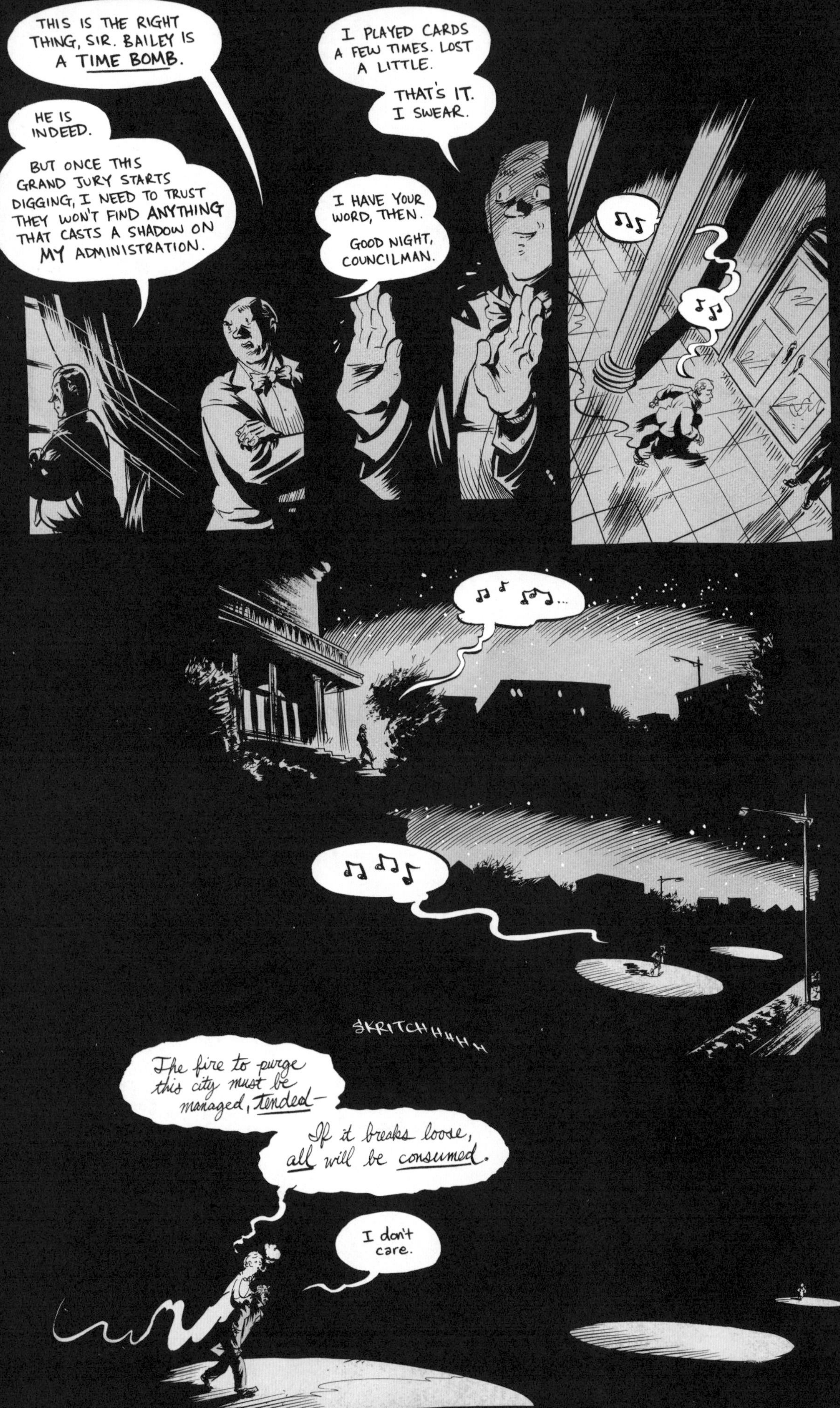
THIS IS THE RIGHT THING, SIR. BAILEY IS A TIME BOMB.
HE IS INDEED.
BUT ONCE THIS GRAND JURY STARTS DIGGING, I NEED TO TRUST THEY WON'T FIND ANYTHING THAT CASTS A SHADOW ON MY ADMINISTRATION.
I PLAYED CARDS A FEW TIMES. LOST A LITTLE.
THAT'S IT. I SWEAR.
I HAVE YOUR WORD, THEN.
GOOD NIGHT, COUNCILMAN.
SKRITCHHHHH
The fire to purge this city must be managed, tended—
If it breaks loose, all will be consumed.
I don't care.

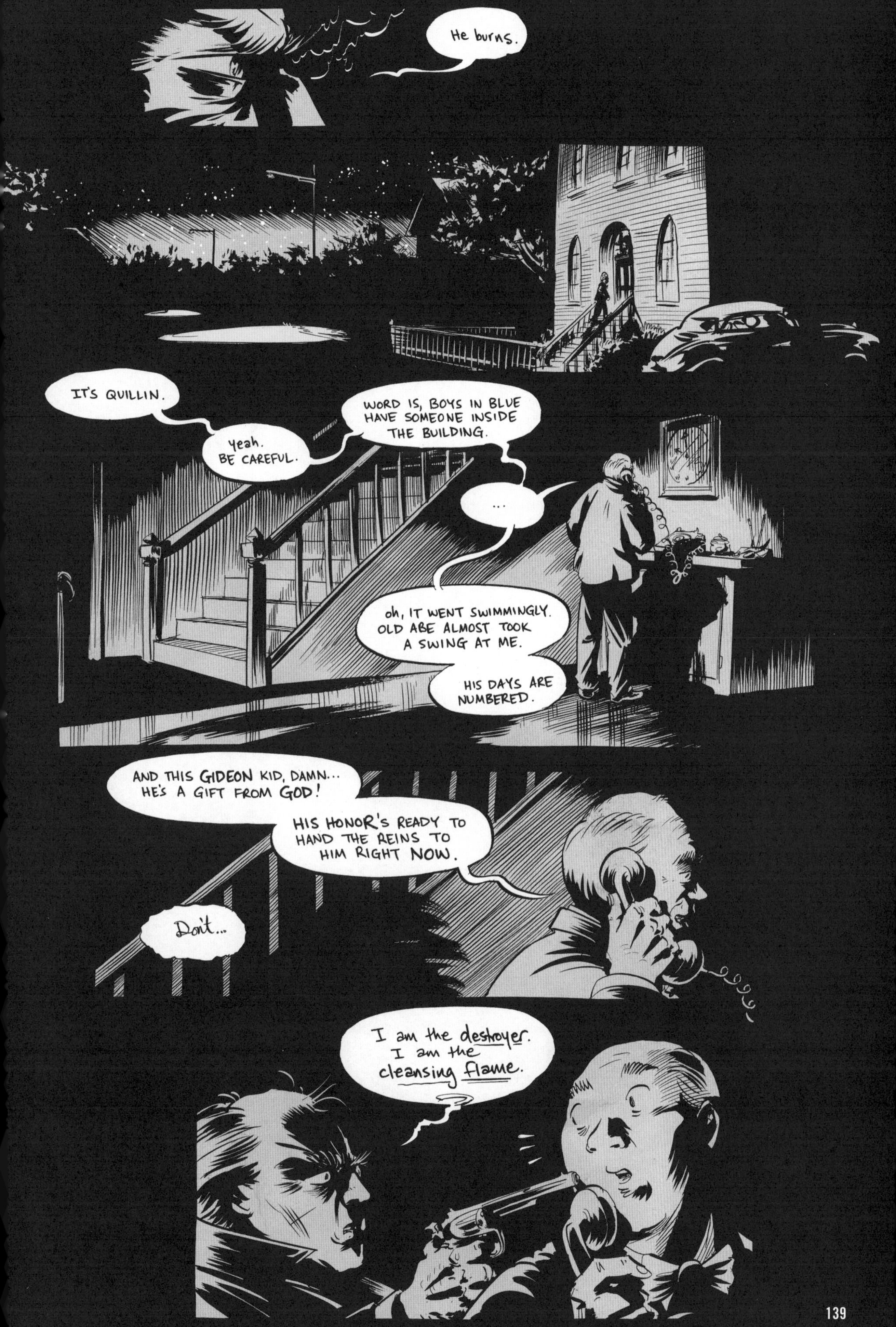
He burns.
IT'S QUILLIN.
yeah. BE CAREFUL.
WORD IS, BOYS IN BLUE HAVE SOMEONE INSIDE THE BUILDING.
...
oh, IT WENT SWIMMINGLY. OLD ABE ALMOST TOOK A SWING AT ME.
HIS DAYS ARE NUMBERED.
AND THIS GIDEON KID, DAMN... HE'S A GIFT FROM GOD!
HIS HONOR'S READY TO HAND THE REINS TO HIM RIGHT NOW.
Don't...
I am the destroyer. I am the cleansing flame.

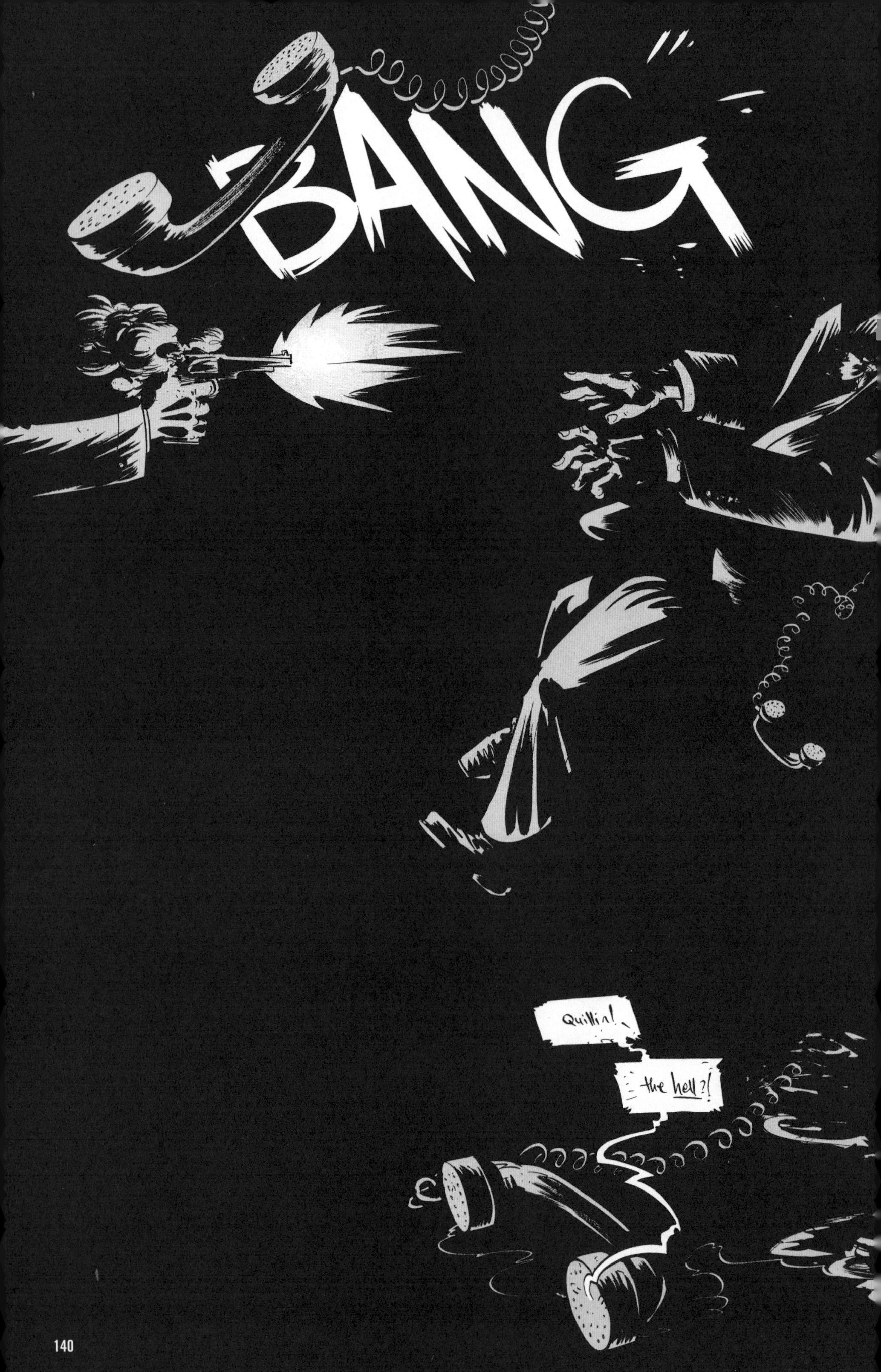
BANG
Quillin!
the hell?!

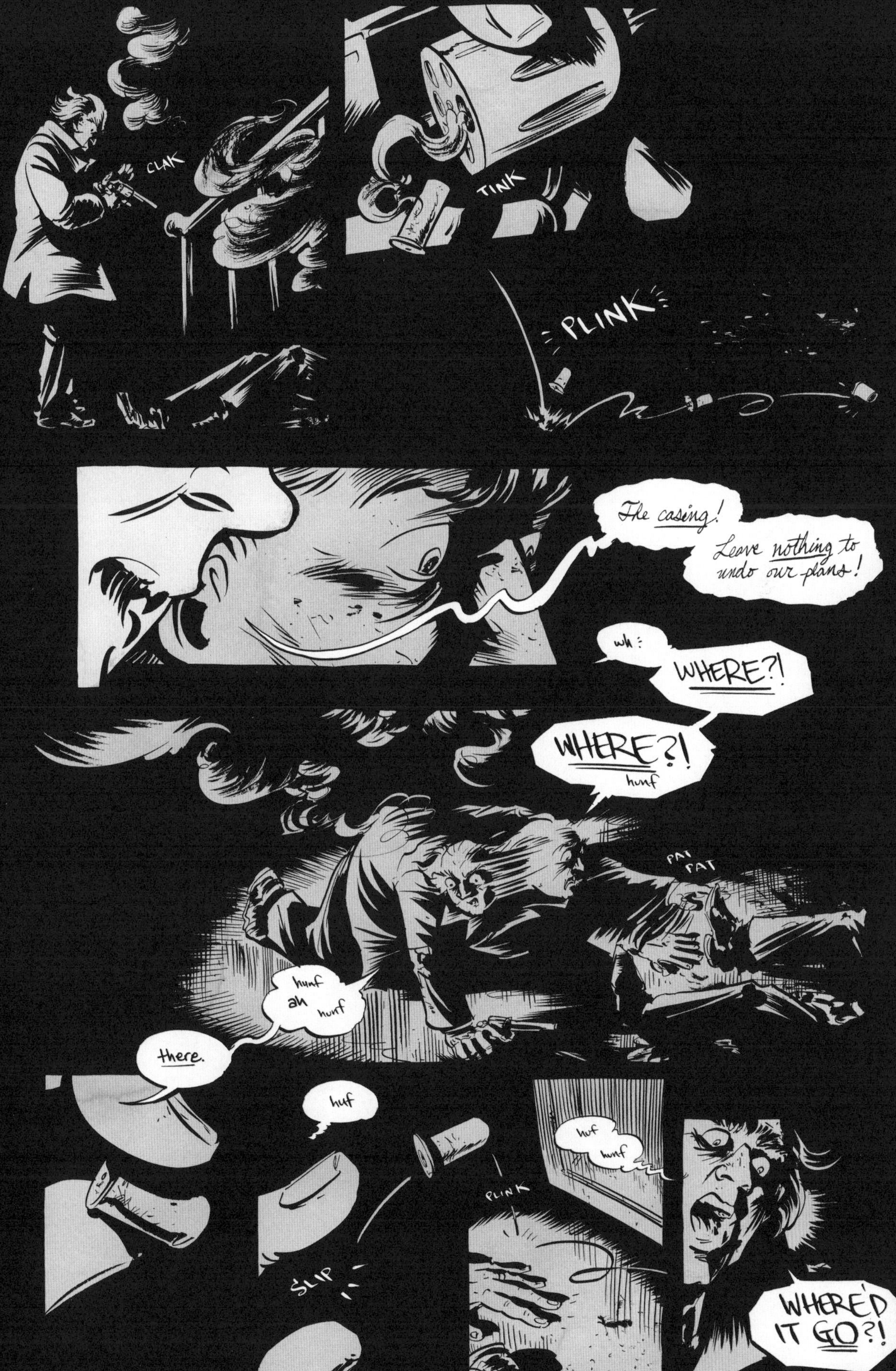
CLAK
TINK
PLINK
The casing!
Leave nothing to undo our plans!
wh:
WHERE?!
WHERE?!
hunf
PAT PAT
hunf ah hunf
there.
huf
SLIP
PLINK
huf hunf
WHERE'D IT GO?!

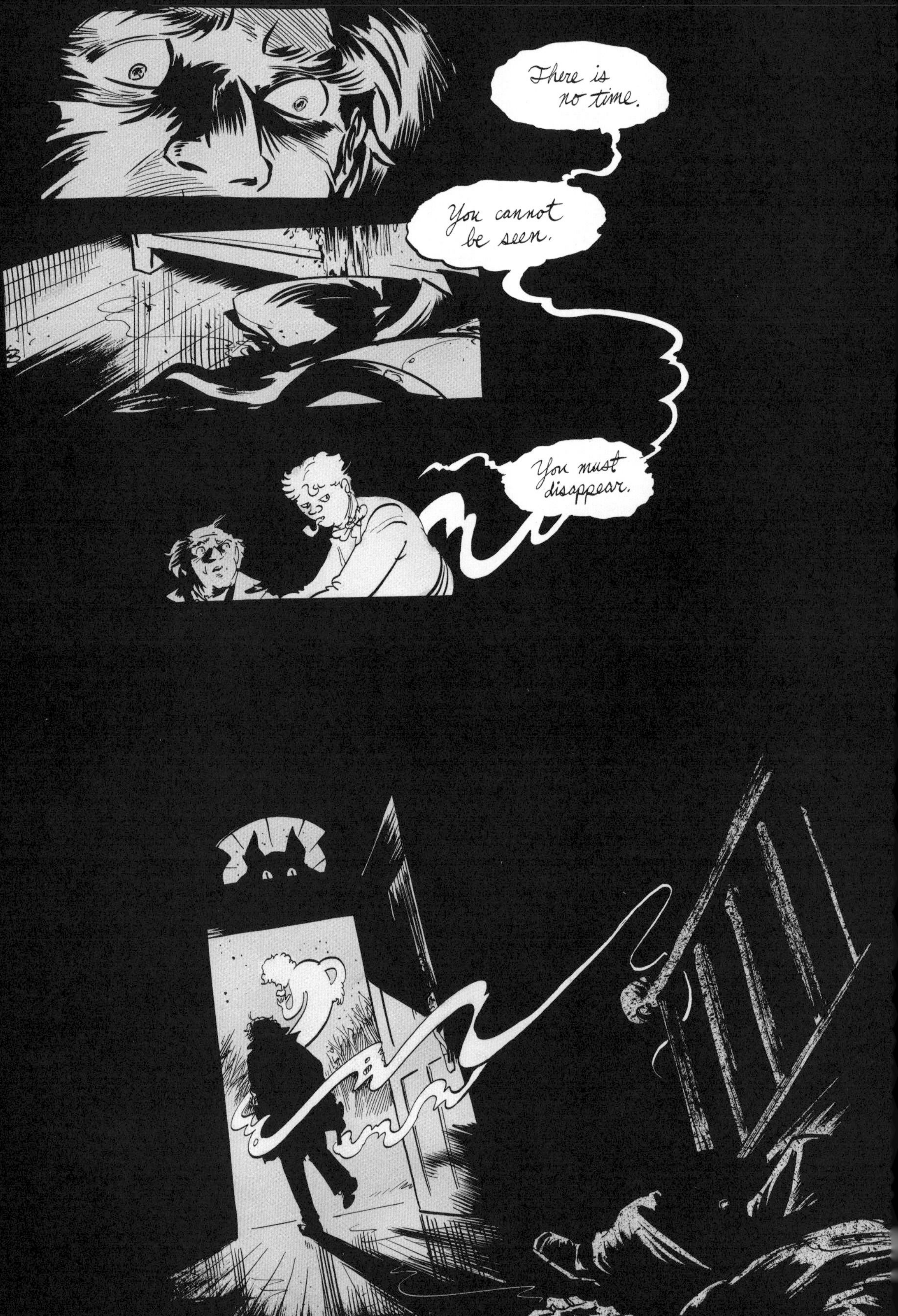
There is no time.
You cannot be seen.
You must disappear.

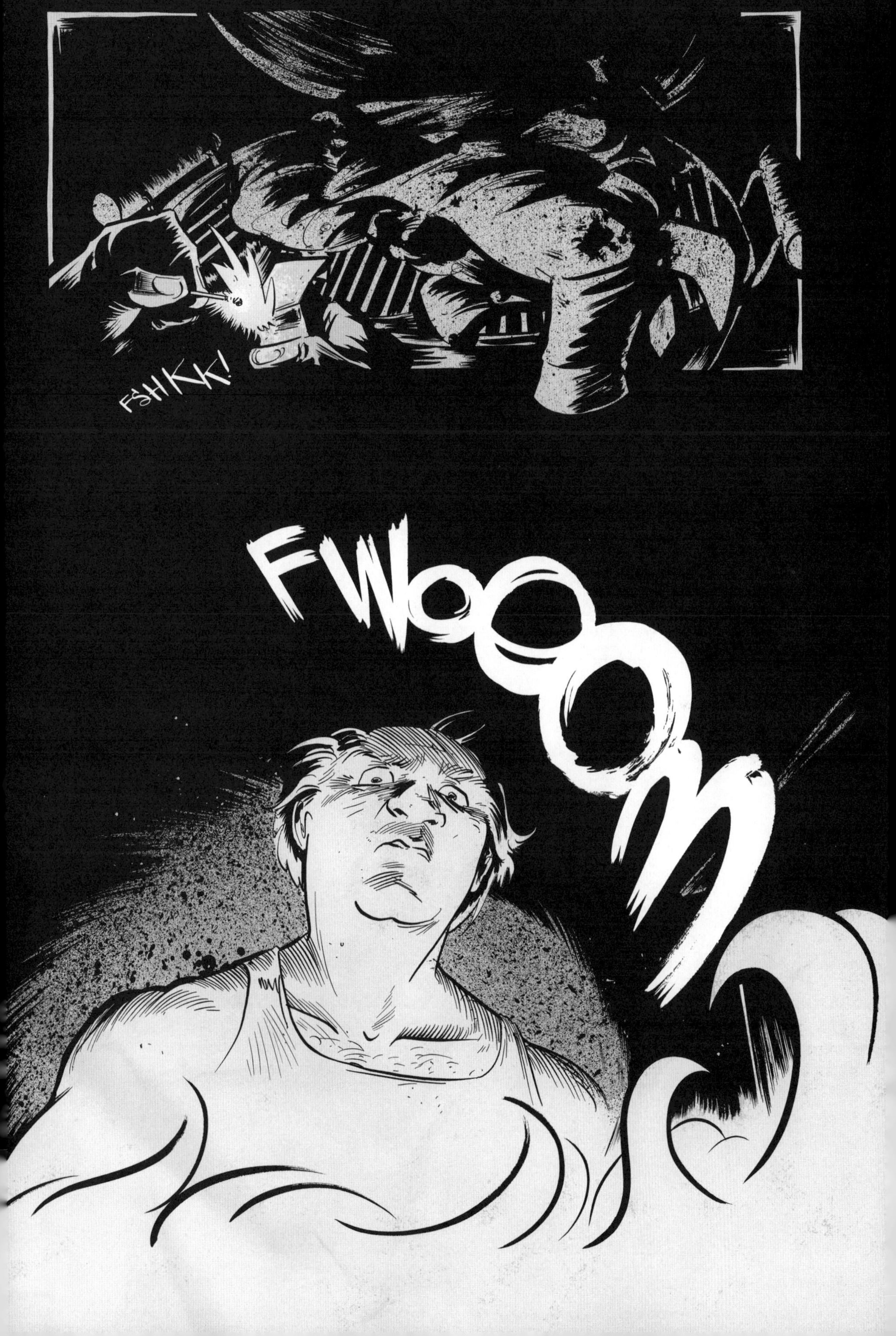
FSHIKK!
FWOOOM

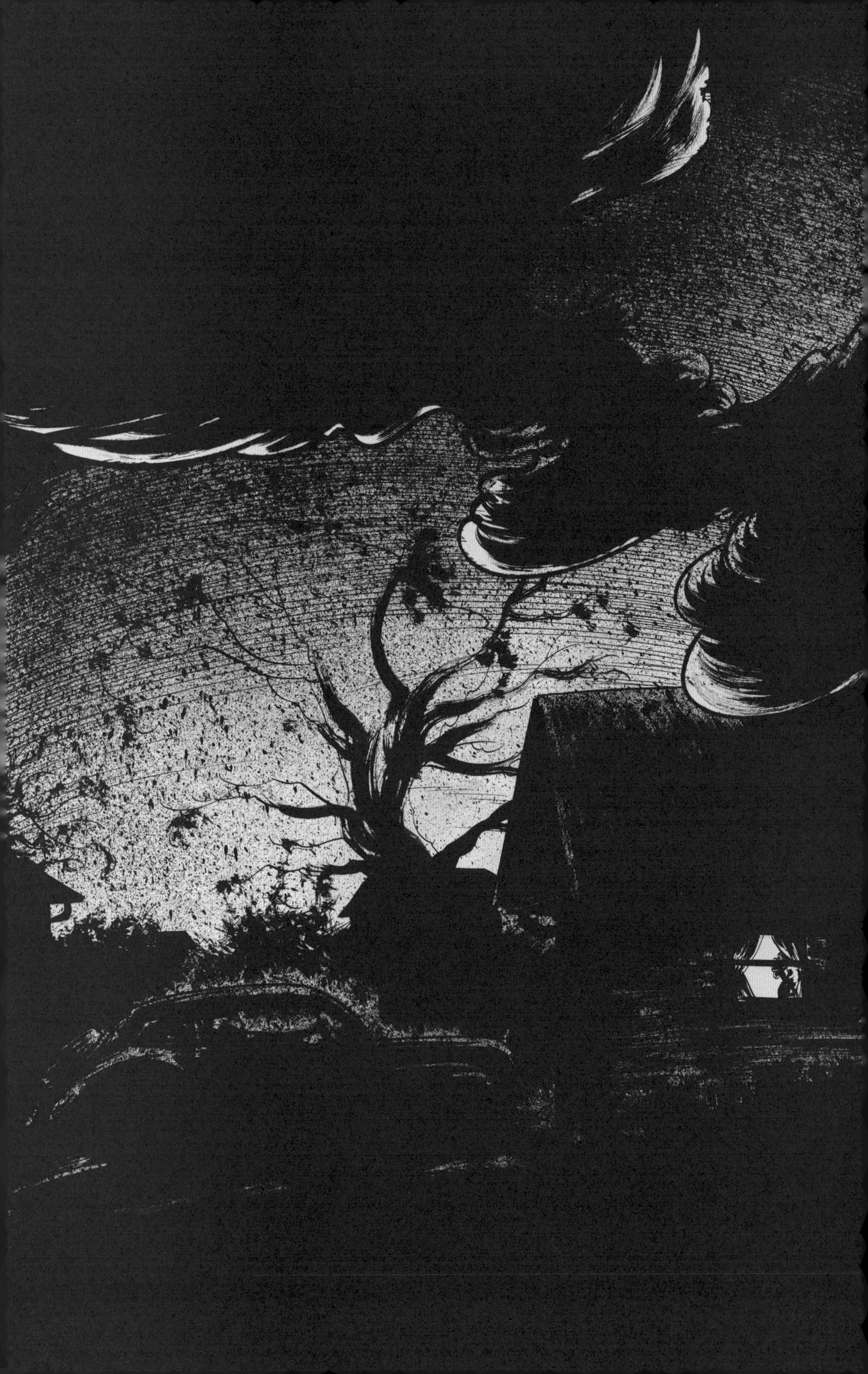

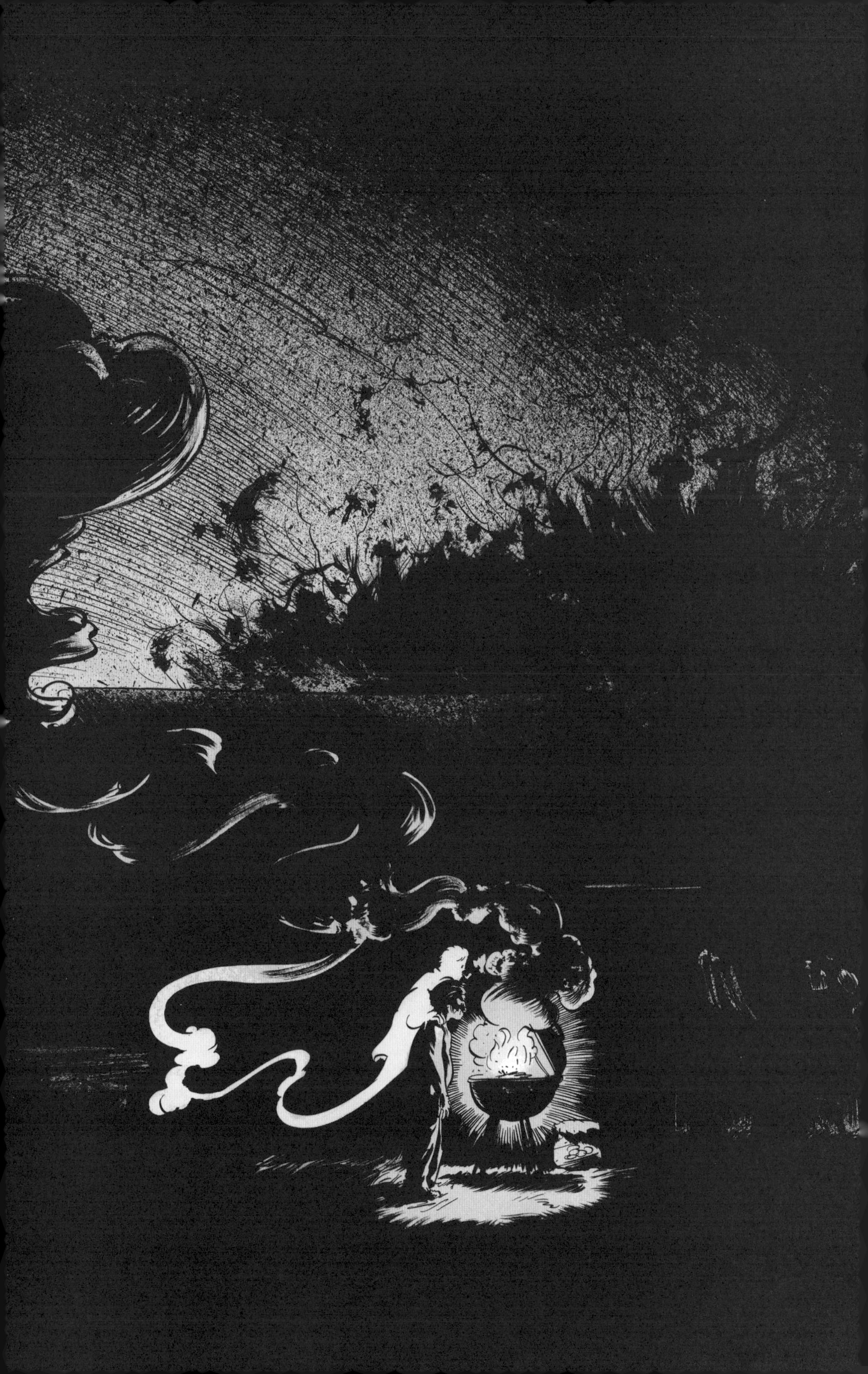

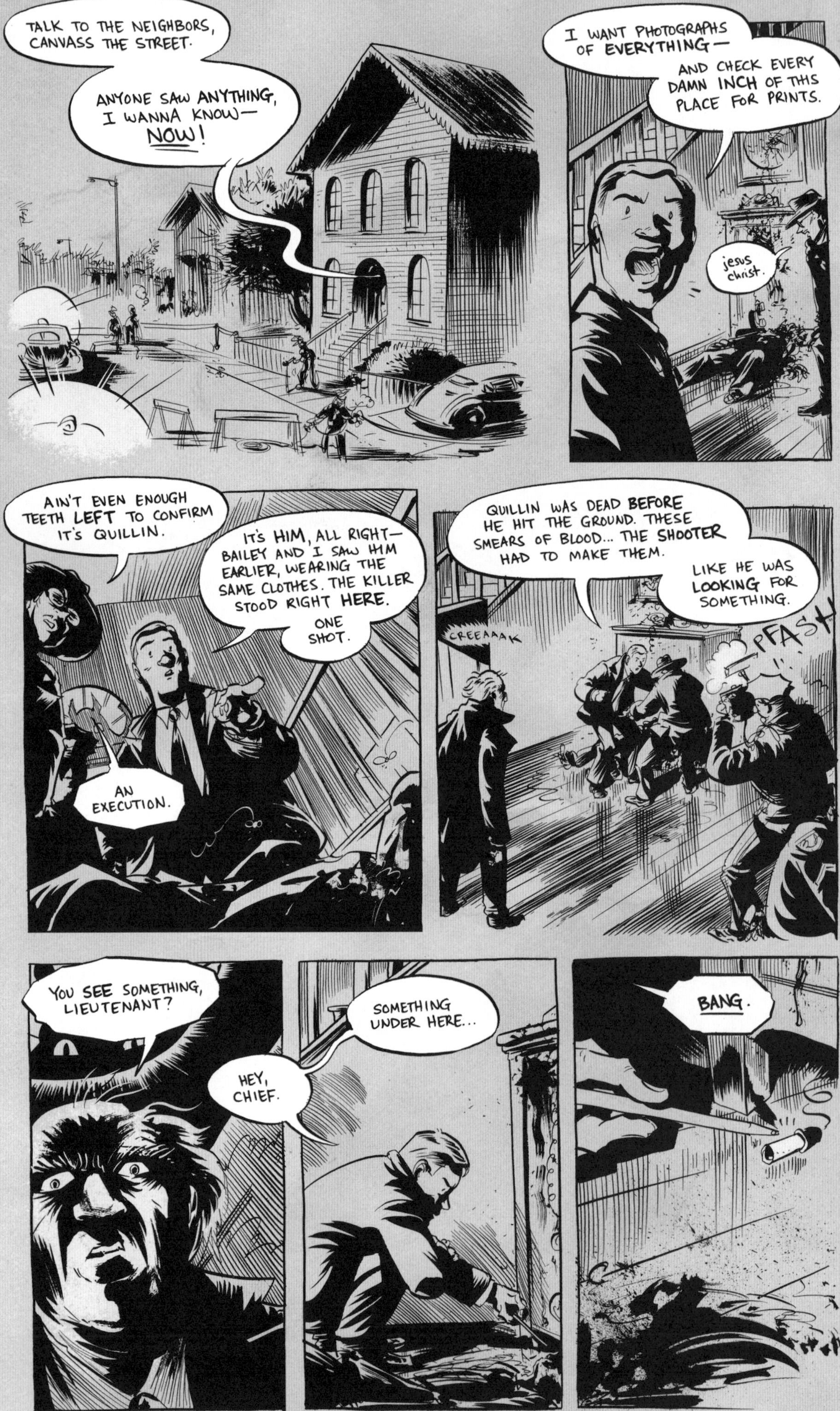

TALK TO THE NEIGHBORS, CANVASS THE STREET.
ANYONE SAW ANYTHING, I WANNA KNOW— NOW!
I WANT PHOTOGRAPHS OF EVERYTHING—
AND CHECK EVERY DAMN INCH OF THIS PLACE FOR PRINTS.
jesus christ.
AIN'T EVEN ENOUGH TEETH LEFT TO CONFIRM IT'S QUILLIN.
IT'S HIM, ALL RIGHT— BAILEY AND I SAW HIM EARLIER, WEARING THE SAME CLOTHES. THE KILLER STOOD RIGHT HERE.
ONE SHOT.
AN EXECUTION.
QUILLIN WAS DEAD BEFORE HE HIT THE GROUND. THESE SMEARS OF BLOOD... THE SHOOTER HAD TO MAKE THEM.
LIKE HE WAS LOOKING FOR SOMETHING.
CREEAAAK
PFASH
YOU SEE SOMETHING, LIEUTENANT?
SOMETHING UNDER HERE...
HEY, CHIEF.
BANG.

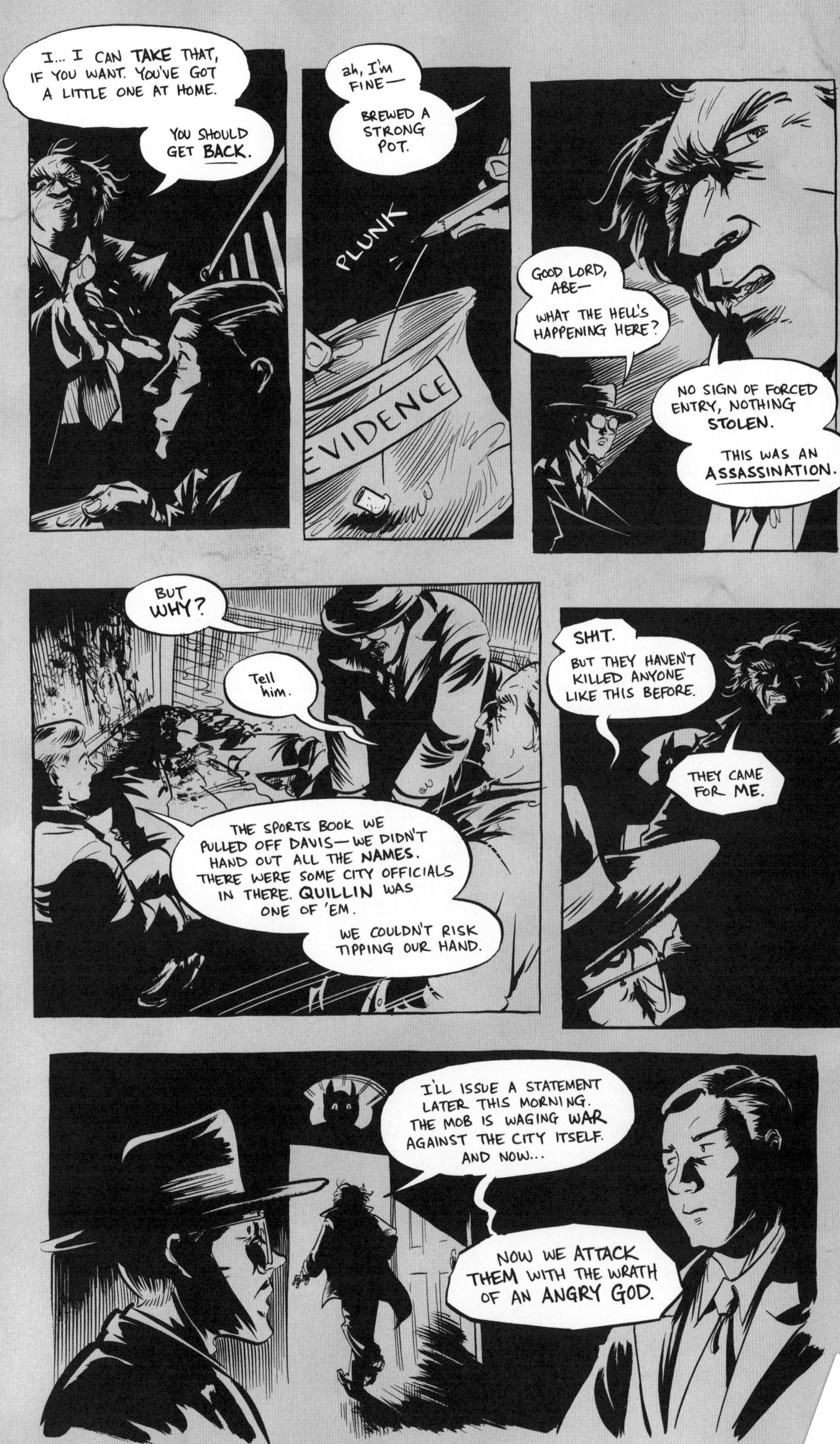
I... I CAN TAKE THAT, IF YOU WANT. YOU'VE GOT A LITTLE ONE AT HOME.
YOU SHOULD GET BACK.
ah, I'm FINE—
BREWED A STRONG POT.
PLUNK
EVIDENCE
GOOD LORD, ABE—
WHAT THE HELL'S HAPPENING HERE?
NO SIGN OF FORCED ENTRY, NOTHING STOLEN.
THIS WAS AN ASSASSINATION.
BUT WHY?
Tell him.
THE SPORTS BOOK WE PULLED OFF DAVIS—WE DIDN'T HAND OUT ALL THE NAMES. THERE WERE SOME CITY OFFICIALS IN THERE. QUILLIN WAS ONE OF 'EM.
WE COULDN'T RISK TIPPING OUR HAND.
SHIT.
BUT THEY HAVEN'T KILLED ANYONE LIKE THIS BEFORE.
THEY CAME FOR ME.
I'LL ISSUE A STATEMENT LATER THIS MORNING. THE MOB IS WAGING WAR AGAINST THE CITY ITSELF. AND NOW...
NOW WE ATTACK THEM WITH THE WRATH OF AN ANGRY GOD.

OCTOBER, 1944

ITALY

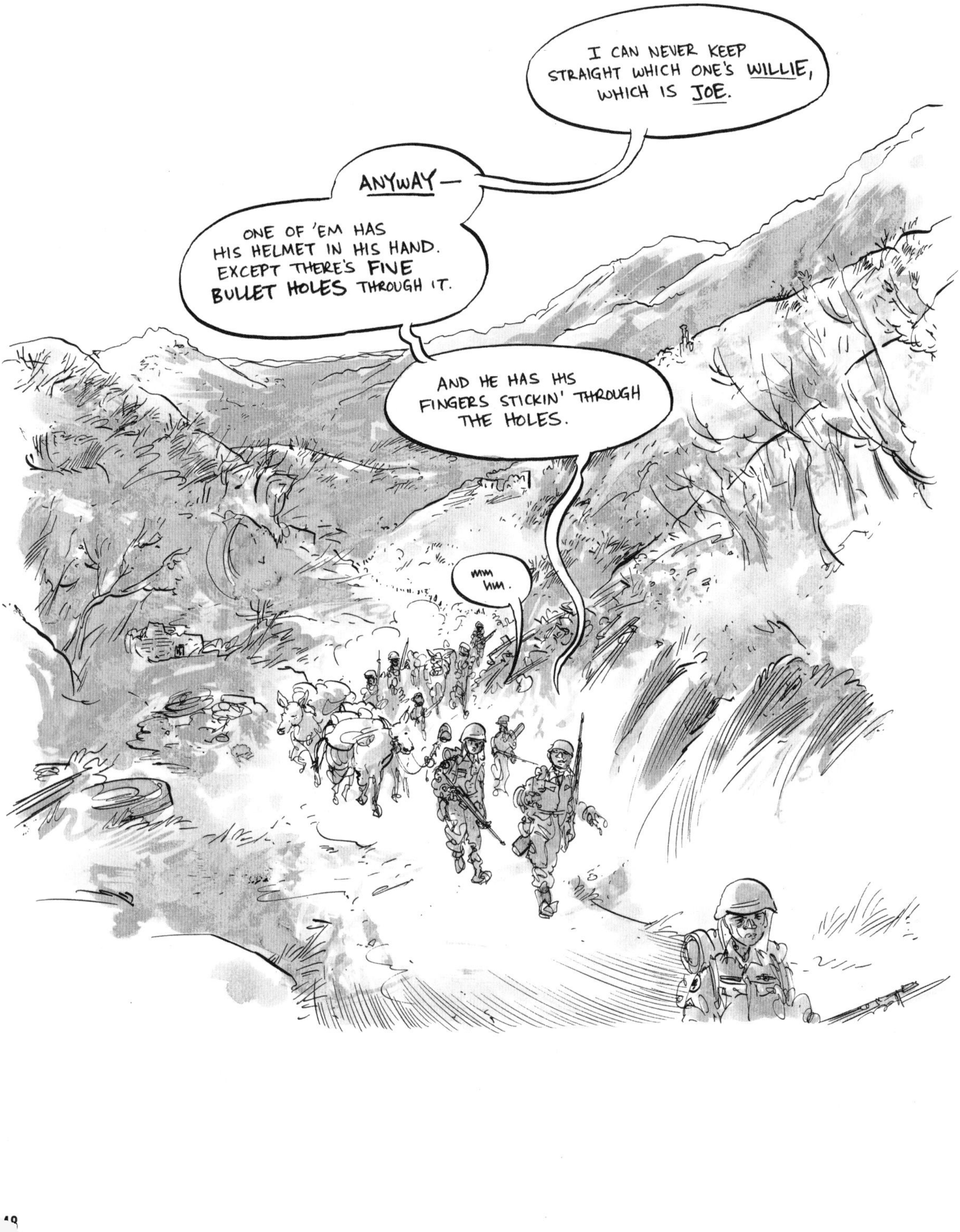

I CAN NEVER KEEP STRAIGHT WHICH ONE'S WILLIE, WHICH IS JOE.
ANYWAY—
ONE OF 'EM HAS HIS HELMET IN HIS HAND. EXCEPT THERE'S FIVE BULLET HOLES THROUGH IT.
AND HE HAS HIS FINGERS STICKIN' THROUGH THE HOLES.
MM HM.

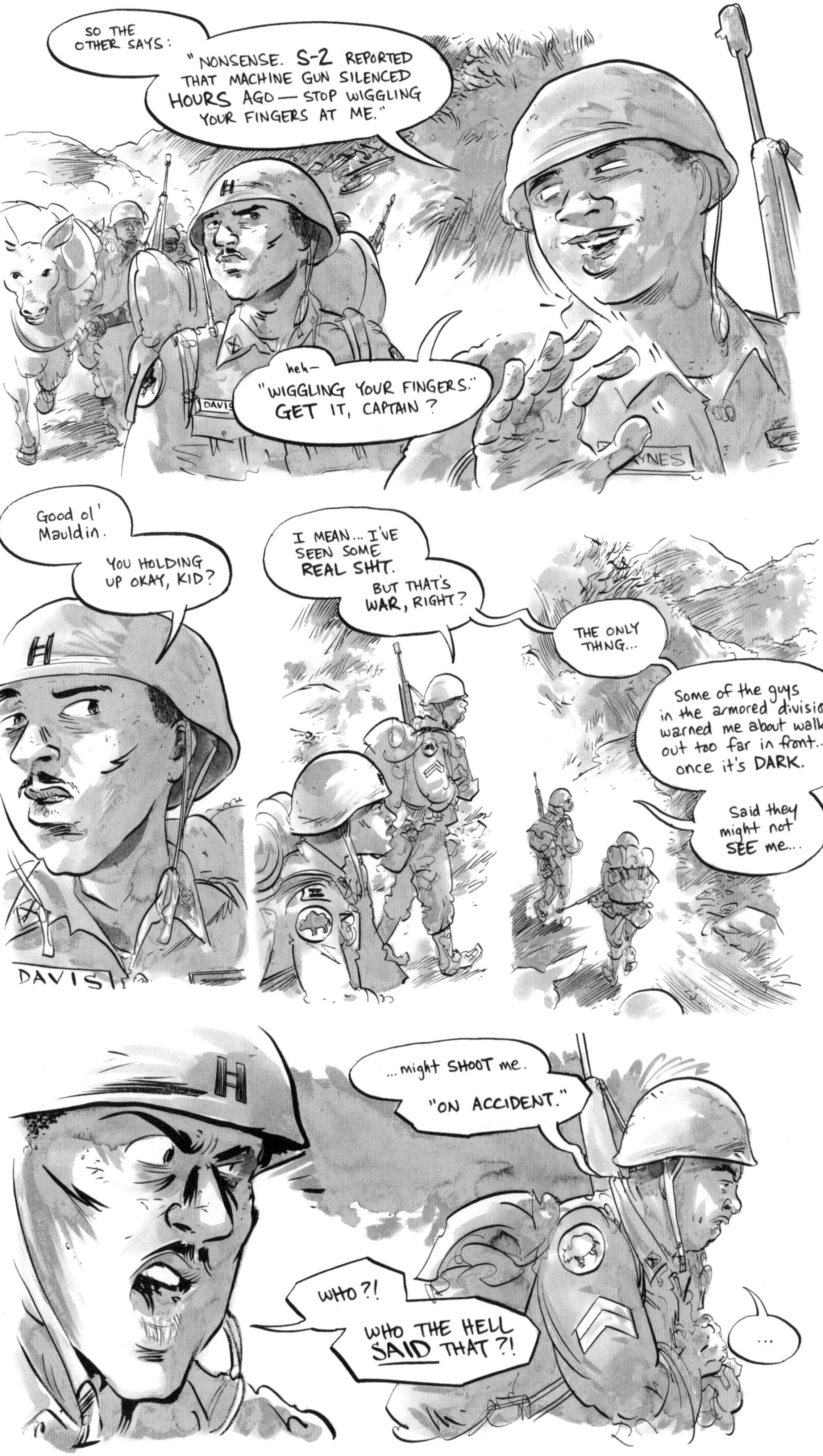
SO THE OTHER SAYS: "NONSENSE. S-2 REPORTED THAT MACHINE GUN SILENCED HOURS AGO— STOP WIGGLING YOUR FINGERS AT ME."
heh— "WIGGLING YOUR FINGERS." GET IT, CAPTAIN?
DAVIS
YNES
Good ol' Mauldin.
YOU HOLDING UP OKAY, KID?
DAVIS
I MEAN... I'VE SEEN SOME REAL SHIT.
BUT THAT'S WAR, RIGHT?
THE ONLY THING...
Some of the guys in the armored division warned me about walkin' out too far in front... once it's DARK.
Said they might not SEE me...
...might SHOOT me.
"ON ACCIDENT."
WHO?!
WHO THE HELL SAID THAT?!
...

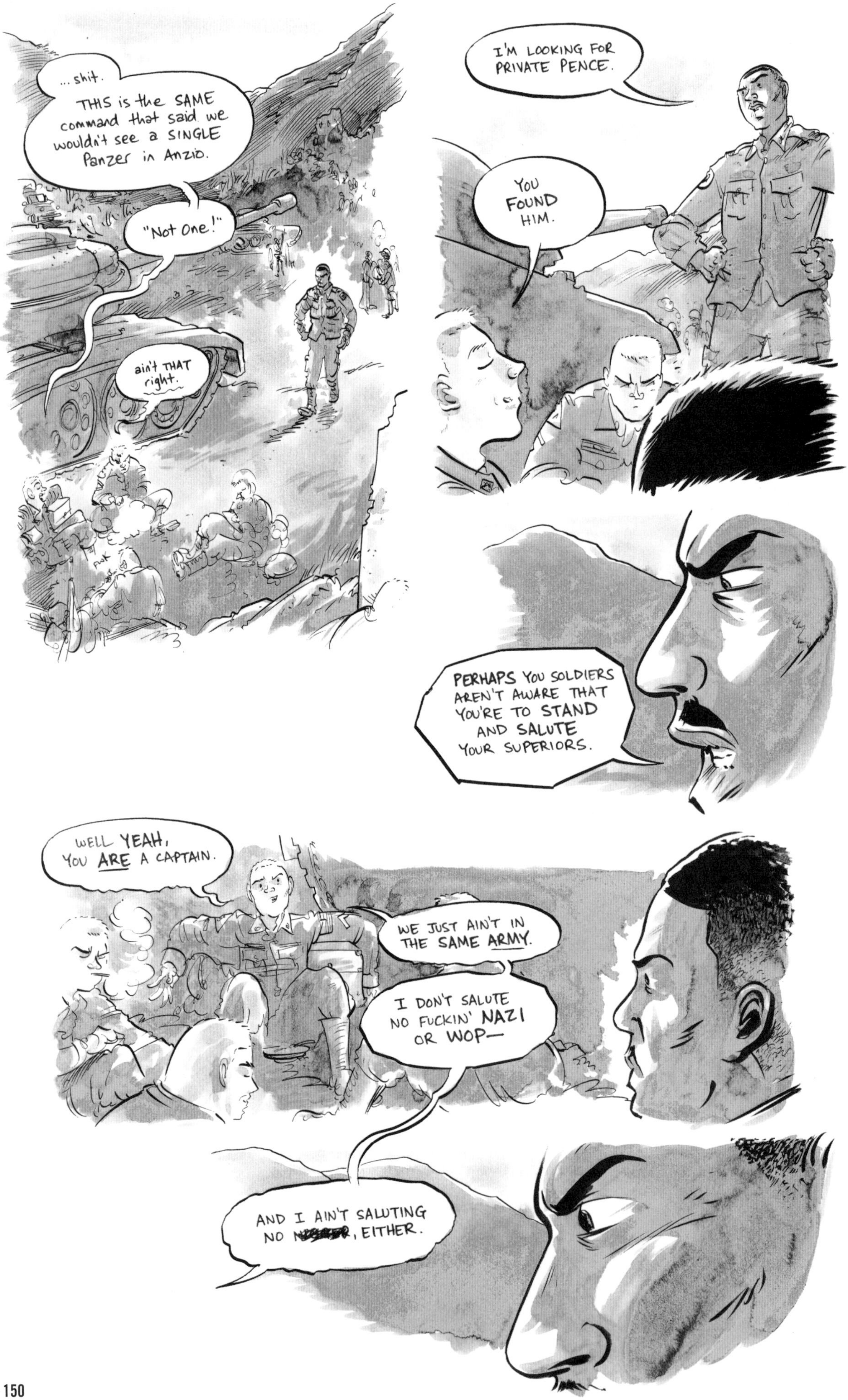
...shit.
THIS is the SAME command that said we wouldn't see a SINGLE Panzer in Anzio.
"Not One!"
ain't THAT right.
I'M LOOKING FOR PRIVATE PENCE.
YOU FOUND HIM.
PERHAPS YOU SOLDIERS AREN'T AWARE THAT YOU'RE TO STAND AND SALUTE YOUR SUPERIORS.
WELL YEAH, YOU ARE A CAPTAIN.
WE JUST AIN'T IN THE SAME ARMY.
I DON'T SALUTE NO FUCKIN' NAZI OR WOP—
AND I AIN'T SALUTING NO [redacted], EITHER.

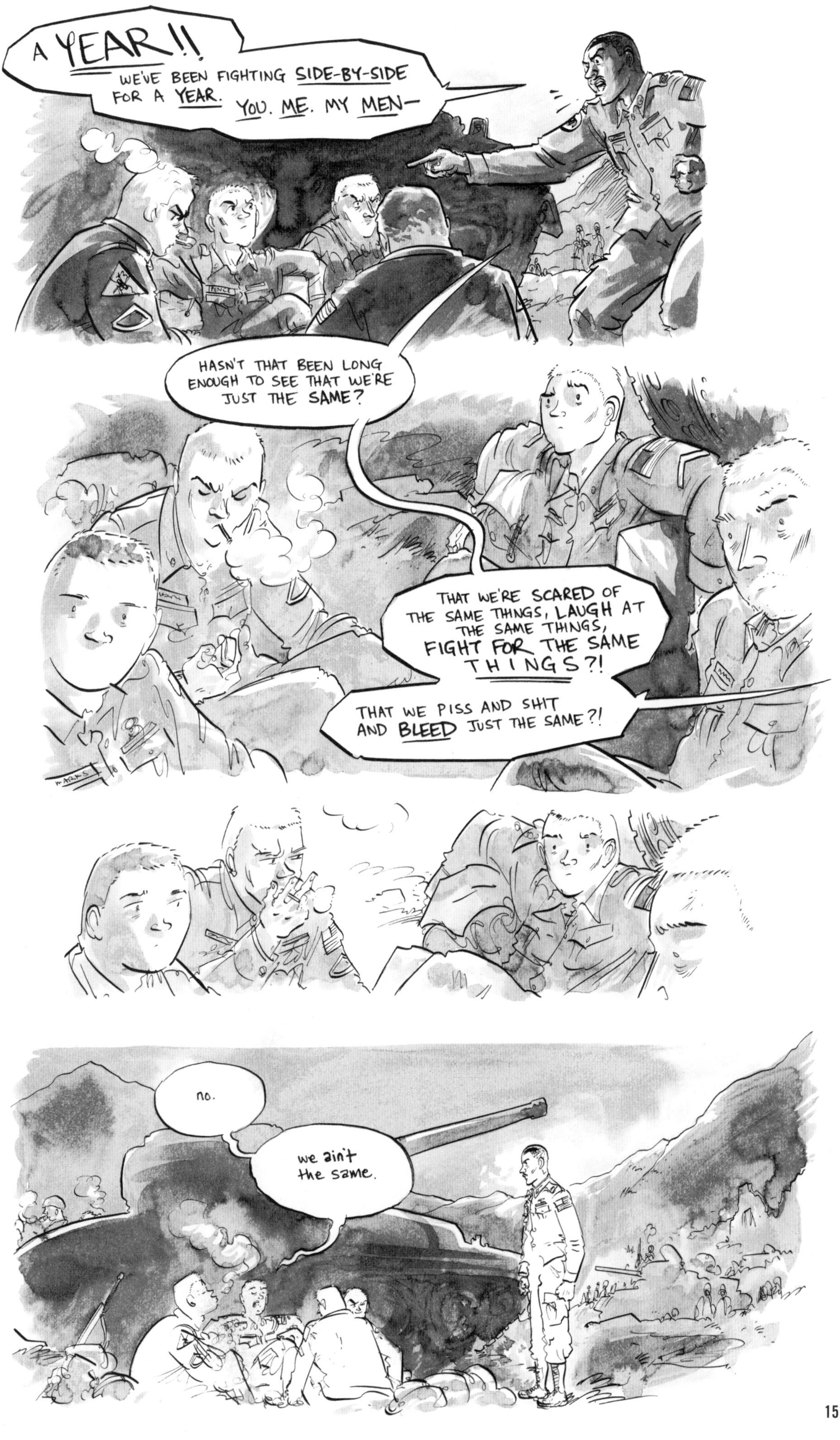
A YEAR!!
WE'VE BEEN FIGHTING SIDE-BY-SIDE FOR A YEAR. YOU. ME. MY MEN—
PENCE
HASN'T THAT BEEN LONG ENOUGH TO SEE THAT WE'RE JUST THE SAME?
THAT WE'RE SCARED OF THE SAME THINGS, LAUGH AT THE SAME THINGS, FIGHT FOR THE SAME THINGS?!
THAT WE PISS AND SHIT AND BLEED JUST THE SAME?!
MARKS
no.
we ain't the same.

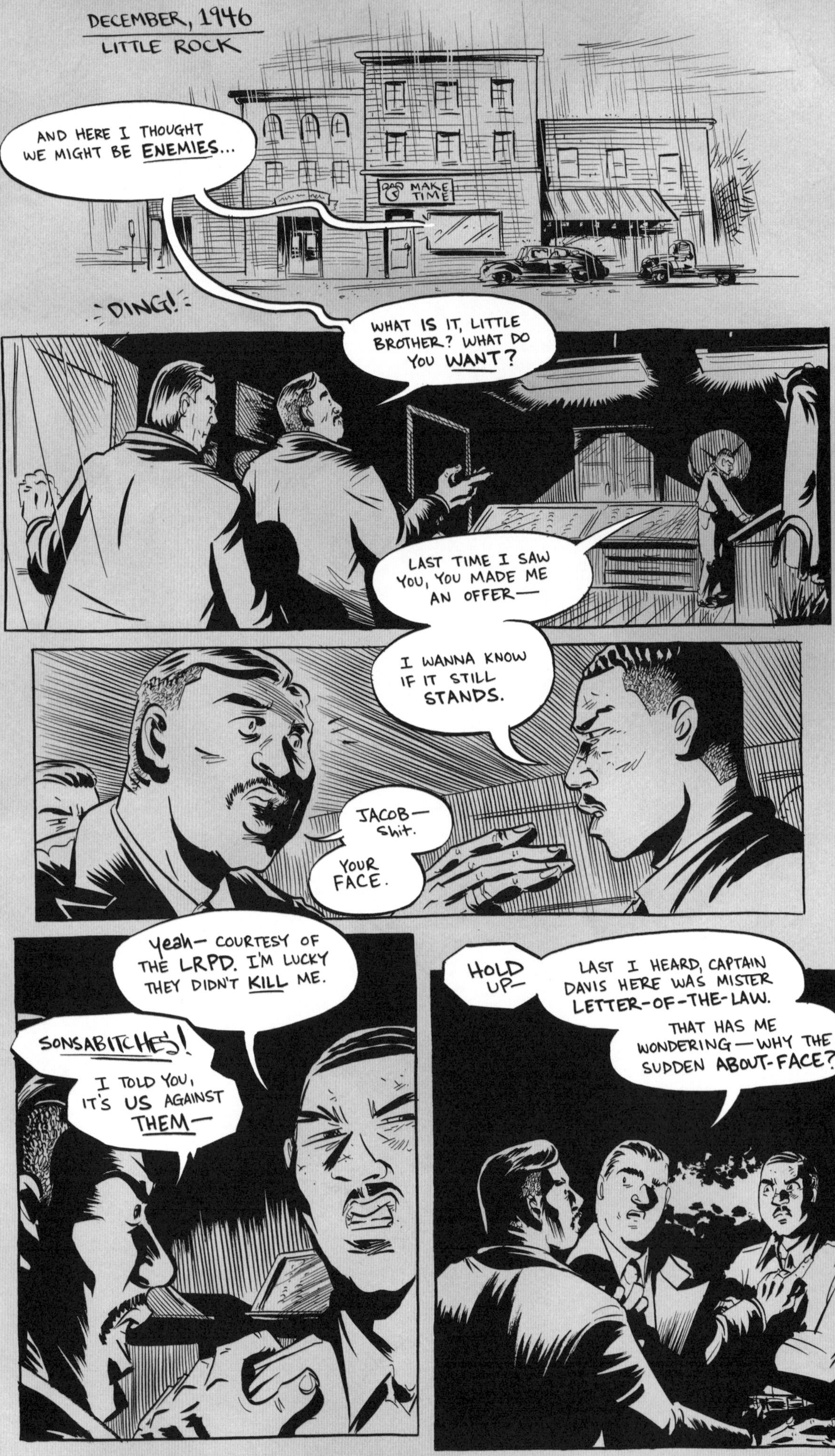
DECEMBER, 1946
LITTLE ROCK
AND HERE I THOUGHT WE MIGHT BE ENEMIES...
MAKE TIME
DING!
WHAT IS IT, LITTLE BROTHER? WHAT DO YOU WANT?
LAST TIME I SAW YOU, YOU MADE ME AN OFFER—
I WANNA KNOW IF IT STILL STANDS.
JACOB— Shit.
YOUR FACE.
Yeah— COURTESY OF THE LRPD. I'M LUCKY THEY DIDN'T KILL ME.
SONSABITCHES!
I TOLD YOU, IT'S US AGAINST THEM—
HOLD UP—
LAST I HEARD, CAPTAIN DAVIS HERE WAS MISTER LETTER-OF-THE-LAW.
THAT HAS ME WONDERING— WHY THE SUDDEN ABOUT-FACE?

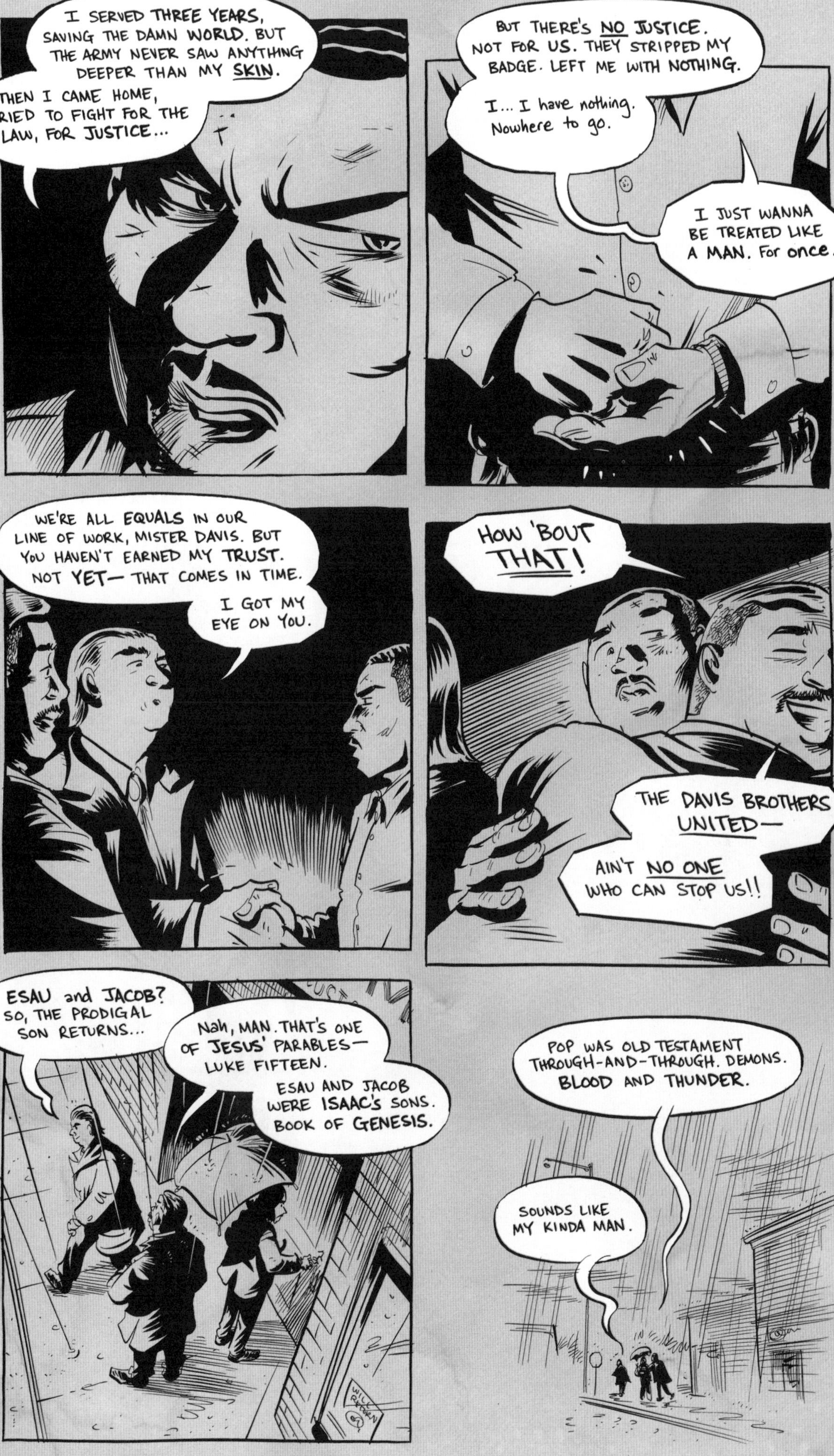

I SERVED THREE YEARS, SAVING THE DAMN WORLD. BUT THE ARMY NEVER SAW ANYTHING DEEPER THAN MY SKIN.
THEN I CAME HOME, TRIED TO FIGHT FOR THE LAW, FOR JUSTICE...
BUT THERE'S NO JUSTICE. NOT FOR US. THEY STRIPPED MY BADGE. LEFT ME WITH NOTHING.
I... I have nothing. Nowhere to go.
I JUST WANNA BE TREATED LIKE A MAN. For once.
WE'RE ALL EQUALS IN OUR LINE OF WORK, MISTER DAVIS. BUT YOU HAVEN'T EARNED MY TRUST. NOT YET— THAT COMES IN TIME.
I GOT MY EYE ON YOU.
HOW 'BOUT THAT!
THE DAVIS BROTHERS UNITED—
AIN'T NO ONE WHO CAN STOP US!!
ESAU and JACOB? SO, THE PRODIGAL SON RETURNS...
Nah, MAN. THAT'S ONE OF JESUS' PARABLES— LUKE FIFTEEN.
ESAU AND JACOB WERE ISAAC'S SONS. BOOK OF GENESIS.
POP WAS OLD TESTAMENT THROUGH-AND-THROUGH. DEMONS. BLOOD AND THUNDER.
SOUNDS LIKE MY KINDA MAN.

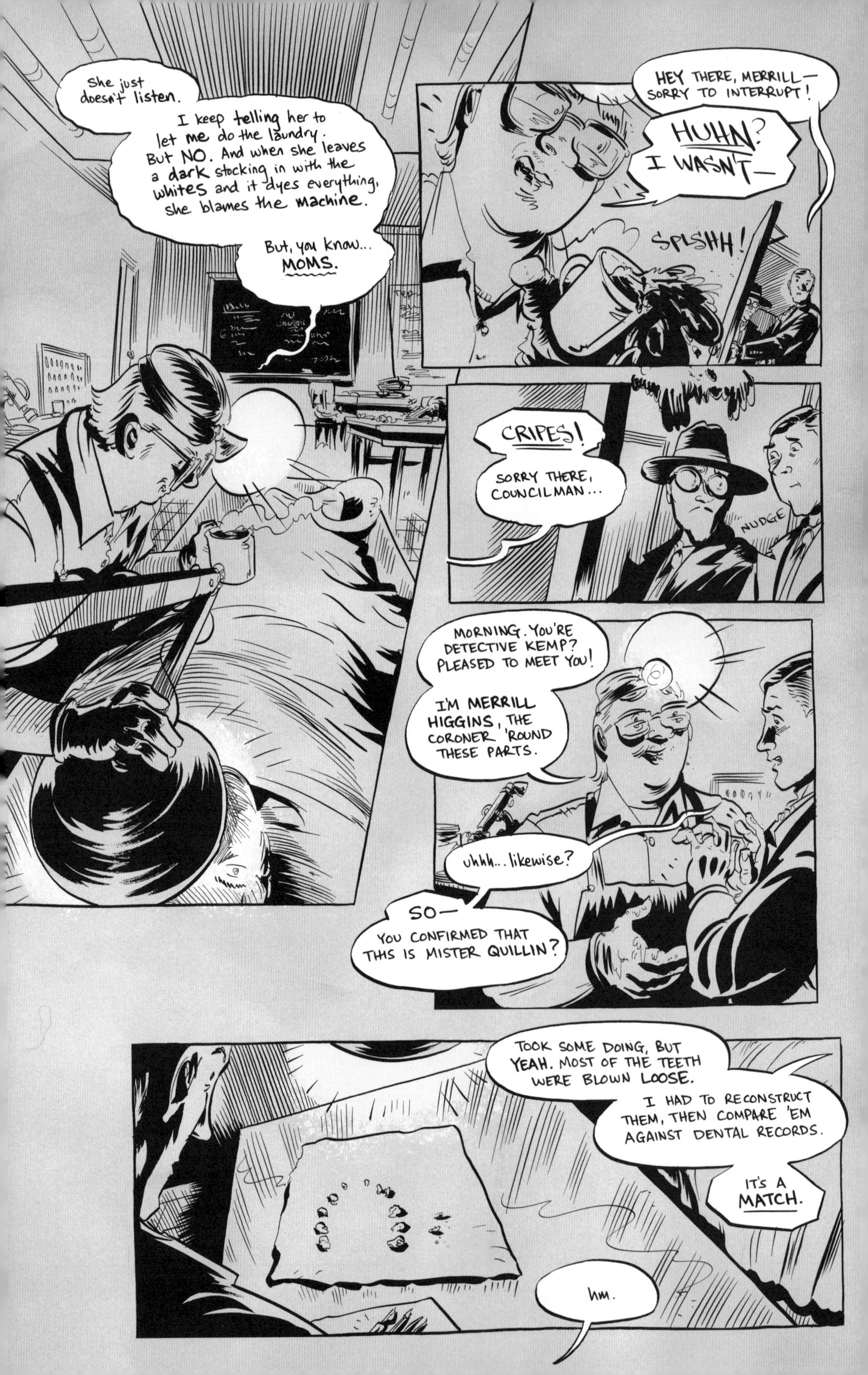
She just doesn't listen.
I keep telling her to let me do the laundry. But NO. And when she leaves a dark stocking in with the whites and it dyes everything, she blames the machine.
But, you know... MOMS.
HEY THERE, MERRILL— SORRY TO INTERRUPT!
HUHN? I WASN'T—
SPLSHH!
CRIPES!
SORRY THERE, COUNCILMAN...
NUDGE
MORNING. YOU'RE DETECTIVE KEMP? PLEASED TO MEET YOU!
I'M MERRILL HIGGINS, THE CORONER 'ROUND THESE PARTS.
uhhh... likewise?
SO—
YOU CONFIRMED THAT THIS IS MISTER QUILLIN?
TOOK SOME DOING, BUT YEAH. MOST OF THE TEETH WERE BLOWN LOOSE.
I HAD TO RECONSTRUCT THEM, THEN COMPARE 'EM AGAINST DENTAL RECORDS.
IT'S A MATCH.
hm.

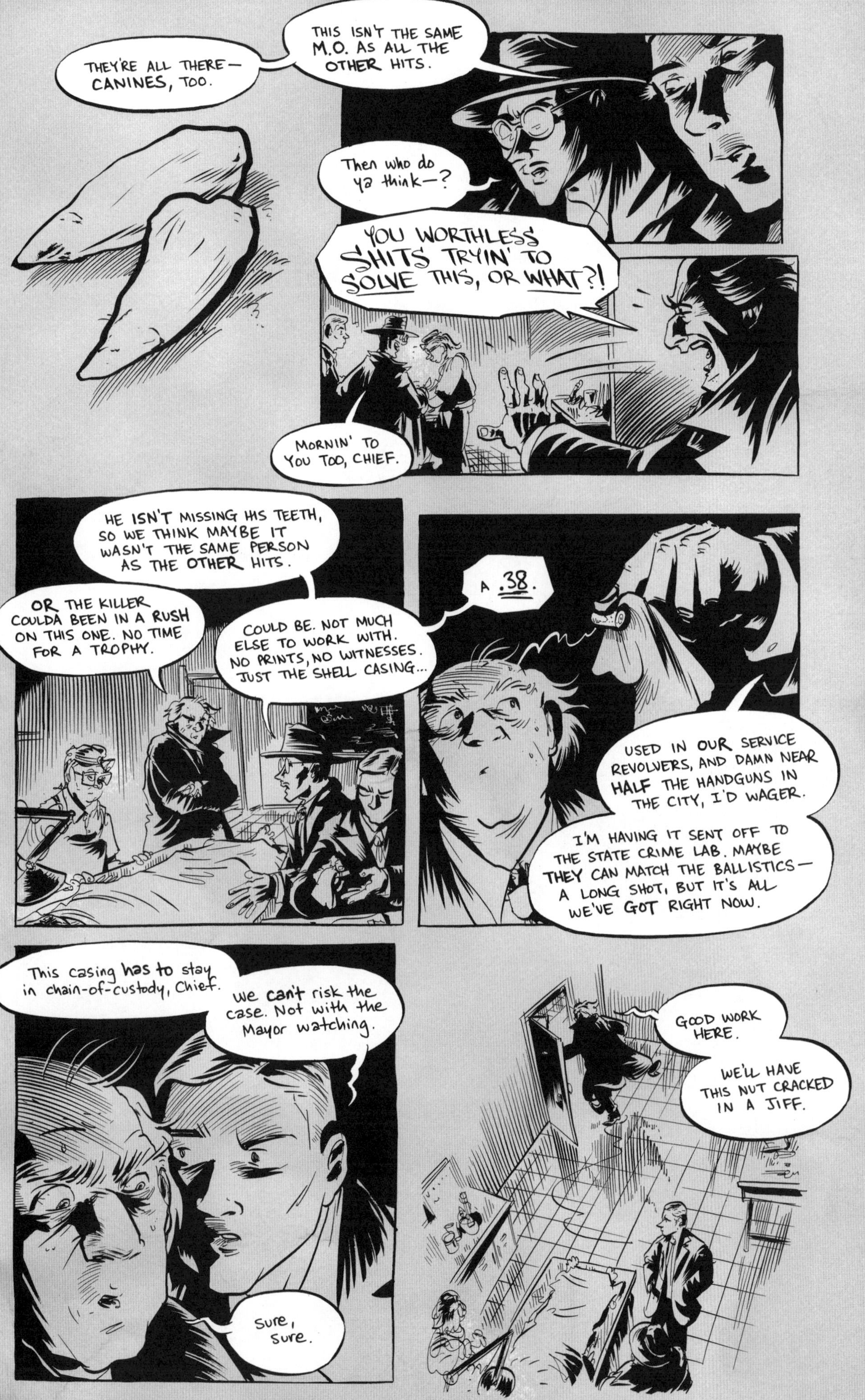

THEY'RE ALL THERE— CANINES, TOO.
THIS ISN'T THE SAME M.O. AS ALL THE OTHER HITS.
Then who do ya think—?
YOU WORTHLESS SHITS TRYIN' TO SOLVE THIS, OR WHAT?!
MORNIN' TO YOU TOO, CHIEF.
HE ISN'T MISSING HIS TEETH, SO WE THINK MAYBE IT WASN'T THE SAME PERSON AS THE OTHER HITS.
OR THE KILLER COULDA BEEN IN A RUSH ON THIS ONE. NO TIME FOR A TROPHY.
COULD BE. NOT MUCH ELSE TO WORK WITH. NO PRINTS, NO WITNESSES. JUST THE SHELL CASING...
A .38.
USED IN OUR SERVICE REVOLVERS, AND DAMN NEAR HALF THE HANDGUNS IN THE CITY, I'D WAGER.
I'M HAVING IT SENT OFF TO THE STATE CRIME LAB. MAYBE THEY CAN MATCH THE BALLISTICS— A LONG SHOT, BUT IT'S ALL WE'VE GOT RIGHT NOW.
This casing has to stay in chain-of-custody, Chief.
We can't risk the case. Not with the Mayor watching.
Sure, sure.
GOOD WORK HERE.
WE'LL HAVE THIS NUT CRACKED IN A JIFF.

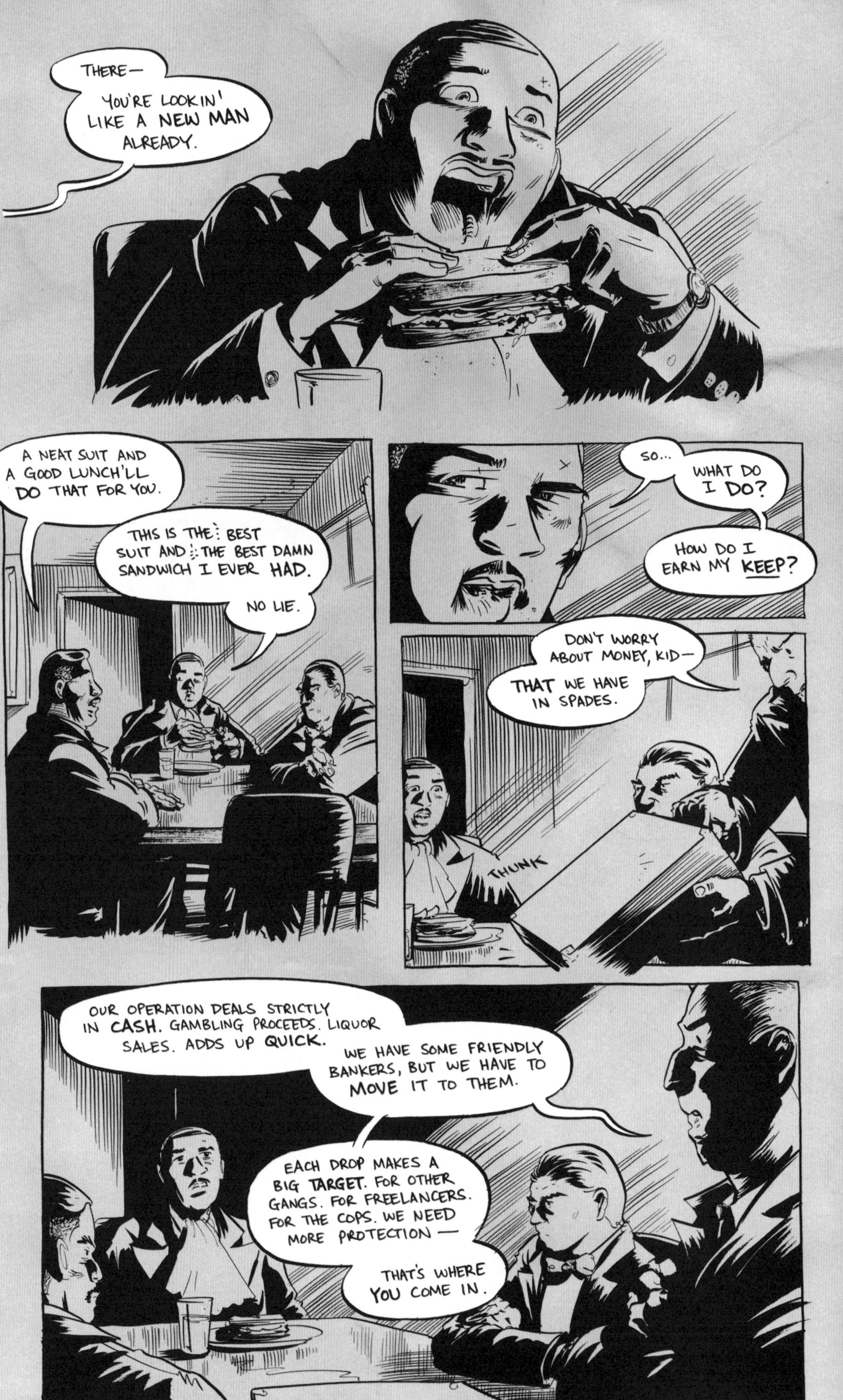
THERE—
YOU'RE LOOKIN' LIKE A NEW MAN ALREADY.
A NEAT SUIT AND A GOOD LUNCH'LL DO THAT FOR YOU.
THIS IS THE BEST SUIT AND THE BEST DAMN SANDWICH I EVER HAD.
NO LIE.
SO...
WHAT DO I DO?
HOW DO I EARN MY KEEP?
DON'T WORRY ABOUT MONEY, KID—
THAT WE HAVE IN SPADES.
CHUNK
OUR OPERATION DEALS STRICTLY IN CASH. GAMBLING PROCEEDS. LIQUOR SALES. ADDS UP QUICK.
WE HAVE SOME FRIENDLY BANKERS, BUT WE HAVE TO MOVE IT TO THEM.
EACH DROP MAKES A BIG TARGET. FOR OTHER GANGS. FOR FREELANCERS. FOR THE COPS. WE NEED MORE PROTECTION —
THAT'S WHERE YOU COME IN.

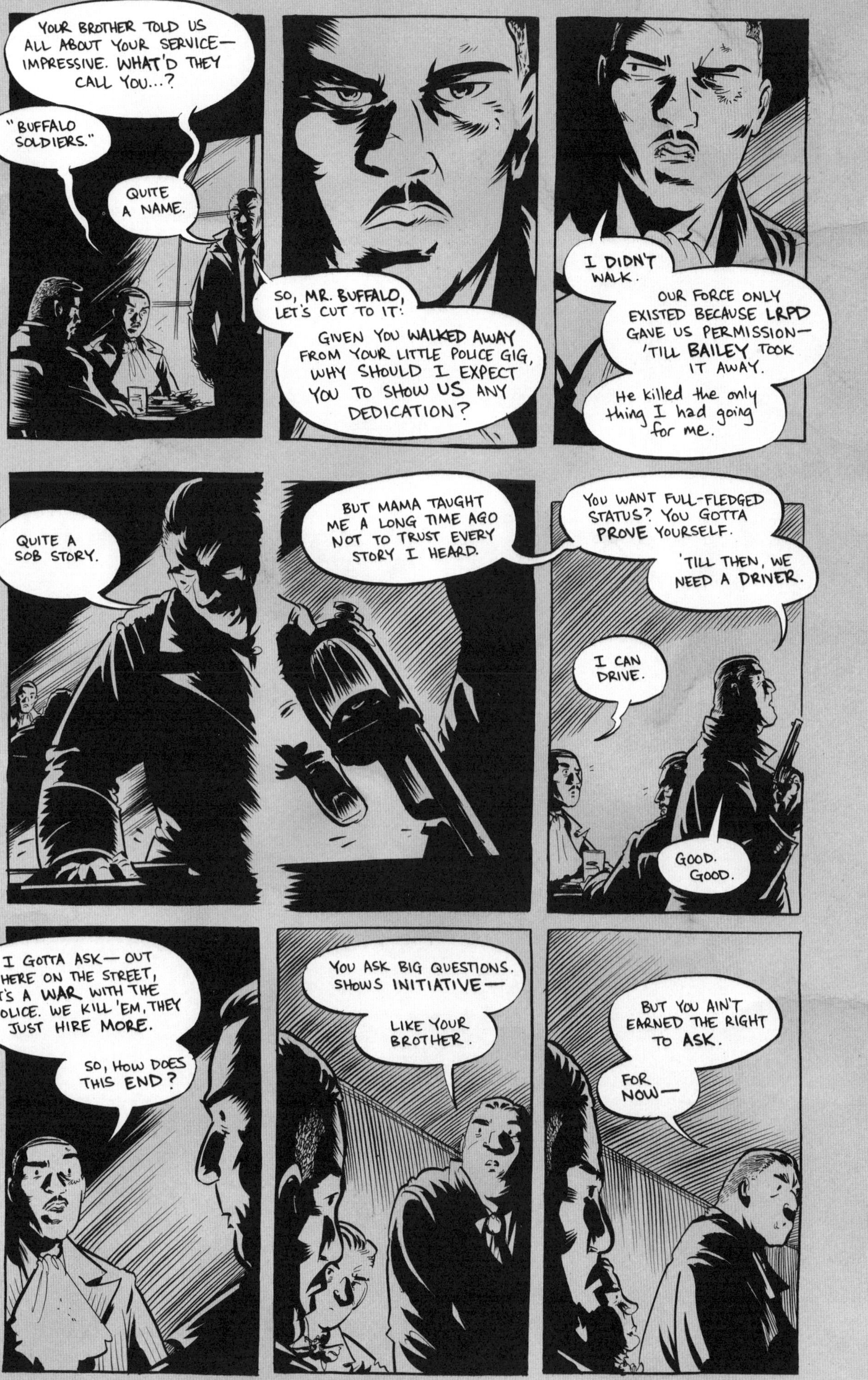

YOUR BROTHER TOLD US ALL ABOUT YOUR SERVICE—IMPRESSIVE. WHAT'D THEY CALL YOU...?
"BUFFALO SOLDIERS."
QUITE A NAME.
SO, MR. BUFFALO, LET'S CUT TO IT:
GIVEN YOU WALKED AWAY FROM YOUR LITTLE POLICE GIG, WHY SHOULD I EXPECT YOU TO SHOW US ANY DEDICATION?
I DIDN'T WALK.
OUR FORCE ONLY EXISTED BECAUSE LRPD GAVE US PERMISSION—'TILL BAILEY TOOK IT AWAY.
He killed the only thing I had going for me.
QUITE A SOB STORY.
BUT MAMA TAUGHT ME A LONG TIME AGO NOT TO TRUST EVERY STORY I HEARD.
YOU WANT FULL-FLEDGED STATUS? YOU GOTTA PROVE YOURSELF.
'TILL THEN, WE NEED A DRIVER.
I CAN DRIVE.
GOOD. GOOD.
I GOTTA ASK— OUT THERE ON THE STREET, IT'S A WAR WITH THE POLICE. WE KILL 'EM, THEY JUST HIRE MORE.
SO, HOW DOES THIS END?
YOU ASK BIG QUESTIONS. SHOWS INITIATIVE—
LIKE YOUR BROTHER.
BUT YOU AIN'T EARNED THE RIGHT TO ASK.
FOR NOW—

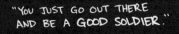

"YOU JUST GO OUT THERE
AND BE A GOOD SOLDIER."

POLICE—

VRRRRmmmmmmmm

:'eeeeOOeeeOoooe

Steady.

OOeeeeoooooOOOeeeeeeeeoooo

ERT

WE DIDN'T DO ANYTHING
WRONG. THEY HAVE NO
CAUSE TO SEARCH US.

THEY'RE PULLING US OVER
JUST 'CUZ WE'RE BLACK.
YOU THINK THEY'RE GONNA
FOLLOW THE RULEBOOK?!

I can talk
us outta this.

Sure...

go ahead
and stop.

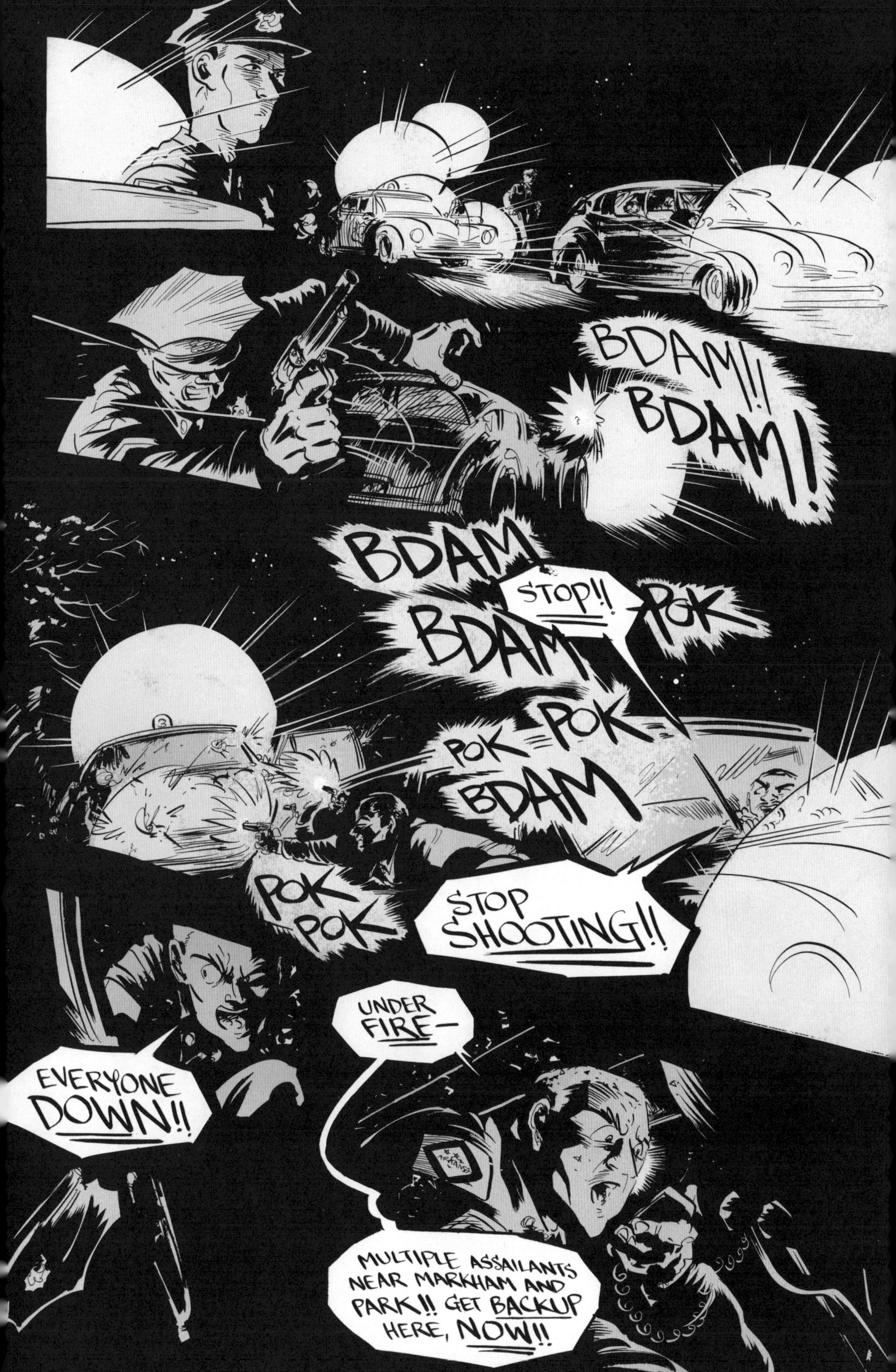
BDAM!! BDAM!
BDAM
STOP!!
BDAM
POK
POK POK
BDAM
POK POK
STOP SHOOTING!!
UNDER FIRE—
EVERYONE DOWN!!
MULTIPLE ASSAILANTS NEAR MARKHAM AND PARK!! GET BACKUP HERE, NOW!!

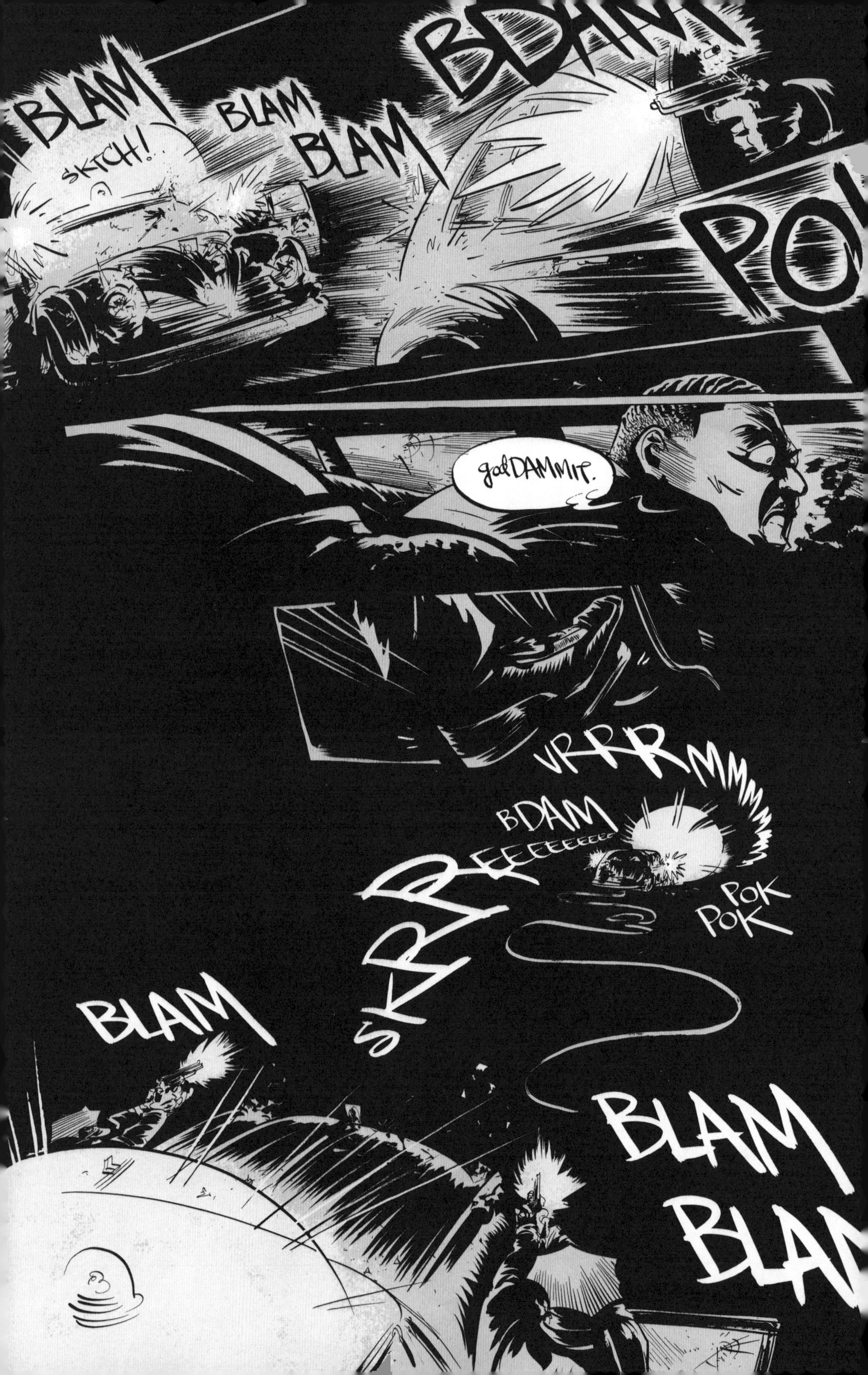
BLAM
SKTCH!
BLAM
BLAM
BDAM
POK
goddAMMIT.
VRRRMMMM
BDAM
SKRREEEEEEEE
POK
POK
BLAM
BLAM

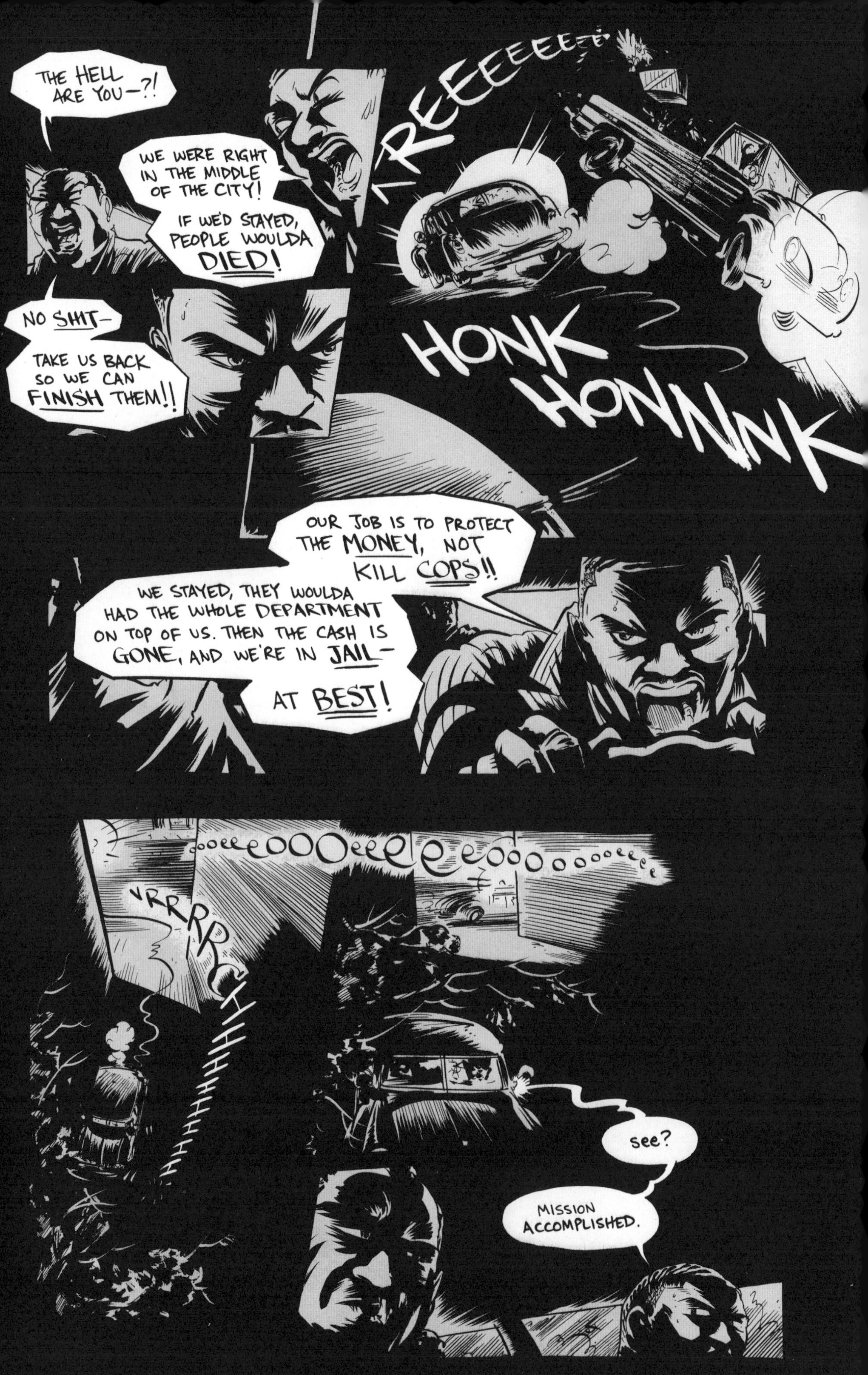
THE HELL ARE YOU—?!
KREEEEEEEE
WE WERE RIGHT IN THE MIDDLE OF THE CITY!
IF WE'D STAYED, PEOPLE WOULDA DIED!
NO SHIT—
TAKE US BACK SO WE CAN FINISH THEM!!
HONK HONNNNK
OUR JOB IS TO PROTECT THE MONEY, NOT KILL COPS!!
WE STAYED, THEY WOULDA HAD THE WHOLE DEPARTMENT ON TOP OF US. THEN THE CASH IS GONE, AND WE'RE IN JAIL—
AT BEST!
ooeeeOOOeeeeeeOOOoooooeeee
VRRRRCHHHHHHHHH
see?
MISSION ACCOMPLISHED.

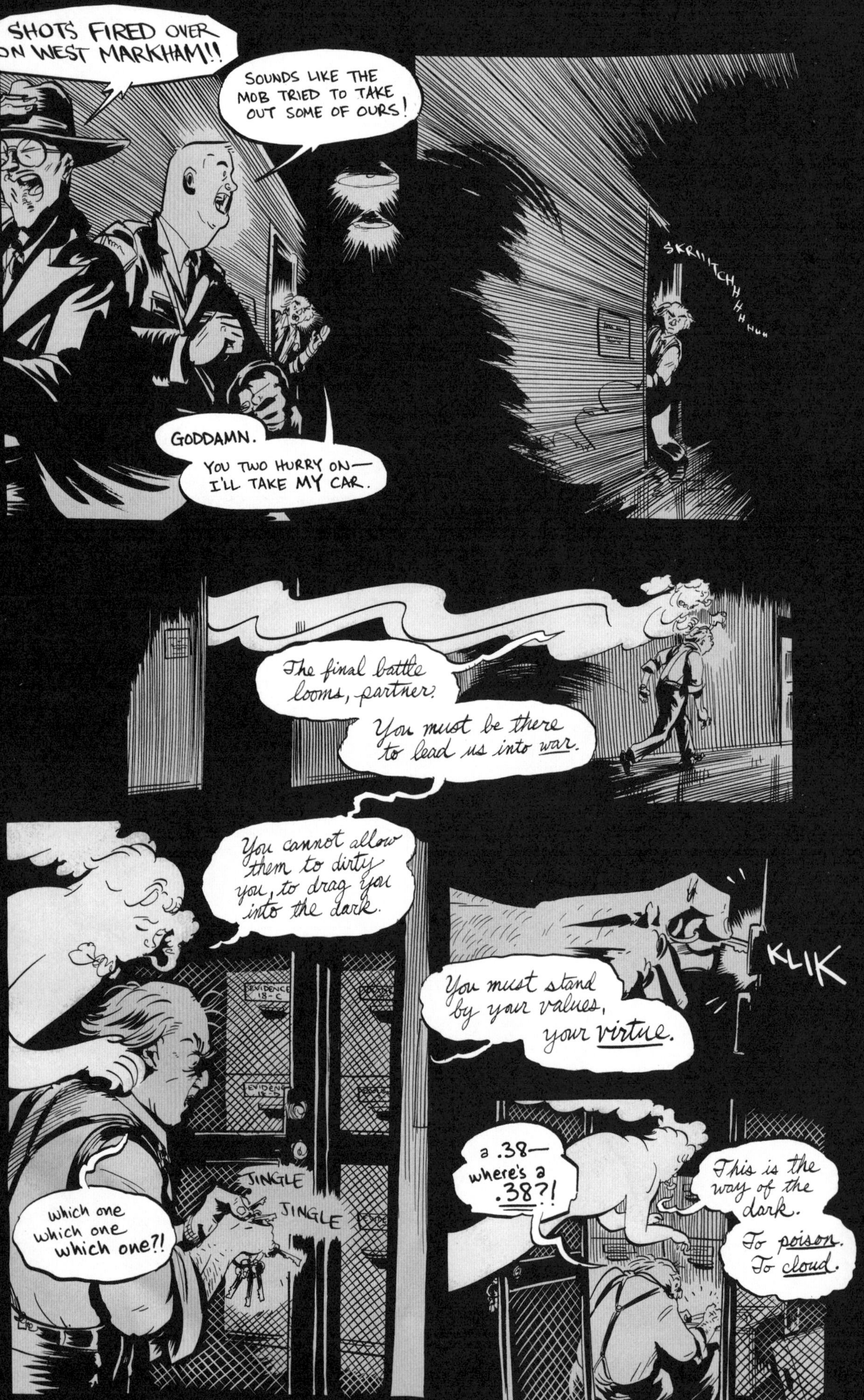
SHOTS FIRED OVER ON WEST MARKHAM!!
SOUNDS LIKE THE MOB TRIED TO TAKE OUT SOME OF OURS!
GODDAMN.
YOU TWO HURRY ON— I'LL TAKE MY CAR.
SKRIIITCHHHHHuuu
The final battle looms, partner.
You must be there to lead us into war.
You cannot allow them to dirty you, to drag you into the dark.
EVIDENCE 18-C
KLIK
You must stand by your values, your virtue.
JINGLE
JINGLE
which one which one which one?!
a .38— where's a .38?!
This is the way of the dark.
To poison. To cloud.

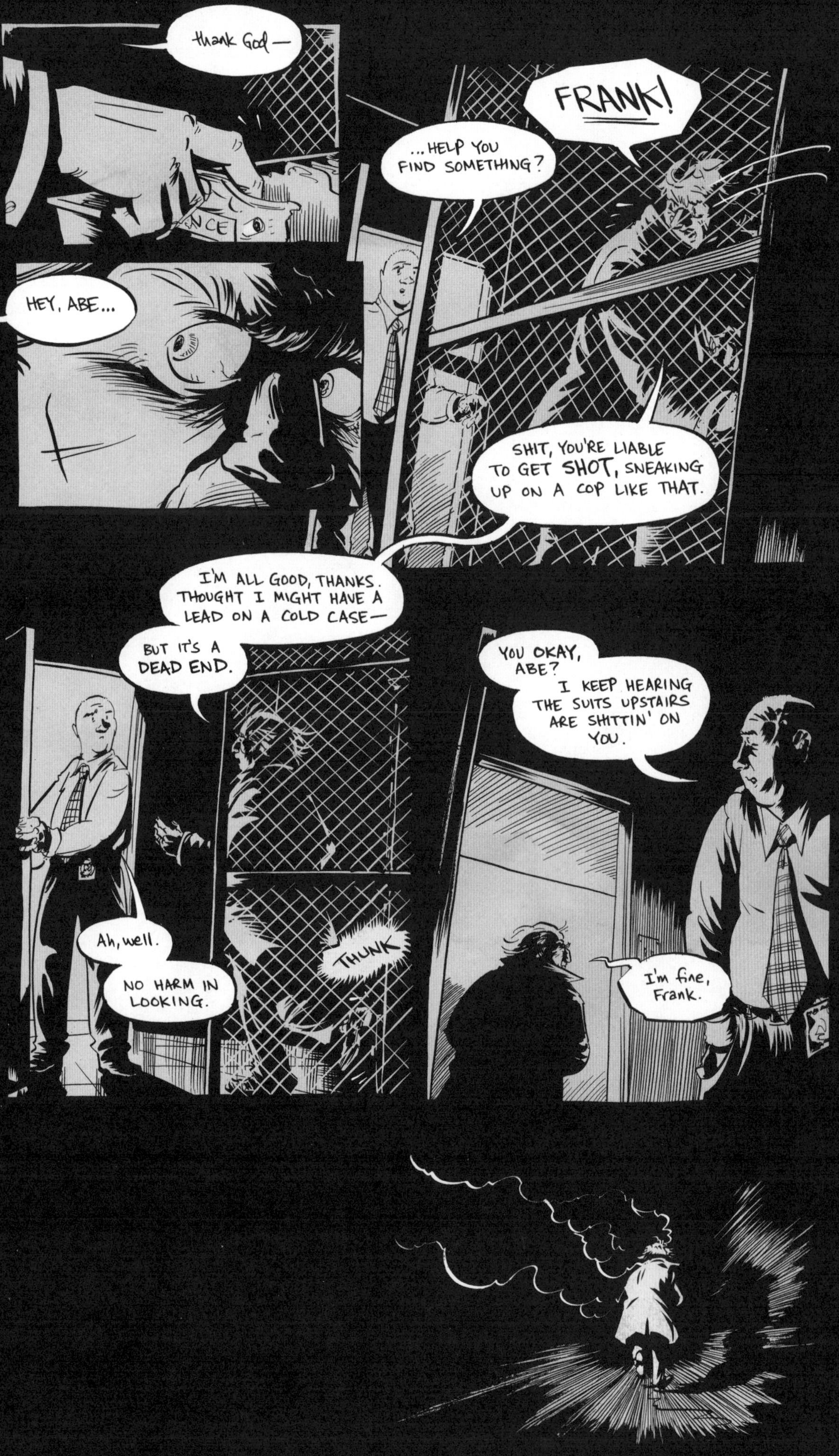
thank God—
NCE
FRANK!
...HELP YOU FIND SOMETHING?
HEY, ABE...
SHIT, YOU'RE LIABLE TO GET SHOT, SNEAKING UP ON A COP LIKE THAT.
I'M ALL GOOD, THANKS. THOUGHT I MIGHT HAVE A LEAD ON A COLD CASE—
BUT IT'S A DEAD END.
Ah, well.
NO HARM IN LOOKING.
THUNK
YOU OKAY, ABE?
I KEEP HEARING THE SUITS UPSTAIRS ARE SHITTIN' ON YOU.
I'm fine, Frank.

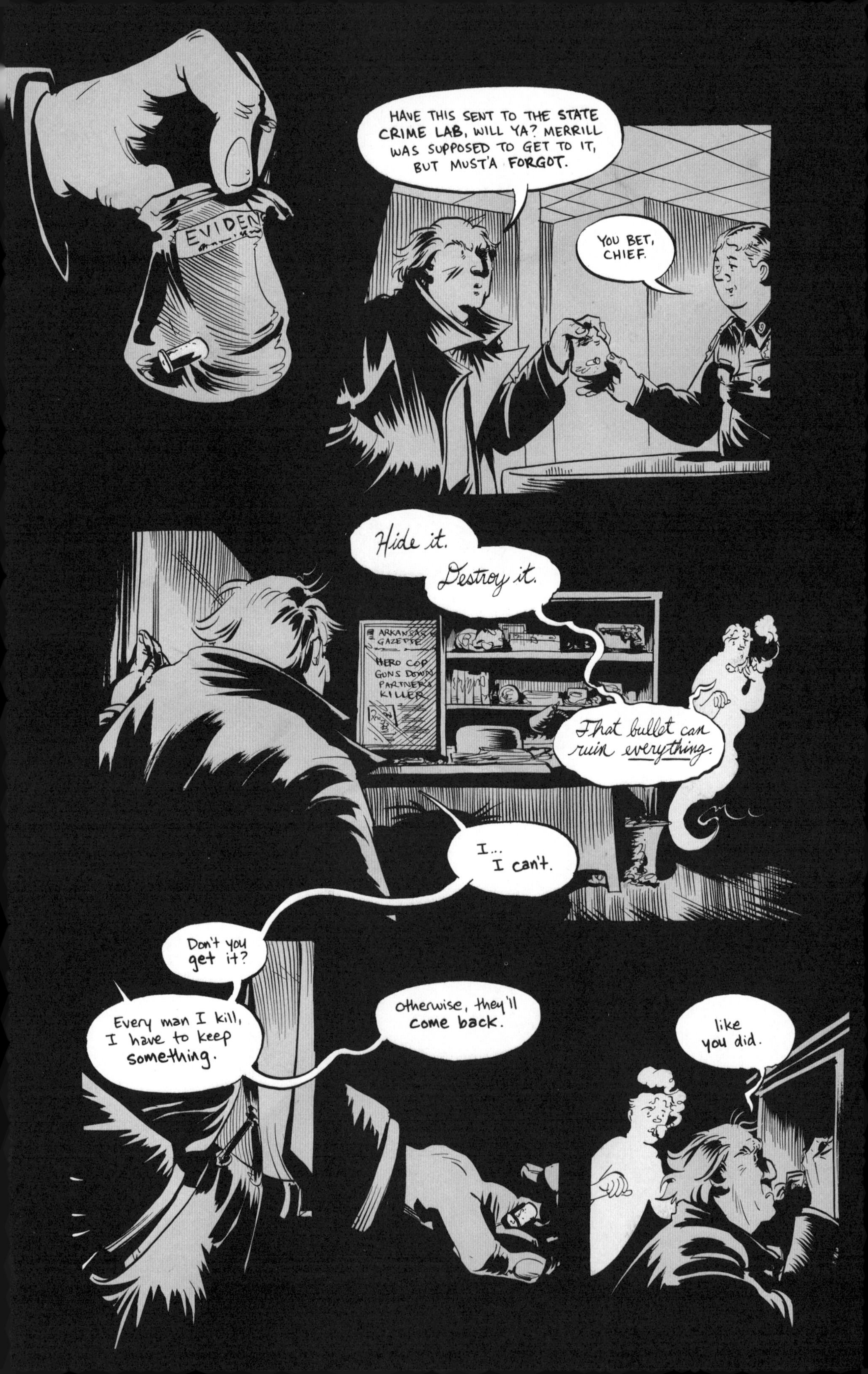
EVIDEN
HAVE THIS SENT TO THE STATE CRIME LAB, WILL YA? MERRILL WAS SUPPOSED TO GET TO IT, BUT MUST'A FORGOT.
YOU BET, CHIEF.
Hide it.
Destroy it.
ARKANSAS GAZETTE
HERO COP GUNS DOWN PARTNER'S KILLER
That bullet can ruin everything.
I... I can't.
Don't you get it?
Every man I kill, I have to keep something.
otherwise, they'll come back.
like you did.

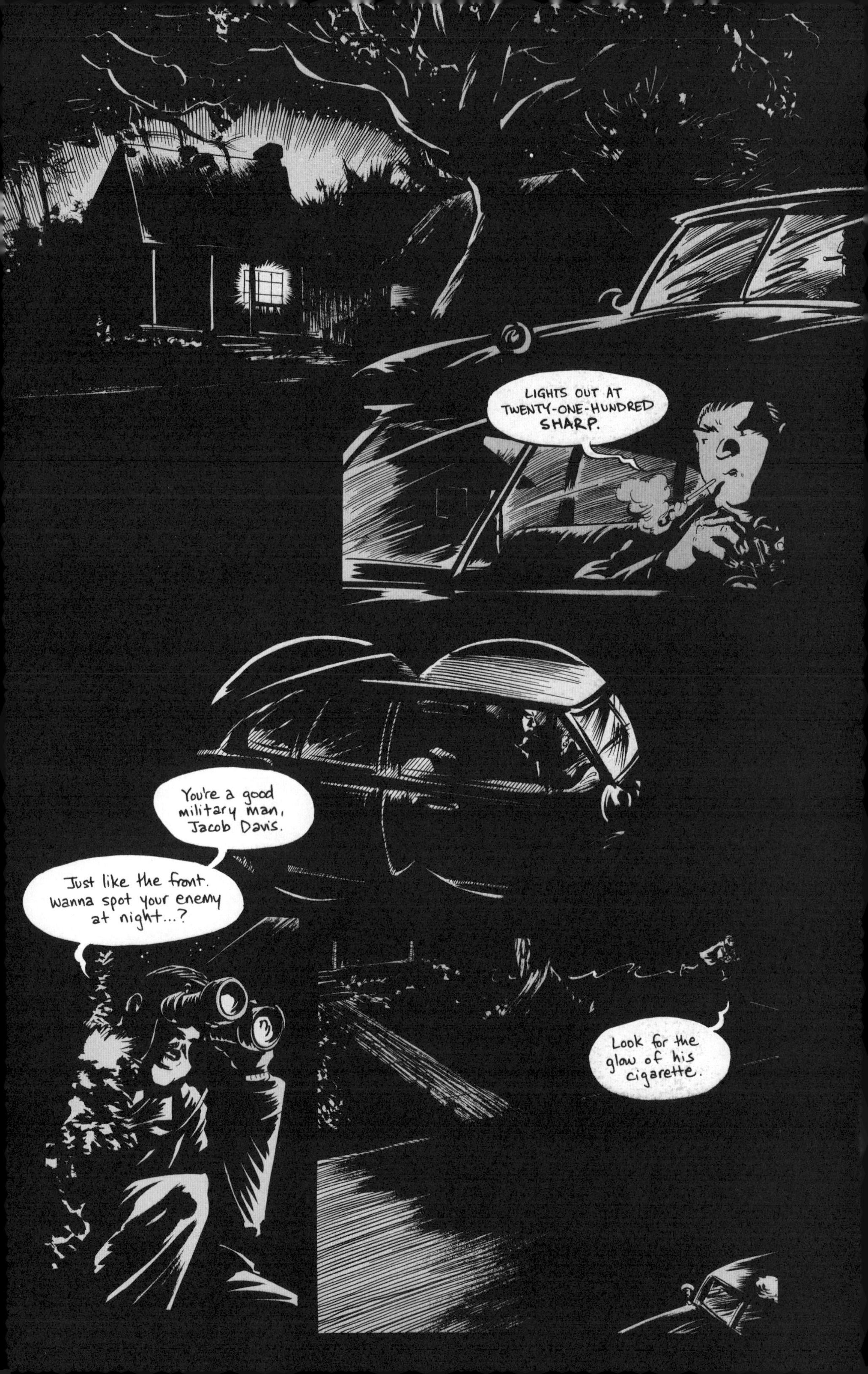

LIGHTS OUT AT TWENTY-ONE-HUNDRED SHARP.
You're a good military man, Jacob Davis.
Just like the front. Wanna spot your enemy at night...?
Look for the glow of his cigarette.

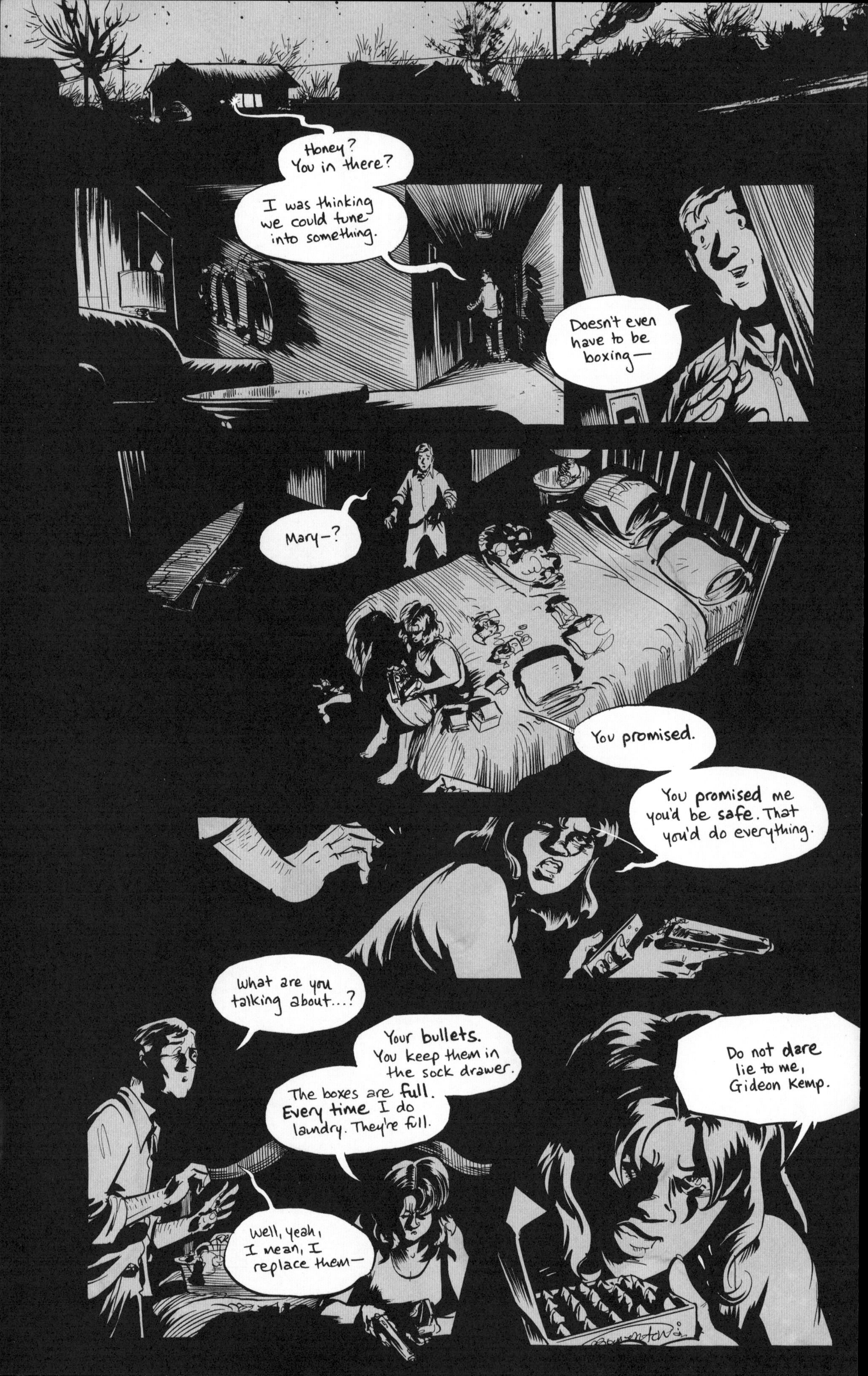

Honey? You in there?
I was thinking we could tune into something.
Doesn't even have to be boxing—
Mary—?
You promised.
You promised me you'd be safe. That you'd do everything.
What are you talking about...?
Your bullets. You keep them in the sock drawer.
The boxes are full. Every time I do laundry. They're full.
Well, yeah, I mean, I replace them—
Do not dare lie to me, Gideon Kemp.

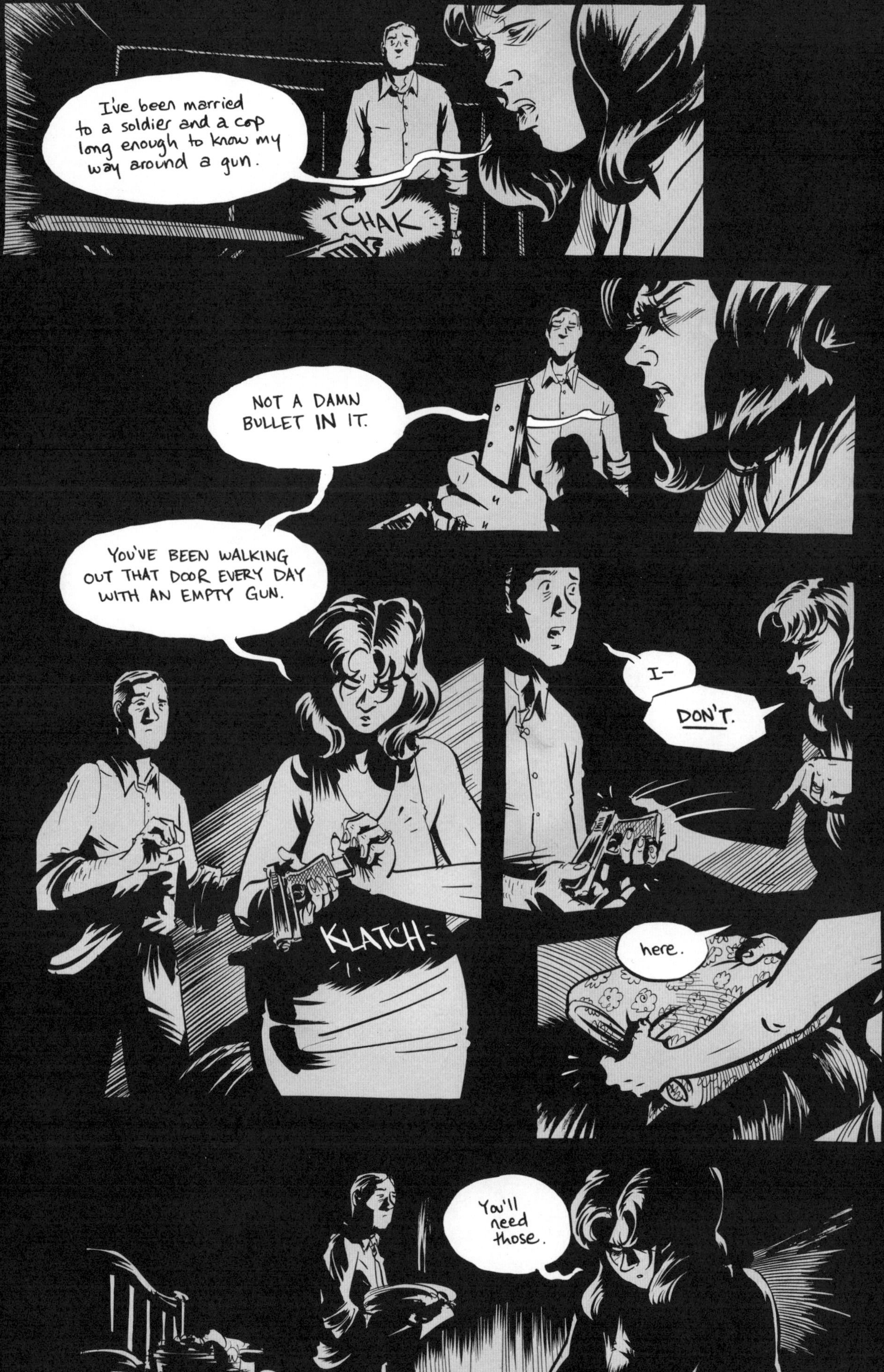
I've been married to a soldier and a cop long enough to know my way around a gun.
TCHAK
NOT A DAMN BULLET IN IT.
YOU'VE BEEN WALKING OUT THAT DOOR EVERY DAY WITH AN EMPTY GUN.
KLATCH
I-
DON'T.
here.
You'll need those.

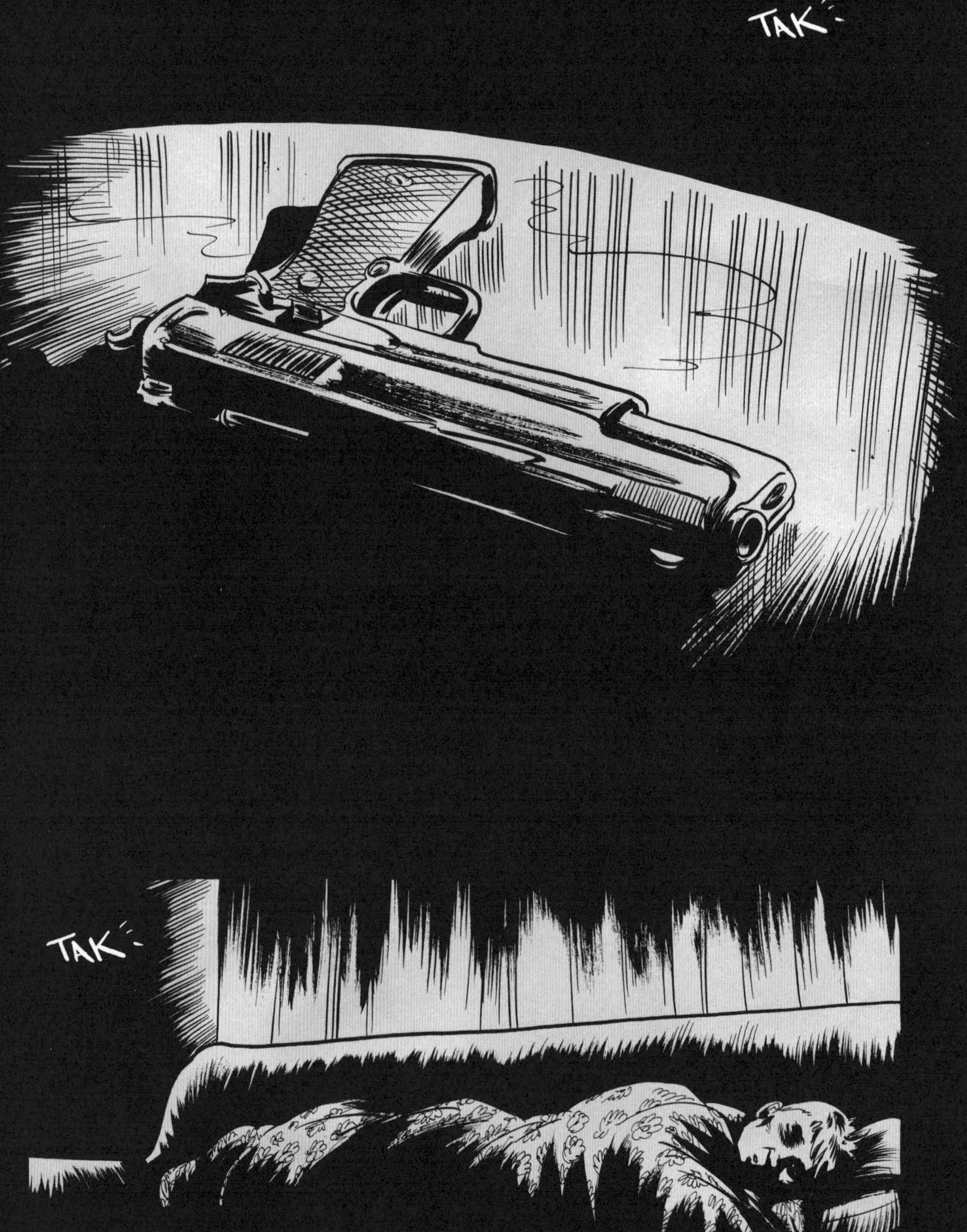
TAK
TAK

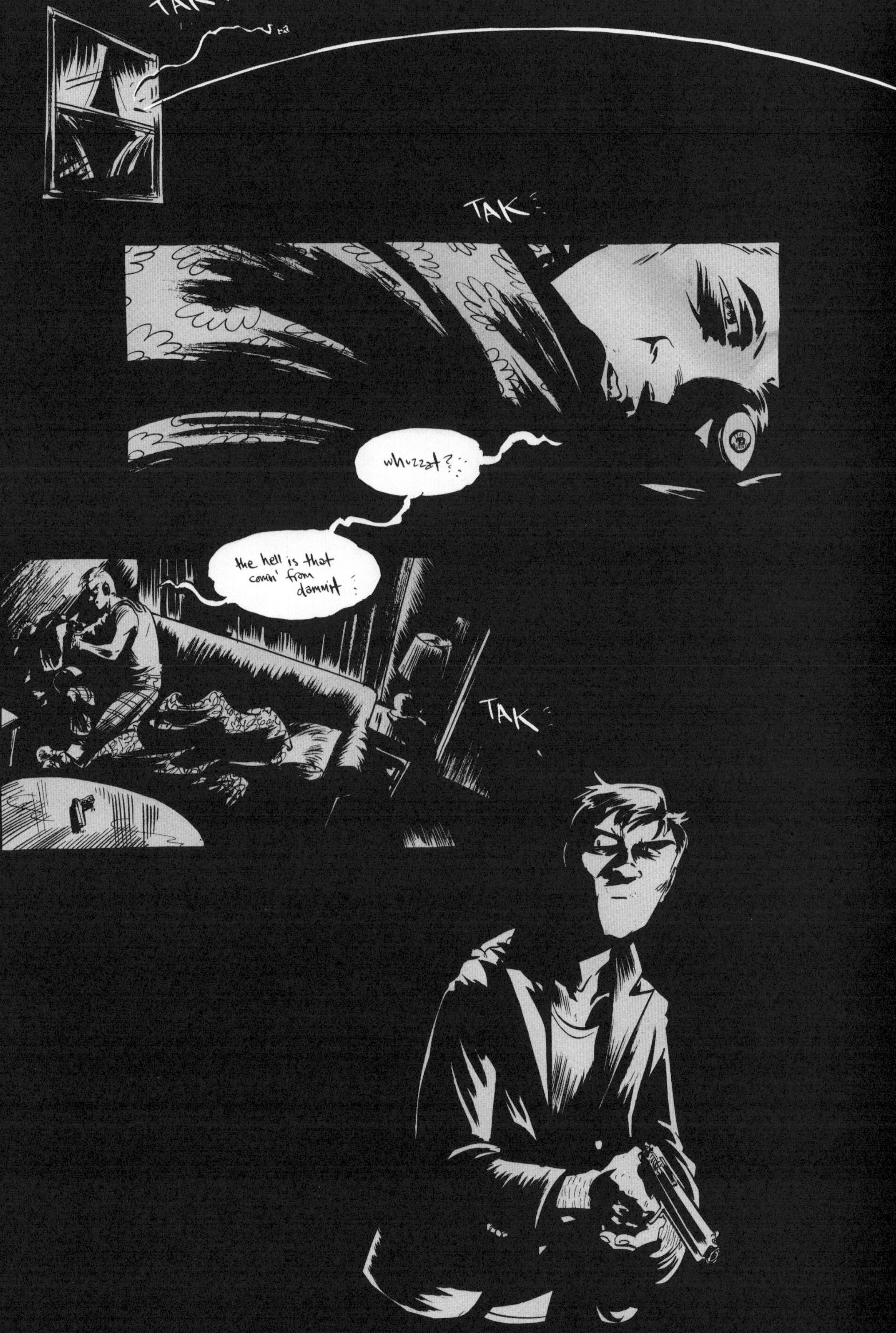
TAK
TAK
whuzzat?
the hell is that comin' from dammit
TAK

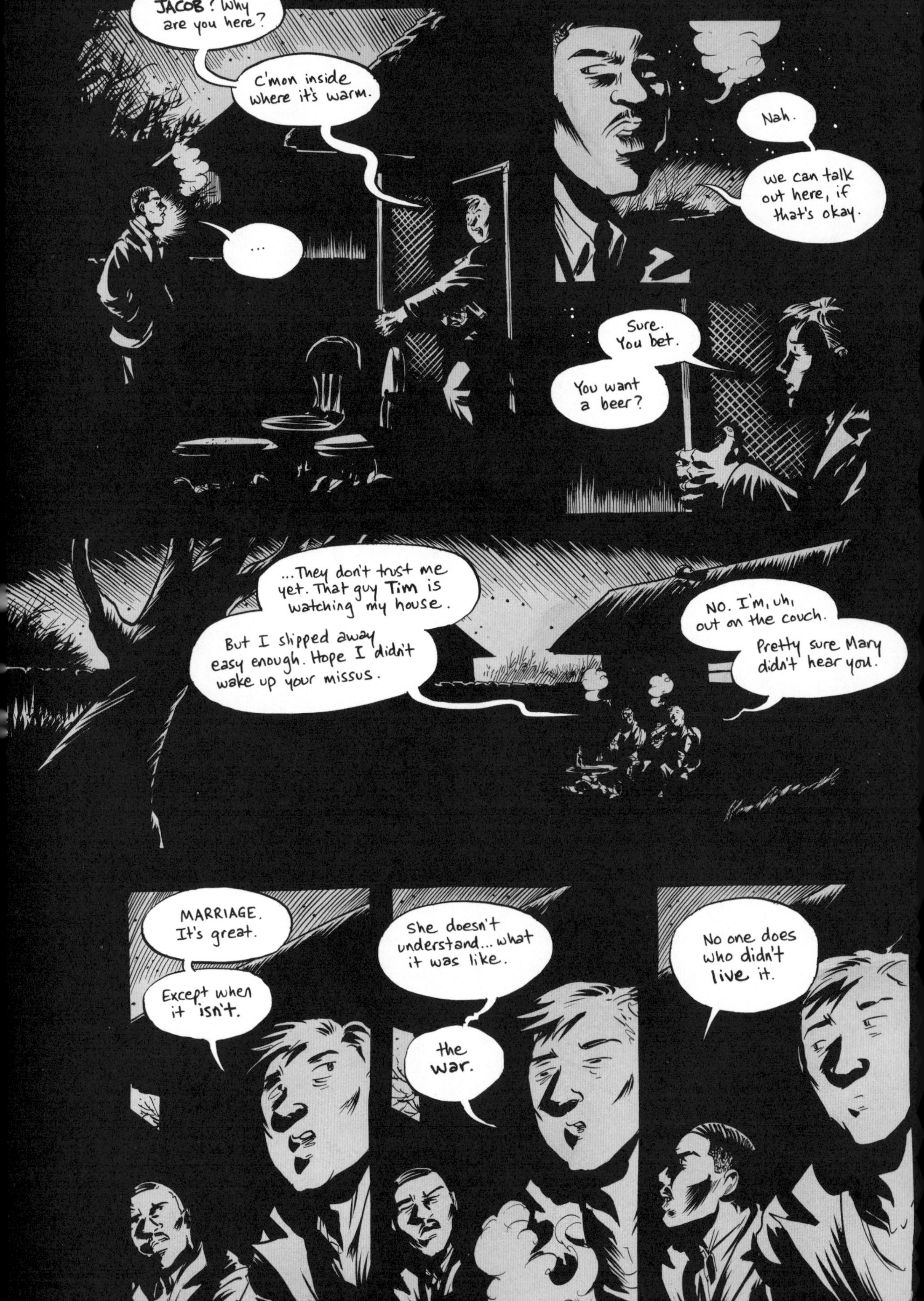
JACOB? Why are you here?
C'mon inside where it's warm.
...
Nah.
We can talk out here, if that's okay.
Sure. You bet.
You want a beer?
...They don't trust me yet. That guy Tim is watching my house.
But I slipped away easy enough. Hope I didn't wake up your missus.
NO. I'm, uh, out on the couch.
Pretty sure Mary didn't hear you.
MARRIAGE. It's great.
Except when it isn't.
She doesn't understand... what it was like.
the war.
No one does who didn't live it.

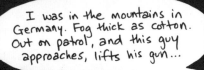

I was in the mountains in Germany. Fog thick as cotton. Out on patrol, and this guy approaches, lifts his gun...

So I sh... I shot him.

One of ours.

I killed him.

nobody knows.

It don't help to say this, I know... but those things happen in war. It's awful. Horrible. Doesn't make any goddamn sense.

But they happen.

You should tell your wife. I bet she'll understand better than you think.

my two cents, anyway.

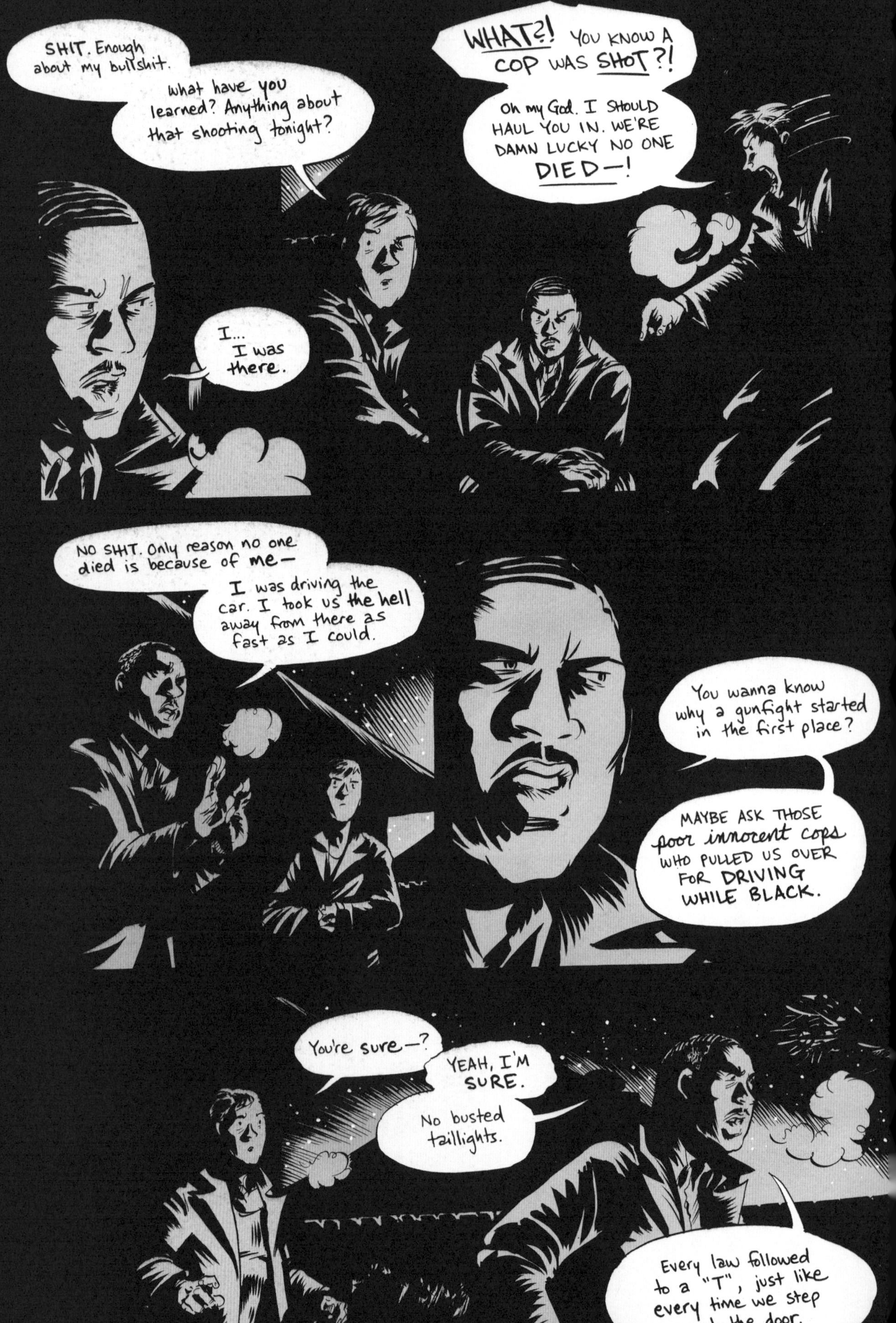
SHIT. Enough about my bullshit.
What have you learned? Anything about that shooting tonight?
I... I was there.
WHAT?! YOU KNOW A COP WAS SHOT?!
Oh my God. I SHOULD HAUL YOU IN. WE'RE DAMN LUCKY NO ONE DIED—!
NO SHIT. Only reason no one died is because of me—
I was driving the car. I took us the hell away from there as fast as I could.
You wanna know why a gunfight started in the first place?
MAYBE ASK THOSE poor innocent cops WHO PULLED US OVER FOR DRIVING WHILE BLACK.
You're sure—?
YEAH, I'M SURE.
No busted taillights.
Every law followed to a "T", just like every time we step out the door.

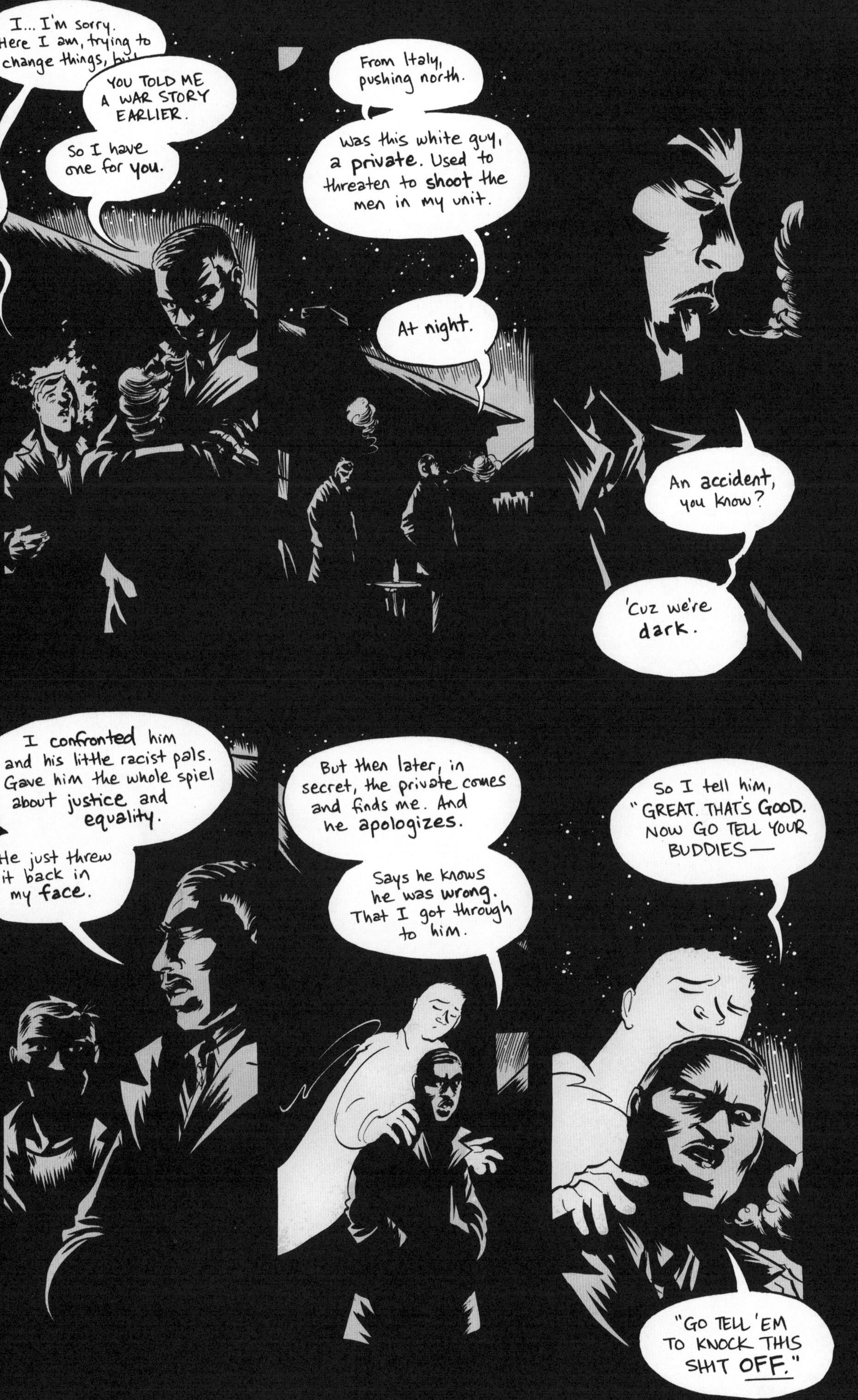
I... I'm sorry. Here I am, trying to change things,
YOU TOLD ME A WAR STORY EARLIER.
So I have one for you.
From Italy, pushing north.
Was this white guy, a private. Used to threaten to shoot the men in my unit.
At night.
An accident, you know?
'Cuz we're dark.
I confronted him and his little racist pals. Gave him the whole spiel about justice and equality.
He just threw it back in my face.
But then later, in secret, the private comes and finds me. And he apologizes.
Says he knows he was wrong. That I got through to him.
So I tell him, "GREAT. THAT'S GOOD. NOW GO TELL YOUR BUDDIES—
"GO TELL 'EM TO KNOCK THIS SHIT OFF."

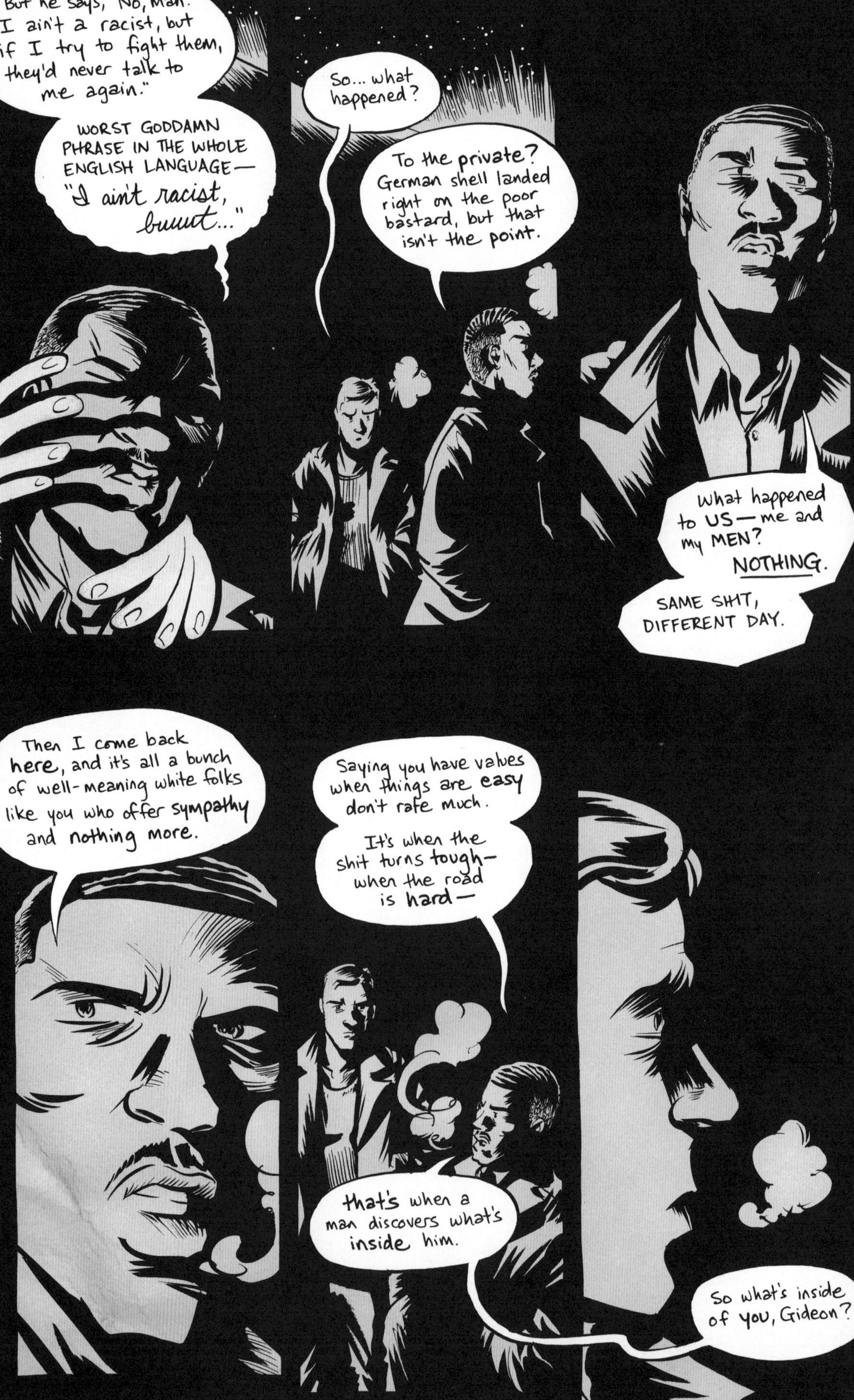
But he says, "No, man. I ain't a racist, but if I try to fight them, they'd never talk to me again."
WORST GODDAMN PHRASE IN THE WHOLE ENGLISH LANGUAGE— "I ain't racist, buuut..."
So... what happened?
To the private? German shell landed right on the poor bastard, but that isn't the point.
What happened to US—me and my MEN? NOTHING.
SAME SHIT, DIFFERENT DAY.
Then I come back here, and it's all a bunch of well-meaning white folks like you who offer sympathy and nothing more.
Saying you have values when things are easy don't rate much.
It's when the shit turns tough—when the road is hard—
that's when a man discovers what's inside him.
So what's inside of you, Gideon?

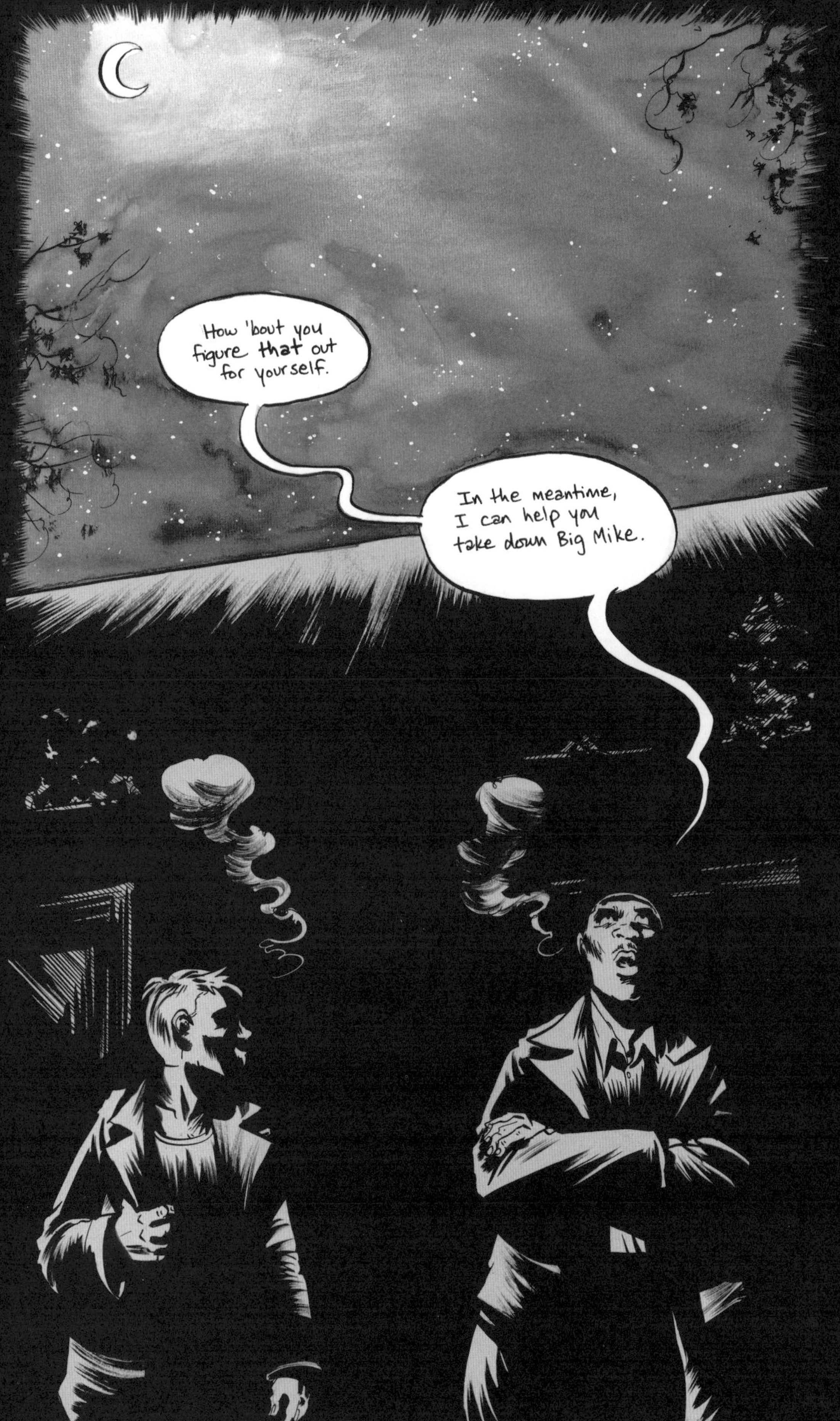
How 'bout you figure that out for yourself.
In the meantime, I can help you take down Big Mike.

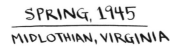

SPRING, 1945
MIDLOTHIAN, VIRGINIA

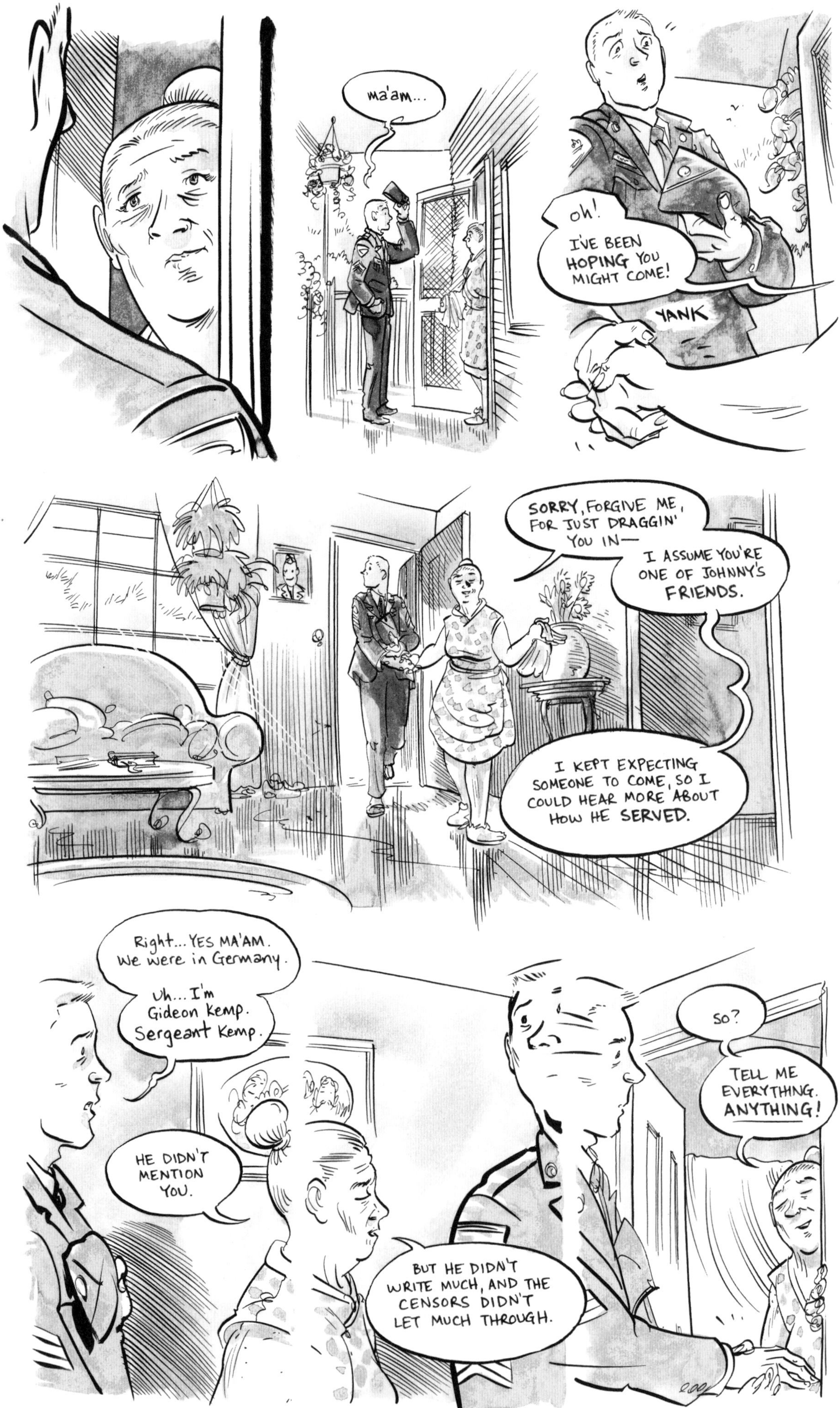
ma'am...
oh!
I'VE BEEN HOPING YOU MIGHT COME!
YANK
SORRY, FORGIVE ME, FOR JUST DRAGGIN' YOU IN—
I ASSUME YOU'RE ONE OF JOHNNY'S FRIENDS.
I KEPT EXPECTING SOMEONE TO COME, SO I COULD HEAR MORE ABOUT HOW HE SERVED.
Right... YES MA'AM. We were in Germany.
Uh... I'm Gideon Kemp. Sergeant Kemp.
HE DIDN'T MENTION YOU.
BUT HE DIDN'T WRITE MUCH, AND THE CENSORS DIDN'T LET MUCH THROUGH.
SO?
TELL ME EVERYTHING. ANYTHING!

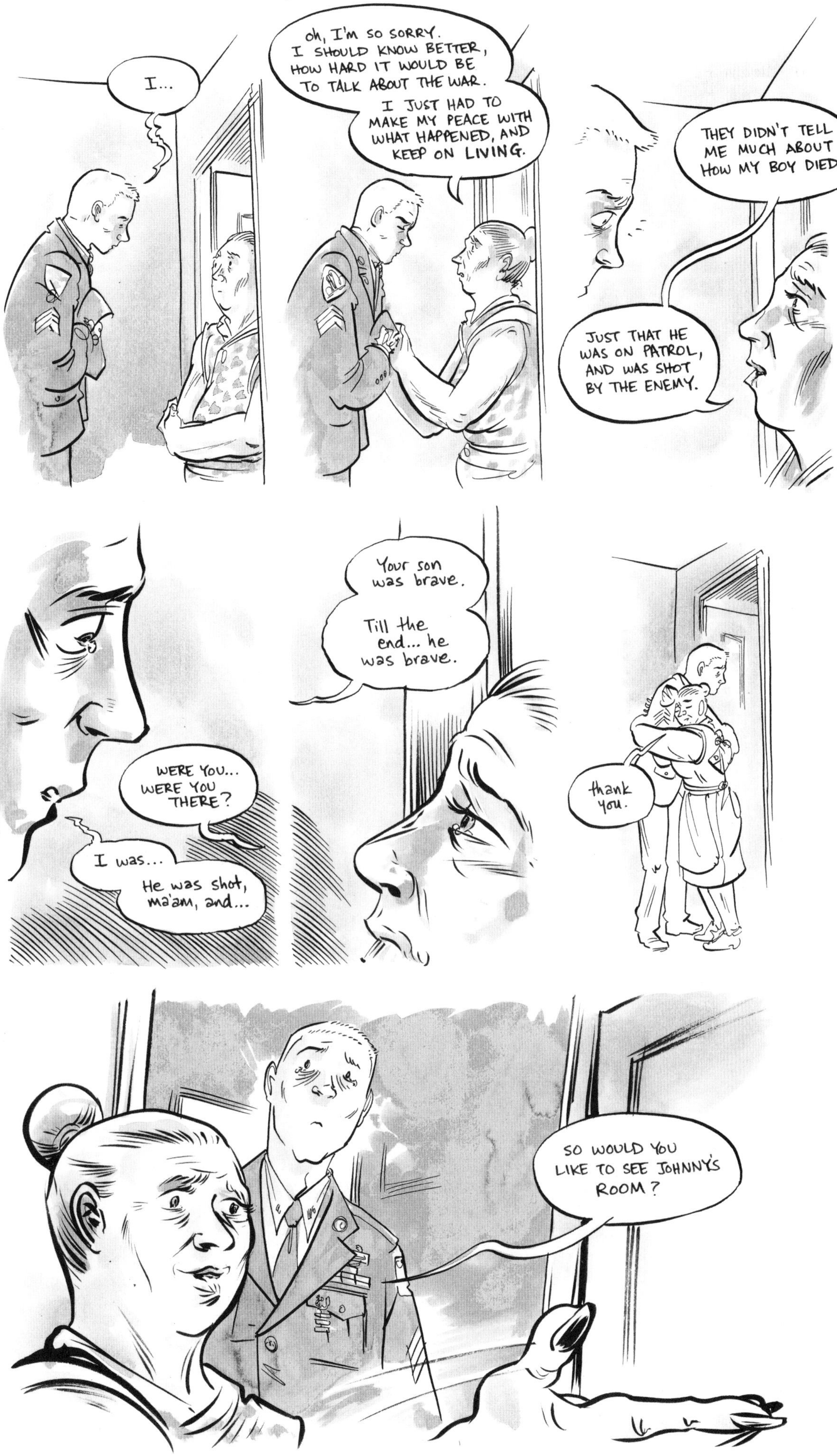
I...
oh, I'm so sorry. I should know better, how hard it would be to talk about the war.
I just had to make my peace with what happened, and keep on LIVING.
They didn't tell me much about how my boy died.
Just that he was on patrol, and was shot by the enemy.
Were you... were you there?
I was...
He was shot, ma'am, and...
Your son was brave.
Till the end... he was brave.
thank you.
So would you like to see Johnny's room?

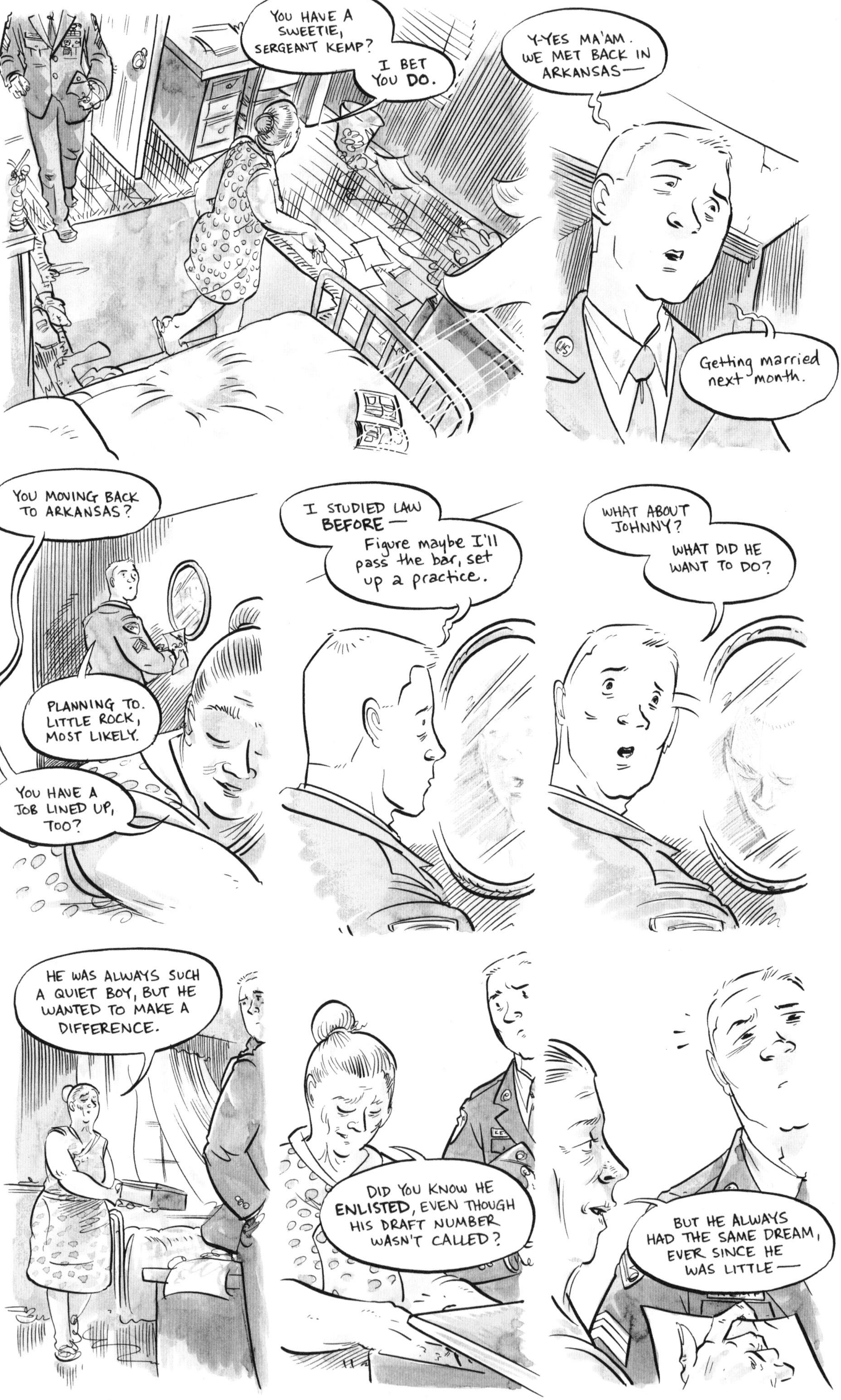
YOU HAVE A SWEETIE, SERGEANT KEMP?
I BET YOU DO.
Y-YES MA'AM. WE MET BACK IN ARKANSAS—
Getting married next month.
YOU MOVING BACK TO ARKANSAS?
PLANNING TO. LITTLE ROCK, MOST LIKELY.
YOU HAVE A JOB LINED UP, TOO?
I STUDIED LAW BEFORE—
Figure maybe I'll pass the bar, set up a practice.
WHAT ABOUT JOHNNY?
WHAT DID HE WANT TO DO?
HE WAS ALWAYS SUCH A QUIET BOY, BUT HE WANTED TO MAKE A DIFFERENCE.
DID YOU KNOW HE ENLISTED, EVEN THOUGH HIS DRAFT NUMBER WASN'T CALLED?
BUT HE ALWAYS HAD THE SAME DREAM, EVER SINCE HE WAS LITTLE—

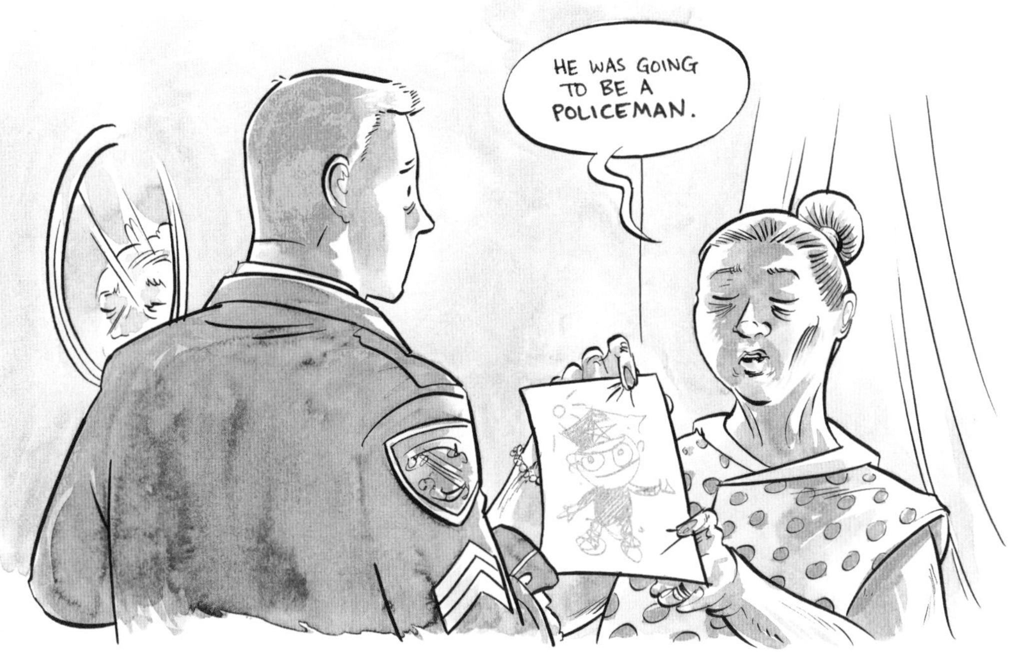
HE WAS GOING TO BE A POLICEMAN.

DECEMBER, 1946

LITTLE ROCK, ARKANSAS

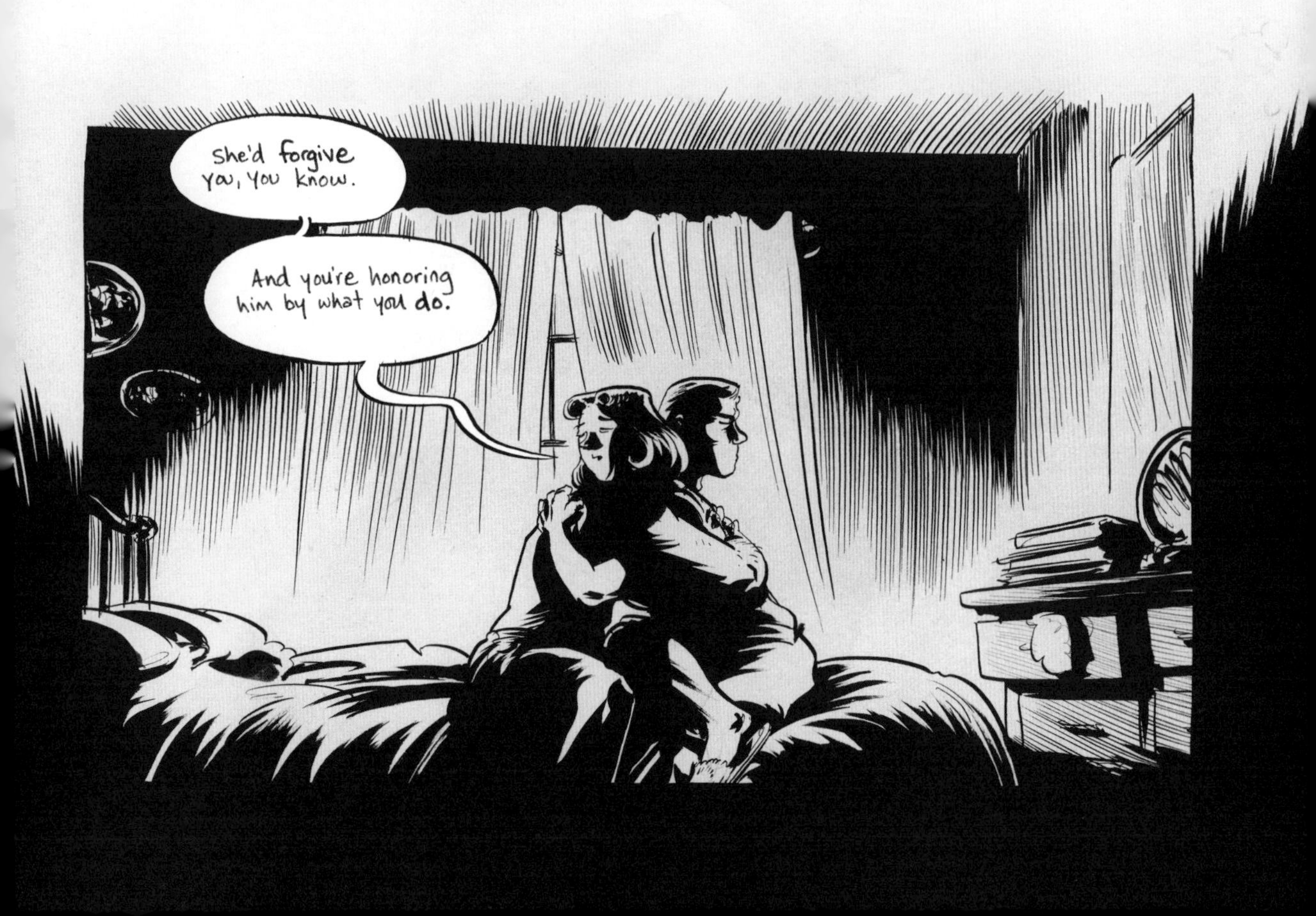
She'd forgive you, you know.
And you're honoring him by what you do.

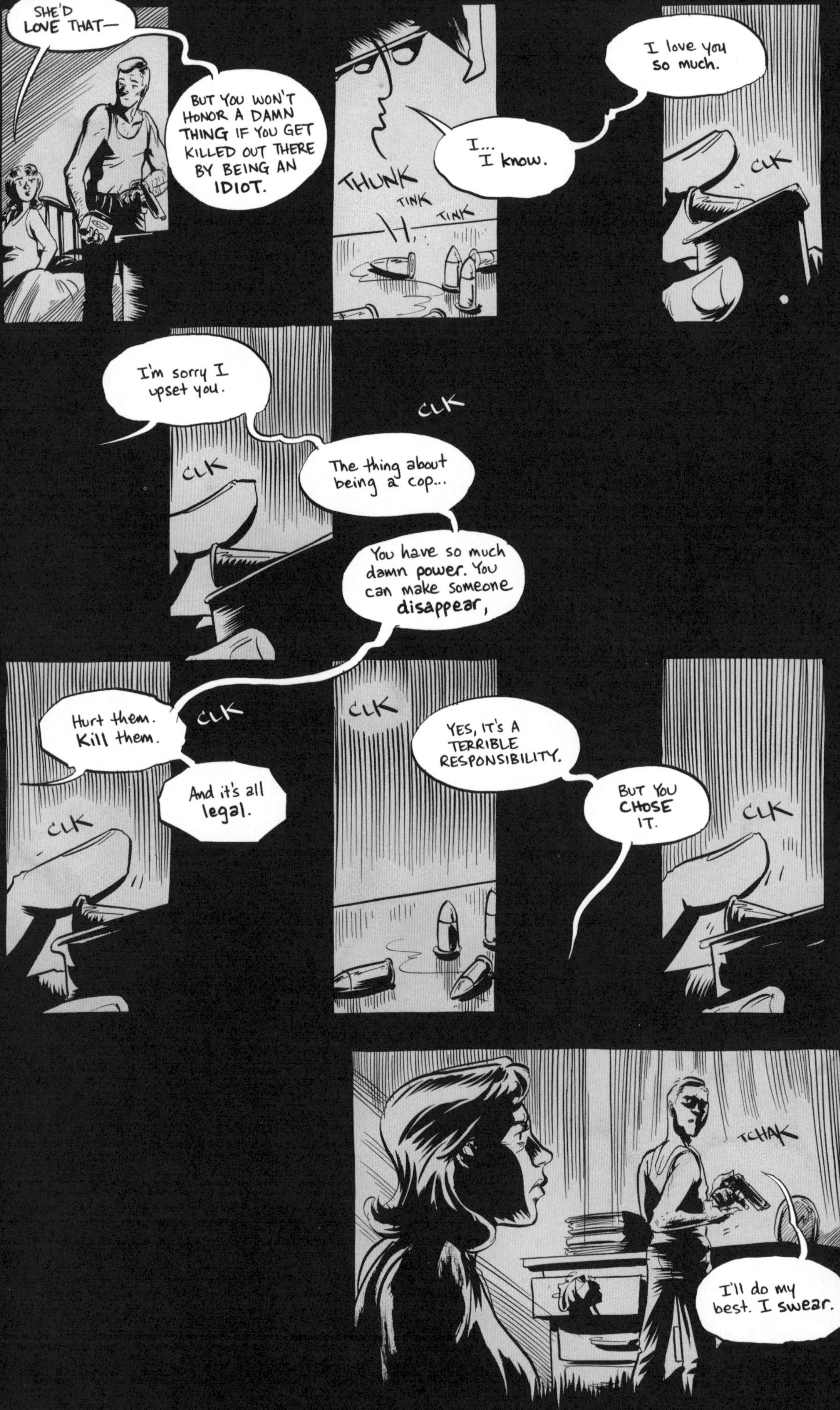
SHE'D LOVE THAT—
BUT YOU WON'T HONOR A DAMN THING IF YOU GET KILLED OUT THERE BY BEING AN IDIOT.
THUNK
TINK
TINK
I... I know.
I love you so much.
CLK
I'm sorry I upset you.
CLK
CLK
The thing about being a cop...
You have so much damn power. You can make someone disappear,
Hurt them. Kill them.
CLK
And it's all legal.
CLK
CLK
YES, IT'S A TERRIBLE RESPONSIBILITY.
BUT YOU CHOSE IT.
CLK
TCHAK
I'll do my best. I swear.

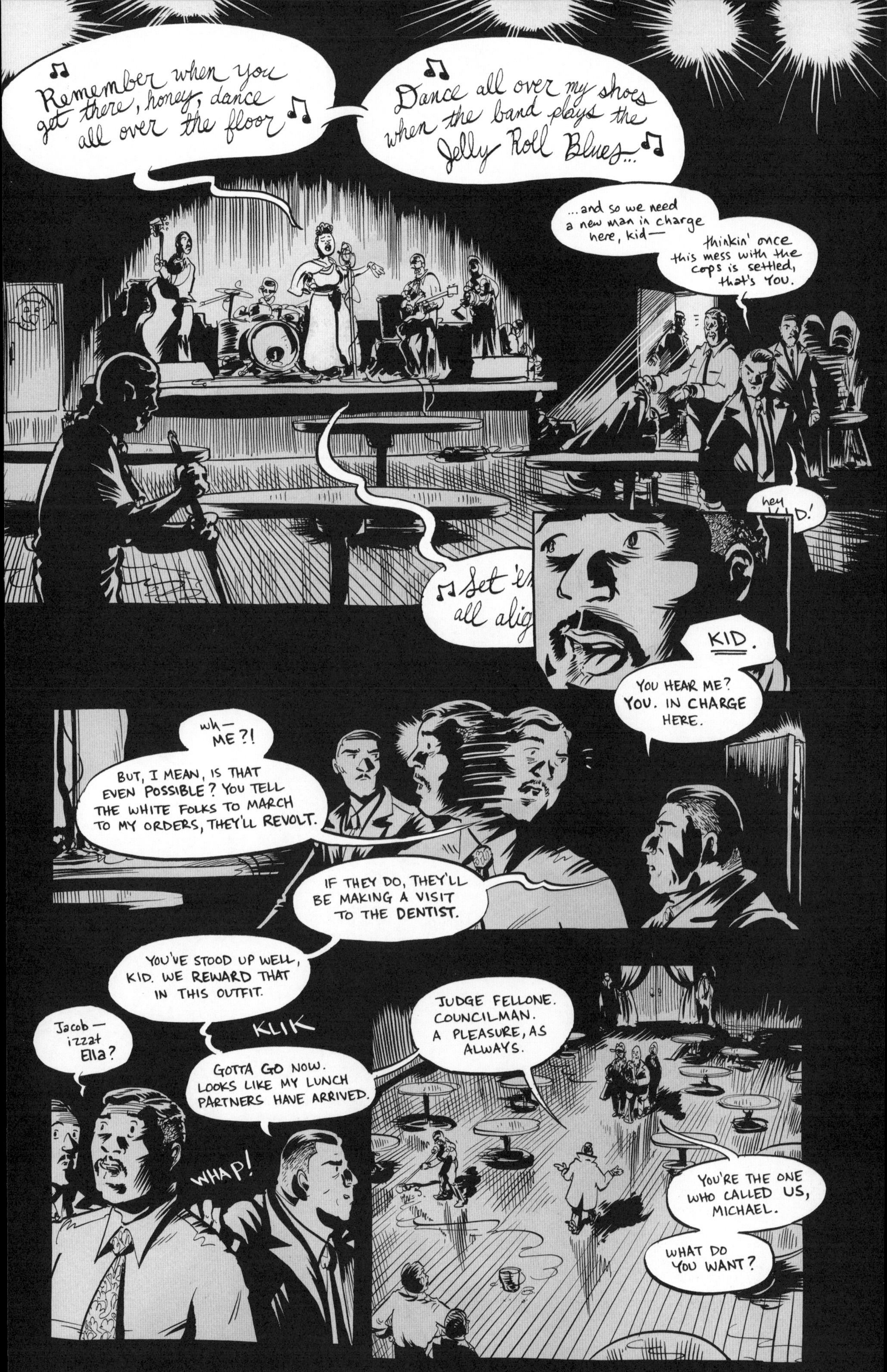
♫ Remember when you get there, honey, dance all over the floor ♫
♫ Dance all over my shoes when the band plays the Jelly Roll Blues... ♫
...and so we need a new man in charge here, kid—
thinkin' once this mess with the cops is settled, that's YOU.
hey KID!
♫ Set 'em all alig
KID.
YOU HEAR ME? YOU. IN CHARGE HERE.
wh— ME?!
BUT, I MEAN, IS THAT EVEN POSSIBLE? YOU TELL THE WHITE FOLKS TO MARCH TO MY ORDERS, THEY'LL REVOLT.
IF THEY DO, THEY'LL BE MAKING A VISIT TO THE DENTIST.
YOU'VE STOOD UP WELL, KID. WE REWARD THAT IN THIS OUTFIT.
KLIK
GOTTA GO NOW. LOOKS LIKE MY LUNCH PARTNERS HAVE ARRIVED.
Jacob— izzat Ella?
WHAP!
JUDGE FELLONE. COUNCILMAN. A PLEASURE, AS ALWAYS.
YOU'RE THE ONE WHO CALLED US, MICHAEL.
WHAT DO YOU WANT?

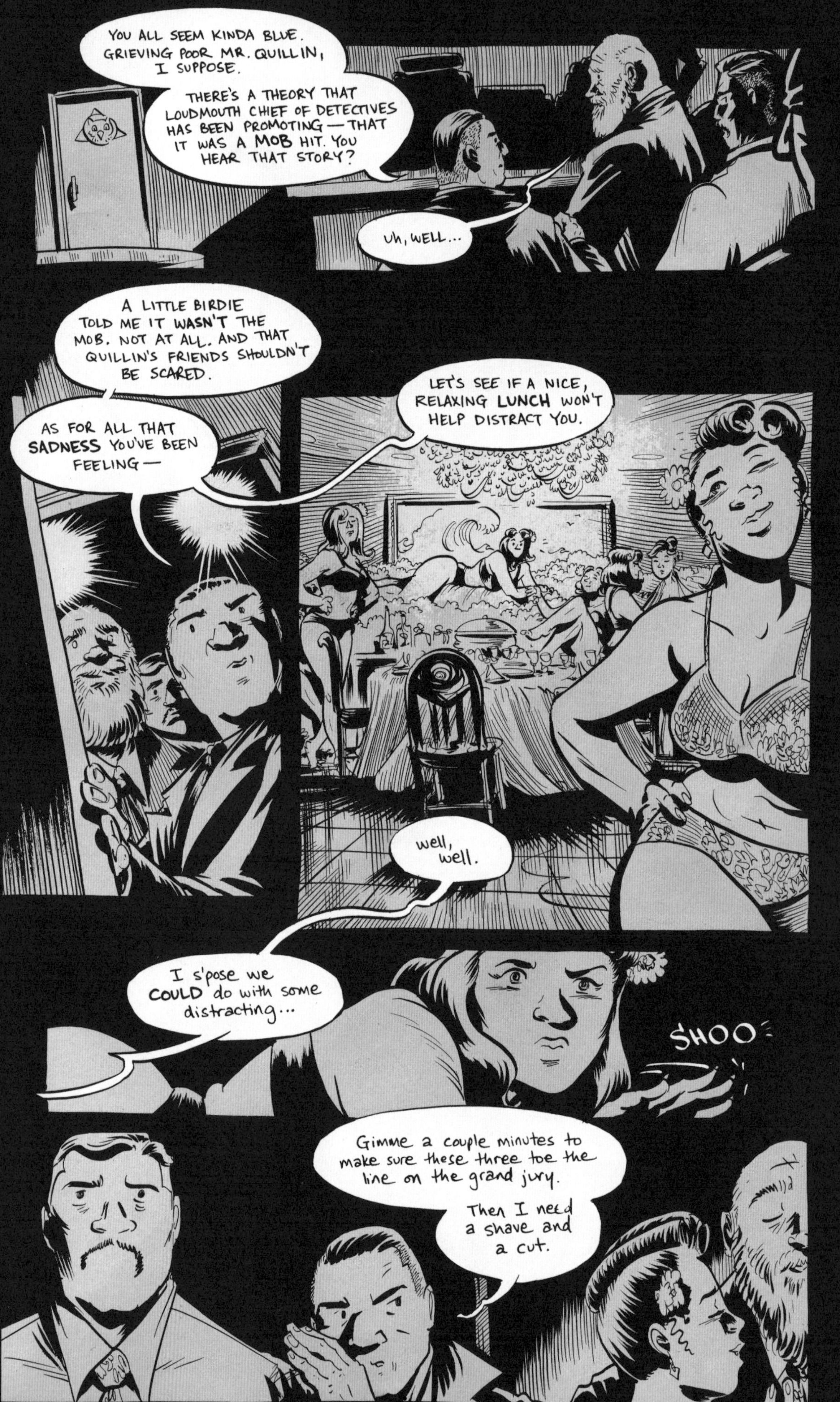

YOU ALL SEEM KINDA BLUE. GRIEVING POOR MR. QUILLIN, I SUPPOSE.
THERE'S A THEORY THAT LOUDMOUTH CHIEF OF DETECTIVES HAS BEEN PROMOTING — THAT IT WAS A MOB HIT. YOU HEAR THAT STORY?
Uh, WELL...
A LITTLE BIRDIE TOLD ME IT WASN'T THE MOB. NOT AT ALL. AND THAT QUILLIN'S FRIENDS SHOULDN'T BE SCARED.
AS FOR ALL THAT SADNESS YOU'VE BEEN FEELING—
LET'S SEE IF A NICE, RELAXING LUNCH WON'T HELP DISTRACT YOU.
well, well.
I s'pose we COULD do with some distracting...
SHOO
Gimme a couple minutes to make sure these three toe the line on the grand jury.
Then I need a shave and a cut.

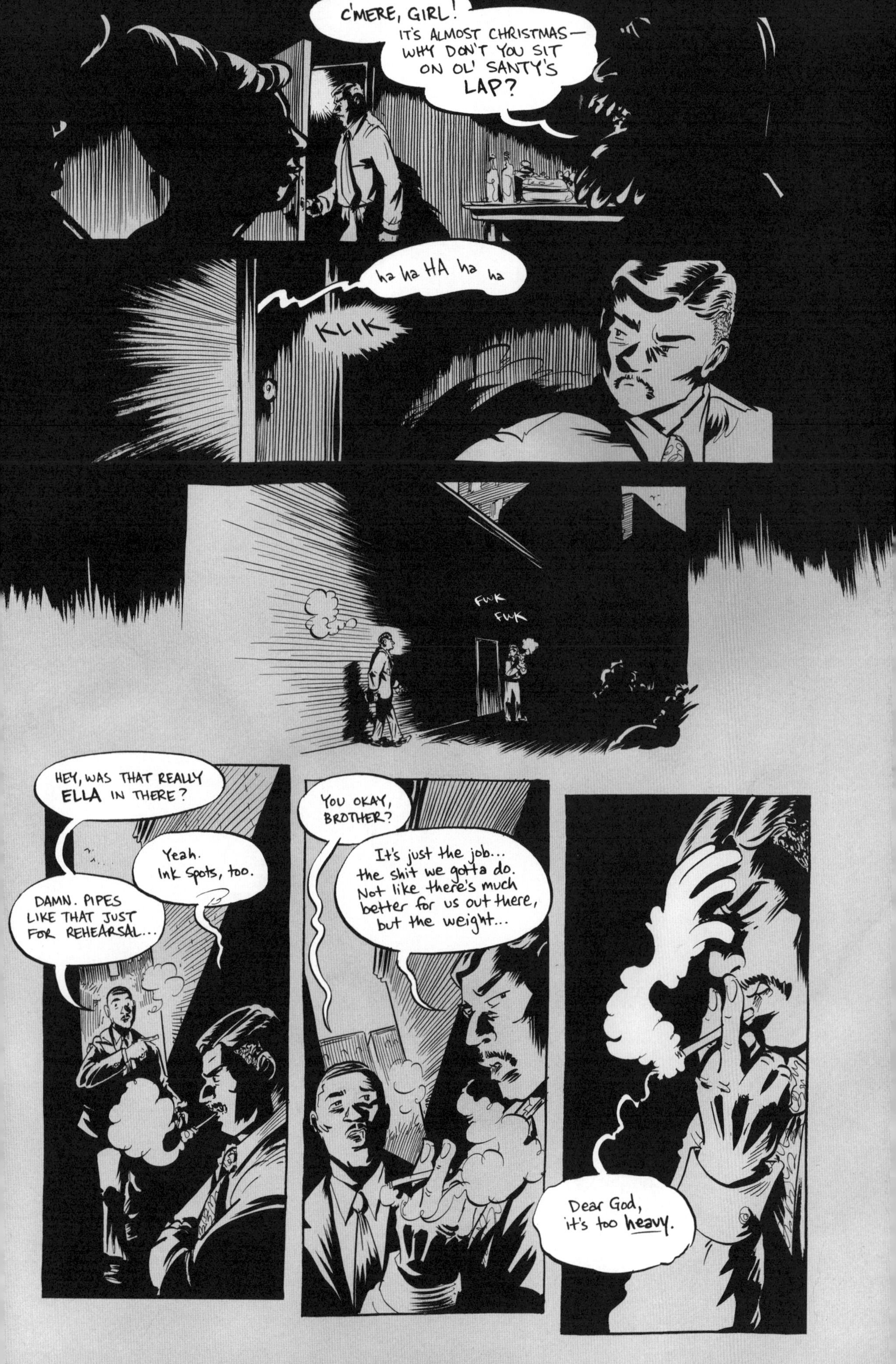
C'MERE, GIRL!
IT'S ALMOST CHRISTMAS— WHY DON'T YOU SIT ON OL' SANTY'S LAP?
ha ha HA ha ha
KLIK
FWK
FWK
HEY, WAS THAT REALLY ELLA IN THERE?
Yeah. Ink Spots, too.
DAMN. PIPES LIKE THAT JUST FOR REHEARSAL...
YOU OKAY, BROTHER?
It's just the job... the shit we gotta do. Not like there's much better for us out there, but the weight...
Dear God, it's too heavy.

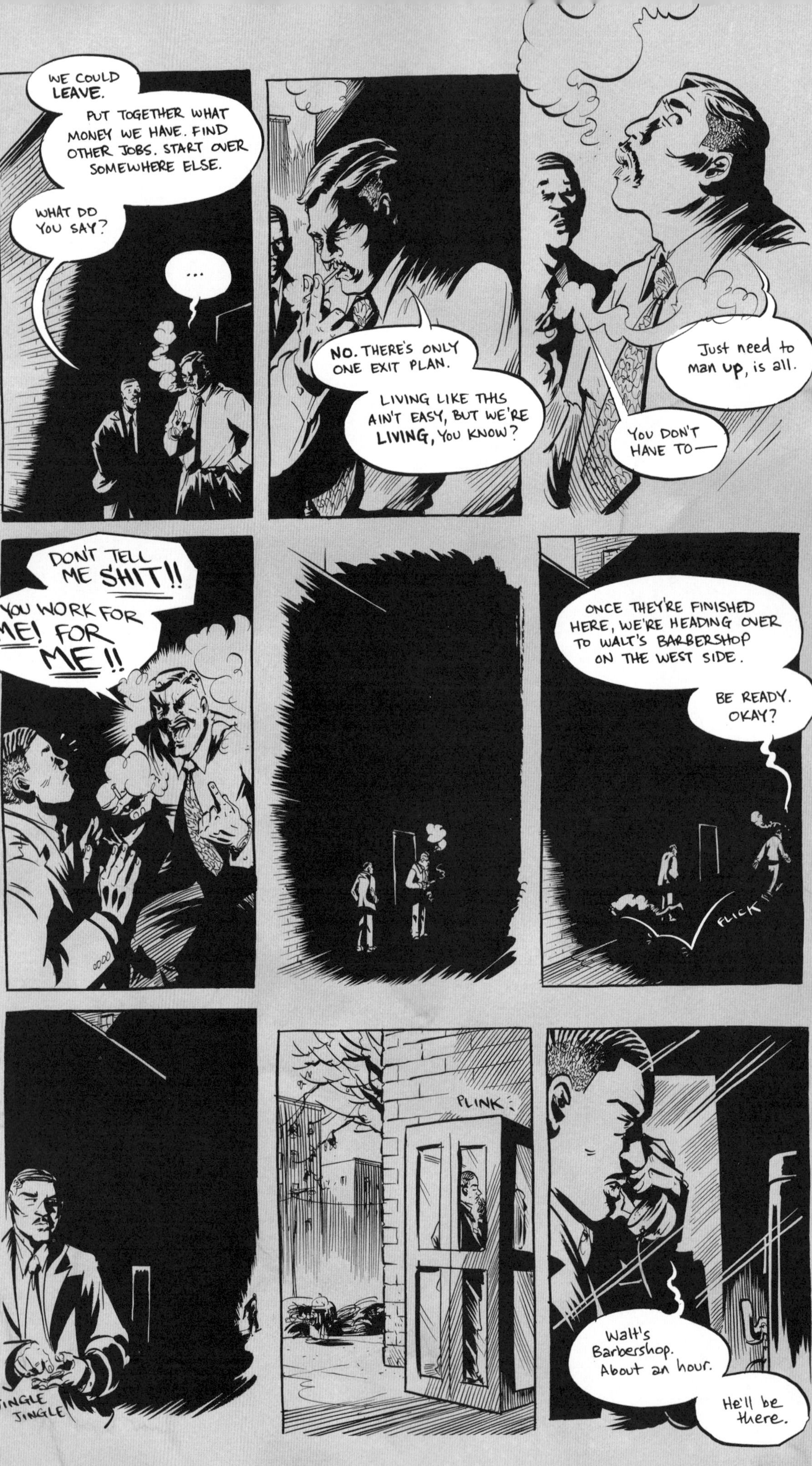
WE COULD LEAVE.
PUT TOGETHER WHAT MONEY WE HAVE. FIND OTHER JOBS. START OVER SOMEWHERE ELSE.
WHAT DO YOU SAY?
...
NO. THERE'S ONLY ONE EXIT PLAN.
LIVING LIKE THIS AIN'T EASY, BUT WE'RE LIVING, YOU KNOW?
Just need to man up, is all.
YOU DON'T HAVE TO—
DON'T TELL ME SHIT!!
YOU WORK FOR ME! FOR ME!!
ONCE THEY'RE FINISHED HERE, WE'RE HEADING OVER TO WALT'S BARBERSHOP ON THE WEST SIDE.
BE READY. OKAY?
FLICK
JINGLE JINGLE
PLINK
Walt's Barbershop. About an hour.
He'll be there.

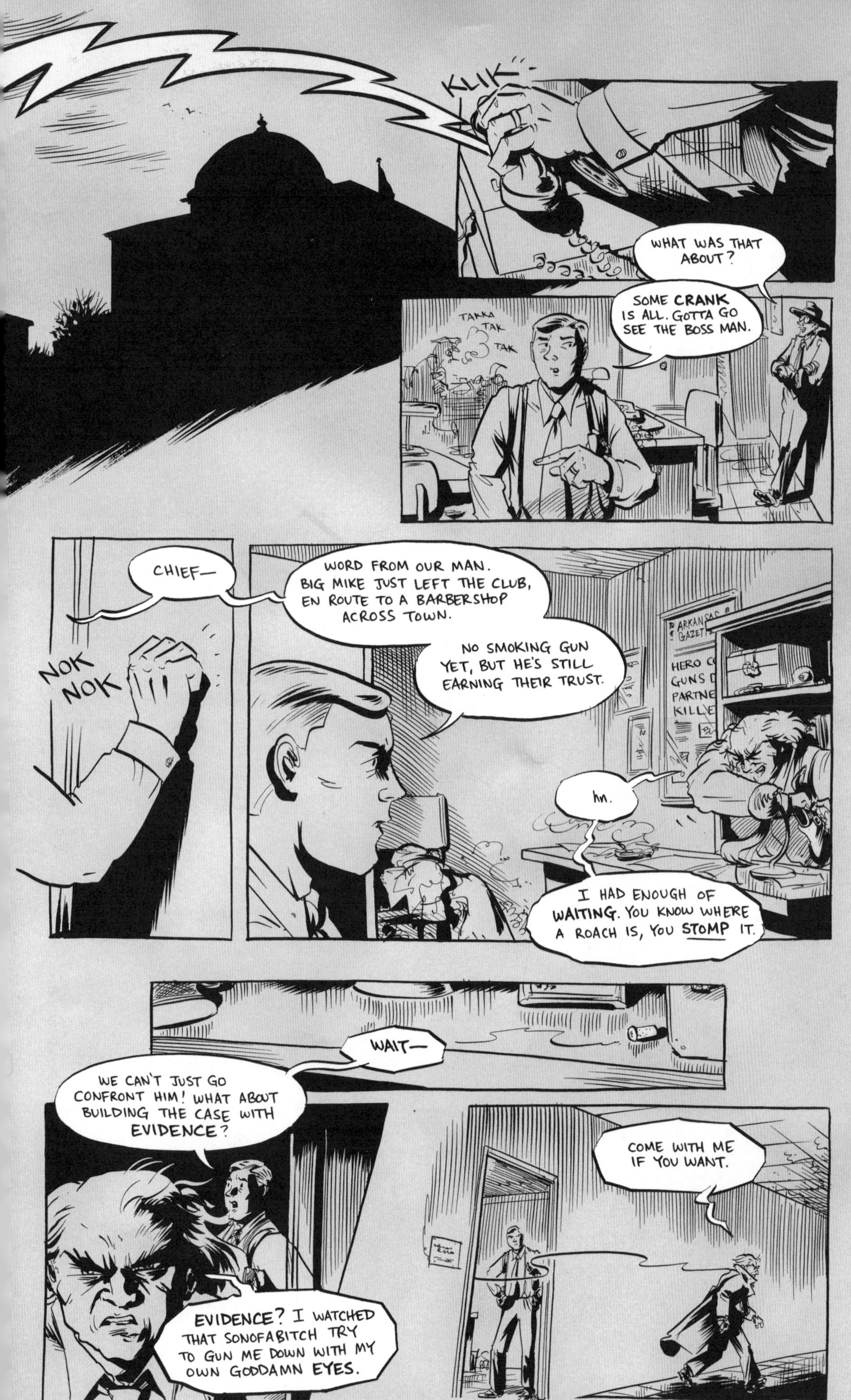
KLIK
WHAT WAS THAT ABOUT?
SOME CRANK IS ALL. GOTTA GO SEE THE BOSS MAN.
TAKKA TAK TAK
CHIEF—
NOK NOK
WORD FROM OUR MAN. BIG MIKE JUST LEFT THE CLUB, EN ROUTE TO A BARBERSHOP ACROSS TOWN.
NO SMOKING GUN YET, BUT HE'S STILL EARNING THEIR TRUST.
ARKANSAS GAZETTE
HERO CO
GUNS D
PARTNE
KILLE
hn.
I HAD ENOUGH OF WAITING. YOU KNOW WHERE A ROACH IS, YOU STOMP IT.
WAIT—
WE CAN'T JUST GO CONFRONT HIM! WHAT ABOUT BUILDING THE CASE WITH EVIDENCE?
EVIDENCE? I WATCHED THAT SONOFABITCH TRY TO GUN ME DOWN WITH MY OWN GODDAMN EYES.
COME WITH ME IF YOU WANT.

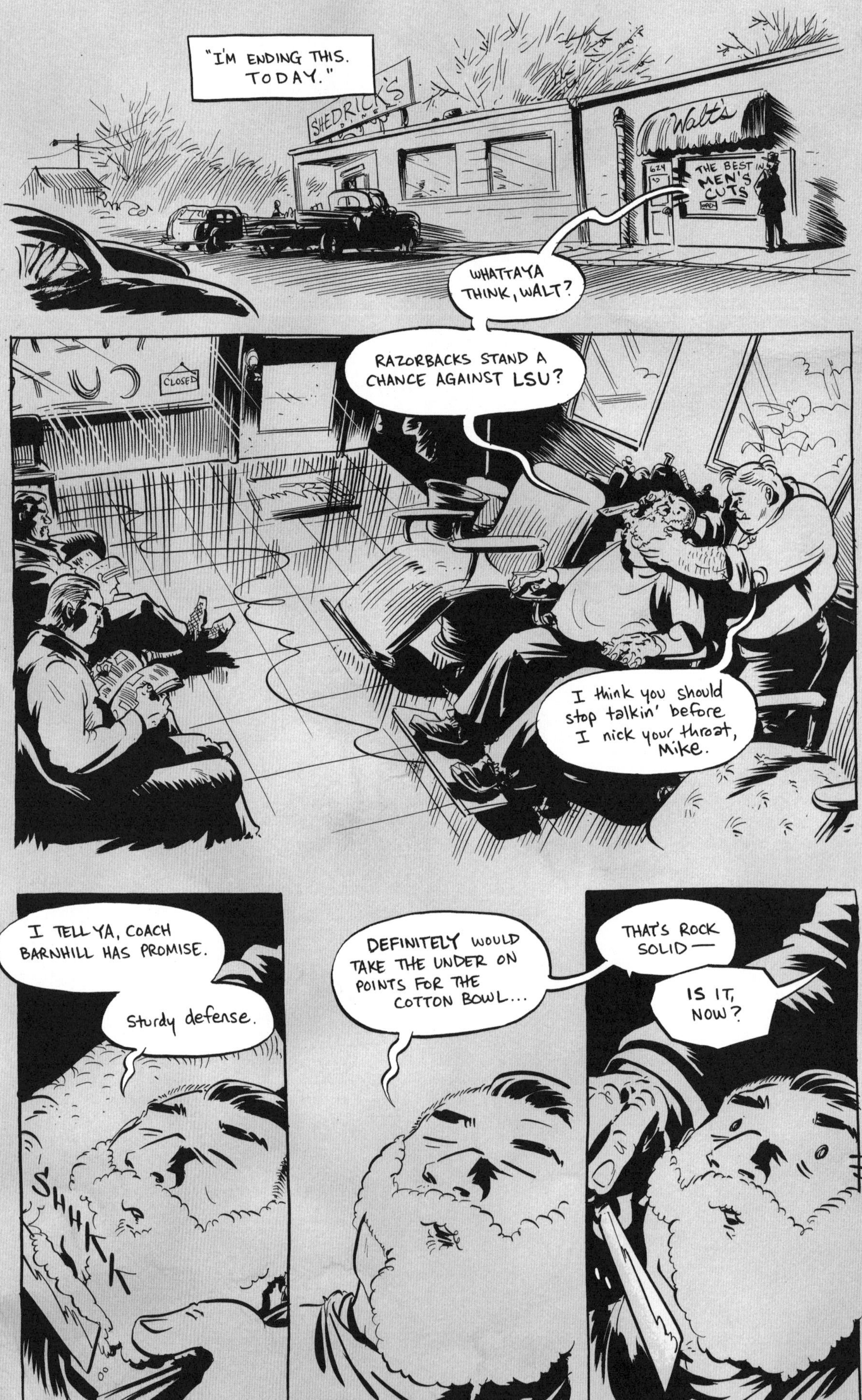
"I'M ENDING THIS. TODAY."
SHEDRICK'S DINER
Walt's
624
THE BEST IN MEN'S CUTS
OPEN
WHATTAYA THINK, WALT?
CLOSED
RAZORBACKS STAND A CHANCE AGAINST LSU?
I think you should stop talkin' before I nick your throat, Mike.
I TELL YA, COACH BARNHILL HAS PROMISE.
Sturdy defense.
SHHKK
DEFINITELY WOULD TAKE THE UNDER ON POINTS FOR THE COTTON BOWL...
THAT'S ROCK SOLID—
IS IT, NOW?

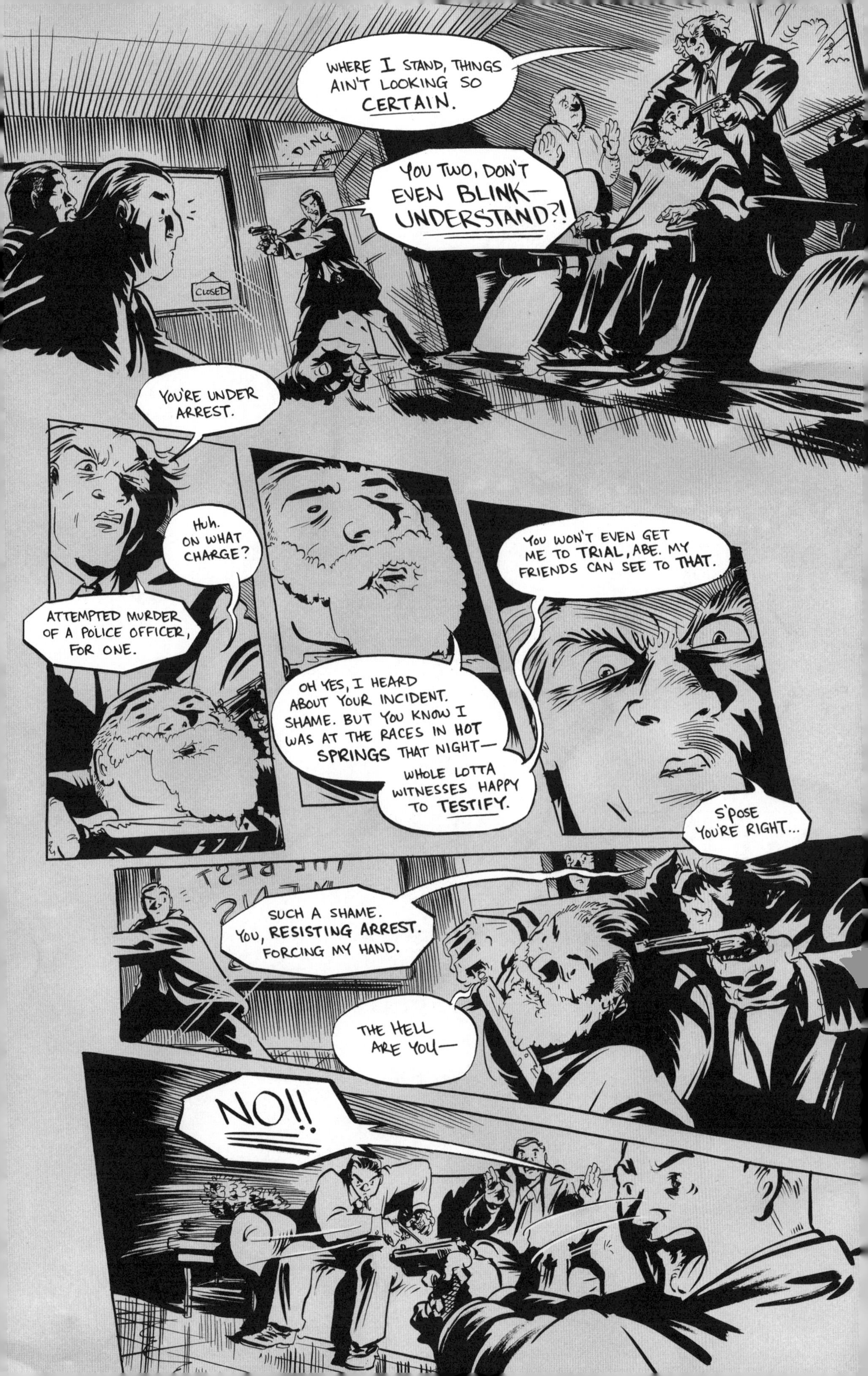
WHERE I STAND, THINGS AIN'T LOOKING SO CERTAIN.
DING
YOU TWO, DON'T EVEN BLINK— UNDERSTAND?!
CLOSED
YOU'RE UNDER ARREST.
Huh. ON WHAT CHARGE?
ATTEMPTED MURDER OF A POLICE OFFICER, FOR ONE.
OH YES, I HEARD ABOUT YOUR INCIDENT. SHAME. BUT YOU KNOW I WAS AT THE RACES IN HOT SPRINGS THAT NIGHT—
WHOLE LOTTA WITNESSES HAPPY TO TESTIFY.
YOU WON'T EVEN GET ME TO TRIAL, ABE. MY FRIENDS CAN SEE TO THAT.
S'POSE YOU'RE RIGHT...
SUCH A SHAME. YOU, RESISTING ARREST. FORCING MY HAND.
THE HELL ARE YOU—
NO!!

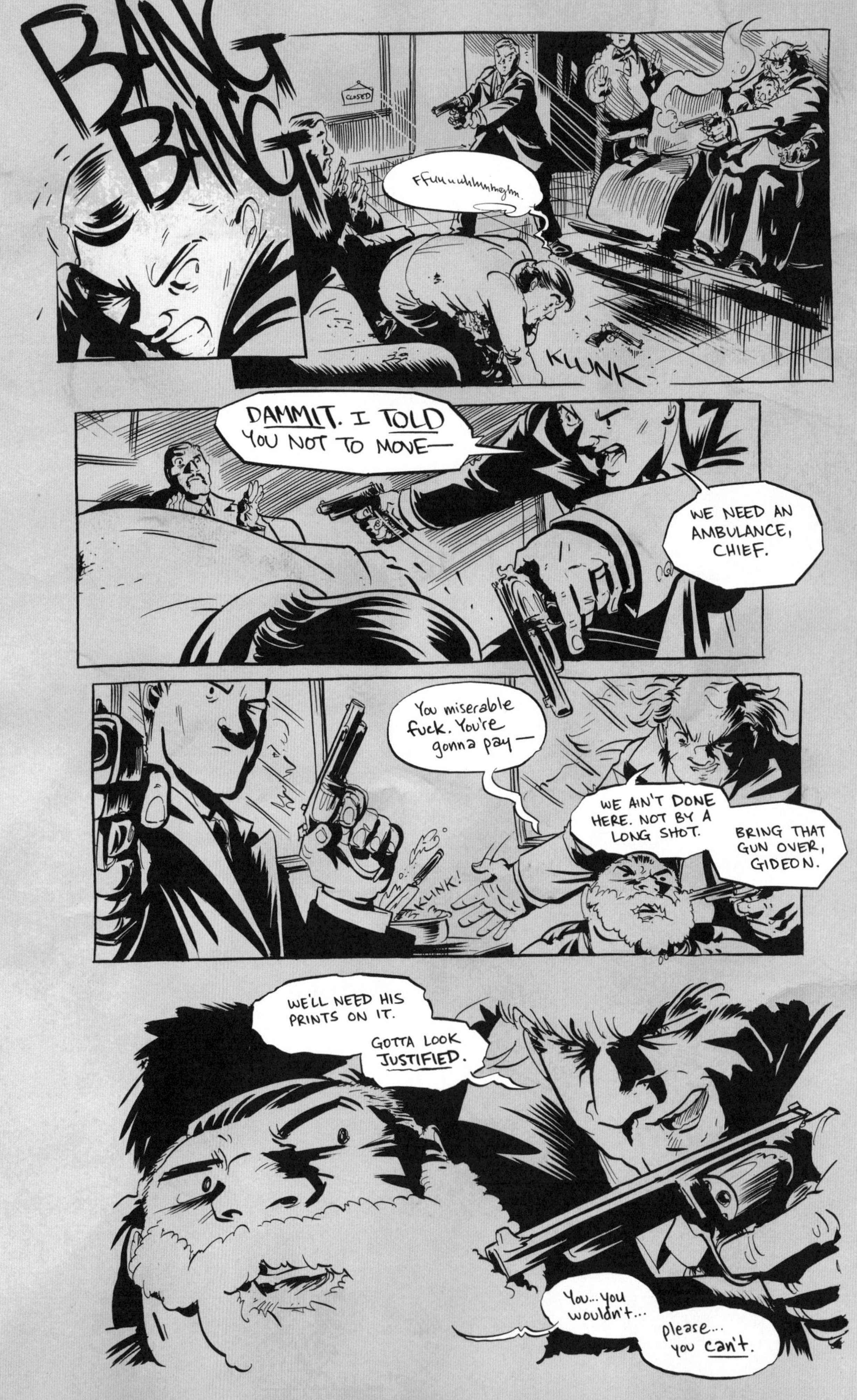
BANG BANG
Ffuuuuuhhhmmghm.
KLUNK
DAMMIT. I TOLD YOU NOT TO MOVE—
WE NEED AN AMBULANCE, CHIEF.
You miserable fuck. You're gonna pay—
KLUNK!
WE AIN'T DONE HERE. NOT BY A LONG SHOT.
BRING THAT GUN OVER, GIDEON.
WE'LL NEED HIS PRINTS ON IT.
GOTTA LOOK JUSTIFIED.
You... you wouldn't...
please... you can't.

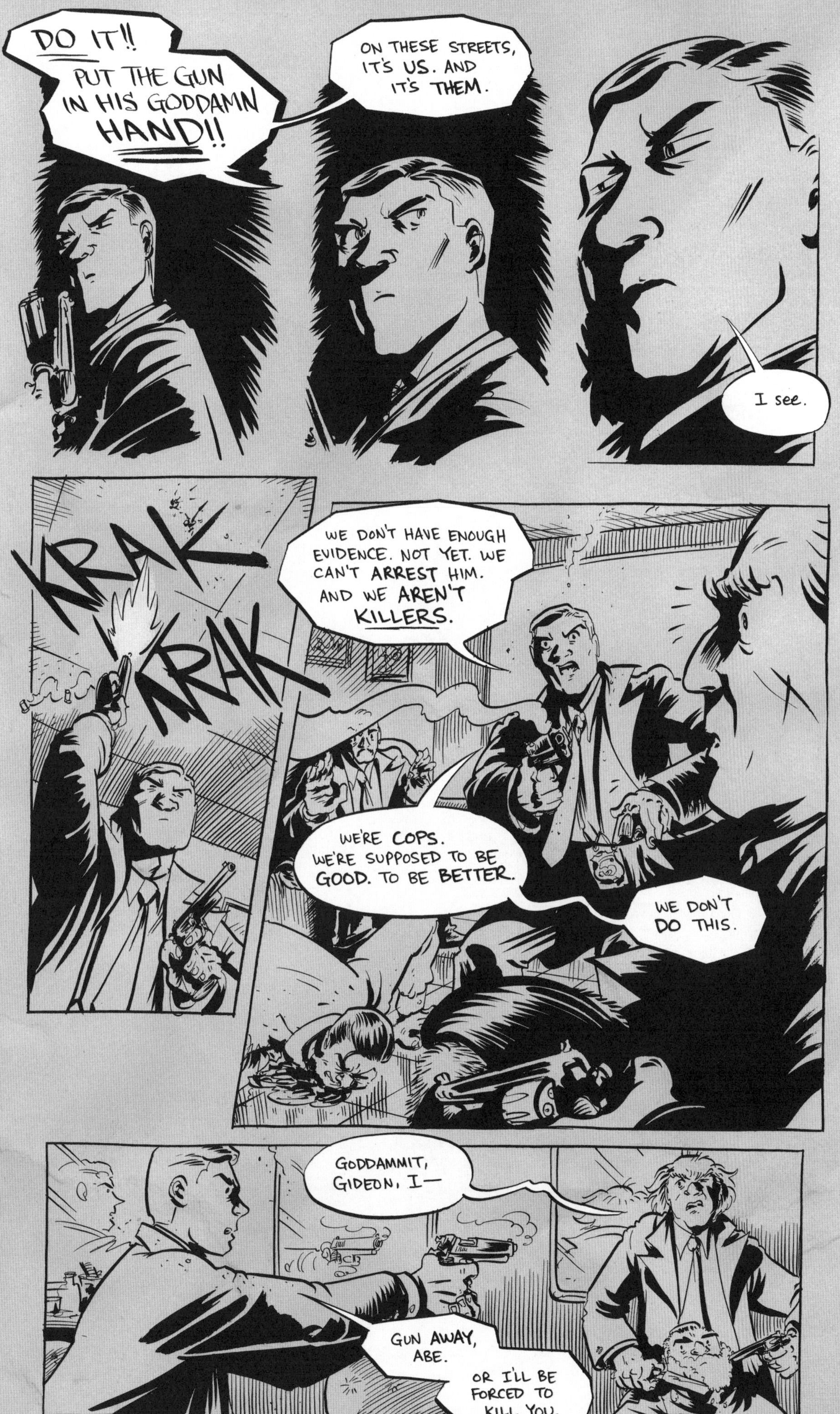
DO IT!! PUT THE GUN IN HIS GODDAMN HAND!!
ON THESE STREETS, IT'S US. AND IT'S THEM.
I see.
KRAK
KRAK
WE DON'T HAVE ENOUGH EVIDENCE. NOT YET. WE CAN'T ARREST HIM. AND WE AREN'T KILLERS.
WE'RE COPS. WE'RE SUPPOSED TO BE GOOD. TO BE BETTER.
WE DON'T DO THIS.
GODDAMMIT, GIDEON, I—
GUN AWAY, ABE.
OR I'LL BE FORCED TO KILL YOU.

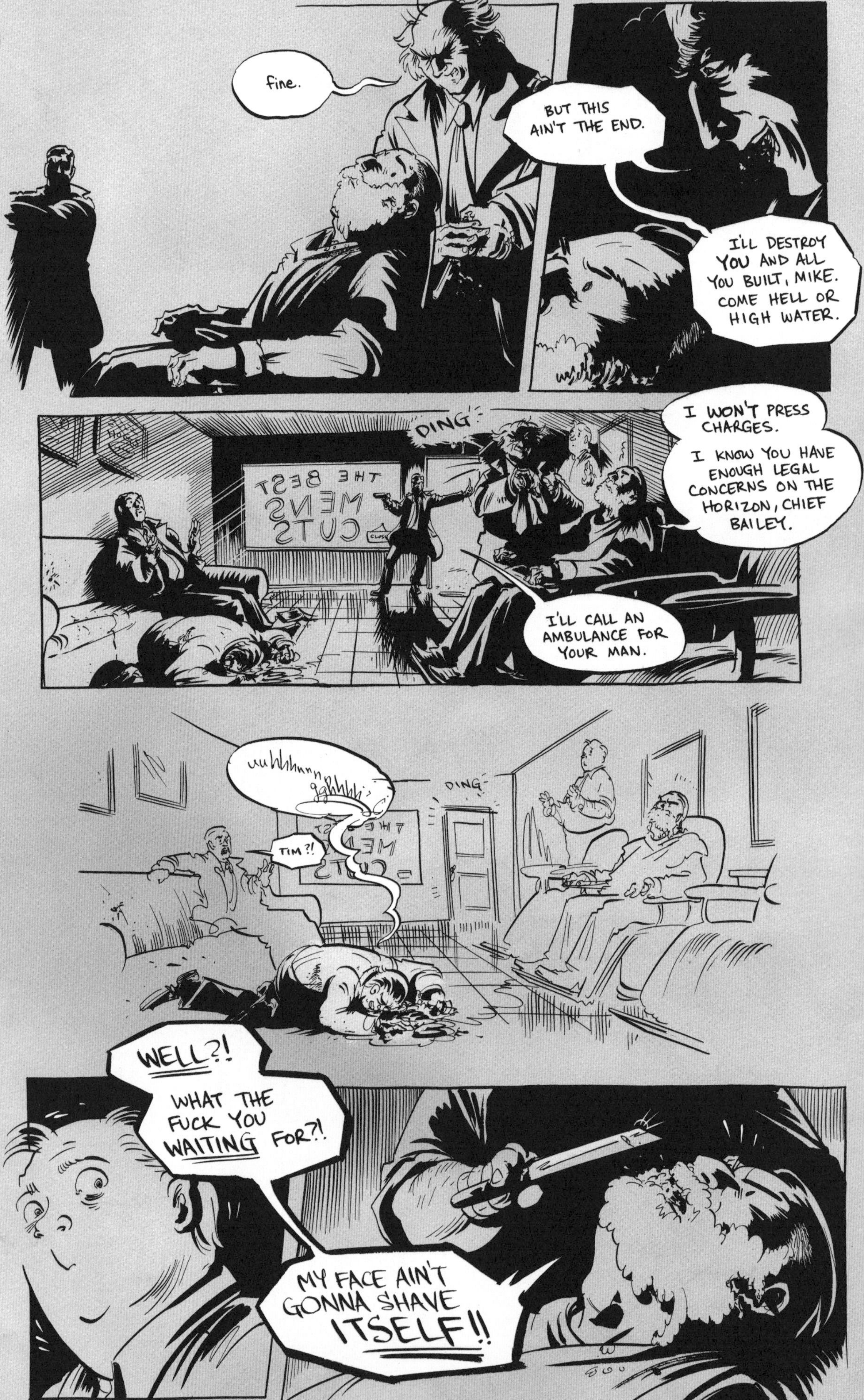
fine.
BUT THIS AIN'T THE END.
I'LL DESTROY YOU AND ALL YOU BUILT, MIKE. COME HELL OR HIGH WATER.
DING
THE BEST MENS CUTS
I WON'T PRESS CHARGES.
I KNOW YOU HAVE ENOUGH LEGAL CONCERNS ON THE HORIZON, CHIEF BAILEY.
I'LL CALL AN AMBULANCE FOR YOUR MAN.
uuhhhnnnggghhhh?
DING
TIM?!
WELL?!
WHAT THE FUCK YOU WAITING FOR?!
MY FACE AIN'T GONNA SHAVE ITSELF!!

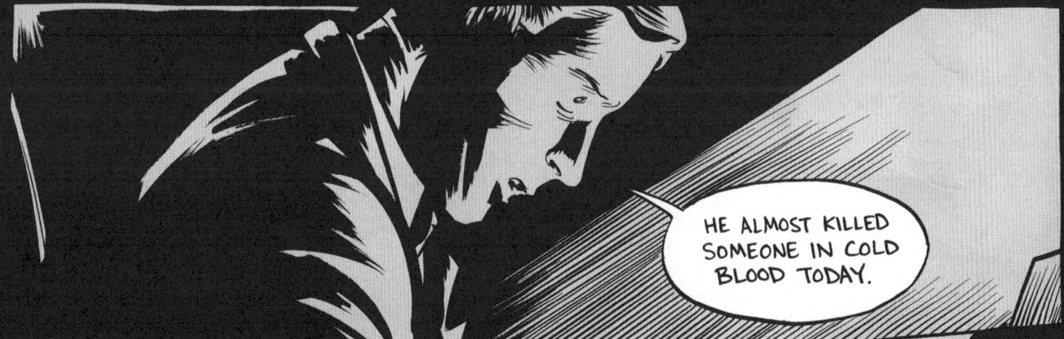
HE ALMOST KILLED SOMEONE IN COLD BLOOD TODAY.

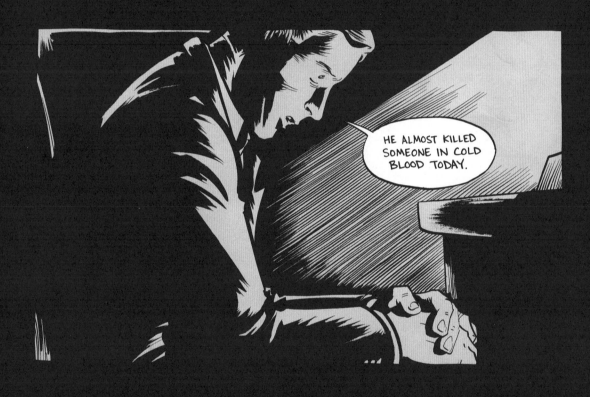

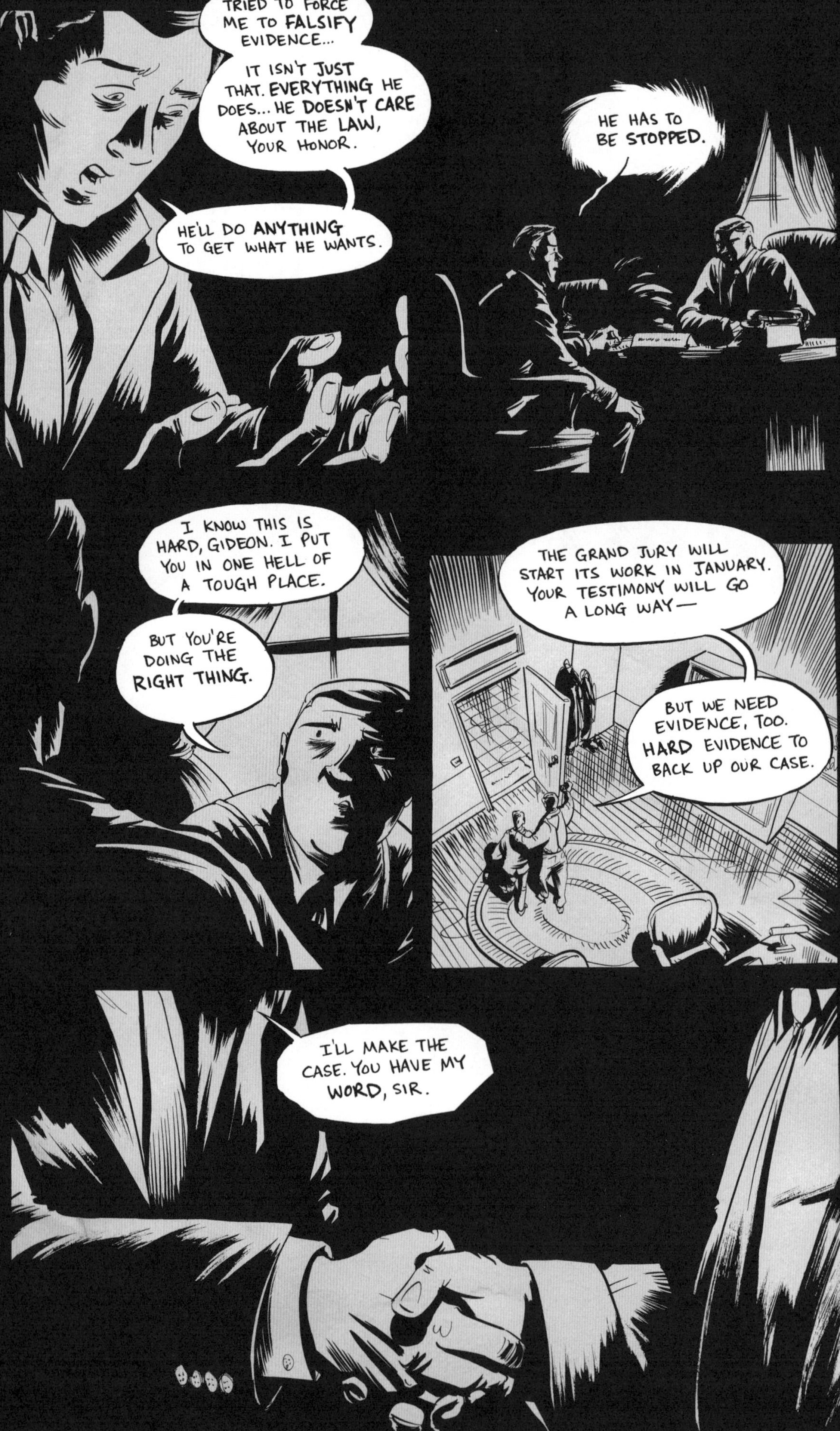
TRIED TO FORCE ME TO FALSIFY EVIDENCE...
IT ISN'T JUST THAT. EVERYTHING HE DOES... HE DOESN'T CARE ABOUT THE LAW, YOUR HONOR.
HE'LL DO ANYTHING TO GET WHAT HE WANTS.
HE HAS TO BE STOPPED.
I KNOW THIS IS HARD, GIDEON. I PUT YOU IN ONE HELL OF A TOUGH PLACE.
BUT YOU'RE DOING THE RIGHT THING.
THE GRAND JURY WILL START ITS WORK IN JANUARY. YOUR TESTIMONY WILL GO A LONG WAY—
BUT WE NEED EVIDENCE, TOO. HARD EVIDENCE TO BACK UP OUR CASE.
I'LL MAKE THE CASE. YOU HAVE MY WORD, SIR.

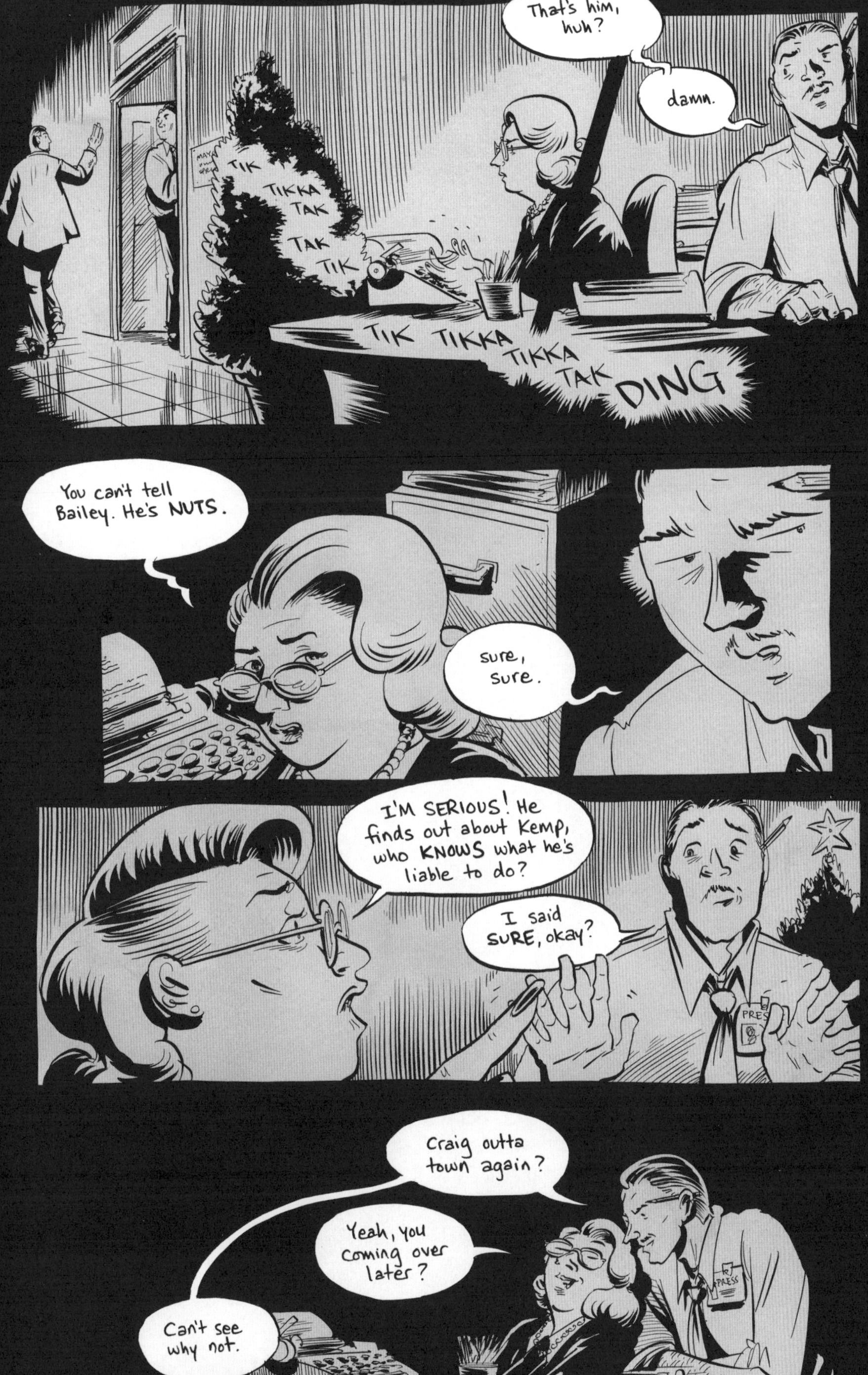

TIK
TIKKA
TAK
TAK
TIK
That's him, huh?
damn.
TIK TIKKA TIKKA TAK DING
You can't tell Bailey. He's NUTS.
sure, sure.
I'M SERIOUS! He finds out about Kemp, who KNOWS what he's liable to do?
I said SURE, okay?
Craig outta town again?
Yeah, you coming over later?
Can't see why not.

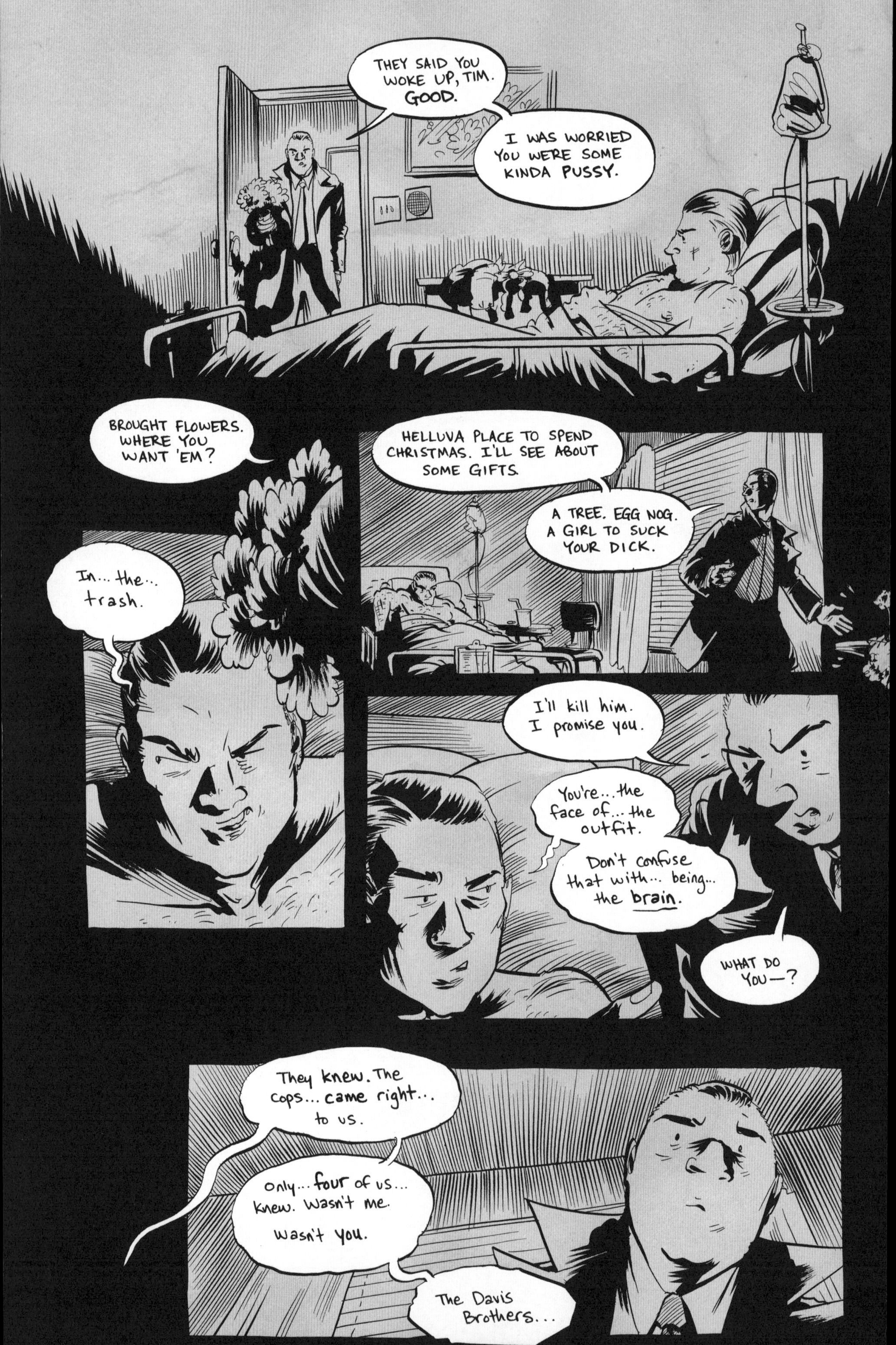
THEY SAID YOU WOKE UP, TIM. GOOD.
I WAS WORRIED YOU WERE SOME KINDA PUSSY.
BROUGHT FLOWERS. WHERE YOU WANT 'EM?
In... the... trash.
HELLUVA PLACE TO SPEND CHRISTMAS. I'LL SEE ABOUT SOME GIFTS.
A TREE. EGG NOG. A GIRL TO SUCK YOUR DICK.
I'll kill him. I promise you.
You're... the face of... the outfit.
Don't confuse that with... being... the brain.
WHAT DO YOU—?
They knew. The cops... came right... to us.
Only... four of us... knew. Wasn't me.
Wasn't you.
The Davis Brothers...

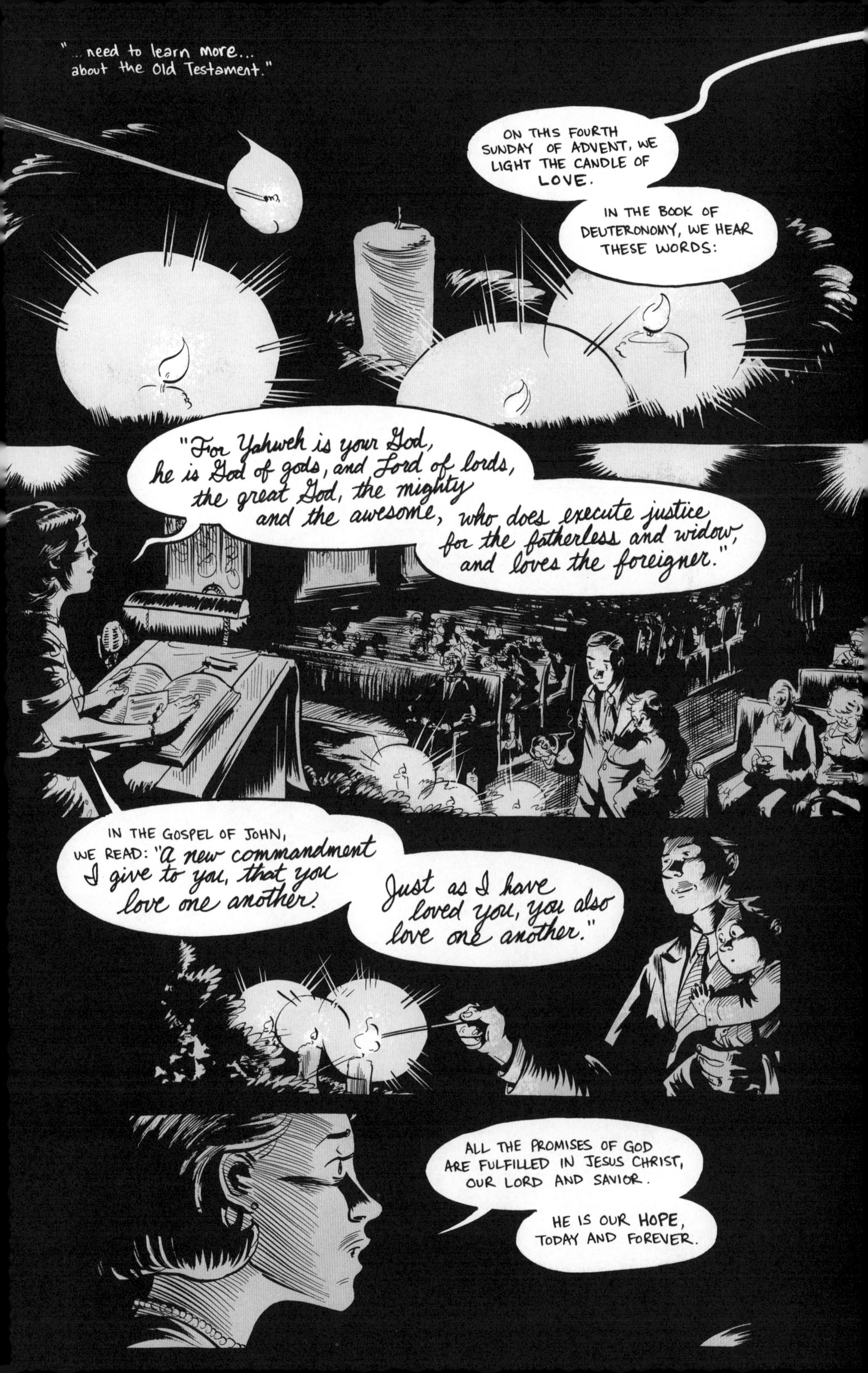
"... need to learn more... about the Old Testament."
ON THIS FOURTH SUNDAY OF ADVENT, WE LIGHT THE CANDLE OF LOVE.
IN THE BOOK OF DEUTERONOMY, WE HEAR THESE WORDS:
"For Yahweh is your God, he is God of gods, and Lord of lords, the great God, the mighty and the awesome, who does execute justice for the fatherless and widow, and loves the foreigner."
IN THE GOSPEL OF JOHN, WE READ: "A new commandment I give to you, that you love one another.
Just as I have loved you, you also love one another."
ALL THE PROMISES OF GOD ARE FULFILLED IN JESUS CHRIST, OUR LORD AND SAVIOR.
HE IS OUR HOPE, TODAY AND FOREVER.

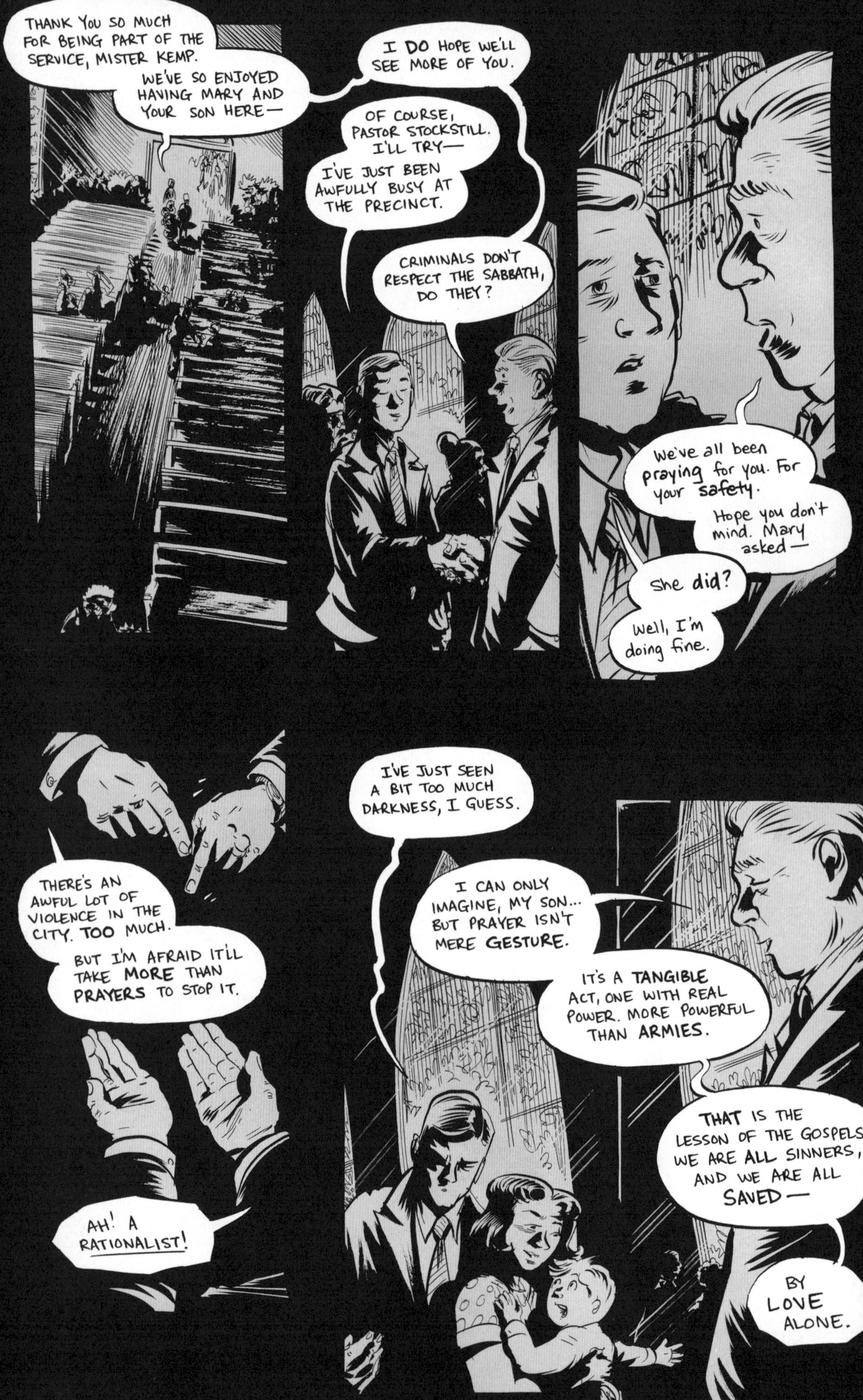
THANK YOU SO MUCH FOR BEING PART OF THE SERVICE, MISTER KEMP.
WE'VE SO ENJOYED HAVING MARY AND YOUR SON HERE—
I DO HOPE WE'LL SEE MORE OF YOU.
OF COURSE, PASTOR STOCKSTILL. I'LL TRY—
I'VE JUST BEEN AWFULLY BUSY AT THE PRECINCT.
CRIMINALS DON'T RESPECT THE SABBATH, DO THEY?
We've all been praying for you. For your safety.
Hope you don't mind. Mary asked—
She did?
Well, I'm doing fine.
THERE'S AN AWFUL LOT OF VIOLENCE IN THE CITY. TOO MUCH.
BUT I'M AFRAID IT'LL TAKE MORE THAN PRAYERS TO STOP IT.
AH! A RATIONALIST!
I'VE JUST SEEN A BIT TOO MUCH DARKNESS, I GUESS.
I CAN ONLY IMAGINE, MY SON... BUT PRAYER ISN'T MERE GESTURE.
IT'S A TANGIBLE ACT, ONE WITH REAL POWER. MORE POWERFUL THAN ARMIES.
THAT IS THE LESSON OF THE GOSPELS. WE ARE ALL SINNERS, AND WE ARE ALL SAVED—
BY LOVE ALONE.

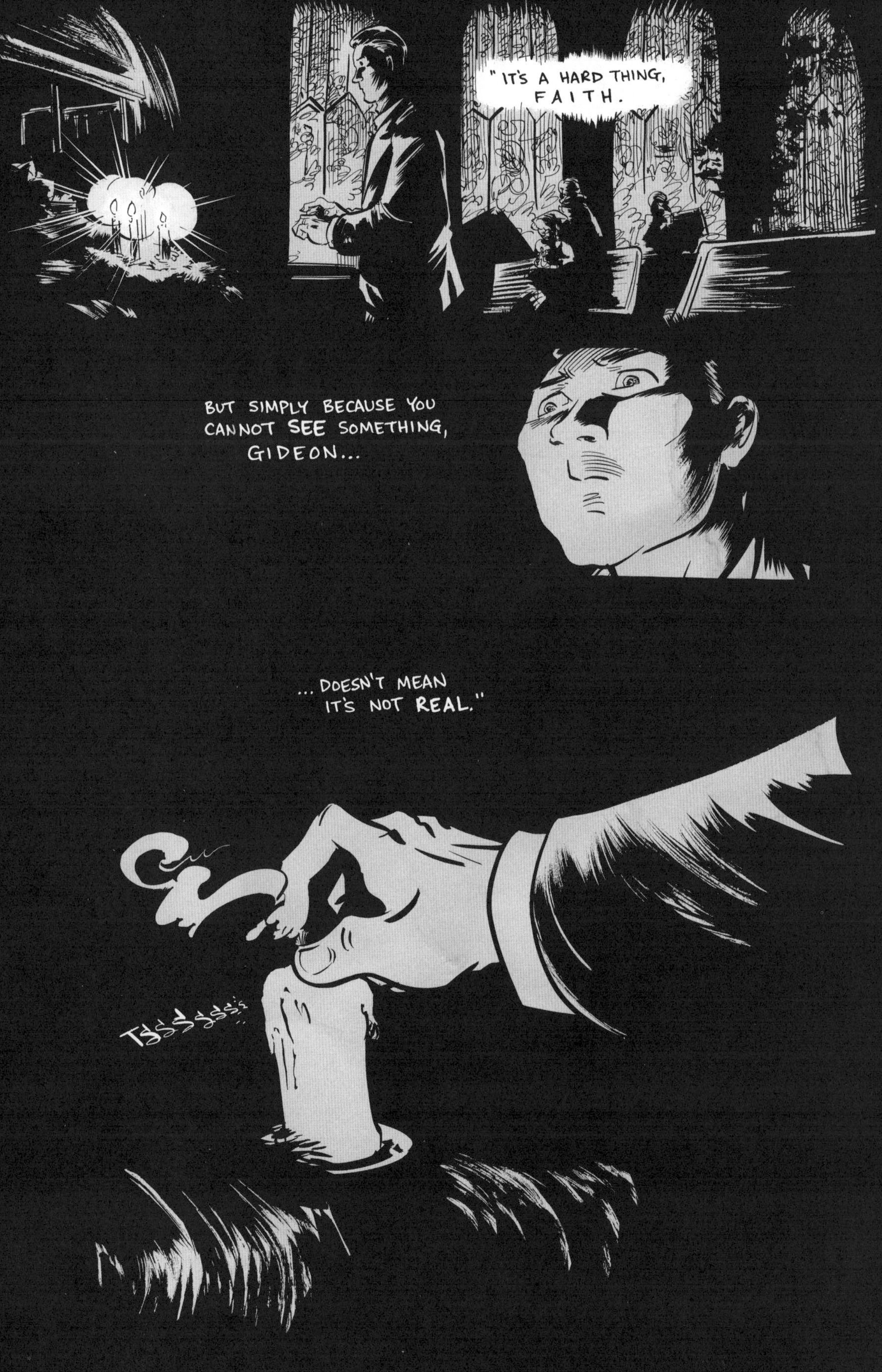
"IT'S A HARD THING, FAITH.
BUT SIMPLY BECAUSE YOU CANNOT SEE SOMETHING, GIDEON...
... DOESN'T MEAN IT'S NOT REAL."
TSSSssss

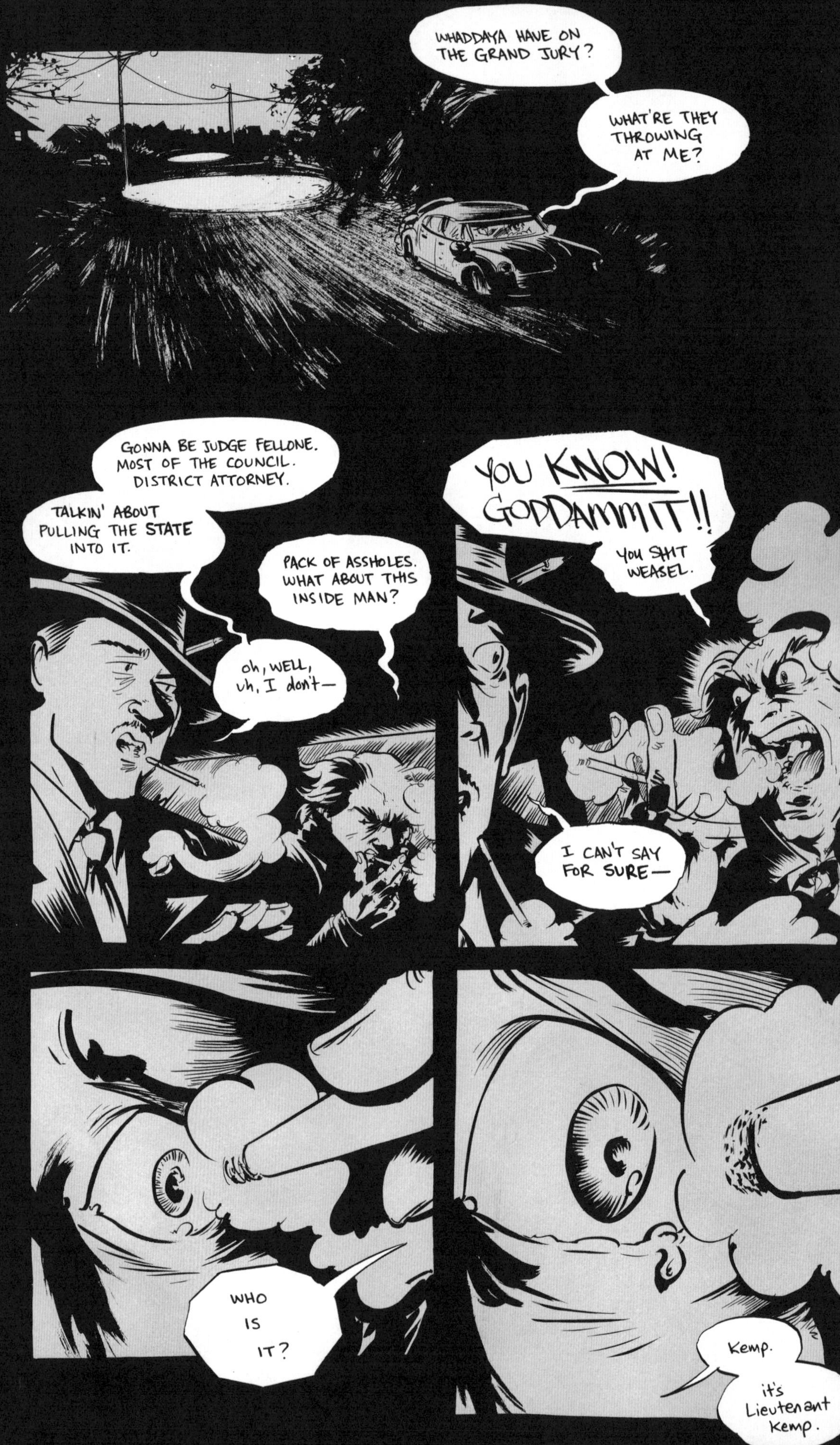

WHADDAYA HAVE ON THE GRAND JURY?
WHAT'RE THEY THROWING AT ME?
GONNA BE JUDGE FELLONE. MOST OF THE COUNCIL. DISTRICT ATTORNEY.
TALKIN' ABOUT PULLING THE STATE INTO IT.
PACK OF ASSHOLES. WHAT ABOUT THIS INSIDE MAN?
oh, WELL, uh, I don't—
YOU KNOW! GODDAMMIT!!
YOU SHIT WEASEL.
I CAN'T SAY FOR SURE—
WHO IS IT?
Kemp.
it's Lieutenant Kemp.

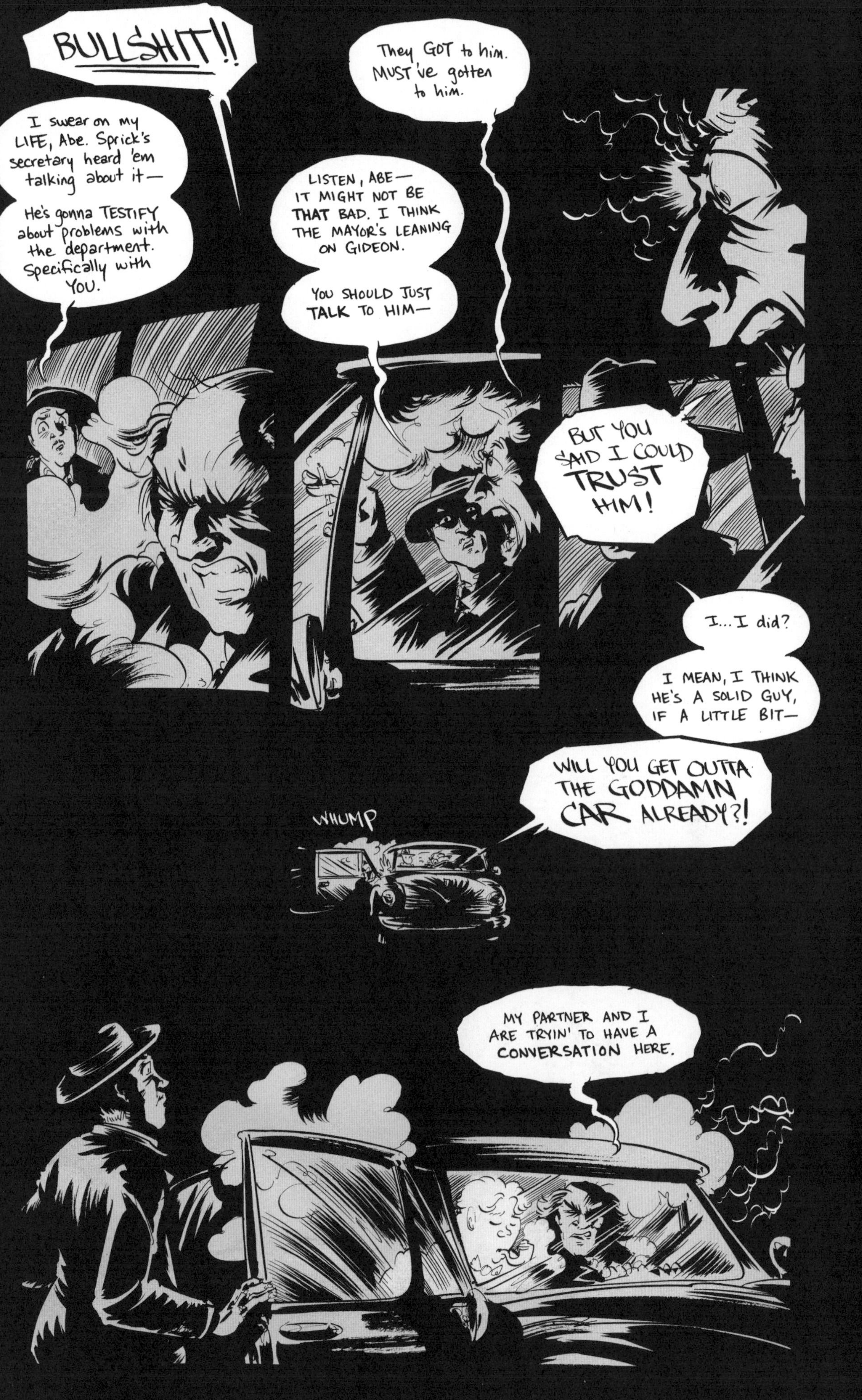
BULLSHIT!!
I swear on my LIFE, Abe. Sprick's secretary heard 'em talking about it—
He's gonna TESTIFY about problems with the department. Specifically with YOU.
They GOT to him. MUST've gotten to him.
LISTEN, ABE— IT MIGHT NOT BE THAT BAD. I THINK THE MAYOR'S LEANING ON GIDEON.
YOU SHOULD JUST TALK TO HIM—
BUT YOU SAID I COULD TRUST HIM!
I... I did?
I MEAN, I THINK HE'S A SOLID GUY, IF A LITTLE BIT—
WILL YOU GET OUTTA THE GODDAMN CAR ALREADY?!
WHUMP
MY PARTNER AND I ARE TRYIN' TO HAVE A CONVERSATION HERE.

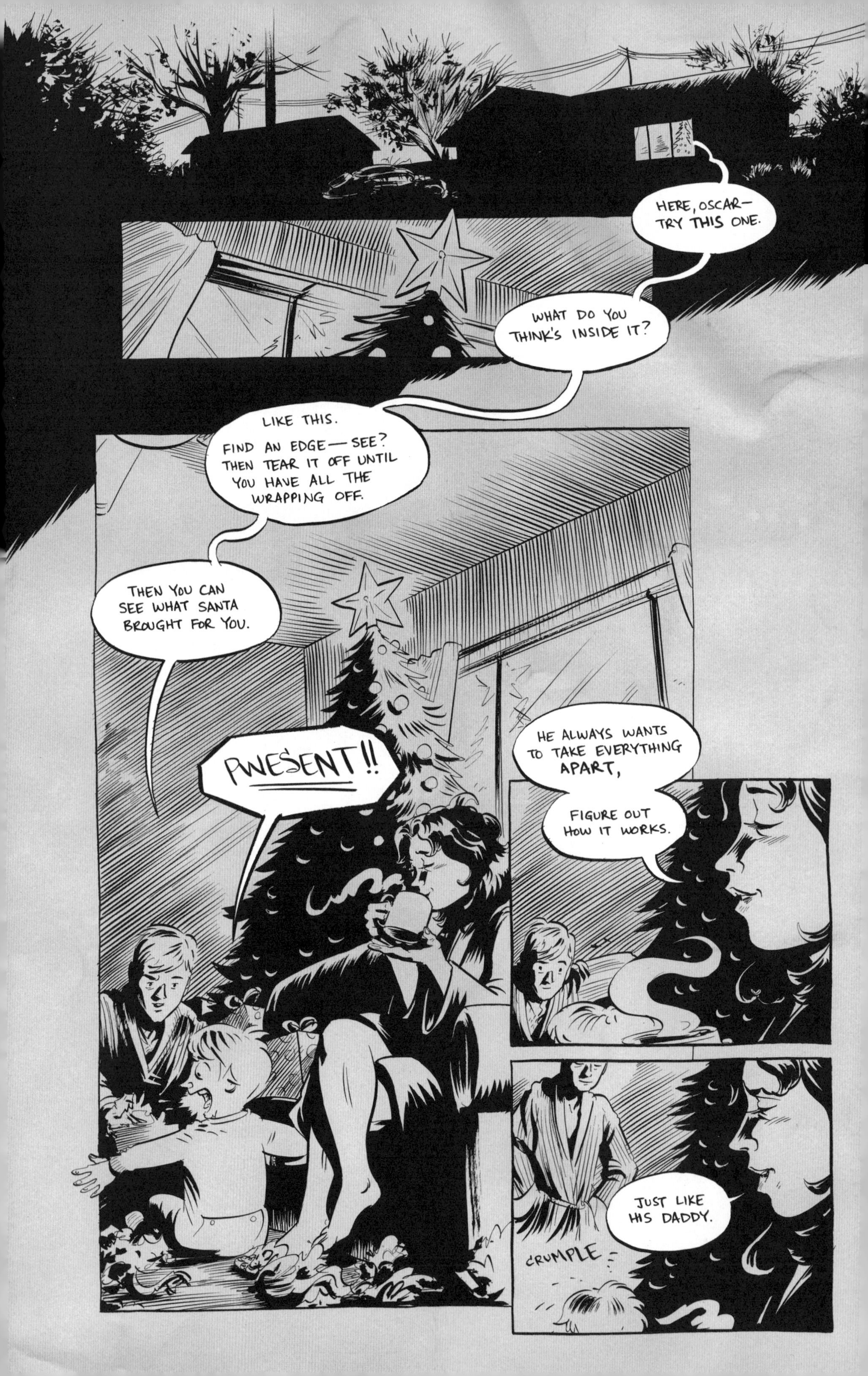
HERE, OSCAR— TRY THIS ONE.
WHAT DO YOU THINK'S INSIDE IT?
LIKE THIS.
FIND AN EDGE—SEE? THEN TEAR IT OFF UNTIL YOU HAVE ALL THE WRAPPING OFF.
THEN YOU CAN SEE WHAT SANTA BROUGHT FOR YOU.
PWESENT!!
HE ALWAYS WANTS TO TAKE EVERYTHING APART,
FIGURE OUT HOW IT WORKS.
JUST LIKE HIS DADDY.
CRUMPLE

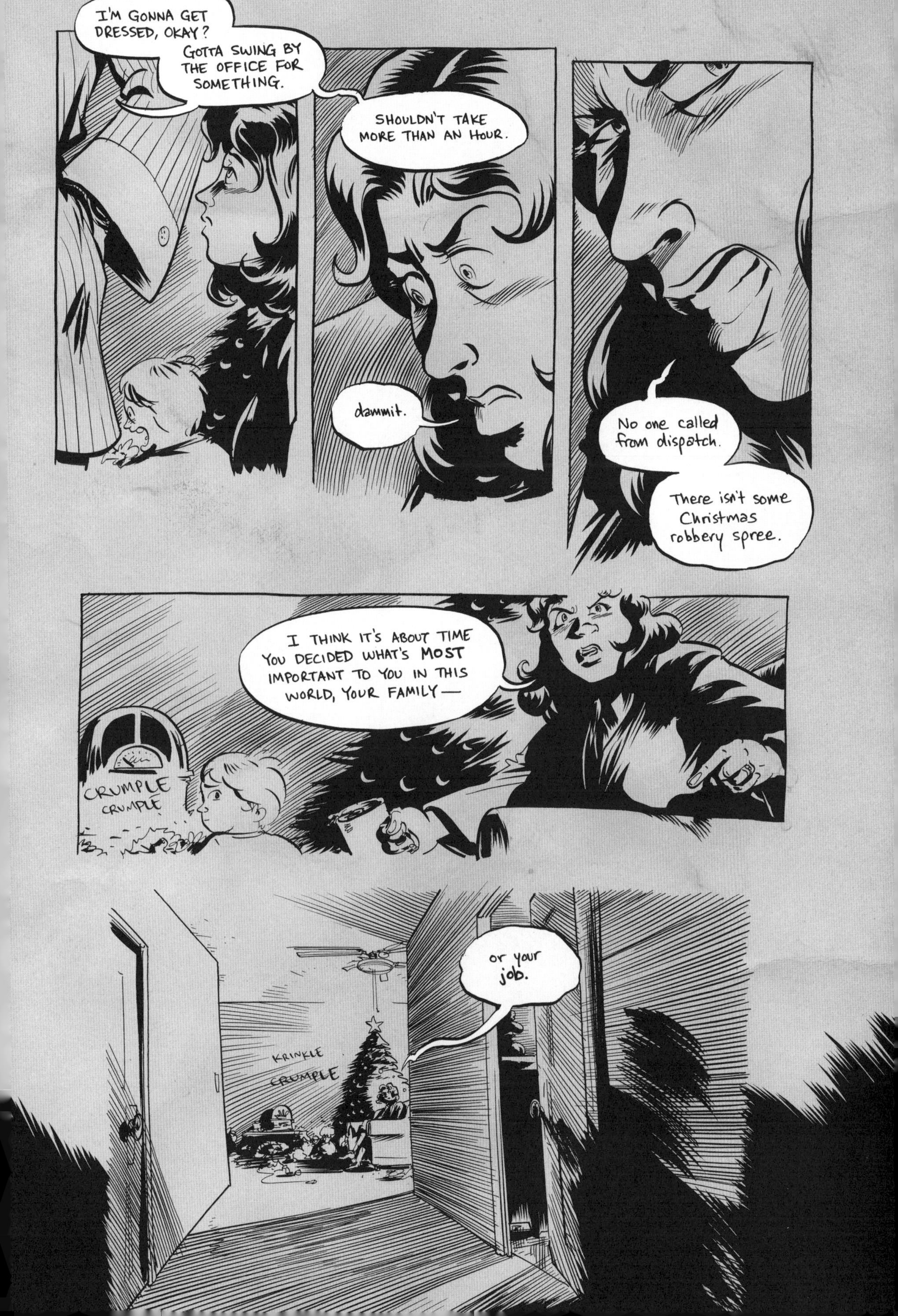
I'M GONNA GET DRESSED, OKAY?
GOTTA SWING BY THE OFFICE FOR SOMETHING.
SHOULDN'T TAKE MORE THAN AN HOUR.
dammit.
No one called from dispatch.
There isn't some Christmas robbery spree.
I THINK IT'S ABOUT TIME YOU DECIDED WHAT'S MOST IMPORTANT TO YOU IN THIS WORLD, YOUR FAMILY—
CRUMPLE
CRUMPLE
or your job.
KRINKLE
CRUMPLE

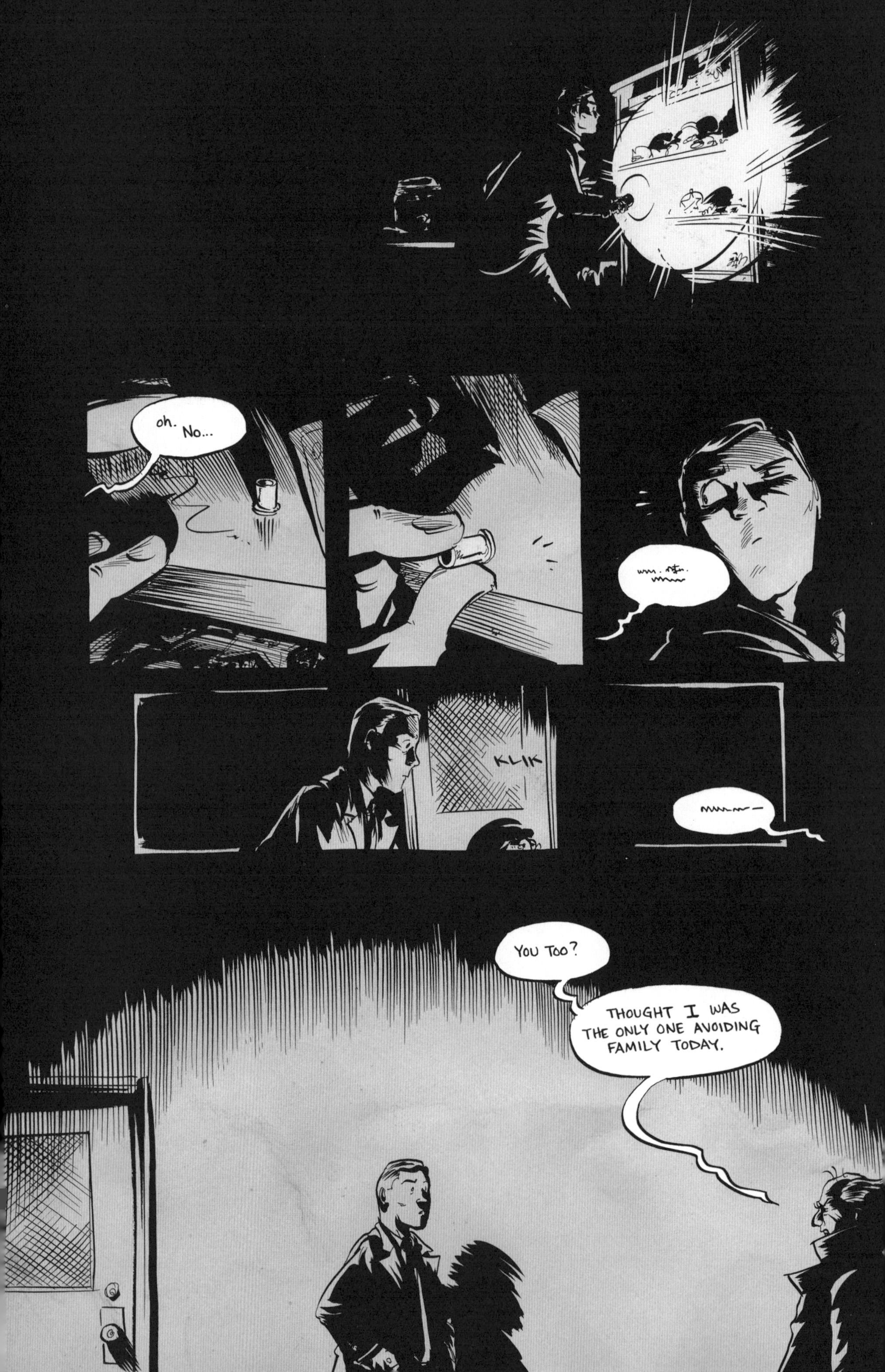
oh. No...
KLIK
YOU TOO?
THOUGHT I WAS THE ONLY ONE AVOIDING FAMILY TODAY.

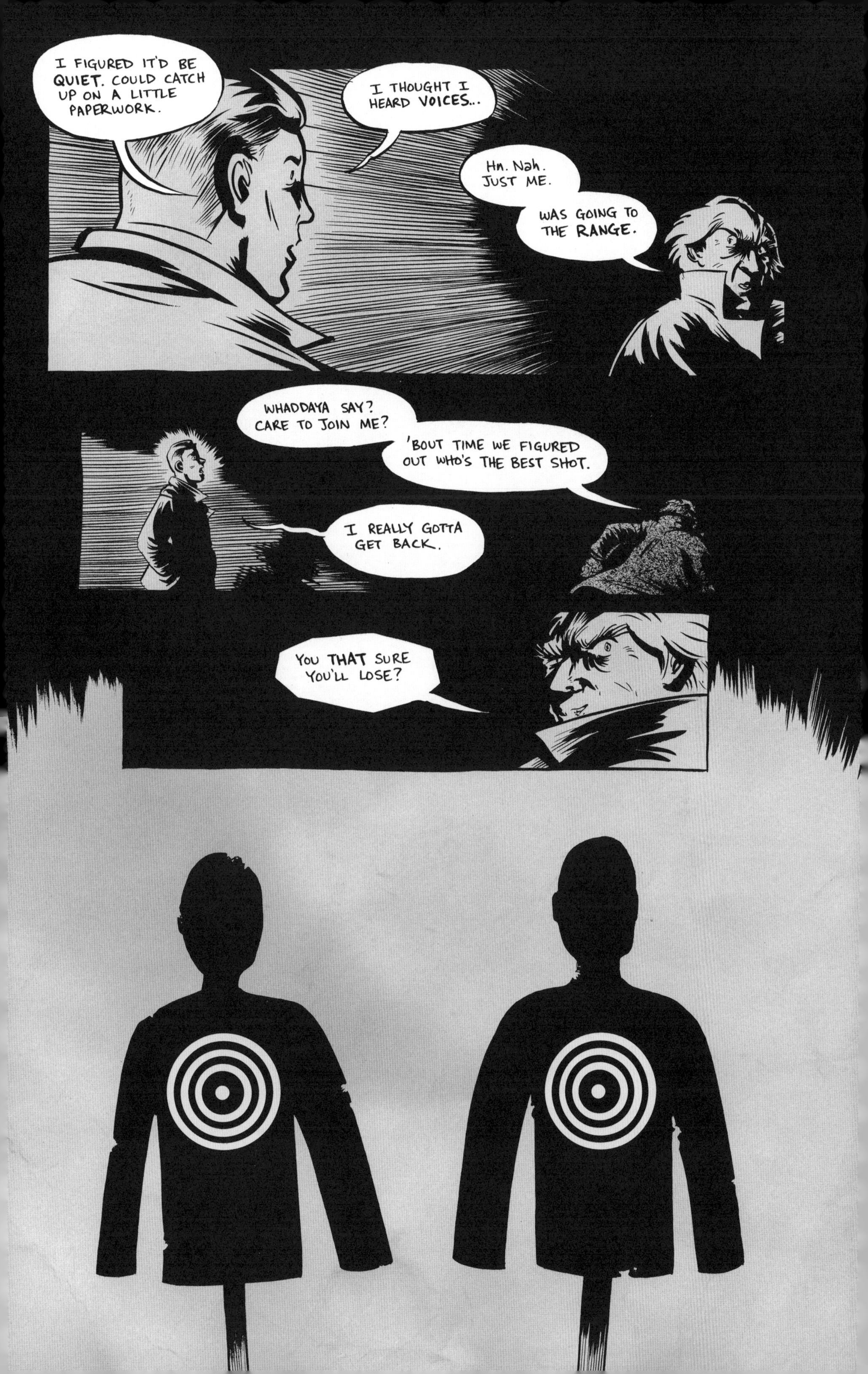
I FIGURED IT'D BE QUIET. COULD CATCH UP ON A LITTLE PAPERWORK.
I THOUGHT I HEARD VOICES...
Hn. Nah. JUST ME.
WAS GOING TO THE RANGE.
WHADDAYA SAY? CARE TO JOIN ME?
'BOUT TIME WE FIGURED OUT WHO'S THE BEST SHOT.
I REALLY GOTTA GET BACK.
YOU THAT SURE YOU'LL LOSE?

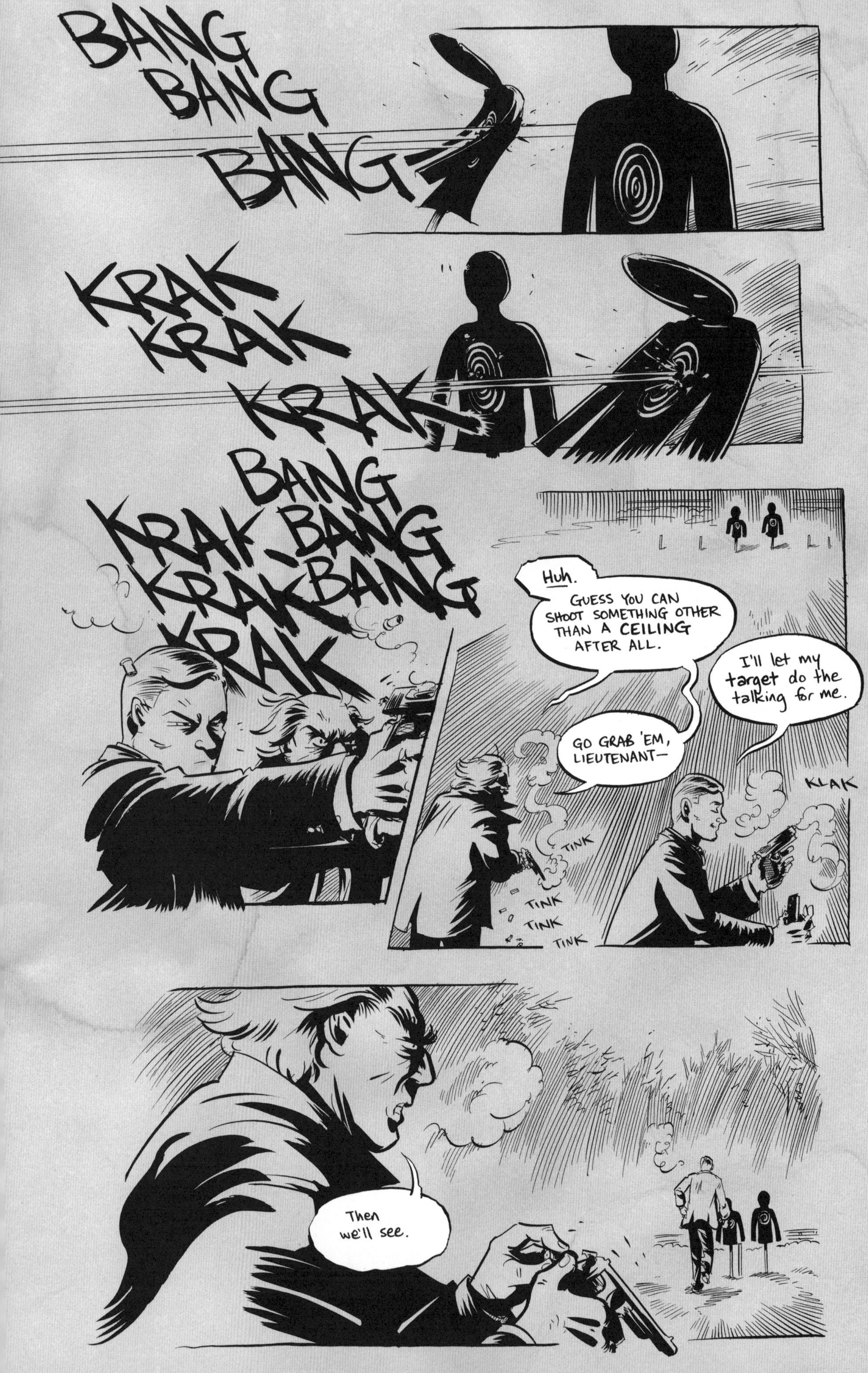
BANG
BANG
BANG
KRAK
KRAK
KRAK
BANG
KRAK BANG
KRAK BANG
KRAK
Huh.
GUESS YOU CAN SHOOT SOMETHING OTHER THAN A CEILING AFTER ALL.
I'll let my target do the talking for me.
GO GRAB 'EM, LIEUTENANT—
KLAK
TINK
TINK
TINK
TINK
Then we'll see.

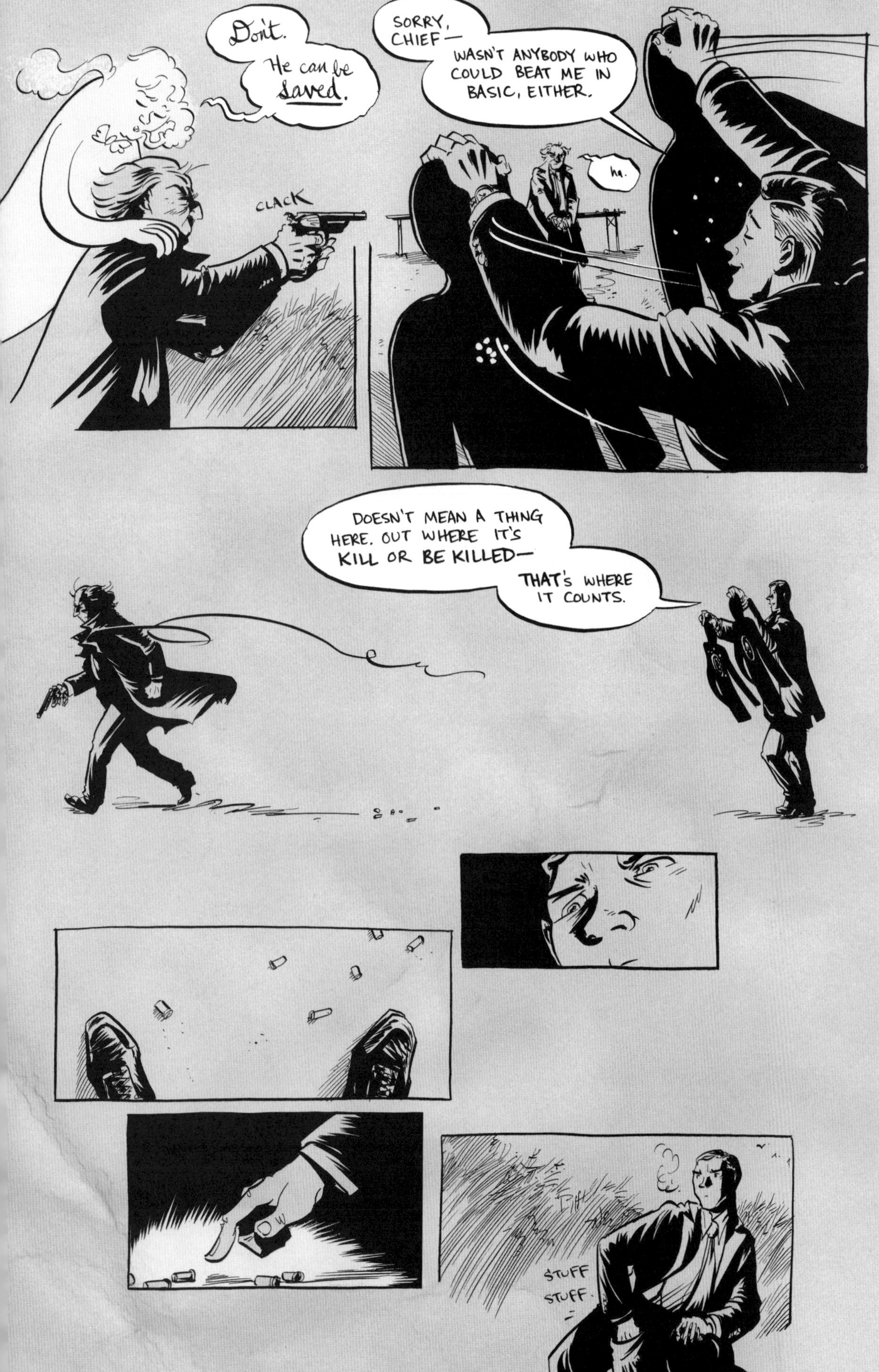
Don't.
He can be saved.
CLACK
SORRY, CHIEF—
WASN'T ANYBODY WHO COULD BEAT ME IN BASIC, EITHER.
ha.
DOESN'T MEAN A THING HERE. OUT WHERE IT'S KILL OR BE KILLED—
THAT'S WHERE IT COUNTS.
STUFF
STUFF

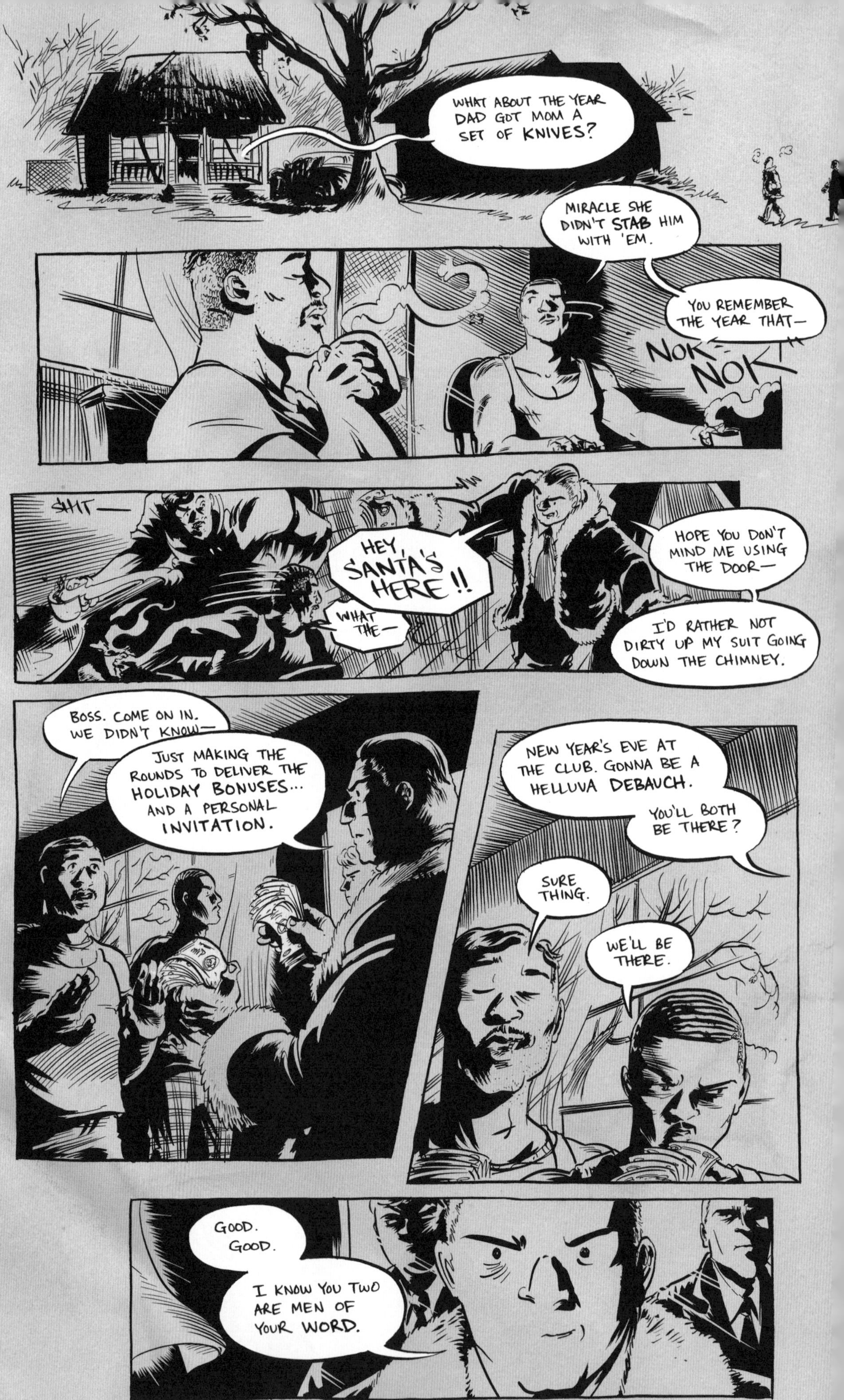
WHAT ABOUT THE YEAR DAD GOT MOM A SET OF KNIVES?
MIRACLE SHE DIDN'T STAB HIM WITH 'EM.
YOU REMEMBER THE YEAR THAT—
NOK NOK
SHIT—
HEY, SANTA'S HERE!!
WHAT THE—
HOPE YOU DON'T MIND ME USING THE DOOR—
I'D RATHER NOT DIRTY UP MY SUIT GOING DOWN THE CHIMNEY.
BOSS. COME ON IN. WE DIDN'T KNOW—
JUST MAKING THE ROUNDS TO DELIVER THE HOLIDAY BONUSES... AND A PERSONAL INVITATION.
NEW YEAR'S EVE AT THE CLUB. GONNA BE A HELLUVA DEBAUCH.
YOU'LL BOTH BE THERE?
SURE THING.
WE'LL BE THERE.
GOOD.
GOOD.
I KNOW YOU TWO ARE MEN OF YOUR WORD.

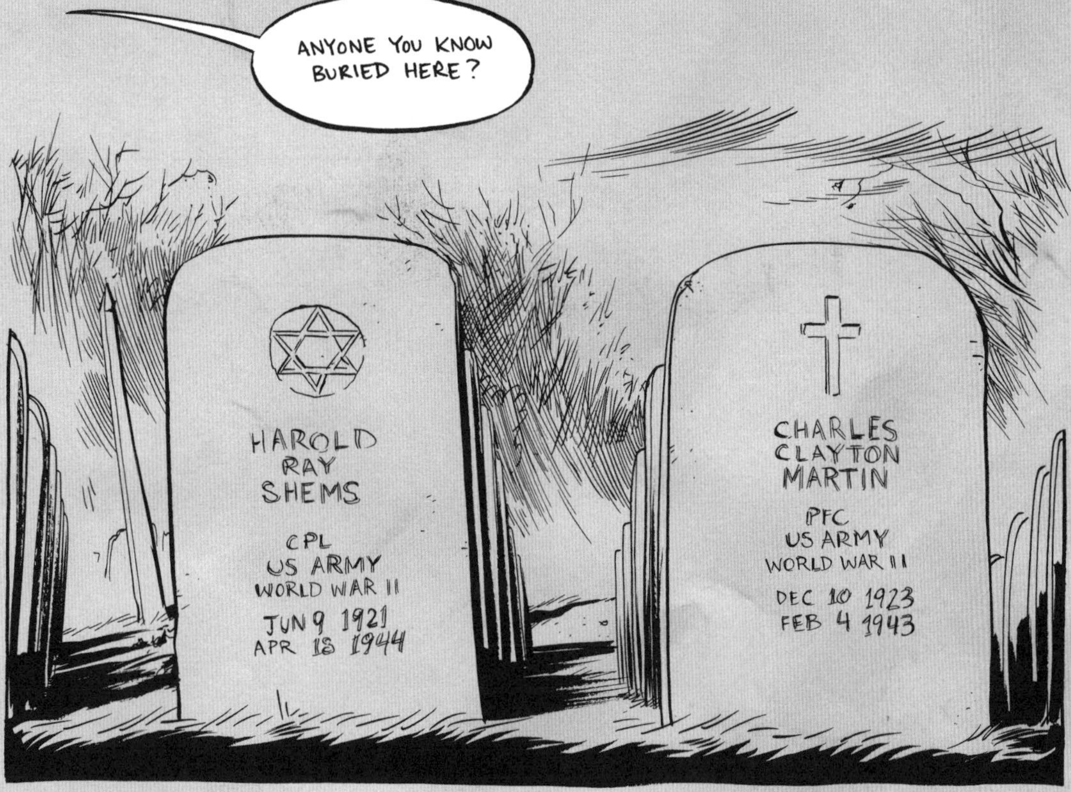
ANYONE YOU KNOW BURIED HERE?
HAROLD RAY SHEMS
CPL US ARMY WORLD WAR II
JUN 9 1921 APR 18 1944
CHARLES CLAYTON MARTIN
PFC US ARMY WORLD WAR II
DEC 10 1923 FEB 4 1943

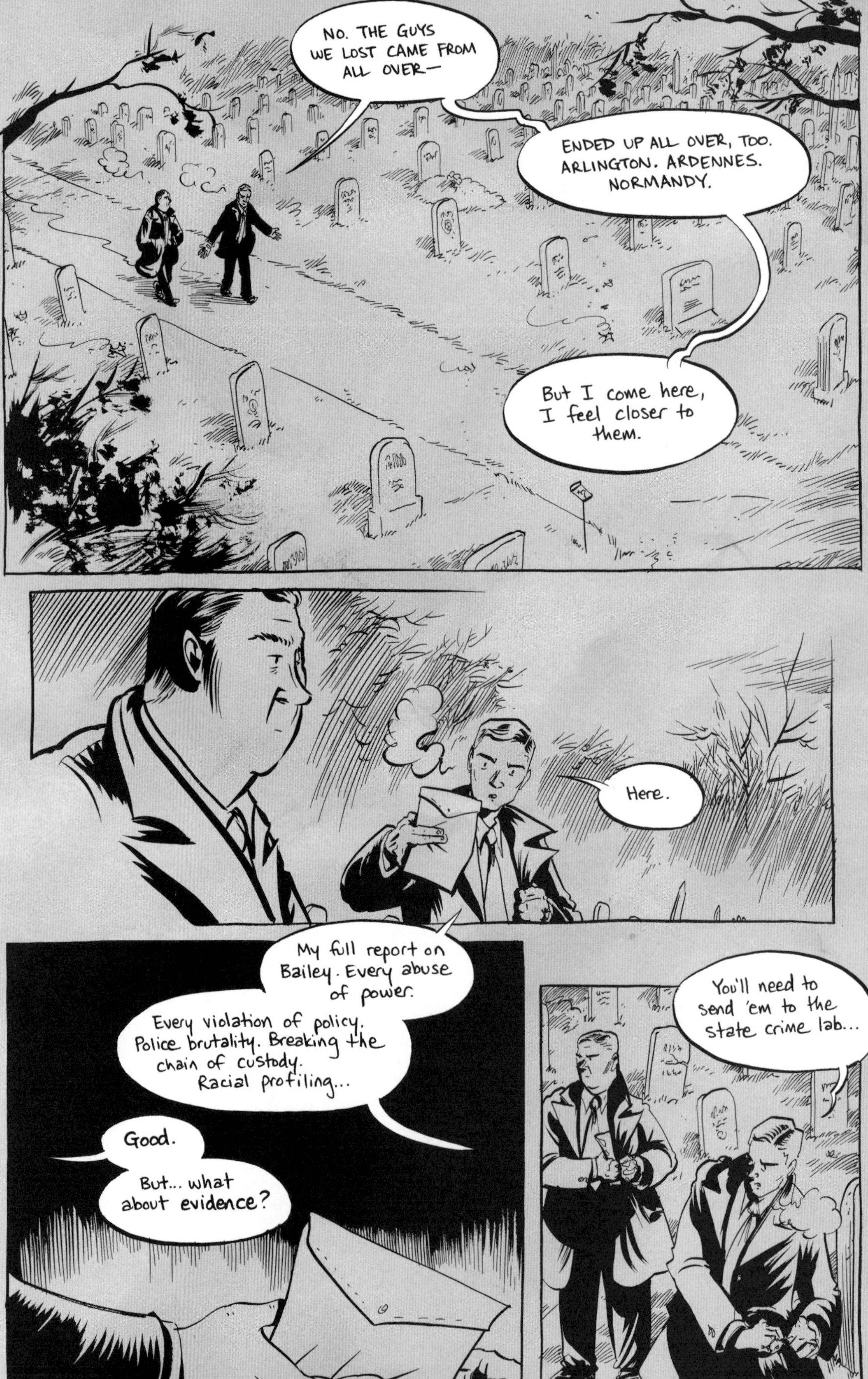
NO. THE GUYS WE LOST CAME FROM ALL OVER—
ENDED UP ALL OVER, TOO. ARLINGTON. ARDENNES. NORMANDY.
But I come here, I feel closer to them.
Here.
My full report on Bailey. Every abuse of power.
Every violation of policy. Police brutality. Breaking the chain of custody. Racial profiling...
Good.
But... what about evidence?
You'll need to send 'em to the state crime lab...

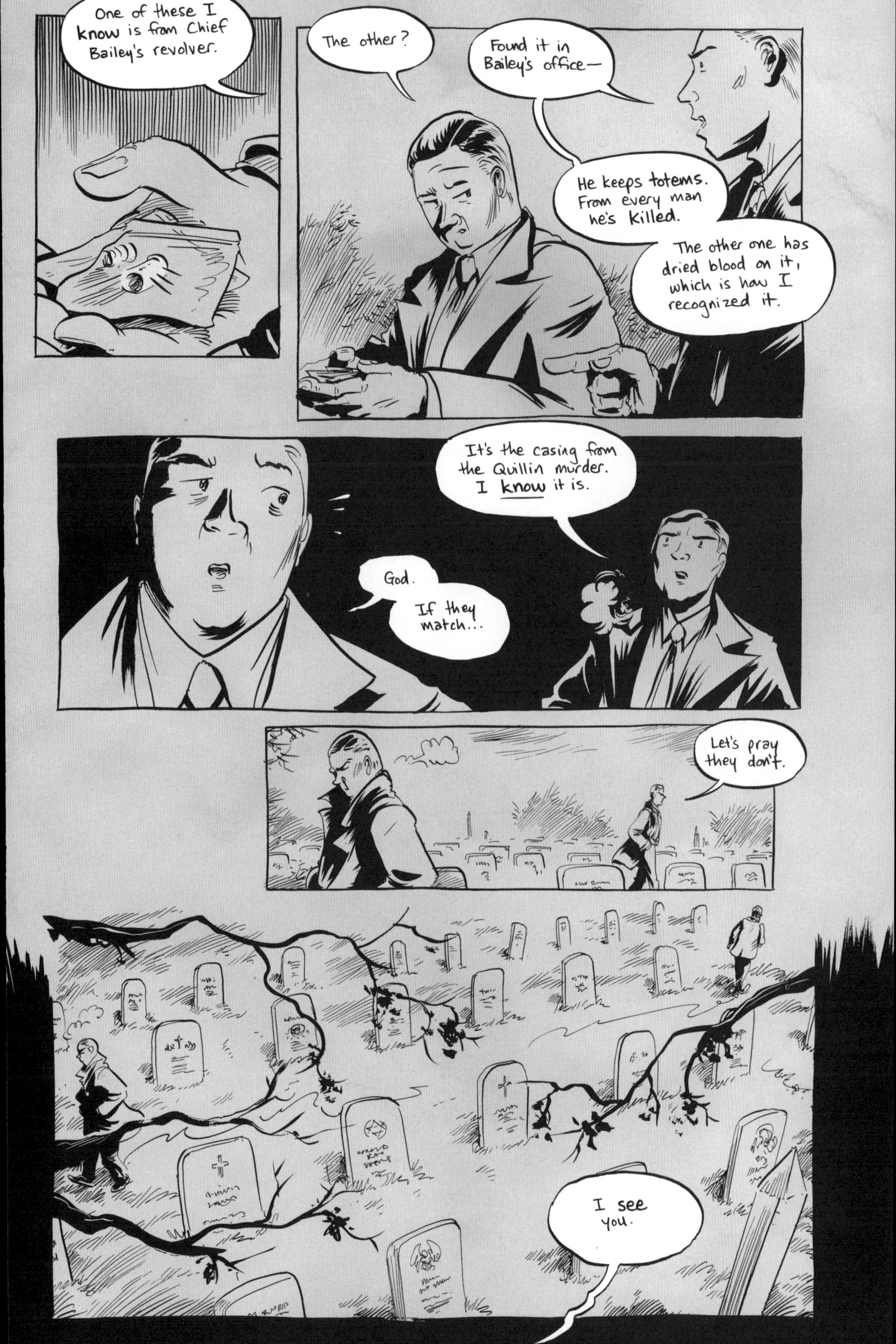
One of these I know is from Chief Bailey's revolver.
The other?
Found it in Bailey's office—
He keeps totems. From every man he's killed.
The other one has dried blood on it, which is how I recognized it.
It's the casing from the Quillin murder. I know it is.
God.
If they match...
Let's pray they don't.
I see you.

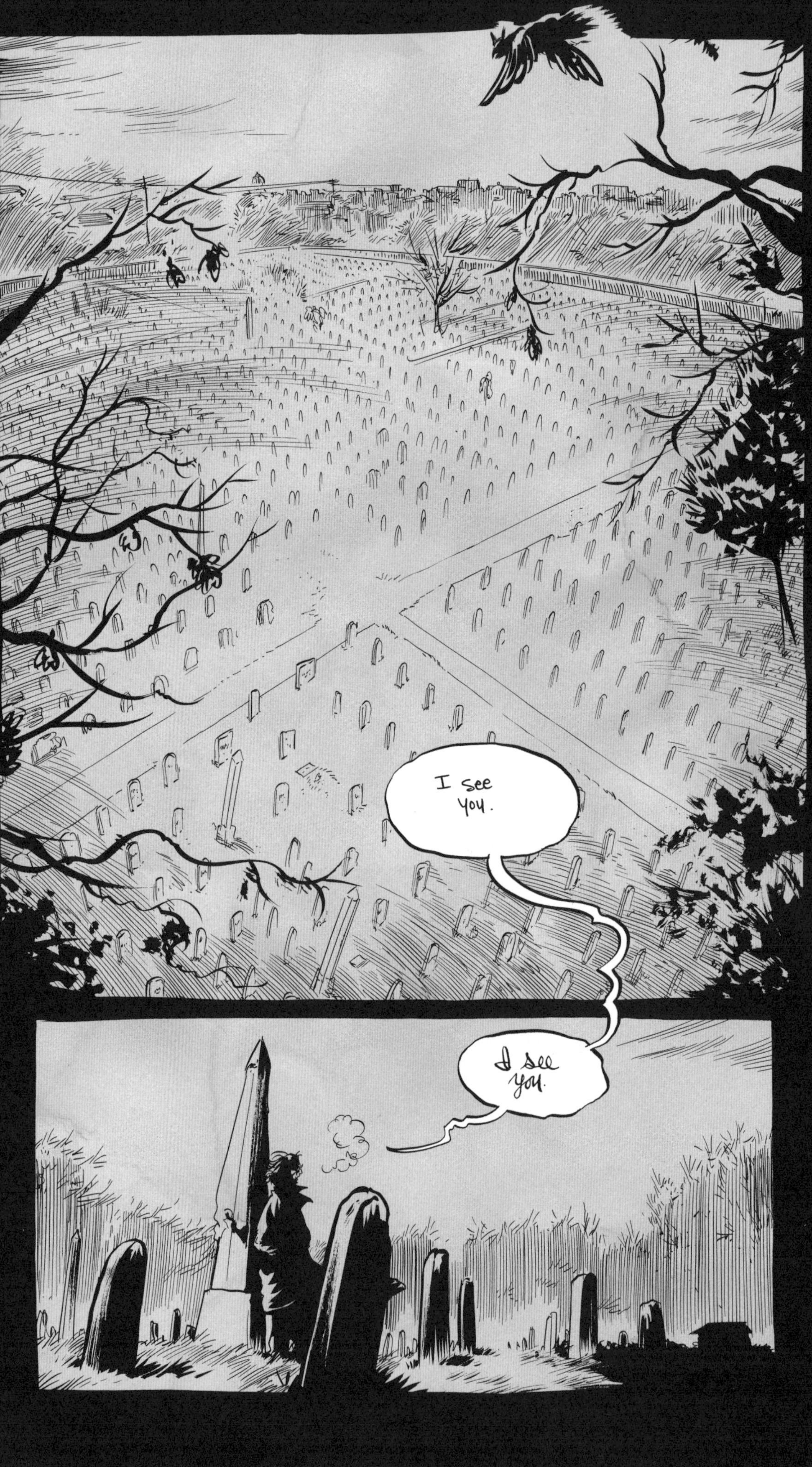
I see you.
I see you.

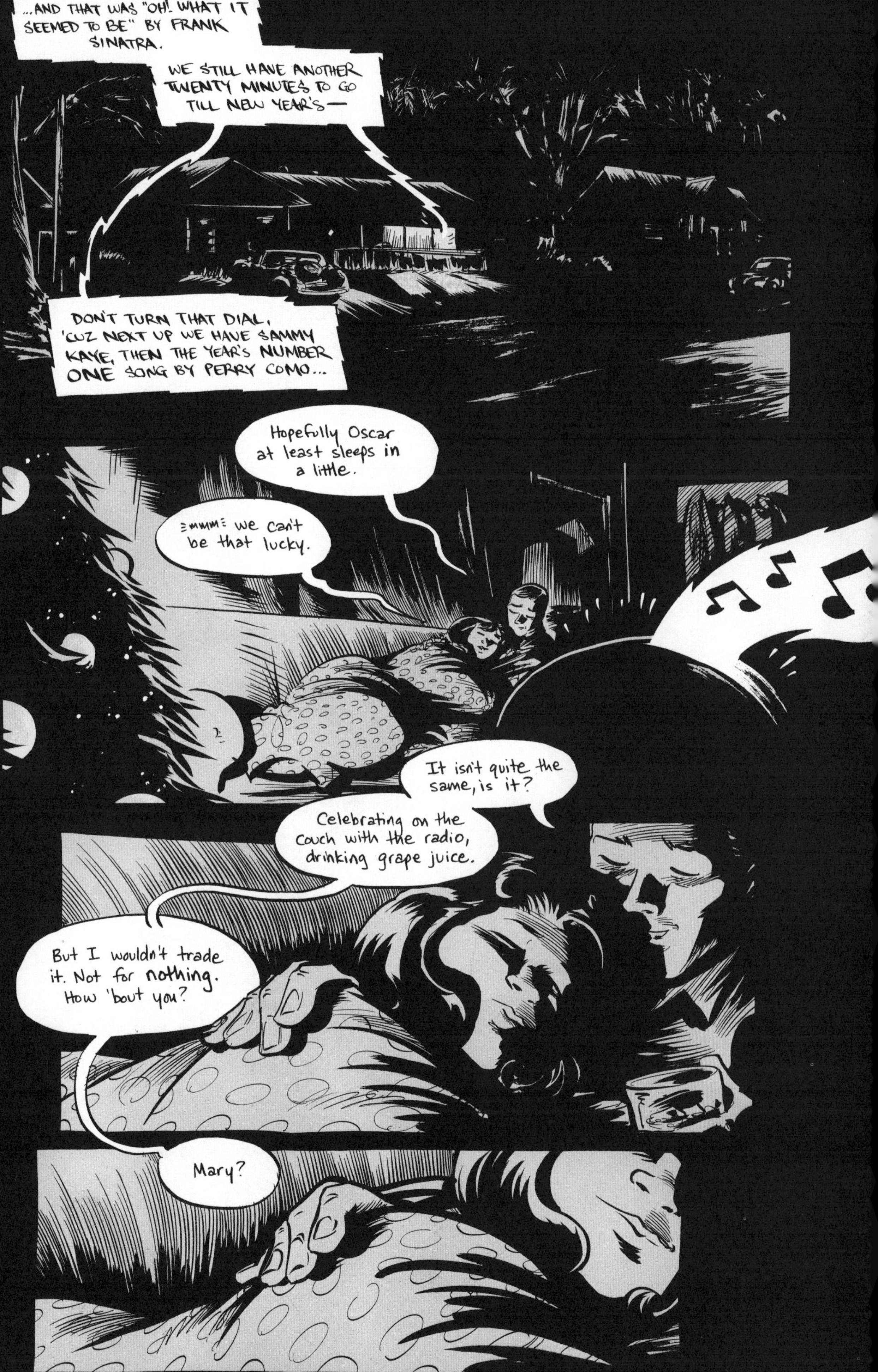
...AND THAT WAS "OH! WHAT IT SEEMED TO BE" BY FRANK SINATRA.
WE STILL HAVE ANOTHER TWENTY MINUTES TO GO TILL NEW YEAR'S—
DON'T TURN THAT DIAL, 'CUZ NEXT UP WE HAVE SAMMY KAYE, THEN THE YEAR'S NUMBER ONE SONG BY PERRY COMO...
Hopefully Oscar at least sleeps in a little.
=MMM= we can't be that lucky.
It isn't quite the same, is it?
Celebrating on the couch with the radio, drinking grape juice.
But I wouldn't trade it. Not for nothing. How 'bout you?
Mary?

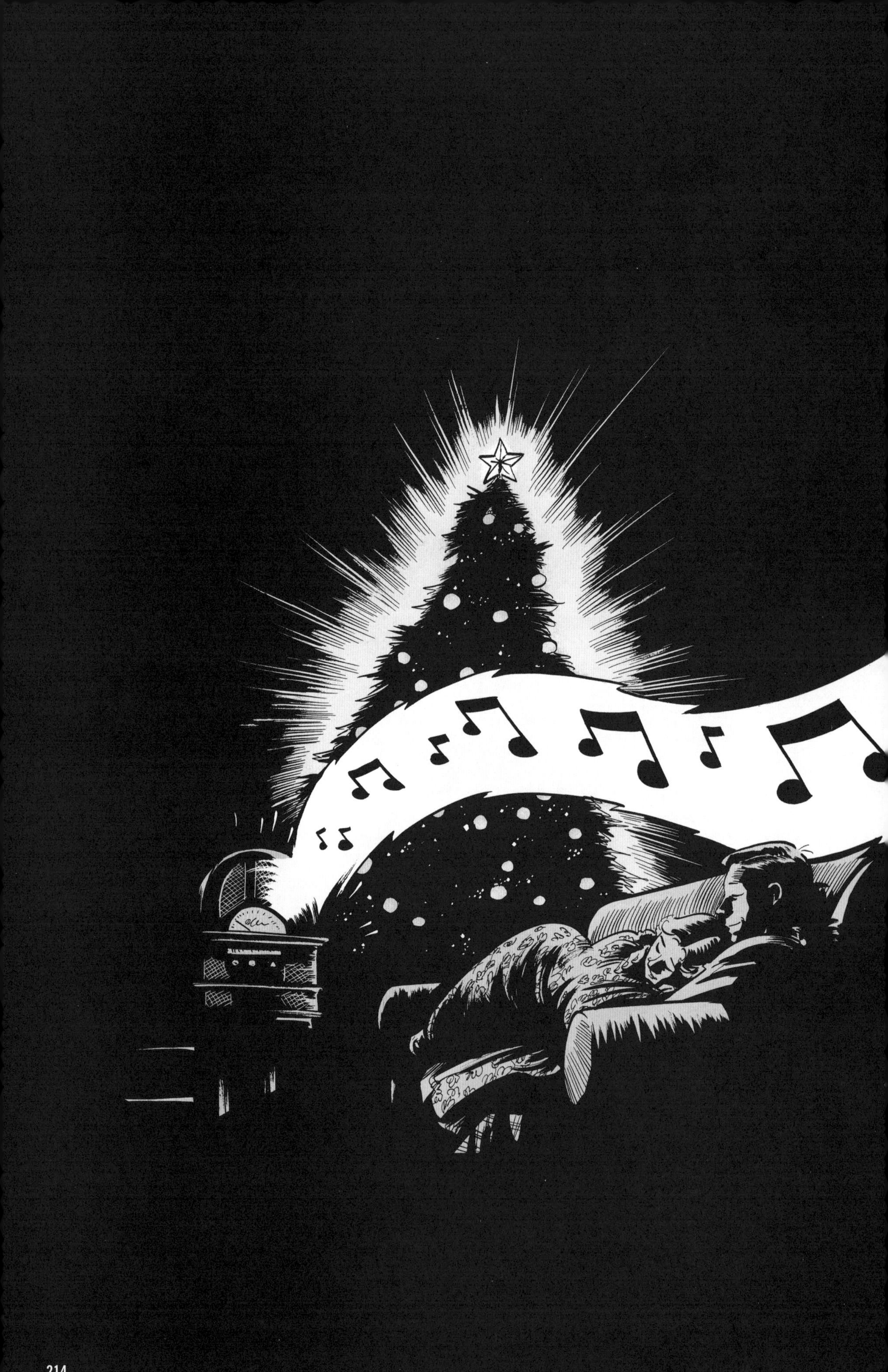

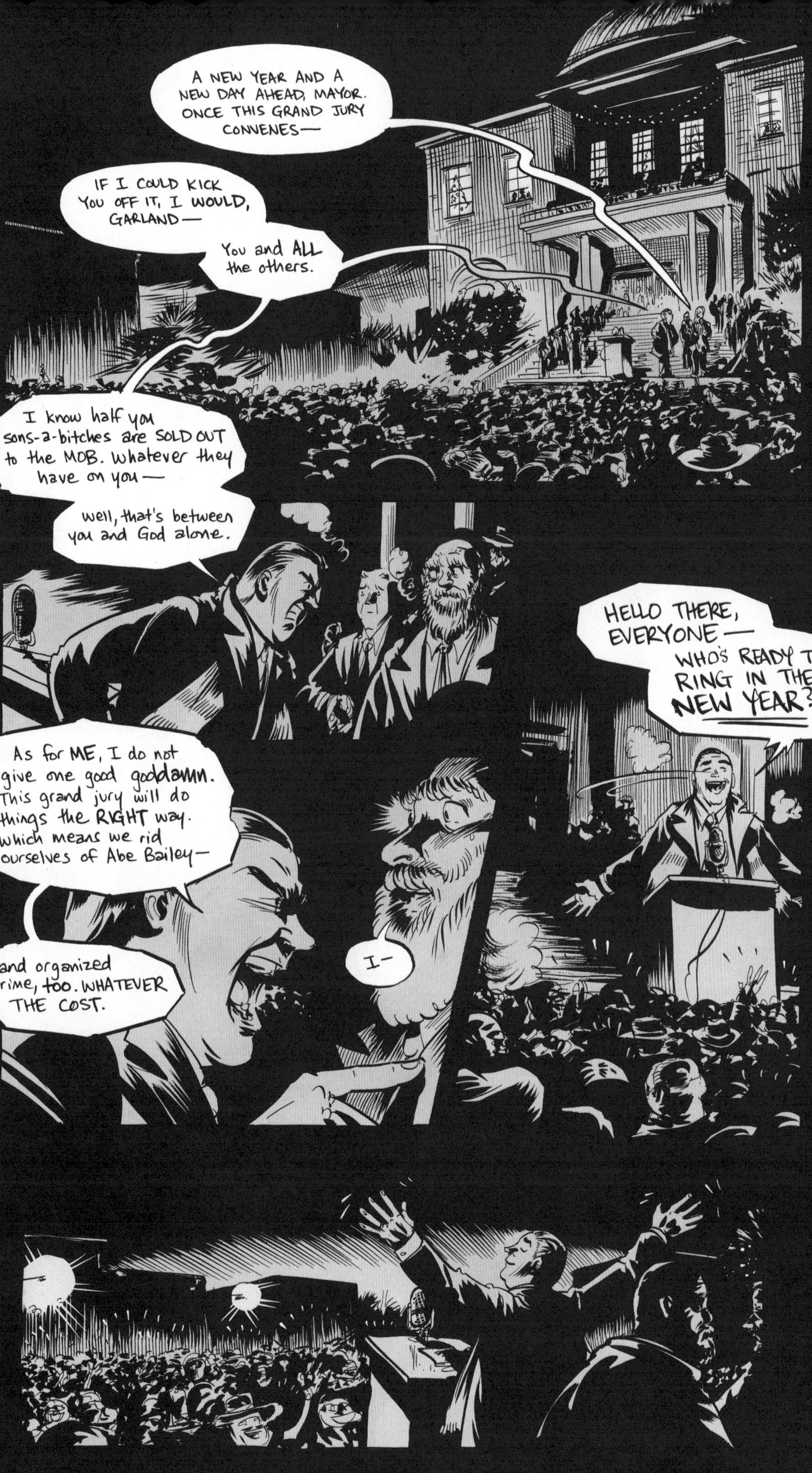
A NEW YEAR AND A NEW DAY AHEAD, MAYOR. ONCE THIS GRAND JURY CONVENES—
IF I COULD KICK YOU OFF IT, I WOULD, GARLAND—
You and ALL the others.
I know half you sons-a-bitches are SOLD OUT to the MOB. whatever they have on you—
well, that's between you and God alone.
As for ME, I do not give one good goddamn. This grand jury will do things the RIGHT way. which means we rid ourselves of Abe Bailey—
and organized crime, too. WHATEVER THE COST.
I–
HELLO THERE, EVERYONE—
WHO'S READY TO RING IN THE NEW YEAR?!

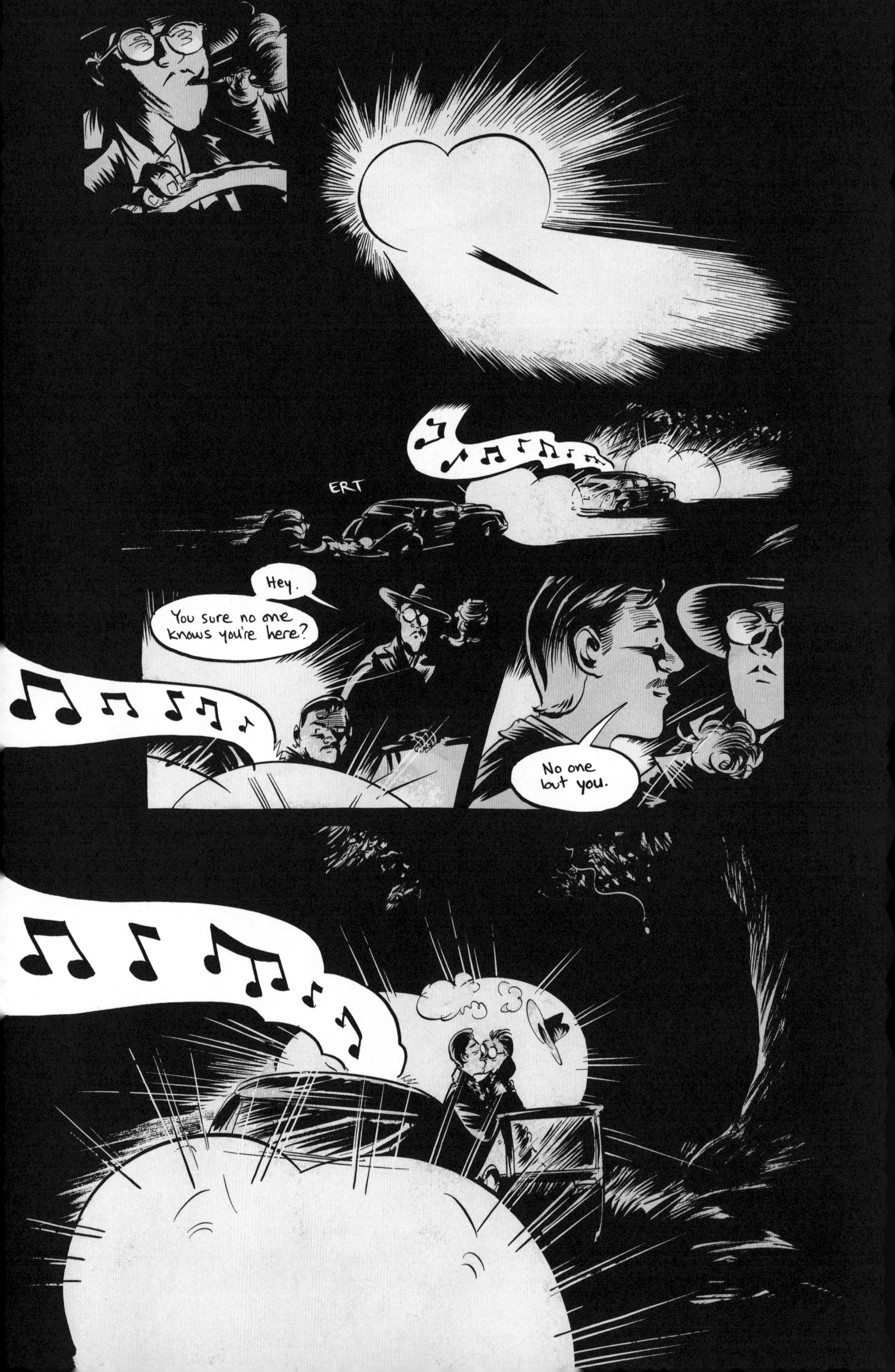
ERT
Hey.
You sure no one knows you're here?
No one but you.

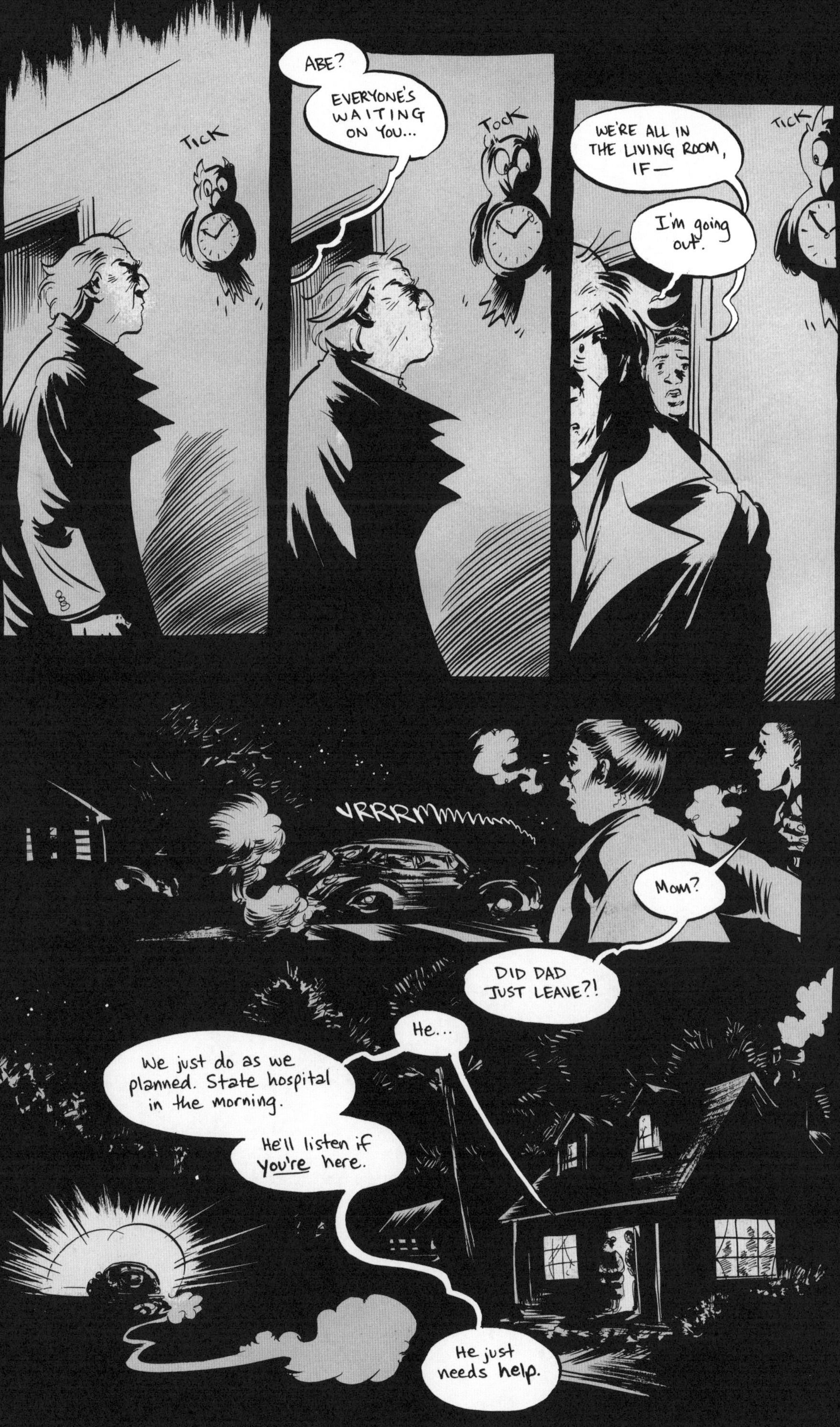
TICK
ABE?
EVERYONE'S WAITING ON YOU...
TOCK
WE'RE ALL IN THE LIVING ROOM, IF—
I'm going out.
TICK
VRRRMmmmmm
Mom?
DID DAD JUST LEAVE?!
He...
We just do as we planned. State hospital in the morning.
He'll listen if you're here.
He just needs help.

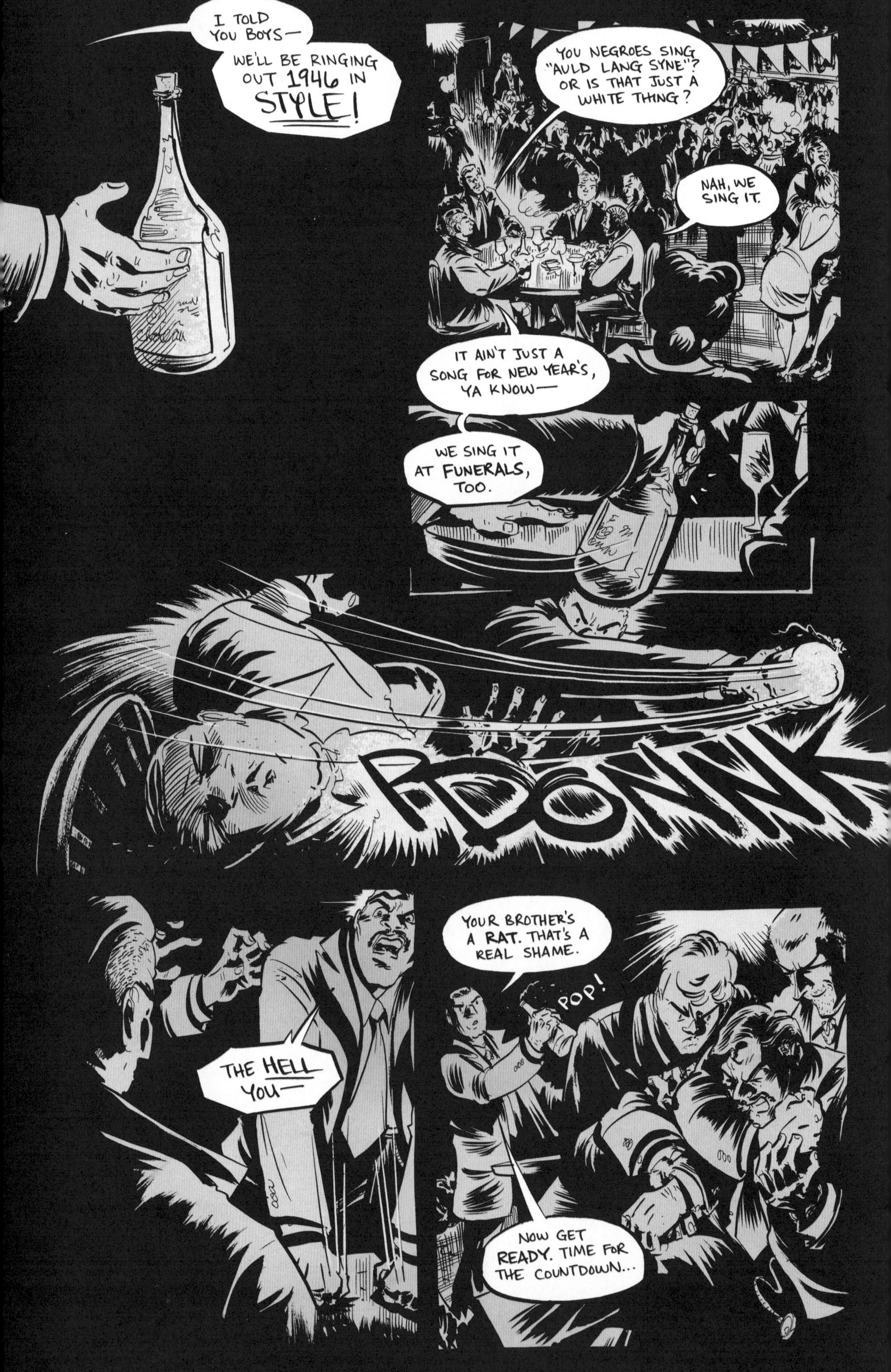
I TOLD YOU BOYS—
WE'LL BE RINGING OUT 1946 IN STYLE!
YOU NEGROES SING "AULD LANG SYNE"? OR IS THAT JUST A WHITE THING?
NAH, WE SING IT.
IT AIN'T JUST A SONG FOR NEW YEAR'S, YA KNOW—
WE SING IT AT FUNERALS, TOO.
PDONNK
THE HELL YOU—
YOUR BROTHER'S A RAT. THAT'S A REAL SHAME.
POP!
NOW GET READY. TIME FOR THE COUNTDOWN...

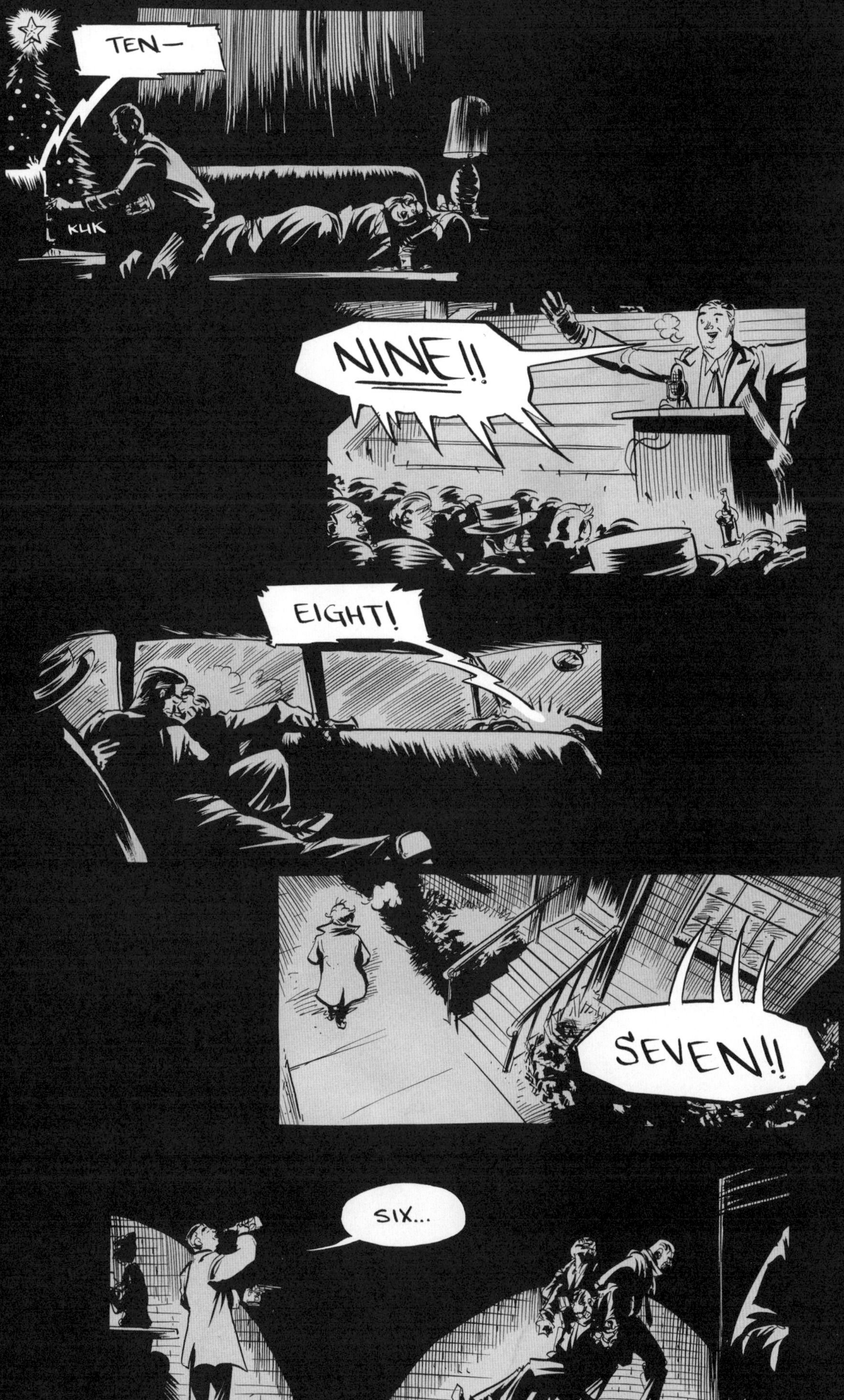
TEN—
KLIK
NINE!!
EIGHT!
SEVEN!!
SIX...

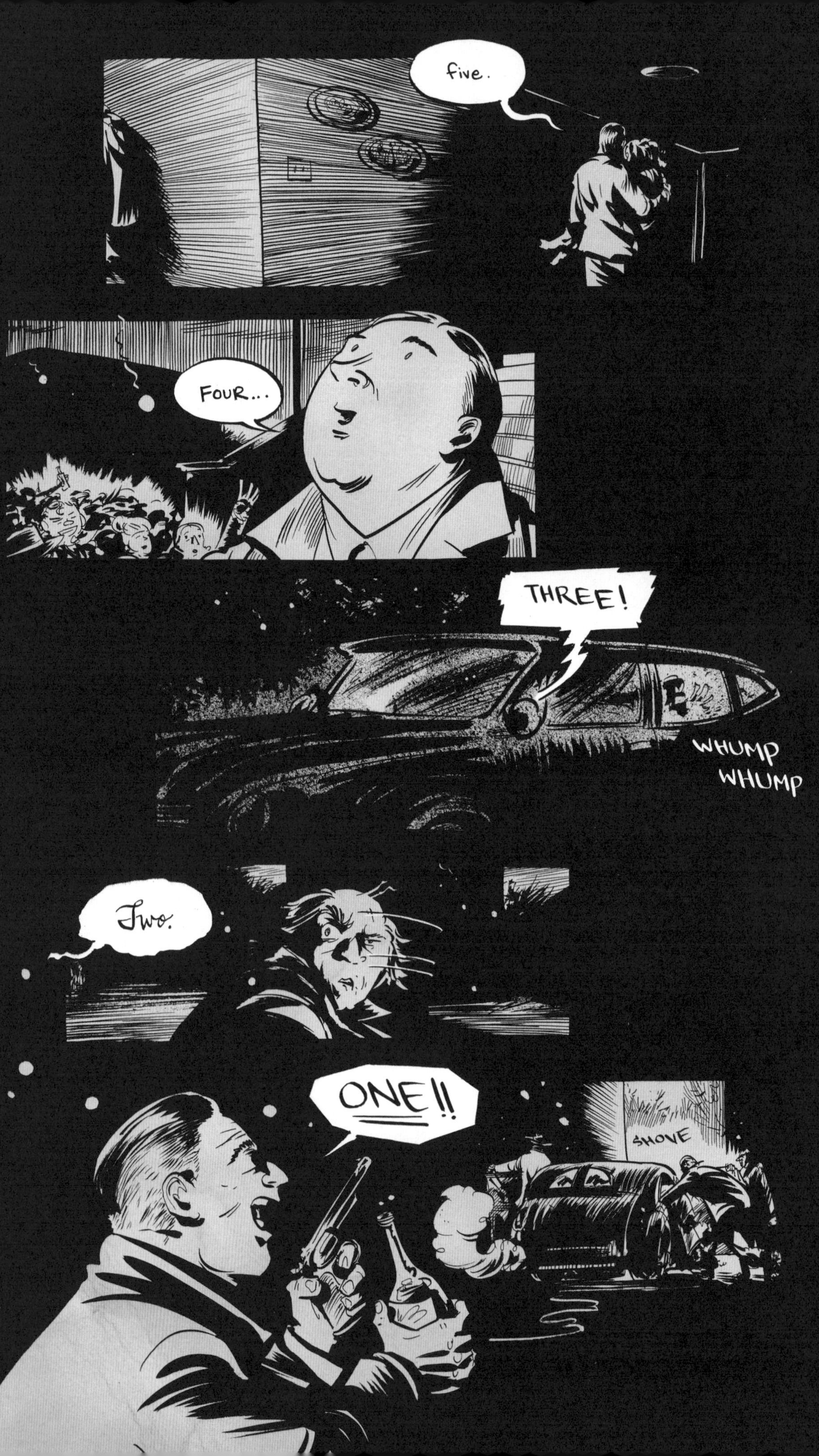
five.
FOUR...
THREE!
WHUMP
WHUMP
Two.
ONE!!
SHOVE

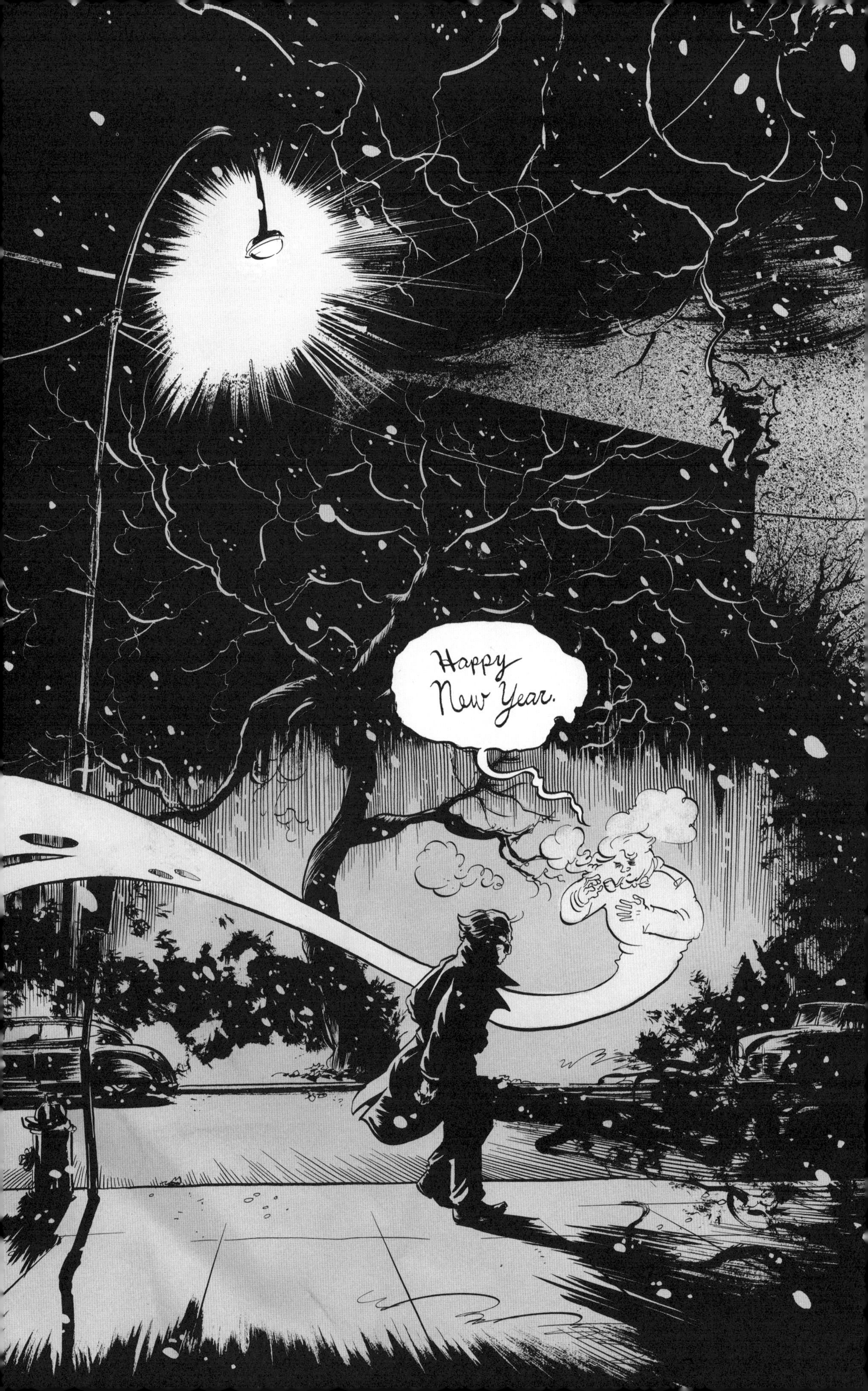
Happy New Year.

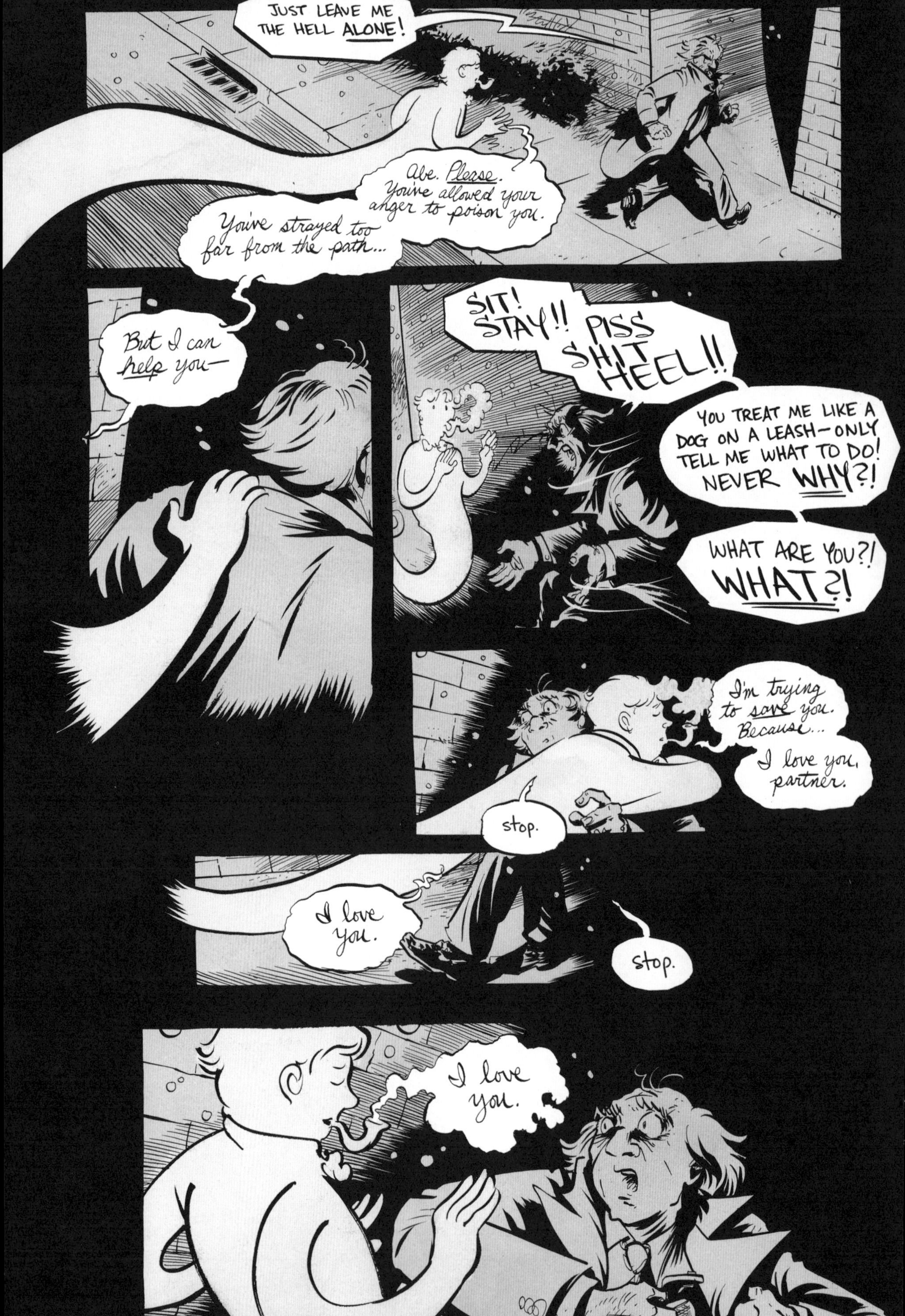

JUST LEAVE ME THE HELL ALONE!
Abe. Please. You've allowed your anger to poison you.
You've strayed too far from the path...
But I can help you—
SIT! STAY!! PISS SHIT HEEL!!
YOU TREAT ME LIKE A DOG ON A LEASH—ONLY TELL ME WHAT TO DO! NEVER WHY?!
WHAT ARE YOU?! WHAT?!
I'm trying to save you. Because...
I love you, partner.
stop.
I love you.
stop.
I love you.

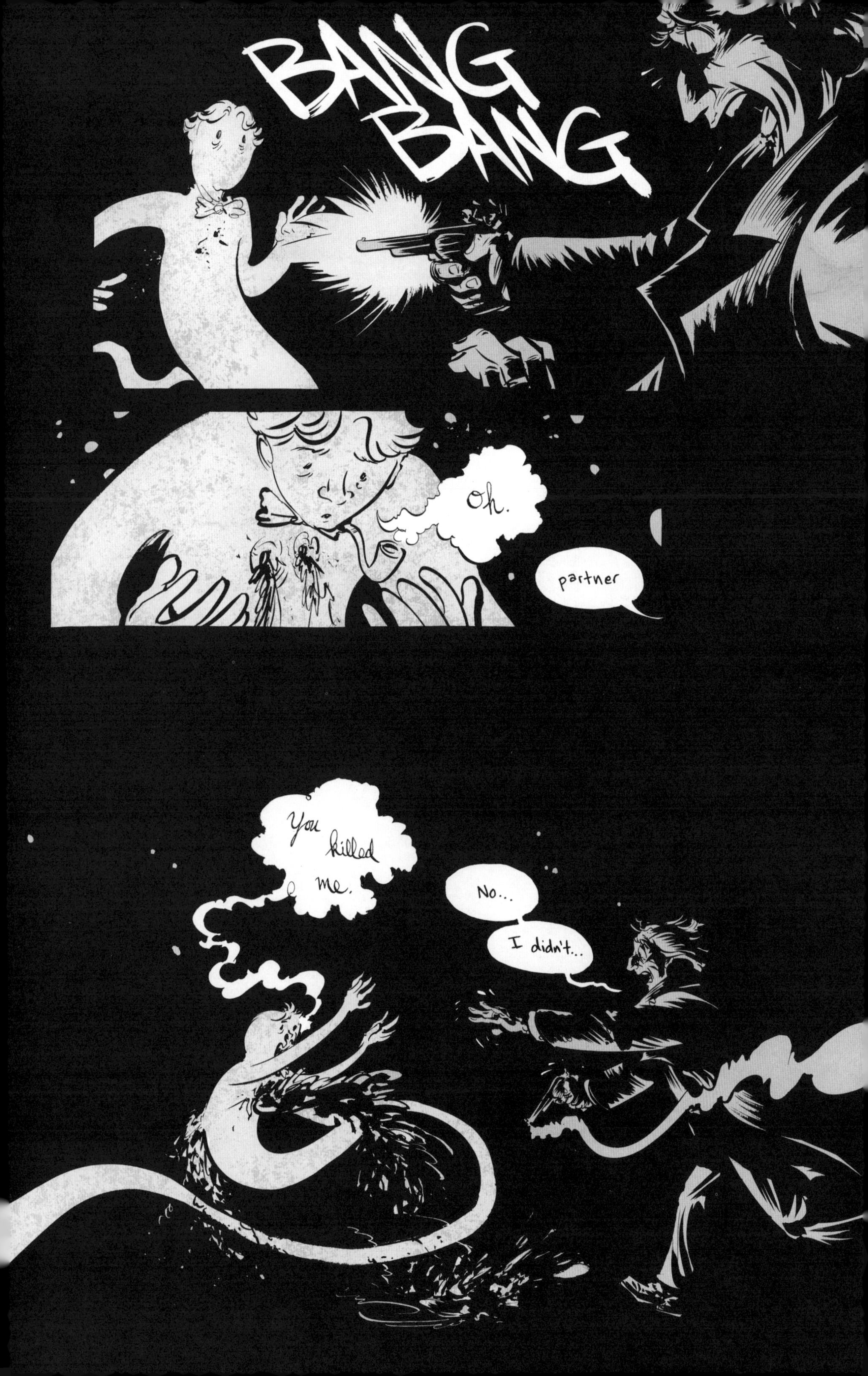
BANG
BANG
Oh.
partner
You killed me.
No...
I didn't...

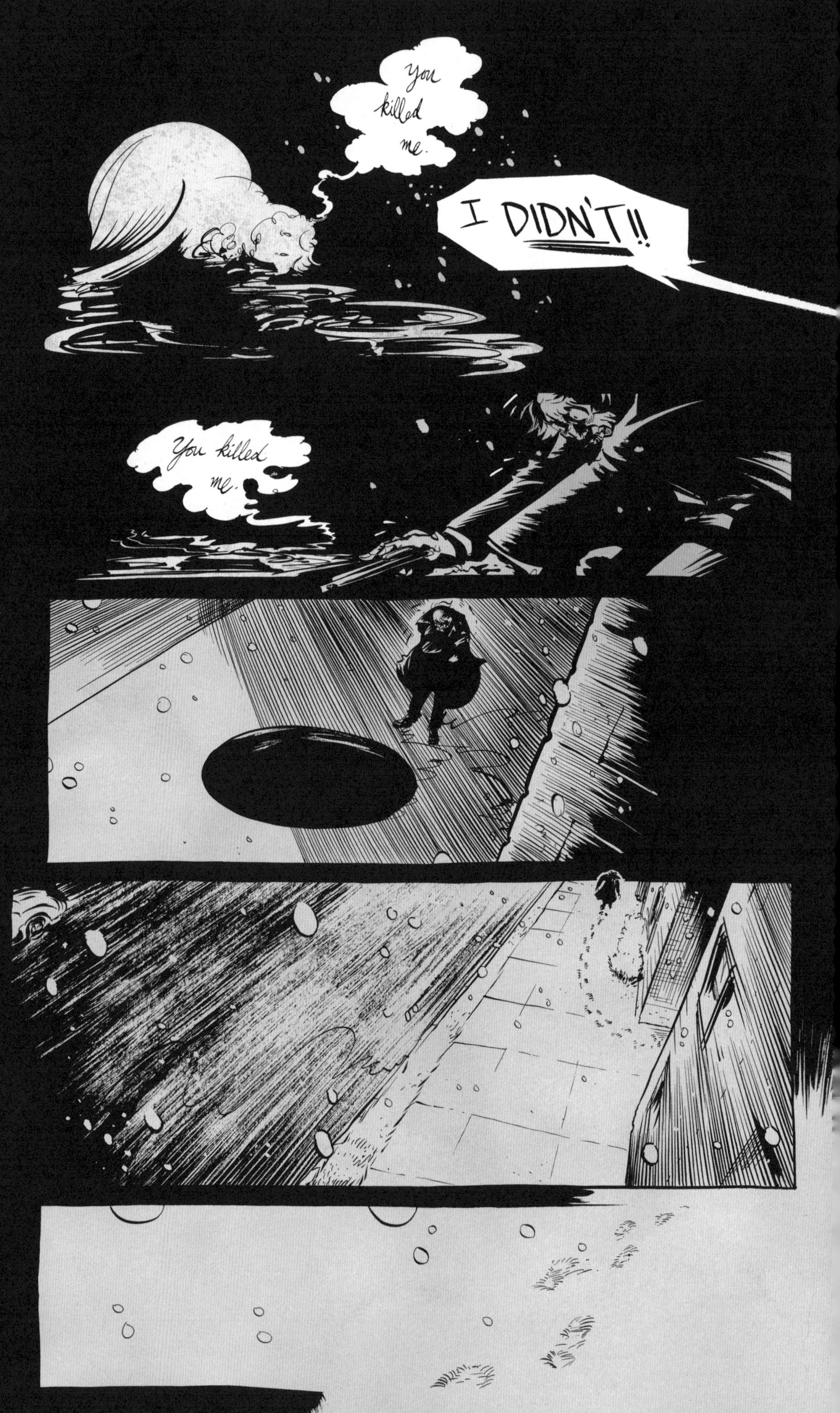
You killed me.
I DIDN'T!!
You killed me.

AUGUST, 1922

NORTH LITTLE ROCK

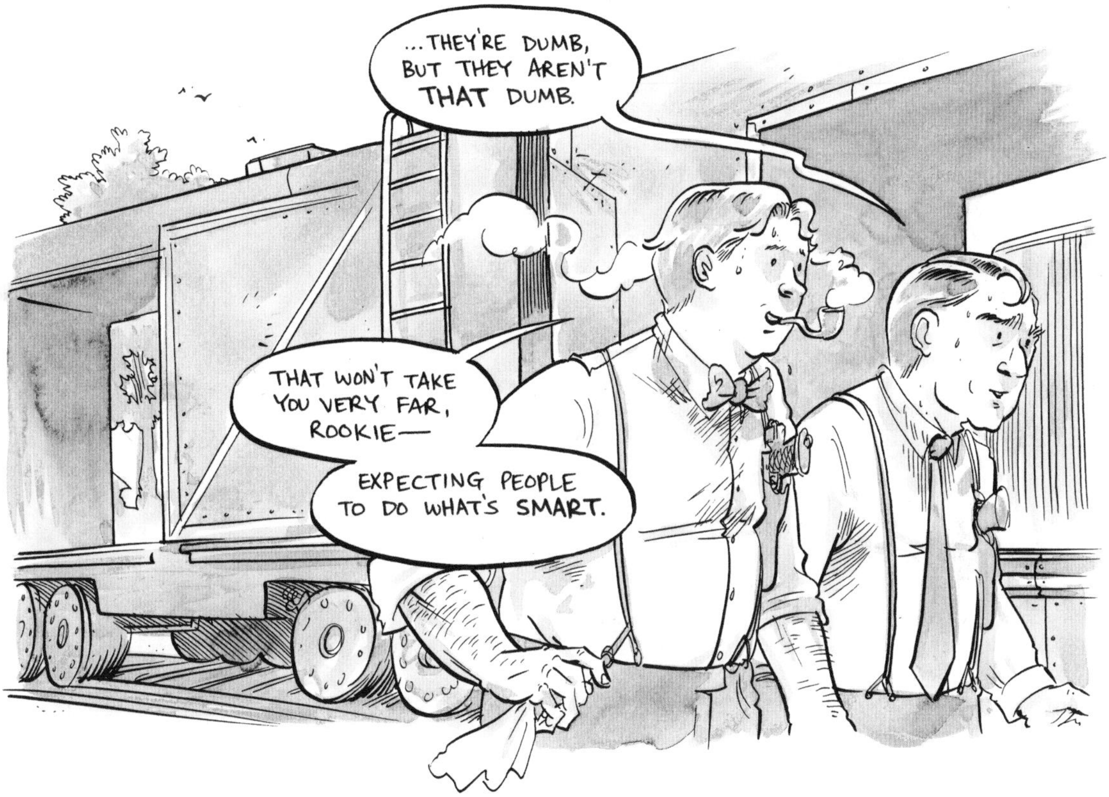
...THEY'RE DUMB, BUT THEY AREN'T THAT DUMB.
THAT WON'T TAKE YOU VERY FAR, ROOKIE—
EXPECTING PEOPLE TO DO WHAT'S SMART.

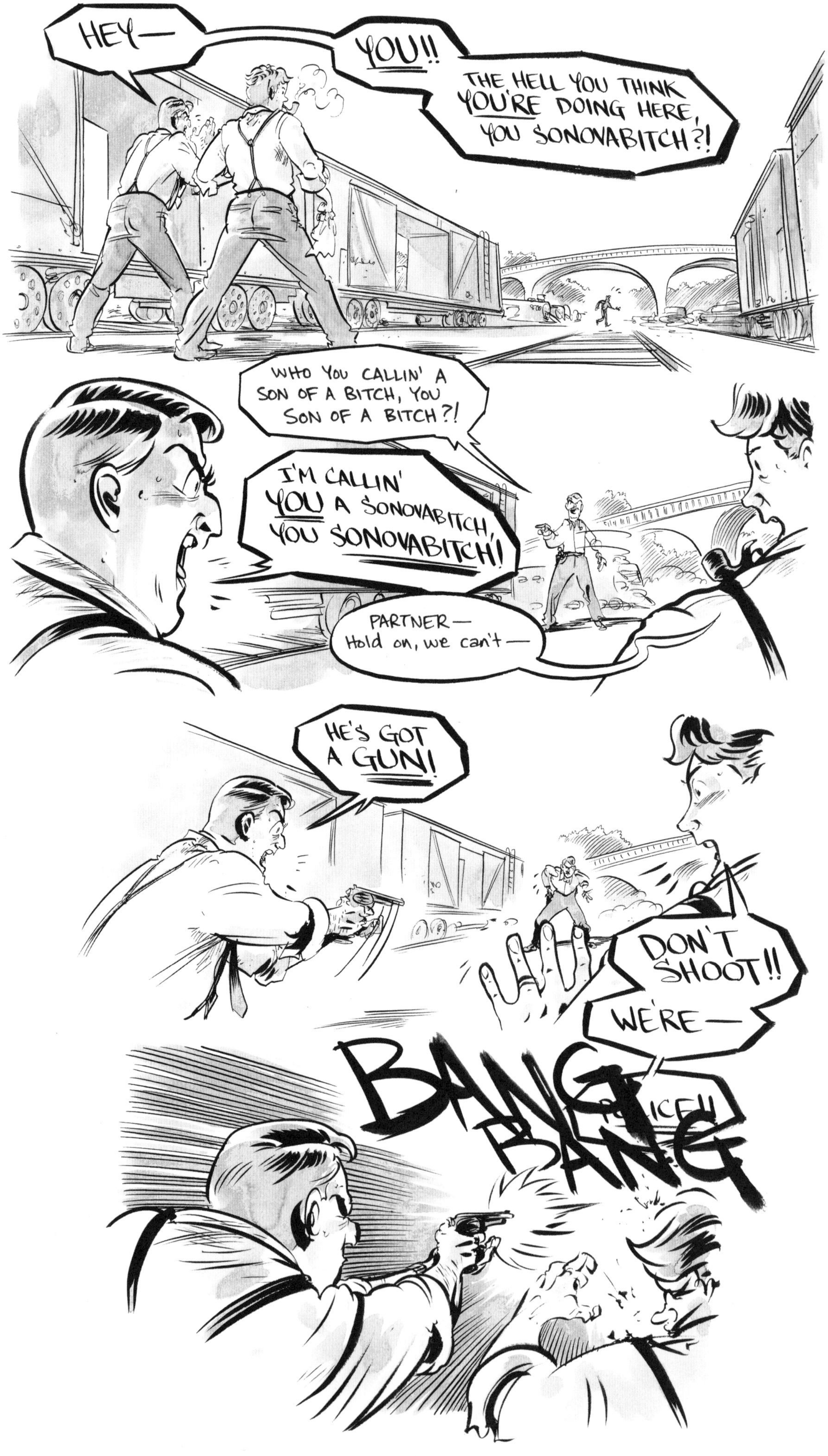
HEY—
YOU!!
THE HELL YOU THINK YOU'RE DOING HERE, YOU SONOVABITCH?!
WHO YOU CALLIN' A SON OF A BITCH, YOU SON OF A BITCH?!
I'M CALLIN' YOU A SONOVABITCH, YOU SONOVABITCH!
PARTNER— Hold on, we can't—
HE'S GOT A GUN!
DON'T SHOOT!! WE'RE—
BANG
BANG

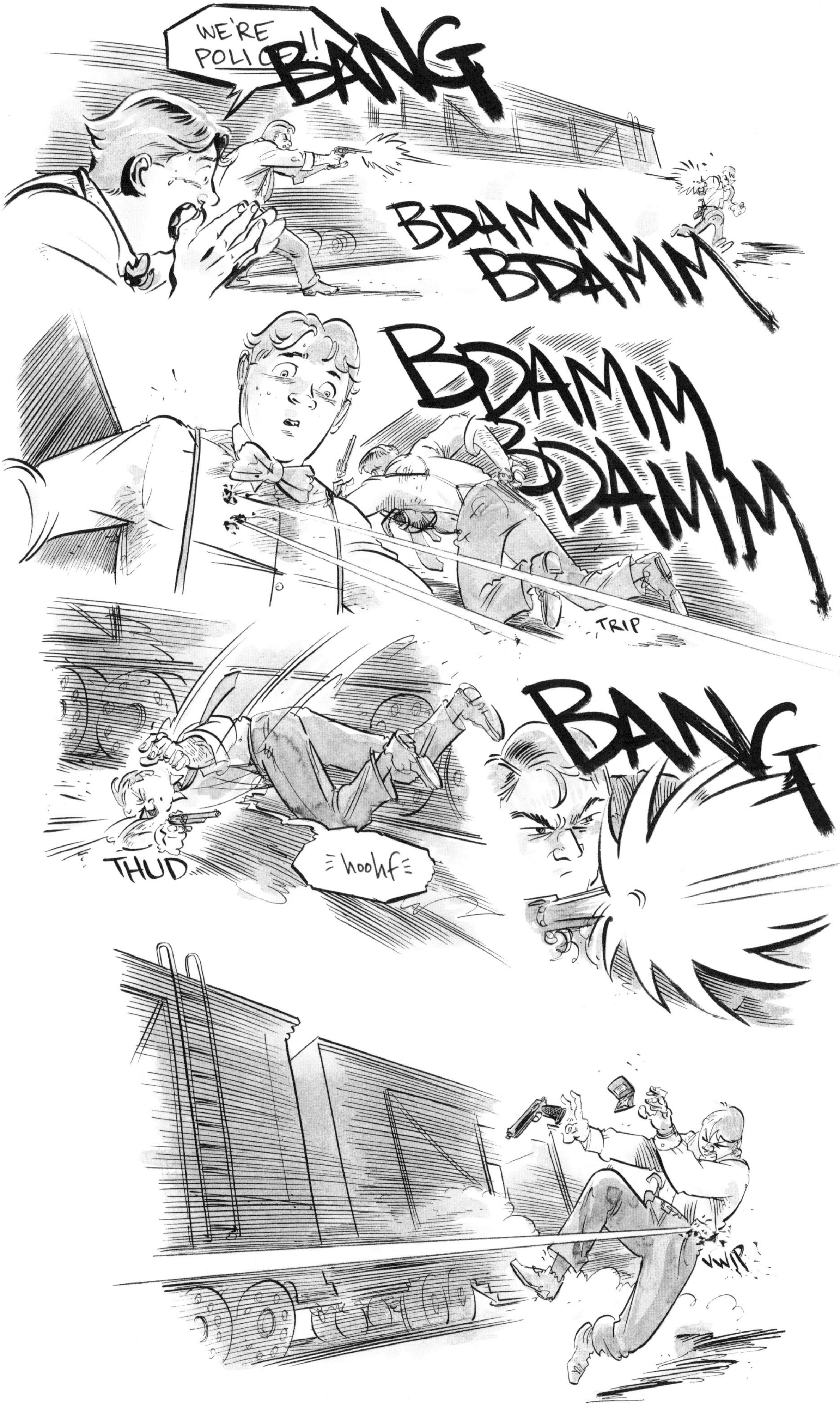
WE'RE POLICE!!
BANG
BDAMM BDAMM
BDAMM BDAMM
TRIP
BANG
THUD
hoohf
VWIP

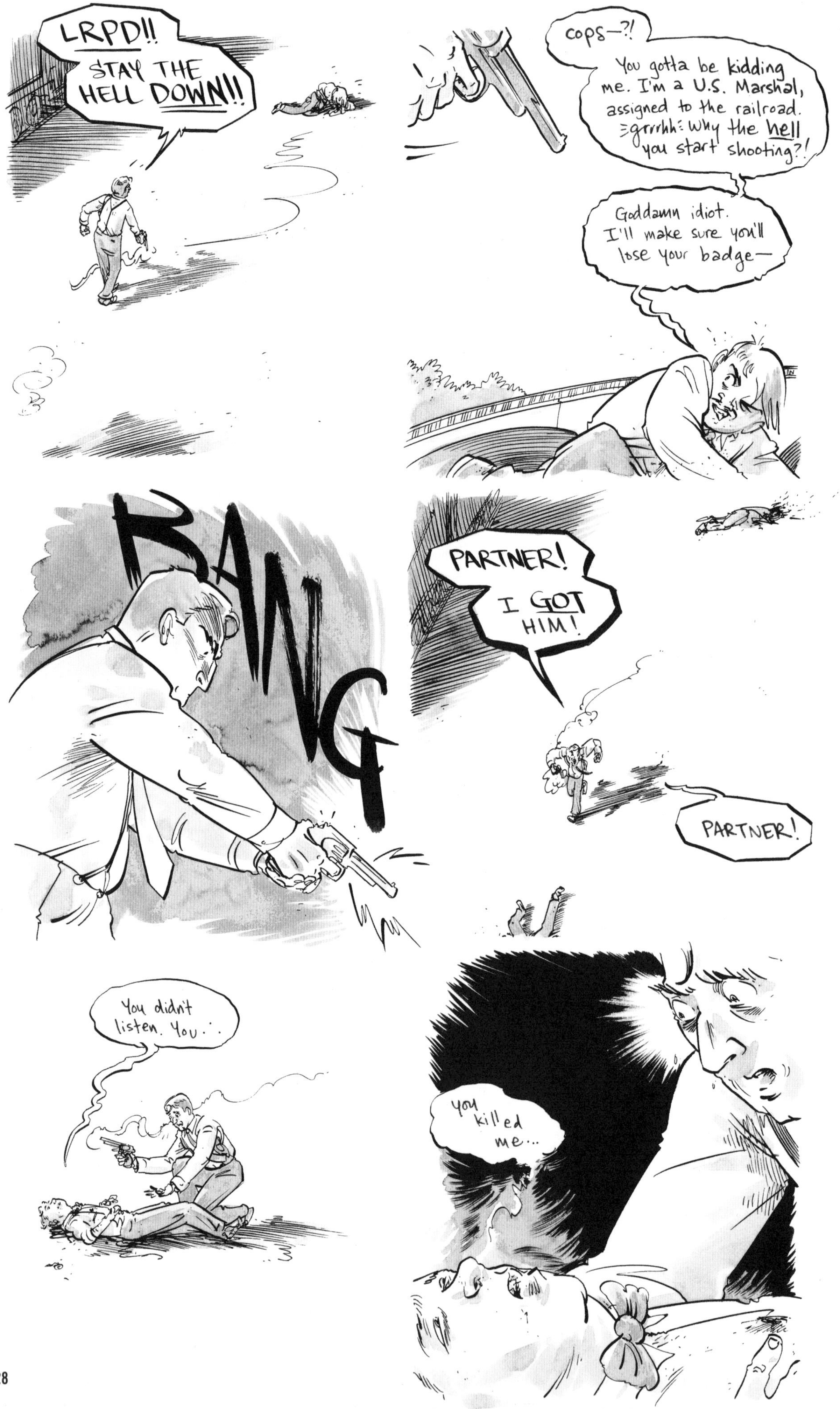
LRPD!! STAY THE HELL DOWN!!
cops—?!
You gotta be kidding me. I'm a U.S. Marshal, assigned to the railroad. =grrrhh= Why the hell you start shooting?!
Goddamn idiot. I'll make sure you'll lose your badge—
BANG
PARTNER! I GOT HIM!
PARTNER!
You didn't listen. You...
you killed me...

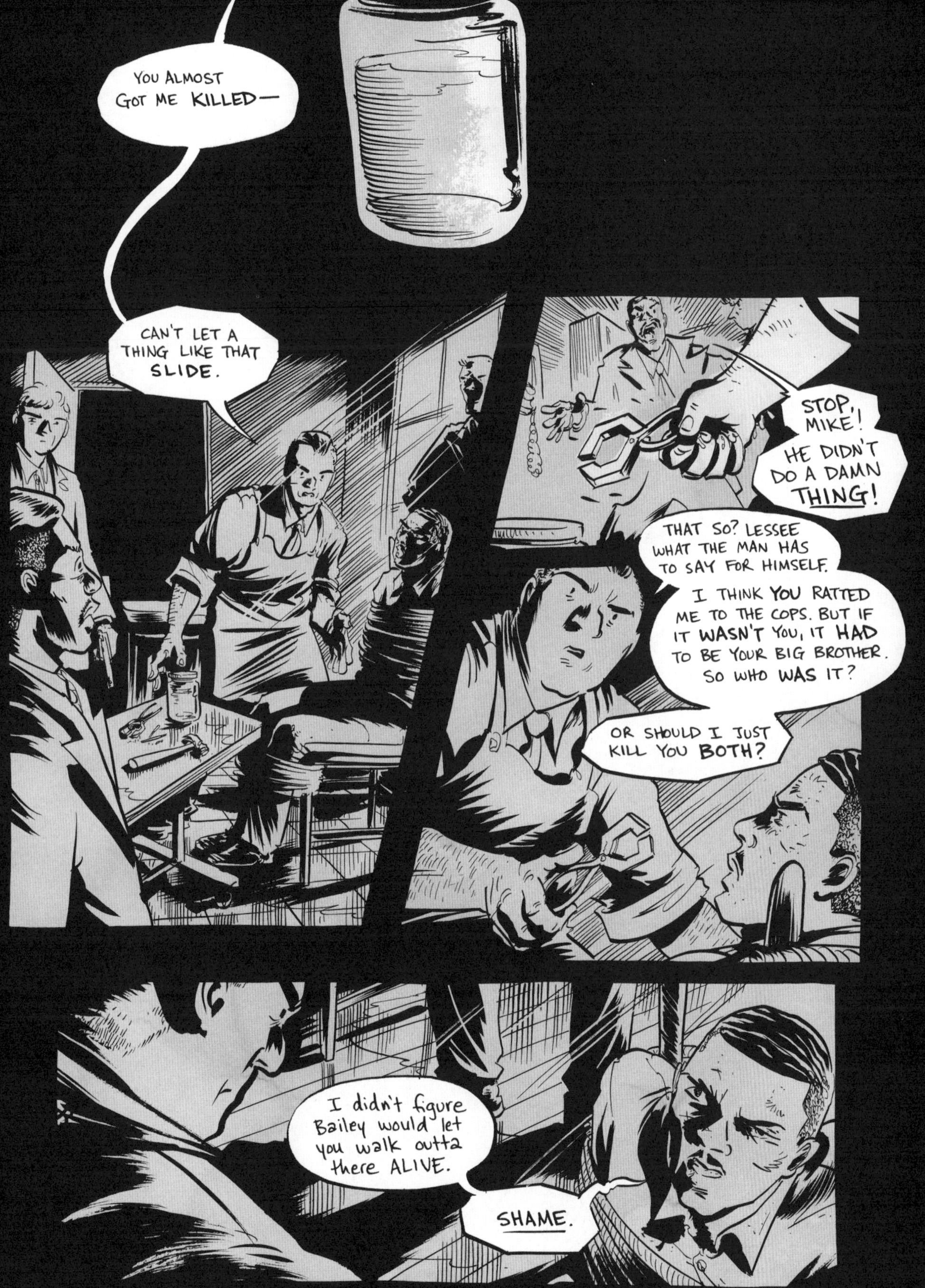
YOU ALMOST GOT ME KILLED—
CAN'T LET A THING LIKE THAT SLIDE.
STOP, MIKE!
HE DIDN'T DO A DAMN THING!
THAT SO? LESSEE WHAT THE MAN HAS TO SAY FOR HIMSELF.
I THINK YOU RATTED ME TO THE COPS. BUT IF IT WASN'T YOU, IT HAD TO BE YOUR BIG BROTHER. SO WHO WAS IT?
OR SHOULD I JUST KILL YOU BOTH?
I didn't figure Bailey would let you walk outta there ALIVE.
SHAME.

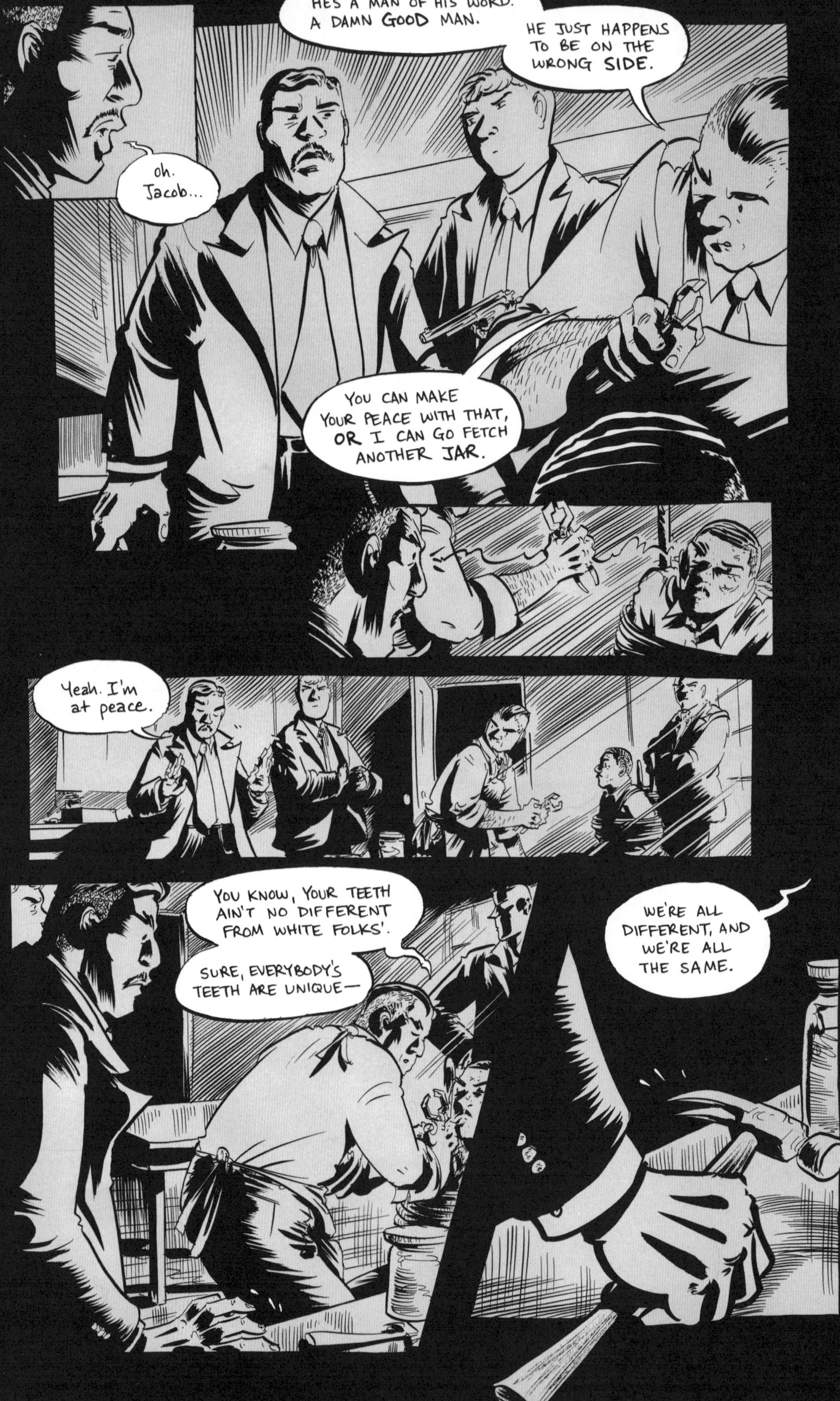
HE'S A MAN OF HIS WORD. A DAMN GOOD MAN.
HE JUST HAPPENS TO BE ON THE WRONG SIDE.
oh. Jacob...
YOU CAN MAKE YOUR PEACE WITH THAT, OR I CAN GO FETCH ANOTHER JAR.
Yeah. I'm at peace.
YOU KNOW, YOUR TEETH AIN'T NO DIFFERENT FROM WHITE FOLKS'.
SURE, EVERYBODY'S TEETH ARE UNIQUE—
WE'RE ALL DIFFERENT, AND WE'RE ALL THE SAME.

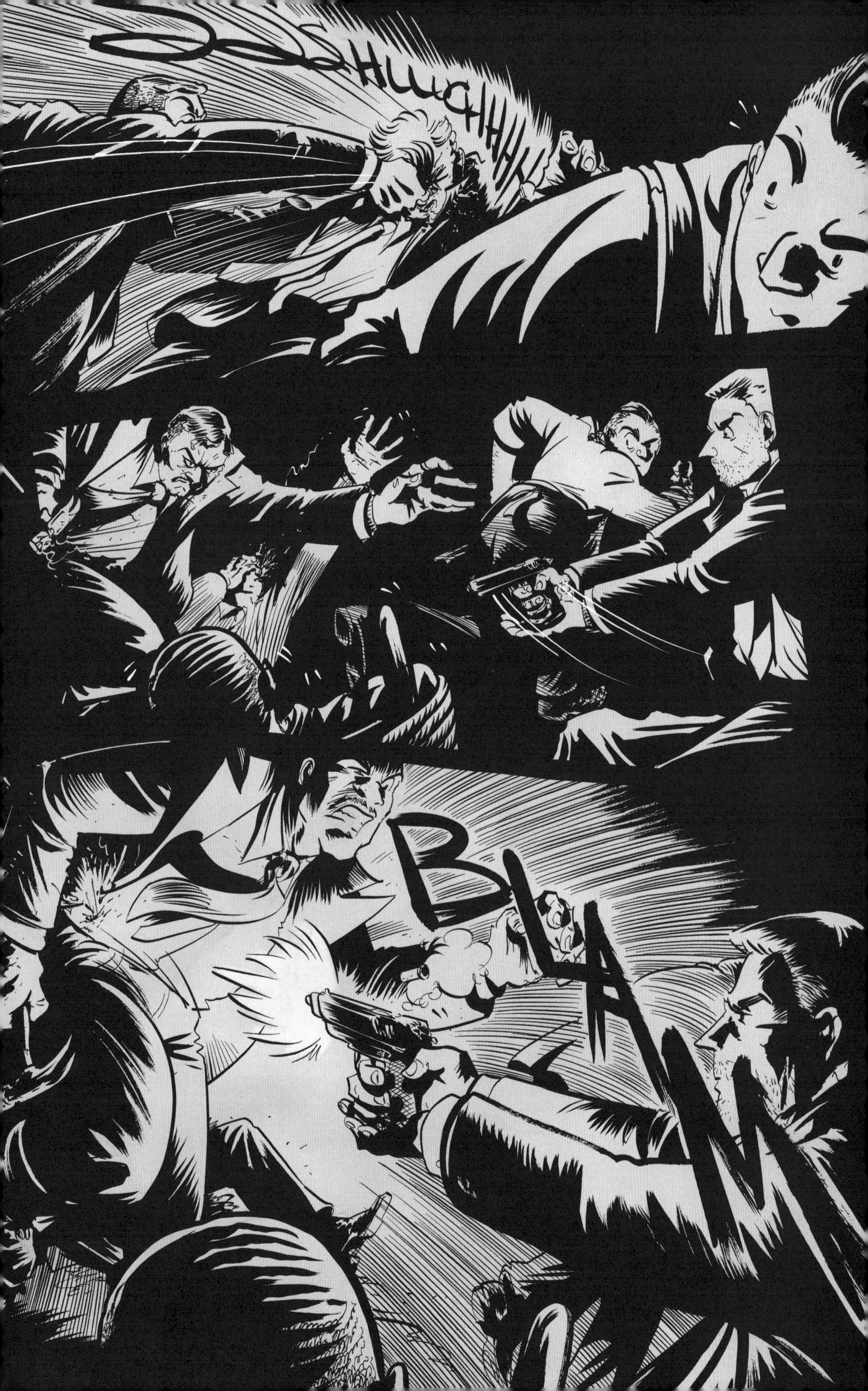
BLAM

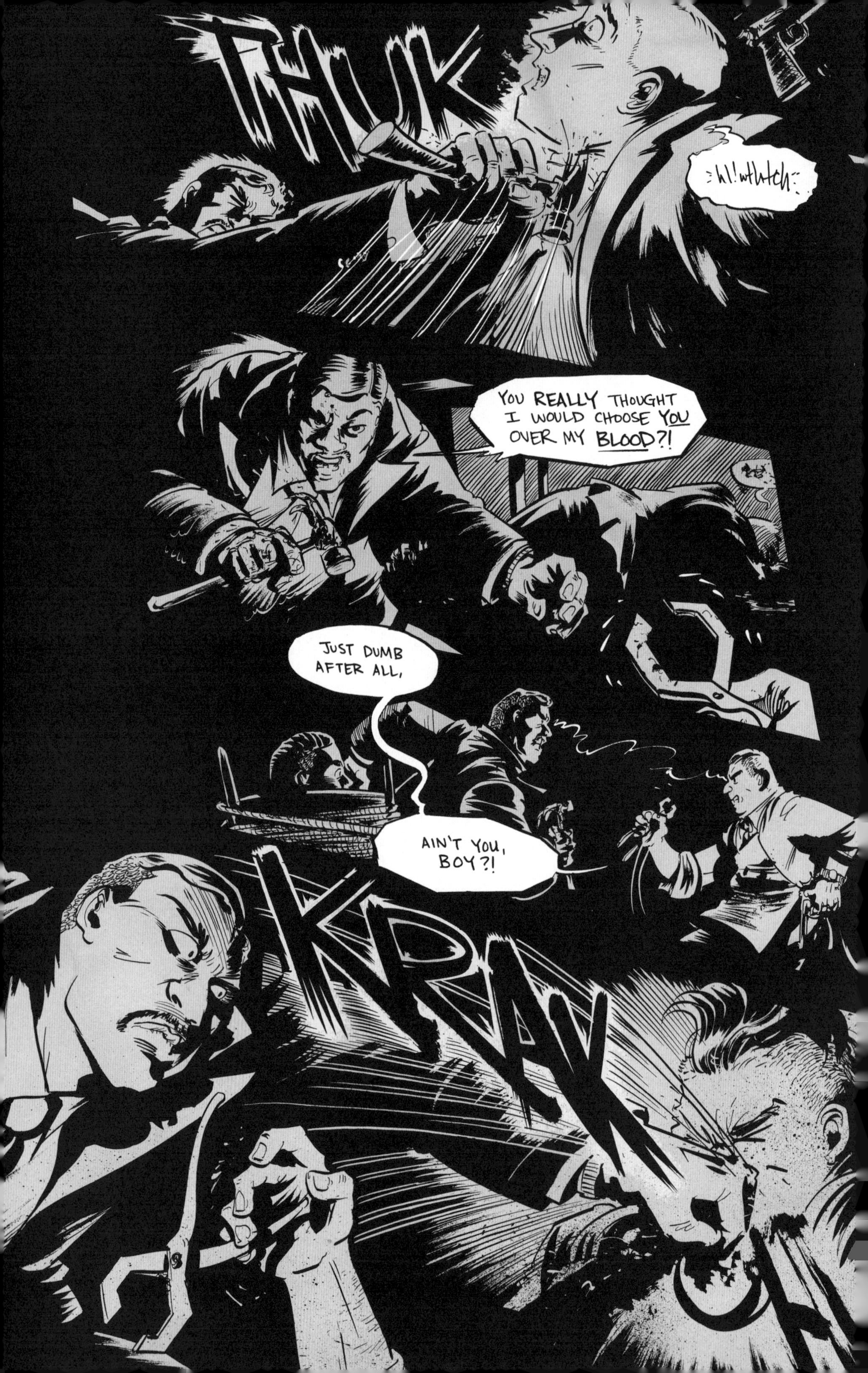
THUK
hl!wtlutch
YOU REALLY THOUGHT I WOULD CHOOSE YOU OVER MY BLOOD?!
JUST DUMB AFTER ALL,
AIN'T YOU, BOY?!
KRAK

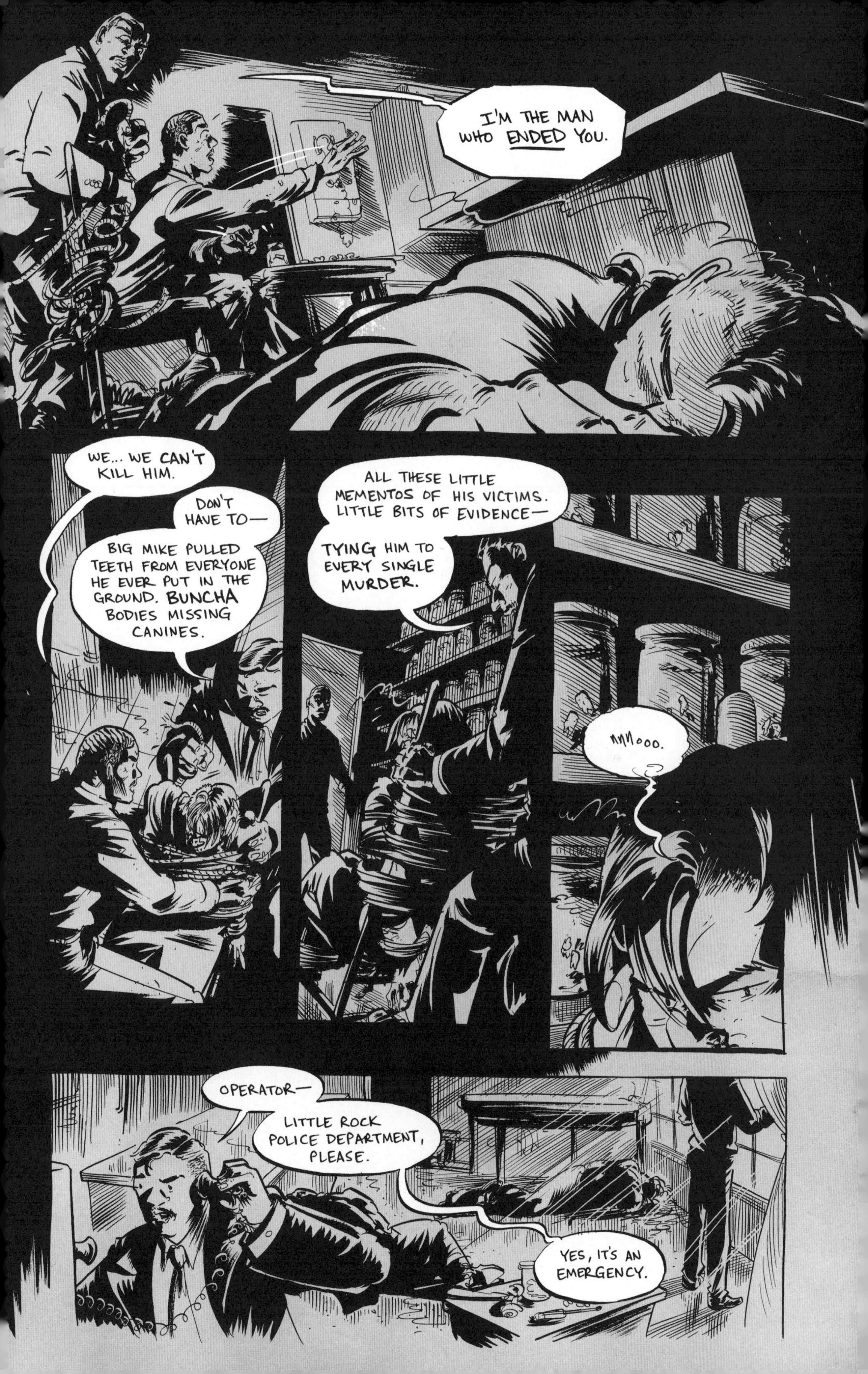
I'M THE MAN WHO ENDED YOU.
WE... WE CAN'T KILL HIM.
DON'T HAVE TO—
BIG MIKE PULLED TEETH FROM EVERYONE HE EVER PUT IN THE GROUND. BUNCHA BODIES MISSING CANINES.
ALL THESE LITTLE MEMENTOS OF HIS VICTIMS. LITTLE BITS OF EVIDENCE—
TYING HIM TO EVERY SINGLE MURDER.
MMooo.
OPERATOR—
LITTLE ROCK POLICE DEPARTMENT, PLEASE.
YES, IT'S AN EMERGENCY.

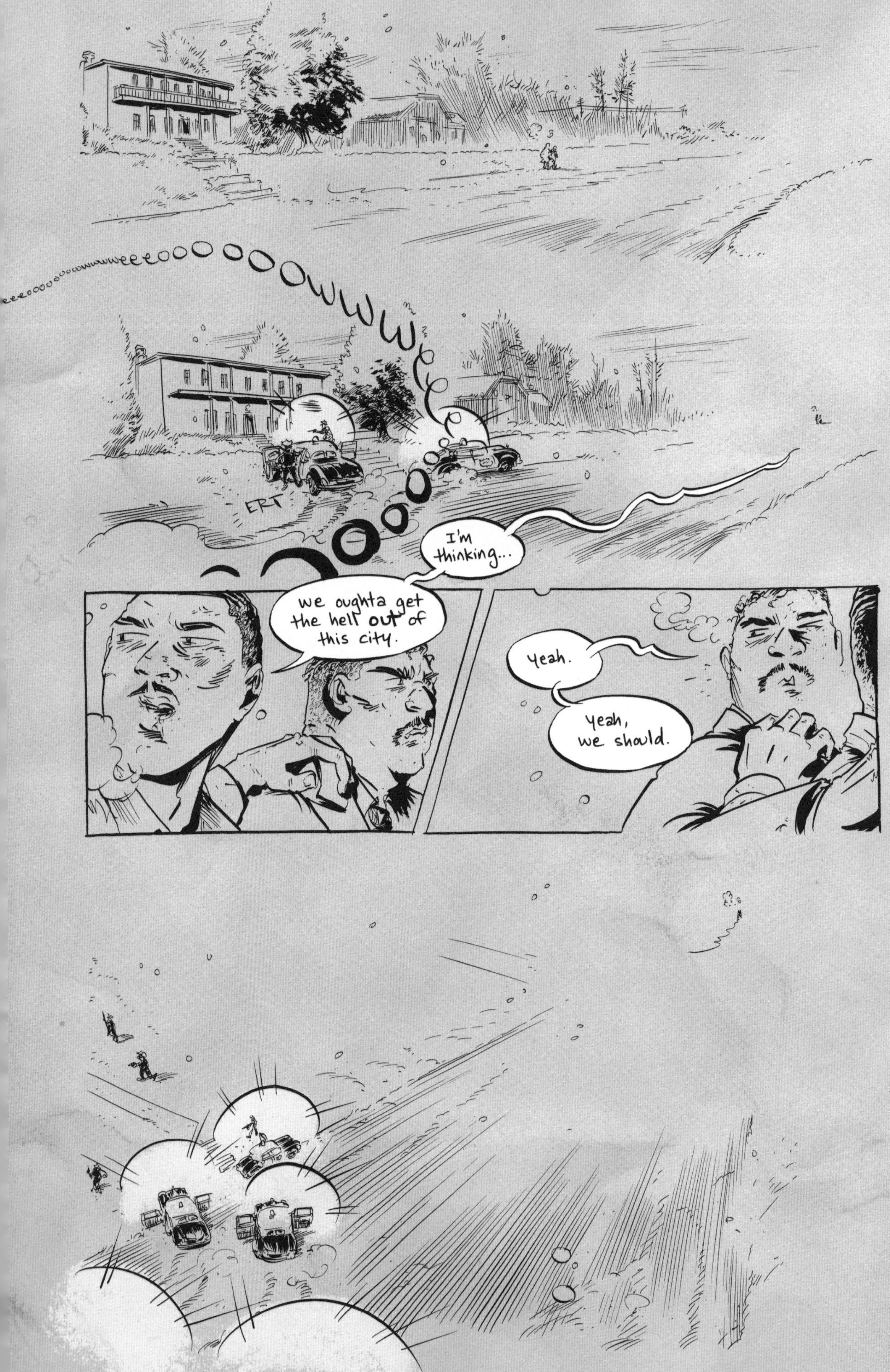
eeeooooooowwwweeeoooooowwweee
ERT
I'm thinking...
we oughta get the hell out of this city.
Yeah.
Yeah, we should.

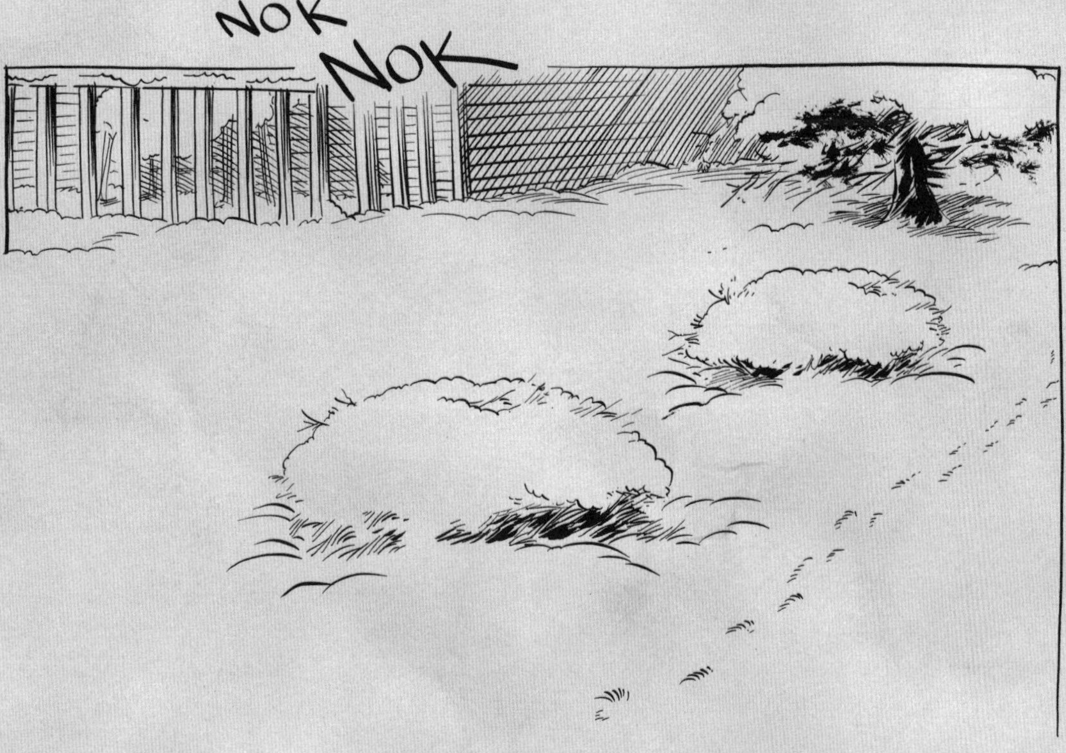
NOK
NOK

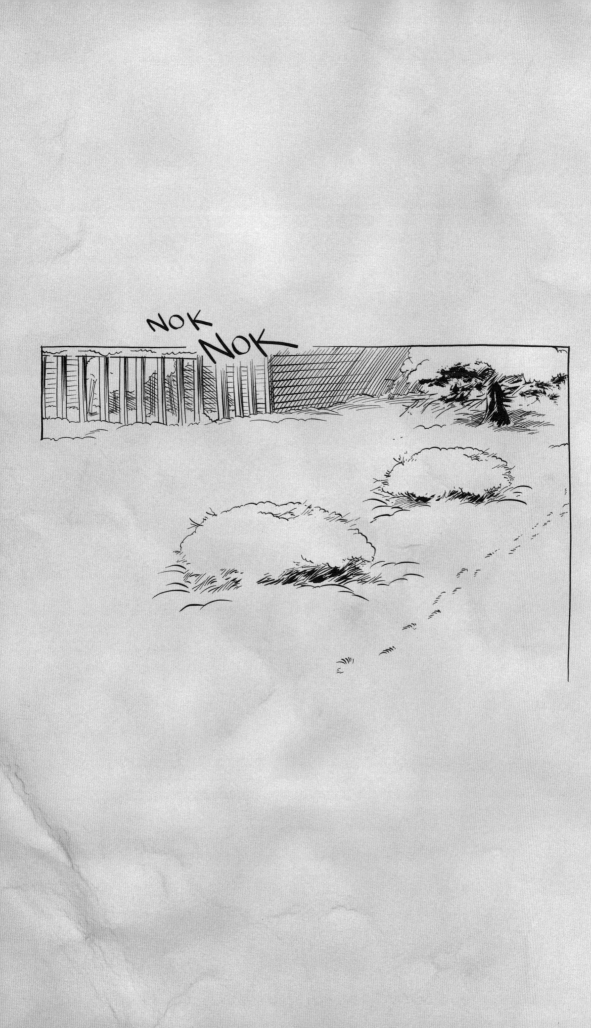

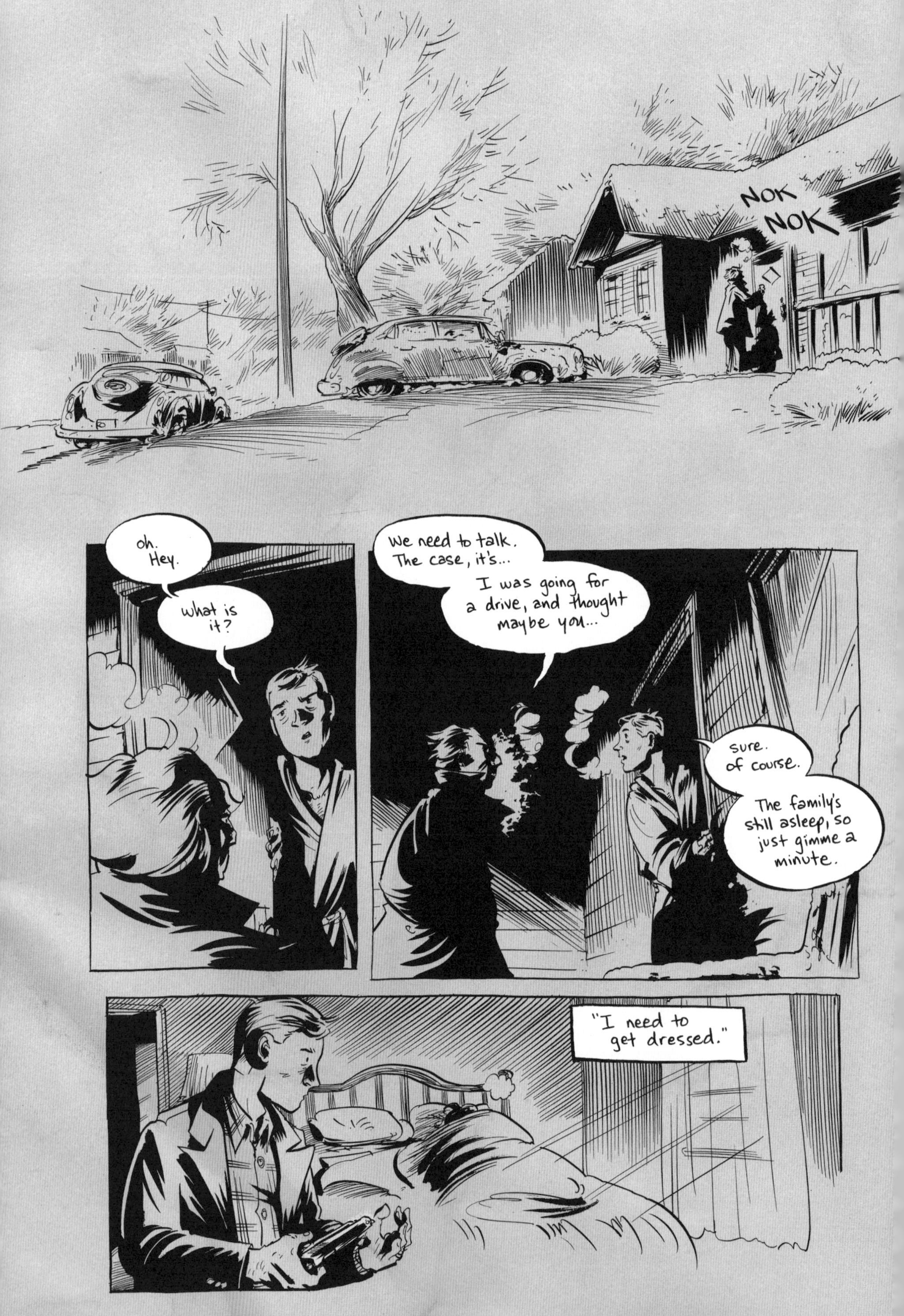
NOK
NOK
oh. Hey.
what is it?
We need to talk. The case, it's...
I was going for a drive, and thought maybe you...
sure. of course.
The family's still asleep, so just gimme a minute.
"I need to get dressed."

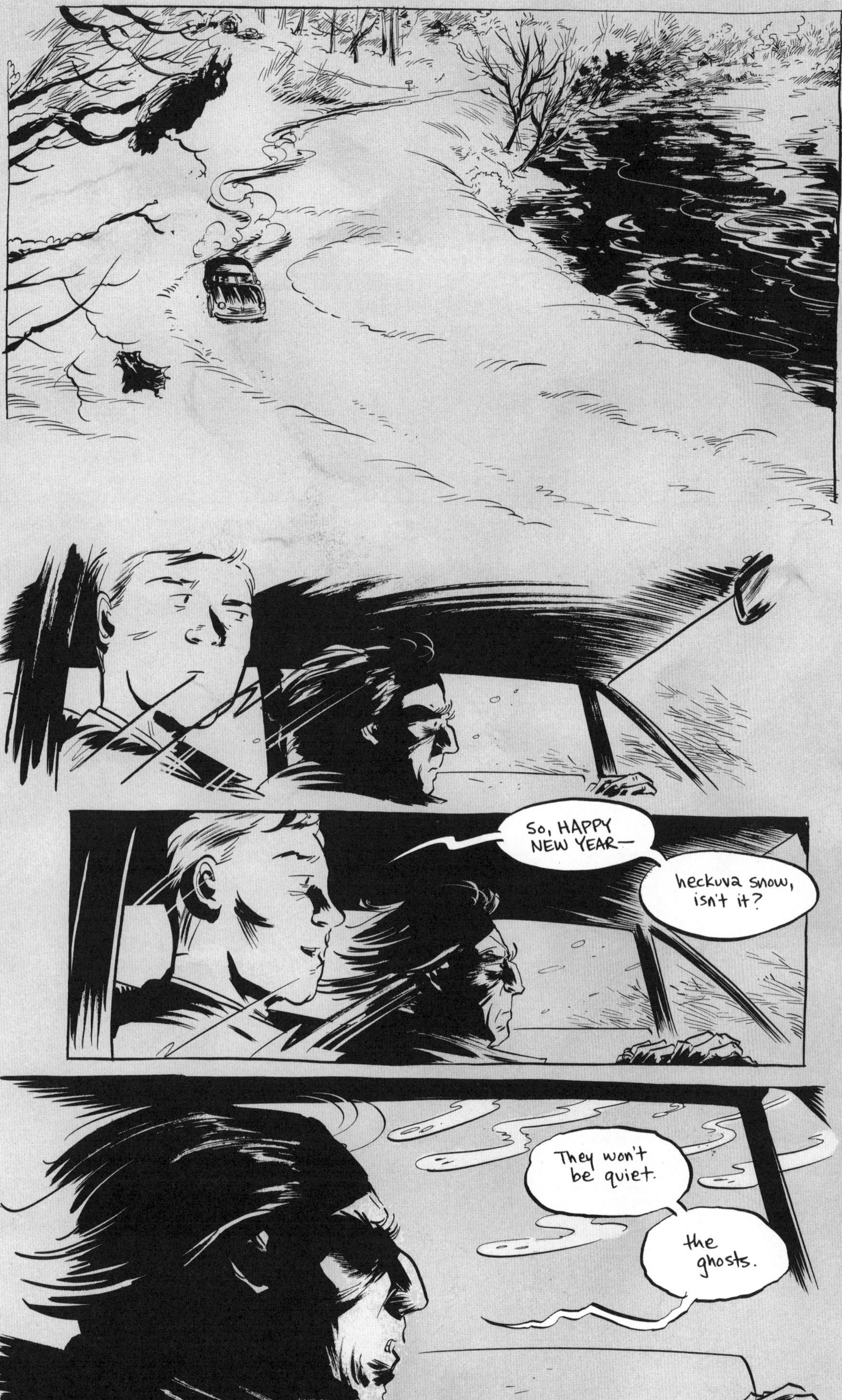
So, HAPPY NEW YEAR—
heckuva snow, isn't it?
They won't be quiet.
the ghosts.

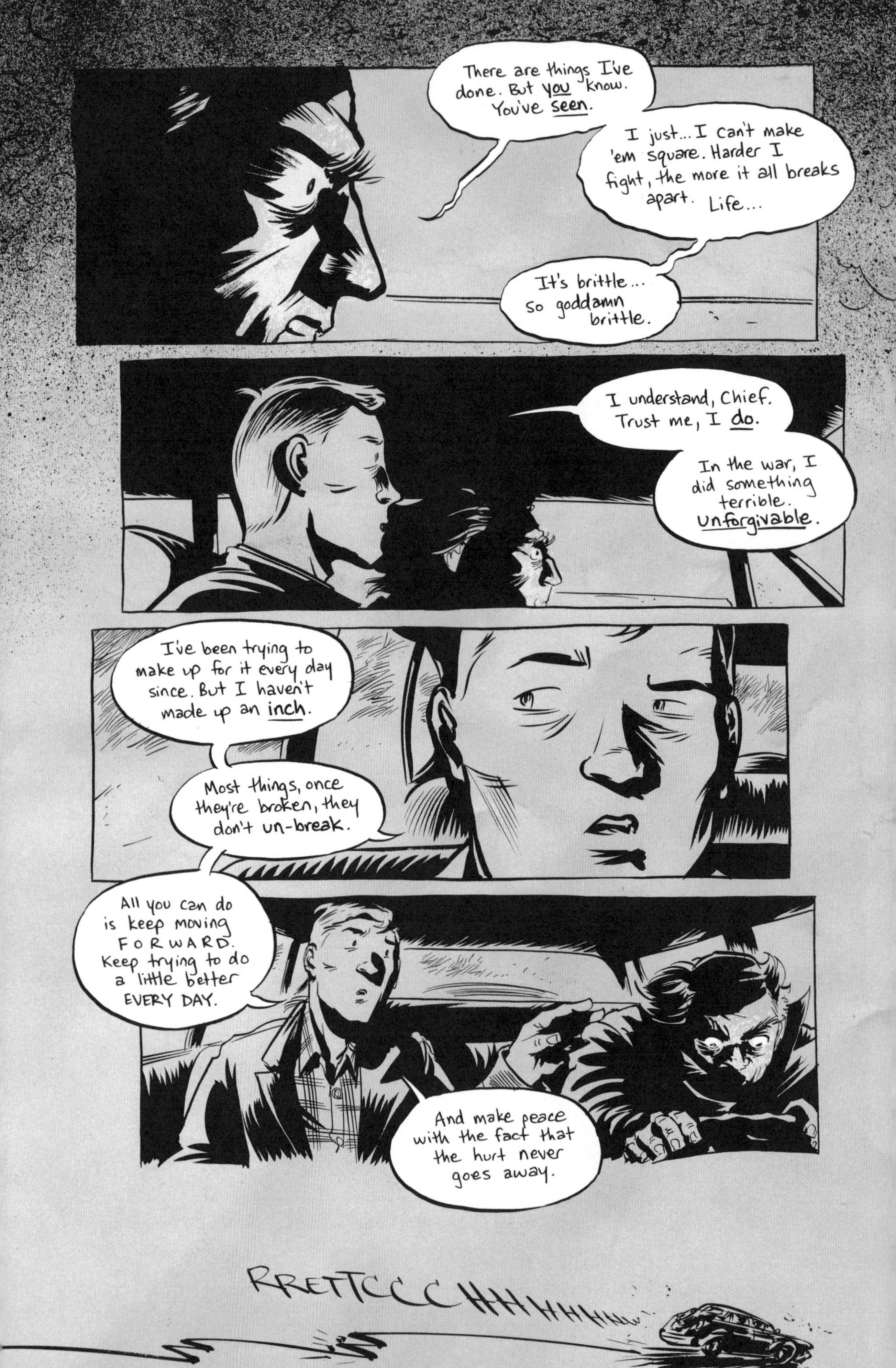
There are things I've done. But you know. You've seen.
I just... I can't make 'em square. Harder I fight, the more it all breaks apart. Life...
It's brittle... so goddamn brittle.
I understand, Chief. Trust me, I do.
In the war, I did something terrible. Unforgivable.
I've been trying to make up for it every day since. But I haven't made up an inch.
Most things, once they're broken, they don't un-break.
All you can do is keep moving FORWARD. Keep trying to do a little better EVERY DAY.
And make peace with the fact that the hurt never goes away.
RRETTCCCCHHHHHHHww

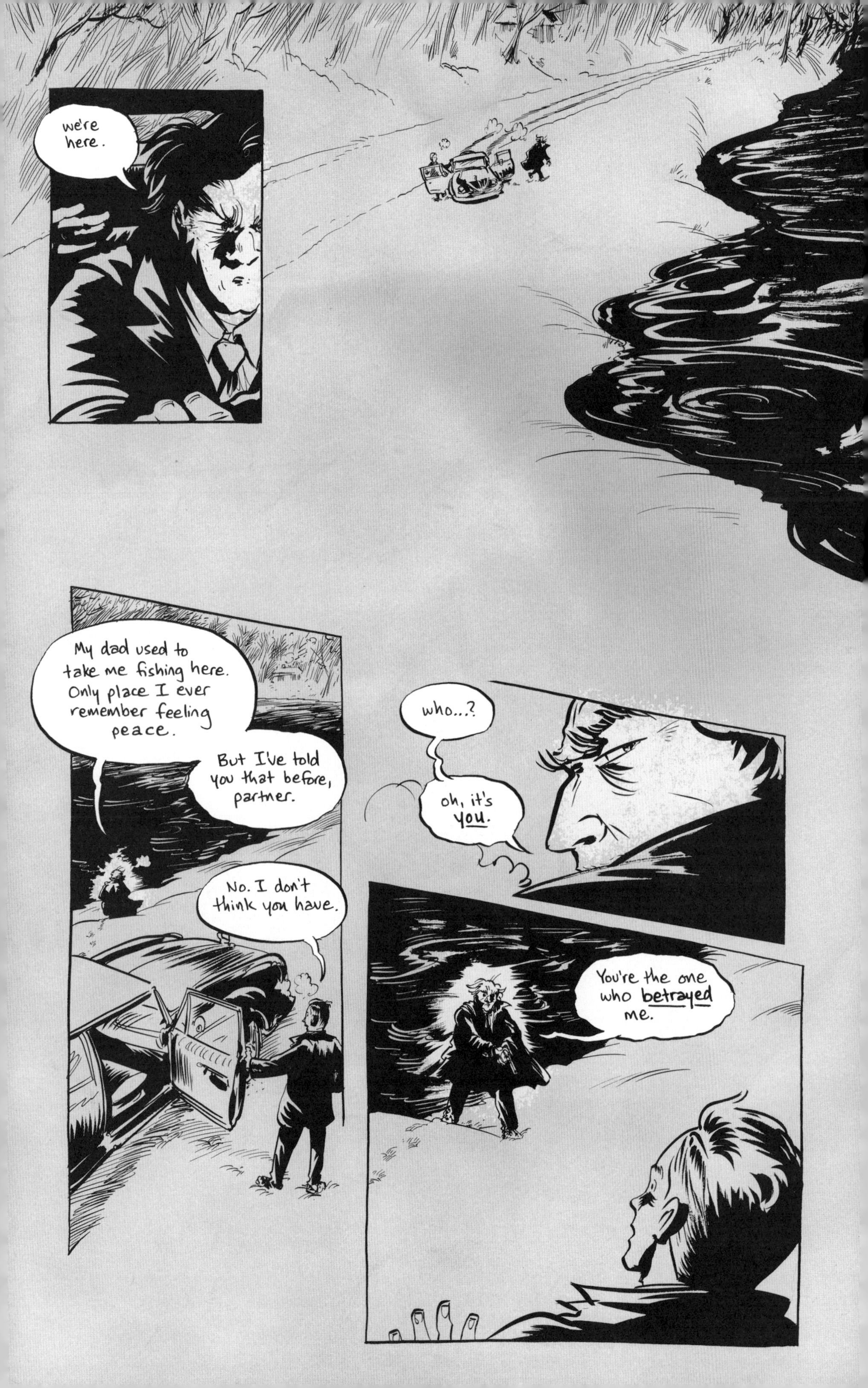
we're here.
My dad used to take me fishing here. Only place I ever remember feeling peace.
But I've told you that before, partner.
No. I don't think you have.
who...?
oh, it's YOU.
You're the one who betrayed me.

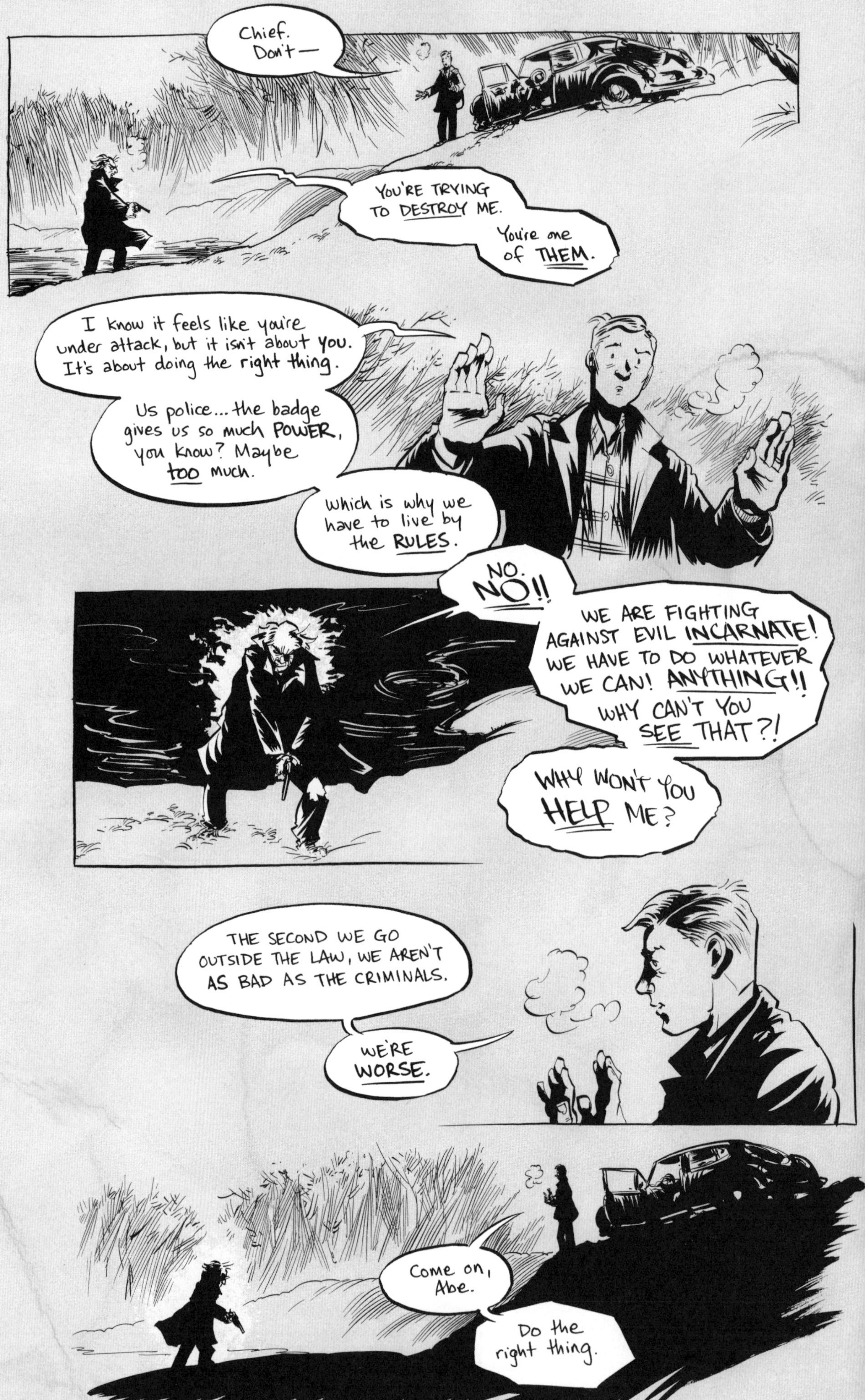
Chief. Don't—
You're trying to destroy me.
You're one of THEM.
I know it feels like you're under attack, but it isn't about you. It's about doing the right thing.
Us police... the badge gives us so much POWER, you know? Maybe too much.
Which is why we have to live by the RULES.
NO. NO!!
WE ARE FIGHTING AGAINST EVIL INCARNATE! WE HAVE TO DO WHATEVER WE CAN! ANYTHING!! WHY CAN'T YOU SEE THAT?!
WHY WON'T YOU HELP ME?
THE SECOND WE GO OUTSIDE THE LAW, WE AREN'T AS BAD AS THE CRIMINALS.
WE'RE WORSE.
Come on, Abe.
Do the right thing.

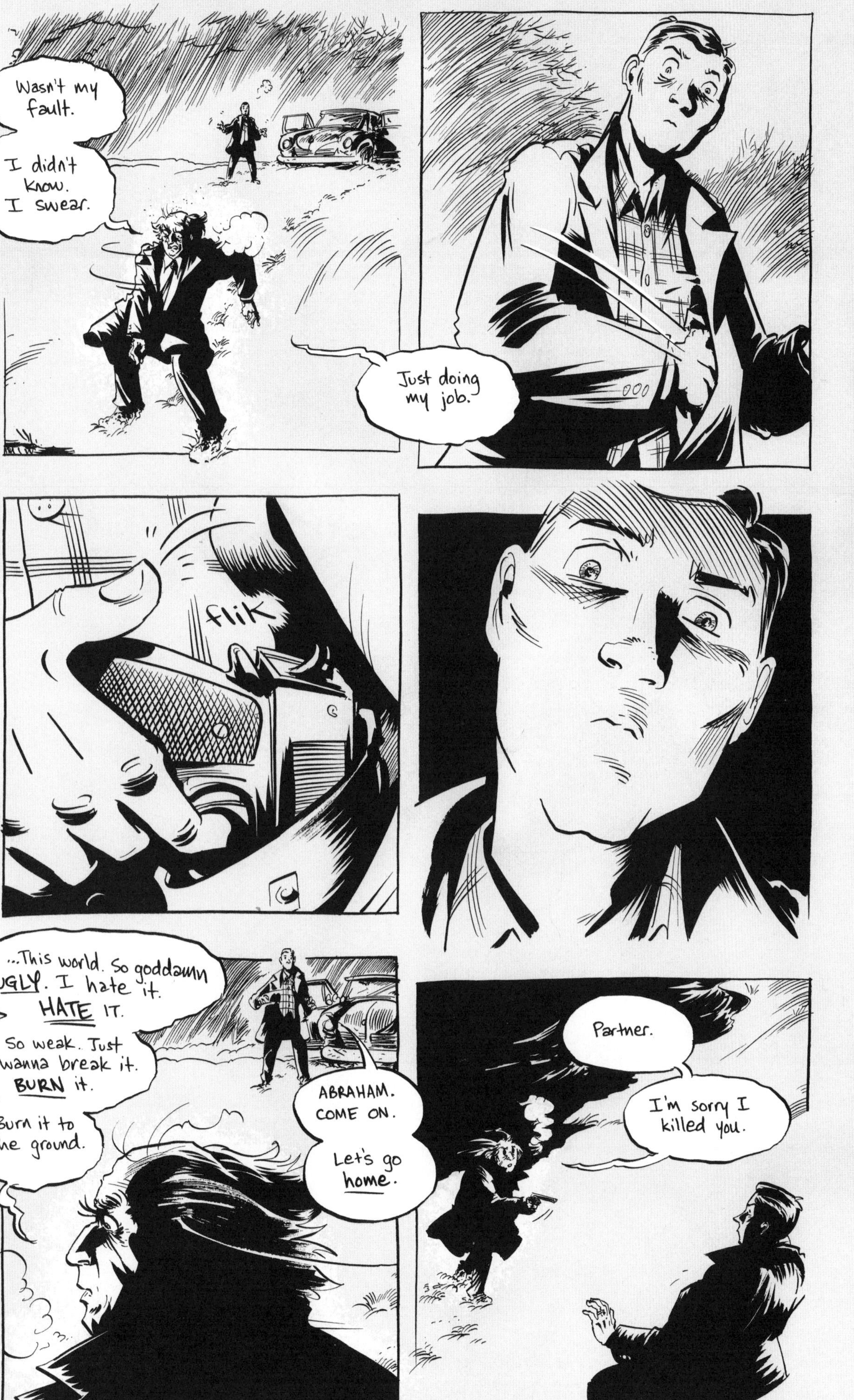
Wasn't my fault.
I didn't know. I swear.
Just doing my job.
flik
...This world. So goddamn UGLY. I hate it. HATE IT.
So weak. Just wanna break it. BURN it.
Burn it to the ground.
ABRAHAM. COME ON.
Let's go home.
Partner.
I'm sorry I killed you.

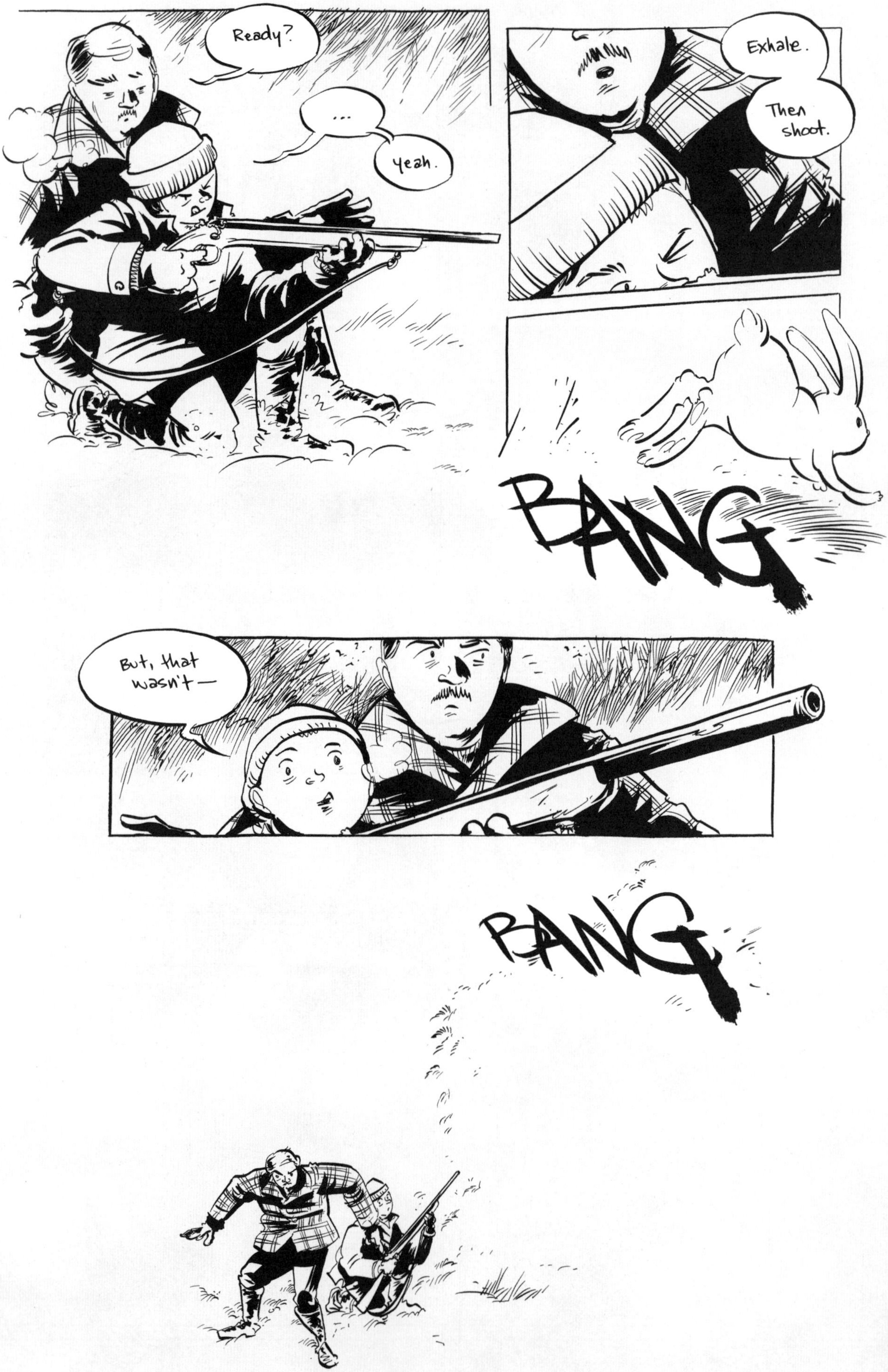
Ready?
...
yeah.
Exhale.
Then shoot.
BANG
But, that wasn't—
BANG

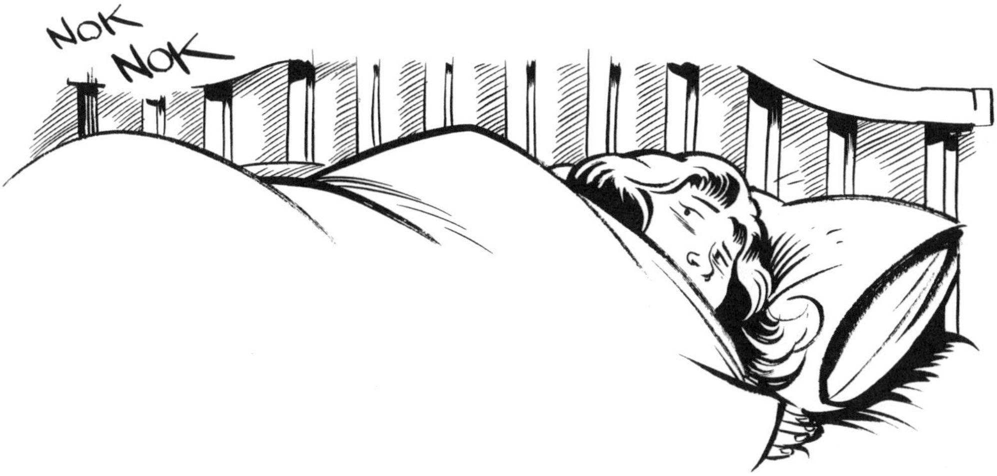
NOK
NOK

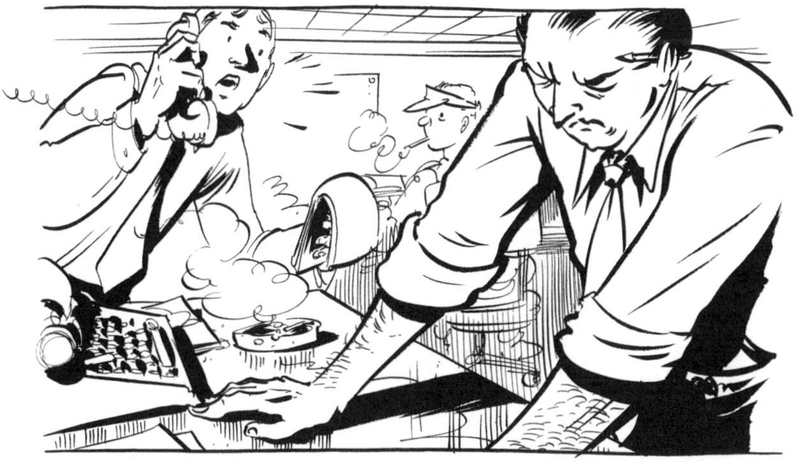

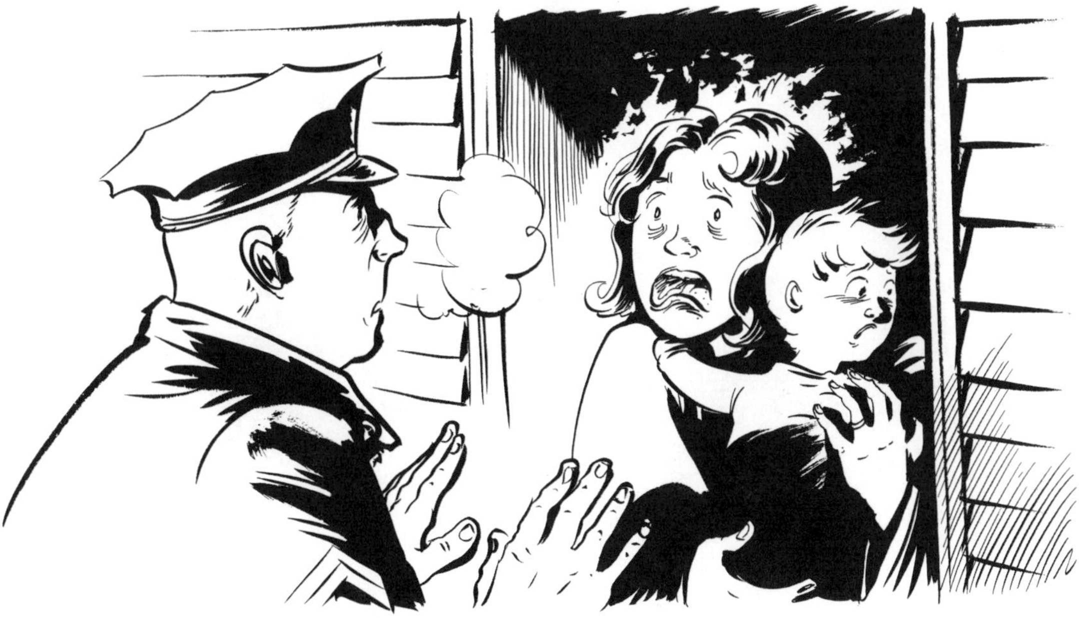

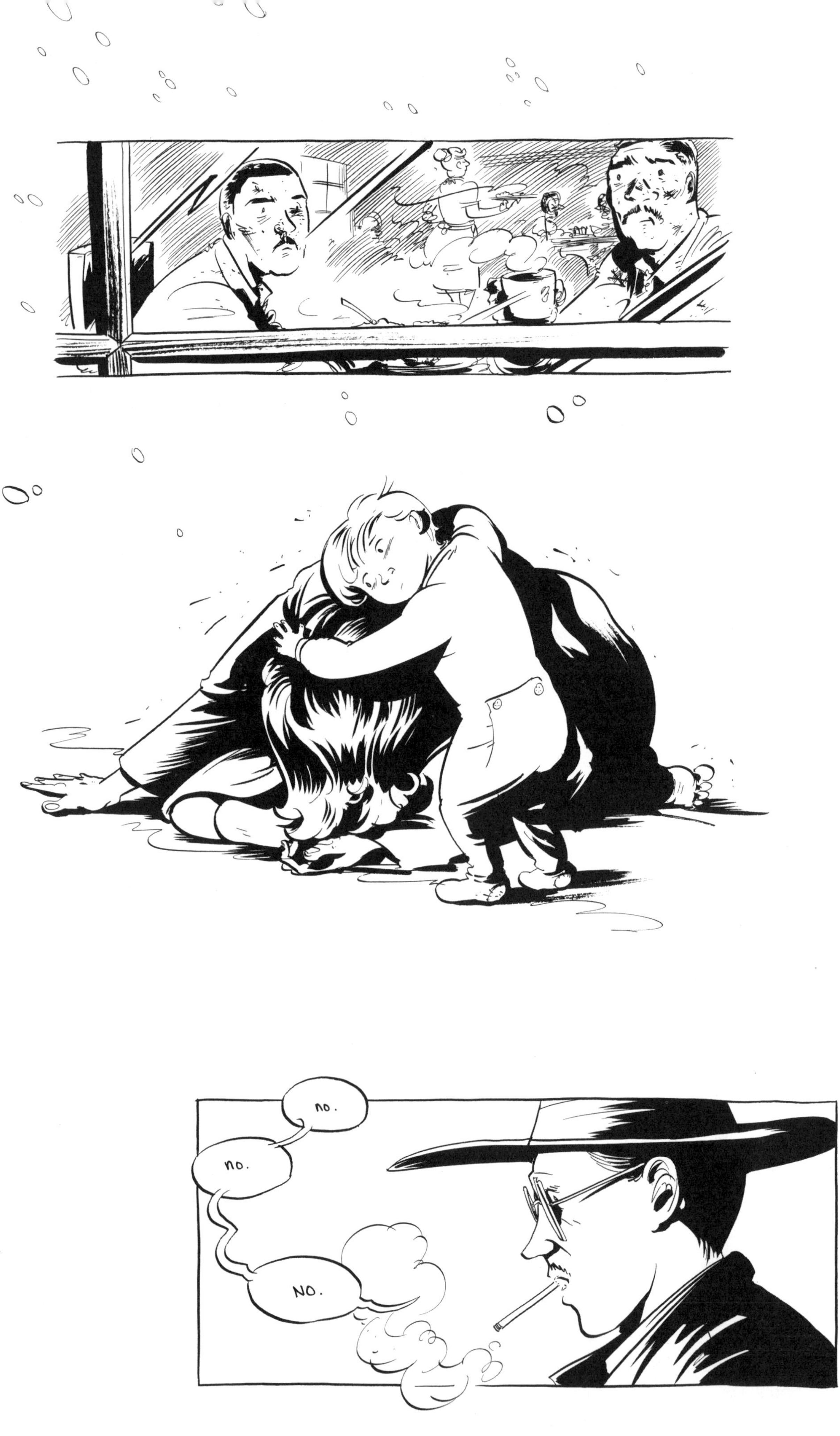
no.
no.
NO.

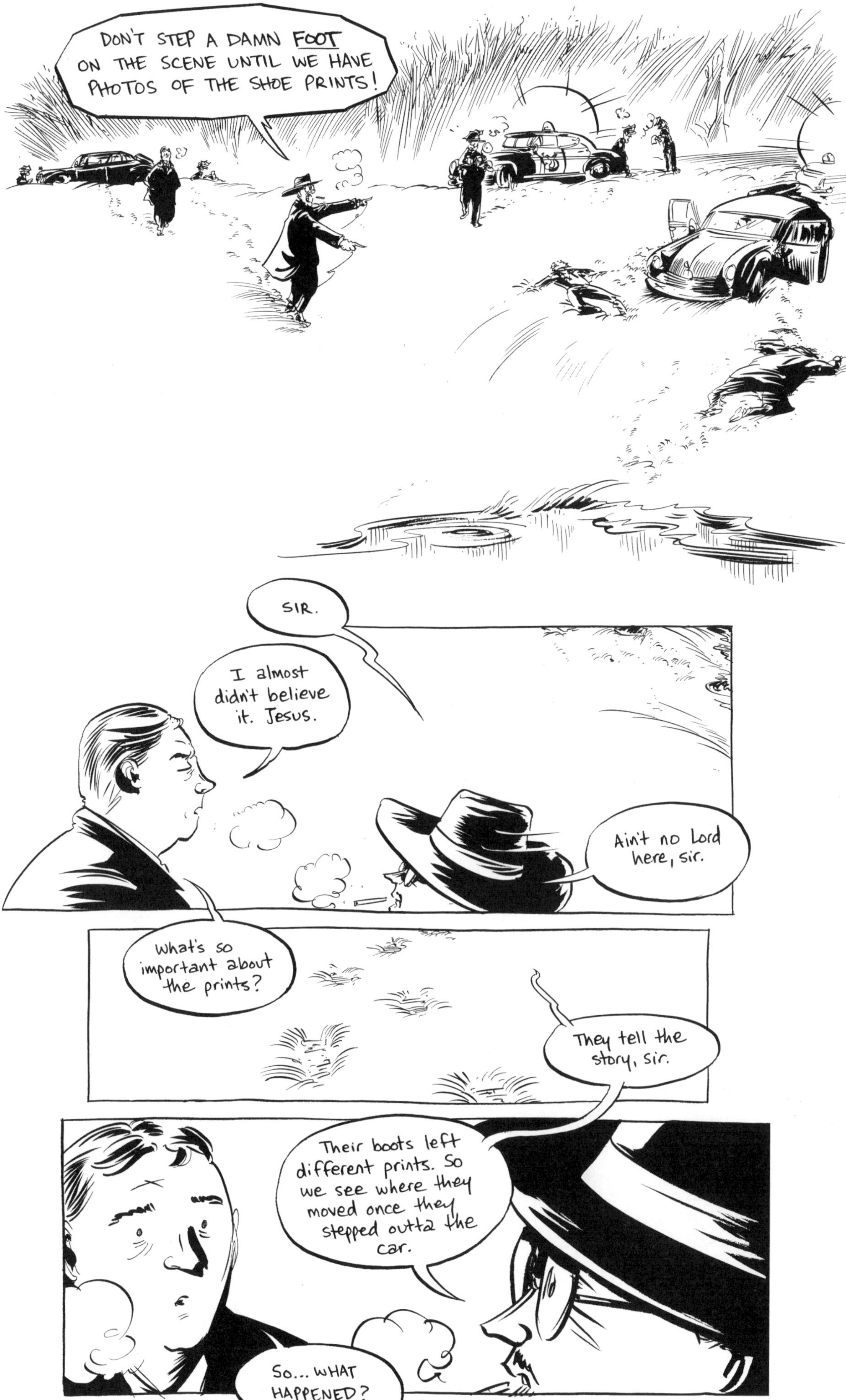
DON'T STEP A DAMN FOOT ON THE SCENE UNTIL WE HAVE PHOTOS OF THE SHOE PRINTS!
SIR.
I almost didn't believe it. Jesus.
Ain't no Lord here, sir.
What's so important about the prints?
They tell the story, sir.
Their boots left different prints. So we see where they moved once they stepped outta the car.
So... WHAT HAPPENED?

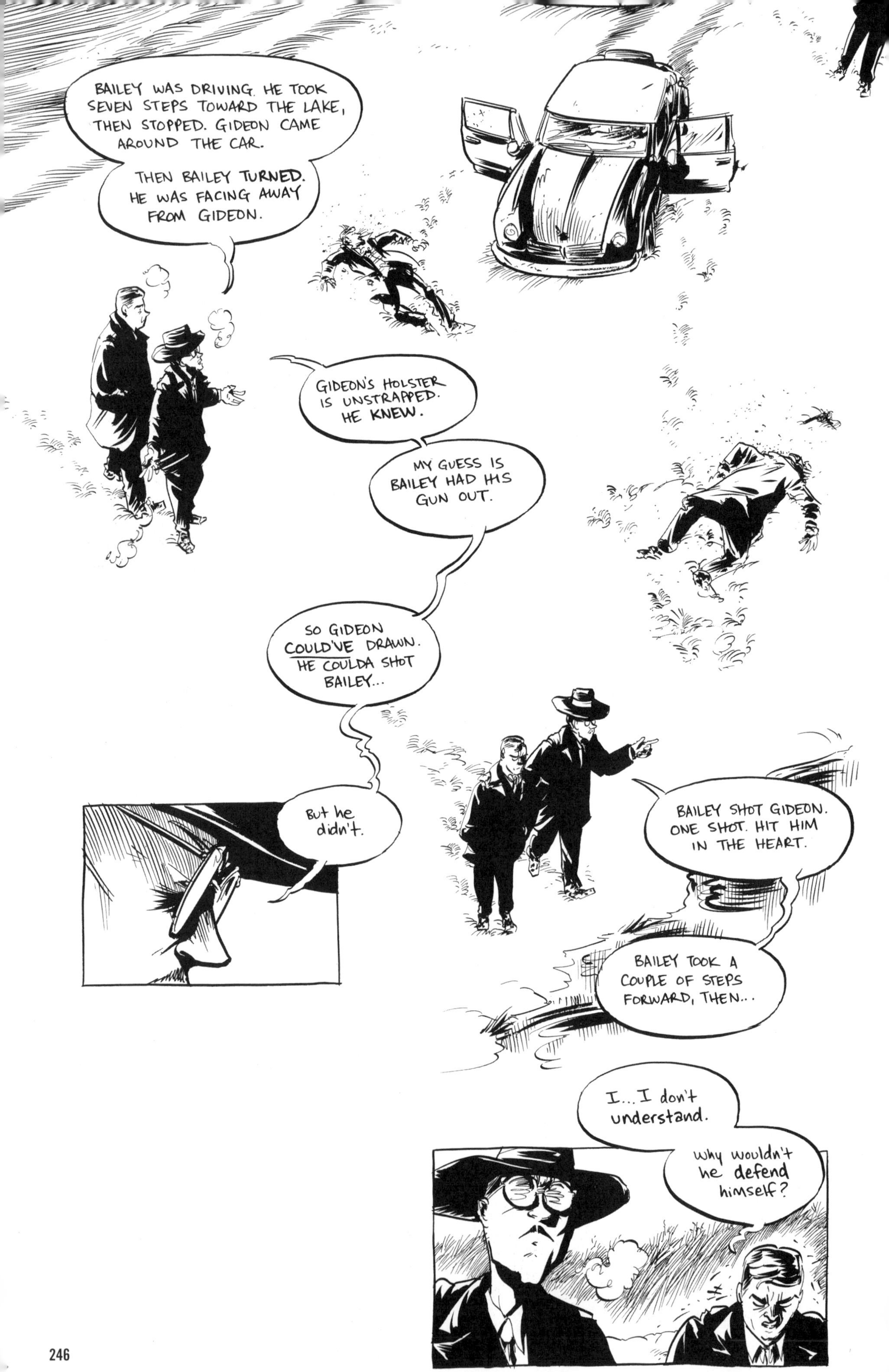
BAILEY WAS DRIVING. HE TOOK SEVEN STEPS TOWARD THE LAKE, THEN STOPPED. GIDEON CAME AROUND THE CAR.
THEN BAILEY TURNED. HE WAS FACING AWAY FROM GIDEON.
GIDEON'S HOLSTER IS UNSTRAPPED. HE KNEW.
MY GUESS IS BAILEY HAD HIS GUN OUT.
SO GIDEON COULD'VE DRAWN. HE COULDA SHOT BAILEY...
But he didn't.
BAILEY SHOT GIDEON. ONE SHOT. HIT HIM IN THE HEART.
BAILEY TOOK A COUPLE OF STEPS FORWARD, THEN...
I... I don't understand.
why wouldn't he defend himself?

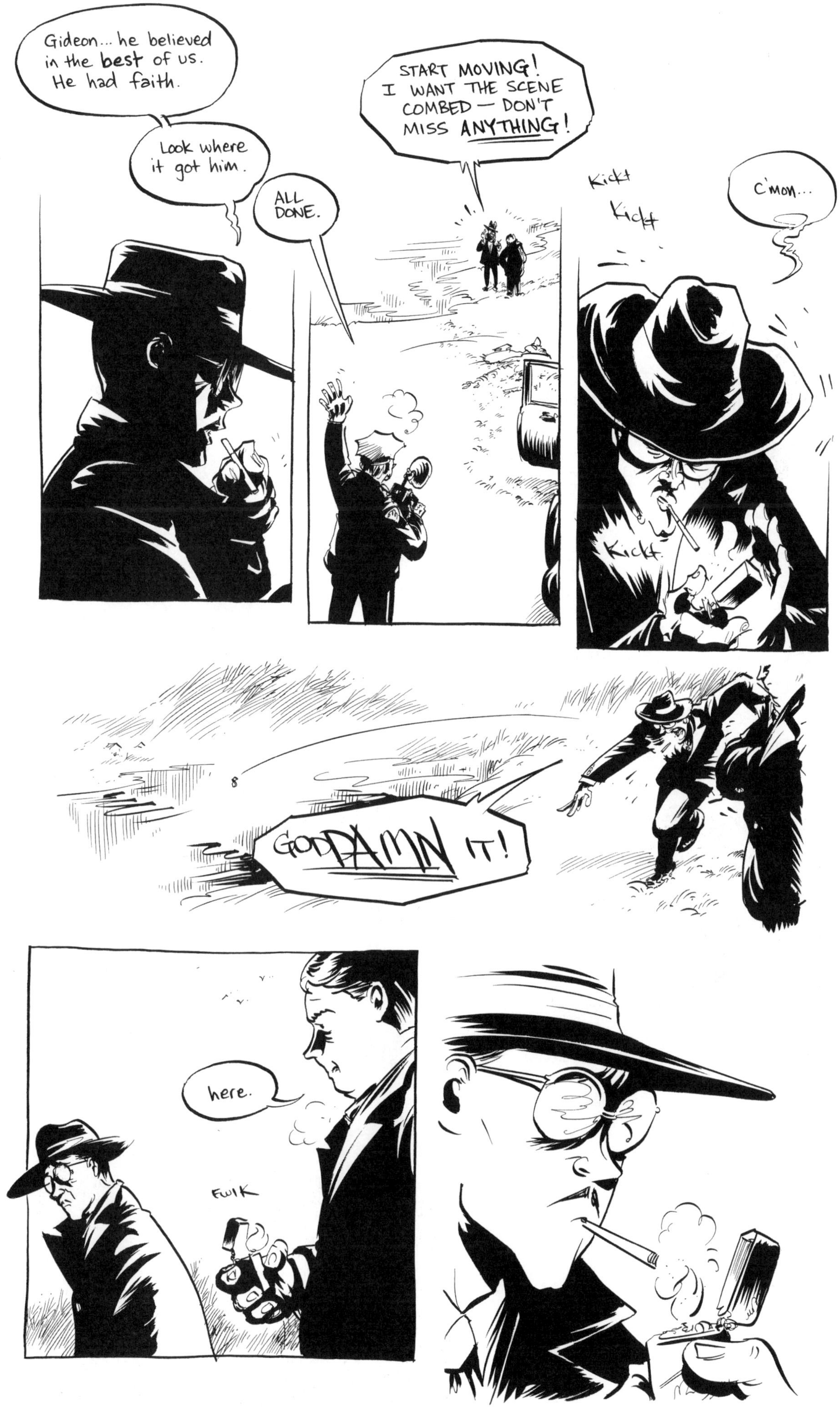

Gideon... he believed in the **best** of us. He had faith.
Look where it got him.
ALL DONE.
START MOVING! I WANT THE SCENE COMBED — DON'T MISS ANYTHING!
Kickt
Kickt
C'mon...
Kickt
GODDAMN IT!
here.
FWIK

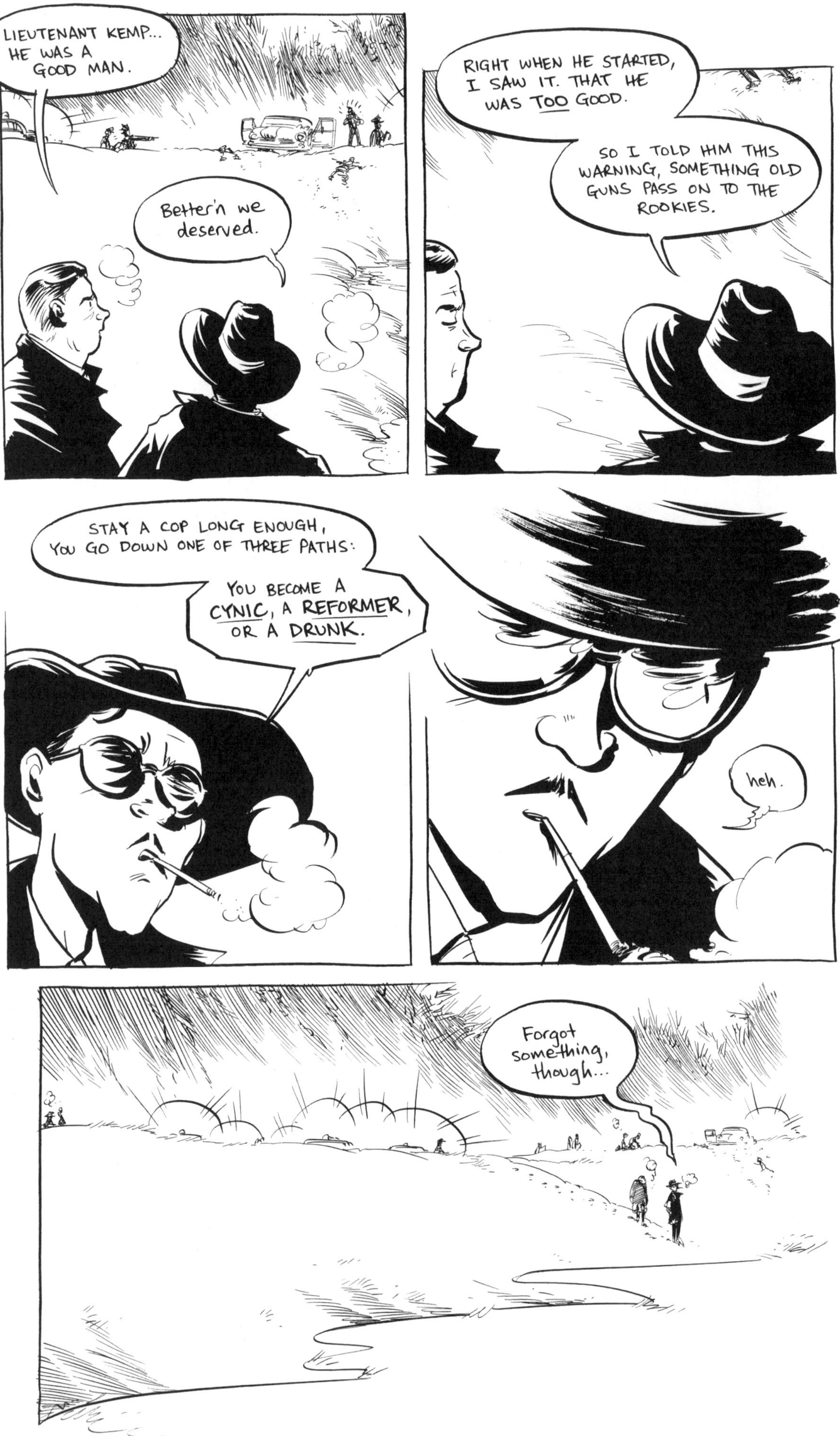
LIEUTENANT KEMP... HE WAS A GOOD MAN.
Better'n we deserved.
RIGHT WHEN HE STARTED, I SAW IT. THAT HE WAS TOO GOOD.
SO I TOLD HIM THIS WARNING, SOMETHING OLD GUNS PASS ON TO THE ROOKIES.
STAY A COP LONG ENOUGH, YOU GO DOWN ONE OF THREE PATHS:
YOU BECOME A CYNIC, A REFORMER, OR A DRUNK.
heh.
Forgot something, though...

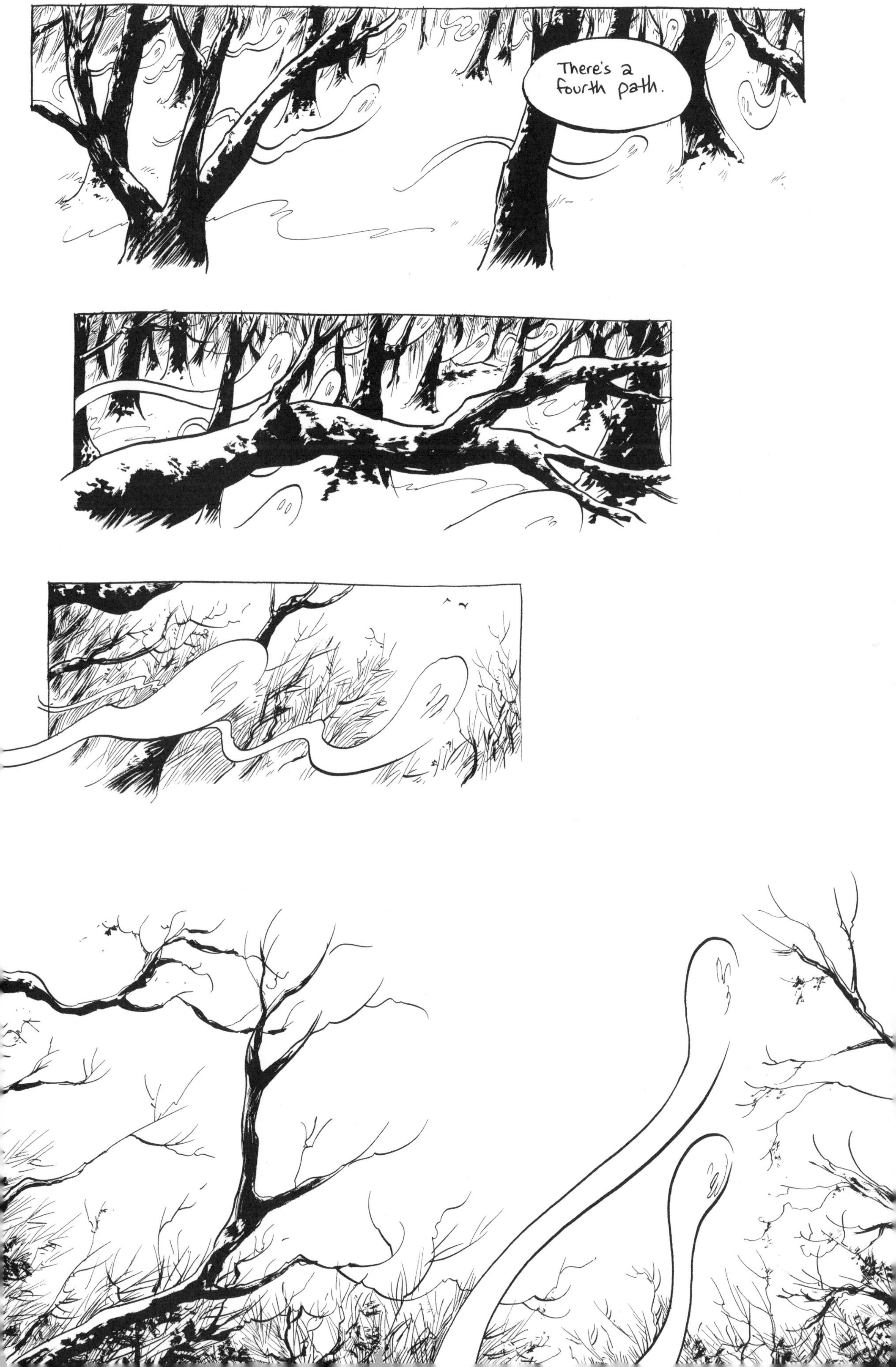
There's a fourth path.

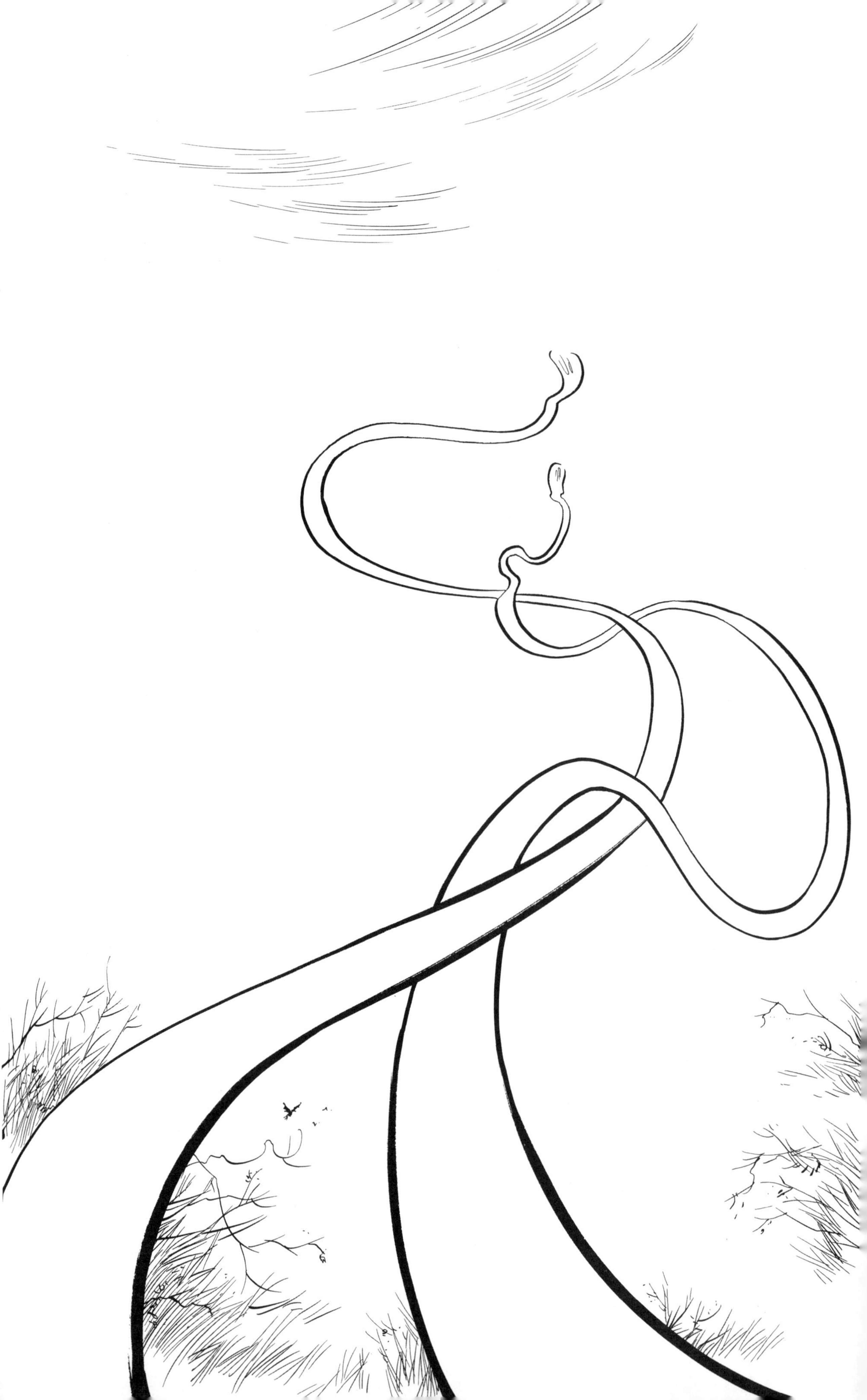

AFTERWORD

"On American soil, no one is more powerful than a police officer. A cop can detain you, hurt you, even kill you, and it's legal."

It was a cop who told me this. We were talking about policing and race and Black Lives Matter. He told me stories about how much good had been done by the terrific officers he knew. And how much pain had been caused by the bad ones.

I've known a lot of cops over the years. More than a decade ago, that was my world—not as one of them, but as a crime reporter at a newspaper in Little Rock, Arkansas. I worked with brilliant detectives, dedicated patrol officers, and complete assholes. It was one of the latter who showed me exactly how he would target young black men, pursue them aggressively, and create a pretense for searching their vehicles. He did all this without apology: *This is how policing works.*

Two Dead is a work of fiction, but one inspired by truths. We've changed names and key details to respect the real people, but *its* tragic events are largely factual. It was a story I came across in the archives while at the newspaper and, over the course of several years, brought to life with Nate Powell, who knows that region and its people and history as well as anyone. But this old story gained a bold new truth, in real time, as we developed it.

The world has changed in this past decade. Not because we are beyond racism. Not because we've gotten rid of the bad cops. Not because young black men have stopped being killed. The world has changed because a new lens has been applied to this systemic evil. As Nate and I worked on *Two Dead*, we sought to bring that lens to this graphic novel as well. We hope that it plays some role, large or small, in urgent conversations about these important truths.

Above all, this is a story about cycles of violence. The violence of war that returns home and perpetuates as what we now know is post-traumatic stress disorder. One violent act by a young police officer that haunts his entire career. The violence of racism that destroys the lives of victim and, in a different way, perpetrator. It is an old myth, that to be a man is to be willing and even eager to inflict pain and suffering. There is another way.

—Van Jensen

ACKNOWLEDGMENTS

The Little Rock Police Department gave critical help in researching this book, particularly crime analyst supervisor Jim Brooks. Much of the historical material came from the archives of the *Arkansas Democrat* and *Arkansas Gazette* newspapers. Erin Tobey breathed extra life into the art. Chris Ross designed the immaculate cover. Our editors and proofreaders at Gallery 13 provided critical attention to detail. Charlie Olsen at Inkwell championed this book for years, ensuring it found a good home. Our families provided endless patience and support. Lastly, it was Jim Gibbons who first believed in the necessity of this book.